Tarnopol Volume
(Ternopil, Ukraine)

Translation of
Tarnopol
(Tarnopol Volume)

The Encyclopaedia of the Jewish Diaspora

Original Book Edited by: Dr. Ph. Korngruen

Originally published in Jerusalem 1955

A Publication of JewishGen, INC
Edmond J. Safra Plaza, 36 Battery Place, New York, NY 10280
646.494.2972 | info@JewishGen.org | www.jewishgen.org

©JewishGen, Inc. 2024. All Rights Reserved
An affiliate of New York's Museum of Jewish Heritage – A Living Memorial to the Holocaust

Tarnopol Volume (Ternopil, Ukraine)

Translation of *Tarnopol (Tarnopol Volume)*

The Encyclopaedia of the Jewish Diaspora

Copyright © 2024 by JewishGen, INC All rights reserved.
First Printing: February 2024, Adar I, 5784
Editor of Original Yizkor Book: Dr. Ph. Korngruen
Project Coordinator and Translator: Moshe Kutten
Cover Design: Irv Osterer
Layout: Jonathan Wind
Name Indexing: Stefanie Holzman

This book may not be reproduced, in whole or in part, including illustrations in any form (beyond that copying permitted by Sections 107 and 108 of the U.S. Copyright Law and except by reviewers for public press), without written permission from the publisher.

JewishGen INC. is not responsible for inaccuracies or omissions in the original work and makes no representations regarding the accuracy of this translation. Digital images of the original book's contents can be seen online at the New York Public Library website or the Yiddish Book Center website.

Library of Congress Control Number (LCCN): 2024930203

ISBN: 978-1-954176-90-4 (hard cover: 358 pages, alk. paper)

About JewishGen.org

JewishGen, an affiliate of the Museum of Jewish Heritage - A Living Memorial to the Holocaust, serves as the global home for Jewish genealogy.

Featuring unparalleled access to 30+ million records, it offers unique search tools, along with opportunities for researchers to connect with others who share similar interests. Award winning resources such as the Family Finder, Discussion Groups, and ViewMate, are relied upon by thousands each day.

In addition, JewishGen's extensive informational, educational and historical offerings, such as the Jewish Communities Database, Yizkor Book translations, InfoFiles, Family Tree of the Jewish People, and KehilaLinks, provide critical insights, first-hand accounts, and context about Jewish communal and familial life throughout the world.

Offered as a free resource, JewishGen.org has facilitated thousands of family connections and success stories, and is currently engaged in an intensive expansion effort that will bring many more records, tools, and resources to its collections.

Please visit https://www.jewishgen.org/ to learn more.

Executive Director: Avraham Groll

About the JewishGen Yizkor Book Project

Yizkor Books (Memorial Books) were traditionally written to memorialize the names of departed family and martyrs during holiday services in the synagogue (a practice that still exists in many synagogues today).

Over the centuries, as a result of countless persecutions and horrific atrocities committed against the Jews, Yizkor Books (Sefer Zikaron in Hebrew) were expanded to include more historical information, such as biographical sketches of famous personalities and descriptions of daily town life.

Following the Holocaust, the idea of remembrance and learning took on an urgent and crucial importance. Survivors of the Holocaust sought out other surviving residents of their former towns to memorialize and document the names and way of life of those who were ruthlessly murdered by the Nazis. These remembrances were documented in Yizkor Books, hundreds of which were published in the first decades after the Holocaust.

Most of these books were published privately, or through Landsmanshaftn (social organizations comprised of members originating from the same European town or region) that still existed, and were often distributed free of charge. Sadly, the languages used to document these crucial histories and links to our past, Yiddish and Hebrew, are no longer commonly understood by a significant percentage of Jews today. As a result, JewishGen has undertaken the sacred responsibility of translating these books into English so that the culture and way of life of these communities will be preserved and transmitted to future generations.

In 1986, a group of farsighted JewishGenners started a project to pool their efforts together in groups based upon their ancestors from each town and donate money to get the Yizkor books of their ancestral towns translated into English. As the translated material became available, it was made accessible for free at www.JewishGen.org/Yizkor. Hardcover copies can be purchased by visiting https://www.jewishgen.org/Yizkor/ybip.html (see below).

It is our hope that the translation of these books into English (and other languages) will assist the countless Jewish family researchers who are so desperately seeking to forge a connection with their heritage.

Director of JewishGen Yizkor Book Project: Lance Ackerfeld

About JewishGen Press

JewishGen Press (formerly the Yizkor Books-in-Print Project) is the publishing division of JewishGen.org, and provides a venue for the publication of non-fiction books pertaining to Jewish genealogy, history, culture, and heritage.

In addition to the Yizkor Book category, publications in the Other Non-Fiction category include Shoah memoirs and research, genealogical research, collections of genealogical and historical materials, biographies, diaries and letters, studies of Jewish experience and cultural life in the past, academic theses, and other books of interest to the Jewish community.

Please visit https://www.jewishgen.org/Yizkor/ybip.html to learn more.

Director of JewishGen Press: Joel Alpert
Managing Editor - Jessica Feinstein
Publications Manager - Susan Rosin

Notes to the Reader

The images in the original book were reproduced from photographs from the time of the first edition. These reproductions were already of poor quality, being pre-war and at least 30 or more years old. As a result, the images in the book are the best achievable.

A reader can view the original scans of the book on the websites listed below.

The original book can be seen online at the Yiddish Book Center website:

https://www.yiddishbookcenter.org/collections/yizkor-books/yzk-nybc314043/korngrin-f-tarnopol

OR

at the New York Public Library Digital Collections website:

https://digitalcollections.nypl.org/items/8d1687d0-356c-0133-62c1-00505686a51c

To obtain a list of Shoah victims from **Tarnopol (Ternopil, Ukraine),** the reader should access the Yad Vashem web site listed below; one can also search for specific family names using family name option. These lists are continually updated by Yad Vashem, so it is worthwhile to periodically search these lists.

There is more valuable information (including the Pages of Testimony, etc.) available on this website: https://yvng.yadvashem.org/

A list of all books available from JewishGen Press along with prices is available at: https://www.jewishgen.org/Yizkor/ybip.html

Dedication

In memory of my grandmother Josephine Pessie Mattel Edelstein (nee Apter) (and my grandfather Shmuel), my great uncle, Heinrikh (and his wife Mania), natives of Ternopil, my great uncle and aunt, Shmuel Baar and Laura-Etka Baar (nee Apter), and their children Richard and Eric natives and residents of Ternopil who perished in the Holocaust.

Moshe Kutten
Project Coordinator and Translator
Coatesville, PA
January, 2024

Photo Credits

Front Cover:

Synagoga — Pozdrwien ie z Tarnopola, attributed to C. Haliczer in Tarnopol between 1899 and 1901. The image was part of a series of regional postcards. Photo has been substantially restored and retouched
Public Domain image: https://commons.wikimedia.org/wiki/File:Tarnopol_%28Ternopil%29_Synagogue.jpg

Back Cover:

Committee of the Cooperative Bank
[Column 360] – Dr. H. Parnas, Eng. Schechter, Eichenbaum, Sperling, and the clerks: Mrs. Horovitz and Gelber

Common grave of the martyrs of Tarnopol
[Column 427]

Committee of the Tarnopol Landsmanschaft in the USA
[Column 366] - From right the left: Top row – S. Marmorek, Dr. Schuster, Dr. Migden, Wunderlikh, Scwarzapel and Atterman
Center row – Dr. Goldwasser, Mrs. Rattenberg, M. Guliger, Racker, Dr. Fish, and Bazas
(No names are given for the front raw)

Map showing Tarnopol
Public domain image https://picryl.com/topics/maps+of+ternopil/maps+of+ternopil+raion

Joseph Perl
[Column 62]

Seal of the Tarnopol Bar-Kochba Organization
[Column 115]

Rabbi Y. K. Landman
[Column 267]

Cover Design by: Irv Osterer

Geopolitical Information

Ternopil, Ukraine is located at 49°33' N 25°35' E and 227 miles WSW of Kyyiv

	Town	District	Province	Country
Before WWI (c. 1900):	Tarnopol	Tarnopol	Galicia	Austrian Empire
Between the wars (c. 1930):	Tarnopol	Tarnopol	Tarnopol	Poland
After WWII (c. 1950):	Ternopol'			Soviet Union
Today (c. 2000):	Ternopil'			Ukraine

Alternate Names for the Town:

Ternopil' [Ukr], Tarnopol [Pol, Yid], Ternopol' [Rus], Tarnepol

Nearby Jewish Communities:

Mikulintsy 10 miles S
Kozliv 10 miles W
Stryyivka 11 miles ENE
Zbarazh 12 miles NE
Ozerna 13 miles WNW
Strusiv 15 miles S
Darakhov 17 miles S
Terebovlya 18 miles SSE
Zaliztsi 19 miles NNW
Kam'yanky 19 miles E
Skalat 20 miles ESE
Novyy Oleksinets 20 miles N
Zolotnyky 21 miles SSW
Burkaniv 21 miles SSW
Zboriv 21 miles WNW
Kozova 21 miles WSW
Vyshhorodok 23 miles NE

Romanivka 23 miles S
Yezezhanka 23 miles WNW
Dolyna 24 miles SSE
Vyshnivchyk 24 miles SSW
Hrymayliv 25 miles SE
Vishnevets 25 miles NNE
Pidvolochys'k 25 miles E
Volochysk 26 miles E
Khorostkiv 27 miles SE
Budaniv 27 miles SSE
Pidhaytsi 28 miles SW
Pidkamin 29 miles NNW
Pomoryany 30 miles W
Ozhyhivtsi 30 miles ENE
Tovste 30 miles SE
Berezhany 30 miles WSW
Yabloniv 30 miles SSE

Jewish Population: 13,468 (in 1880), 13,999 (in 1931)

Map of Ukraine showing the location of **Ternopil**

Table of Contents

Initial pages		3

Historical Chapters

The History of the Jews in Ternopil	Dr. N. M. Gelber	7
The History of the Zionist Movement in Ternopil Before the First World War	Dr. Ph. Korngruen	72
Dr. Israel Waldman (A Biographic Note)		96
The "Young Zionism" in Austria	Meir Khartiner	97
Memories from the period 1914-1919	Dr. Khaim Gilad (Shmeterling)	103
Ternopil During the First World War	Sh. Ansky	107
From an Austrian to a Ukrainian Regime	Ben-Tzion Fett	109
During the Days of the Ukrainian Regime	A. Weisglass	113
Memories of A Jewish-Ukrainian Soldier	Moshe Guliger	114
The Zionist Movement During the Years 1919-1939	Dr. Tzvi Parnas	118

Parties and Youth-Movements

Parties

The Zionist Labor Party "Hit'akhdut" ["Union"]	Arye Avnon - Bronstein	139
"Poalei Tzion" ["Workers of Zion"]	Tzvi Weisbersht, Dr. A. Avishur (Werber)	143
The Z. P. S – "Bund" - The Jewish Socialist Party	Arnold Himelbrandt & Israel Grinberg	144
"HaMizrakhi"	Tova Sanhedrai (Dimend)	146
"Tif'eret Hadat" ["The Splendor of Religion"] and "Agudat Israel"	Dr. Hillel Zeidman	150

Youth Movements

"HeKhalutz" ["The Pioneer"] – A Turning Point for the Ternopil's Youth	A. Mesh	153
"HaShomer HaTzair" ["The Young Guard"]	Avraham Amernet	159
"HaNoar HaTzioni" ["The Zionist Youth"]	A. Dolin	163
"Gordonia"	Arye Avnon-Bronstein	165
"Histradrut HaNoar HaLomed" ["The Union of Young Students"] – "HaShakhar" ["The Dawn"]	A. Dolin	167

"Histadrut HaNoar HaLomed" ["The Union of Young Students"] – "Kadima" ["Forward"]	Khaim Harari (Goldberg)	169

The Religious Life

The Rabbis of Ternopil During the 18th and 19th Centuries	Dr. Hillel Zeidman	172
R' Ya'akov Kapil Landman ZTz"L	Rabbi Zusia Landman	177
Ternopil – A City of "Minkhat Khinukh" - ["Offering of Education"]	Dr. S. B. Feldman	178
Haredi Jews in Ternopil	Hillel Zeidman	180

The Synagogues in Ternopil

The Old Synagogue	Engineer, Architect Zeev Porat (Oks)	184
Houses of Prayer and Batei Midrash	Dr. Hillel Zeidman	186
Cantors and Cantorship	M. Sh. Geshuri	189

Educational and Cultural Institutions

Hebrew Educational Institutions in Ternopil		
"Tarbut" ["Culture"] School	Mordekhai Deutsch	194
"Tarbut" Association and its Activities	Nathan Ostern	197
The Kindergarten of "Tarbut"	Masha Ostern	200
The Jewish Theater in Ternopil	Dr. Moshe Fiol	202
Wolfstahl Family		
"Wolfstahl Orchestra"	M. Sh. Geshuri	205
Khone Wolfstahl	Karl Rothaus	206

Folklore Chapters

As Told by the People	A. Landfish	211
Words in the Name of their Sayer [Verbatim Quotation]	M. Deutsch	213
To the Khupa	Meir Khartiner	214
Ternopil Throughout the Year	Avner Avnon-Bronstein	218

The Sports Clubs in Ternopil

The Athletic and Physical Culture Zionist Association – "Beitar"	A. Landfish	227
The Sports Club "Yehuda"	Dov Niman	228

Economy and Welfare

On the Economic and Social Image of Ternopil	Dr. Tzvi Parnas	231

Destruction and Holocaust

Yizkor	Meir Khartiner	252
Ternopil During the Second World War	Avraham Oks	253
From the Depths…	Slomia Luft (Oks)	269
My Experiences in Ternopil Ghetto	Janet Margolis	275
Common Grave of the Martyrs of Ternopil		285

Name Index – Original Page Numbers 286

Name Index - English Edition 334

This is a translation from:

Tarnopol

(Tarnopol Volume)

The Encyclopedia of the Jewish Diaspora, Poland Series,
Published in Jerusalem 1955 (474 cols., H,Y, E)
Ed. Dr. Ph. Korngruen

49°33' / 25°35'

Acknowledgments

Project Coordinator:

Moshe Kutten

This material is made available by JewishGen, Inc. and the Yizkor Book Project for the purpose of fulfilling our mission of disseminating information about the Holocaust and destroyed Jewish communities. This material may not be copied, sold or bartered without JewishGen, Inc.'s permission. Rights may be reserved by the copyright holder.

JewishGen, Inc. makes no representations regarding the accuracy of the translation. The reader may wish to refer to the original material for verification. JewishGen is not responsible for inaccuracies or omissions in the original work and cannot rewrite or edit the text to correct inaccuracies and/or omissions. Our mission is to produce a translation of the original work and we cannot verify the accuracy of statements or alter facts cited.

אנציקלופדיה של גלויות

ספרי זכרון לארצות הגולה ועדותיה

סידרת פולין

הוצאת חברה אנציקלופדיה של גלויות בע"מ
ירושלים

Encyclopaedia of the Jewish Diaspora
A Memorial Library of Countries and Communities

POLAND SERIES

Tarnopol Volume

Edited by
Dr. PH. KOENGRUEN

Published by
ENCYCLOPAEDIA OF THE JEWISH DIASPORA CO., LTD.
Jerusalem – Tel-Aviv

יו"ר חברת אנציקלופדיה של גלויות
ד. בּרלס, ירושלים

כל הזכויות שמורות
לחברת אנציקלופדיה של גלויות בע"מ
ירושלים, רחוב סוכרת בית 4 טלפון 6850
All Rights Reserved ● Printed in Israel
סדר הדפוס בדפוס "צבי", תל־אביב
גלופות: צינקוגרפיה י. ריבלינסקי, תל־אביב
אדר תשט"ו ● פברואר 1955

Tarnopol Volume

Encyclopedia of the Jewish Diaspora
(A Memorial Library of Countries and Communities)

Poland Series

Ternopil Volume

Edited By: Dr. Ph. Korngruen

Published by

the Encyclopedia of the Jewish Diaspora Company Ltd.

Jerusalem – Tel-Aviv

Chairman of the Encyclopedia of the Jewish Diaspora Company

Kh. Barles, Jerusalem

All rights reserved

The Encyclopedia of the Jewish Diaspora Ltd.
Jerusalem, 6 Se'adia Gaon Street, Tel.: 3259
All Rights reserved, Printed in Israel
Arranged and published at "Sefer" Printing Ltd., Tel Aviv
Engravings and Zincography by Y. Rindzonski, Tel Aviv
Adar 5715, February 1955

Members of the Committee

of the

Ternopil Volume:

A. Oks, Dr. Sh Amernat, Y. Biler, A. Goldberg
B. Goligher, Dr. Kh. Gilad (Shmertling), A Dolin
Eng. M. Hamer, Dr. H. Zeidman, M. Khartiner, Dvora Levion
Y. A. Mesh, Ben-Tzion Pet, Dr. Tz. Parnas, Dr. Korngruen
A. Kornblit

Editorial Secretary- Meir Kuzhan

Corrections of Errors and Omissions

[All corrections and omissions have been incorporated in the translated book]

[Forward by] the Editorial Committee

After a great deal of effort, we offer the readers the Yizkor book for the famed community of Ternopil. This magnificent city yielded numerous Torah scholars and prominent people of wisdom and action and captured an honorable and paramount place in the history of our people.

The mission to publish the book was not easy, as most of Ternopil Jewry was annihilated in the Holocaust. Lives were not the only thing that was terminated. All the government and municipal archives, archives of the community executive committee and political parties, and the documentation of many other institutions that our city was blessed with were destructed. There wasn't even one document we could have relied on to reconstruct the past.

Therefore, we had to rely on memory, which is flawed by nature. We also encountered difficulties with memories because only a few activists who could give us details survived. We had to rely on these few activists and officials to recount their actions and tell us about the diversity of the institutions where they served. Hence, the articles and memories brought herewith may not be sufficiently thorough for the subjects they are meant to cover. For that reason, the description of many of the life aspects is somewhat lacking, and at the same time, other areas comprise an abundance of material. All of the shortcomings were known to us. We did our best to circumvent them. If we have not always succeeded, we cannot be blamed for it.

The material presented in the book is arranged chronologically. We started from the day the city was established, proceeded through the period when Jews settled in it and, ended with the destruction of the Jewish community by the Nazis.

The historian N. M. Gelber wrote the history of the Jewish Ternopil specifically for this book. He relied on the information found in archival materials that had not been published as of yet. This article sheds new light on some periods of Ternopil's history, particularly the Enlightenment period. We trust that the new material was fully and correctly presented herewith. Due to the historical and cultural importance of the phenomena of the Enlightenment movement, this material would be valuable not only for Ternopil historians but also for those who want to explore the roots of the Enlightenment movement with its various manifestations.

We allocated a central location in the book to the discussion about National Movement in Ternopil. We described the 20th century history of our city from that National Movement's point of view since it was the one, which had the principal effect on our lives, and because it shaped our history in that century. It is important to note here that Ternopil contributed significantly to the consolidation of the idea of our national dream. A historian could find compelling details about the beginning of the National Movement in Poland and its development routes in the articles of Dr. Ph. Korngruen, Meir Khartiner, and Dr. Tzvi Parnas.

We did not ignore the other movements, such as the assimilation movement, Zh. P. S. [Jewish Socialist Party] and others, whose influence was substantial, during some of the periods in the city's history. We also did not disregard lesser affairs, such as folklore and popular folklore songs. We did our best to make sure that nothing worth mentioning was missing. We strove to highlight the unique character of Jewish Ternopil as a vibrant city, always alert, fighting, zealous, stubborn, extreme in its conduct, and joyful-but- serious at the same time. In our mind, Ternopil was not just a geographic location or just a regular place where Jews lived their entire life from birth to death. In our memory, mind, and heart, Ternopil occupies a very unique image. Our wish of resurrecting that Ternopil on the pages of this book was our guiding principle in our work.

We paid particular attention to the period of the Holocaust. With awe and reverence, we collected all of the relevant material concerning that period from the miraculously surviving eyewitnesses, and based on some documents, memories, and letters that we managed to collect, laid down that section of the book. The reader will find in that chapter a comprehensive and accurate description of the Ternopil Ghetto. That section contains a description of the daily life in the ghetto, the suffering, and the ghetto destruction. That section is also available in Yiddish for the benefit of the readers in the US who are not proficient in Hebrew.

We, the remnants of our generation who live in this critical time, took it upon ourselves to preserve the historical information so valuable to the history of the Ternopil glorious community. We collected remnants of ruins, broken tablets, fragments of creative works, and personal memories from daily life before they would disappear into the oblivious abyss.

We trust that the readers would forgive us for any flaws as our good intention and dedication invested in this holy work would stand in our favor.

We must thank all of the people who participated and helped us to publish this book. We are thankful for the people who provided us with material or advice and those who helped by doing. We would like to thank the people and natives of Ternopil in Israel and the US, particularly Dr. Tzvi Heller, who represented the Ternopil Jewry at the Polish Sejm. As such, he was rooted in the life of his people and their problems. He extended his kind help to us in the resurrection of whole chapters and isolated details from the not-so-distant past, which, to our dismay, became so farfetched.

The Old Synagogue of Ternopil

Historical Chapters

[Columns 21 - 22]

The History of the Jews in Ternopil

By Dr. N. M. Gelber

Translated by Moshe Kutten

A.

Ternopil was established in 1540 by the *Voivode* [military leader] of Krakow and *Hetman* Jan Tarnowski[1]. The objective was to protect the province from the relentless attacks and invasions by the Tatars and Wallachians under their leader *Hospodar* [supreme ruler]. When he was appointed the *Voivode* of Reisyn (Rus'), and *Hetman* of Poland, Tarnowski grasped the extent of the great suffering of that province during the invasions. He began to construct a defense line at the borders of Reisyn after recapturing the city of Pokutia from the Wallachian *Hospodar*, Patrila, in the 1931 battle near Obertyn and winning against the Muscovites in the 1535 battle near Starodub. As part of the system of fortifications, he built the fort-city Ternopil and built a fortified castle in it. His son, Jan Krzysztof, improved the castle-fort and strengthened the city fortifications. As early as 1540, King Sigismund I, awarded Tarnowski the "first privilege" that included special rights concerning the city of Ternopil. Jacob Bodzianowski was elected as the first mayor (*wojt*) of Ternopil. The privilege was renewed in 1548, which validated the Ternopil as governed by the Magdeburgian law. In 1550, King Sigismund-Augustus added a regulation to the city privileges, under which merchants and waggoneers traveling to Volhynia [Volhyn] from Halych, Kolomyia, and Koropets, to pass through Ternopil and pay custom. His intention was to develop the city trade-wise.

In 1566, King Sigismund-Augustus awarded Ternopil the "Emporium Right" ([declaration that a city is a principal] center of commerce), comparable to Lviv's privilege. That privilege contributed substantially to the development of Ternopil as a trade center in Eastern Poland.

Following the death of Jan Krzysztof, his son-in-law, Prince Konstanty [Wasyl] Ostrogski, and his descendants inherited the city. The family devoted special attention to widening and strengthening the castle and the fort. By enlarging and widening the castle-fort, they created a sanctuary for the local population during the invasions of the Taters, which eventually took place in 1575 and 1589.

The Polish [deputy] Chancellor, Tomasz Zamoyski, gained ownership of Ternopil in 1621 by marrying Katarzyna Ostrogska Zamoyski. He often resided in the castle and invested considerable efforts to improve it. He hosted the Polish Crown Prince, Wladyslaw, when the latter passed through Ternopil on his way back to Poland following his win [over the Turks] near Khotyn.

However, the city residents did not enjoy peace for much longer. Despite the improvement made to the castle and its fortifications[2], the city endured tremendous suffering resulting from the invasions of the Cossacks and Tatars in 1648 and 1653. As a result, nearly the entire city and its castle were destroyed.

The city and the fortifications were rebuilt by the new owner of Ternopil. Aleksander Koniecpolski. That was indicated in a legal document (*Lustracja*) from 1672. However, the city was attacked again in the same year by the Turkish army, during its advance towards Lviv and surrendered immediately.

In 1675, the Turkish armies under the command of Ibrahim Shishman Pasha camped in the city. However, these armies were forced to retreat due to the fierce resistance

[Column 23]

by the Polish forces situated at Terebovlya's fort. The Turks were forced to retreat beyond the Zbruch River. While retreating, the Turks set fire to the castle, destroyed its fortifications, and bombed the forts. The city lay in its ruins for several years.

The city became the property of the House of Sobieski in 1690. Queen Marie Casimire Louise [Polish – Maria Kazhimiera d'Arquien] rebuilt the castle and did much to restore the city. The Tatars attacked the Ternopil for the last time in 1694 but did not manage to conquer it.

The Potocki's [pronounced – Potowtski in Polish] purchased the city from the Sobieski family and kept it until the beginning of the 19th century. During their ownership, Ternopil suffered from the invasions by the Russian and other confederations, established during the second half of the 18th century. In 1770, a severe pandemic decimated most of the population. One of the city's new owners, Count Franciszek Korytowvski, eliminated the fortifications and rebuilt the castle as a modern palace.

[In 1772 after the first partition of Poland], the city came under Austrian rule. The situation was improved then in many aspects. It became a paramount trade center, and its development accelerated.

During 1800 – 1815, the city of Ternopil and its district came under Russian rule and were governed by the Russian Senator Theyls. In 1815, Ternopil returned to Austrian hands. It remained private until 1843 when all privileges of its previous owners were eliminated[3].

B.

Verified details about the establishment and the beginning of the Jewish community in Ternopil are not available. It is logical to assume that Jews settled in the city a short time after it was established. Ternopil was located, at that time, on the main road from Lviv, through Winniki, Pidhayatta [Podhajce], and Zolochiv-Zboriv to Ternopil, Myukulyntsi [Mikulince], Terebovlya, Kopychintsi, Zaliztsi [Zalozce], and Chortkiv. The road continued through Bukovina [or Wallachia] to Iasi [Yasi] in Romania and from there southward to Istanbul [Constantinople]. Many merchant convoys from Poland to Wallachia and Turkey passed through Ternopil, and therefore, it attracted many Jews. It is also logical to assume that the city's owners were interested in the economic development and awarded the Jews additional rights to attract them. We learn from the statute that Tarnowski awarded the city in 1550 that he allowed Jews to settle anywhere in the city except in the market square. It is mentioned in archive documents that Jews visited the fairs in Lviv in 1635. In one such document, the merchant Barukh Davidovitz (son of David) from Ternopil was mentioned giving a person named Gzhagozh Sheremedez [in Lviv] two promissory notes [*Obligi*] totaling 2000 guldens. The document stated that the latter did not pay back the debt despite his commitment[4].

A prosperous Jewish community, with a stable organization and creditable institutions, existed at Ternopil since as early as the years of the pogroms (1648 – 1657) [Also called Khemilintzki's Uprising].

Rabbi Meir, son of

[Column 24]

Yitzkhak Tarnopoller wrote in his book "Maor HaKatan" ["The Little Light"] (Fuerth, 5457 [1697]), about his family running away, in his childhood, from his town Ternopil in 5408 [1648]. He called Ternopil "Our Capital Community – Ternopil".

Tombstone in Ternopil Cemetery from the 17th Century

    Rabbi Meir Yitzkhak Tarnopoller was born in Ternopil in 1636. His father was wealthy and was one of the distinguished people in the community. When the Cossacks reached Ternopil, he escaped with his parents. Most of his family was annihilated. They wandered around with his father from place to place during the entire summer. They returned to Ternopil in the winter of 1649 and found their house in ruins and their belongings destroyed. When the Cossacks invasions renewed, the family was forced to leave the city and run away again. During the wonderings, his father died, and his mother was left to take care of three orphans: Aharon, Meir, and Gelah (a girl). Meir reached the center of Poland and studied in Lublin with the Maggid, Rabbi Israel Heschel, and [Rabbi] Shmuel Keidanover. When the Russians invaded Lublin and destroyed the Lublin community, Meir escaped with the Rabbis and the students to Moravia. During these wanderings, he met the daughter of R' Khaim Zelig, son of Nathanel, who was previously a cantor in Lviv. R, Khaim moved from Moravia to Fürth and served as a cantor there. R' Meir moved with him and resided in Fürth for seventeen years.

[Column 25]

Later on, he was nominated as a Rabbi in Oettingen. R' Meir authored a book of sermons about the Torah – "HaMaor HaKatan". Since he was not blessed with sons, he wished to publish his sermons in print to immortalize his name. Fürth's Rabbi – Shmuel son of Feibish, Bamberg's Rabbi – Menakhem Mendil Ashkenazi, and Chief Rabbi of Ansbach – Yisaskhar Barman, relied on the book. R' Meir died in 1696. The book was published by his father-in-law R' Khaim in 1697[5].

We know from the same period that during the Cossacks Wars and later during the Swedes' Wars, the Jews in Ternopil were obligated to defend the city like the rest of the residents. They were armed with rifles and gunpowder like the Christians. Sometimes, they also had to operate cannons. That obligation was also imposed on the Jews in other cities in Podolia, such as Husiatyn, Terebovlia [Trembobla], Chortkiv, Buchach, as well as in Polish cities such as Przemys [Pshemishel], Rzeszów [Reisha], and Lviv[6].

The privileges awarded by the king for building the synagogue included the following rules: It should be constructed from stones, and at a time of an enemy attack, it could be used as a citadel. The Jews were obligated to include gun shooting slots in the synagogue walls, allowing shooting in all directions. The Jews were also obligated to purchase a cannon. Defending the synagogue when an enemy approached the city was mainly the responsibility of the Jewish Artisan's Union. For that purpose, they were positioned in their own forts and own gates[7] under the command of the synagogue commander, nicknamed "*Hetman Zhidovsky*" [the Jewish commander].

The known traveler Ulrich [von] Werdum passed through Ternopil and stayed overnight there on 27 November 1671, during his travel in Poland. He wrote in his journal: "The papists ([Roman] Catholics) have a large stone-built church in the city. The Ruthenians – have three churches, and the Jews, who are numerous here and live in their own quarter (the best in town), have a synagogue built from such a beautiful stone, which I have not seen anywhere else in Poland[8].

From his writings, we learn that the Jews resided in their own separate quarter, as early as the second half of the seventeenth century, and that their state was so prosperous that they could afford to erect a synagogue, outstanding in its architecture and beauty.

That synagogue was probably built in the first half of the century. It was constructed as a citadel. Its defense obligation was imposed on the Jewish population. The interior and external appearances were similar to the synagogue at Husiatyn, which was also built in the same period. Perhaps the two were designed by the same architect.

After the events of 1648 [Cossacks and Tatars invasions], the economic situations of the Jews worsened by such an extent that the "*Sejmic Ruski*" [Red Ruthenia regional Sejm] that conferred in Halych in 1675, asked the Sejm to eliminate the poll-tax:

"*bo calemi w Buczaczu, Ternopolu, Podhajcach i po wszystkiem wojwodztwie indzicj zgineli miastami przez co tak wielkiej nic moga wystarczyc sumy*" (*akta grodzkie i ziemskic, tom XXIV nr. 205 p. 398*) ["Due to the fact that many Jews were murdered in the towns of Buczacz, Ternopol, and Pidhaitsi, the remaining minority cannot pay the great sums of the poll-tax (Town and Land Records, Volume XXIV no. 205 p. 398)".

Since the city's "Jewish Statute" was destroyed in the seventeenth century's wars, Ternopil's owner, *Voivode* [warlord] from Kyiv, Joseph Potowtski, who resided then in Stanislaw [Ivano-Frankivsk], approved a copy of that statute. As known, Ternopil belonged to the Sobieski family (who also owned Brody) before Potowtski. In 1699 Ya'akov [Polish - Jacub] Sobieski [father of King John III Sobieski] awarded the Jews new rights (on top of their old rights).

[Column 26]

Bronze "Menorah" from the Seventeenth Century in the Old Synagogue

[Column 27]

The principles of the former regulations were included in the new statute received from Joseph Potowtski, and new rights were added similar to those in the statute awarded by Potowtski to Stanislawow's Jews.

According to the statute from 1740, Jews were allowed to reside in any area of the city. There were also allowed to trade anywhere and anytime (except Sundays, Saturdays, and Catholic holidays). They were allowed to engage in any craft as long as they would not infringe on the privileges of the Christian crafts guilds. Jewish craftsmen had to register with the municipal craft guilds. However, since they could not participate in the guilds' customary religious processions, they had to pay the treasury of the guilds the sums paid by the Christian craftsmen when they were absent. The Jews were also exempt from attending the church services but were obligated to pay the candle and other taxes. The Jewish butchers were allocated particular locations in the market square. The butchers received half of the municipal slaughtering allotment by paying the palace two stones (an old Polish weight measure, approximately 12 kilograms) of milk by every butcher. Otherwise, the Jews were free of any other obligations to the city owner, except for the following:

- They had to pay a tax for road maintenance (*Szarwark*).

Bronze wash basin from the 17th Century, in the Old Synagogue

[Column 28]

- They had the same obligations toward the palace authorities imposed on the rest of the city residents.

- They had to man half of the guard shifts.

- Homeowners had to pay the palace the following taxes: On a home located in the market square – 18 guldens per year; On a home located on any other street in the city – 10 guldens; On a home located on [another house's] yard-4 guldens and 15 groszy; Tenants had to pay 1 gulden and 15 groszy per year.

- The Jews were obligated to pay general taxes like the rest of the residents.

The statute also regulated the legal jurisdiction under which cases involving Jews were heard as follows: Court cases between a Jew and a gentile had to be held at the palace courts (the type of the court was dependent on the type of the case). Like in other private cities, court cases between two Jews were first litigated by the rabbinical court. Appeals were handled in front of a palace official (governor) and attended by a *parnas* [official / leader] of the Jewish community.

The Rabbi and his home, cantor's and caretaker's houses, hospital, synagogue, and four adjacent houses, a ritual bathhouse, and the cemetery (in Mikuliniatski suburb) were exempt from taxes. The Jews were allowed to hold funerals on Christian holidays, provided they kept totally quiet and there was no yelling. On holidays they were allowed to open their stores but only after the conclusion of the prayers in the churches.

The Jews were allowed to own taverns and trade in all sorts of spirits in locations allocated to them by the palace authorities. To trade in spirits, they had to pay a "Drinking Tax" (*czopowe*) to the city's owner. The Jews were allowed to build houses, wine warehouses, and beer brewers. They were also allowed to trade in various goods (such as gold, silver, fabrics, furs, leathers, and all sorts of haberdasheries). They were not allowed to own a store near homes, only in the market square (*rynek*).

The Jews were allowed to sell their houses and did not have to get a special permit for that purpose. In cases of a fire, either in homes in their community or Christian homes, they were obligated to put it out. The Christians had the same obligation toward the Jews.

Like in all the other cities owned by Sobieski and Potowtski, Ternopil's Jews were given the right the participate in the municipal elections.

The above-mentioned statute[9] was also approved by Potowtski 's heir, his son Stephen Potowtski, in Zhbarazh on 13 April 1752,

[Columns 29-30]

after the death of Joseph Potowtski (who died on 19 May 1751).

During ownership by Joseph Potowtski, Poland suffered from anarchy resulting from the battles between Stanislaw Leszczynski and King Frederick Augustus, who was forced to abdicate the throne. Potowtski, who wished to stay neutral, was drugged by his wife, Victoria (nee Leszczynski), to join Leszczynski's camp. His involvement brought Ternopil into the whirlpool of war. The city mainly suffered from the invasion of the Russian army under the command of the Hesse-Homburg prince.

The Jewish community flourished economically during the ownership of the Potowtski Family. The Jews concentrated the trade of grain and cattle in their hands and took command of the fairs in Ternopil. The economic prominence of the city grew, principally when the Lviv-Ternopil- Staniv trade route was blocked by Turk, Kalil Pasha. He closed the border with Podolia (held by the Turks for 27 years) by positioning forts on the Dniester and Zbruch Rivers. On the eastern side of the border, the Polish cut off the roads leading toward Kamenetz Podolsk. As a result, the entire trade concentrated in Ternopil province, mainly in the city itself. The border opened after the Peace Treaty of Karlovitske (1699) when Podolia returned to Poland. This change resulted in a flow of many Jews from Lviv province. That led to the strengthening of the Sabbatian movement among the newcomers, who belonged to the poor class and who came to Ternopil to seek a livelihood.

C.

In the second half of the 17th century, after the calamity of 1648 – 1649 and the many wars during the period 1648 – 1660, which befallen the population of the eastern provinces of Poland, the inner life in the Jewish community also gradually crystallized.

Organizationally, the Jewish community was affiliated with the Jewish organization of Reisyn, which was headed by the two Jewish communities of Lviv [one inside the walled city and one that lay on the outskirts]. These communities ruled all other Jewish communities in the province. The war period depleted the two Lviv communities. The communities in Reisyn, such as the ones of Zhovkva, Lesko, Buchach, Brody, and also Ternopil, strove to free themselves from the rule of Lviv communities. A quarrel for the nomination of the state rabbi erupted between the Lviv Jewish community candidates and the candidates of Buchach and Ternopil. Ternopil's candidate was never elected.

Many Jews left Lviv and its surroundings settled in the eastern province and joined the Jewish communities there. During that period, the Jewish population in Ternopil also increased. The Ternopil community was organized like other Jewish communities in Poland. The community branches (*przykahlki*) in Kozliv, Kopychyntsi, and Bavoriv were affiliated with the Ternopil community. We only have limited information about the lives in the community at that time. We do know that a poll tax of 524 guldens was imposed on the Ternopil community. That poll tax was part of the total of 3141 guldens and 7 groszy, which was imposed on the entire state of Reisyn[10]. It was said that "the allotment was decided upon "by the Jewish leadership"[11]. In 1728, a trustee of the "Council of Four Lands", Mordekhai BABa"D of Brody, wrote to the state treasury registrar, Haslavski, that according to the division of the poll tax imposed on the Reisyn province, Halych's Jews were allotted 200 guldens instead of 100 guldens. Therefore, he asked Haslavski to correct the error and impose the excess 100 guldens on Ternopil Jews[12].

Among the prominent figures in Ternopil, R' Israel, son of Shmuel, was famous. He was the ABD [Head of the rabbinical court] in Lublin. He was called "the chief supervisor over all the Jews, particularly those in the Polish Kingdom, and a *parnas* [activist] of the "Council of Four Lands". As part of that role, he signed off on all of the Council's obligations. He participated in the Council's sessions in 5431 (1671), 5433 (1673), 5438 (1678), 5440 (1680), 5441 (1681), and 5443 (1683)[13].

Shmuel of Ternopil was one of the best students and the cousin of Gaon R' David, son of Shmuel HaLevi, the author of the book "Turei Zahav" ["Columns of Gold"]. He served as the ABD [Head of the Rabbinical Court] in Ludmir and Lutsk. It was said about him that: "He was the leader among the geniuses and wise men of his generation, and that no committee or advisement excluded him"[14].

Among the rabbis of Ternopil in that period, we know of Rabbi Yehoshua Heschel, the son of the ABD and leader of the community of Brody, Rabbi Yitzkhak BABa"D. BABa"D family was one of the most prominent families in Brody and held key positions in the life of the Brody community and in the Jewish autonomy in the Kingdom of Poland. The father of R' Yehoshua Heschel, Gaon R' Yitzkhak Krakover, a decedent of Gaon R' Heschel, ABD of Krakow. The latter served as the Rabbi in Brodzany and later on, until he died in Brody in 1704. He was respected and loved by all residents. His house served as a place for discussing all the affairs of the community because the population considered him the "father of the community". Because his sons were called "Bnei ABD" [the sons of the ABD] the honorific BABa"D was added to their name. In Polish, the sons of the rabbis were called Rabbinowicz . He laid down the foundation for the famed family known around Poland and the entire state of Reisyn.

His sons, except R' Yehoshua Heschel, did not want to dedicate themselves to becoming rabbis.

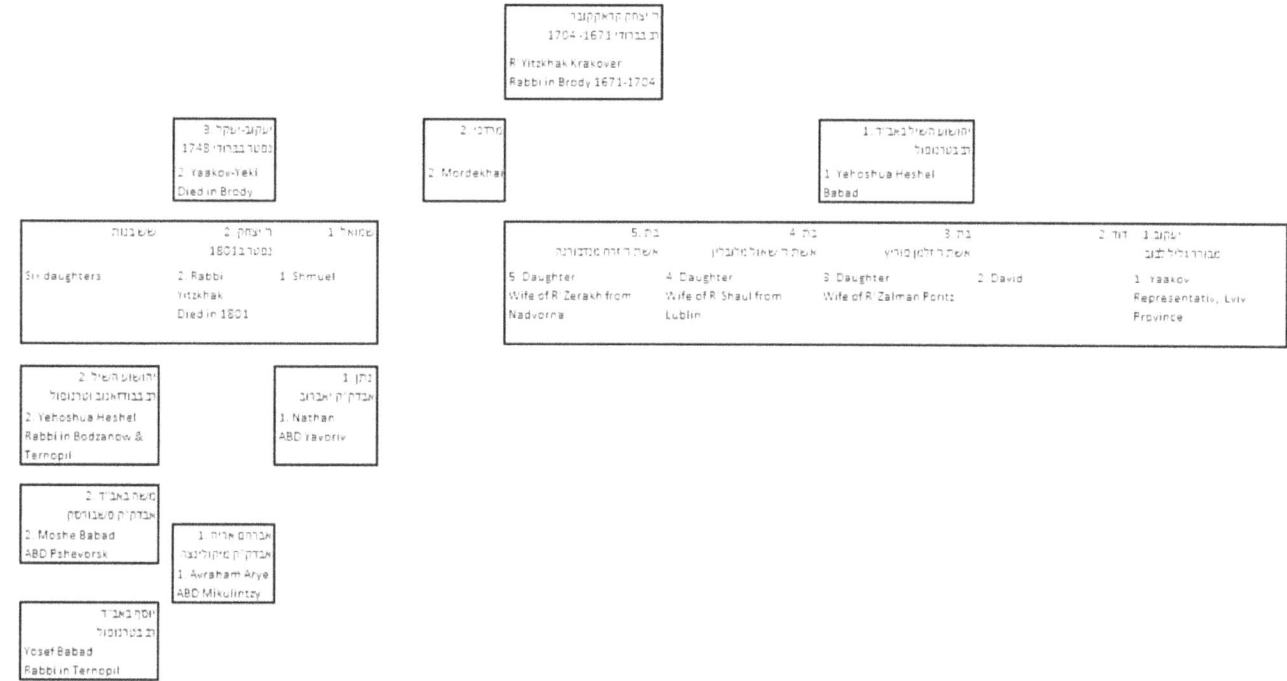

Family Tree of BABa"D Family

After they completed their studies – and when it came to their education, R' Yitzkhak was very strict – they got married and worked in commerce. R' Yitzkhak left four daughters[15] and three sons.

His eldest son, R' Yehoshua Heschel, ABD of the holy community of Ternopil, participated in 5471 (1711) in the meeting of the "Va'ad HaMedina" [Jewish "State Council"] in Yarichyv. On 11 Iyar, he gave his consent for the book "Mikhtav Eliyahu" ["Elijah's Letter"], by Rabbi Eliyahu, son of Arye-Leib from Kovrin. In 5478 (1718), he was fired from his rabbinical position due to a conflict in his community. R' Arye-Leib, son of Shaul (1671 – 1755) was nominated to replace R' Heschel, under the appeal by R' Gershon Nathan, son of Betsalel, the head of the Council of Reisyn.

R' Arye-Leib was the son-in-law of the scholar Tzvi Ashkenazi[16]. According to his brother-in-law, Emden[17], the scholar Arye-Leib "bought" Tzvi Ashkenazi to be his son-in-law by providing him with a hefty dowry (1700 guldens). Arye-Leib preferred him as a groom for his daughter over the fine young sons of exceedingly-rich people in central and eastern Europe. The latter perused him, trying to lure his daughter for free or even by paying him. His other son-in-law said about him that "despite Sara being exceedingly beautiful and learned, Arye-Leib preferred a pedigree over grandeur and wealth. He incurred significant expenses and also paid for the food for several years. At the same time, the father of the groom only helped by providing clothing and gifts".

After Gershon son of Nathan who was the son of the tax collector, Betsalel from Zhovkva, [Zholkova],

contacted Ya'avetz [Rabbi Ya'akov son of Tzvi Ashkenazi]. Ya'avetz made an effort "to find R' Arye-Leib a respectable position in Ternopil, where another rabbi [Rabbi Heschel] was serving at that time. According to Ya'avetz, Rabbi Heschel "had to let go because he used a fierce hand in his rulings". One of Arye-Leib's relatives was rejected by Rabbi Heschel with the excuse that he was not a scholar and was not fit to be a teacher. That event bought R' Heschel many enemies in the province, including people from the Arye-Leib's family, originally his followers and helpers. They began to resist him since (according to their opinion) he hurt his own followers to benefit himself. They did not rest until Rabbi Heschel was fired. "They did to him as he did to their follower"[18].

After residing for some time in Dukla, Rabbi Heschel became a rabbi in 1724 in Rzeszow [Reisha][19] and then returned to the throne of the rabbinate in Ternopil. He succeeded to reclaim his prominent position in the community and the Jewish autonomy authorities. Obviously, he got the support of his family in Brody, which played a substantial role in the life of Polish Jewry.

He participated as a representative in the 5491 (1731) session [of the "Council of the Four Lands"] in Yaroslav on 3 Tishrei. His relations with the people of the Jewish community probably improved. We find evidence to that in his *Haskama* [approbation] for the book "Meri Tzvi" about the [Talmudic tractate] Yevamot, by Tzvi Hirsh Luria from Lithuania (Zhovkova, 5504 [1743/4]) contained the phrase:" The flag of love is hoisted by the province of Podolia people, may G-d guard them.". His two sons also occupied prominent positions in the Jewish public life. His son Ya'akov was a representative of the Podolia province in the session of the "Council of Four Lands" held in Tyszowce on 8 Elul 5502 (1742)[20]. His other son was one of the honorable people in Ternopil[21].

After Yehoshua Heschel, R' Ya'akov, son of R' Yitzkhak Landau, was elected to serve as a rabbi. When R' Ya'akov served as the rabbi in Tarla[22], he signed a proclamation issued in Brody 26 Sivan, 55125 (1754) against the Sabbatians. He died in 1777. At the same period, Shmuel son of Ya'akov[23], served as a *parnas* [community leader-official].

In 5552 (1792), R' Shmuel, son of Rabbi Moshe-Pinkhas[24] Falkenfeld (1737 – 1806) was elected to serve as the rabbi in Ternopil. Earlier, he served as the rabbi in Bilgorajand and later on in Przeworsk. He served in Ternopil, where he died in 1788.

After the death of Rabbi Meir of Przeworsk in 1789, the community leaders decided to invite [Rabbi] Shmuel Falkenfeld, who was already known throughout the diaspora as a scholar. However, R' Shmuel preferred Ternopil, for which he had been already elected as its rabbi. He served there until 1801 when he was invited by the Poznan community to inherit the rabbinical throne after his brother Yosef's death. Rabbi Yosef was a rabbi in Przeworsk [Pshevorsk] there during 1780 – 1801[25].

During his reign in Ternopil, he published "Beit Shmuel Akharon" (Novidor, 1796), a response to "Shulkhan Arukh".

After him, R' Yehoshua-Heschel, son of Yitzkhak, son of Ya'akov-Yekl BABa"D of Brody, was elected as a rabbi. Rabbi Yehoshua was the grandson of Ya'akov-Heschel, the brother of the Rabbi from Ternopil, Yehoshua-Heschel BABa"D. R' Yehoshua was born in Brody in 5514 (1754). His father R' Yitzkhak, was the son of Ya'akov-Yekl BABa"D, and the son-in-law of *parnas* [community official-activist] of the "Council of the Four Lands", R' Avraham Kheimesh from Lublin, who was a leading merchant and one of the honorable people of Brody community. R' Yitzkhak followed his father, R' Ya'akov BABa"D, and was greatly involved in the affairs of the Jewish community.

[Columns 35-36]

He gave his two sons R' Nathan, who later became a rabbi in Yavorov, and Yehoshua-Heschel, an exemplary education. During his youth, Rabbi Yehoshua-Heschel was a rabbi in Budzaniv [Budzanow] and, from 1801, a rabbi in Ternopil. To his credit, we should mention that he gave his consent to the school founded by the enlightened Yosef Perl. In 1828 he was invited to serve as a rabbi in Lublin but decided to return to his rabbinical position in Ternopil, a short time later. He stayed in Ternopil until his death in 1828. He was the author of the book "Sefer Yehoshua" ["The Book of Yehoshua"], a Responsa to "Shulkhan Arukh", Zhovkova, 1829.

The economic situation did not change in the 18th century compared to the situation at the end of the 17th century. Besides local merchants and nobles who came to the month-long fairs in Ternopil, came also people from the rest of Reisyn cities, especially Brody merchants who purchased the goods and industrial products for wholesale selling in the fairs in Germany and Silesia. Only towards the division of Poland (in 1772), the situation worsened due to political events.

In the census held on 12 February 1765, 1161 Jews and 85 children younger than a year old were counted. In the affiliated branches, the following numbers were recorded: Kossiv-46 and one child, Kopychintsi – 40 and 8 children, and Bobrov - 17 and one child. In sixty-five villages that belonged to Ternopil, 416 Jews and 42 children less than one–year–old were counted. In the entire district, 1680 Jews and 137 children younger than one–year–old, were counted. In the province of Terebovlia [Trembowla] – (*powiat trembowelski*) a total of 7018 Jews and 516 children younger than one year (altogether 7534) were counted[26].

Due to the spreading of Frankism in the Podolia province, it would be logical to assume that a branch of the movement existed in Ternopil. However, none of the Frankish Jews who converted to Christianity after the debate in Lviv in 1759 came from Ternopil.

D.

The year 1772 was a turning point in the history of Reisyn Jews in general and the Jews in Ternopil with it. The annexation of these areas to the Habsburg Kingdom made them into a state called "Galitsia and Lodomeria". Obviously, that development also brought many changes in the lives of the Jews.

On the Austrian officialdom, which arrived to accept the new asset that Austria obtained as a result of the first partition of Poland, Ternopil made an impression of a sizable city (like many other cities such as Brody, Sambir, Taroslav, Przemys [Pshemishel], Drohobych, Tarnow, Biala, and, Podgozha, as opposed to many other towns). They particularly emphasized the economic role that the Ternopil fairs played, as well as the importance of the crafts held by the Christian residents - shoemaking, tanning, and by the Jewish residents – tailoring, and baking. They obviously pointed out the role of Jews in the wholesale and retail trade, leasing, and production of spirits drinks.

The sudden change affected the Jews throughout Galitsia. The Austrian authorities wished to convert the Jews to citizens of Austria in a blink of an eye and to accustom them to the new conditions. A wave of instructions, decrees, and regulations flooded Galitsia's Jews. The Jews were initially embarrassed, however, when they recuperated, they began to show a definitive resistance to the regime's intentions. With time, the authorities came to the conclusion that they would not be able to cause far-reaching changes in the lives of the Jews by purely bureaucratic means. The fate of Ternopil's Jews was, of course, similar to the fate of the rest of the Jews in Galitsia.

Despite recognizing the importance of the Jews to the economy, many officials did not hesitate to include in their reports, statements about the Jews such as the following: The Jews - "*wenn ihen das Märkeln, und Schleichhandel nicht mehr gelingt, sich endlich aufs Betrügen, Stehlen und Rauben verlegen.*" ["if you no longer succeed in fooling or sneaking, you will finally focus on deceiving, stealing, and robbing."]. On the other hand, the officials indicated that due to the low standard of living of the Jewish population, they constituted an economic factor, due to their ability to compete with both the other city dwellers and the farmers. In Lviv, the average annual budget of a Jew was 30 guldens. In the eastern province – in cities such as Ternopil and Zalishchyky, an average Jew spent in one month what an average Christian resident spent in one week.

The cities and towns of Ternopil, Gezimalov, Skalat, Zbarazh, Mikolintsy and their surroundings became a special district (XVII *Tarnopoler Kreis* [Ternopil District]). The city owner and the Jews tried to protect their rights. However, they were not successful for long. The new authorities wished to implement the same policies toward the Jews in the entire country, initially just administratively but, later on, also economically. The Austrian authorities considered the elimination of the Jewish bartenders, an important issue. They conducted a survey among the eighteen district heads in Galitsia. Only eight, including the district head of Ternopil, agreed to the government proposal. The authorities relied on the example of a similar decree in Bukovina[27], where the abolishment was beneficial, and based on that example they hoped that their plan might force the Jewish bartenders

[Columns 37-38]

in Galitsia to seek employment in productive professions[28].

From the start of the Austrian conquest, the Jews bore a heavy tax burden they could not pay. In December 1776, the community representatives, Shimon-Leibel, Hirsh-Shimon, and Mikhael-Yosef submitted an application on behalf of the

Ternopil's Jews to eliminate the debt incurred in the poll-tax. They also sought an obligation to be paid for the food supplied to the military by Ternopil Jews[29]. However, the authorities rejected the request. In January 1778, the community asked to reduce the annual tax, totaling 4000 florins, imposed on the Jews of Ternopil and Zbarazh. In March 1778, the Jewish community submitted a request to modify the property and employment tax imposed on the Jews of Ternopil. After the authorities rejected these applications[30], the community leaders appealed to the governor's office in Lviv. However, the central authorities rejected the appeal since the requests seemed unjustified. On the contrary, the district authorities requested to submit a detailed report on the economic situation and the properties of the Jews in Ternopil, which they could use as a basis for rejecting the appeal[31].

All the attempts during the reign of Empress Maria-Theresa did nothing to improve the economic life of Galitsia Jews. It is, therefore, no wonder that the economic situation during the reign of Emperor Joseph II worsened to such an extent that the authorities faced a difficult dilemma – how to improve the shaky and worsening standing of the Jewish population. Joseph II, who held physiocratic economic and political views, tried to resolve the Jewish problem by agricultural settlement.

In 1781, the Galtisian representative was asked to award the Jews government lands to cultivate by themselves. In 1782, a regulation was issued from Vienna that Jewish agriculturalists would only pay half of the marriage- tax, and later on, would be exempt from paying the tax altogether. The preparations for the first Jewish colony began in spring 1785. The preparations were completed with a settlement in Spring 1786 (in the village of Dombrovka near Nowy Sacz). Later on, the second colony of Neu Babyulon [New Babylon], near the city of Bolechiv, was established along with other small colonies, here and there, none of which lasted for a long time.

According to the government plan, out of 1410 settlers from throughout Galitsia, the community of Tarnopol had to provide 84. However, only 79 families actually settled. The Jewish communities in the areas of the settlements had to cover the expenses (based on a budget of 250 florins per family.

Seventy-nine families from Ternopil resided in their settlements as of the end of October 1803[32]. These results, which were included in the report by the Galitsian governor office from 12 July 1792, did not satisfy the central authorities. The ministers of the following districts fulfilled their settlement quota ("*Sich bei dieser Unternehmung vorzüglich ausgezeichnet haben*" ["excelled in fulfilling that requirement"]): Sambor, Stryy, Zhovkva, Zalshitzki, and Zamosc. The following districts managed to fulfill their quota, despite numerous obstacles: Rzeszów, Tarnow, Sendetz[?], Buchania, and Myslenice. Unlike the ministers of the districts listed above, the district minister of Ternopil (like the district ministers of Lviv, Zolochiv, and Stanislaw) received a harsh reprimand and a warning to immediately settle the required number of Jewish families and collect, from the community, the annual contribution of 62 florins and 30 kreuzers per family[33]. However, all of the reprimands and warnings did not bear fruit. In 1882, only 10 families remained in their settlements. All of these families were fully supported by the community[34].

Like all other Galitsia districts and cities, the heavy tax burden caused a deterioration in the economy of the Jewish population in Ternopil. In addition to the "Tolerance-Tax" [a tax that Jews had to pay to be "tolerated"], the Jews were obligated to pay paid all sorts of other fees and taxes. Most of the Jews made a living as bartenders. Often, the number of Jewish families was the same as the number of taverns.

[Columns 39-40]

The government did not object to that since forbidding the Jews from working as bartenders meant a reduction in the treasury's revenues.

In terms of tax collection, Ternopil was considered one of the large communities during the initial period of the Austrian regime. The large communities were allowed to appoint, for the purpose of Kosher meat tax collection, a dedicated official with an annual salary of 200 florins and a Jewish clerk earning 350 florins annually[35].

A "Tolerance Tax" of 11,395 florins was imposed on 2279 Jewish families of the Ternopil district in 1790 alone. Only 10,227 florins were actually collected, resulting in a debt of 1,168 florins. A debt of 482 florins was also carried over from 1789[36]. The authorities in Lviv then suspected that the communities bribed the officials to postpone the payment of the debts. The suspicion grew particularly after the community asked to leave the district office in Ternopil, at the same time when the authorities were contemplating moving it from there in October 1790. The communities accounts were audited to investigate whether the officials received any gifts.

An additional factor that contributed to the deterioration of the economic situation of Ternopil's Jews in that era resulted from the declaration of Brody as a free city (*zollpolitik*). The result was that the merchants in Brody, who were the main customers in fairs, stopped attending the fairs at Ternopil, which adversely affected the economy of the city and the Jews of Ternopil. Therefore, the city owner, Seweryn Potowtski, submitted an application in the name of all Ternopil residents to the Viennese government at the end of October 1781. In that application, he asked: "Pease show us kindness, and allow Brody merchants to attend the month-long fairs". The appeal included a request that the merchants pay the consumption tax (*konsum zalle*) only on the sold goods and a transit tax on unsold goods" (that was not allowed according to the tax regulations of Galitsia from 1778 (paragraph 58).

In a report from November 1781, the [district] commission announced (in support of Ternopil's request) that paragraph 58 was meant to be applied only to merchants coming from abroad, Therefore, the government should allow Brody merchants to attend the fairs in Ternopil. The commission further explained that although Brody's people were considered residents of an excluded [free] region (*ausgeschlossens Gebiet*), they were still subjects of the emperor, and as such, they should enjoy the privileges enjoyed by other citizens. The emperor accepted the commission proposal based on his court presentation of the appeal[37].

According to a political census (*politische Conscription*) held by the Galitsian governor in 1788, the district of Ternopil (the city and the 8 affiliated communities) contained 2596 Jewish families. These families consisted of 2485 men, 2548 women, 1055 boys and 935 girls above the age of one year, and 2123 boys and 1960 girls younger than one year. In addition, the census counted 678 male helpers and 678 female helpers, 69 registered male beggars, and 148 female beggars. Altogether – 6380 males and 6374 females. According to the census, there were 1530 families of type 1, 981 of type 2, 111 of type 3, and 575 poor families.

We learn about the growth of the Jewish population by comparing its numbers to those of 1765 when the last Polish census took place[38].

Jews worked mostly as bartenders or in retail commerce. However, the number of Jewish artisans, other than tailors or bakers, continued to grow, and the number of Jews employed in other occupations became substantial.

The Patent from 9 February, 1784 [a constitution of the Austrian Empire promulgated in the form of letters patent] included the prohibition of the production and sale of mead, liquors, and beer by Jews and set the deadline date as the beginning of 1787. The decree included an exception for city Jews who had personally worked as bartenders at their homes, as of 5 November 1784. The permit was provided only to them for life and it was not transferable. It also required a special license from the district offices. The decree meant an economic disaster for thousands of Jews throughout Galitsia.

The community leaders of Lviv decided to submit an appeal to Vienna, contesting the decree. The leaders submitted that appeal in the name of all the Jews in the state. Though orders had been already issued, the governor recommended approving the appeal stating that implementing the decree would leave thousands of Jews without the means to make a living. That would force them to seek employment in despicable professions. The governor recommended delaying the implementation of the decree by three years and allowing the Jews already employed in the sale of liquors to continue their employment in that profession for life. The governor claimed that the government should not blame the Jews for causing drunkenness among the peasants. He stated that the blame should be placed on the estate owners who leased the taverns to the Jews to increase their revenues by all means possible. The authorities in Vienna did not accept these claims, stating that the Jews had a sufficient amount of time since 1772 to seek other occupations. Nevertheless, they submitted a request to the emperor to postpone the implementation of the decree until the end of 1787. To avoid bad publicity, they suggested not publicizing the delay. The emperor rejected the claim and ordered on 29 January 1787 to immediately execute the decree without any delay.

[Columns 41-42]

The emperor declared that estate owners who would not strictly implement the decree, and hold on to Jewish lessees, would be punished[39].

In 1791, the authorities prohibited the Jews from residing in villages and leasing taverns, brewers, and flour mills there. That decree harshly hurt the Jews economically. The communities in Galitsia, including Ternopil, sent a delegation to Vienna who submitted a written request to annul that decree. Their application was rejected by the authorities. They used the excuse that the Jews were not allowed to nominate their own representatives without a license from the government[40].

Despite the severe punishments, the Jews found ways to continue selling liquors in the villages. They succeeded to such an extent that many years later, in 1828, the authorities found it necessary to contact the district ministers to explain why the Jews violated the prohibition so frequently? The authorities asked for means that should be taken to combat that phenomenon. The district minister of Ternopil understood well what his officials understood - that the Jewish bartenders are not allowed to work in other professions. He recommended abolishing the ban, particularly since the Jews were not exploiting the peasants like in the previous generations. He stated that if the prohibition cannot be abolished, the Jews who violate it should be deported out of the country[41]. The truth was that this prohibition was not enforced in all cases because the estate owners were interested in owning taverns and liquor distillers, and they were the ones that helped the Jews evade this decree.

In addition to the displacement of the Jews from their traditional occupations, the authorities imposed compulsory army service and new taxes. One such tax was the candle tax, which was imposed according to the suggestion by the school supervisor, Hertz Homberg, who received 2% of that revenue.

The tax burden kept increasing year after year and oppressed the Jews in Ternopil.

Therefore, the Jewish population breathed a sigh of relief when Ternopil and its district were transferred to Russia in 1809.

In 1788, Hertz Homberg opened the first [secular] Jewish school (*Jüdische Normalschule*) in Ternopil. Hirsh Eizenshtetter, who received an annual salary of 200 florins, was employed as a teacher in the school[42].

In 1806, all of the Jewish schools in Galitsia, including the school in Ternopil, were abolished. During the same period, the enlightened Yosef Perl began his efforts to establish a Jewish school based on his views about Jewish education.

Perl was not a fan or follower of Hertz Homberg the "enlightenment pioneer" in Galitsia, and his [assimilating] entourage. He did not communicate with him personally and absolutely objected to Homberg's educational method [which did not have any Jewish content]. That method was resented by the Jews. In his youth, Perl saw with his own eyes that Homberg's school, "which was founded by an order from the top in 1786", did not have any influence. Perl himself did not study in any elementary school.

In 1729, when Perl was still a young man, he accompanied the Ternopil district's rabbi, R' Shmuel, son of Moshe-Pinkhas Falkenfeld in his visit to the home of Polish noble Franciszek Korytowski (owner of the Plotitz estate and later the owner of Ternopil). The Polish noble asked the rabbi: "why aren't the Jewish people interested in general education and why are most of their teachings religious in nature?" The noble also asked: "why weren't the Jews involved in agriculture and why didn't they wish to be like the rest of the people?"[43]

These questions did not leave any impression on the rabbi and the Jewish community leaders since they all adhered to their tradition and customs and considered those questions by Christians to be antisemitic in nature.

However, Perl himself, was still a young man then, "whose heart was still open and full of feeling". He did not think that the questions were antisemitic. He considered the questions by the Christians as coming from true concern, and the wish of transforming the Jews to be educated and happy people. That view motivated him to study and become proficient in general secular sciences and languages. He was already thinking about the need to establish a secular school for the Jewish youth. Since he frequented Vienna for his business, he began his efforts there, during the years 1808 – 1809[44], to receive a government permit for a school. However, the war [The "War of the Fifth Coalition" was a European conflict - a part of the Napoleonic Wars] put his efforts on hold.

[Columns 43-44]

E.

The 1809 war between Austria and Napoleonic France ended with a treaty signed on 14 October 1909 in Schönbrunn, Austria. According to the treaty, Austria lost western and southern areas. It also lost substantial areas in Eastern and Western Galitsia to Napoleon's allies, the Russians and the Duchy of Warsaw. The Duchy of Warsaw annexed the districts of Krakow and Zamość (altogether an area of 961 million square miles). Russia received an area in Eastern Galitsia originally annexed by Austria during the First Polish Partition (with a population of about 400,000 people). It was agreed that the final borders would be determined by representatives of Austria and Russia. Russia, which was interested in getting a foothold in eastern Galitsia for a long time, was finally given its wish.

On 9 October 1809, the Austrian delegation to mark the borders was chosen in the emperor's bureau. The delegation consisted of two commissioners: Field marshal Friedrich-Heinrich Graf Bellegrada, and Graf Christian Wurmser, who was the civil governor of Galitsia during the period 1806 – 1809. The advisor and the head of the presidential commission in Lviv, Ernest Bogopel Kortum, a true bureaucrat from the period of the Austrian regime, joined the delegation as an official and secretary for special services. His office was relocated to Bielsko-Biala, as Lviv was still held by the Russian army.

Colonel Stavitski was sent as the Russian representative. It was decided, by the representatives of both countries, as early as 11 November 1909, that the district of Ternopil would be handed over to Russia. The district minister was then Baron von Dykeh. The Russian forces headed by Prince Golitsyn took over the Ternopil district on 15 December 1809.

The entire province was officially transferred to Russia on 15 June 1810. Its total size was 121 million square meters, 65 million of that was from the Ternopil district, 2 million square miles from parts of the Zolochiv district, Berezhany (7 msm), and Zalishchyky (47 msm). The province included 7 cities[45], 25 towns, and 484 villages (altogether 516 settlements). It contained a population of 349,015 people, 60,508 houses, 54,711 horses, 9 mules, 38,030 oxen, 35,028 cows, and 98,453 sheep. Overall, it was a valuable asset. There were two estate holdings of the Austrian government in the province. The first, the estate of Ust'ye / Biskopia, was valued at an estimated 3,523,934 florins. The other was part of the village Biala near Chortkiv, valued at 122,500 florins. [Before the war], the Jewish Ignaz Bronstein wanted to purchase the latter[46]. He offered a third of its value, so Emperor Franz [Joseph] ordered to cease the negotiations since the offer demonstrated disrespect for the kingdom.

Following province's official handover and the retreat of the Austrian armies from their bases, the Russian civil representative, Senator Ignazi Theyls arrived at Ternopil on May 10, 1810. He was tasked to organize the civil administration and was nominated as the provincial governor.

On 11 May 1810, Theyls published a proclamation, on his own initiative but in the name of the Russian government, that the Russian Tzar would like to award his new subjects the rights enjoyed by other nations under his rule. Disputes erupted between him and the Austrian representative, Baron von Dykeh, so the latter left Ternopil in 1810.

In fact, the population was satisfied with the new regime after the oppressive regime of the Austrian bureaucracy. Theyls, who ruled Ternopil for more than 5 years (from 15 June 1810 until 6 August 1815), first made an effort to organize his administration according to the Russian format, employed in other Russian states. Before coming to Ternopil, he served as the governor of the Bialystok District, which was annexed by Russia in 1807. Therefore, Theyls had substantial administrative experience. He was an ethnic German from Courland and was very familiar with the structure of the Prussian and Austrian administrations. He tried his best not to abolish the administrative bodies of Austria at once. He actually kept the district offices but nominated Russian officers to replace the Austrian emperor's officials (*Hauptmann*). Unlike the Austrian officialdom, he strove to maintain good relations with the Polish nobility, because he considered that the best way to bolster the Russian rule. Based on that principle, he established the "Ternopil Committee" ("*komitet Tarnopolsky*"), which consisted mainly of Polish nobles, as the highest-ranked ruling body. He also awarded the lower-ranked positions to Poles and set Polish as the official language of verbal and written communication with the population, replacing German. By implementing these changes, he managed to gain the support of the Poles.

[Columns 45-46]

The Polish Mikhael Starzynski, a member of the Polish Sejm and the assistant to Governor Theyls in Bialystok, was nominated to be the assistant of the governor Theyls in Ternopil. His role was to mediate between the Russian authorities and the Polish nobility. Despite the above-mentioned liberal steps, the main objective of the Russians was to eventually annex the province to Russia.

On 29 July 1810, an official ceremony of the swearing of the population to be loyal to the Russian Tzar was conducted in Ternopil. The Jewish population was sworn in the big synagogue in Ternopil.

The province was partitioned into three counties: Terebovlia [Trembowla], Ternopil, and Zalishchyky, each headed by a "*Gorodnitzi*"[?]. In Zalishchyky – Pavel Bartosiewicz, In Terebovlia – Jan Hilferding, and in Ternopil – Zankovski. The committee bureau in Ternopil consisted of four departments handling civil, judicial, political, and governmental affairs. An office of Senator Theyls was located in Ternopil near the district committee bureau.

To gain the support of the Polish nobility, besides the district committee and offices, another institution – the "Nobility Marshal" (*marszalek szlachjty*) was established. The noble marshal was selected from among the estate owners in the three counties, nominated by Theyls, and approved by the Tzar.

Franciszek Korytowski, who bought Ternopil from the Potowtski family in the 19th century, was elected governor of Ternopil county.

There were no major changes in the administrative area. In fact, the same administration institutes remained from the Austrian regime. One change was introduced in the organization of the Judicial system - a municipal court was established in the city of Ternopil. The court consisted of the mayor and four advisors – two Christians and two Jewish. The Russians did not introduce any major changes in the taxes. In terms of taxes on Jews, the "Tolerance Tax" and the "Class-Tax" (*klasowy*) remained, both with a 50% addition. These taxes were in addition to other taxes and fees imposed on the Jews during Austrian rule. Unlike the custom during the Austrian regime, the collection of Jewish taxes was not leased. The authorities did not evaluate the ability of the taxpayers to pay the taxes. Instead, evaluation committees consisting of the population representative were tasked to do that. Taxes were paid directly to the government treasuries. To prove the superiority of their financial administration over the Austrian financial administration (which went bankrupt in 1811) the authorities collected only paper currencies according to the exchange rate of two paper Rubles per Rubel coin.

Compulsory military service was imposed only on the Christian population. In general, the Jews enjoyed reprieves that were not available during Austrian rule. There were 13 Jewish communities in the county of Ternopil, where no changes were imposed by the Russians. It is no wonder, therefore, that the Jews liked Governor Theyls. Thanks to his efforts, the Russian government abolished all the restrictions the Austrians imposed on the Jews and allowed them the freedom of purchasing homes and lands. Moreover, it approved all purchases even in cases when the sellers were Christians[47]. During that period, Ternopil and Zalishchyky Jews purchased, with the approval of the Russian government, 57 houses from the Christians[48].

At that period, there was not even a single school in the entire province of Ternopil[49]. Two government schools in Ternopil and Zalishchyky were closed to save money. Yosef Perl decided then to renew his efforts to establish a Jewish school.

Yosef Perl was the most prominent figure in the life of the Jewish public at that time. He was born in 21 Kheshvan 5534 (1773) in Ternopil. His father, R' Todros was a wine merchant, and for some time, the lessee of the Meat-Tax[50] and mills in Ternopil. As a pious Jew and a stubborn "*Mitnaged*" [Opponent to Hassidism] he gave his son a traditional education.

Yosef, who worked in his father's business, used to travel to Hungary where he bought wines and Vienna where he sold honey, milk, wax, and agricultural products. Later on, he partnered with his father and his brother-in-law, R' Yitzkhak-Leib Atlas. He also was a lease holder, which acquired him some opponents in the city who complained to the authorities that he oppressed the citizens[51]. He succeeded in his businesses and amassed a vast fortune.

In his youth, he aquatinted himself with the traditional Haredi *melamed's* [religious teachers] and the teaching methods in the *Kheders*. The stories of Sheftel Horowitz made great impressions on Yosef Perl in his youth. Horowitz authored the book: "Vavei Ha'Amudim" ["Columns with Vav-Shaped - Struts" - The holy temple contained columns headed by struts in the shape of the Hebrew letter Vav] about his father the SHLAH [Yeshaia ben Avraham Ha-Levi Horowitz, known as the SHELAH after his book "Shnei Lukhot HaBrit" ["The Two Tablets of the Covenant"]. In the book, Horwitz stated that his father was jealous of the Sephardic Jews in Amsterdam who maintained the school "Etz Khaim" ["Tree of Life"]. In that school students, learned religious [and modern] studies according to an organized curriculum and teaching methods.

[Columns 47-48]

Since reading the book, Yosef Perl dreamt about establishing a similar school in Ternopil[52]. Besides the Talmud and the rabbinic literature, he studied Kaballah books and became a Hassidic Jew, much to the displeasure of his father. The latter accepted him as a partner in his businesses to distance him from the Hassidim and Hassidism.

In 1801, Perl traveled to Brody on his father's business and met the enlightened poet Dov Ginsburg (1776 – 1811) there. Under the poet's influence, Perl became close to the enlightened circles. During his trip to Brody, Lviv, and Zhovkva, he got to know Mendel Lefin, Nakhman Kromkhel, S. Y. Rappaport, Ya'akov Shmuel Bik, Yitzkhak Erter, and Shimshon Blokh.

Perl studied languages and secular sciences leaving Hassidism entirely and becoming its enemy. However, he did not abandon tradition, although he was not pious or Haredi. He insisted on keeping realistic commandments and was an opponent of the Brody's [assimilating] enlightened, who abandoned tradition and religion altogether. These differences of opinion were the reason for the hatred Brody's enlightened felt towards him. As mentioned in Dr. Letris's book[53]: "He resented the people in Brody and its leaders. While Perl came to know his advocate and admirer, Dov Ginsburg, Brody people complained and talked about the fact that they disagreed with Ginsburg's opinion".

As mentioned above, in 1809, Perl took the first steps while in Vienna, to secure a permit to establish a Jewish school based on his teaching philosophy. However, war events put an end to his efforts then. He renewed his efforts during the Russian rule. Undoubtfully, Yosef Perl was helped by the enlightened author Mendel Lefin (1749 – 1826), who resided in Brody and Ternopil at the time. After all, it was Lefin, who proposed in 1792 to establish a Jewish school as part of his plan for remedying the Jewish situation. The plan was formed, in the Polish Sejm in 1788 – 1792, under the initiative of Adam Czartoryski, for the "Committee for the Solution to the Jewish Problem". Lefin considered establishing Jewish schools as the most effective mean to change the lifestyle of Polish Jews. The schools were meant to direct the Jews towards becoming useful citizens by remedying their social and professional status[54]. Perl's ideas, mentioned in his memorandums during the Russian rule and later on to the Austrian authorities, were similar to Menakhem Lefin's proposal.

In 1812, he alerted the Jews in Ternopil about the need to establish the school. In his proclamation, he announced that: "Anybody who is not blinded or dazzled [by religious views], must admit that the traditional education and teaching of the Jewish children are harming their bodies and souls. The influence of the *melameds* and their helpers is absolutely harmful. It is a miracle that we can still find decent and educated people among the Jews". In his proclamation, Perl mentioned R' Yeshaia Horowitz, the author of SHELAH ["Shnei Lukhot Ha'Brit"], who commented on the sorry state of the Jewish education in Poland and demanded to emulate the Jews in Amsterdam, who established schools where the Jewish youths enjoyed systematic and organized modern schooling. The [district] governors also showed their interest in improving the poor state of education among the Jews and tried to improve it. The Russian Tzar, in his order form 9 December 1804, promised: "that improvements in the education of the Jewish youths would be executed with fatherly love". He recognized that [a modern] education can lift the Jewish nation from its degraded state. The Tzar indicated that the time had come for actions by taking advantage of the encouragement given by various elements in the society. Perl discussed his views with many people, who expressed willingness to help, according to their ability, to establish an educational institution. He also found many influential supporters among the Christians, who were willing to contribute to that effort. Perl announced that he had already purchased an appropriate land on Zbarazh Street. He turned to Ternopil Jews to contribute, each according to his ability, to the construction of the building. At the end of his proclamation, Perl proposed to form a committee to manage the project[55].

Perl turned to Korytowski, whom he knew from his youth when the latter served as the Ternopil [district] governor, and at the end of the Russian rule, as the governor of the entire province. He requested that Korytowski help finance a Jewish school. It is logical to assume that Korytowski assisted him in his lobbying Senator Theyls.

In his memorandum[56] issued in 1812, Perl expressed his negative view of the traditional Jewish pedagogical methods. He described, in detail, the essence of the education in the Jewish *Kheders*, including their physical appearance, the *melameds*, and their teaching method. He gave a gloomy picture [of the traditional Jewish education system]. Perl judged the people involved with the traditional Jewish education field harshly and called them – "people with no integrity, loafers, who lack any pedagogical training and general knowledge". Perl mentioned that the only exceptions were those *melameds* who taught Gemarah, which required good skills. Despite its inadequacy, that education system involved substantial costs (maintenance of *Kheders* buildings, teaching tools, salaries for the *melameds* and their assistants, etc. …).

Despite Perl's objection to the education in the *Kheders*, he was not a fan of the pedagogical methods of Hertz Homberg and his teachers, who generally lack knowledge and education. Perl called them "lustful gangs". He considered them "the new anti-Semites" who "poison the youth and trample with their feet, everything good"[57]. Perl's objectives were not to educate scholars, but people with practical knowledge, good Jewish citizens with good virtues, by "teachers who are loyal friends

[Columns 49-50]

of our nation". He considered the Talmud as a basis for the tradition and insisted on teaching it in his school. He also proposed that the students were to be tested on their Talmud knowledge every half a year by the district rabbi. He adopted fierce criticism against the extremist views of Homberg's teachers regarding religious studies.

Perl was interested in pedagogic literature and searched for the golden path for the Jewish school that would meet the requirements of the Jewish people. His view was that the school should blend general and Jewish studies without violating the principles of the Jewish religion. His opinion was that the school's objective was to teach the students practical professions.

Senator Theyls received Perl's proposal amiably because of the desire of the Russian government to gain the support of all parts of the population, including the Jews.

Theyls particularly liked the plan laid out in Perl's memorandum from 1812. In that memorandum, Perl explained the shortcomings of the traditional education system on one side and the deficiencies of the schools founded by Homberg on the other. Theyls also liked the way Perl expanded on his views about pedagogical methods, based on a gradual approach of acceptance rather than through enforcement.

In his memorandum, Perl indicated that the curriculum for boys should be based on the Jewish tradition and the Hebrew language. He recommended having a house of prayer at the school, like the one established by Israel Jakobson (1768 – 1828) in his school in Seesen am Hartz. His view was that a house of prayer would enhance the parents' trust in the school. In addition, any revenues from the house of prayer could contribute school's budget. In establishing that house of prayer, he later laid down the foundation for a modern synagogue in Ternopil. Prayers in that synagogue were conducted silently, as opposed to other Galitsian synagogues, in which it was customary to shout while praying. The district rabbi gave several sermons during the year in that synagogue[58].

According to Perl's memorandum, the proposed school would contain four classes, and studies would last eight years [for boys]. The teaching language would be German. The Hebrew studies would include grammar, the bible (with German commentary and translation), and starting with the third year, Mishna with light commentary. Besides Yiddish writing, the general studies would include reading, arithmetic, calligraphy, and accounting. Beginning with the fourth year the curriculum would also include household and farming management, natural history, geography, and rhetoric. Studies would include French and Polish and also Italian and music electives. Perl also intended to establish an additional class for school graduates who wished to become proficient in rabbinical studies. Perl suggested that a city rabbi or a Talmud scholar[58] would teach that class.

Perl proposed that the learning for girls would be five years long (ages 5 – 10). The curriculum would include only German and Russian, as well as some religious studies and ethics, Yiddish writing, household management, arithmetic, and handcraft.

Perl insisted that the teachers would meet the requirements of an appropriate level. He also insisted that the teachers would receive wages that would enable adequate livelihood. He proposed that the school budget would be covered by a minor raise in the Meat-Tax, and tuition imposed on the wealthy children. The poor children would be exempted from paying tuition. An overseeing committee would consist of municipal representatives, the Ternopil school committee members, and the school principal.

The construction of the building commenced following Theyls' approval. It was financed by contributions from Christian philanthropists and wealthy Ternopil Jews, particularly merchants, whose economic situation improved remarkably during the Russian rule (their trade with Russia brought substantial revenues). Perl himself, whose wealth increased substantially during that period "due to profitable businesses"[59], contributed large sums. Money was also secured from the sale of seats in the house of prayer. Perl provided the school with six rooms in his private home until the completion of the construction. The school opened in September 1813 with 16 students[60].

In 1814, the number of students grew to 24, and in the following year to 36. The school building was inaugurated on the holiday of Shavuot [September] 1815. It contained a house of prayer with 130 seats for men and 63 for women.

Ya'akov Neiman was nominated as principal[61]. The teachers were: Moshe Friehling[62], and two Talmud teachers – Yitzkhak Mikhael Munies[63], and Meir Koreh. The latter was replaced in 1816 by Shimon Reis.

[Columns 51-52]

After Neiman left the school in 1817, no new principal was nominated. Only in 1820, Perl agreed to take on himself the management of the school. Moshe Friehling was nominated as the acting principal.

A fourth teacher, Moshe L. Shulbaum, who was previously a teacher in Dynow, was nominated as the fourth teacher in the school.

In 1814, a teacher of the Polish language and crafts, Elizhbieta Shyemanovska, joined a teacher of the girls' class. The Hebrew author Aryeh Leib Kinderfreind[64] served as a teacher in the school for a few years (1788 – Zamosc [Zamoshetz], 1837 – Brody).

In 1815, Perl published a pamphlet in German containing a review of the curriculum and teaching methods:

"*Kurze Übersicht des in der Tarnopler Freyschule israelitischen Freyschule eigngefuehrten Lehrplans, nach dem der Unterricht, in allen Classen dieser Schule, ertheilt wird. Zur Befriedigung derjenigen, die von dieser Lehranstalt eine genauere Kenntnis zu haben wuenschen herausgegeben.*" ["A short review of the curriculum of the Ternopil Free Jewish Day School, according to which the instruction in all classes of this school is given. Published for the satisfaction of those who wish to know more about this school."].

Perl drew special attention to the religious studies portion of the curriculum, as he appreciated the importance of the Talmud in the Jewish people's life. The school also issued a pamphlet about the rules of behavior in the school:

"*Verhaltungmassregln für die Schüler des Tarnopoler iaralitischen Freyinstituts, wie solche sich in ihrem ganzen Betrugen, sowohl zu Hause als beim Gebete, wie auch in der Schule, vor, waehrend und nach dem Unterrrichte aufzfuehren haben. Gezogen aus den Schulgesetzen, zur bequemen Uebersicht der Buchdrueker und Buchhaendler*" ["Rules of conduct for the students of Ternopil Free Jewish Day School regulate how the students should behave at home, in prayer, and at school, before, during, and after the lessons. Taken from the school laws, for a convenient overview of book printers and book dealers."], (1815)

Perl also edited and published the textbooks for the school since the textbooks for the general school have not suited to the needs of the Jewish school in Ternopil[65].

The Russian authorities greatly appreciated Perl's work and treated him with extraordinary fondness. Therefore, it is no wonder that Tzar Alexander I awarded him, on 20 September 1816 (a year after Ternopil was returned to Austria), a gold medal as an appreciation for his educational and cultural work during the Russian conquest[66].

In addition to his educational work, Perl devoted time to literacy work. During the years 1814 – 1816, he published a Hebrew magazine for the youth called "Tzir Ne'eman" ["Faithful Envoy"].

With these projects, Perl laid down the foundation for the fame of Jewish Ternopil as an important center of the enlightened movement processes in Galitsia for 33 years.

According to the Austrian-Russian treaty agreement, signed in Vienna on 3 May 1815, Russia returned (paragraph I) the entire Ternopil province to Austria. That paragraph was added (as paragraph V) to the final treaty agreement of the Viennese Congress on 9 June 1815.

F.

After the Viennese Congress signed the final agreement, the Austrian authorities ordered the Austrian governor in Galitsia, Baron Frantz Hauer, to make all the necessary preparations for the transfer of the Ternopil province back to Austria. However, Senator Theyls, who had never accepted his government's relinquishment of the Ternopil province, did not forgive the Tzar, or mainly the Tzar's advisors, for allowing the Tzar to make such a shameful Russian policy mistake. He acted on his own and imposed many difficulties during the implementation of the province return. He notified the Lviv representative of the Austrian governor that he had not received any instructions from Saint Petersburg about the transfer of the province. He had notified Lviv that the instructions for the transfer had been received only on July 25th, 1815,

Companies of the Austrian army entered Ternopil on July 30th, 1815. A proclamation by Theyls about the transfer of the province was issued on August 6th. The formal transfer of the province to Austria was completed with the hoisting of the Austrian national emblems on the government buildings.

In the negotiations between the Austrian representatives and Theyls, the latter did not show any courtesy. He demanded to receive the sums of money of all taxes for which the due dates were before June 20th. However, the Austrian representatives refused to forego these quite substantial sums.

As in any other transition period, the Jews suffered the most. The Cossacks oppressed them, the customs inspectors harassed them with accusations that they were smuggling goods, and extorted money from them. Theyls responded to the Austrian complaints about these attacks that he issued specific rules about people who were violating the law. The Austrians, who had already encountered his negative stance, did everything they could to get rid of him as soon as possible.

The accounting agreement with the Russian administration was signed on August 19th, 1815. Senator Theyls and the chairman of the Ternopil's committee, Baumgarten left the city on August 22nd.

[Columns 53-54]

With that, the Russian rule ended, and Ternopil became an Austrian city again.

After the transfer of Ternopil to Austria, the Jews continued to pay the same taxes they had paid under Russian rule. The Jews were requested to pay a meat tax of 120,808 florins and a candle tax of 96,108 florins from November 1st, 1815 to October 31st, 1816[67].

The community submitted a request to reduce the supplement on the Tolerance Tax by 90,046 florins because the leased taxes provided the government with a sum of 104,564 florins, which was budgeted. By doing that, there were sufficient amounts left to cover the Tolerance Tax. The request was denied by the government[68].

A more complicated issue was the houses purchased during the Russian rule. In 1805, a decree was issued which forbade Jews in towns and cities of Galitsia, except Brody, from purchasing houses. The decree also disallowed Jews to purchase houses owned by Christians who wanted to sell their houses, which they originally bought from Jews, back to Jews. During the Russian rule, the authorities did not enforce the ban and approved every purchase made by Jews.

On 16 December 1816, the governor's office in Lviv issued a regulation, which required all the homeowners who bought the houses [from Christians during the Russian rule] to sell them back to Christians.

After the regulation has been publicized, 57 homeowners in Ternopil and Zalishchyky submitted a request to approve the houses they bought during the Russian rule from Christian sellers. The homeowners supported their request by the claim that the Russians annulled the Austrian laws concerning the Jews and approved the purchases.

Galitsia governor in Lviv was convinced by these claims and proposed to allow the Jews to keep the houses they owned, beyond the letter of the law. He stated that the request would be approved for purchases that had been registered and approved, with the Ternopil's real-estate register, before 6th August 1816 [should be 1815?], and in Zalishchyky before August 8th, 1816 [should be 1815?].

The central authorities did not agree with the governor's proposal. They only approved the house purchase by Ya'akov Neiman, who was the principal in Perl's school, because of his rights in education.

However, after negotiations, the central authorities acceded and allowed the homeowners to keep their houses for life. However, the houses would have to eventually be sold only to Christians[69].

The following Court bureau's resolution was announced on 14 April 1818: "Jews residing in Ternopil district, who acquired Christian houses during the Russian rule, and registered their purchase by 6 August 1815 in Ternopil and by 8 August 1815, in Zalishchyky (the dates by which the province was returned to Austria), and thus formalized their legal ownership of their house, are hereby receiving a confirmation of their legal ownership for life. However, if the house is sold, it must be sold only to Christians"[70]. That was how the painful problem was solved.

Additional problems arose besides the issue of house ownership. There were cases that the Russian authorities awarded Jews to occupy professions forbidden for them by the Austrian regime. For example, the Austrians did not allow Jews to own printing houses (except in Lviv). During the Russian conquest, in 1812, Nakhman Finlish, a relative of Yosef Perl, was awarded the privilege to establish a German-Hebrew printing house in Ternopil[71]. That printing house was established because of the closure of the Hebrew printing house in Zbarazh, which existed for only one year – 1811. When the printing house was transferred to Ternopil in 5573 [1812], it was owned by the two partners, Ya'akov Auerbakh and Nakhman Finlish. The printer R' Benyamin son of Avigdor from Zbarazh was also connected to that printing house. The first Hebrew book printed in Ternopil was probably the book [by Yitzkhak son of Yehuda Halevi]: "Pa'ane'akh Raza" ["Decode the Enigma"] (5571 [1810/11]). The following attribution appeared at the end of the book: "The workers from Zbarazh at the new printing house in the holy community of Ternopil". The workers were Mordekhai, son of Tzvi-Hirsh, and the young man Arye-Leib, son of David. Finlish, who leaned toward enlightenment, became the partner of Yosef Perl, who printed in his printing house the calendar and several pamphlets. Starting 5574 [1813], the ownership of the printing house was transferred wholly to Finlish and his partner left the business"[72].

Nakhman Finlish requested [the Austrian authorities] to approve the privilege awarded to him by the Russians. The Austrian government approved his request on July 1st, although, according to the specific regulations, "a Jew is allowed to work in that profession [printing] only in Lviv"[73].

Life returned to normal slowly. Ternopil was a major community (*hauptgemeindeh*). The following towns were affiliated with the city: Strusiv, Tovste [Tluste], Tarnoruda, Kopychintsi, Dolina [Yanov], and several small Jewish settlements in surrounding villages.

A committee of three members headed the community. The members were elected for three years. The election was held on 15 September, every three years. The people who were allowed to participate in the election were heads of families who purchased a minimum number of candles throughout the year prior (a candle tax was imposed in Ternopil for lighting seven or more candles). The voting right was contingent upon the knowledge of the German language (reading and writing).

[Columns 55-56]

It was also contingent on paying the candle tax (in Ternopil - for at least 10 candles in the year before the election).

The community leaders received – depending on the ability of the community – an annual salary. In addition, they enjoyed exemptions from the meat tax and the candle tax, everything according to the views of the district minister.

Besides the community leaders, there were other positions in the community, which were filled by an election. These positions included the heads of *Khevra Kadishah* [burial society], the synagogue *gabbai* [administrator], *gabbai* of the hospital, assessors, and accountants. The community administration also included the positions of the secretary, rabbi, *dayanim* [religious judges], and caretakers. The community administration had the authority to represent the Jewish population and defend its rights. It was authorized to sign contracts, handle assistance to the needy, keep an accurate population registry and vital records, collect taxes for which the community leased the collection, supervise the community property, and manage community affairs.

The three *Parnases* [activists – leaders] of the community at that time were Nakhman Finlish, Mendel Cohenberg, and M. Goldberg. The five members of the community committee were: Avish Goldhaber, Menakhem Dinish, Shlomo Shraga, Pinkhas Horwitz, and Zelig Perl.

The rabbinate was headed by Yehoshua-Heschel BABa"D, who was also the district rabbi (*Kreiz-Rabiner*). He enjoyed an annual salary of 225 florins paid by the Ternopil community and its affiliated communities. Besides his salary, he also received special payments for registering births, marriages, and deaths (according to 3 categories: I – 7.5 kreuzers, II – 15 kreuzers, and III – 30 kreuzers), and a fee for certificates. He was exempt from paying any community tax.

The economic state of Ternopil's Jews did not change much [after the takeover by the Austrians]. According to the census from 1824, there were 364 retail merchants, 205 bartenders, and 8 tobacco goods merchants (*trafickanten*). There were 884 merchants in the city of Ternopil alone. Among the 76 large stores registered in Ternopil, 75 were owned by Jews. The number of craftsmen is unknown. In the same year, there were 11,997 Jewish residents and 197,267 Christians.

Most of Perl's effort was dedicated to his school. Upon the takeover by the Austrians, he first strove to obtain a permit from the Austrian authorities. Lviv provincial government's adviser, Alovisi Stutterheim, who received the Ternopil district [from the Russians] and later became the district minister, investigated the state of the school and recommended the governor to approve the request[74]. Nakhman Finlish and Ya'akov Neiman also lobbied on behalf of the school in Lviv immediately after Ternopil returned to Austria.

Following Stutterheim's s initiative, the official overseeing the education committee, Franz Kratter, and the president of the provincial government, Baron Franz Hauer (during his stay in Ternopil in September 1816), visited the school. Stutterheim himself witnessed the students' examination on 19 September 1816. He immediately sent a detailed report to Lviv about his impressions. In his report, Baron Hauer praised the teaching method and the knowledge level of the students.

Perl himself, and his friends in Lviv, did not sit idle and continued their lobbying efforts with the authorities. On 19 October 1815, the provincial government sent a report to the Education Committee (*Studien – Kommission*) in Vienna, in which the following was written: "When the Ternopil and Chortkiv districts were annexed by the Russians, all the schools that were in existence during the Austrian regime, were abolished.

In contrast, a "free Jewish school" (*Israelitische Freyschule*) was established in Ternopil thanks to Yosef Perl's lobbying effort and the assistance by the Russian senator Von Theyls. The school was actually established based on the structure of an Austrian upper-level elementary school (*Hauptschule*). Its objective and program are oriented toward fostering the moral and religious education of the Jewish youth. In addition to the regular classes of an elementary school, they study in that school business and Polish and French languages. An appropriate and sturdy school building was erected. The school is supported by contributions, charity donations, allocations from the kosher meat tax, and Ternopil municipal taxes, which were approved by Senator Theyls to benefit the school enterprise. Von Stutterheim, appointed as the district minister, investigated that educational institution, after the transfer of the province, and recommends approving its continuation"[75].

From the Crown Court's presentation, which was attached in the report's margin, we learn that the provincial government proposed to approve the school as a private school. The approval would be contingent upon having only certified teachers teaching in the school. They also qualified their recommendation on the condition that the school would be operated under the school laws and that the examinations would be public. The provincial government also stated that the school should be placed under the state inspector general, similar to the school in Brody. The province government president, Hauer, supported the provincial government's recommendation with the justification that the German language studies would be more extensive in that school than in the Christian school. He attended an examination and was convinced about the high level of the school. The provincial government's proposal was approved, and the school was recognized under the proposed conditions.

In the meantime, the financial state of the school worsened during the years 1816 – 1817. The principal position was eliminated, and Polish and craft teachers were laid off. The wages were not paid on time, and the deficit grew larger and larger. Until March of 1817, 25,000 florins were invested in the building and furniture.

Perl himself contributed 18,000 florins of his own money. He decided to turn to the government for help, to improve the situation. In a memorandum from 26 March 1817[76], Perl declared that he was willing to hand over the school building and the house of prayer in exchange for the following: 1) A fund of 2000 florins would be established by the community, the interest from which (6%) would support three scholarships, annually.

[Columns 57-58]

2) Perl would receive 3000 florins cash for a period of 5 to 8 years. He would also receive another 800 Rubles he borrowed from the Zbarazh community to finance the construction of the building. 3) Perl would head the school and the praying house for life. He would hire the teachers and would also be allowed to select his successor. 4) Perl and the teachers would be exempt from paying the community taxes. This was supposed to eliminate the possibilities for conflicts. Conflicts could erupt if the management team of the community would fall into the hands of zealots who could harass the enlightened teachers. Perl proposed to establish a school fund which would be financed by the following: a) An addition to the kosher meat tax (the community would collect 2 florins and 15 kreutzers for every bull, 1 florin and 30 kreutzers for a cow, and 7.5 kreutzers for every calf, lamb, and goat); b) from annual tuition of 4 – 9 florins for every student. Poor students would be exempt from paying tuition. According to Perl, the cost budget (for 7 general education teachers, 2 Talmud studies teachers, one assistant, and two caretakers) would be 3,105 florins. He proposed to convert the school from being a private school, to a state-run elementary school, with public privileges under the supervision of the Ternopil Jewish community.

Perl also proposed some changes in the curriculum, such as: adding the study of Italian, drawing, etc. Perl stated in his memorandum that the heads of the community agree to his proposal,

The provincial government supported Perl's proposals before the Learning Commission (*Studien-kommission*) and highlighted Perl's educational accomplishments among Galitsia's Jews and recommended awarding him a medium golden medal. The Learning Commission passed the memorandum to the Emperor's Bureau with an extensive review of its position, clearly emphasizing that Perl intended to convert his school to a public school. The Learning Commission recognized the need to establish a budgetary fund (*Dotationsfund*) with the participation of the Jewish population in Ternopil and the adjacent communities. They recognized the importance of that fund to build a school building that meets the requirements of the school law. However, the commission objected to any addition to the meat tax, which might harm the revenues from that tax. The commission recommended that the deficit in the budget would be covered by voluntary donations from the communities. If that could be accomplished the commission agreed to convert the school to a German-Jewish public upper elementary school (Oeffentliche Deutsche jügische Hauptschule) according to the proposal outlined by Perl and under his management.

Emperor Franz I accepted the commission's recommendations and approved the following resolution in Hermannstadt, in 1817:

"I agree that the Jewish school in Ternopil founded a few years ago, would continue to operate as a Jewish public upper elementary school. My approval is contingent on the establishment of a fund- without relying on canny pressure or coercion and without any addition to the state taxes imposed on the Jews. In terms of governmental supervision, school management, teachers, and study subjects, the school should be organized similarly to the Christian schools. Obviously, instead of the Christian religion studies, the school will teach the Jewish religion. It is, therefore, necessary to allow the Jews to teach subjects that are not taught in the Christian schools. Perl may become the principal of the school. Christian children will not attend the Jewish school"[77].

After Perl had received the approval, he signed an agreement with the Ternopil community on 23 January 1818. In that agreement. Perl transferred the ownership of the school and the house of prayer to the community according to the terms mentioned earlier. Similar agreements were signed with the adjacent communities: Hrymayliv [Gzhimalov], Skalat, Myukulyntsi [Mikulnitza], and Terebovlia [Trembowla]. They were obligated to collect allocations from the meat tax for the school. In return, they were allowed to send their children to school by paying the regular tuition. On 22 December 1819, the community in Zbarazh joined these agreements[78].

On 12 September 1818, the provincial government authorized the "certificate of foundation", which served as the juridical basis for the school. It also contained the approval of the agreements between Perl and the Ternopil community and the adjacent communities mentioned above. The certificate also included the emperor's resolution from 11 September 1817.

After the approval of the "certificate of foundation", Perl received the medal of honor in the shape of a medium golden medal. In 1820, the emperor certified the award of the medal of honor. Along with that, the emperor appointed Perl as the principal of the school with the authority to appoint his successor and the teachers under the approval of the appropriate authority[79].

[Columns 59-60]

When the school became a state public school, it became necessary to adapt its building to conform to the requirements of the state general education system. It was also required to adjust the duration of the studies to four years (for ages 7 – 14). That change resulted in the reduction of Jewish studies.

Perl was not satisfied with the achievement from 8 November 1819. During a stay in Vienna, he visited the chairman of the Learning Commission and gave him a letter with a 60-page memorandum[80]. In that memorandum, Perl described the poor state of Jewish education, particularly in the *kheders*. He repeated the things he wrote in his 1812 memorandum to Senator Theyls. His proposal included the following: a) Abolishment of the education in the *kheders*, b) Formation of schools like the one in Ternopil, where the studies of the Hebrew language and its grammar, the German translated Torah and Talmud are integrated with the general elementary school studies.

He insisted that the Talmud studies would be taught in a way for the students to derive practical benefits. These schools should only employ certified teachers. The uncertified teachers should not be allowed to privately teach students.

Perl proposed to form an assembly (*Synode* [Knesset]) consisting of "cultured and enlightened people of the Jewish nation". The assembly could serve as the representative of the Jewish people towards the government (*als Organ des Jüdischen Volkes bei der Regierung* [an organization of the Jewish people in the government]). That assembly would manage the Jewish religious affairs and supervise the Jewish education system and its institutions.

In an accompanying letter, Perl expressed his opinion that such an assembly could greatly benefit the government by managing the vital records, which was in a state of neglect in Galitsia. It could also provide official explanations about the religious laws and customs. With the help of the assembly, the government could nominate educated rabbis. They could explain the importance of enlisting in the army and similar matters and guide the Jewish masses (which were incited by zealot rabbis, who objected to any improvements in education}. The assembly could also educate the Jews towards forming a positive attitude towards the government.

As usual, Vianna inquired with the provincial governor about his opinion on that matter. The governor raised a concern that the Jews in Galitsia would consider the proposals as an attempt to enforce a religious reform. He warned particularly about possible resistance to the proposition to abolish traditional religious studies and the proposal to establish a Jewish assembly that in fact did smell like a religious reform. For these reasons, the governor did not support the entire proposal. However, he did support the gradual establishment of Ternopil-like schools. He proposed to place the schools not under the supervision of an assembly but the state inspector. He stated that the government should avoid exerting any pressure and coercion. He suggested that the budget should be covered by local sources and not by imposing new taxes.

Vienna authorities accepted the opinion of the governor[81]. They introduced a change – the supervision would be handled by the bureaucracy of state schools.

In the end, nothing came out of Perl's proposal, although, at the request of the governor, Perl stayed in Lviv for a whole year. The governor organized a meeting of the Jewish leaders in Galitsia. The meeting was organized in connection with the new statute for Galatia's Jews. Perl was among the activists who participated in the meeting and proposed various changes[82].

While in Lviv, Perl spoke to Lviv's Rabbi Orenstein about the entablement of moderately oriented schools that incorporate many concerns of the pious Jews. However, his discussions with the rabbi were in vain. The rabbi, in his extreme zealotry, rejected any attempt at a compromise[83].

In his order from 22 January 1820, concerning the changes that were about to be introduced with the new Jewish regulations, the emperor emphasized that in addition to religious studies, the Jewish youth must study in the Christian schools.

On 17 July 1820, Perl turned to the governor with a proposal to establish a [secondary elementary or middle] school in Brody based on Ternopil's example. Perl stated that, in his opinion, such a school was needed there in light of the opening of the Re'ali school [a 2 years Jewish high school]. He noted his belief that, following the establishment of such a school in Brody, it would be easier to establish similar schools in the rest of the cities since Brody served as an example in all other areas. Though the governor valued Perl's aspiration to elevate the education level among the Jews, he rejected the proposal.

In 1821, the issue of the prohibition of traditional attire was on the agenda. The attire question was discussed as part of the changes associated with the implementation of the new Jewish regulations in Austria and particularly in Galitsia. The provincial government proposed, based on the initiative by several wealthy Jews, to disallow the Jews to wear their traditional attire. That was proposed to be enforced before the final decision about the new Jewish regulations.

In 1821, Perl decided to take advantage of the government's attention to Jewish affairs and proposed "an excellent plan for the Jewish schools' reorganization, which were previously abolished". Perl suggested placing the schools under the supervision of the kingdom. He also proposed to allow Jews to send their children to state high schools since he believed that education was the only way by which the state of Jews could be remedied. He also believed that education could lead to the adaption of the Jews to the state's requirements could be achieved.

In his memorandum, Perl repeated his proposal from 1819 to establish a permanent Jewish assembly, consisting of enlightened and dependable people, as the representatives of the Jewish people. Perl proposed that the assembly manage all Jewish affairs, supervise the education system, and represent it towards the state.

[Column 61]

The Viennese government did not accept his plan. It only allowed the Jews to establish, at their expense, Ternopil-like elementary schools, that would be placed under the supervision of the Catholic school system. A short while later, the government agreed that these schools would be placed under the supervision of the district offices[84].

Perl demanded to abolish the examinations about the book "Bnei Tzion" ["Children of Zion"] by Hertz Homberg [1812] that Jews who wished to marry were required to pass. He claimed that it was not logical to put obstacles to marriage. He claimed that it was especially true since the Jewish and the Christian schools could not absorb all the Jewish children. It was also because Jews were not inclined to send their children to these schools anyway. Perl's offer was rejected.

In 1825 – 1826, the government offices in Vienna recommended the establishment of a rabbinical academy based on the example of the academy in Padoa. The Galitsia governor expressed his opinion that the requirement to also study in a Christian academic school would destroy the trust of the Jews in their rabbis. In his opinion rabbis should be requested to show that they had studied in the school in Ternopil.

The governor asked Perl for his opinion on that matter. Perl objected to the idea since most of the rabbis and *melameds* "lack general education" and therefore, the time has not come to establish such an institution[85]. Perl himself intended to establish a special general studies seminary for rabbis and to nominate Rabbi Sh. Y. Rapoport [SHI"R] to head it, but the plan did not materialize because of lack of financial means. Also, the candidacy of SHI"R ceased to be topical, as the latter accepted a position with a meat-tax leasing company in Brody. Perl was upset because he considered it an injustice that SHI"R "consented to allow his name to be used [by a tax leasing company] and agreed work to rob an entire Jewish community". Perl would not call the tax leasing occupation any other name. Generally, Perl considered it "inappropriate for SHI"R to run around in Brody with the butchers"[86].

In 1826, Perl came up with an idea to widen the scope of the school and remove it from the format of regular schools. He planned to establish an institution where students who did not wish to devote themselves to craftmanship or study in colleges could study advanced Hebrew and general education subjects. He intended to nominate a teacher for the Hebrew studies to head the institution and also serve as a preacher in the house of prayer.

In October of the same year, Perl complained to the authorities, that he would not be able to publish textbooks since there were no other schools like the one in Ternopil, elsewhere in Galitsia.

At the same period, the authorities contacted Perl with a question as to whether he would be able

[Column 62]

Yosef Perl

to add a seminary for Jewish teachers to his school. Perl agreed, and in 1833, Perl added another wing to the building and planned to establish the seminary. However, the plan did not come to fruition[87].

In 1833, when a proposal was submitted to the court bureau in Vienna to establish a Jewish philosophy seminary (*Israelitische poilosophische Lehranstalt in Galizien*), the authorities requested Perl's opinion. Perl submitted a counter-proposal to establish a rabbinical seminary of six years of studies of the following subjects: Bible, Mishnah, Jerusalem and Babylonian Talmud's, Poskim [Prominent rabbis' *Halakha* rulings, *Midrashim* [Prominent rabbis' commentaries of the bible and *Halakha*], religious books, Hebrew grammar, style and interpretation, translations, theory of logic, rhetoric and homiletics.

Besides the Jewish studies, Perl proposed to include the following general studies subjects: German language, calligraphy, arithmetic, style theory, general history, geography, natural history, mathematics, accounting, Polish and French languages.

[Columns 63-64]

To cover the budget, Perl proposed the following: a) To collect 1800 florins from the fund of the schools abolished in 1806. b) To annul the decree of examinations as a condition for getting a marriage license, and instead, require to pay a fee to the school fund. C) To impose an obligation on Ternopil Jews who did not send their children to the Jewish school to pay tuition.

His proposals about the budget were rejected by the Viennese Learning Commission[88], and with that, the whole program failed.

Perl was convinced that only a total revamp of elementary education would result in an improvement in the lives of the Jews in Galitsia and advance their standing with the government. He also took care of the vocational education of the youth. Like other enlightened people of his generation, headed by Menakhem Lefin, he understood that the social and professional composition of the Jews must be changed. They had to divorce themselves from occupations in retail mercantilism and peddling. Many should be employed in the production process- craftsmanship and industry, the latter of which began to capture a prominent position in the Galitsian economy during his time.

Perl considered that one of the crucial causes for the poor economic state was the crowding of the Jews in the big cities, especially in Lviv. Jews flocked to Lviv in the hope of finding easier life. His phrase: "*Je mehr Juden in Lemberg desto mehr decrees in Lande.*" ["the more Jews in Lviv, the more decrees in the country"][89], was an accurate description of reality.

In his memorandum to Theyls and the Austrian authorities, Perl first spoke about the need to train the Jewish youth In craftsmanship. For that purpose, he established a special laboratory in his school. He also planned to conduct courses in crafts and establish a special class for that purpose. However, that plan was never materialized.

Perl used the annual profit of 120 florins, derived from the fund of 2000 florins, established as part of the "letter of the foundation' of the school, to place students from his school, who showed tendencies towards craftsmanship, in workshops of Christian craftsmen in Ternopil, Lviv, and even Vienna. Perl chose professions for that program that were not common among the Jews such as locksmithing, tinsmithing, and carpentry. Despite the difficulties and the resistance of the Christian crafts' guilds, the program had some successes. Three locksmiths, two blacksmiths, one glove maker, one builder, and several tinsmiths were trained by that program.

Realizing the possibility for broader activities in that field, Perl developed a plan in 1828 to establish "*Verein yur Verbreitung nütlicher Gewerbe unter der Galityischen Judenschaft*" ["an association for disseminating industry and useful crafts among the Jews in Galitsia"]. He planned to establish the association on the sixtieth birthday of Emperor Franz I (9 February 1828). Perl developed the plan together with R' Mordekhai-Berish Margaliot, who was a member of the commerce court and an agent of a credit union.

On 9th February 1828, Perl and Margaliot were summoned for an interview with the Galitsian commissioner, Prince Lobkowitz. They submitted him a memorandum containing the plan for the establishment of the association. They also proposed to widen the scope of the association to include agriculture[90].

Lobkowitz allowed them to convene a founding meeting, which took place on 12 March 1828. The following prominent people participated in that conference: Dr. Ya'akov Rappoport, D. Epstein, Nathan Kolischer, Dr. Kolischer, and Hertz Ettinger - all of them from Lviv. After the level of membership dues was determined, a committee of three members was established to prepare the association's bylaws.

Perl and Margaliot lobbied for the approval of the bylaws and were seen by Chancellor Metternich (on 1st June 1829).

On 24 July 1832, the court bureau prepared a report[91] about the plan. The report stated that: "Perl proposed to establish an association to disseminate useful crafts among the Jews. According to the association bylaws, a member could join the association by paying a membership fee of 200 florins or upon undertaking a 5% lien on one's real estate assets. Jews from outside of Austria would be allowed to become members of the association[92]. The association was obligated to place poor children who wanted to learn a useful craft and who possessed the required skills, in workshops of craftsmen. That would guarantee appropriate training. The association would cover the living and clothing expenses of the students. It would also pay the required tuition and the craftsmen's guild taxes".

According to the report, wealthy members of the Jewish community had already joined the association and committed to paying the required membership fees. The sum collected became available for the association management, which consisted of the members of the commerce court in Lviv, Markus Margaliot, and others. The association would begin its activities when its capital reached twenty thousand florins.

On 11 April 1833, ten months after the lecture by the court bureau was submitted, the emperor ordered to submit the proposal to the police minister - Sedlintzky. He was tasked with providing his opinion about the association should be established and whether there were no issues associated with its establishment.

Sedlintzky turned, on 4 May 1933, to Lviv's head of police,

[Columns 65-66]

Von Sakher, and asked for his opinion about the association bylaws. The head of police was requested to submit a report about Yosef Perl, his personality, mindset, and standing among the Jews. He was also asked as to whether the association should be allowed to be formed. Sedlintzky received the report two months later and submitted his presentation in writing to the emperor on 8 March 1834[93].

The view of the head of the Lviv police, as detailed in the report, was that the state should not oppose the establishment of the association. He stated that "the establishment of the association was desirable for political and administrative reasons. He also articulated that the association would contribute greatly to the civil assimilation rapprochement of the Jews, including in matters related to the police. That was particularly important since the Jews were politically supportive of the regime. However, he recommended objecting to the second paragraph of the proposed bylaws according to which Jews outside Austrian could join the association. He suggested that government commissars would participate in all association gatherings to protect the interests of the kingdom. The state was interested that its Jewish citizens would assimilate within the general population and become a part of it. That could be achieved by religious, moral, and intellectual education. They could also be directed to occupations that would benefit them and the civil society as a whole. The proposed association would be one of the positive means that would enable achieving that goal. Therefore, he stated that there should be no concern about the establishment of the association, particularly since its members obligated themselves to cover all expenses and would not be a burden on the government. The person who submitted the proposal, Yosef Perl, possessed the appropriate education and had a good name among his people. He was capable and well-positioned to execute the plan and head the association. As a result, Sedlintzky recommended the emperor to approve the establishment of the association, with the change proposed by Lviv's police, which would only allow Jews residing in Galitsia to participate. He also noted that a government commissar reporting to the Galitsian government should always attend the association gatherings".

Despite the recommendation by the police minister, the emperor did not approve the plan. The founders probably failed to raise the necessary sums, and the approval of the request was postponed for years. The approval was finally given on 11 April 1848[94], nine years after Perl passed away.

Although Perl did not succeed in accomplishing all of his educational plans, he exerted a significant influence over the education field's development. Pioneers in many life fields came out from among the school's students: Expert physicians, orthopedic surgeons, and talented teachers who established similar schools outside of Austria,

Based on the example of the school in Ternopil, the following schools were established by its students or under their influence: In 1822, in Uman; in 1927, by Betzalel Stern in Odesa, and Kishinev. Even the famous principal of the Jewish school in Brody, H. Reitman, was a student in the school. It is no wonder that the orthodox Jews were not pleased with his deeds. They considered Perl a person who disseminated impiousness and resisted him with all of their might. Against their resistance, the enlightened called him; "provides food to those hungry for wisdom"[95].

The orthodox Jews conducted a fierce war against Perl and his school, not only in Ternopil. A short while after Ternopil was returned to Austria, Lviv's Rabbi Ya'akov Orenstein announced a public boycott against the schools in Brody. He claimed that the "city was known, for quite some time, to be an incited city", and that "Ternopil already established a school where the youth is unfortunately educated in foreign languages and sciences"[96]. "The school's graduates marry women from Lviv and spread "these foreign ideas" among the youth in Lviv. They incite the youth to read books in foreign languages and get accustomed to foreign customs. To prevent this evil, we announce this big boycott on any heads of families who would wed their son or daughter to people from those two cities". The curses tied to that big boycott were listed at the end of the proclamation. That was how the war was declared against Yosef Perl and his school by the orthodoxy, joined later on by the Hassidim.

In Ternopil itself, people who resisted and boycotted Perl and his school did not walk on the street where the school and the house of prayer were located. The Rabbi of Ternopil, Yehoshua-Heschel BABa"D, and his family also came out against Perl. The rabbi came out often, verbally and in writing that it was forbidden to send children to attend the school.

The community of Zhbarazh submitted an appeal to the authorities in 1819, when the school was awarded a status of a principal Jewish school. The appeal was rejected by Governor Hauer since it was not signed by the heads of the communities but by "Hassidim who object to any form of education"[97].

On August 1827, 23 *Batei Midrash* in Ternopil[98] renewed their resistance to the school and submitted a letter of protest. However, the governor rejected it by claiming that the letter was submitted by Hassidim circles who object to any form of education.

The fiercest resistance came from Rabbi

[Columns 67-68]

Tzvi Eikhenstein aka Zhidachover and his Hassidim. Rabbi Eikhenstein resided then in Podkamin, and he declared a boycott on the enlightened people of Ternopil in 1822[99].

Perl did not sit quietly and decided to take revenge. He found out that an "association against the Jewish school in Ternopil" was founded at that time. He also found out that the head of the "harmful sect of Hassidim, Hirsh Eikhenstein, was invited by the heads of the Zhbarazh community to come and stay in Zhbarazh". On 2 January 1827, Perl persuaded the authorities to warn the heads of the Zhbarazh community that the visit by the rabbi from Zhidachev violated the law (announced by the governor in 1824). The authorities were familiar with Rabbi Eikhenstein from the 1818 case of the smuggling of Hassidic books to Galitsia (in collaboration with the Russian Jew, Ya'akov-Meir). They also knew about him from the letter sent by Rabbi Naphtali from Ropshitz. In that letter, Rabbi Naphtali detailed Rabbi Eikhenstein's "bad thoughts" (At the time, Perl was asked by the authorities to explain the content of the letter). The authorities instructed the Zhbarazh community that if the "misleading" Rabbi shows up in Zhbarazh, they must demand to show them his passport or a trip license. If he would not have one, he must be returned "the way they return prisoners". Even if he had such a certificate and could not explain the reason for his visit, he should be expelled"[100].

In the war against the school, his rivals used all means. Every time the meat tax was raised, they directed the resentment of the masses against the school since part of the addition to the kosher meat tax was given to the school.

The situation became serious on 6th of January when a raise in the meat tax was announced. Somebody declared a boycott, which forbade the Jews from eating meat. Perl's enemies blamed him before the district minister. The district minister threatened Perl that he would close the school[101]. Perl then turned to Lviv, and there, his friends convinced the government commission to annul the threats, and the school continued operating.

Among Perl's rivals, there were some people for the benefit of whom Perl previously lobbied with the authorities. They paid him back with "defaming, cursing, despising, insulting and swearing." They did not hesitate from "slandering him with the authorities"[102]. Perl was not surprised by their actions. He said that "he knows nature of people, and he did not expect gratitude". He knew that every beginning would be difficult, even when it came to disseminating education that fitted the time.

Even though Perl's rivals did not hesitate to defame him before the authorities and the Jewish masses, Perl remained the central figure in Galitsia Jewry and the authorities turned to him for advisement on matters related to the Jews.

The authorities consisted of highly-ranked officials with modern views who understood well what was happening in Judaism. They considered Perl as a reformer with broad horizons.

Perl's educational work was also respected abroad by Jews and non-Jews. An unnamed observer described Perl as someone who "acts according to his individual views, and by that, he pushes aside any objectivity". That observer described Perl with a few appropriate sentences: "Perl is assertive, possesses credible principles, knows what he wants, and fight stubbornly and vigorously over his will. However, he was capable of wasting his virtues uselessly on implementing an idea he likes, for an imaginary benefit for the people"[103].

G.

Perl's literary fight against Hassidism[104], began as early as 1812 – 1820 when he collected material for a book about the Hassidim and their customs.

On 2 December 1816, Perl sent from Lviv a manuscript to the Galitsian commissioner, Frantz von Hauer, whom he knew from the latter stay in Ternopil. He named it: "*Über das Wesen der Sekte Chassidim, aus ihren eignen Schriften gezogen*" ["About the nature of the Hassidim sect, drawn from their own writings"].

Based on sources from the Hassidic writings, Perl described the historical evolution of Hassidism, its essence, and various sects, and provided details about the prominent leaders who outlined the ways of its development. Perl's approach was rational. He placed the blame for the gloomy cultural and spiritual condition of the Jewish masses on Hassidim.

In the memorandum attached to the manuscript, Perl explained that he wanted, for a long time, to publish an essay based on the Hassidic literature describing the Hassidic cult's customs and its principles. His desire "to awaken his nation from its deep sleep" drove him to do so. Only the fear of persecution by the Hassidim prevented him from carrying out his idea earlier. However, getting to know the commissioner and his willingness to support any enterprise aimed at elevating the cultural and moral standing of the Jews gave him the courage to act. When the commissioner published his instructions against the zealots' antics – who declared a boycott against the enlightened in Lviv in 1816, and following the orthodoxy outburst associated with the opening of the Re'ali school in Brody,

[Columns 69-70]

Perl decided to print his essay to alert the government about how deeply Hassidim was rooted among his people. He claimed that the goal of "instilling enlightenment among the Jews", which was in line with the government's policy, could only be achieved with the demise of Hassidism. Perl detailed the reasons for his essay and asked the commissioner to grant him a permit to dedicate the book to him.

In December 1815, the commissioner sent the manuscript to the police minister in Vienna, Graf Sedlintzky, accompanied by an informative report about Perl[105]. He stated that he would not allow Perl to dedicate the essay to him because, as a state commissioner, he would not want to alienate a specific group, even though its zealous principles were against the kingdom's will.

When Sedlentzky received the opinions of the censors for Jewish affairs and religious affairs, he notified Lviv that he would not provide a permit to publish the essay. He indicated that the reason was that it may evoke a negative reaction from the non-Jewish enlightened camp, and on the other hand, would not influence the un-cultured Jews who were not versed in the German language.

Based on those opinions, Sedlentzky ordered to conduct a thorough investigation of the Kabbalah and Hassidic books and to place the Hassidim under the supervision of the police, to choke that evil in its roots.

For his part, Hauer sent a copy of the manuscript to all the district ministers, so that they could familiarize themselves with the essence of Hassidism. Perl, who had received the notification of the prohibition to publish his essay, gave it to the Jewish historian Peter Beer. The latter who was about to publish his book, "Geschichte der Lehren und Meinungen aller bestandenen und noch bestehenden religiösen Sekten der Juden" ["History of the teachings and opinions of all past and existing Jewish religious sects"]. The historian made use of the article in the chapter - "Chassidim oder Beschttianers" ["Hassidim and the followers of the BESHT][106].

The historical documentation proves that Perl did not intend to "snitch". We should also note that Perl was a Hassid in his youth. He knew Hassidism for all its shortcomings, superstitious beliefs, and nonsenses that prevailed in it, from his personal experience. Perl witnessed the phenomena in the courts of the Rebbes [Hassidic Rabbis], who were brainwashing the masses and acting to strengthen their ignorance. That was why he found it necessary to alert people about the danger of Hassidim to his people and the state. Perl particularly resented the zealotry of the Rebbes, who allowed themselves to violate the orders and laws of the state. As an enlightened person, he considered that injustice against the kingdom.

In his book "Megaleh Tmirin" ["The Revealer of Secrets"] (Vianna 1819), which was the first satirical literary creation in the history of modern Hebrew literature, Perl reached a peak in his harsh criticism of Hassidim. Perl wrote the book in a format of letters exchanged between two Hassidim - the *Gabbai* [of a prominent Hassidic Admor], Rabbi Zelig Latitzover, and his friend Zeinvel Verkhibekker. Perl used a distorted form of the Hebrew language, imitating the language used in the Hassidic books of the period[107]. Perl wrote the book under the influence of the satires of Crotus Rubianus and Ulrikh von Hutten - "Epistolae Obscurorum Virorum" ["The Letters of Obscure Men"] (1515 – 1517).

The letters dealt with matters of making a living, Hassidism, and their acts. It described the fights of Hassidim against the governor regime, whom they called "the witzer gubernator" [a governor joker]. The Hassidim claimed that the governor hated them since he had received [what the Hassidim called] "the Bukh" [a secular book in Yiddish – as opposed to a religious – holy book] [108], [Perl's], a German written book that defamed Hassidism. The story in the book revolves around the theft of the [Perl's] German essay from the governor. The theft was carried out with the help of the maid of the vice governor and underworld thugs. The *Gabbai* and his friend intended to burn it. They hoped to find a picture of the author in the essay. They believed that it would have been enough for the rebbe to look at the picture to cause the death of the author. However, according to the story, the theft was discovered, and the rabbi was forced to flee to Eretz Israel.

The main plot is entwined with stories about the harassment of the enlightened by the Hassidim, and hegemonizing of the *Mitnagdim* [Opponents] (Rabbis who opposed Hassidism) by the Rebbes. The book describes how the rebbes loaned their followers money with an exorbitant rate of interest for "*pidyonot*" ["soul redemptions"] they administered and lived a life of luxury. The book faithfully describes the economic and social life of Galitsia Jews at the beginning of the 19th century, including all means of making a living in occupations based on "hot air" without a solid basis and in manners detached from the market reality.

"Megaleh Tmirin" made an enormous impression and aroused hatred among the Hassidim. Therefore, it is hardly surprising that the Rabbi of Ruzhyn called Perl – "The Second Yosef, Son of Miryam" (Perls' mother was Miryam).

Perl also wrote his second book - "Bokhen Tzaddik" ["The Test of the Righteous"] (Prague 1938) in the form of correspondence (between Ovadyah Ben Petakhya, a name Perl used as a pseudonym for the author of the book, and his friend R' Moshe Umanir). The book mocks not only the Hassidim. Unlike "Megaleh Tmirin", which only presents Hassidim in a negative light, in this book, Perl describes the faults in the Jewish society in Galitsia in general, pointing to the need to return to nature and work the land. The location of the plot is Avdari[109], or Brody. On one side, Perl resented Brody and its rabbis, preachers, and "*Lomdei Sheur*" [people who devote their lives to studying Torah and Talmud]. On the other side, he also disliked the enlightened people (whom the masses called- "Epikoroses" [people who maintain that there is no divine providence]).

[Column 71]

Jewish characters in Galitsia at the first half of the 19th Century

The satire was particularly aimed at the Brody enlightened who boasted about their wisdom and education when in fact, they had received all of their education from catalogs, novels, plays, and mediocre encyclopedias. They talk against studying Torah and demand that Jews become agriculturalists and craftsmen. However, their hidden agenda was to get rid of potential competitors. He blames them for discussing politics, medicine, and legal affairs without really knowing anything about those subjects. Perl claims that no honest men can be found in Brody (he called it Avdari in his book), even among the educated people and the rest of the residents. He claims that the merchants sell inferior and counterfeit goods and go bankrupt to get rich.

Their head and soul are in their businesses and they do not deal with the needs of the public faithfully. The innkeepers and the owners of taverns hold rooms for prostitutes and shelter thieves and smugglers. They mix their wine with water and toxic potions. The money exchanger, middlemen, and the slaughterers, *melamed's*, and craftsmen

[Column 72]

are crooks and swindlers. Perl blames the flattery to the wealthy, pursuit of a life of luxury, and the comfortable life of the Tzaddikim [righteous), for the prevalent corruption.

R' Ovadya leaves Galitsia, moves to Crimea, and witnesses the Jewish colonies established there in 1805. He imagines that he is in Eretz Israel. After seeing the Jewish settlements in Crimea, he concludes that the only way to change the Jews to become a productive element of society is by returning to working the land.

The book "Bokhen Tzaddik" angered Brody enlightened people. One of them published a harsh criticism of the author in the magazine "Allgemeine Zeitung des Judentums" ["General Newspaper of Judaism"]. He accused the author of imitating Perl's book -"Megaleh Tmirin" and daring to defame the entire Jewish public in Galitsia, particularly in Brody. The author blamed the big merchants for dishonesty. The anonymous author of the article assumed that the book's author was somebody who opposed enlightenment. However, a short while later, an enlightened person published an article signed by M. L. K. and revealed that "Bokhen Tzaddik" was also authored by Perl[110]. That article was full of praises for the book[111].

From Perl's writings, it is clear that Perl considered Hassidism a movement that did not want to and could not extricate the Jewish masses from the poor social and cultural state they were in.

[Columns 73-74]

However, he did not consider the enlightened camp an active and stable element to execute that historic process either.

There is no doubt that Perl valued cooperation with the government administration. That was also the view held by people of his generation, and one cannot consider his views as ingratiating to the authorities.

Through that collaboration, Perl meant to improve the state of the Jews and their legal standing and place education on a sound foundation fitting the period. He considered it his duty to alert the authorities, whom he trusted, about the faults in the Jewish lives and the need to correct them or eliminate them altogether.

For their part, the authorities asked Perl for his opinion about matters associated with Gaitsian Jews. There is no denial that Perl exaggerated, not once, in his patriotism. He did not refrain from sending memorandums that emitted a smell of "dedication [to the state]". However, it is unjust to say that Perl "snitched" intentionally, as Dr. Mahler claimed in his book "Der Kampf Zwischen un Khassidut in Galitisye" ["The struggle between enlightenment and Hassidism in Galtisia"][112].

Perl, the enlightened and *Mitnaged* [A person who opposed Hassidism], saw where Hassidism was leading by taking control of the communities. Rabbis who did not yield to the will of the [Hassidic] rebbes did not endure. All the positions in the communities – the slaughterers, *mohels*, and *gabbais*, were captured by Hassidim, who used their power to oppress their opponents[113]. The Hassidim resisted any attempt to improve the Jewish education system. They sabotaged any effort toward changes in the Jewish economic and social lifestyle. Their main objective was to prevent any undermining of their mastery over the masses.

Perl, who acquired European and traditional Jewish education, did not come to terms with that situation principally because he realized that those who were "connected" in the courts of the rebbes were using the "holy war" to accumulate wealth for themselves. Perl knew to distinguish between the Hassidim of the generation of R' Levi-Yitzkhak of Berdichev, who excelled in "praying, charity and freeing of captives by paying ransom"[114], and the Hassidism of his generation who were unscrupulous faithless crooks, whose only goal was to extort money from their followers, rich and poor.

Perl's position about the Hassidism movement was manifested in 1837 when Karl Seyfarth (who presented himself as the representative of Sigfrid Yustus the First, "King of Jerusalem and High Priest") came out calling the Jewish community to establish a state of Israel and the Kingdom of Zion[115]. On 10 July 1837, the Galitsia Commission turned to Perl, through the district minister in Ternopil, requesting that he provide his opinion about Seyfarth's proclamation. On 27 October 1837, Perl submitted a comprehensive report, which was transferred to the police minister Sedlintzky. In his report, Perl expressed his opinion that Seyfarth[116] did not exert any influence on Galitsian Jews because his views were foreign to them.

In his memorandum, Perl provided a comprehensive review of Galitsian Jews. He divided them into the following four groups: a) the masses, b) the pious-zealots, c) the Hassidim, and d) the enlightened (whose numbers were small). According to Perl, the masses were incapable of thinking or acting independently. He hesitated between the pious and the Hassidim, whose views about the arrival of the Messiah were the same, and there were no chances for Seyfarth to find followers among them. Perl stated that he might be able to find fans among the Hassidim if he adjusted his enterprise according to the interests of the sect and their rebbes since the Hassidim would agree to divert from the religious laws to advance their standing. However, Perl claimed that none of the Hassidim would join Seyfarth's movement for two reasons: 1) Seyfarth's plan would undermine the Hassidim's standing and also because it might reduce the revenues of the charity of Rabbi Meir Ba'al HaNess [R' Meir, "Master of the Miracles", one of the greatest of the Tannaim of the fourth generation], which mainly benefited the rebbes. 2) Seyfarth's views stood opposite to the Jewish tradition ["Return to Zion" would only be accomplished upon the arrival of the Messiah].

Perl fiercely opposed the collection of money for the "Meir Ba'al HaNess charity". He insisted that the custom of placing collection boxes in synagogues benefited only the rebbes rather than the settlements in Eretz Israel [which the charity claimed to help]. Perl authored a booklet named "Katit Le'Maor" ["Virgin Oil for Lighting"] as early as in 1822, in which he expressed his opposition to the boxes of Meir Ba'al HaNess charity. He requested a permit to publish the booklet in 1829. Graf Sedlintzky transferred the request to Galitsia's commissioner - Prince Lobkowitz and asked for his opinion. Perl was requested to submit a German translation of the booklet and a copy of the Hassidic proclamations

[Columns 75-76]

calling for handouts to the Meir Ba'al HaNess charity[117]. The matter was dragged on for several years. Perl received the permit only in 1836. The memorandum was published in the same year (5596) in [periodical of the enlightened movement] "Kerem Khemed" ["Vineyard of Delight"] under the title "Three letter-cards about the charity of R' Meir Ba'al HaNess"[118]. In 1836, when Perl was working on the memorandum regarding Seyfarth's (Sigfrid Yustus's) proclamation, he came across a confidential fundraising effort. The fundraising aimed to cover the cost of the trial in Ust'ye-Zelenoye [Ushitze][119] and the needs of the court of Rebbe Israel of Rozhin. The most amount of money from Galitsia came from the districts of Sanok, Jaslo, and Tarnow. Tzvi Hirsh Mesharet was the one who collected these sums. Only small sums of money were collected in the rest of the districts including Lviv. In the Ternopil district, only the activist David Parnas from Yanov [Dolina] contributed 50 florins. However, the faithful follower of R' Israel Rozhiner, R' Yitzkhak Fishler, an exceptionally wealthy man from Borshchiv and the partner of David Parnas, collected large sums of money. It is reasonable to assume that about forty to fifty thousand florins were collected and sent to Russia[120]. According to Perl, the Jew who murdered the two informers resided in Galitsia [the murder that R' Israel of Rozhin was accused of]. Perl claimed that the murderer received money from Fishler for his living expenses and the expenses of his wife, who remained in Russia.

Based on Perl's memorandum, all the district ministers were requested to investigate "the harmful acts by the Hassidim sect"[121].

Out of his hatred for the Hassidim, Perl demanded that the libraries in the *Batei HaMidrash* - "Shilkhen" and Kleizlekh" be closed. He requested that the books be transferred to his school's library, which he had planned to establish. He also requested to shut down the Mikveh's [ritual emersion baths], which have been eliminated in Jewish communities in France, England, and Italy and existed only in Poland. He claimed that the Hassidim go to the Mikveh's supposedly for ritual bathing purposes, but in fact, they come for "discussions" and "small talk", and thereby, they were late for the prayers[122].

Perl's hatred for the Hassidim grew even stronger with the election of Ternopil rabbi at the beginning of 1838. That event resulted in a serious dispute with the Hassidim.

H.

In 5597 (1837), R' Yehoshua Heschel BABa"D, an aged man of 82, who served as the city rabbi for about forty years, left his rabbinical position for an unknown reason (to this day). According to the custom in pious communities, a rabbinical judge would have been nominated as the deputy rabbi. Perl seized the opportunity to elect a modern and educated rabbi as in the communities of Germany and Italy. On his initiative, the district minister, Karl von Sakher, requested that the community invite candidates for the rabbinical position of Ternopil through an announcement in the newspapers[123].

When R' Aharon Frenkel responded to the announcement as the first candidate, Perl advised his friend, Rabbi Sh. Y. Rappaport [SHI"R], to present his candidacy. Thirty-six government-appointed arbitrators were tasked with electing the rabbi. They elected SHI"R with 33 votes. On 23 Kislev 5697 (7 December 1936), SHI"R received the nomination letter on behalf of the Ternopil community.

A harsh dispute erupted just after his election. Disparaging documents against SHI"R and Perl were distributed from Lviv and Ternopil. SHI"R also received threatening letters, which warned him against coming to Ternopil. However, when he received the nomination letter from the district office, he trusted the power of Perl and the protection by the district office so he arrived at Ternopil on Shabbat eve, 16 Shevat (11 February 1838). Perl and one of Ternopil's prominent leaders, traveled to Lviv to accompany him. In Ternopil, the honorable people came out "in chariots and as horsemen" [Genesis 50:9] to greet him in great honor[124].

Nakhman Kromkhel [a Jewish Galician philosopher, theologian, and historian], who moved from Zhovkva to Ternopil in 1837, understood that in light of the then-current situation in Galitsia, the time has not come yet for an enlightened and educated rabbi of the type of SHI"R, and therefore he initially objected

[Columns 77-78]

to SHI"R's candidacy[125].

The election of SHI"R was welcomed enthusiastically by the enlightened camp. People like Samuel David Luzzatto, Shalom Cohen, Yosef Almantzi, and Yehuda Yetlis sent the rabbi congratulating letters or praised him in poems[126]. Out of their bitter resistance, the zealots immediately announced a boycott of the pharmacy of Mikhael Perl (Perl's son).

SHI"R gave a sermon at the big synagogue on the first Shabbat, and in the house of prayer of Perl's school on the second Shabbat. The zealots, headed by Hassid Zilberfeld, started a dissention. They turned to Brody's maggid, R' Shlomo Kluger, requesting that he would not recognize SHI"R as the rabbi. The district minister von Sakher was convinced that Lviv's Rabbi, Ya'akov Orenstein, encouraged the dissention. In his report to the governor, from 7 June 1838 the district manager specifically reported: *"(Orenstein) geniesst er den Ruf der Sekte (Chassidim) zugethan zu sein und hat auch bei den Tarnopoler Händeln die Hand im Spiele, und ich bin gewiss, dass die hier bestehenden Chassidim schulen nie ins Leben getreten wären, wenn er nilhtjenen Juden, die darin Minian abhalten, willig das Zeugnis ihrer Unbedenklichkeit ausgestellt hätte."*[127] ["Orenstein enjoys the reputation of being associated with the Hassidic sect and he also had a hand in the Tarnopol dealings. I am sure that the Hassidic schools existing here would have never come into existence if he had not willingly issued the certificate of their harmlessness to those Jews who attend a *minyan* there."].

The opponents of SHI"R gathered in the two *Batei Midrash* and vilified his name. After the gathering, the district minister, who supported the enlightened, closed down the *Batei Midrash*.

The fire of the dispute flared up and penetrated every layer of the population. An objective observer who stayed in Ternopil at the time wrote: "The city seems to be in a state of emergency. It looks like it is under attack by its enemies[128]. Resentment dominates, and the rabbi's affair is the subject of all conversations. It takes center stage in conversations in all circles, in the city streets, and among families at home behind the curtains, regardless of age and religion, Jews and Christians alike, men and women, and young men and young women. Quarrels divided families, children beat their friends, who claimed that the rabbi was not a scholar, and the parties resorted to indecent means in their war. No wonder that the hatred grew more and more".

Boycotts were announced daily, and clashes were frequent. Many people were arrested and brought to trial. The municipality found it necessary to publish, on 16 March 1838, a proclamation against the assaults as they disrupted the public order. The government announced that it would not allow calling Aharon Frankel, whom it did not recognize, a rabbi. Any action he took on religious matters, including boycotts, was declared null and void. The municipality called on Aharon Frankel and his associates publicly to cease their shameful actions and avoid disruption of the public order. The government warned Aharon Frenkel and his followers that refusal to obey the request would bring about criminal punishment. "Anybody who would cooperate with them, participates in assaults, or helps propagate the boycott, would be punished with a fine of fifty thalers or by flogging"[129].

The situation became unbearable in the summer of 1838 when the 83 years old Rabbi Yehoshua-Heschel BABa"D died. The zealots spread rumors that the rabbi died from sorrow and shame and that SHI"R caused his death. At about that time, SHI"R moved to the old synagogue and took the place of Rabbi BABa"D, which further angered the zealots. They covered the walls of the synagogue with defamation writings. When SHI"R ascended to the Torah, the Hassidim welcomed him with laughter. On one of the Shabbats, he found his seat covered with tar. In addition to their antics, the Hassidim announced that the synagogue became a place of impurity. They dirtied the stairs to the ark and the pulpit with tar and mud. The enlightened submitted a complaint against some of the zealots, and one of the zealots was sentenced to flogging in public. Other zealots were sentenced to jail terms[130].

Perl decided to calm things down. On the Shabbat of the weekly portion Netzavim, he gave a speech at the house of prayer in the school. It was given in Yiddish, spiced with jokes, like the ways of the preachers, and included 56 quotations from the Bible, Mishnah, rabbinical sermons, and books[131]. In his sermon, Perl pointed out the damage inflicted on the community by the fraudulent accusations and quarrels. He stated that these quarrels could cause damage to the entire Jewish population. He brought as an example the controversy about

[Columns 79-80]

the country's central rabbinate in the 1780s. That controversy resulted in the abolishment of Jewish autonomy[132]. He reminded the audience that Rabbi Yehoshua-Heschel BABa"D was elected when Rabbi Falkenfeld (his predecessor) was still alive. The masses and the leaders lobbied the district officials to leave Rabbi Falkenfeld in his position. They also asked BABa"D not to come. When they heard that he decided to come, despite their request, they sent a special envoy to him in Zaloshitz [Dzialoszyce], who warned the rabbi not to come. However, the rabbi did not heed these requests and threats. Perl, who was the head of the community at that time, tried to calm everyone down. He asked the district minister not to get involved and treated Rabbi BABa"D with respect. It is not appropriate to provide details, in this article, about how they deceived Rabbi Falkenfeld and convinced him to leave Ternopil. If a dispute had not erupted then, it was because there were only a small number "of nice and pious Jews, as well as strangers" in Ternopil at the time. SHI"R received a substantial majority of the votes. After the election, the rabbinical judges came to Perl and told him about their wish to send the elected rabbi a congratulatory letter. However, Perl prevented them from doing so. A few days before SHI"R's arrival, the rabbinical judges expressed their willingness to cooperate with him despite the rumors spread by his opponents that he was never a rabbi but just a merchant. The vocal among them expected to receive money. However, when the rabbi came and did not give them any money, they spread fraudulent lies about him. Suddenly, the rabbinical judges refused to come to the rabbi. Perl emphasized in his speech that he knew SHI"R and can testify that he was G-d fearing person and an outstanding scholar. He added that the rabbi received his ordination from the Gaon Rabbi R' Ya'akov [of] Lissa [R' Ya'akov Lorberbaum]. *Beit HaMidrash*, which was closed by the authorities, served as the center for the inciters who defamed SHI"R. They turned the place into a den of criminals. Perl turned to the people who imposed the boycotts with harsh words. He told them that their actions were not according to the laws of the Torah. These vocal people were, in actuality, villains who extort money fraudulently. He ended his sermon with the following words: "Whoever is not attracted by their lies would remain a free person. Please do not surrender to the will of these despicable people, whose only objective in life is to extort money".

Perl's sermon did not achieve its purpose. It did not relieve the tension and did not calm down the people. On the contrary, the zealots expanded their activities. On Friday, 12 October 1838, a Hassid, Melekh Apter, disguised himself as a rabbi and along with several other Jews, passed through the Jewish quarter and cursed SHI"R. At the same time, the zealots gathered around SHI"R's apartment, played music, danced, and yelled: "Rabbi, send out your daughters so that we can have fun". Among the gathering people, there was someone by the name of Hertz Brody who dressed up like Yosef Perl with two medals on his chest. When the district manager heard of these antics, he ordered to arrest Apter and punish him with 150 lashes[133].

The controversy was not to SHI"R's liking. He was especially angry with his enlightened friends in Brody, R' Yehoshua Heschel Schorr[134], and his brother Mendel. They published the affair in articles in the Jewish newspapers in Germany in Dr. Jost's "Annalen" ["Annals"], Dr. Fuerst's "Orient", and Dr. Phillipson's "Algemeineh Tzeitung des Judentums" ["The General Gazette of Judaism"].

Perl was full of bitterness and disappointment about the events in his city. He finally understood that the fire of the dispute was ignited by the "*Klei HaKodesh*" [people who serve the masses on religious matters], and by people who were incited by the Hassidim. They pursued their own gain. He then wrote a memorandum about the actions of the rebbes, slaughterers, and *mohels*. He submitted it on 6 July 1838 to District Minister Sakher, requesting to transfer it to the Governor.

In an accompanying letter, Perl pointed to the scandals that erupted under the influence of the Hassidim. He described their antics against SHI"R and about the *mohels* who refused to circumcise the sons of SHI"R's followers. He stated that the antics carried one objective: to keep the Jews away from education and to sink the masses into the abyss of ignorance. Being ignorant would make it easier to enforce surrender to the will of the rebbes, who exploit them and get rich at their expense. It is not the zealotry and superstitions that drove the Hassidim to do these things, but the interests of their leaders. They aimed at imposing the rule of the rebbes over the entire Galitsian Jewry against the Torah and the state laws. The rebbes' regime caused a deadly disaster. Therefore, the state should end that situation using appropriate means[135].

in that memorandum[136], Perl mentioned that he devoted his fortune and all of his energy to improving the cultural state of Galitsian Jews and founded the school for that purpose. While he enjoyed the fruits of school, which educated exemplary students, he was fearful to witness to watch how the Hassidim undermined any effort aimed at improving the state of the Jews. Due to his illness, he could only describe how the Hassidim attracted Galitsian Jews, caught them in their net, and took control over their lives.

His description follows: "The Hassidim subjugated the rabbis under their control. The Hassidim slandered rabbis who opposed them and spread rumors that they were secular. The rebbes' followers bully the rabbis until they left them with no choice but to travel to the Rebbe and ask for his forgiveness if they wanted to continue their work as a rabbi. When the authorities issued a harsh regulation against the Hassidim, they managed to sway the rabbis to declare a favorable opinion of them.

[Columns 81-82]

They pressured the rabbis to testify in favor of the Hassidim. The pressure caused the government to change the interpretation of the regulations mentioned above.

The slaughterers, who play a major role among the *Klei HaKodesh*, belong to one of the Hassidim dynasties for quite some time now. Candidates for that occupation study with Hassidic slaughterers. They are accepted to their position by the community with the community rabbi's approval. In cases where the community or the lessee of the Kosher meat refuses to accept them, the Hassidim announce a boycott against them and forbid buying the meat they handle as *Trefah* [non-kosher].

The rebbes use the slaughterers to pressure the Jewish communities. The Kosher meat lessees, meat suppliers, and whole communities were largely dependent on the Hassidim. If not satisfied, the latter could declare that a random animal is *Trefah* or make it *Trefah* purposely. The slaughterers are, in fact, the "foot soldiers", agents, and spies manipulated by the rebbes. The emissaries sent by the rebbes to visit a community always stay at the slaughterer's home. The slaughterers are going around in the villages slaughtering animals there. The meat tax is not paid in these cases, in violation of the laws from 1789 and 1810. The rebbes also manipulate the *mohels*. There are many cases when the *mohels* refused to circumcise children of the "*Mitnagdim*" [people who oppose the Hassidim].

By taking control over the rabbis, slaughterers, and *mohels*, the Hassidim managed to subdue the Galician Jewry to their will. If that situation lingers on, there would be no force that could bring the Jews closer to the rest of the residents in Galitsia due to the separatism tendencies and intolerance of the Hassidim".

Perl stated that to remedy that gloomy situation the authorities should abolish the regulations from 1789 about the rabbis, slaughterers, and *mohels*. Those regulations forbade to nominate rabbis that do not know German. According to a regulation from 1846, it was not even allowed to nominate a rabbi who had not studied philosophy and pedagogy. There were only three district rabbis that fulfilled the requirements of the law: Rabbi Tzvi Hirsh Khayut in Zhovkva, Mikhael Kristianpoller in Brody, and Shlomo-Leib in Ternopil. Sixteen other district rabbis and 200 local rabbis have no general education and are among those who hate it.

The district rabbis Khayut, Kristianpoller, and Rapoport, were all persecuted by the zealots. Rabbi Kristianpoller had to protect Maggid Shlomo Kluger, who provoked Galitsian rabbis to rally against him. The rabbis announced that he was a heretic and unbeliever. He survived only due to the support of Brody's privileged families:

Kalir, Nathanzon, and Bernstein. Rabbi Khayut had to spend his entire fortune, which he inherited from his father, to "keep the mouth of the haters shut". The story about Rabbi Rapoport is especially bitter since he did not have behind him a powerful and wealthy family who could appease his haters.

The administration did not supervise the rabbis. It did not support the enlightened either. Because the administration had never disqualified a rabbi due to offenses against the law, enlightened Jews were not seeking rabbinical positions.

Due to the insufficient regular salaries, the rabbis were dependent on gifts. That situation resulted in corruption and dependence on the people of the community. In his memorandum, Perl detailed some proposals to remedy the situation as follows: "a) The rabbis' salaries should be sufficient to make a living according to their status and be determined by the law. The costs associated with that should be covered by the community taxes, proportional to the values of people's properties. b) The rabbis should be assigned the supervision over the *Kheders*, and authorize them to test the *melameds* and award them certificates. c) The district offices should make sure that the elected rabbis provide proof of the studies in German schools, even if they do not have certificates. d) Rabbis should be elected for life, rather than three years, which is the current custom. e) When the community does not have a rabbi, it should return the salary money to the district office. The money should serve as the foundation fund for a rabbinical college. f) Salaries for the slaughterers should be funded by the community, eliminating the special tax collected for slaughtering and salt. g) The costs of the communities should be covered by a proportional tax and not by indirect taxes since it is not fair that the poor would pay the same amount as the wealthy. Only through rabbis who can guide the people, it would be possible to instill the will for education, and feelings of respect and discipline towards the laws".

The governor responded on July 23, to the district minister von-Sakher that it would be difficult to root out the harmful influences of the Hassidic sect. The facts mentioned by Perl about taking control over the rabbis, slaughterers, *mohels*, and other "*Klei HaKodesh*" were correct, and it was possible to draw beneficial conclusions from them. Perl's recommendation provided additional proof that his intentions were to help the state administration. However, the government is not able to execute them. Concerning the rabbis, the governor stated that the authorities would have to wait for the new regulations on Jewish affairs planned for in the entire kingdom. The governor also claimed that the kingdom could not accomplish the recommendation offered by Perl since Perl himself admitted that that were no appropriate rabbinical candidates at that time.

Perl's recommendations, regarding the slaughterers and *mohels*, would be considered when the negotiations about it would commence.

Perl's memorandum was his "swan song". It did not cause the stir he hoped for. The disappointment reached him again, with no hopes for any improvements. Under that mood, he advised his friend SHI"R to lobby for his candidacy for the rabbinical position vacated in Prague in 1838.

In the fall of 1838, Perl became seriously ill and received treatment by Dr. Rapoport in Lviv[137]. In September 1839, it became clear

[Column 83]

that he could not be cured. He passed away on Simkhat Torah (on 1st October 1839) at 7 a.m. He left one son, Mikhael, a pharmacist, and two daughters. His daughter Sheindel married Finlish[138], a native of Jaroslaw [Yaroslav], who later moved to Ternopil. The other daughter, who was married to Ashkenazi, was a teacher who managed the girls' classes in her father's school.

In his will, he bequeathed 6000 florins to Jewish artisans. He left the school and its library to the Ternopil community and nominated his son Mikhael as the school principal.

When the Hassidim heard about his death, they began to dance with joy. Government representatives participated in his funeral, and Rabbi Sh. Y. Rapoport (SHI"R) eulogized him at the cemetery[139].

His generation already recognized his rights as a pioneer of the enlightenment movement and Jewish education. They saw him as their Israel Jacobson[140] [A Jewish German banker, considered the precursor of Reform Judaism]. Perl was the first educator who merged general education and Jewish studies and established his school as a Jewish public school.

The Jewish journalism dedicated eulogizing articles to him[141]. In Vienna, he was eulogized by Maggid Noah Mannheimer[142].

After Perl's death, SHI"R remained without his protector, and his situation deteriorated.

Tomb of Yosef Perl

[Column 84]

Hassidim gathered in front of his house on the first night of the Shavuot holiday of 1840[143]. They threw rocks into his apartment, broke the windows, and tried to break into the apartment to hit the hiding rabbi. Only the Dragon Battalion, sent by the district minister von Sakher, managed to subdue the riot. After that scandal, the rabbi decided to leave the rabbinical position in Ternopil.

SHI"R was elected to the rabbinical position in Prague in the summer of 5599 [1840] through the lobbying and recommendation by Shlomo Rosenthal, Samuel-David Luzzatto, and Sh. L. Goldenberg, owner of "Kerem Khemed". The Maggid of Prague, Dr. Mikhael Zaks, managed to convince Moshe Landau (the grandson of R' Yekhezkel Landau, the author of "Nodah BeYehudah], who was among the heads of the Prague community to elect him. However, the government did not approve SHI"R's election due to all the defamation letters that the Hassidim in Ternopil sent against him. Only in 1840, the government approved the election of SHI"R as the head of the rabbinical court (*Oberjurist*) in Prague, thanks to the lobbying by the district minister, von Sakher.

[Columns 85-86]

SHI"R left Ternopil on 15 July 1840. His friends accompanied him to Zolochiv, and others went with him to Lviv. That was "a gloomy and painful farewell"[144].

With that, the SHI"R rabbinical affair in Ternopil, one of the gloomiest chapters in the history of the city and Galitsian Jewry, came to an end.

I.

From the beginning of the emergence of the Enlightenment Movement of Mendelson's school of thought, Ternopil captured a central role in Galitsia thanks to Yosef Perl, the undisputed spiritual leader of the enlightened there. However, we should not ignore the fact that the first "rays of enlightenment" penetrated Ternopil only after 1801, when Perl became an adversary of Hassidism and came to know the poet from Brody, David Ginsburg (1776 – 1811). The latter came to Ternopil on business. Perl invited him to his home as a teacher. During the two years (1801 – 1803)) that Ginsburg stayed in Ternopil, Perl became enlightened. Through Ginsburg, Perl connected with the leaders of the Enlightenment Movement in Brody, Lviv, and Zhovkva. However, from his first steps as an enlightened person, he remained moderate in his views about religion and secularism. With those views, he was different from the enlightened people in Brody, who distinguished themselves in their extremism. Only in his fight with Hassidism did Perl know no bounds. Before the 1848 Austrian Revolution, when Hassidism with its rebbes and their followers began to capture key positions and take control over the Jewish communities, it was difficult for Perl to accept.

Ternopil became a center of enlightenment, thanks to the school established by Yosef Perl and the group of teachers who taught there. Perl and the teachers formed the first circle of enlightened people in the city. Over time, the best of the Jews joined that small circle. Under the guidance of Yosef Perl, that club devoted its effort to disseminate the enlightenment ideas, based on the fundamentals of the Jewish tradition, resisting "agnosticism for its own sake", in which most of Brody's and Lviv's enlightened people were famous for.

Enlightenment in Ternopil carried a practical and less theoretical character. Its followers did not necessarily hold any particular view on the whole set of problems in Judaism. Despite their harsh fight against the Hassidim and their rebbes, or perhaps because of the experiences in that fight, they recognized the reality and appreciated the power of tradition in the life of the Jewish people. It was that view that motivated Perl to establish a house of prayer in his school and to dedicate special attention to the religious education in his institution.

The circle of enlightened people in Ternopil, who concentrated around Perl, was initially small, although it did have significant influence within the Jewish population, who recognized him as the undisputed leader and the guardian of the ideas of the Galitsian enlightenment. Ternopil lucked the human material. In that, it differed from Brody. Brody maintained tight business connections with Germany and Austria, even before the Enlightenment Movement, and its merchants were exposed to the cultural life in these countries. In Ternopil, the enlightenment advancement was initiated from within, with the expansion of the school and the activities of the teachers, who served as the enlightenment pioneers. The objectives of Ternopil's enlightened people were to facilitate the acquisition of European education for their people, raise the level of craftsmanship among them, and bring the Jews closer to the general population. Perl did not have a far-reaching or revolutionary spiritual plan to achieve those goals. He aimed to keep the Jews anchored around the historic religious basis without any changes or improvements. When it came to praying, he aimed at improving the ritual externally and introducing aesthetics and grace to the worship of G-d. He wanted to free the worshipers from the noisy and market-like atmosphere that prevailed in the synagogues in Poland and Galitsia at the time. That was also one of the factors that led to his immense hatred towards Hassidism, which he fought using the weapon of literary satire and destructive ridicule.

The enlightened people of Ternopil saw it as a historical privilege that fate chose them to be the first to start the fight against the zealots and Hassidim. by establishing the school and its house of prayer, which they considered a German-style "improved" synagogue. Although the Rapoport affair drugged them into the "fires of war" and fierce brawls, they considered the courage of electing an educated rabbi and a famous researcher such as SHI"R - a touchstone for the enlightenment movement in their city.

As a result of their effort, Perl and the school teachers succeeded to widen the ranks of the enlightened circle and establish a club of authors and people of letters although, in Ternopil, there were no prominent enlightened figures like Ya'akov Shmuel Bik, Berish Blumenfeld, Zeev Bukhner, Israel Bodek, Hirsh Bodek, Yitzkhak Erter, or the brothers Schorr – all famous authors. There were also no wealthy patrons of the kind of Alexander-Ziskind Kalir, Brotziner-Trakhtenberg, Inlander, Mordekhai Uspitz, Shalom Kromkhel, the brothers Hertzenstein, Ya'akovka Landau, M. Nirenstein, or Nathanzon – all backers of Brody's enlightenment. The circle of Ternopil enlightened included Shmuel-Leib Goldenberg, Yitzkhak Mikhael Munis, Moshe Khaim Katz, and Aba'leh Horwitz.

Shmuel-Leib Goldenberg (1807 -1846), was a native of Bolekhiv [Bolekhov] and a descendant of a rich family. He married a daughter of a wealthy family in Ternopil and did not have to work for a living. He dedicated his life to studying and reading books. He was one of Perl's most loyal friends. He corresponded about Judaic sciences with SHI"R, Reggio, Sh. D. Luzzatto, Dr. Geiger, Dr. Leopold Tzuntz, and Dr. Mikhael Zaks. Immediately after the journal "Bikurei Ha'Itim" ["The First Fruits of the Time"] ceased its publication in the summer of 1932, Goldenberg, who had already lived in Ternopil, began to publish the journal "Kerem Khemed". He conducted negotiations in Vienna, as early as 1830, with I. Sh. Reggio, Sh. D. Luzzatto, and the printer Anton Schmidt in Vienna. On 30 November 1830, he turned to Reggio with a proposal to publish a new journal.

[Columns 87-88]

Reggio stated that he intended to continue publishing "Bikurei Ha'Itim". In the meantime, Goldenberg came to Vienna and negotiated with the printer. The latter agreed to publish, at his own expense, a volume containing letters about literary and science matters.

The first volume was published in March 1833. It contained 40 letters about "wisdom and science"[145]. Goldenberg, who came from an enlightened family (his father R' Hirsh) was one of the first enlightened leaders in Bolekhiv), corresponded with the heads of the Enlightenment Movement in Galitsia, Austria, Germany, and Italy. He was among the first Galitsian enlightened people to connect with the enlightened people in Italy. He managed to acquire friends from among the heads of the Enlightenment Movement and persuade them to participate in his journal (which was just a collection of letters), with his cordial and flattering style. That was how he became the intermediary between the enlightened people in Galitsia and Western Europe. He provided information to Italy's enlightened people about the Hebrew publications in Galitsia and biographies of the figures in Galitisa's enlightenment.

Among the people who participated in "Kerem Khemed", the following people should be mentioned: Yekhezkel Dobbes, Yitzkhak Munis, Avraham Goldenberg from Ternopil, Ya'akov Shmuel Bik, Dr. Yitzkhak Erter from Brody, and Y. L. Meizes.

During 1833 – 1843, Goldenberg published seven volumes. Some were published in the printing house of Anton Adler von Schmidt in Vienna and five in Prague. These volumes contained an abundance of material about Judaic sciences. The first "gate" of R' Nakhman Kromkhel's "Moreh Nevukhei HaZman" ["Guide for the Perplexed of the Time"], named "HaSamim" ["The Drugs"], was published in one of the volumes (The entire book was published posthumously).

Yosef Perl participated only in the second volume published in 1836. He published research aimed to prove that R;' Meir Ba'al HaNes was not the Tannai R' Meir mentioned in the Mishnah. Dr. Yitzkhak Erter published an article about "Hassidism and wisdom". SHI"R participated in "Kerem Khemed" as well, during his service in Ternopil[146], and to a greater extent in the volumes published in Prague. Authors from outside of Galitsia also participated in "Kerem Khemed". Among them Avraham Geiger, Leopold Tzuntz, Leopold Löw [Lef], Aharon Khorin, Mordekhai Shmuel Ghirondi, Shmuel Vitah Dalla Volta from Mantua, Hillel Dalla Torre, I. Sh. Reggio, Aharon Yelink, Simkha Pinsker, David Kassel, and others.

The publishing of "Kerem Khemed" ceased for 11 years with the death of Goldenberg on 10 January 1846[147]. However, it renewed its publication by Shneur Zaks (Sachs) in Berlin in 1854. Two volumes were published (1854 – 1856).

[Yitzkhak] Mikhael Munis was the first teacher in Perl's school for Talmud and the Hebrew language. He was a great scholar and one of the fiercest opponents of Hassidism. Munis worked in Perl's school for almost 25 years and educated many students. He did not write much but corresponded directly with RIVAL[148], collected proverbs of Maggid R' Ya'akov from Dubno, and published a book about his life. In that book, he added the philosophical article "The wisdom of proverbs and poetry". In 1842 he traveled to central Europe and Prussia to promote his book. He wrote about himself: "I have obtained certificates from famous scholars, the geniuses of the land, and learned people in their courts. They all praised me and adorned me with a splendorous wreath, claiming that I deserve to be a rabbi"[149]. Among his writings, the article "Question and Answer about Customs", published in M. Mohar's journal "Yerushalayim"[150], is well known. In that article, he provided the meanings and history of Jewish customs. One of the customs expanded upon was the lighting of the candles during the holiday of Lag BaOmer in memory of the soul of R' Shimon Bar Yokhai. Munis published the Hebrew translation of four letters sent to Euler about matters in physics[151]. He also expanded about the blessing, "LeHakhniso BiVrito Shel Avraham Avinu" [circumcision blessing - "Bring him into the covenant of Avraham, our father"] in "Kerem Khemed". In 1839 he was set to publish an article about aesthetics[152]. He was also favored by the heads of the Enlightenment Movement in Galitsia and Russia[153].

The influence of Ternopil's enlightenment grew during the years that R' Menakhem Mendel Lefin of Sasiv, the "Socrates" of the Galitsian Enlightenment Movement, stayed in Ternopil (1817 – 1826). Lefin contributed greatly to the new spiritual lives and had a significant influence on the emergence of the enlightenment. He maintained a sincere friendship with the entire circle of enlightened people and showed great interest in their spiritual progress[154]. He resided in Yosef Perl's home and gathered around him the enlightened people of Ternopil who thirstily listened to his teaching. Lefin was imbued with popular spirit. He recognized the importance of the people's language in the development of the enlightenment and came out against the "official" enlightenment views that were guided by the slogans coined by its heads in Berlin and aimed only at disseminating the general culture. In that respect, Lefin exerted a strong influence

[Columns 89-90]

on the enlightened people of Brody and Ternopil. Thanks to him, the Galitsian and the Russian Enlightenment Movements took a different direction from the Enlightenment Movement in Berlin. Lefin fought against the piling of rhetoric, fastidious explanations, and ignorance about the Torah and sciences…

Lefin advocated the popular Hebrew language of the Mishnah and demanded that enlightened people would deepen their education and knowledge. Lefin's friendship with Perl did not prevent him from criticizing Perl's style of writing in the book "Megaleh Tmirin".

Lefin translated the book of Proverbs to Yiddish in Ternopil and printed it in 5576 (1816) with commentaries. That translation invoked a fierce resistance among the enlightened circles. Translation of the bible to Yiddish required substantial courage among the enlightened circles since most of the enlightened people considered the objective of the enlightenment was to bring the Jews closer to the languages of the civilized world. They advocated the use of the German language, or at least, in countries where the spoken language was not German, the language of the nation among which the Jews resided. The enlightened Tuvia Gutman, son of Tzvi-Hirsh Fedder, a native of Przedborz (Krakow District], lived in Ternopil at the end of his life and died there on 9 Tamuz (23 June), 1817. He was a merchant and a proofreader for Torah scrolls, Tefilin, and Mezuzot. For years, he served as a wandering teacher[155]. He was an enlightenment zealot and a man of quarrel. He became enraged when Lefin published the translation for Proverbs in Yiddish. Fedder claimed that Lefin "showed contempt toward the preacher of the right, and spitted in the face of the eloquent speaker". Fedder respected Lefin, whom he considered the spiritual successor of Mendelson, and as someone who symbolized the exalted ideal of the enlightenment. Precisely because of that view, he could not forgive Lefin for his "crime of the Yiddish translation". He wanted Lefin to educate the people of his generation on the civilized language – German. He published a pamphlet named "Kol Mekhatzetzim" ["The Archers' Voice"], a satire full of personal sarcastic remarks about Lefin. The proofreading sheets that Fedder sent to Brody reached Ya'akov Shmuel Bik, who was hurt by the fact that Fedder offended Lefin. He turned to Fedder and asked him, in his name and the name of Lefin's admirers, not to print the pamphlet. He warned him that he would not acquire honor by publishing it.

Fedder responded that he did not mean to disrespect Lefin's character, he only went against the translation. He stated that he would not be deterred by threats, as he was used to being oppressed by other people. He said that he would avoid publishing the book if Lefin admirers would refund him the printing costs. Brody's enlightened people sent him 100 rubles and the book was not published at the time. The book was later published by. A. M. Mohar, when Lefin and Fedder were not among the living[156].

That literary episode passed without causing a severe quarrel within the enlightened camp.

In Ternopil, Lefin completed his German written book "Nachlass eines Sonderlinges Zu Abdera" ["The Literary Estate of a Crank from Abdera"], which he devoted to princess Isabella Czartoryski. That book was never published and remained as a manuscript in the library of Perl's school.

Besides the Czartoryski family who admired Lefin, he had other friends among the Polish nobility in Ternopil and its environs. In particular, he maintained close friendly relations with the counts Bobrovsky and Korytowsky.

Lefin translated "Moreh Nevokhim" ["The Guide for the Perplexed"] by the RAMBAM to Hebrew of the Mishnah, in Ternopil. He kept busy with that translation till the end of his life.

Lefin celebrated his seventieth birthday in Ternopil in 5579 (1818/19). During one of the enlightened bashes, Lefin addressed R' Nakhman Kromkhel, without him being present and demanded that he cease his silence. He said that Kromkhel should "Enlighten your people from your chamber by holding on to the authors' pen".

Lefin died at the age of seventy-seven on 6 Tamuz 5586 [1826], in Ternopil. He died "lonely, without a wife or children, leaving his treasures to his friends such as the scholar Ya'akov Shmuel Bik from Brody[157]. His death hit his friend, Yosef Perl, hard. The latter paid R' Zalman Masita to say Kadish after Lefin for the whole year. In addition, he gave 27 rubles to the poor who attended Lefin's funeral and asked the teacher Freihling to copy Lefin's will and preserve the original in a safe location[158].

As mentioned, R' Kromkhel settled in Ternopil in 1838. Before that he resided in Zhovkova until 1836. From there, he moved to Brody. His financial state in Brody forced him to move to Ternopil and reside with his elder daughter

[Column 91]

Kona (the wife of the physician Dr. Nathan Horwitz). In Brody, he completed his life's project – the book "Moreh Nevokhei HaZman" ["Guiding the Perplexed of the Time"]. In Ternopil, he relaxed and copied chapters from his book. His home in Ternopil served as a place where the enlightened from the city and surroundings gathered. Kromkhel became "the glory of the city and its ornament". When Kromkhel stayed in Ternopil, he got an offer for the rabbinical position in Berlin, which he rejected. In Ternopil, he witnessed the attacks by the zealots and Hasidim on Sh. Y. Rapoport. RANAK [R' Nakhman Kromkhel] was a peaceful man and was against the nomination of SHI"R to the rabbinical position in Ternopil foreseeing the fights in the community that SHI"R's election would bring about. He also considered the nomination as an infringement on the tenure of the old rabbi R' Heschel BABa"D. He, therefore, objected to Perl's appeal, who advised the district minister to demand from the Ternopil community to elect a new rabbi. He fought against the nomination of SHI"R.

However, when SHI"R was elected, he came to terms with it and sent SHI"R a letter in which he congratulated him and wished him success. Kromkhel wrote to him: "Get Stronger. Do not lose, even for a minute, your peace of mind. Be diligent in removing any cause that may inhibit peace between you and the less fortunate in your community[159].

RANAK possessed views based on historical prospection. He objected to the fight against zealotry and Hassidism in the ferocity and fanatism way it was conducted and did not take an active role in it. Despite that, his influence over the enlightened people in Ternopil strengthened.

Tomb of Rabbi Nachman Kromkhel

[Column 92]

He died in Ternopil on July 31, 1840. On the thirtieth day anniversary of his death, a memorial was held at the house of prayer of Perl's school. Yitzkhak Mikhael Munis spoke about his personality and his spiritual life work[160].

Another figure from among the enlightened people who shaped Ternopil's spiritual-cultural image was Perl's student, Betsalel Stern (1798 – 1853), who served as one of the primary spokesmen during Perl's battle with the Hassidim during the period 1816 – 1828. In 1828 he moved to Odesa to serve as the principal of the Jewish school founded by Brody enlightened people. He became one of the leaders of the Enlightenment Movement there.

Another graduate from Perl's school, Hirsh Reitmann (1804 – 1866) was one of the activists in the enlightened club[161]. Later on, Hirsh moved to Brody and became the principal at the first Jewish elementary school there.

Zeev Dement (1830 – 1897), a graduate of Perl's school, authored poems in Hebrew, German, Polish, and Yiddish. He served as a correspondent of the journals "Ben Khanania" and "Allgemeine Zeitung Des Judentums" for many years. He moved to Brody in the 1870s and was appointed as the principal of the Jewish school there.

Dr. Nathan Horwitz, born in Brody on February 3 1799, moved to Ternopil after graduating from his medical school and worked there until his death on 22 January 1857. He was the son-in-law of Nakhman Kromkhel. His wife Kona (who died in Ternopil on 10 September 1857), was an enlightened woman. Her brother, Avraham Kromkhel, put her in his book "Even Rishona" ["First Stone"] (Vienna, 1871). In that book, she argued with her father and Rabbi Tzvi-Hirsh Khayut about [the philosopher] Spinoza. Dr. Horwitz tried his hand at writing. He translated the "Song of Songs" to German and added a scientific commentary. Dr, Nathan participated in the journal "HaTzfira" ["The Siren"] of Dr. Meir Letris. After Perl's death, he wrote a biographic review about Perl in the Jewish-German calendar of Y. Bush in Vienna[162]. He and the other physician Dr. Frenkelfeld, and the first Jewish lawyers in Ternopil, Dr. Kolischer, Dr. Alex Friehling, the son

[Columns 93-94]

of the teacher Moshe Friehling), and Dr. Yosef Blumenfeld, were, during those years, the only Jewish figures with academic education.

Moshe Shmuel Weisstein (1802 – 1881) was among the enlightened people. He was known by his literary pseudonym MESHOSH. Weisstein was a wise and learned man (his contemporaries called him a "Talmudic Scholar"). He was one of the biggest fans of Perl and Sh. Y. Rapoport and stood by SHI"R as a loyal friend during his entire rabbinical service in Ternopil[163].

Eliyahu Mordekhai Werbel, a graduate of Perl's school, was one of the enlightened people in Ternopil (born in Ternopil on 16 August 1805 and died in Odesa on 9 August 1880). In 1837 he was offered a position of a teacher at the Jewish school of Odesa, headed by Betsalel Stern (also a graduate of Perl's school). Other enlightened people were the teacher Moshe Khaim Katz, Aba'le Horwitz, one of the authors of "HaTsfira" of Meir L Letris, and Karl Flohen (born in 1800), who was a teacher in Perl's school. He was nominated as the Jewish population registrar in the 1840s.

Among the young enlightened, Shaul Katriel Horwitz excelled. He wrote poems when he was only 15 years old. He translated and provided a commentary about the prophets Nakhum and Ovadiah. That commentary was published in a limited quantity. He was one of the participants in [the enlightened journal] "Kokhavei Yitzkhak" ["Stars of Yitzkhak"] in the years 1847 – 1848[163]. On 23 May 1856, he published a letter in "Kokhavei Yitzkhak", in which he declared that all of his essays, poems, and commentaries mentioned above, were written at a young age and were handed for publication for the readers, hurriedly and frivolously. He asked that people consider them a childish act, which he regretted. The editor of "Kokhavei Yitzkhak", M. A. Stern, remarked that nevertheless, the writings deserve appreciation and recognition[164].

Yekhezkel Dukash, also one of the young enlightened, was a learned person with a comprehensive general education. He excelled in his talent for esthetic and belonged to the club of Goldenberg, the editor of "Kerem Khemed". Dukash published in that journal a letter he sent to I. Sh. Reggio, the spokesman of the Italian Jewish enlightened, about the sun[165].

Among the participants in "Kokhavei Yitzkhak", was also Yosef Benyamin Grass, who was a known enlightened figure in Ternopil. He moved to Lviv, later on. Grass wrote poems and translated poems of Lviv's Rabbi-Preacher Bernard Levenstein. He also published articles in the Journals "HaShakhar" of Peretz Smolenskin, "HaCramel", and Shulbaum's "HaEt" ["The Time"].

Khaim, son of Nathan Garfinkel, was born in Ternopil in 1827. He was also among the enlightened who tried their hand in rhyming and participated in "Kokhavei Yitzkhak". He left his native city and settled in Brody, where he died in 1880.

Menakhem Mendel, son of Moshe Landau (1836 – 1863) was also from among the people who participated in "Kokhavei Yitzkhak". He was born in Ternopil but resided in Kolomiya, where he later died.

People from that generation of enlightened included Shalom Grass, who also participated in Kokhavei Yitzkak", and Shlomo-Tzvi, son of Simkha Hirsh, who was born in Ternopil in 1834. He was one of the leading enlightened people and authored two books about the fate of the Jewish nation: a) "Netzakh Israel" ["Eternal Strength of Israel"], (Lyck [Elk], 5626 [1865/6]). b) "Korot Israel" ["The History of the Jewish Nation"], (Part A – Vienna, 5633 [1872/3], Part B – Ternopil, 5636 [1875/6]). He also wanted to publish a book containing the nouns in the bible but ran out of time. Hirsh established a *Beit Midrash* for praying by the name of "Gomlei Khesed" ["Benefactors"].

The following people belonged to a different kind of enlightened people who participated in the magazines of Smolenskin and David Gordon:

Manish, son of Moshe Landau, was born in Ternopil in 1852. He was a famous merchant who started his literary work with poems published at "Kokhavei Yitzkhak" (issues 35, 36). Later on, Manish participated in the journals "HaShakhar" ["The Dawn"] and "HaMaggid" ["The Preacher"]. He died in Ternopil in 1919.

Nathan Valerstein was born in Ternopil in 1853 and died in Kozova in 1911. His father, Mordekhai-Shmuel, was among the first enlightened people in Ternopil. The latter educated his son traditionally. However, he also provided him with general education. He published articles about the Jewish public life in Ternopil and its surrounding in the journals "HaShakhar, "HaMaggid", "HaEt" ["The Time"], and "Ivri Anokhi" ["I am Jewish"].

A productive author was Berish Goldenberg. He was born in 1825 in Vyshnivets (near Kremenets). Berish served as a teacher in Botosani, and from there he came to Ternopil as a Hebrew teacher in Perl's school. He worked there until his death on 5 June 1898. He began his literary work at "Kokhavei Yitzkhak" in 1845. While in Ternopil, he published the Hebrew journal "Nogah HaYare'akh" ["Moonlight"], which was published in Lviv during the years 1872 – 1873 (11 issues), and later on in 1880 in Ternopil (4 issues). A circle of Galitsian enlightened and Hebrew authors concentrated around him. In 1866 he published a comprehensive bibliography named "Ohel Yosef" ["Yosef's Tent"] about Yosef Perl and his school. In 1868 he translated into Hebrew the speech of the famous Galitsian politician, Dr. Franciszek Smolska, about the "Jewish Question". Smolska gave the speech at the Galitsian Sejm in 1898. Goldenberg also dealt with commentaries to the Torah and linguistics. In 1898 his linguistic book "Or Khasdash" ["New Light"] was published in Drohobitz (1898). He also published articles on the syntax of the Hebrew language, and commentaries about the Torah. His publications in German were: "Der Einfluss der semitischen auf die indogermanischen Sprachen"["The influence of the Semites on the Indo-European languages"], (1880); "Die religiösen Ideen der Alten und ihr Einfluss auf die hebräische Sprache vom hebräischen Standpunkte aus beleuchtet" ["The religious ideas of the ancients and their influence on the Hebrew language illuminated from the Hebrew point of view"], (1880);

[Columns 95-96]

"Die Assimilation der Juden" ["The Assimilation of the Jews"], (1883), "Gebräuche der alten Hebräer" ["Customs of the Ancient Hebrews"], (1885). [As demonstrated by these articles], a retreat from the aspiration of complete assimilation was felt among the epigones of the Enlightenment Movement, during the 1870s.

In 1875, the Ternopil's enlightened, Eliyahu Auerbakh[166], published [an article] that in the history of the Jews, the national consciousness (*Stammesbewustsien*) was stronger and more persistent than the religion. Even in ancient times, the religious factor was not the leading factor. He claimed that all the Jewish holidays bear the imprint of national memories. The national element also prevailed over religion in the laws of the "Jewish Great Assembly". In that way, the men of the "Great Knesset [Assembly]" wanted to preserve the unique attributes of the Jewish nation, and guard it against assimilation among other nations. In Auerbakh's opinion, the decisive factor was the national one, and therefore, it should be highlighted more than the Jewish religion. Auerbakh was already influenced by the journal "HaShakhar" of Smolenskin, whose ideas began to penetrate the enlightened circles in Galitsia and Ternopil.

J.

For the Ternopil's Jews, the period before the 1848 Austrian Revolution was marked by the fierce struggle between two camps: the zealots and Hassidim on one side and the enlightened on the other. The election of Rabbi Sh. Y. Rapoport amplified the tension between the camps, which did not subside after the latter left the city. With the passing of Perl, a personality who succeeded to win over the people in the community despite the difficulties and obstacles was gone. The school management was passed over to Yosef Perl's son, Mikhael, who followed his father's wishes and began his pharmacy studies. According to

Mikhael's sister, Sheindel Finlish, her father "made a mistake, which was difficult to forgive to a man like him. He did not explore nor question whether Jews were permitted to work in that profession[167]. For him, the only proof that the profession was allowed was a Jewish pharmacist he had met in Vienna. That pharmacist probably inherited an old privilege. It was enough for my good father, who always said that any old question had an answer. He did not consult with others and encouraged my brother to study". R' Nathan Kolischer[168] from Lviv, saw that Mr. Perl educated his son to be a pharmacist, also sent his son to study pharmacy sciences[169].

Mikhael Perl studied to be a pharmacist as an apprentice based on a permit of the emperor bureau with the pharmacist Christian Holstein in Zalishchyky, who provided him with a graduation certificate. He then continued his studies in Vienna in 1827. In the meantime, a small obstacle emerged. Somebody snitched about Nathan Kolischer that his son was studying pharmacy without a permit. During the investigation, the authorities found out that another youth, Mikhael Perl, was studying pharmacy in Vienna. The Viennese police investigated the matter and handed the emperor the following report on 4 August 1827:

"Among the pharmacy students, there was a Jewish student named Perl. According to Perl, he studied with the pharmacist Christian Holstein in Zalishchyky under an apprenticeship permit. He received a graduation certification there. That certificate allowed him to continue his pharmacy studies in Vienna. If Perl could pass the tests, he would be allowed to establish and own a pharmacy"[170].

Based on that report, the emperor issued a confidential direction (*Allerhöchstes Reservat*), in which he ordered to investigate "whether there was a directive allowing the Jews to own a pharmacy. If there was such a directive, he ordered to find relevant reasons for abolishing it and forbid the Jews from owning pharmacies"[171].

Based on the recommendation by the authorities, and thanks to his special privileges, Yosef Perl received a special permit from the emperor, allowing his son to complete his studies and to own a pharmacy after his graduation. When Mikhael Perl returned to Ternopil, he established and operated a pharmacy in 1832. That was the first pharmacy in Austria owned by a Jew.

According to his father's will, Mikhael managed the school after Yosef Perl's death. Mikhael's sister, Mrs. Ashkenazi, managed the girls' classes in the school[172]. However, Mikhael did not hold any essential roles in the community like his father. The progressive Jews succeeded to maintain leadership over the community until 1858, Despite the resistance by the zealots and the Hassidim. Only then, did the zealots managed to capture the lead and hold on to it for several years[173].

During the years 1843 – 1844, the public standing of the Jews as residents of the city underwent a major change. In September 1843, the Ternopil community submitted a request to grant the Jews the right to be elected to the municipal council. The Governor's response was received on 1 December 1843[174]. In his response, he emphasized that there were no

[Columns 97-98]

restrictions concerning the Jews' right to vote and to be elected to the city council. He stated that the community did not need any special privilege or permit. He declared that there was nothing that prevented the authorities from approving the request brought to their attention by the Jews. According to the law, Jewish homeowners and people who had legitimate occupations were allowed to receive citizenship. The municipality was allowed to award citizenship to others if they were found to be deserving of it. To obtain the right to be elected, the homeowners had to prove that they had successfully graduated from an elementary school. However, that condition did not apply to the right to vote. Every Jewish homeowner or Jew who held a civil trade was allowed to vote in the election for the city council. 150 people registered to become citizens, based on that declaration, and swore an allegiance oath. Twenty people from that group were elected to the city council, however, they were not allowed to vote [as members of the council].

In 1845, Ternopil, which was until then a privately owned city, became a free "state city". Ternopil's Jews celebrated that occasion with a ball. The district minister, Von Sakher, the municipal physician, Dr. Fibotzki, nobles, clergies, and other distinguished Jewish and non-Jewish people participated in that party. The speakers emphasized unity among the city residents, regardless of religion. In general, the ball's objective was "to promote reconciliation among the religions and classes. Everybody approved the speeches that were adhered to that spirit"[175].

After Sh. Y. Rapoport vacated the rabbinical position, the Jewish community considered the candidacy of Dr. Moritz Steinshneider[176] for that position. However, that never materialized, probably due to the refusal by the latter to move from Berlin to Ternopil[177].

When Galitsia Jews sensed that the Royal House of Habsburg intended to introduce liberal regime changes, they began to worry about improving their political situation and lobbied the authorities

[Columns 99-100]

to abolish the special taxes imposed on the Jews. Ternopil's community joined that political effort.

The heads of the large Jewish communities in Galitsia gathered in Lviv in 1847. In that gathering, they decided to submit a petition to the government, describing the sad state of the Jews. Since a joined petition of all the communities was not allowed, it was decided that each community would submit a separate petition.

The Lviv community sent its petition to Vienna on August 22, 1847. The Brody community – on 19 October of the same year, and the communities of Stansilawow [called today Ivano-Frankivsk], Stryy, and Sambir – on 25 October.

Ternopil sent its petition on the 1st of October 1847. The petition, written as a memorandum, was comprehensive and well-edited. It was sent directly to Emperor Ferdinand[178]. The memorandum contained an accurate review of the social and constitutional state of the city's population, the city's economic importance, and the special status granted to the city as early as during the days of Polish rule. Since Galicia was under Austrian rule, the city occupied a special place in the government discussions. As part of the imperial Patent, issued on 7 May 1789, Austria determined that, based on the principles of the "Toleration" policy, any disparities between the Jews and Christians had to be eliminated. And the Jews should be granted the same rights enjoyed by other subjects. None of the promises was fulfilled during the fifty years that passed since then. According to the Patent, equal obligations have been imposed on the Jews (similar to those imposed on the rest of the citizens), along with equal rights. However, over time, additional state, municipal, and community obligations were imposed unequally on the Jews.

The Jews were obligated to fulfill all military service requirements and pay the direct and indirect tax obligations. In addition, special taxes (candle and Kosher meat taxes) were imposed unequally on the Jews.

Following the description of the candle tax burden (from which only four thousand families were exempted, and about eleven thousand families paid only half), the memorandum continued to note that the promise, from June 8, 1813, to eliminate the candle tax was not fulfilled. The income tax was imposed, but the candle tax was not eliminated.

"Not once the poor, which the authorities exploited without a pity, had to spend his Shabbat in the dark, hungry, and in pain since he could afford to pay the pennies for a dinner for his family, and, at the same time, pay the tax collector lessee for a permit to light a candle on Shabbat. The poor often had to panhandle for the pennies that he had to pay the tax collector lessee to avoid confiscation of the straw mattress or the pillows".

The meat tax was not less oppressive. In 1824, the tax quota was set to 836,000 guldens annually. More than a million guldens were actually collected.

In 1847 45,000 Jewish families were counted, containing 325,000 people. They paid 1,400,000 guldens to the government (4-5 guldens per person). Those taxes burdened mainly the poor population, forcing it to decrease the consumption of meat because they could not pay the tax. The poverty level among the Jews was well known to everybody. Those who violated the [tax] law faced severe punishments which shamed the honorable Jew.

The burden of the municipal taxes on the Jews was heavier than the one imposed on the Christians since the Jews constituted the majority of the population in the cities. In addition to the municipal taxes, the Jews had the cover the expenses of their communities.

Despite the fact that following the abolishment of the Jewish schools in 1806, the money from the Jewish schools' funds, totaling 259,088 guldens (132,460 florins in banknotes and 126,628 in debt notes) went to fund the general schools, the government tended not to support the Jewish schools established later in the communities of Ternopil, Brody, and Lviv. In several other communities, private schools existed, which could not become public schools due to a lack of funding.

The general hospital did not accept Jewish patients, and, therefore, the Jews had to maintain their own hospitals, which did not receive any financial support from the state or the cities and towns.

The Jews were also bound by constitutional restrictions. They were not allowed to be employed by the state or in municipal services. They were not allowed to be elected to the municipal councils, and although the imperial directive from 16 November 1784 allowed to employ Jewish physicians, there were no Jewish physicians in service for the state, except a small number of municipal physicians. There were Jews who were employed in the government services as advisors at the commerce courts, police supervisors, and in Brody and Lviv, as mail carriers. There were only three Jewish lawyers in Galitsia, and no permits to work in that profession was awarded since 1832.

In the army, Jews were not allowed to become officers, despite the praises issued by Prince Karl about the actions of the Jewish soldiers during the latest wars.

It was well known that Jews were prohibited from purchasing houses, lands, and plots, as well as pharmacies. They were also not allowed to lease mines, mills, and the like.

From the description highlighted in the memorandum, it was clear that the Jews in Galitsia were oppressed by the burden of the taxes and the restrictions imposed on them. The Jews had to seek all sorts of tricks to make a living for their families. The people live in indescribable poverty and hunger,

[Columns 101-102]

therefore, the situation calls for changes.

In December 1847, the imperial court lecturer presented a report about the memorandum. That report included the conclusion that the appeals [by the Galitsia's Jewish communities] resulted from the elimination of the candles tax in Bohemia. The appeals aimed at the abolishment of the tax in Galitsia too. The handling of the appeals was handed over to the Treasury Bureau (*Hofkammer*). The bureau's response was issued following the publication of the constitution on 25 April 1848. That response stated that the matter was assigned to the parliament and therefore, the handling of the appeals had to wait for a decision by the "Assembly of the Nations Representatives"[179].

The 13th of March 1848 revolution brought freedom to the nations under Austrian rule. However, it did not immediately change the state of Jews, whose leaders demanded equal rights. The constitution provided for freedom of religious worship, but it did not address the problems involved with the legal and civil restrictions. The decision about those matters was postponed until the convening of parliament.

When demonstrations of the Sympathy Movement took place in Galitsia in support of the slogans of the Viennese revolution, battalions of civil guards that included Jewish companies rose. In Ternopil, where the Jews constituted a majority, a company of Jewish guards was also established.

In the election to the Austrian parliament, Ternopil Jews, who constituted a majority in the city, decided to elect a Jewish representative from among themselves. Their choice was unlike Brody Jews, who selected the Viennese Rabbi Noah Mannheimer to demonstrate their Germanism and to reconcile their unity with the Jews of the West.

In Ternopil, the Jews elected a representative by the name of Karmin in the Jewish district. However, for some unknown reasons, he gave up his mandate a few weeks after being elected[180].

During those years (1846 – 1849), Dr. Ya'akov Atlas, Perl's brother law, headed the Jewish community[181]. From 1834 To 1847, he was a physician in Ternopil. He was among the founders and organizers of the Jewish hospital. He was also a member of the city council. When he headed the community, he strived to renew the community's image by establishing institutions that fit the time.

When the "Kremsier Parliament" issued a resolution on 5 October 1848 that abolished all special taxes imposed on the Jews, the financial sources that supported the Jewish schools dried out. These sources paid for the wages and expenses of the rabbis, rabbinical judges, and the rest of the community's officials.

A delegation of rabbis appeared in Vienna before the Minister of Religions and Education, Graf Tehun. They described the desperate financial situation that the Jewish communities were facing. Tehun instructed them to provide him with the list of rabbis and officials to call on them for advisement. However, he later canceled the project.

In the meantime, The Jewish communities of Ternopil, Lviv, and Brody managed to obtain a permit to collect a meat tax to allow maintaining of their schools[182]. In that manner, the Ternopil community escaped a severe financial crisis. In Ternopil, the community also obtained an exclusive license to sell yeasts. The sale helped support the budget for the wages and expenses of the people serving in the synagogue. During those years, there were only two rabbinical judges in Ternopil. Their wages amounted to 1,575 florins.

The issue of the meat tax was on the agenda for many years. The finance ministry demanded a complete abolishment of that tax, however, its efforts were in vain because the communities favored its continuation and because the interior and the religions and education ministries supported their position. The community at Ternopil, who also explored various other sources to cover its budget, claimed that it would not be possible to do it in a less burdening way than the meat tax[183].

A cholera epidemic struck the city in 1848. The Jews established a committee for mutual aid, consisting of sixty members who did much to alleviate the situation among the general population[184].

When the authorities allowed the Jews to acquire real estate in 1850, 35 families submitted applications allowing them to purchase houses and estates. The following are the families whose application was approved: 1. Ziskind Rosenstein[185], 2. Dr. Ya'akov Atlas[186], 3. Aba Aberman, 4. Meshulam Aberman, a merchant and an estate lessee, 5. Salo Weinbau, a merchant, 6. Israel Fogel, 7. Israel Sapir, 8. Betzalel Sapir, 9. Perlmutter, 10. Eisenberg, 11. Khmilenker, an estate lessee, 12. Kittel, 13. Stein, 14. Breitbein, and 15. Berl Lorber[187].

In the period following 1848, changes took place in the organization of the elementary school established by Perl. At the end of the 1850s, the size of the school had to be increased. A separate school for girls had to be established. For that purpose, the community asked to raise the meat tax to secure the proceeds required to maintain the school. The financial ministry objected to approving the application, claiming principally that it was not desirable to raise the meat tax, which was just abolished. According to the ministry's view,

[Columns 103-104]

there should not be any special regulations for a specific religious community, against the principle of equal rights.

Against that, the interior ministry claimed that it also objected to the tax that burdened the poor classes, however, they should not change the status quo, since there was no other way to secure the revenues needed for the Jewish communities. Even in the case of reorganization of the communities, there were no other means to maintain the community institutions but the kosher meat tax.

In the end, the community did not receive the license to raise the meat tax, and the matter dragged on for many more years[188].

Perl's school was renamed starting in 1860: "Israelitische Haupt und Mäadchenschule" ["The Jewish Main and Girl's School"]. The Jewish studies were reduced, particularly in the girls' classes. The Talmud studies ended as early as 1855. The curriculum was adjusted according to the program in the state schools and from the Jews studies, only the religious studies (2 hours a week), and the study of the Hebrew language (11 hours a week) remained.

In 1869, 656 students studied in the school, taught by 8 teachers whose wages rose to 3868 florins annually.

The teachers took care of the poor students and established a company to supply their clothing. They organized Hannukah balls for that purpose[189]. The teachers who were active at that time were: Imanuel Perl, who managed the school after the death of Mikhael Perl, later on, Karl Flohen, Moshe Friehling, who received a medal of excellence for his pedagogic service, Phillip Liebling, Hirsh Glassgal (who transferred in 1844 to the elementary school established in Lviv by Rabbi Cohen). Among other teachers we should mention David Korngruen, Mesuta, Moritz Meirovitz, and Steinshneider.

In 1866, 90 Jewish students studied in the [state] high school[190], and in 1911 – 135 students out of 662 students were Jewish. 89 Jewish students studied in the science and math high school [The Realit Gymnasium] out of 213 students.

Various charity organizations were established in the 1860s[191], such as "Gemilut Khasadim" ["Bestowing Kindness"] and the craftsmen association "Yad Kharutzim" ["Arm of the Diligents"]. Under the initiative and lobbying of Zeev-Wolf Sapir, a new building was built for the "Talmud Torah" religious school, in which 300 students studied[192]. In 1870, the association "Khesed VeEmet" ["Grace and Truth"] was founded under the initiative of the rich man, Avraham Kutner. The association was headed by Shmuel Weinstein. Mikhael Perl founded the Association "Provide Clothing and Shoes for the School Students in Hannukah"[193]. The community also maintained a Jewish hospital containing 40 beds.

Rabbi Yosef BABa"D (1800 – 1875) served as the Ternopil rabbi beginning in the 1860s. He previously served as a rabbi in Sniatyn and Bohorodchany. He was known as a great scholar. He authored the book - "Minkhat Khinukh" ["Offering of Education"], which was published in three parts starting in 1869. The book contained a commentary on the book "Sefer HaKhinukh" ["The Book of Education"] by Aharon HaLevi (Ra'aH) of Barcelona.

The Jews had representatives in the city council. According to the law of the municipalities approved by the Galitsian Sejm in 1868, there were, in the 36 members city council, eleven Catholics, seven Greek-Catholics, and eighteen Jews.

The Jewish population grew from 11,000 people (52% of the total population) in 1869 to 13,648 (52.2%), 13,842 in 1890 (50.5%), to 13,495 (44.2%) in 1900, 14,000 in 1910 (the last year that the census was conducted by the Austrian regime), and 16,320 people in 1921.

During the period 1900 - 1910, the number of Jews decreased due to the worsening of the economic situation, which drove many of them to immigrate to America.

As a result of imposing equal rights for Austrian Jews, they were imposed the obligation of compulsory military service. As early as 1846 – 1849, several Jews enlisted in the professional army in the rank of officers, veterinarians, and military clerks[194]. In 1852,

[Column 105]

66 Jews were recruited to the army in the district of Ternopil, compared to 640 Christians.

A process of assimilation with the Polish culture, among the Jewish intelligentsia in Ternopil, began in the 1860s'. The Jewish intelligentsia maintained a common political platform with the Poles. Most of the Jewish youth that studied in the state schools and universities were subjected to Polish influence.

The following Jews participated in the Polish uprising, which took place in 1863: 1. Adolf Epstein - was nominated by the Polish national government for the position of commissioner. He participated in the battles alongside the Polish rebels. The Austrians caught him and sentenced him to jail time. Later on, Adolf moved to Chernivtsi [Yiddish - Tschernovitz] and was engaged in literary work. 2. Frankfurter Mikhael was a pharmacist, who joined the rebels when he was still a high school student, and took part in several battles[195].

Direct elections to the Viennese Parliament were held in Austria in 1873. The Jewish Organization "Shomer Israel" ["Guardian of Israel"] decided to enter the campaign as an independent party. They arrived at their decision since the Polish Sejm, under the influence of the Poles, did not send even a single Jewish representative to the Austrian Parliament.

Dr. Julius Kolischer and Dr. Emil Bik headed the central election campaign. "Shomer Israel" came out with the slogan that the Jews support the observance of the constitution and the Viennese centralism. In Ternopil, Dr. Yosef Cohen, the president of "Shomer Israel", was nominated as the candidate of the organization, however, the Poles impeded his election.

The Jews in Ternopil voted for the Jewish candidate, Dr. Yekeles in 1879 but the Pole Cherkevski was elected.

1880 was a turning point in the national policy towards the Jews. Taaffe-Donayevski's cabinet handed over the rule of Galitsia to the Poles. The Polish faction in the Austrian Parliament decided the fate of the Jewish representation in the Austrian Parliament and the Galitsian Sejm. Although the Jews constituted 11% of the population in Galitsia, they did not receive the parliamentary representation they deserved.

The heads of the "Shomer Israel" organization allied with the Poles and subjugated the Jewish representation to their will.

In the same period, the progressive circles decided to nominate a modern preacher who possessed an academic education to a preacher position in Perl's house of prayer. They also decided that he would also be principal of the school aside from his duties as a preacher. In 1890, Dr. Shimon Dankovitz was among the pioneers of assimilation with the Poles. He was also a warrior who participated in the Polish Uprising of 1863. He was nominated for the same positions as his predecessor[196].

Dr. Dankovitz was a fascinating personality who possessed a high cultural level. He was born in 1841 in Czestochowa, studied medicine in Warsaw, and took advanced studies in Jewish sciences with Dr. Mordekhai Yastrov who then served as a preacher in Warsaw. He also studied for some time at the rabbinical Beit Hamidrash in Bratslav. When he returned to Warsaw, he joined a club of young Jews,

[Column 106]

I. Rienthal

who were sympathizers of the Polish national movement on the eve of the 1863 Polish Uprising. He caused a storm with his lecture about the Jewish question (in 1860), in which he proved that the Jews were still a nation although they lost their homeland.

When the uprising erupted, he joined the rebels' companies and participated in the battles. When [he was injured]

[Column 107]

he was smuggled out to Krakow. After he recovered, he made a living by teaching Hebrew. Under the lobbying by the progressives in the Jewish committee, who knew him from his activities during the uprising, he was nominated in 1867 to the position of a preacher at the [Lviv's] Temple Synagogue. During 1880 – 1886 he served as a rabbi in Shotz [Suceava] and in other communities in Bohemia. In 1886 – 1889 he became the Chief Rabbi of Bulgarian Jews and later on, a rabbi in Meveh?. In 1889, after the death of [Rabbi] Bernhard Lowenstein he tried to replace him as the preacher in Lviv, but failed. A short time later, he was appointed a preacher in Ternopil, however, he stayed in Ternopil only a short time[197]. After him came to Ternopil as a religion teacher, preacher, and principal of Perl's school, Shmuel Taubles, who was previously during the years 1889 – 1892 the rabbi of the community of Bzenec in Moravia. After him, the teacher Philip Liebling was nominated as the principal of the school, and after him, the secretary of Ternopil community David Korngruen, served as the school principal until the break of World War I[198].

David Korngruen

In the 1880s', the National Jewish movement commenced, and the frenzy encircled the Jewish intelligentsia circles in Lviv and the big provincial towns. It also resonated in Ternopil.

The slogans of the Zionist movement that had already substantially crystallized in Lviv also penetrated the Jewish youth in Ternopil. Clandestine students' associations have been established. Lectures and courses about Jewish history and the Hebrew language were held. Intense debates about the Jewish problems took place there. All the associations established at the end of the 1880s' maintained relations with the "Zion" associations in Lviv.

The propaganda tour of Dr. Birenbaum in Galitsia cities awoke the youth and resulted in the widening of the Zionist activity. The "Zion" association in Lviv sent weekly speakers and lecturers to the provincial towns, including Ternopil.

On 29 August 1893, the first public gathering, organized by Yosef Otsheret, took place. Mordekhai Aharonfreiz and Yehoshua Thon gave speeches at that gathering about the Zionist idea and the Jewish settlements in Eretz Israel. A preparatory committee for the establishment of a Zionist organization was elected in that gathering. The members of the committee were" Yosef Otsheret, Mentel, lawyer Yoakhim Binder, Adolf Kerpel, Shenkar, Wachs, M. A. Rapoport, A. Hartman, lawyer

[Column 108]

Betzalel Boistein, Ya'akov Halperin, and Israel Hertband[199].

The association "Beni Tzion" ["The sons of Zion"] was established. Three hundred members joined, most of whom were from the middle class and local intelligentsia. Two lawyers, the philosopher Dr. Taubles (the religion teacher), and two university students joined as well. Podles, the student who established a library and a reading hall, was very active during the initial period. Hebrew language courses taught by the known enlightened and grammarian Berish Goldenberg were held immediately after the establishment of the association.

In 1894, the first Hannukah Maccabim ball took place. Carl Shtandt, David Maltz, and Dr. Taubles spoke in that ball. The latter joined the assimilators' camp later on and persecuted the Zionists in the schools.

With the number of members growing, the association rented a large home in the city square and held a festive housewarming ball. Rabbi Israel Parnas opened the party and called for unity. Aharon Karpel spoke about assimilation and the damage it brought to Judaism. In his speech, the preaching rabbi, Dr. Taubles, emphasized the value of the Hebrew language for women[200].

The association continued to grow, and the Zionists' influence on the public life of the Jews in Ternopil became apparent. The courses and lectures about Jewish literature and history, which were held for years, played a major and important role in the Zionist education of the Hebrew youth.

Ternopil's representatives participated in the conference union of the organizations that were active in settling in Eretz Israel and Syria. Ternopil's representatives also attended the deliberations of the "Zion" organization in Austria. Ternopil's representative, Mendel Pomerantz, was elected to the management committee.

Ternopil's representatives also participated in the second conference of Galitsia's Zionists, which took place in Lviv on 2 – 4th of September 1894. Y. D. Rodnik reported about the "Bnei Zion" association in Ternopil. He was also elected to the presidency of the conference. Pomerantz was elected to the national committee.

Ternopil's Zionists began to capture an important position in the Zionist movement and the Jewish Ternopil became one of its forts.

Author's Notes:

1. Jan Tarnowski (1488 – 1561) excelled as a military commander. He participated in the battles with the Tatars and the Muscovites, starting in 1521. During 1517 – 1521 Jan traveled to western Europe, Syria, and Egypt [he made a pilgrimage to the Holy Land during that trip]. In 1521 he helped the Hungarian King Ludvik in his war with Turkey. In 1931, he fought as the head of the Polish army against Turkey, Wallachia, and Moscow
He was from among the proponents of the Habsburgs. He was also known as a military author. His book "Consilium Rationis Bellicae" ["Council of the War Case"], Tarnow 1558, was used as a war sciences textbook for several generations. He stood in opposition to King Sigismund-Augustus.
2. The palace fortification constituted a sturdy fort separated from the city by a moat and a stone-made levee covered by an oak grate. At the edges of the levee, on the city side, stone citadels were erected. They were fitted with gun shooting slits. Bridges hanging on chains above the moats and levees linked the castle and the city at a time of need. A two-story castle stood within the fort, containing several halls and residential rooms. The castle building was also outfitted with gun shooting slits. An arsenal containing a substantial number of rifles, gunpowder, lead, and cannons was located in the yard.

3. "Przywileje królów i właścicieli miasta Tarnopola" ["Privileges of the Kings and Owners of the City of Tarnopol"], Dr. Jan Leniak, 1932.
4. Dr. Majer Balaban: "Zydzi Lwowscy" ["The Jews of Lviv"] p. 371.
5. The "Orient", 1848, pp. 478 – 480.
6. In one of his answers (Responsa 43), R' Meir indicated that at the time of the Tatars' attacks, every resident in Volhynia was obligated to fight on the front, by the order of the Duke (*Voivode*). Jews were trained on shooting. The same obligation was also imposed in Reisyn [Belarus].
7. In 1672 the following was written in the city record: "*Musztra Zydzi równo z chrześcijanami powinni odprawować, z muszkietem pewnym stawać, kul wedlug potrzeby, knotow i prochow stawac, pod wina trzech grzywien na zamek naleząca*" ["Jews are obligated to train with muskets, and if needed, also bullets, wicks and gunpowder. Any avoidance is subject to fines by the authorities."] (Finkel Ludwik: "Miasto Ternopol w r. 1672" ["The city of Tarnopol in 1672". Rocznik Kolka: "Naukowegi Tarnopolskiego za rok, 1892", str. 127 ["Annals of Tarnopol Scientific Collection for the Year 1892", p. 127].
8. Mentioned in the Polish translation of the book by Xawery Liske: "Cudzoziemcy w Polsce" ["Foreigners in Poland"], Lviv 1876 p. 159.
9. A copy of the statute is located in an archive and library of the Duke Bavorovski in Lviv: "Ksiegi lawnicze tarnopolskie z lat 1738 do 1788" ["Ternopil Law Books from 1738 to 1748"].
10. Israel Halperin: "Pinkas Va'ad Arba HaAratzot" ["The Ledger of the Council of Four Lands"], Tel Aviv, 5705 (1944 / 45), No. 43, p. 271, 5561 (1800/01).
11. Va'ad Arba HaAratzot" ["The Council of Four Lands"].
12. Israel Halperin: "The Ledger of the Council of Four Lands", p. 310, book 5619 (1848/9), No. 51, XLIX, a letter from 16 September 1728.
13. Israel Halperin: "The Ledger of the Council of Four Lands", pp. 126, 143, 163, 165, 168, 177, and 181.
14. Khaim-Nathan Dembitzer: "Klilat Yofi" ["Beauty in Perfection"], Krakow 1888. Part A p. 58/b.
15. Rabbi Yitzkhak Krakover's daughter, Sara, was married to [Head of the Rabbinical Court] Skalat, Rabbi Wolf, the father of the activist of the "Council of Four Lands" and the last Jewish leader of the state of Reisyn, R' Yisaskhar Berish. Rabbi Wolf of Skalat was also the grandfather of the first and the only state Rabbi of Gaitsia during the Austria rule, R' Arye-Leib Bernstein (grandfather of Professor Dr. Tzvi Peretz Khayut). The second daughter of Rabbi Yitzkhak Krakover was the wife of Rabbi Yitzkhak ABD Iziaslav [Zaslav], R' Yosef Kharif. Among other sons-in-law, we should also mention Rabbi Moshe-Shaul, ABD Kalish, and later on Zhuravne, and Rabbi Moshe from Brisk, Lithuania.
16. The husband of his eldest daughter, Miryam, about him: Dembitzer - Klilat Yofi, part A, pp. 131 – 132.
17. Ya'akov Emden – "Megilat Sefer" ["The book Scroll"], David Kahana Publishing, Warsaw 1896, p. 65.
18. [Yaakvov Emeden's] "Megillat Sefer", pp. 67-68.
19. R' Arye-Leib was a rabbi in Rzeszów [Reisha], up to 1728, and then in Glogow during 1734 – 1739. While in Glogow, He declared a boycott against the RAMKHAL [Rabbi Moshe Khaim Luzzatto]. During that period, he also served as a rabbi in Lviv and its district. In 1740, he was selected as the Rabbi of Amsterdam and took an active role in the conflict between Eibeschitz and Emden. His correspondence on that affair was published in Ya'akov Emden's books "Sfat Emmett" ["The Language of Truth"] and "Hit'abkut" ["Wrestling"].
(Also see Y. Halperin: "Pinkas Va'ad Arba HaAratzot", pp. 345 – 349, 355 – 358, 361 – 362, 364 – 371, 374 – 376, 378 – 379, 408, 411, and 477).
Arye-Leib died on the seventh day of Passover 5515 (2 April 1755). His brother-in-law, Ya'akov Emden, who did not appreciate Arye-Leib in his memory book, changed his mind in his eulogy about him where he said: "I found myself obligated to eulogize and cry after him not only because I was his brother-in-law, but more so because he suffered because of me and what I said" (Pamphlet "She'agat Arye" ["Lion's Roar"], Amsterdam, 5515 1754/55] and a quote in Y. Halperin: "Pinkas Va'ad Arba HaAratzot", p. 345, Note 12).
20. Y. Halperin "Pinkas Va'ad Arba HaAratzot", p. 334, book 5657 [1896/7].
21. Among his three daughters, one was married to Zalman Portis, the son of the famous activist of the Va'ad Arba HarArzot, Dr. Yitzkhak Portis ( ). The second daughter married the leader from Lublin, Avraham Kheimesh, and the third Married the leader, Zoralth from Nadvorna.
22. Yitzkhak, son of Tzvi-Hirsh HaLevi Landau, was a rabbi in Tarla and from 1719 a rabbi in Afta. During 1729 – 1738 he was a rabbi in Zhovkva and then the province in Lviv. Starting 1754, he served as the ABD [Head of Rabbinical Court] in Krakow. In the controversy between Eibeschitz and Emden, he favored Eibeschitz. He died in Krakow in 1767. During his service in Tarla, he saw the certificate from 1726 in the "Historisheh Shriften" [" Historical Writings"], YIVO B' II 643 (Dr. Refael Mahler: "Documenten Tzu der Geshikhte fon di Va'adei HaGlilot in Poilen" ["Documents of the History of the Provincial Committees in Poland"]. Also printed in the Ledger of the "Va'ad Arba Ha'aratzot", p. 303, 5606 [1845/6].
23. He signed on the census of 1765 as Szmujlo Jakubowicz.
24. Moshe-Pinkhas, son of Avraham R' Kheimesh of Lublin (who was the last *parnas* – [activist-official] of the "Council of the Four Lands"), was the son-in-law of Israel-Isrel from Zhovkova, who was also a *parnas* of the "Council of Four Lands". After serving as a rabbi in Svirzh, he was nominated to be the rabbi in Zhovkova in 5506 (1746). In 1751 he threw his support in Zhovkova in favor of Eibeschitz.
25. R' Yosef, the son-in-law of R' Yekhezkel Landau (author of "Nodah Be'Yehuda") was a rabbi in Yavorov, Vyskov, Sokal, and since 1780 until he died in Poznan. Since he issued judgments against the Prussian laws, he was punished by the authorities with a

fine of a thousand thalers in cash. He died in the month of Adar 5561 [February 1801] (Shlomo Buber: "Kehila Ne'emena" p. 69-70).
26. Dr. Majer Balaban: "Spis Zydow i Karaitow ziemi Halickiej i powiatu Trembowelskiego i Kolomyjskiego w r. 1765" ["Census of Jews and Karaites in the Halych Land and Trembowel and Kolomyjski Counties in 1765"], Krakow, 1909, pp. 14 – 15.
27. N. M. Gelber: "The History of the Jews in Bukovina in the Years 1773 – 1785", "Tzion", 5702 [1941/2].
28. Actually, the central authorities in Vienna planned to push for an Industrialization program, which the commission in Galitsia was against, particularly Graf Brigido and his advisor Kortum. The latter thought that industrialization would not bear any results unless the Jews were not expelled from the cities. Kortum wrote the following in 1768:
"*Bekanntlich ist der Jude in Galizien alles. Er ist Bürger. Er ist der Fuss, das principale der städtischen Bevölkerung. Sein Esprit de Corps setzt ihn schon allein in den Stand, alles was Industrie heisst um sich her zu verdrängen. Die Erfahrung redet dafür. Immer war er der Ausbreitung der städtischen Industrie hinderlich. Aber seitdem den Juden alle Arten von bürgerlichen Gewerben freigegeben worden - ohne Mittel, die ihre Anzahl Jemals vermindern können und bei der überwiegenden Wahrscheinlichkeit ihre Menge von Jahr zu Jahr zu wachsen zu sehen- verschwindet auch die Möglichkeit des Gedankens in Städten wo Juden wohnen, fremde Fabricanten und Handwerker auch bei aller Unterstützung mit guten Erfolg anzusiedeln.*" ["As commonly known, the Jew is the basis for life in Galicia. He is a citizen but of lowest class, which is the basis of the urban population. His community comradeship [*ésprit de corps*] alone enables him to drive out everything around him that has to do with urban industry. The experience speaks for itself. The Jew has always been a hindrance to the expansion of urban industry. Since all sorts of civic trades have become available for Jews, there are no means by which we can reduce their numbers. There is an overwhelming probability that their numbers will grow from year to year. Therefore, the possibility of successful settling of foreign fabricants and craftsmen, in cities where Jews live - diminishes, even with all the support."].
(Bericht vom Dezember 27 1785. Archiv des Ministeriums des Inneren", Wien V.G. ["Report of December 27 1785. Archives of the Interior Ministry", Vienna V.G.], Carton 2968 from 12 February 1768.
29. Archive of the Interior Ministry (A. d. N. d. J.), Protokolle Galitsien [Galitsian Protocols] 1776, December No. 30.
30. Ibid, 1778, January No. 28, March, No. 9.
31. Ibid, June No. 29, Vienna.
32. N. M. Gelber "Statistic fon di yiden in Poilen, sof 18 yarhundert" ["Statistics of the Jews in Poland at the end of the 18th century"], Shriftn fur ekanamik on statistic" ['Writings on Economics and Statistics"], YIVO volume, Berlin 1928, p. 188.
33. IV T. 1, Judenansiedlung {Jewish Settlements] c.a. 1792, carton 2580.
34. Archiv des Ministeriums für Innere's, Wien. [Archive of the Interior Ministry, Vienna], Galitzien IV T., ex 1822.
35. Archiv des Ministeriums für Inneres, (Wien), [Archive of the Interior Ministry, Vienna], IV T., ad Carton T. 11 e. a. 1787, Carton 2658 No. 147.
36. Anton Mosler served as the district minister during those years. IV T. 11, Carton 2658.
37. Hofkammer-Archiv, Wien, im Archiw des K.u.K Ungarn u. Galizien [Imperial and Royal archive of Hungary and Galitsia], fasc. 57 as 5, January 1782.
38. Slightly different numbers are mentioned in the census from 1791 - Archiv des Ministeriums für Inneres. Wien [Archive of the Interior Ministry, Vienna], IV T., ad Carton 2580 (1792 -1804).
39. The following is the content of his decision:
"*Sämtliche Schänkarenden sind den Juden in Galizien ohne mindeste Termin-Verlängerung sofort abzunehmen. Die Dominien aber, die wieder diesen Verbot derlei jüdische Pächter beibehalten, sind mit der bestimmten Geldstrafe ohne alle Rücksicht anzusehen. Wien 29.1.1787. Josef* ["Jews are to be removed from all taverns in Galicia immediately without any extension of the deadline. The estate owners, who would again violate this ban on those Jewish lessees, are to be fined without any consideration. Vienna, January 29, 1787. Emperor Josef II"].
Archiv des Ministeriums des Innern, Wien IV T. 11 Carton 2568 (1786 – 1792) Nr. 37.
Also see - Mikhael Stöger: "Darstellung der gesetzlichen Verfassung der galizischen Juden" ["Representation of the legal constitution of the Galician Jews"], Lemberg [Lviv], 1833 I pp. 154 – 159.
40. Protokoll Galizien 1791 – 1793 Dezember, Nr. 159.
41. IV T. 1 Galizien, Carton 2580 (1792 – 1804), Fasc. 277 – 278 (1828 – 1848).
42. In the rest of the district communities the following people served as teachers:
    1. Yeshaia Rosenbush in Zbarazh (his annual wage -150 florins).
    2. Levi Tornauer in Hrymailiv [Grzylavow] (200 florins).
    3. Khaim Handek in Myukulyntsi [Mikulince] (150 florin).
    4. Aharon Balk in Terebovlia [Trembowla] (150 florins).
    5. Hirsh Urban in Budzaniv (150 florins).
43. Korytowski's letter from 25 March 1812, was published by Israel Weinlez' "Historische Schriften", YIVO, Vol. I, p. 811
44. Archiv des Ministeriums für Unterricht und Kultur [Archive of the Ministry of Education and Culture], Wien 23, a ad 70 ex Mai 1816 Isr. Freischule zu Tarnopol.
45. The cities were: In the district of Ternopil - Ternopil, Terebovlia [Trembowla], Zbarazh, Skalat, and Husiatyn, and in the district of Zalishchyky - Zalishchyky and Yazlovets. The towns were: In the district of Ternopil - Myukulyntsi [Mikulince], Strusiv, Hrymailiv [Grzymalow], Khorostkiv, Kopychintsi, Yablonovy, Suchostav, Dolina [Yanov], Budzaniv, and Ihrovytsy. [No district is mentioned for the following additional towns:] Borshchiv Ustechko, Khorostkiv, Zvebyhorod, Horodok, Yahilnytsya, Ozeryani [Borshchiv subdistrict], Korolowka, Krzywcza, Korerintza, Pidbuzh, Skala, Tovste [Tluste], Ust'ye, and Biskopia.

46. Yitzkhak Iganz Bronstein was the son-in-law of Ternopil District's rabbi, R' Shmuel Falkenfeld. During the Russian regime in Ternopil, he purchased the Zalishchyky's estates. He converted to Christianity in 1815. He acquired for himself the title Baron Bavari which was later approved by the Austrian government in 1918. His wife, Rachel, daughter of Rabbi Falkenfeld, refused to convert to Christianity and remained Jewish with her two daughters. She was buried in the Jewish cemetery in Zalishchyky. The daughter of his son Leon – Malvina, was married to Victor Bilinski and was the mother of the famous Austro-Polish scholar and politician, Dr. Leon Bilinski (1846 – 1923).
47. Archiv des Ministeriums des Innern IV T. (1815 – 1828) ad. 115, April 1818 (32420 / 3665): "Grundbesitze der Tarnopoler Juden" ["Land ownership of the Ternopil Jews"].
48. Staatsarchiv Wien [State Archive, Vianna] SA / 1545, 25 February, 1818, "Hausbesitz Tarnopol "["Ternopil – Ownerships].
49. A report of the Austrian Commissioner in Ternopil, Stutterheim, from 21 November 1815, as quoted at:
    Jan Leszczynski: "Rzady rosyjskie w Kraju Tarnopol-skim 1809 – 1815, ["Russian rule in The Tarnopol Region 1809 – 1815"]. Krakow-Warsaw 1903].
    (monogarfie w zakresie Dziejow Nowozytnych Wydawca Szymon Askenazy) Vol. III p. 138, 254 ["Monographs on Modern History" - publisher Szymon Askenazy, Vol. III, P. 138, 254].
50. He was a stern lease holder. In 1820, four Jews submitted a complaint against him.
    Archiv Min d. Innern, Wien, Protokoll Galizien 1820.
    Also, the archive of the commissioner in Lviv: "Protocol Präsidialakten" ["Protocol Presidential File"], 1820 No. 3488.
51. His sermon from 1838. Parts of the sermon were published in the book by Weinlez: "Yosef Perl's Yiddish Writings", p. LXIII.
52. Dr. Nathan Horwitz: "Joseph Perl, Eine biographische Skizze" ["Yosef Perl, A Biographical Sketch"]. J. Busch: "Kalender und Jahrbuch der Israeliten", ["Calendar and Yearbook of the Jews"], 1846 / 47, Vienna, p. 216 – 217.
53. Dr. M. Letris: Memory in the Vienna book, 1869, pp. 98 – 99.
54. N. M. Gelber's article about Mendel Lefin, in his book: "Aus zwei Jahrhunderten" ["From two Centuries"].
55. Published in Dr. Philip Friedman's article: "Yosef Perl Vi a Bildungestuer un zein shul in Tarnopol" ["Yosef Perl as an Educator and his School in Ternopil"], YIVO Bletter [YIVO Journal], 1948, Actn un Documenten [Acts and documents], pp. 188 – 189.
56. Ibid pp. 132 – 137.
57. As he mentioned in his letter from November 11 1826, to Leon Landau in Odesa Published in Wienlez p. XVII.
58.
   1. According to the report of the first school's principal – Neiman. A manuscript in Perl's library in Ternopil. It is quoted in the article by Dr. Philip Friedman (mentioned above [in note 55]), p. 141.
   2. Perl's letter to Leon Landau in Odesa from November 9, 1826. The letter was published in I. Weinlez: "Yosef Perl's Yiddish Writings", p. XVII.
59. Dr. Horowitz: "Jahrbuch Busch" V., p. 217
60. The students were 1. Betsalel, 2. Khana Mirel Stern, 3 and 4. Two Perl's children, 5. Yosef Hirsh, 6. Yitzkhak Dinish, 7. David Tzvi, 8. Leah Frantsoiz, 9. Lipa, 10. Yehoshua, 11. Yokheved, 12. Rakhel Atlas, 13. Falk Regel, 14. Moshe Kohenberg, 15. Leib Bronstein, and 16. Yitzkhak-Hirsh Weintraub.
61. Neiman managed the school until 1817. After Ternopil ed to Austrian hands in 1816, he lobbied the Austrian authorities about school matters.
62. Born in Kolikiv in 1779. He was a German, French and Hebrew teacher. In 21 September 1854, the celebrated his anniversary with the school in splendor. He received a medal of excellence - "Goldenes Verdienskeiz". Algemeine Zeitung Des Judentums [Jewish General Newspaper], 1854, 534.
63. Yitzkhak Mikhael Meniyes was a Hebrew author who participated in "Kerem Khemed", in which he published the translation of four letters by Euler about physics and an article about the blessing "Bring him into the covenant of Avraham our father" (II pamphlet 23).
    He also published scientific news under his name, Shmuel-Leib Goldenberg. He published the article "Questions and Answers about Customs" in "Yerushalayim", Zhovkva, 1844. He was a known Torah scholar. He served in Perl's school for more than 25 years. He died in Ternopil in the summer of 1844. He left a Hebrew translation of Euler's letters, the book "Mishlei Ya'akov from Dubna" ["Proverbs of Ya'akov from Dubna"], and a book about esthetics.
    Written about him in the "Orient" p. 407, and in Allgemeine Zeitung des Judentums", 1846, pp. 105 – 106.
    He corresponded with the RIVAL [Yitzkahk Ber Levinzon]. His letters were published in "Be'er Yitzkak" ["Yitzkhak Well"], EWarsaw 1899, pp. 90, 105, 121 – 122.
64. Aryeh Leib Kinderfreind was the student and trainee of the Hebrew author Ya'akov Gelber-Eikhenbaum, the author of the poem collection "Shirim Shonim" ["Miscalenous Songs"], Lviv 1834. He was a very skilled linguist. He wished to help another teacher, Yitzkahk Erter, join the school. The latter came to Ternopil for that purpose, but for some reason, his hiring never materialized.
65. The reason why the students learn the "Deutsche-Yudeshe Shparkh" ["German-Jewish language"] was explained in one of the textbooks: "Since the Jews do not have their own language, they always use the language of the nation they reside with. However, for the written language, they use Hebrew letters, particularly, that is the custom used by the Jews who speak German. Since the five books of the Torah and Psalms were translated recently into German, using the Hebrew letters, it was useful for the youth to study form these books for religious studies." (Dr. Friedman p. 163 – 164).
66. After the liberation of Ternopil, a fable was circulated in Russia that [Tzar] Alexander the 1st said (ostensibly) that "because of that Jew (Perl), it was hard for him to give Ternopil up".
    Dr. M. Weissberg: "Die neu hebräische Aufklärungs-literatur in Galizien, (Monatsschrift für Geschichte und Wissenschaft des

Judentums)", 1928, Heft 1-2 p. 83 ["The New Hebrew Enlightenment Literature in Galicia, (monthly journal for the history and Judaic studies"), 1928, issue 1-2 p.83].
67. IV. T. 2 carton 2661 ad. 238, July 1816.
68. IV. T. 2 carton 2661, No. 158. January 1816.
69. Staatsarchiv, Wien SA/1545, 25 February 1818.
70. Archiv des Ministeriums für Innern IV. T. 1, 15 April 1818.
71. According to Dr. Horowitz, in his biographic review about Perl:
Since Ternopil was separated from Lviv, Perl obtained a permit to establish a printing business there. He later sold it to Finlish. The Yiddish translation of the book of Proverbs by Mendel Lefin was printed in that printing house in 1813. Perl's calendar for the years 5574 [1813/14], 5575 [1814/15], and 5576 [1814/15], the book "Rosh Emuna" ["The Pinnacle of Faith"] by Abarbanel, and the Perl school's publications were also printed there.
72. The article by Dr. Meir Balaban about the Hebraic publishing in Poland in "Soncino Blätter" III, H. 1, and the article by A. M. Haberman: "The Hebraic publisher in Ternopil, and the list of published books", published in "Alim" ["Leafs"] for bibliography, Vienna, 5695 [1935], pp. 24 – 31.
73. IV. T. 7, Carton 2627.
74. Archiv des Ministeriums für Kultus und Unterricht, Wien [Archives of the Ministry of Culture and Education, Vienna], 23 a ad. 70 ex., May 1816.
75. Archiv des Ministeriums für Kultus [Archive of the Ministry of Culture], 23 a, 1816 ("Israelitische Freyschule zu Tarnopol" ["Ternopil Free Jewish Day School"]).
76. Archiv des Ministeriums für Kultus und Unterricht, Wien [Archives of the Ministry of Culture and Education, Vienna] SA/6265 ad 21 August 1817, "Israelitische Freyschule zu Tarnopol und deren Erhebung zur Hauptschule" ["The Jewish Free Day school and its upgrade to a secondary school"].
77. Archiv des Ministeriums für Kultus und Unterricht, 23a, 213 ex September 1817.
78. The delay was caused by the resistance of the people in the community, most of whom were Hassidim, who did not want to pay an ongoing contribution. Because the community leaders and a few prominent Jewish families joined the agreement, the authorities in Vienna were encouraged to direct the provincial government to approve the agreement, against the Hassidim's will. Zhbarazh community committed itself to contributing an amount of 450 florins annually.
Archiv des Ministeriums für Kultus und Unterricht, SA/8173, 20 December 1819.
79. The resolution by the emperor was worded as follows:
"*Ich genehmige, dass zu Tarnopol gemäss den von der Studien Commission, gemachten Anträgen eine Israelitische Hauptschule errichtet werde und ernenne zum Direktor derselben den Joseph Perl, welchen Ich zugleich die Erlaubniss erteilte, seinen Stellvertreter und seinen Nachfolger, wie auch taugliche Lehrer, Solange er das Amt eines Direktors besorgen wird, unter Bestätigung der ordentlichen Behörde zu ernennen. In Anschnung der gemachten ansehnlichen Aufopferungen und des bezeigten lobenswerthen Eifers verleihe Ich dem Joseph Perl die mittlere Goldene Ehrenmedaille mit Ohr und Band um Deren Ueberkommung sich an Mein Oberstkammerant zu wenden Ist*" ["I authorize the establishment of a Jewish secondary school in Ternopil according to the proposal made by the Studies Commission and appoint Joseph Perl as director of the same. I also grant him a permit, for as long as he holds the position of a principal (with the approval of the proper authority), to appoint his deputy, his successor, and qualified teachers. In recognition of the considerable sacrifices made and the praiseworthy zeal shown, I award Joseph Perl the Medium Golden Medal of Honor with Ear and Ribbon, the code for which, will be addressed by my Upper-Bureau]. Troppau 16 November 1820.FRANZ
Perl's annual salary, as the principal of the school, was 600 florins. However, he refused to receive it (Dr. Horowitz Jahrbuch V pp. 219 – 220).
80. "Die Erziehung der jüdischen Jugend in Galizien wie sie ist und wie sein sollte." ["The education of the Jewish youths in Galicia as it is and as it should be"], Archiv des Ministeriums für Kultus und Unterricht, Wien SA/ 5049, 1826, 16 August. Also found in the file: 23 A 5213 October 1830.
81. Archiv des Ministeriums für Kultus und Unterricht und Kultus, SA/5049.
82. Dr. Horowitz pp. 223 – 224.
83. M. Weissberg MS f. G. u. W. d. J. 1927, p. 83.
84. Archiv des Ministeriums für Innern, V T 1, "Duldung der Juden in Galizien" ["Tolerance of Jews in Galicia"], 1815 – 1828.
85. IV T 1, 1815 – 1828, kt. 781/179 February 1826.
86. In his letter to SHI"R from 30 November 1825, published at I. Weinlez, pg. XXXIV.
87. Archiv Ministeriums für Kultus und Unterricht, 23 E, 169, 5 July 1836.
88. Archiv des Ministeriums für Kultus und Unterricht, 23 a, 14 July 1833, Z. 12049.
H. Reitman who published, after the death of Perl, the review: "Joseph Perl und die Schule zu Tarnopol" ["Yosef Perl and his School in Ternopil"], In the journal of Dr. Avraham Neiger: "Wissenschaftliche Zeitschrift für Jüdische Theologie" ["Scientific Journal for Jewish Theology"], pp. 312 – 318, 1839. He writes that the proposal was submitted by Perl in 1836, however, archival documents show that it was actually submitted as early as 1833.
89. From his letter from 20 February 1826 to Friehling, published by I. Weinlez p. XLIX.
90. Archive of the Galitsian Commission in Lviv: Fasc. 11 Juden Algemeine Sachen, Nr. 14690, 1830.
91. Staatsarchiv Wein, S. A. 4200 ex 4 July 1832.

92. The Viennese government objected to that paragraph for the fear that it would "*die Einschleichung fremder Individuen erleichtert werde*" ["facilitate the incursion of alien individuals"]. The government changed the paragraph to read that only wealthy members can join the association.
93. "*Vortrag über den Vorschlag des Direktors der israelitischen Hauptschule zu Tarnopol Joseph Perl wegen Gründung eines Vereines zur Verbreitung nützlicher Gewerbe unter d. galizischen Judenschaft*" ["Lecture on the proposal of the director of the Jewish secondary school in Tarnopol, Joseph Perl, regarding the establishment of an association for the expansion of useful trades among the Galician Jews"].
    Archiv des Ministeriums des Innern: Polizeiakten [Archive of the Ministry of the Interior: Police files] No. 3348.
94. Gerson Wolf: Joseph Wertheimer, Vienna 1860, p. 105.
95. Dr. Aharon Paries from Lviv: "The history of SHI"R in [the periodical] "HaShakhar" ["The Dawn"], 5629 [1868/9], p. 26.
96. The translation to German of the full text of two boycotts. One boycott of SHI"R (Sh. Y. Rappoport), Avraham-Banyamin-Tzvi Natkis, Yehuda Pestor and Yitzkhak Erter. The second boycott of Brody and Ternopil were attached to the file:
    Archiv des Ministeriums für Kultus und Unterricht, IV T 5, ad 26, September 1816.
97.
98. Archiv des Ministeriums für Kultus, ad ex 194, November 1819.
99. Akt 106 ex August 1827.
100. Dr. P. Friedman: Di Ershte Kampen Tzwishen Haskalah un-Hassidim in Galitsye – Fun Nanten Avar" ["The First Battles between Haskalah [Enlightenment] and Hassidim in Galicia - from the Recent Past"]. Vilna, booklet 4.
101. Dr. J. Nakht: "Ein unveröffentlichtes Aktenstück von Josef Perl" ["An unpublished document of Josef Perl"], M.G. W. d. J., 1927 [pp.] 308 – 311.
102. Dr. P. Friedman "Yosef Perl vi a bildungs-tuer un zein shul ein Tarnopol" ["Joseph Pearl as an educator and his school in Tarnopol"], YIVO Bletter [YIVO Journal], 1948 pp. 171-172.
103. In his sermon on Shabbat Nitzavim Torah portion, 1838. Published by I. Weinlez p. 8.
104. "Die Juden in Galizien" ["The Jews in Galitsia"], Lepzig, 1845 p. 21.
105. A unique impression, which he never forgot, made on him the riot by the Hassidim, in 1815, when they broke into the new school building and broke the glasses and destroyed the windows (B. Goldenberg, "Ohel Yosef, Toldot Perl VeBeit Sifro" ["Yosef's Tent. The History of Perl and his School"], Lviv, 1866, p. 4.
106. Archiv des Ministeriums für Inneres, Wien, Polizeiakten [Police Records] e.a., 1816 Nr. 2328.
107. Brünn [Brno], 1823 Volume II pp. 197 -259
    Beer specifically wrote that he received from Yosef Perl from Ternopil and from the preacher Nishka Hassidic books, and that he made significant use of the essay that Perl had sent him (Vol. II p. 205).
108. The manuscript was sent to the censor as early as 1816.
109. According to Dr. Nathan Neteh Horwitz (Jahrbuch V, p. 222), this is about the book by Peter Beer. However, Beer's book. However, that book was published in 1823, while "Megaleh Tmirin" was published in 1816. Undoubtfully, this is about the article: "Uber das Wesen der Sekte der Chassidim" which Perl submitted to Hauer in 1816. According to Dr. Philip Friedman (in his article "Di Ershte Kampfn Tzwishen Haskalah un-Hassidism" in "Fun Naetn Avar", Vilnius, 1838, pp. 261 – 263). Perl possebly referred to the Polish translation "Shivkhei BESHT" ["Praises of the BESHT"], about which Shmuel Bik wrote on 15 Iyar 5579 (1819) to Mendel Lefin, who resided in Ternopil at that time. According to Bik, the translation was popular among the Polish nobility.
110. Allgemeine Zeitung des Judentums, 1839, No.. 32, p. 46-47.
111. Allgemeine Zeitung Des Judentums, 1839 No. 90 (21.9) pp. 483 – 484, 92 (5.10) pp 511 – 512).
112. It is interesting that in Jost's "Israelitische Annalen", published after Perl's death, an article appeared in which the following was said about the book "Bokhen Tzaddik":
    "*Seine jüngste Schrift verdient der Vergessenheit übergeben zu werden. In diesem Buche werden zum Theile harmlose und dem und ruhige Personen ohne Grund angegriffen und dem Tadel preisgegeben auch die Galizier mit Unrecht öffentlich blossgestellt, so dass er allgemeinen Umwillen auf sich zog und man ihn hasste wegen seiner Träume und Reden. Daher hat den auch sein Tod nicht den erwarteten Eindruck gemacht und weniger Trauer erregt als wir anfangs vermuteten. Ja, wir haben selbst zu unserrem Leidwesen hören müssen, dass seine früheren Verehrer jetzt sein Ableben als Glück betrachten.*
    So hat sein Alter Manches Werk seiner Jugend verdorben. Ja, seine Schrift hat das Volk um mehrere Stufen zurückgeworfen in dem es danach die Aufklärung beurtheilt und noch stärker zu vermeiden strebt. Nicht blos das gemeine Gesindel der Chassidim, welche am Abend über seinem Grabe (!) vom Branntwein berauscht herumsprangen und in roher Freude über den Tod ihres Feindes an diesem Ort des Friedens sich tummelten, sondern wir gesagt auch viele Bessergesinnte theilen die Ansicht, dass Buch besser nicht geschrieben wäre" ["His most recent work deserves to be destined to oblivion. In this book, harmless and calm people are attacked without reason. The book unjustly exposed in public the faults of the Galicians. Thus, he attracted general displeasure, and people despised him because of his dreams and speeches. Therefore, his death did not generate the expected impression and caused less grief than one can expect. We were sorry to hear that his former admirers have cheered the news of his death. Thus his age has spoiled many works of his youth. Yes, his writing has set the people back several years in judging the Enlightenment Movement. His latest work caused people to avoid enlightenment even more than before.
    The Rebbe and his followers, the Hassidim, danced around intoxicated on his grave (!), a place of peace. They romped in a raw joy over the death of their enemy. Many open-minded people just shared the opinion that it would have been better if the book had not been written"].
    (Israelitische Annalen 1839 Nr. 44 p. 346).
    A few years ago, an unknown manuscript written by Yosef Perl (from his school library in Ternopil), written in the format of stories

of Rabbi Nakhman of Bratslav (in the books "Shivkhei Ha'RAN ["Praises of Rabbi Nakhman from Bratslav"], and "Likutei MAHARAN" ["Collection of Rabbi Nakhman's Teachings"]). The manuscript is in Jerusalem and would be published soon after the publishing of the Yizkor Book. It would include an introduction and scientific commentary by H. Shemrock, one of the workers at the general Jewish archive in Jerusalem.

113. New York, 1942, p. 30.
Dr. Mahler describes the Hassidic rebbes and their followers as people who hated the lessees of the tax collection and considered themselves as savior and faithful warriors for the benefit of the masses. He ignored the fact that there were tax collection lessees, even among the Hassidim, who exploited people like other lessees. We should not forget that there were also enlightened people who detested the lessees and their methods.

114. The same Hassidim and rebbes who fought against the tax collection lessees did not shy away from trying to get collection leases for themselves and their followers. In a letter from 1833 to SHADAL [Samuel David Luzzatto], Sh. Y. Rappaport [SHI"R] wrote about the details of his fight to secure the position of a secretary in a kosher meat tax collecting corporation. He had to fight against the lessees who objected to his candidacy because they were from "an evil Hassidic sect" (Ben Tzion Dinaburg, SHI"R's Letters, "Tzion", Booklets a and b, Jerusalem, 5687 [1926/7], p. 49).

115. His sermon in the House of Prayer in Ternopil in 1838 (see Weinlez, p. LIX [59]).

116. More about him in N. M. Gelber's book: "Vorgeschichte des Zionismus" ["From the Prehistory of Zionism"], Vienna, 1927, pp. 92 – 124.

117. l.c.p. 117 – 124.

118. Dr. R. Mahler p. 216, Addendum VII.

119. "Kerem Khemed", 5596 [1835/6] II, pp. 16 – 36.

120. In Ust'ye-Zelenoye [Ushitze] (Podolia), two informers, Yitzkhak Oksman and Shmuel Schwartzman, were killed based on the decision by the district communities and with the agreement of Rabbi Israel of Rozhin. The trial required huge sums of money (R' Shaul Gintsburg: "Ma'aseh Ushitz ["The Story of Ust'ye"] published in "Historisheh Verk" ["Historical Works"], volume 3, New York 1837).

121. Dr. R. Mahler pp. 178 – 180 and Addendum VIII. Copies of those documents were also found in the Archive of the Ministry of Interior in Vienna (IV T I Fasc. 278). In connection with the escape of Rabbi Israel Friedman [of Rozhin] to Bokovina see N. B. Gelber's book: "Aus zwei Jahrhundreten" ["From Two Centuries"], Vienna 1924 p.p. 116 - 121: Zur Geschichte der Dynastic Sadogora" ["On the history of the Dynasty of Sadogora"]

122. The assumption by Dr. Mahler that R' Israel Friedman [of Rozhin] was arrested because of Perl's memorandum (the content of which was given to Podolia governor, Lashkarev), is unsubstantiated. Despite the harsh accusations, the central authorities in Austria refused to extradite him to Russia when he escaped to Bukovina in 1841, despite Russia's forceful requests.

123. Perl's memorandum and the authorities' instructions were published in Dr. R. Mahler's book, Addendum X, 1-50. pp. 232 – 237. Perl justified his request to eliminate the ritual baths by claiming that underage sex solicitations occurred there. He witnessed such an event in 1790 when he was still visiting the baths. The RIVAL [Rabbi Yitzkhak Ber Levinzon] reported about a similar case in Radyvyliv [Radzivilov], in 1820, in his letter to Perl (see the article by Dr. Simkha Katz in "Moznaim", Tel Aviv, 5712 [1951/2], issue a-c, pp. 266 – 276).

124. According to the notes by [Leopold Ritter von] Sakher-Masoch, who served in the government in Galitsia at the time: "Tages Notizen" ["Daily Notes"] v. 28. V. 1838. Archiv Ministeriums des Innern, Polizeiakten [Police Files] Fasc. 1460.

125. An article about the election and arrival [of SHI"R] in Ternopil: Algemeine Zeitung, 1838 No. 22 (20.II) p. 88, No. 23 (22.II), p. 91. In the article from 20 February 1838, (signed Mektram), the following was written about the Hassidim and the zealous'

126. outrage:
"Was für ein Zetergeschrei für einen Wehruf, als ob die Welt untergange hat das Gelichter der Fanatiker ausgestossen, als die Wahl desselben (S. I. Rappaport) abgestimmt wurde. Ein gellender Schrei Der Wut, der Entrüstung enrfuhr ihnen. Sie glaubten dadurch ihn einzuschüchtern, seine innere Berufsstimme zu betäuben, damit er entweder ab-geschreckt werde oder wenigstens nach seiner Erwählung nichts zu ihrem Nachteile unternehme, was ihnen bei so Vielen schon gelang." ["What a clamor for a cry of defiance, as if the world is coming to an end. The response by the fanatics, following the election of the same (S. I. Rappaport). They sounded a shrill cry of rage and indignation. They believed that by intimidating him and silencing his inner professional voice, he would either be deterred or at least do nothing to their disadvantage, which they had already succeeded in doing to many other people."].

127. A. Poros, "Toldot HaRav R' Shlomo Yehuda Leib Rappaport" ["The History of Rabbi Shlomo Yehuda Rappaport'], "HaShakhar" ["The Dawn"], (in a special pagination), pp. 37 – 40.

128. In an article from 22 February 1838, Ternopil role was specifically mentioned:
"Tarnopol scheint von allen anderen Gemeinden Galiziens vom Schicksal ausersehen in siegreichen Kampfe gegen Orthodoxie und Chassidismus ihren Mitschwestern mit glänzende Beispiele Vorauszugehen." ["Ternopil seems to have been destined by fate to precede its sister-cities by providing shining examples in its victorious struggle against Orthodoxy and Hassidism."]. (Allgemeine Zeitung des Judentums., 1838, p. 91).

129. Dr. Mahler addendum IX p. 229.

130. Die Juden in Galizien, Leipzig, 1845, pp. 38 – 41.

131. The proclamation in the file: "Tages Notizen Sakher-Masoch, Polizeiakten [Daily Notes Sakher-Masoch, Police Files], Fasc. 1460.

132. In the archive of the Ministry of Religious Affairs and Education, IV T 27662 ad 5/838, I found the following report about the controversy in Ternopil:
"TARNOPOL – ZWIST.

Die erfolgte Wahl des als hebräischen Litteraten Lemberger Israeliten Salomon Leib Rappaport zum Tarnopoler Rabbiner und die im polizeilichen Wege Verfügte Sperrung der dortigen seit jeher bestehenden fanatisshen Partei, hat zu Ausbrüchen des leidenschaftlichen Hasses gegen den neuen Rabbiner u. d. Schuldirektor Perl Anlass gegeben. Die schändlichen Auftritte der Chassidim verursachten die Versperrung einiger.

Der Führer dieser Umtriebe namens Silberfeld wurde zu achttägigen Arreste verurteilt. Was die Winkelbethäuser betrifft, wird nur erzahlt von einer Brodyer alten Frau, wie es zu ofters zu solchen überraschenden Szenen kam, dass Inmitten der grössten Andacht war man den plötzlichen Eindringen von Polizisten ausgesetzt die die betenden auseinander trieben, die Wohnung und die Teilnehmer mit schwerer Strafe belegten" ["The TERNOPIL DISPUTE. The election of the Lviv Jew, Salomon Leib Rappaport, a Hebrew literary figure, as the rabbi of Ternopil and the police blocking off the fanatical party that had always existed there, gave rise to outbursts of passionate hatred against the new rabbi and the school director Perl. The disgraceful performances of the Hasidim caused the blocking of some.

The leader of these activities, named Silberfeld, was sentenced to an eight-day jail term. An old woman from Brody said that there were often some surprising scenes in their houses of prayer - amid the greatest devotion, the worshipers were often surprised by a sudden intrusion of policemen, who dispersed the praying people and punished the participants with severe punishment."].

133. Portions are published in the book by I. Weinlez: "Yosef Perl's Yiddishe Ktavim" ["Yosef Perl's Yiddish Writings"], pp. LXV – LVII.
134. See N. M. Gelber's book: Aus zwei Jahrhundreten" ["From Two Centuries"], Vianna, 1924.
135. Tages Notizen Sakher- Masoch, Polizeiakten [Daily Notes, Sakher-Masoch, Police Files] Fasc. 1460, from 23 October 1838.
136. Yehoshua Heschel was the permanent correspondent of the magazine "Algemeineh Tzeitung des Judentums" ["The General Gazette of Judaism"] from 1835. The advisor Krieg wrote about him in a report of Lviv's police from 28 September 1835: "*H. Schorr ist der jüngere Sohn des Brodyer Handelsmannes Schacher Schorr. Er hat kein Gewerbe, beschäftigt sich mit Lektüre, soll eitel und eingebildet sein und unter Juden als Schönheit gelten.*" ["H. Schorr is the younger son of the Brody merchant Schacher Schorr. He has no trade and occupies himself with reading. He is said to be vain and conceited, and is considered a fine man among the Jews."]. Weiner Polizei-Archiv [Vienna Police Archive], Fasc. Nr. 1478.
137. Dr. Mahler, Addendum XI, pp. 238-239.
138. Dr. Mahler, pp. 193 – 201.
139. Even in Lviv, while being ill, he was involved in public affairs. He met with Lviv's enlightened and proposed that they build a modern synagogue. He told them to turn to the emperor for help. His proposal was accepted, and Dr. Rapoport initiated the planning for building the Temple Synagogue in Lviv.
140. Her husband was probably the relative of the printing house's owner in Ternopil, Nakhman Finlish, one of Perl's friends. I received from his daughter Sheindel compelling correspondence from 1821 – 1825 with her friend, Moshe Inlender, a known enlightened in Brody. These letters were supposed to be published shortly with an introduction and note, after the publishing of the Yizkor book.
141. An article by Sh. L. Goldenberg in the "Orient", 1840, pp. 267 – 270.
142. Dr. Jost's Isrelitische Annalen, 1839, No. 44 (1.IX).
    Dr. Julius Heinrich Dessauer: Geschichte der Israeliten, Braslaw, 1870, p. 532.
    Dr. Leopold Löw called him "Mendelson of Galitsia". He claimed that thanks to Perl's school, "Ternopil became one of the centers of the enlightenment, or the Athens' Galitsia": Ben Chanania, 1861, No. 13.
143. "Kerem Khemed", 5601 [1841/42], pp. 163 -169.
    The German monthly journal in Lviv "Mnemosyne" [the source of the name - in Greek mythology, the goddess of memory] published in 1839, 12/X, an article of appreciation about Perl. The article was later published in "Allgermeine Zeitung des Judentums", 1839, No.r. 99, 103.
    Obituaries were published in "Israelitische Annalen" as early as in 1839. One Obituary is particularly interesting. This obituary, which is full of personal stinging remarks, was published by Y. H. Schorr in Dr. Jost's '", 1839, No. 44 p. 346: "*Er war in der That ein vortrefflicher Mann wiewohl wir uns nicht verhehlen, und zu unserem Schmerz gestehen müssen, dass auch er seine Fehler hatte und menschliche Unvollkommenheiten an sich trug. Zunächst ist zu bedauern, dass es ihm an geordneter Schulbildung gebrach und er in keiner Sprache sich eigentlich gut und richtig ausdrückte.*" ["Indeed, he was an excellent man, although we must not hide and painfully admit that he also had his faults and human imperfections. First of all, it is to be regretted that he lacked a proper school education and that he did not express himself well and correctly in any language."].
    Later on, Schorr published his criticism on Perl's book "Bokhen Tzaddik". The enlightened Schorr could not forgive Perl, who insulted Brody enlightened and its merchants in that book.
144. Published in the "Orient", 1840, p. 355.
145. According to the custom, people stay awake that night and read the "Tiqun of Leil Shavuot." ["Rectification for Shavuot Holiday Night."]. SHI"R followed that custom. SHI"R woke up the next morning, tired from a lack of sleep, and asked the young cantor, Yehoshua Abrass, to sing some Niguneim [traditional melodies] for him to relieve his sleepiness. A zealot Hassid who heard the melodies in the street shouted: "They are playing Christian song at the rabbi's house". Pandemonium ensued and the Hassidim attacked the rabbis' house (Poris, pp. 46 – 47).
146. An article by Sh. L. Goldenberg, "Orient", 1840, pp. 260 – 261.
147. Hirsh Goldenberg, a person with a broad general education, knew Greek well. He turned to SHI"R to inquire about as to whether his translation of a word borrowed from Greek in his article about Nathan from Rome [Rabbi Nathan, son of Yekhiel], is correct.
148. SHI"R connected with Ternopil's enlightened, during his years as a Rabbi in Ternopil through the journal "Algemeineh Tzeitung des Judentums" ["The General Gazette of Judaism"].

The following article appeared in 7 April 1838, Vol. 52., p. 165,

"Seitdem Rapaport in Tarnopol ist, haben sich die sonst isolierten und zersprengten jüdischen Gelehrten in der hiesigen Gemeinde zu einem Gelehrtenkreis um ihn gesammelt uzw. Samuel Goldenberg, Isaak Monies der neueste und naivste hebräische Parabeldicher, der Ordensritter Joseph Perl, Moses Chaim Katz, Lehrer an der Perl Schule, Dr. Horowitz, Arzt schrieb in der "Zephira."" ["Since Rapaport has been in Ternopil, the otherwise isolated and scattered Jewish scholars in the local community have gathered around him to form a circle of scholars. Samuel Goldenberg, Isaac Monies, the newest and most naive Hebrew parabolic poet, the knight Joseph Perl, Moses Chaim Katz, teacher at Perl's school, Dr. Horowitz, physician, who wrote in "Tzphira.""].

149. A eulogy article by Hirsh Reitman in "Algemeineh Tzeitung des Judentums", 1846, pp. 104 – 105.
150. See "Be'er Yitzkhak", a book containing the correspondence between Yitzhak Levinzon and scholars of his period in different times, Warsaw, 1899, p. 90.
151. A letter from 24 Sivan, 5602 [June 2, 1842], p. 90.
152. Zhovkova, 1844, p. 9 – 21
153. "Kerem Khemed" II, No. 23.
154. "Igrot SHADAL" ["Shmuel David Luzzatto's Letters], Krakow, 1900, p. 93.
155. Dov Ber Nathanzon, "Sefer Zikhronot" ["Book of Memories"], Warsaw. 1875, p. 8.
156. According to the letters of Sheindel Finlish, the daughter of Yosef Perl. The letters were supposed to be published in "Reshumot" [the gazette of record for the State of Israel], after the publishing of this Yizkor book.
157. Fedder wrote rhetorically. Among his writings we need to mention the following: 1."Sefer Bayit Ne'eman" ["The Book of the Faithful Home"] (Berlin 1794). 2. "Beit Tuvya" ["The House of Tuvya"] about grammar (the manuscript was lost). 3. "Lahat HaKherev HaMit'hapekhet" ["The Flame of the Turning Sword"] (Vilnius 1866) written against the erroneous commentaries by Aharon Wolfson to the Books of Kings, and that of Yitzkhak Aikhel in his book "Seder Tfila" ["The Order of Prayer"]. 4. "Zohar Khadash LePurim" ["New Allure for Purim"], a humorist parody for the holiday of Purim written in the language of the Zohar, printed by Moshe Tenenbaum from Ternopil in Shaltiel Gerber's "Otzar HaSifrut" ["The Literary Treasure"], Yaroslav, 1888/9 (1889/90). Tenenbaum had many unpublished letters of Fedder. A. B. Gotlober published his poems (1877) in his journal "HaBoker Or" ["Morning Light"].
158. Ya'akov Shmuel Bik wrote about him after his death: "The poet R' Tuvyahu Fedder, may he rest in peace, was hated during his life for his custom of fiddling with his rhetorical sword on his thigh like a commander in the army when a rival or a cripple passed by. However, Bik respected him as a poet and wrote about him that "when the sun of [Yehuda Leib] Ben Ze'ev has set, the sun of Tuvyahu shined" ("Kerem Khemed", I, p. 96), Letris – "Mikhtavim BeIvrit" ["Letters in Hebrew"], p. 123.
159. Dr. Shlomo Rubin – Introduction to the book "Malkhut Shaddai" ["Kingdom of Heaven"] (Part 3 of the Hebrew translation of "Moreh Nevokhim" by M. M. Lefin)
In the monthly magazine "Nogah HaYare'akh" ["Moonlight"] by Berish Goldenberg from Ternopil, Lviv, 5632 (1871/2), issue 4-5, p. 27, remark.
160. Yosef Perl's copy book, in his library in Ternopil. The following is the writing on his Lefin's gravestone: "Here buried, the old exalted scholar, our teacher, Menakhem Mendel Lefin who was born in Satanov in 5509 [1749]. He authored the books - "Igerot HaKhokhmah"[Letters of Wisdom"], "Sefer Refuat Ha'Am" ["The Book of Popular Healing"], "Sefer K?eshbon HaNefesh" ["The Book of Moral Accounting"], "Sefer Makhkimat Peti ["Book of Making the Foolish Wise"], and "Elon Moreh" ["An introduction to Moreh Nevokhim"], in addition to other delightful essays. He authored commentaries for the books of Lamentations and Ecclesiastes, as well as Sifrei Emet [Psalms, Proverbs, and Job]. He also rewrote [translated into Mishnaic Hebrew] the book "Moreh Nevokhim" ["The Guide of the Perplexed"]. He passed away on Tuesday, 6 Tamuz 5586 [1826].
161. Published by Dr. Sh. Rabidowitz: "Kitvei RANAK" [RANAK's Writings"], Berlin, 5684 [1923/4], p. 430. The relations between RANAK and SHI"R soured when SHI"R tried to secure the rabbinical position in Prague. Rabbi Tzvi Hirsh Khayut also applied for the same position, and RANAK supported him. SHI"R left Ternopil on 14 Tamuz 5600 [15 July 1840], and RANAK died on the first of AV 5600 [31 July 1840]. After RANAK's death, SHI"R published a eulogy in which he highlighted his admiration for his late teacher.
162. Israelitische Annalen, 1840, No. 36, pp. 301 – 302, No. 39, p. 328.
163. Reitman published the first review of Perl's school: "Perl und die Schule zu Ternopil" (Dr. Abraham Geiger's: Wissenschaftliche Zeitschrift für jüdische Theologie ["Perl and the Ternopil School" (Dr. Abraham Geiger's: "Scientific Journal for Jewish Theology"] , 1838, p. 316).
164. "Kalender und Jahrbuch für Israeliten" ["Jewish Calendar and Yearbook"], Bd. V, Vienna, 1846, pp. 209 -232.
165.
  1. Participated in the journal "HaMaggid" of David Gordon: "HaIvri" in Brody.
  2. In "Kokhavei Yitzkhak" Volume X, he published a translation of the poem "Der Jude von Kampf" ["The Jew of Struggle"], the story "HaZe'ev VeHaro'eh" ["The Wolf and the Shepherd"], and two articles with commentaries to the Bible.
166. "Kokhavei Yitzkhak" XXII pp. 78 – 79.
167. From the date 13 Shvat 5690 (11 February 1930), [the Hebrew date in the article 18 Shvat 5504 seems to be an error], "Kerem Khemed" I, issue 30. The answer by Reggio was published in issue 31.
168. "Neuzeit" ["Modern Age"] (Vienna), 1875, No. 42, p. 341.
169. According to paragraph 31 of the 1785 "Jewish Regulations", Jews were allowed to hold any profession which they were forbidden to hold under special laws. There was no prohibition for a Jew to be a pharmacist or to own a pharmacy. However, years later, a regulation was issued according to which it was forbidden for a Jew to be a pharmacist or to own a pharmacy.

170. Among the leaders of the Lviv's community. A friend of Yosef Perl.
171. The letter from Sheindel Finlish in Ternopil to Moshe Inlander in Brody from 29 February 1824 (From the collection of her letter that the author has).
172. Staatarchiv Wien: Kabinetsakten [State Archive, Vienna, Government Cabinet Files], 1827, No. 395.
173. Ibid.
174. Allgemeine Zeitung des Judentums, 1844.
  Dr. Julius Barasch's article: "Wanderung durch Krakau, Galizien, Bukowina, Moldau und Wallachei" ["Wanderings through Krakow, Galitsia, Bukovina, Moldavia and Wallachia", pp. 439 – 441.
175. "Neuzeit" (Vienna), 1862, 1/VIII.
176. The archive of the commission in Lviv, Gubernialdekret [Governor's decree], v. 1.XII.1843, Zl.967.
  The following is the full text:
  "*Ueber das im September 1843 unmittelbar beim hohen Landes-gubernium angebrachte Gesuch der Tarnopoler israelitischen Gemeinde um Ertheilung der Wahlfähigkeit gum städitischen Ausschusse an einzelne Judemeinde-Glieder ist mit hohem Dekret v. 1 Dezember 1843 Z. 70966 anher bedeutet worden, dass sowoklm in Betreff des Bürgerrechts der Juden als auch in Betreff ihrer passiven u. aktiven Wahlfähigkeit zum städtischen Ausschuss sich lediglich nach jenem Gesetye zu benehmen sei, welches unterm 5 Oktober 1792 Z. 29081 bekanntgegeben wurde und dass jeder Zweifel in dieser Bezichhung durch die neueste ah. Entscheidung gelöst, sonach ohne weitere Anstände nach dieser Vorschrift zu verfahren sei, ferner, dass die Judengemeinde hierzu weder eines eigenen Privilegiums noch einer besonderen Bew lligung bedürfe und dass ihr das was sie anspricht unter keinem Vorwande vorenthalten werden kann. Rücksiehtlich der allgemein besorgten Beeinträchtigung der christlichen Bevölkerung wurde im bezogenen hohen Dekrete insbesonders bemerkt, dass diese Besorgnis bei genauer Betrachtung des Sachverhältnisses schwinde, denn das Gersetz bestimmt, dass nur jene Juden das Bürgerrecht anzusprechen berechtigt sind, die Besitzer von bürgerlichen Realitäten oder Gewerben sind, an solche aber, die nicht zu dieser Kategoric gehören spricht das Gesetz aus, dass die Magistrate nicht verhalten werden sollen, das Bürgerecht zu verleihen. Es bleibt daher ywar dem Magistrate freigestellt, auch Juden der letzten Kathegori, wenn sie in sonstiger Beyiehung, desselben würdig erscheinen, sloches zu verleihen. chieht es aber nicht über die Verweigerung beim Kreisamte beschweren. Durch die Erlangung des Bürgerrechts allein werden aber die Juden noch nicht zu Ausschussmännern wahlfähig sondern hierzu müssen sie nicht blos Inhaber einer Realität oder eines Gewerbes sein, sondern nebstbei auch beine höhere Bildung besitzen, unerlässlich aber nachweisen dass sie Normalschule mit gutem Erfolge zurückgelegt haben. Hieraus ergiebt sich schon, dass die Zahl derjenigen, die zum Ausschusse wahlfähig erscheinen, keineswegegs bedeutend sein kann und dass nicht zu besorgen sie, dass Leute ohne alle Vorbildung in dem Ausschuss gewählt werden könnten. Dass dagegen die Stimmfähigkeit kein Nachteil, und vielmehr zu wünschen sei, dass Juden auch bei der Wahl christlicher Ausschussmänner ihre Stimmen abgeben, ergiebt sich daraus, da sie von der Moralität und Fähigkeit christlicher Ausschussmänner ebensogut untterrichtet sind als die Letztern u. die Würde eines Ausschussmännes nicht gerne einem Individuum zuwenden werden das kein Vertrauen verdient, daher mit Grund zu erwarten ist, dass tauglichere Individuen in den in den Ausschuss gewählt werden dürfen wenn die Jüdischen Mitbürger mitwählen, als wenn sie von der Stimmgebung ausgeschlossen sind. Bei den Christen ist zum Bürgerrechte sowohl als zur Wahlfähigkeit, weder der Besitz einer Realität noch eines bürgerlichen Gewerbes vom Gesetze gefordert. Es können daher Aerzte, Lehrer Pensionisten Künstler und dgl. Individuen ohne Realitäten zu besitzen, Bürger und Ausschussmänner sein, so bald sie nur ihren fixen Wohnsiz in der betreffenden Stadt aufschlagen. Die Tendenz des Gesetzes geht vorzüglich auf die Würdigkeit des Charakters und die höhere Inteligenz, daher es besonders angedeutet ist das Lehr-Personale für den Anschluss zu gewinnen und die Lehrer and den Haupt-und Normal-Trivialschulen haben auch wesentliches Interesse zum Ausschusse zu gehören und die Vermögens-Gebahrung der Städte zu Kontrollieren, da nach den neuesten Bestimmungen die Stadtkassen die Gehalte, Pensionen und Schulauslagen theils ganz theils grösstenteils zu tragen haben. Es ist Kaum zu zweifeln, dass auch die Jüdischen Stimmführer sich füur solche Individuen entscheiden werden, wenn sie durch Charakter und Intelligenz dessen würdig erscheinen.*"
  ["The following is the response to the application of the Tarnopol Jewish community to grant individual members of the Jewish community the right to vote in the municipal committee, which was submitted directly to the high state governorate in September 1843: The High Decree no. 70966, from December 1, 1843, states that in the matter related to the civil rights and the right to vote or be elected to the municipal council, it is only necessary to act according to the law, which regulates the right of the Jews to obtain citizenship and their right to vote and be elected to the municipal council. The law (item 29081) was promulgated on October 5, 1792. Any doubt in this matter should be resolved by the most recent High Decree no. 70966. Furthermore, the Jewish community requires neither a special privilege nor a special permit for these rights. Any of those rights cannot be withheld from the Jews under any pretext. Concerning the general concern that the Christian population would be adversely affected - it was noted in the High Decree that this concern is should be extinguished if the facts of the matter at hand, are examined more closely. The law stipulates that only those Jews who are owners of civic real estate or those who possess trades are entitled to apply for citizenship. Law - item 29081 states that the magistrates should not be required to grant citizenship to those Jews who do not belong to these categories. The magistrates are free to confer the right of citizenship on Jews of these categories if they appear worthy of it in other respects. A refusal to grant citizenship can be contested by submitting an appeal to the district office. However, the acquisition of citizenship alone is not sufficient for a Jew to be eligible to be elected as a council member. To be elected, Jewish citizens must have higher education. They need to prove that they have successfully completed general schooling. Imposing those conditions means that the number of Jews who are eligible to be elected to the committee can by no means be significant. Therefore, there is no reason to worry that people without education could be elected to the committee. Awarding the Jews the right to vote should not be considered a disadvantage. The public, as a whole, benefits when the Jews are allowed to cast their votes in the election of Christian council members. The Jews are just as informed of the morality and ability required from a council member. They would not award the

honor associated with the role of a council member to an individual who does not deserve their trust. It is therefore reasonable to assume that more suitable individuals may be elected to the committee if the Jewish citizens are allowed to vote, than if they are excluded from voting. In the case of Christians, neither the requirement of possession of real estate nor of a civil trade is required by law for civil rights or the ability to vote. Physicians, teachers, pensioners, artists and the like can be citizens and council members without possessing real estate, as soon as they set up their permanent residence in the city in question. The law's objective meant to address the worthiness of characters of the council members and ensure that they possess high intelligence. Therefore, it encourages the teaching staff of the general elementary schools to run for council membership. The law also encourages ownership of the real estate. That allows according to the latest regulations, the people who pay the taxes and the city treasuries a better control over the school budgets (salaries, pensions, and school expenses) either partially or completely."].

177. "Orient", 1845, p. 118.
178. Allgemeine Zeitung des Judentums, 1845, p. 688
179. The cantor of the house of prayer, Yehoshua Arbass, from among the well-known cantors of that period (Born in Brody in 1820, and was the student of Zulzer), also left Ternopil after he served there during the years 1837 – 1844, He was accepted as a cantor in the Temple Synagogue that was established then in Lviv.
180. The archive of the Governate Commission in Lviv. Fasc. 11, Juden Allgemeine Sach? No. 728.
181. The archive of the Galitsian Governate Commission, Fasc. 11/2, Juden.
182. I. Busch-Letteris: "Oesterreichisches Zentralblatt für Glaubensfreiheit, Cultur und Literatur" ["Austrian central newspaper for freedom of faith, culture, and literature"], Vienna 1848, No. 22.
183. His sister, Tauba, was the wife of Mikheel Perl. She died in 1867 at the age of 64 ("Neuzeit", 1867, p. 399).
184. Archiv des Ministeriums für Innern IV T. 11, ZI 23472 c.a. 1854.
185. Staatsarchiv, Vienna, 1860, ZI 2796.
186. "Orient" 1848, p. 185.
187. An estate lessee in the district of Ternopil in 1852, paid an annual tax of 1700 florins for his estate.
188. He submitted a request in 1856, to allow him to purchase the house of the heirs of Arzem Pirutzki. Graf Agnor Golokhovski and the justice minister Bakh supported the request and provided recommendations. The emperor gave the permit to register the property under the name of Dr. Atlas on 8 February 1856 ([Archiv des Ministerium für Innern] IV T/2 2310/57).
189. Archiv des Ministeriums für Innern IV, T/2 Besitz c.a. 1850 – 1860.
190. Staatarchiv 2796 / 1860.
191. "", 1859, p. 91.
192. "Neuzeit" 1866. Demant: "Briefe aus Galizien" ["Letters from Galitsia"] p. 43.
    The high level of the school's teachers is highlighted in the article as follows: *"Der grössere Teil hat wissenschaftliche Bildung und bringt die Freistunden mit dem Studieren der Klassiker zu oder ruht sich von der Arbeit aus in der biblischen Exegese order im Labyrint des Talmuds lustwandelnd"* ["The majority of them have a scientific education and they spend their free time studying the classics, resting from their work in biblical interpretation, or wandering in the labyrinth of the Talmud".
193. In 1866, the community's rich man, Meir Bik, who did not have any heirs, passed away. He left a fortune of 160,000 florins. From that he left a quarter to his late wife's family. He banished his own family from the inheritance ("Neuzeit", 1866, No. 1 p. 5). It is unknown what happened to the rest of the property and as to whether it was left for social needs).
194. The report was published in "Neuzeit", 1875, No. 38 p. 306.
195. Articles in the Journal "HaShakhar" ["The Dawn"], third issue, p. 2, 5631 [1870/71] p. 2, 5632 [1871/72] pp. 88 and 181.
196. The following is the list of Jewish officers and physicians who served in the professional Austrian army during 1849 – 1911
    Officers:
    1. Shpeizer Aharon, born in Ternopil in 1826. Recruited in 1846. 1866 – He served as a Second Lieutenant, 1875 – Lieutenant (*Aberlieutenant*), 1883 – Captain (*Haftman*). Participated in the war against the Hungarians (1848). Died in Fagaras in 1892.
    2. Grold (Goldberg) Yosef. Born in Ternopil in 1868. 1891 – Second Lieutenant in a calvary battalion, 1895 – Lieutenant.
    3. Rapoport Aharon. Born in 1859. Graduated from an officer school (*Kadettenschule*), 1879 – Second Lieutenant. Left the army in 1882.
    4. Rapoport Johan. Born in 1856. 1879 – Second Lieutenant.
    5. Shapel Marian Igen (Shmuel Markus). Born in 1863. A graduate of the officers' school in Lubzov (?). 1888 – Second Lieutenant, 1899 – Lieutenant. Left the army in 1897.
    6. Wahl Heinrikh. Born in 1859. A graduate of an officers' school. 1878 – Second Lieutenant. Participated in the war in Bosnia (1878). 1883 – Lieutenant. Committed suicide in 1888.
    7. Emil Adler von Kolischer. Born in Ternopil on 20 September 1856. His father, Karl Kolischer and his mother Rosa (maiden name Kornfeld). Served in the army from 1879. He was awarded a noble title in 1909 by Emperor Franz Joseph 1. Died in 1909 with the rank of Field Marshal.

    Physicians:

    8. Reis Markus. Born in Ternopil in 1814. Served as a deputy physician (*unterärtzit*) during 1851 – 1859.
    9. Dr. Ya'akov Hirshhorn. Born in 1848. In 1879 – he served as a Senior Physician (*überärtzit*), 1892 – Regiment Physician (*regimentärtzit*), 1899 – Staff Physician (*stabestärtzit*), 1909 – Senior Staff Physician] (über*stabestärtzit*).

10. Dr. Shimon Freudenthal, born in 1849. In 1882 he served as a Senior Physician, 1885 – Regiment Physician, and 1909 – Staff Physician.
11. Dr. Oscar Lazarus, born in 1872. In 1879 he served as a Senior Physician, and in 1900 -1905 as a Regiment Physician.
12. Dr. Kantz Wilhelm, born in 1863. In 1889 he served as a Senior Physician, and in 1892 – as a Regiment Physician.
13. Dr. Goldberg Adolf, born in 1822. In 1849 he served as a Physician. Participated in the wars of 1859 and 1866. In 1877 he served as a Regiment Physician. Died in 1888 in Brasov.
14. Marmurek Yosef, born in 1838 in Ternopil. During 1859 – 1861 he served as a Deputy Physician.
15. Perl Mikhael, born in 1835, served as a Deputy Physician in 1862.
16. Freudenthal Shlomo, born in 1832. During 1857 – 1871 he served as a Military Physician. Participated in the wars of 1859 and 1866. Died in Braslaw.
17. Dr. Yosef Finlesh, born in 1840. In 1860 he served as a Physician. In 1880 – as a Regiment Physician. Participated in the wars of 1866 and 1878. Died in Vienna in 1892.
18. Dr. Finlesh Yosef, born in 1843 in Ternopil. In 1864 he served as a Deputy Physician. In 1874 – as a Senior Physician. In 1880 – as a Regiment Physician. Died in 1894, in Nei-Markt . Participated in the wars of 1866 and 1878.
19. Dr. Zilberman Herman, born in 1838. Served as a Senior Physician. Was taken as a prisoner of war during the Prussia-Austria war. Died in Theresienstadt [Terezin] in 1867.

Veterinarians

20. Tau Yosef, born in 1847. Served as a Deputy Veterinarian (*untertierärtzit*) during 1878 – 1880.

Adminstrators

21. David Shponberg, born in 1851. In 1883 served as a Accountant- Lieutenant (*rechnungsleutnant*) in 1888 –Accountant Senior Lieutenant (*rechnungsüberoberleutnant*) and in 1895 –accountant captain (*rechnungshauptmann*). Died in Lviv in 1907.
22. Weinberg Julius, born in 1830. In 1863 he served as an Accountant Officer, in 1880 – 1891 he served as an Accountant Senior Officer. He died in Vienna in 1899.

This list was organized based on:
Moritz Frühling: "Biographisches Handbuch der in der K. u. K. Oesterr. Ung. Armee und Kriegsmarine aktiv gedienten Offiyiere, Aerzte, Truppen-Rechnungsführer und sonstigen Militärbeamten Jüdischen Stammes" ["Biographical Handbook of Officers, Physicians, Troop Accountants and Other Military Officials of Jewish Origin Serving in the Imperial and Royal Hungarian Army and Navy"], Vienna 1911.

197. Dr. N. M. Gelber: "Die Juden und der polnische Aufstand 1863" ["The Jews and the Polish Uprising of 1863"], Vienna 1923, p. 221.
198. Rabbi Dr. Sh. D. Tauber served before him for a short time. Rabbi Tauber came from Iasi. In 1889 he eulogized, in the house of prayer, the Lviv's Rabbi Bernhard Lowenstein from Ternopil. He was offered the rabbinical position in Belovar Croatia (Ch D. Lippe's Lexicon, 1899, p. 368).
199. Lippe's Lexicon, Chapter D, Vienna 1899, p. 368.
200. During 1918 – 1919, Dr. Shalom Okser managed the school. During 1919 – 1935, Mark Gotfried, and during 1935 – 1939 – the school teacher Mrs. Rakhel Kita'ee. During the last period, the school staff included 11 teachers (8 females and 3 males). The number of students grew in 1936 – 1937 to 378 students.
201. "Przyszlosc", 1893, No. 23, P. 261.
202. "HaMaggid", 1891, Issue 4, p. 372.

The History of the Zionist Movement in Ternopil Before the First World War

In memory and honor of the academic Zionist association "Bar Kokhba" in Ternopil

By Dr. Ph. Korngruen

Translated by Moshe Kutten

The Zionist Movement in Ternopil was born, like in other Galitsia cities, a few years before Herzl, under the influence of the Russian association "Khibat Tzion" ["Affection for Zion"].

In the beginning, it was not a direct influence and it was not based on organizational relations. The miraculous word - "Zion", floated in the air and awoke the yearnings, which had been dormant for generations. It did influence the unaffiliated Jews who did not assimilate into the non-Jewish culture around them. The Zionist movement was established in Galitsia under the organization "A'havat Tzion" ["Love of Zion"]. A few years before Herzl it was formed as an organization under the leadership of Dr. Avraham Zaltz, and Dr. Z. Bromberg-Bitokovski. The center was in Terniv [Ternov], in Western Galitsia. A short time later, the organization established branches in Lviv and many provincial cities in Galitsia. The organization set a goal for itself to found a settlement for Galitsia's Jews in Eretz Israel. The people of "Ahavat Tzion" began to recruit members and collect monies from them. A branch of "A'havat Tzion" was also established in Ternopil and its members paid two kreuzers monthly. A prominent figure, rabbinical judge R' Israel Parnas, headed the branch. The heyday lasted only about one to two years, thanks to one Aliya candidate from the Ternopil area who expressed his wish to settle in "Makhnayim", in Eretz Israel. "Makhanayim" received a financial assistance from the Odesa's [Zionist] committee. The name of Baron Edmond de Rothschild was also mentioned vaguely in connection with the place. The pioneer, named Pollak, made Aliya with his family and settled in Eretz Israel. However, he came back as he went. He was a simple man, a city dweller who was not physically able to work the land and lucked any attributes required for a pioneer. When he came back, the glamour and shine of the movement dimmed for a while. It took a few years for the case to be forgotten and for the people who opposed Zionism to stop using it as proof that the Galitsian Jews cannot be accustomed to working the land. The case succeeded to weaken the movement, and the "Khibat Tzion" in Galitsia never reached the level fitting the importance of Galitsia's Jewry.

The Ternopil branch of "Ahavat Tzion" (initially located in one of the *Batei Midrash*), united later with the political Zionist Union. It concentrated around its youths who were on their way out of the Hassidic kloiz, towards enlightenment and assimilation. These youths constituted the initial crowd to whom the movement addressed its efforts and sent a group of intellectuals to talk to. Most of these intellectuals were university students who arrived at the Zionist view in their own original way. Even before Herzl, they acquired the Zionist views based on Jewish nationalism and the recognition that the Jews constituted, like all other nations, a separate ethnic entity. They recognized that as s separate national unit, they were entitled to live as an independent nation in their homeland with its people dispersed throughout the world. As a national unit, they have the right to develop a national religion, language, economic life, and culture. Among these pioneering activists, we should mention the names of Adolf Shtandt, Shlomo Shiller, the two brothers Korkis, Gershon Zipper, Markus Braude, and Dr. Yehoshua Thon.

Herzl's appearance unified all of these scattered elements and formed them into the "Jewish-State-in-the-making". Herzl's book "Medinat HaYehudim" ["The Jewish State"], left an enormous impression on the Ternopil's youth. However, from [its publication] in 1895 till the First [Zionist] Congress [in 1897], no major event occurred under its influence. Nobody from Ternopil attended the First Zionist Congress. The Jewish intelligentsia was in the midst of a vigorous assimilation process, which was pretty advanced. The orthodox Jews [and the Hassidim] opposed the Zionist idea and the concept of a Jewish State. On the other side, the Jewish proletarians began drifting in the direction of socialism, which constituted also a type of assimilation then. But the name Herzl and the aspiration for an independent Jewish state were carried in the air, fired up the imagination, and conquered the minds. Herzl introduced the positive element into the debate about the future of the Jewish nation that intensified with the Dreyfus Court Martial. That element meant the categorial demand for a solution to the Jewish question by establishing an independent state for the Jewish people.

[Columns 111-112]

In Ternopil, the academic Zionist association "Bar Kokhba", formed in 1902, took it on itself to fulfill the idea of Herzl. As a matter of fact, the association was formed without its formal name in 1897, the same year of the First Zionist Congress. It was born as a club of the students of the local high schools, like the old state Dominican gymnasium, the Re'ali school, and the Teachers seminary. The Polish name of the club was Kolko ["The Little Club"]. It was operated clandestinely and kept secret from the teachers and the authorities, which was then at the hand of the Poles.

In Ternopil, the academic Zionist association "Bar Kokhba", formed in 1902, took it on itself to fulfill the idea of Herzl. As a matter of fact, the association was formed without its formal name in 1897, the same year of the First Zionist Congress. It was born as a club of the students of the local high schools, like the old state Dominican gymnasium, the Re'ali school, and the teacher seminary. The Polish name of the club was "Kolko" ["The Little Club"]. It operated clandestinely and was kept secret from the teachers and the Polish authorities.

The founding general assembly was held in a park belonging to the Ternopil Catholic church but was open for the public. On sabbaths, Jews used to sit there dressed with home clothing and slippers, and the park was therefore called - "Der Pantoffeln-Garten" ("The Slippers' Garden"). The "official" name of the garden was *Die Geistlichen Garten* (The Priests' Garden). It did not have a Polish name. About twenty youths of ages 18 – 20 gathered there in one of the afternoons, at the end of July or beginning of August 1902. They occupied just a few benches in the corners. Some were standing, and some others were sitting on the grass. The "old" man in the bunch, Avraham Pomerantz, stood or sat in the center. He was about twenty-four years old because he was late to graduate from his studies at the gymnasium of Berezhany. He did finally graduate along with the youngsters among us, who had just graduated. There were three layers in the group: The "elders" who graduated two years before (1900), the "middle" ones who graduated in 1901, and the "youngsters" (*"Frish Gebakeneh Akademiker"* [Yiddish for "Fresh Baked Academics"]), the graduates from 1902. Everybody in the group, without exception, came out of the "Student Club" (*"Kolko Stdudenekie"*), namely "The Club of the Zionist Gymnasium Students". The club was founded by Avraham Pomerantz, Wolf Beltukh, Izidor Tzin, Israel Waldman, and Nathan Nussbaum in 1897, immediately following the First Zionist Congress in Basel. Students who joined that club were the students who were accepted to the high school, most of whom were 14 – 15 years old. They were not accepted to the club easily because the club founder, Avraham Pomerantz, was conservative and cautious. He feared to take most of the students because they came from assimilating families. The source of the assimilation was the first modern Jewish school founded by Yosef Perl z"l. He used all sorts of subterfuges to get rid of these students. These students finally gave up, stopped attending the club, and formed their own Zionist youth club. Izidor then intervened and unified the "elders", students of the seventh and the eighth-graders, with the younger fifth and the sixth graders. The club operated underground because of the fear of snitching by the assimilating students, the Polish patriots among them, and by students from earlier generations.

When I graduated from high school, I headed a youth organization that contained hundreds of members. It was organized in age groups and operated under exceptional discipline and enormous enthusiasm. In five years, we eradicated the assimilation tendencies, without any remnants, out of the studying youths and poured the foundation on which the Zionist life in Eastern Galitsia was founded. The members Waldman, Pomerantz, and Tzin were expelled from high school (received a *Consilium Abeundi* [Latin for "advised to leave"]). They were expelled due to their involvement in "politics" that went against the state (the Poles thought that anybody who opposed them was also against the Austrian state). However, that did not frighten us. We continue to assemble, read Zionist literature, and newspapers. We debated, studied Hebrew and Jewish history, listened to lectures, and gave other lectures. The central circle gathered every Saturday afternoon at one of the halls of Perl's school (from all places), under the disguise of an "advanced studies class".

In 1900, the founders went to the university. However, their number was too scant for founding an association. In 1901, some additional members joined, however, the activists among them, went to the technical university in Lviv under the direct influence of Herzl's book "Altneiland" ["The Old New Land"]. In the book, Herzl relayed the vision of a Jewish state built by technical progress. A new state would require engineers, surveyors, chemists, and architects. Only in 1902, a sufficient number of members collected and dared to fulfill our dream of establishing the "Bar Kokhba" association. The following people participated in the founding gathering: Avraham Pomerantz, Nathan Nussbaum, Yosef Reitman, Mark Reitman, Israel Waldman, Mark Zlateks, Philip Korngruen, Aba Auerbakh, Leon Horwitz, Yehuda Friedman, Ya'akov, Retzenstein, Henryk

Regenbogen, Albin Mueller, Izik Nussbaum, Shabtai Fogel, Zusia Dizenfeld, Avraham Gruenberg, Ya'akov Likhtigfeld, David (Dzionio) Katz, Kaminker-Wakhman, Wilhelm Landau, Bernard Winkler, and Avraham Sas. We should also add the following members who could not participate for various reasons: Wolf Beltukh, Karl Unter, Alexander Rapoport, Izidor Tzin, and Zigmont Broiner. By mentioning them, we save these young people's names from oblivion. In 1902, they were all considered "veterans Zionist activists" from the days of the First Zionist Congress, or even two years before that. We were all the disciples of Theodor Herzl, who swore allegiance to the flag of the Jewish state in Eretz Israel. Indeed, we were "political Zionists" in the spirit of our great leader - Herzl's books -"Der Judenstaat" ["The Jewish State"] and "Altneuland". We were enthused not by words or speeches. We were imbued with a great vision to devote our lives to the international Zionist Movement. We desired to conquer the hearts of our people for our homeland and conquer our homeland for the people. We considered our people the unique historical, ethnic, religious, and cultural unit that it was. We aimed to return to the ancient and beautiful Jewry. We aspired to develop all the national forces and march the people of Israel toward independence in its country as equal members of the new nations. Since there was no university in Ternopil, we had to name our association: "The Jewish Youth Association Bar Kokhba'". However, from our by-laws, it was clear that we were not similar to other associations.

Paragraph number 3 of the by-laws reads:

[Columns 113-114]

The Founders of the Academic Zionist Association "Bar-Kokhba" in Ternopil (1902)

Sitting: First Row - Israel Waldman, F. Ziltz, M. Zlateks, Mark Reitman, Razenstein
Second Row: Yehuda Freidman, Leon Horwitz, Abraham Pomerantz, I. Nussbaum, Aba Auerbakh, Ph. Korengruen
Standing: First Row – D. Katz, Yacob Lichtigfeld, Abraham Gruenberg, Z. Wiesenfeld, Fogel, Isaac Nussbaum, Albin Mueller Henryk Regenbogen
Second Row – Abraham Sas, Bernhard Winkler, Wilhelm Kaminker-Wakhman

"The association's goal, which does not have any local political aspiration, are as follows: multi-facets development of all spiritual and physical energies of its members, cultivation of the knowledge of literature, Jewish history, and the Hebrew language, and development of the social lives".

Paragraph 4 reads as follows: "To achieve our goals, we will operate to - a) Establish a library b) Conduct recitation, lectures, and debates about general sciences, and particularly about literature and Jewish history c) Conduct lessons of the Hebrew language for all members d) Learn gymnastic and fencing by all members e) Arrange meetings, games, and social parties".

That modest program was a framework by which we could introduce the entire Zionist program without colliding with the government, which had already begun to look at our activity suspiciously. Galitsian Poles were not interested in having Jews with national aspirations, possessing Hebraic and Yiddish culture amongst them. They especially resented proud Jews, standing tall, self-respecting with the power to defend their civil and national rights in the Austrian state.

In fact, we created a complete academic Zionist corporation in all of its fine details. In choosing the name of the last hero of the State of Israel - Bar Kokhba, we meant to emphasize the emotional connection between the end of our independence in our land and the beginning of our strive to free independent lives in our ancient homeland. We made ourselves available to Herzl and the Galitsian Zionist Movement, without any doubts or hesitations. We accepted, with love, anything that was required of us: propaganda work, publicity, and later on, political activity, organization of general and Jewish cultural events, or just a mundane work of collection of donations, guarding and ushering at Zionist gatherings, distribution of announcements and newspapers, participation in a fight for defending the honor of Israel in duels or just a brawl. "Bar Kokhba" association members did all of that in a spirit of total volunteerism and complete discipline. There were never such occurrences when members avoided fulfilling any role, even the very difficult ones.

[Column 115]

The members of "Bar Kokhba" were always in the locations they were requested to be in - ready for action. At the same time, they were elegant, polite, social, helpful, and friendly. They generated respect for themselves, the nation of Israel, and particularly for their association. We wore a blue and white ribbon (the Zionist symbol), and green – which was the symbol of the academic association for the days of vacation (*Ferial Verbindung*). Its edges were golden to state that our association does not shy away from a battle. Fencing played a major role in the lives of Austrian universities. At the university in Vienna and the Technion in Lviv, we needed, more than once, to protect, by force, the honor of the Jewish student against the antisemitic Germans and the "National Democratic" Poles. The very existence of organized groups who were capable to respond, not only with convincing explanations in debates but also by hand and sword, carried a positive effect and lifted the level of appreciation for the Jews in the eyes of the non-Jews. Every one of our "brothers" wore a symbol on his lapel – a small porcelain armor with the acronym of the words "*Vivat, Floreat, Crescat*" [Latin for "Live, Grow, and Flourish".

Our steering committee ("The Convent") met at least once a week and in some urgent cases, even more often. The topics discussed in the meetings were: a) Current events in the world and the Jewish world b) local issues, such as Daily Zionist activities; Establishment of Zionist organizations and associations in Ternopil and in 20 towns that belonged to the Ternopil "District Committee"; Establishment of Youth organizations and gymnastic associations for men, women, and children; Establishment and support for Jewish school; c) Organization of lectures, balls, and parties at the public and private parks.

The Seal of the "Bar Kokhba" Organization
[The Hebrew words around the seal:
"The Association of the Academic Zionists "Bar Kokhba" in Ternopil"]

The "steering committee" determined the direction of our activities. They would select a member or a few members to execute a specific mission. We did not insist that all the activities were carried out under our name - "Bar Kokhba". We were satisfied with the results provided that the activity would take place with the active participation of our members who devoted their time, efforts, and skills. The Zionist activities took place quietly and were executed efficiently by the association, which ensured that anybody who successfully organized a worthwhile event would be helped. Our influence was felt in the Jewish street. We controlled the entire learning youth and the youth who came from orthodox homes. Our predecessors were assimilators who distanced themselves from Jewish lives,

[Column 116]

while we looked for a connection with them. A new phenomenon appeared – the pride of belonging to the Jewish nation. Our predecessors, the older physicians, and lawyers were ashamed of their Jewishness and they were afraid to admit it openly.

The first stage [of our activity] lasted only about two to three months. It involved administrative preparations, arranging an apartment, furniture, and other similar things. For a short while, we operated out of the house of our first fencing teacher, our comrade Ziltz. Later on, we moved our "shack" to the house of Rafael Greenspan, on Train Street, where we rented a large room. The house contained two rooms. The other room was the owner's unused tavern. We did not disturb the owner, particularly since he was deaf. We moved our Hebraic, Yiddish, and general library to that room. Hundreds of books were borrowed by members and even non-members. We stayed in that apartment until 1914.

We strove to have every leader ("senior"), who served for a 6 months session, add his own new and unique activity to the regular activities of the association and the Zionist movement. The first leader – Avraham Pomerantz, organized a wonderful inauguration ball of our association in the Ternopil municipal meeting hall. It was the first time, the Jews dared to request the city council (consisting of only 1/3 Jews, the other 1/3 were Poles and 1/3 Ukrainians) to use the meeting hall. Avraham Pomerantz opened the gathering, which was also attended by non-Jewish city councilors. I gave the opening programmatic speech, which I wrote in consultation with the association members, and the honorary member Mrs. Roza Pomerantz, the sister of our first president. The Pomerantz family brought political Zionism to Ternopil. at the Pomerantz house, I read Herzl's book - "The Jewish State", for the first time. Roza Pomerantz (who later married [Isaak] Meltzer), was a sharp, learned, and vigorous woman. She was the Chairwoman of the Ternopil "District Committee", and the representative of the Central Committee in Lviv, headed by Adolf Shtandt. [In 1922 she became the first Jewish woman elected to the Sejm]. The Zionist movement was still at its beginning. There were already representatives of the movement in the provincial cities of the Ternopil's district, but everything was still in its infancy.

The first leader ("senior") was Avraham Pomerantz. His vice ("co-senior") was Israel Waldman. I served as the secretary. I was therefore tasked with the honor to give the programmatic speech. A year earlier, I organized the first gathering of the high school graduates from the entire Eastern Galitsia, which assembled in Ternopil in 1901. I managed the conference and authored the program (chapters from the protocol of that conference are published in this book – see page 143).

The second "senior" (from October 1902 – to April 1903) was Nathan Nussbaum. His project was the "Toynbee Hall" (a Jewish university for the masses).

[Columns 117-118]

A ball took place every Saturday night and on holidays, at the hall of the craftsmen association "Yad Kharutizim" ["Hand of the Diligent"]. Each ball included a scientific lecture, mostly on a Jewish subject, a musical show, and a recitation from Jewish literature in Yiddish, Polish, or German. The cost of the ticket was kept low, just to cover the expenses. The turnout was so great that we had to arrange two shows in one evening, just after the first ball. The speeches were given twice and so were the musical performances and the recitation.

A Group of Students with their Instructor, Ph. Korngruen (1903)

About 1200 – 1400 visitors attended weekly the hall in "Yad Kharutzim". That allowed us to establish the "university for the masses" where Jewish culture, science, philosophy, art, and literature were taught. Nussbaum invested a tremendous effort in managing that project. "Bar Kokhba's" members worked as ushers, cashiers, and pasters of posters. Only in the winter of 1903 - 4, we succeeded in renting a more spacious hall called "*Armon*" (*Schloss*-Castle), containing enough seats for the crowd that flocked to our balls. That cultural institution operated and progressed until the break of WW I. In addition to its cultural value, the event served as a colossal stage for Zionist propaganda.

The third "senior" was Wilhelm Landau. During the election, the youngsters staged a mini-rebellion. They also wanted to be elected as "seniors". That created some tension during the election (the first and the last time in "Bar Kokhba's" history). I was elected as the "vice-senior" at that election. A grand party, which took place in the city park, was etched and remained in my memory from that period. That was the first time that the park was allocated to a private organization to hold a celebration. The revenues from that celebration were all devoted to charity and for the benefit of the Zionist fund. That celebration in the large city park turned into a tradition since then, like the "Toynbee Hall". The second tradition was the "Maccabees Balls" (*Makabäer-Abend*) in the wintertime. It was incumbent upon us to have these balls as extraordinary celebrations. While during regular propaganda events, public lectures, and the like, local forces appeared, the custom was that in the "Maccabees balls" only "stars" participated. That included the speakers, musicians, and reciters. Speakers from Lviv, Vienna, and Krakow, such as Adolf Shtandt, Markus Braude, Dr. Leon Reikh, and the like, appeared. So did singers from the opera in Lviv and famous actors from various theaters. it was considered a great privilege when a local speaker, such as Israel Waldman or Philip Korngruen, was allowed to deliver the introductory or closing speech. After each ball, everyone in town could hardly wait to see what other innovations can our association come up with next.

Yosef Rietman, one of the "elders", served as a "senior" in the winter of 1903-04. His vice was Moshe Fisher from amongst the "youngsters". The tension between the camps evaporated and never returned. Our activities at that period included: maintenance of the library, supervision of the "Young Students" youth movement, assisting in Zionist activities and propaganda throughout the district, the great "Maccabees Balls", and "Toynbee Hall" event in front of a crowd of more than a thousand people. A new activity was added that winter – The "Representative Ball" of the "Bar Kokhba" academic association. That was an unforgettable experience. The preparations for that ball lasted for months. Any member who did not know how to dance was ordered by the "co-senior" to learn that skill, otherwise, they would have been severely reprimanded or even "kicked out" of the association. Before the ball, the "co-senior" inspected the members and anybody who was not properly dressed was sent home to correct anything amiss in their elegance. All of that effort was done for a purpose: so that none of the invited guests (such as the neighboring estate owners, their lessees, and assimilating physicians) would say that the Jewish students were bums who did not know how to dress or behave properly in an elegant company. The preparations for the ball, which included flower deliveries or drawing names of dancers on small cards, became quite an experience in the life of the members. The "co-senior" would stand in the middle of the hall during the dance with a group of youths. He stood there just to make sure that none of the ladies was missing a "cavalier". (The custom of coming as a pair and dancing with the same partner the whole night, did not exist at the time). He would signal the "reserves" with whom they should dance so that nobody could say they were bored at the ball of "Bar Kokhba". The "out-of-this-world" organizers, Tzvi Regenbogen, Zigmont Broiner, and Moshe Fisher, organized the quadrille, mazur, and lancier dances. They rehearsed the dances in advance so that everything would work outright. It was an unforgettable experience that was etched in the memory of all participants.

A new Jewish society was emerging due to Zionist activities. It was based on a profound change of values, and education for a self-recognition of self-worth as a Jewish person, with the head, held high.

Obviously, the romantic aspect was not lacking. People used to say that in Ternopil – "*nad "Bar-Kokhba" rozbila sie bania milosci*" (a bubble of love burst above "Bar-Kokhba"). That was a joyful gang, lively and vibrant, full of jokes and humor, healthy, beautiful, noisy, and adventurous at times, however, always impeccable in two areas: Zionism and "Bar Kokhba".

All of the [Zionist] movements in Galitsia were, basically, movements of students.

[Columns 119-120]

The influence of "our doctor", even if he had not yet graduated from high school, was a crucial impact on the family. It was especially true in Ternopil (perhaps also in Brody and before that Buchach). The large movements within the Galitsian Jewry in the 19th century were: enlightenment, assimilation, Hassidim, and in the end – Zionism that the movements were formed not only as a method, world view, and high philosophy (remember "Morei Nevokhai HaZman" ["Guide for the Perplexed of the Time"]), but they also became parties, supported by fighting figures: Perl, Erter, Lefin, Shmuel Yehuda Rapoport (SHIR), and Nakhman Kromkhel – all native or residents of Ternopil (in any case, they are all buried in its cemetery). The militant enlightenment could not have found more stubborn rivals as the Ternopil's Hassidim, rebbes, and rabbis. The assimilation movement was not as aggressive anywhere else, and Zionism did not penetrate the hearts of the masses as much as in Ternopil. There were almost no indifferent people in Ternopil. Regardless of who they were, they were committed with their heart and soul. They were like the climate in their city – hot in the summer and cold in the winter. Even the "National Democrats" Poles were zealous, and the Ukrainians – radicals. Ternopil people tended not to compromise in their public life either, and most of them were in the opposition. However, their opposition was also creative since people liked to act, and create tangible things. They hated hollow rhetoric more than anything else. When it came to speeches, the audiences in Ternopil were very "spoiled". A speaker who wanted to have a listening audience had to speak on the matter using literary language. He also had to quote from ancient and modern scholars and spice his speech with fireworks of ideas and humor. Among the locals, only two figures managed to secure an affectionate audience – Israel Waldman and Philip Korngruen although, or because each had his own style.

During the period of Herzl's Zionist leadership, "Bar Kokhba" participated not only in the local Zionist activities, but also in the activities of the Zionist Union, which included all currents, classes, and views. However, "Bar Kokhba" had its own view when it came to Zionism's fundamental historical, theoretical, and political issues. We considered Herzl as our leader. When it came to Herzl's leadership, there was not only an organizational discipline but also boundless and unconditional love, respect, and admiration. In the battle between Herzl and the Political Zionists on one side and the Practical Zionists on the other, we obviously supported Herzl, although, there were only a few who understood the reasons for that fight. We followed the notion that when it came to [Eretz Israel] settlement, Herzl was more practical than the "insignificant practical activities" [of the Practical Zionists]. The most Practical Zionist – Baron Rothchild, was a Political Zionist, just like Herzl. In Herzl's fight with [the author] Akhad Ha'Am, we supported Herzl, unlike the people from Brody, under the influence of Khaim Tartokover, who supported Akhad Ha'Am (although not against Herzl). The debate between the Political, Practical, and Cultural Zionism deepened our ideological Zionism and brought us to a more unified Synthetic Zionist thinking [the name Synthetic Zionism was given to the unified approach in the 10th Zionist Congress]. With that concept, politics, settlement in Eretz Israel, and the language and cultures were all included as a unified approach as parts of the "Jewish State in the making". In the fight between the Democratic Faction in the [Zionist] Congress (that included Dr. Khaim Weitzman, Martin Buber, Berthold Feibel, George Halperin, Yitzkhak Gruenbaum, and Alfred Nossig) against Herzl, we supported the latter. We did not do much for the "Jewish Settlement Fund", as we were still high school students. However, we became fond immediately of the KKL-JNF.

The standing of "Bar Kokhba" became stronger and stronger, not only in the city of Ternopil itself, but also in the district towns of Jezierzany, Zalozce, Zbarazh, Pidvolochysk, Mikulince, Terebovila, Kopychyntsi, Chortkiv, Tluste, Zalishchyky, Kozlov, Skala, and Husiatyn. It was also strengthened in the villages around these towns. Jews who lived in these villages were not just owners of taverns and shopkeepers, but they were also estate owners and lessees, agronomists, managers of the estate of Polish nobles, clerks, and experts in the brewery of liquor and beer. That was a fairly diversified and wealthy crowd. The Ternopil district committee, headed by Roza Pomerantz in 1901, managed the Zionist propaganda in the district towns and villages.

I headed the [Zionist committee in the] Ternopil district from 1902 to 1908. Dr. Israel Waldman[1], served in that position from 1908 to 1911, when all of the district committees were abolished. The management of the Zionist activities was transferred then to the Zionist Union Committee in Lviv and to the Central Galitsia's [Zionist] Secretariat. Before 1912, every district committee (including the Ternopil district) sent two representatives, who were elected in the district assemblies, to participate in the Central Galitsia's Secretariat. We always tried to send a representative to participate in the Secretariat. During the period between 1903 and 1911, three of our members participated: Waldman, who was elected as a member of Tz. K. [The Galitsian Zionist Central Committee], myself (Dr. Ph. Korngruen), and Moshe Fisher as representatives of the Ternopil district. From 1911 – to 1914, another member from the district was elected, and I continued to participate in the central committee in Lviv as the chairman of the Jewish schools in Galitsia and Bukovina. Therefore, three or four members from our association were part of the leadership team of the national Zionist Union in Galitsia. We, like all of the members of the Tz. K., were responsible for the politics of the national Zionist Union in Austria in general and in particular in Galitsia. We were tasked with work and the responsibility but also received the honor.

[Columns 121-122]

I brought the details in the introduction to explain our position in the hierarchy of the Zionist Union. The Union built itself as a vigorous organization able and willing to rule over all aspects of Jewish lives and the hegemony in the Jewish Street. The old patriarchally and liberal world, the world of dreams which all of us – the Zionists, but also the Poles, Ukrainians, and even the Socialists lived in, began to break apart. It broke apart faster than any of us expected. We faced a new historical reality and were forced to participate in it. The Russian volcano began to emit smoke and shake the earth. Then came the 1905 Russian Revolution. Its echoes reverberated throughout the entire world, mainly in the Austrian Empire, which embodied about 20 nations and languages. Like always, the revolution was accompanied by pogroms. When Landau was the "senior" or a short time before that, we received the news about the riots in Kishinev. The responses by the Jewish nation and the shock to the

Kishinev pogrom were fiercer than the ones that came after later pogroms, including the Nazi Holocaust. Kishinev removed the facemask from the face of humanity and opened our eyes to see the abyss gaping at our feet. Kishinev's pogrom transformed our aspiration for auto-emancipation to seeking self-defense in the simplest sense of the word. It startled us and demonstrated the fast-approaching Holocaust. However, at the time, we could not foresee the magnitude and the fact that it would occur during the lifetime of the generation that witnessed and protested the riots in Kishinev. The only one who forecasted the Holocaust was Herzl. The prophet saw the destruction of the Russian, Polish, Galitsian, Romanian, and Hungarian Jewry. The vision of that destruction did not leave him even for a moment. It pushed him to negotiate with [the Russians] Pleva and Vita, which brought him to St. Petersburg, risking his life. When Herzl realized that Eretz Israel could not serve as an immediate refuge for his nation, he began to negotiate with England about Uganda. Herzl believed then that Uganda could serve as a "night shelter" for the Nation of Israel on its way to its own state in Eretz Israel. Today it is pointless to argue who was right. Our history continued on its own path: we bereaved a third of our nation, but we acquired a state in our homeland. That was how fate maneuvered our ship.

"Bar Kokhba" position was clear. After Kishinev, we organized protest demonstrations in all the district towns. I was tasked with organizing the demonstrations. Waldman delivered the speech in Ternopil. I delivered speeches in towns of the district, such as Berezhany, based on the recommendation by the Tz. K., which did not have sufficient speakers to deliver speeches to all of Galitsia towns. Berezhany's Zionists turned to "Bar Kokhba" to send them Waldman or me since they needed a "veteran speaker" ("ein älterer Redner"). They claimed that many rabbis, lawyers, and physicians resided in the city and requested to have a "serious" speaker, [preferably] with a white-haired beard. That request came at the time when the eldest member of "Bar Kokhba", Israel Waldman, was only 22 years old, and the other "old" speaker was twenty years old me.

When they saw me, they could not hide their awful disappointment. However, following the speech, which was etched in the memory of the people in Berezhany for many years to come, three thousand Jews burst into tears. The eagerness for self-defense engulfed the listeners and the organizers relented.

The Sixth [Zionist] Congress, named the "Uganda Congress" in Zionist history, despaired us. Strangely enough, despite our love for Herzl, and despite the understanding of his reasonings and his pure Zionist intentions, we all joined the opposition camp without any exception. Us, the Galitsians, and particularly, the people from Ternopil, and especially the members of "Bar Kokhba" were not under the influence of Ussishkin and the people of Kharkiv [Kharkov]. The opposite is true. We could not forgive them for the problems they caused Herzl for decades. It took years until we agreed to welcome Ussishkin, in his visit to Lviv, on the occasion of the first Eretz-Israeli exhibition (If I am not mistaken in 1912). However, for us, Zionism meant the existence of the Jewish nation. We could not come to terms with the existence of the Jewish nation in a location other than Eretz Israel. We were already a nation, and we heard about what Nordau expressed so nicely in one of the Congresses: "A nation can wait. It involves sorrow, but not shame". In the state gathering in Lviv, we supported the proposal by Adolf Shtandt, among all the other alternatives: a) Herzl without Zion b) Zion without Herzl c) Uganda even with Herzl. We insisted on one requirement: Zion with Herzl. "Bar Kokhba" members advocated that requirement without any exception. We did not have even one pro territorialism [advocating an alternative to Eretz Israel] person, and we never participated in efforts of the followers of Zangwill and Nossig who were looking for homeland [other than Eretz Israel].

I was elected as a "senior" for the summer 1904 semester. In the meantime, the number of members grew, since every high school's matriculation exam brought a new cadre of new members. These new members were under supervision for several years in one of the gymnasium's or high schools' clubs. Their identity [as Zionists] was known to all, or at least to the schools' principals. We accepted people with an academic degree from the outside skeptically. Such a candidate had to go through a six-month trial period as a guest. He had to visit us at the "shack", where we lived so that the members get the chance to get to know him. He had to study Jewish history and endear himself on the members since only two votes against him would be sufficient to derail his acceptance. The essence of our strength was grounded on our unity and our camaraderie among us.

During the summer semesters of 1903 (Landau and Korngruen served as "senior" and "co-senior" respectively), and 1904 (Korngruen and Izik Nussbaum), the following members were accepted: Feller, Werber, Yosef Tirkes, Ya'akov Tzin, Kron, Bekerman, Alexander Koenigsberg, Yitzkhak Shapiro, Emanuel Stein, Ze'ev (Wilhelm) Beigel, Moshe Fisher, as well as Meir Khartiner, who devoted a lot of effort to "Hebrew-tize" our members, and was always considered our friend.

[Columns 123-124]

We did not consider them "new members." From among them, we selected committee members, secretaries, treasurers, and especially librarians for our expanding library. The trio - Bekerman – Sas - Koenigsberg served as the librarian for three years.

The 1904 summer semester was a little unique and, to a certain extent, it constituted a turn towards democratization. G-d forbid the change did not tarnish the "Bar Kokhba" association and its formal, close, noble, and academic character. It had to do more with the roles that the time and circumstances had presented us with. I was relieved from my work with students. I was too busy with propaganda work in the city and the district and management of the association. However, now I could hand over that holy mission to loyal [younger] hands. After me, the supervision role over the high school students was given to Ya'akov Tzin and Wilhelm Beigel, and later on, to Khaim Shmertling and Max Schleicher. Khaim and Max were still students when I served as the "senior".

On Lag BaOmer [Jewish holiday], I said goodbye to my work with the Zionist education of the youth. All the members of the "clubs" (organized by their classes), walked to the forest near the village Gaia Vilieka [Velyki Hai?]. We all met and gathered there, about 300 members strong. I lectured about Lag BaOmer being the holiday to commemorate Shimon bar Kokhba (in the meantime, my version about the holiday was scientifically verified over the years). We then returned to the city, group after group, like an army to defend the nation, and take over the homeland. At that time, it did not occur to me that some of these young men were destined to serve as members of the "Hagana" and Israel Defense Force and participate in our independence war.

Peculiar guests arrived at the hall of "Bar Kokhba" at that time. The pogroms in Russia, which occurred as a reaction against the revolutionary movement, resulted in the flight of people involved with workers' organizations and the revolution. There were Zionist activists among them, particularly socialistic Zionists, as well as Hebrew teachers from among the Russian intelligentsia. Our comrades from Skala, Husiatyn, Podwolocyska, and Zbarazh, towns near the borders, used their influence with the Austrian and Russian gendarmeries at the Russian-Austrian border to help the refugees "steal the border". They knew our address. Their first visit on the Austrian side was to "Bar Kokhba" in Ternopil. We revived and strengthened them, and employed them as propagandists. There were good speakers among them, some excellent, and also Hebrew teachers. I remember a person named Yakobson – a speaker par excellence, who resided in Ternopil and made a living as a Zionist preacher. I also remember a person named Abramson, who served as the secretary of Ussishkin. The most important guest was a worker and organizer by the name of Tabachnik. He brought a new spirit with him and began organizing the local workers, apprentices of craftsmen, and stores' salesclerks, under the flag of "Poalei Tzion" ["Workers of Zion"]. The first workers' gatherings, which were organized by Tabachnik to join the Zionist movement, took place at the hall of the academic Zionist movement – "Bar Kokhba" in Ternopil.

Debates among us about Socialism and Zionism continued throughout the entire summer of 1904. A new group that wished to unify the two organizations emerged. The debate also moved to the streets, public gatherings, and coffee shops (e.g. the famous Dreifinger's dairy on Perl's Street). Khartiner, Yosef Sirkes, and his brother Moritz, debated with the members of the Galitsian "Bund", the Z.P.S ["Jewish Socialistic Party"] and P.P.S. [Polish Socialist Party], neither without convincing the other side. However, the group of workers and the shops' clerks continued to grow. As mentioned, the initial gatherings aimed to explain the ideology of "Poalei Tzion" and the workers' meetings (to discuss the establishment of a brunch of "Poalei Tzion" in Ternopil - they already had a brunch in Vienna) were held at the apartment of the academic association "Bar Kokhba". They were helped by and operated under the initiative of "Bar Kokhba's" "senior" that winter semester). In the winter of 1904, the group was strong enough to afford to rent their own apartment in the house of Gelman on Sobieski Street. They formally established a [brunch of the] association "Poalei Tzion". The association just began to consolidate and seize its own standing within the Jewish Congress and the socialistic "International Workers' Federation". The theoretical debate within our own association took the shape of a deep scientific review, and many members, including the "senior", were caught on to the idea of uniting the two ideologies: Zionism and Socialism. A review and study of the socialistic literature, particularly the "Capital" by Karl Marks, was initiated. The ideology began to take root in the Jewish street. We hadn't yet adopted that view, expressed by the proverb – "We are Zionists because we are socialistic". The members of "Bar Kokhba only embraced it years later, under the influence of Daniel Pasmanik and Kaplansky. We were Zionists without any restraint. Zionism for us meant a Jewish State. It was clear to us that our state would be based on social justice - an example for the whole world. In our state, the Jewish wealth and the Jewish labor would cooperate, based on equal rights and obligations, and individual freedom. There would be no coercion or exploitation. There would be no slavery and no blood spilling. Sorting out the relationship between the Zionist ideology and socialism became an urgent and decisive factor in our war against assimilation. At the end of the 19th century and the beginning of the 20th century, socialism became the last refuge and fortress of the previous intellectual generation of Galitsian Jews – the generation of assimilation. The Jewish intelligentsia found a treasure of fresh ideas in socialism, which were not available to their predecessors' assimilators (our parents' generation during 1850 – 1890). Our initial reaction was: "If socialism would unify all the nations in the world, abolish all the nationalities, and remove

[Columns 125-126]

all the divides between one person to another – what is the need for the nation of Israel, and what is the use for a unique State of Israel? Wouldn't it be better to join the socialistic "Fourth Class", who aspires to build a new world, thus bringing to an end the "Jewish Question" along with many other "questions"? Our feeling was that the ideology was nothing but disguised assimilation. Fixing the world should not require the disappearance of our ancient high-culture nation - the creator of the social ideas. The appearance of the "Bund" led to the establishment of the Jewish Z.P.S. - Zydowska Socjalistyczna ["Jewish Socialistic Party"], (1905). That constituted a weak response against the attraction by the P.P.S. ["Polish Socialistic Party"] and the most radical and dangerous threat to our national survival - the assimilation of the Jewish proletariat.

The fierce battle between Zionism and socialism began as early as [the beginning of] 1904. However, in the summer semester of 1904, it ceased for several months, since on July 4th, 1904, Herzl died. Our world darkened., and the beauty in our life vanished. The astonishing belief in the great leader died with him. The confidence and complacency that he would do whatever was necessary changed to a feeling of melancholy and grave responsibility for keeping his plan alive. Lives became gloomy, the glitter erased. We remained a force without a leader, crippled for at least several months. We devoted the time to gatherings of mourning and sobbing. The members of "Bar Kokhba" led by their "senior" cried like after the father of each one of them and the father of all of them. In Ternopil, Waldman spoke for the first time in the old synagogue. The orthodox people and the Hassidim did not dare resist the appearance of a shaved enlightened man standing by the Holy Ark. I visited all of the district towns. The crises dissipated slowly, and we got back to our work on implementing Herzl's plan and widening the membership of the Zionist Union.

In 1904, Zigmont Broiner, a zealous Zionist from a veteran assimilation family and the son of a teacher in Perl's school, was elected as the "senior". A more peculiar event occurred when I was elected, by the first members of "Poalei Tzion" in Ternopil, as the chairman of their association. As a result, I became the Eastern Galitsia representative of the "Poalei Tzion" association.

According to our tradition, "senior" Zigmont Broiner added a new activity to our regular and routine activities. During Zigmont's reign, a calendar of the association was published. I managed to preserve a handwritten version of that calendar, copied for me by the members of "Bar Kokhba". That copy survived World War I but was burnt during World War II. That was a small booklet, which included the civil and Jewish calendars. The calendar also contained a collection of articles: "Zionism" by Israel Waldman, "About Zion – Visions" by Meir Khartiner (translated from Hebrew by Yehuda Friedman), "Inventions and fabrications" by Philip Korngruen, "The Zionist Union" by Yehuda Friedman, and "Silvester of Emigrants" by Israel Waldman.

At the end of the calendar, a chronology representing the entire Jewish history of approximately 5000 years. The chronology listed milestones, considered important by Korngruen and Khartiner, from the point of view of the Jewish people and nation. That chronology got lost. I only remember the last three dates: 135 BC, the fall of "Beitar" [last standing stronghold of the Bar Kokhba revolt] and the death of Bar Kokhba, 1895 – the emergence of Theodor Herzl and his book "The Jewish State", 1897 – the First Zionist Congress in Basel, Herzl – the president of the revived nation.

Israel Waldman was the 1905 summer semester's "senior". His special project was the establishment of a Polish Zionist weekly newspaper named "Słowo Żydowski" ["Jewish World"]. That newspaper was published continuously, under his editorial and management, until the break of the First World War. Obviously, the members of "Bar Kokhba" helped him, not only in writing articles, collecting news, and translating from Hebrew, German, and other languages but also in editing, distribution, shipping, collecting subscription fees, etc… The newspaper's administration was located in our apartment for many years. The newspaper acquired great importance as a mouthpiece for national Jewish politics. Our involvement in the newspaper grew by leaps and bounds under the management of Israel Waldman.

The second project initiated by Israel Waldman was the establishment of a society for athletics and physical culture named "Beitar" [Named after the last stronghold of Bar Kokhba's revolt]. Thanks to his connections with Ukrainian politicians, Israel Waldman got a permit to use a gym named "Bractwo Mieszcannńskie". He hired a Ukrainian gym instructor named Tchubati. It is interesting to note that a similar institution, named "Dror" ["Freedom"], was established in Lviv by a "Bar Kokhba's" member, Izidor Tzin. The latter devoted his life to the physical education of the youth. He educated a whole generation of instructors, gymnasts, and athletes in Galitsia. Many of the students made Aliya to Eretz Israel as physical education teachers, athletes, or mere pioneers and soldiers.

I do not recall who was elected as the "senior" for the winter semester of 1905 - 06. If I am not mistaken, it was Munio (Imanuel) Stein. During that semester, a turning point in the direction of Labor-Zionism took place within the "Bar Kokhba" association itself. It was associated with the visit of Dr. Daniel Pasmanik. I do not remember whether Dr. Pasternak came to Ternopil before the "anti-Uganda" Zionist Congress in the summer of 1905 in Bazel, or after that historical congress. Meir Khartiner attended that congress as a correspondent of the Galitsian "HaTzfira" ["The Epoch"] magazine. Besides telegrams, If I am not mistaken, Meir sent letters from Galitsia to the monthly magazine "HaHed" ["The Echo"].

Khartiner and I participated in the Seventh Zionist Congress. Khartiner represented the magazine "HaTzfira", Warsaw, and I, the youth newspapers "Moria", Lviv, and other magazines.

[Columns 127-128]

The Visit to Ternopil by Dr. Daniel Pasmanik, Honorary Member of the Organization

From Left to right – sitting: First Row – A. Beigel, Landau, M. Khartiner, Brauner
Second Row - Fisher, J. Nussbaum, D. Stein, Dr. Daniel Pasmanik, Pomerantz, Korngruen, J. Waldman
Standing: First Row – Horwitz, Shapiro, Sas, Gruenberg, Mueller, Koenigsberg, Beckerman, Friedamn
Second Row – Kron, Jacob Tzin, Joseph Sirkes, Werber, Feler, Rapaport

"Bar Kokhba" association did not send representatives to the Zionist Congress for two reasons: First - because none of us was old enough to be eligible, and second - because we did not have enough money for the trip. Traveling on public or Union funds was not customary at the time. I covered my own travel expenses. When I returned to Ternopil, I submitted a detailed report to our steering committee (convent) headed by Israel Waldman.

Dr. Daniel Pasmanik visited Ternopil on behalf of the "Poalei Tzion" union in the winter of 1905-06. He conducted two lectures about the relationship between Zionism and Socialism described from the point of view of the Jewish proletariat. The "Bar Kokhba" association organized the lectures, and both turned into a sensation. Dr. Daniel Pasmanik brought up the theory that the Jewish proletariat would not be able to integrate into the natural and essential proletarianization process. He laid down proof that when the industry covert from handwork to machine work, people would expel the Jews from the factories, and the local proletariat would replace them. He claimed that the Jewish proletariat would find itself on the outside in the final war between labor and wealth unless it would acquire a homeland for itself, where it could become the local proletariat. The picture pained by Dr. Pasmanik was horrific. The Jewish wealth in the diaspora would be nationalized by the local proletariat (i.e. - Russian, Polish, English, or German proletariats) and the Jewish proletariat would find itself alone with no wealth of its own unless it would establish the relation between wealth and labor in its own state. For our Jewish proletariat, the war between wealth and labor would only be valid in our own state, where a national framework for creating its own modern Hebrew culture would be developed. That theory seemed to us at the time, as a great discovery, we waited for, for a long time. It proved that the host nations would confiscate Jewish wealth and expel the Jewish workers. Jews would find themselves again outside of society's framework. Thus, whatever happened to the Jews at the end of the feudalistic period, would also happen to them during the socialistic revolution. The only conclusion was that even for the Jewish proletariat, the only way to survival was the "Jewish State".

The academic association "Bar Kokhba" published Dr. Daniel Pasmanik's two lectures and nominated him as an honorary member.

[Columns 129-130]

All that is left from that entire fascinating episode is the description presented on these pages. The torrent of history flooded those fascinating days during which endless dreams were woven.

The flirtation between "Bar Kokhba" people and the Zionist Workers' Organization [that was how the name "Poalei Tzion" was interpreted), lasted about two years. Whatever happened there, is not part of "Bar Kokhba's" history. It belongs to the history of the "HaNoar HaOved" movement and the leftist parties. The German poet expressed what can be said about that:

"*Leicht bei einander leben die Gedanken Doch eng im Raume stossen sich die Sachen*"

["Thoughts live easily together but things bump into each other in a crowded space"]

"Poalei Tzion" party demanded that its members with academic education leave the Zionist Union and join the International Jewish Socialist Workers' Party. We found ourselves at a crossroad, and we refused to leave "Bar Kokhba", renounce our aspiration, and dilute the Jewish character of the party, although the party assured us that it would encompass the entire nation [in the future]. The roads of the Zionist intelligentsia and the Zionist workers separated. They had not found a common ground until today.

In the meantime, things advanced very quickly in Galitsian Zionist politics. A new question emerged: "Should the Zionists participate as Zionists in the battle for the Jewish National rights in the diaspora, or should a new party be formed for that purpose? Perhaps the whole issue is not of any interest to the Zionists. Perhaps each member should be free to choose their own political position as a Galitsian, Austrian, Czech, or Polish Jew?" That question was a subject of fierce debate within the Zionist movement. Until 1906, the question was just a subject for a theoretical debate, albite fierce. Other issues of more political importance were on the agenda – problems with a real urgent value. First, there was the issue of Herzl's attitude towards state politics. Today, 50 years later, we understand his position. There is no doubt that the initial call for the Zionists to take over the Jewish communities came from Herzl. There are no doubts about that part of the [Zionist] politics. People claimed that his intention was not directed at Terebovlia and Kopychyntsi, and not even the city of Ternopil. It was directed at the five largest communities, which were authorized to vote for the directorate of the J.C.A. ["The Jewish Colonization

Association"]. The directorate controlled the multi-million dollar estate of Baron de Hirsch. If I am not mistaken, the communities were - Vienna, Paris, London, Frankfurt (or Budapest), and Brussels (or Amsterdam). However, the call was worded generally. It was clear that by taking over the communities, the Zionists would control Judaism and the Jewish financial institutions. Internally they would be able to impose taxes to benefit the Zionist ideology of "the Return to Zion". They would also be able to represent Eretz Israel's Judaism externally. For the same reason, Herzl supported having Zionist representatives in the parliaments of each country, or at least one Zionist representative in each parliament. Herzl's view was that even a single representative could serve as a speaker of the movement towards the world and the ruling classes of these countries. However, it is doubtful that Herzl advocated participation in the local political battles and the use of the Zionist factions in the parliaments for the day-to-day needs of the Jewish masses in the diaspora. He also did not advocate the establishment of Jewish curia's [blocks of voters with certain characteristics], or the founding of Yiddish schools, which could be considered as elements of autonomy. That would have led inadvertently to resistance by the governments that Herzl needed their help to realize his unique [Zion] plan.

Herzl had only one criterion – whatever advanced us towards the goal of a Jewish State was good and had to be done. Whatever distanced us from achieving that objective was not good, and we had to avoid doing it. Today, it is difficult to know how Herzl would have reacted when, due to the historical development, the debate ceased to be theoretical and when reality forced us to act.

The other important issue was the contrasts between the Austrian Jews and the Galitsian Jews. In the 19th century, Viennese Jews held the hegemony, and the Jewish representatives to the Austrian parliament came from them. However, at the end of the 19th century and the first years of the 20th century, the centers of mass, of both the Zionists and the assimilators, moved to Lviv, Galitsia. The prominent leaders and the representatives of the assimilators were Dr. Emil Bik and Shmuel (Shmelkeh) di Horowitz. The leaders of the Zionists were the members of the Central Zionist Committee who published the weekly "Voskhud" ["The East"] and "Pshishlashtesh" ("The Future"). They were mainly - Dr. Max Braude, Gershon Zipper (who returned to political work after seven-year hiatus), and Adolf Shtandt. The assimilators gang was supported by the Galitsian Polish government. They made a fortune from the franchises awarded to them by the Poles as a reward for bringing Jewish votes during the election. That gang kept a "quid pro quo" relations with the Jewish community leaders in the provincial towns who supplied the votes in exchange for money, permits, and franchises. The Zionist youth supported the Tz. K. [Galitsian Zionist Central Committee]. The Central Committee relied on the academic youth organizations and Zionist associations established throughout Galitsia under various names. With that situation, the community leaders did not face any danger from the old generation, which maintained a strange coalition with the semi-apostates on one side and the rebbes and their Hasidim on the other. The election law was based on the principle of curia's (such as universities, chambers of commerce, age cohorts, and people who pay high taxes). Therefore, the number of eligible voters was limited and since voting was not done secretly, voters were subjected to all means of influence, cooptation, and pressure. Adding another curia would not have changed the situation much since the number of those additional votes would be limited.

[Columns 131-132]

Any attempt to widen the voting rights encountered a resistance from many sides. Those with the interests and privileges protected their political standing against election majorization. All the small minorities, such as the Western Ukrainians and the Ruthenians, feared it. The Poles resisted the widening of voting rights because it could have made them a powerless minority, losing their position as the ruling class.

The situation of the Galitsian Jews, who resided there in masses, was more complicated. It was the logical and inevitable result of the objective conditions that prevailed there. Galitsia, a substantial part of Poland, which fell to Austrian hands during the partitions of Poland in the 18th century, was populated by three nations: More than three million Poles, about the same numbers of Western Ukrainians (Ruthenian), most of them Catholics (Unitarians), and close to a million Jews. The Poles were the rulers, by tradition and customs developed over hundreds of years. The Poles were the intelligentsia, and they owned the fields, forests, and big estates. They developed mutual support relations with the Habsburgs. The Poles, along with the Germans from the western part of the monarchy, served as the pillars for the ruling dynasty and the entire Austrian government. For their support, "Vienna" let them rule in Galitsia, as in their own Polish territory. The Ukrainians also advanced, with the help of "Vienna", for self-explanatory reasons. According to the Polish theory, the Poles constituted, "along with the Jews", the majority in Galitsia. The concept of "Poles of Moses religion", did not have any basis in real life. In actuality, the Poles' attitude toward the Jews could be summarized as follows: a) The Jews are not members of a separate nation like other nations in the Austrian empire, since they do not have their own language or a national school. They also do not constitute a separate economic unit (like the Slovenians). They are considered as "Poles" when they are useful in promoting the Poles and Polish rights in Galitsia. However, b) The Jews are not "Poles", since they are foreign (they have a different religion), insofar as their own rights. c) The Jews must support the Polish interests. They must vote for Poles in the parliamentary election and support any quota favoring the Poles. d) The Poles, are not obligated to give anything back to the Jews, as a group.

At the end of the 19th century and beginning of the 20th century, the hegemony transferred or began to transfer from the nobles, the owners of the large estates, who were linked to the Jews via business connections, and dependent on Jewish capital, to the National Democrats (N. D. Narodowa Demokracja) – consisting of the urban intelligentsia and the middle-class farmers – the two natural competitors of the Jews. The "National Democrats" strove to take over commerce, industry, craftsmanship, brokerage, peddling, Inn ownership, and in general, any influence on finances and economy, from the hands of the Jews and also take over any control of science, the arts, and journalism. A tragic situation emerged: The Jews were humiliated to the level of second-class citizens, and the Jewish nation was perceived as a religious cult. As a result, Jewish immigration to America reached humongous dimensions. Whole towns began to empty out of their Jews, who first moved to the provincial cities and from there to the capital city of Lviv. The Jewish leaders of that period, such as Dr. Emil Bik, Shmelkeh di Horowitz, Dr. Lowenstein, and Dr, Kolischer from Lviv, came to terms with that situation. They accepted the role of representing the Galitsian Jews as "Poles of Moses religion". They handed over the Jewish votes in all the elections to the central Galitsian government, and in return, receive for themselves, and their supporters, all the rights, privileges, and jobs. Similar characters in the provincial cities and small towns like Gal in Ternopil, Roikh in Stanisławów [now Ivano-Frankivsk], Dr. Guld in Zolochiv, and Pirstein in Drohobych, the suppliers of the "Polish Orientation Seal" in the provincial cities -the community leaders, powerful, and wealthy, who came and went into the offices of district governors, and other government offices. They helped individuals, once and a while, mainly their relatives, and tripped their rivals. They were always surrounded by political gangsters and thugs. The latter received their wages in cash or other money-worth compensation (such as flour from the mill of M. Gal in Ternopil, cart-full wood, or potatoes). The right to vote reform awarded to the masses could directly harm the position of the old leaders, who served as arbitrators between the Polish governors and the Jewish masses. It could have undermined the power position of the aggressive community leaders who had total control over the communities. The Jewish intelligentsia was in favor of widening the voting rights for the same reasons it was rejected by the community leaders. All the Jewish parties - the Zionists, Z. P. S (the Galitsian "Bund"), and the Jewish faction of the P. P. S., met at that same point. The Social-Democrats organized large gatherings, in which "Poalei Tzion" participated for the first time. "Poalei Zion" requested that in addition to the four dimensions of the general right-to-vote (general, equal, direct, and secret elections), on adding a fifth dimension -"proportionality". That principle would ensure that small nations would not fall victim to the ruling nations. Initially, the rest of the parties were angry at "Poalei Tzion" because they violated the workers' unity by bringing up an additional request. However, when the Viennese government, to everybody's surprise, announced in response to the demonstrations (in the confidential support of the Poalei Tzion" central headquarter in Vienna), that it intends to enact a five-dimensional election law, "Poalei Tzion" acquired the name of experienced politicians because they were the only ones that foresaw the future.

[Columns 133-134]

However, in 1905-06, it was still far from the active participation in the election of the "Poalei Tzion" faction in "Bar Kohkba", since the new law was approved in the parliament only in 1907. The first election based on that law was held only in the summer of 1907. The debates about whether the Zionists should participate in the election continued endlessly. The debates took place in our gatherings, meetings, and conferences. Who knows whether we would have been able to bring about the revolution that we have caused if not for a faithful event? That event resulted in the cessation of the quarrels and pushed us to jump into the torrent water of national politics.

At the beginning of 1906, Dr. Emil Bik, the leader of the assimilators and a proponent of the subjugation to the Poles, died.

Poster of the Macabbi Party in Kozliv [formally Kozlov] The Speaker: Philip Korngruen.

[Columns 135-136]

    He was an honest man with a Jewish heart. However, as an apprentice of the enlightenment period, which took the form of half-Germen, half-Polish assimilation, he did not understand that the Jews could be grouped as a unique ethnic unit in Austria, like other nations in the Austrian Empire. Bik was a representative in the Austrian parliament from the Zolokhiv, or if I am not mistaken, the Zolochiv-Brody region. He kept one of the "Jewish mandates" – meaning one of the mandates reserved by the Polish governors for "their Jews" (as the Jews constituted a majority in those two cities). With the death of Dr. Emil Bik, another Jewish representative, who would agree to the "Votes for Poland" arrangement, had to be elected. The government initially thought of nominating Dr. Kolischer as its candidate. He was a prominent, honest, learned, and economics expert. He called for a gathering in Brody, in which he intended to explain to his listeners - his platform. However, Zionists, headed by the Tartokover brothers, members of a local prominent and honorable Zionist family, showed up at the same gatherings. Among the Zionists, Dr. Gershon Zipper, then a lawyer from Lviv, also participated. Together, they debated and "destroyed" Kolischer, who panicked and ran away from the debate. The government was forced to select another local aggressive [assimilator] who would not be easily frightened. It fell to Dr. Guld, the head of the community and mayor of Zolochiv, to take the place of Dr. Bik

    The gathering in Brody caused a stir within Galitsian Judaism. It was the first time Zionism and assimilation faced each other in a political battle. It seemed that the Jewish masses considered the Zionists as their natural leaders, not only in affairs related to Zionism but also in all other questions on the agenda of the Jewish world. A new phrase was coined, which was expressed by one German word: "Gegenvortarbeit" ["Present Work" – or "culture work" as opposed to "real work" in Eretz Israel]. The concept of "Tzionistishe Landespolitic" ["National Zionist Politics"] was coined several years later.

    Two Zionist figures urged us to participate in the election, even before the new law was enacted: the first, Dr. Markus Braude, a vigorous man with organization, initiative, and quick decision skills, and the second, Dr. Gerson Zipper, one of the first Zionists who was silent for approximately six years, and reappeared like a meteor. The latter captured the leadership steering wheel of the Zionist Union away from the sensitive and delicate Stand. Under the pressure of these two Zionist figures and some local Zionists, the Zionists nominated a candidate, opposing the assimilators, in almost every city. In the Zolochiv-Brody region, they nominated Adolf Shtandt as their candidate. The battle between the Zionists and the assimilators on the right to represent the Jewish nation towards the non-Jewish world began. Even though there were no real chances for a Zionist to win, there were several reasons for nominating Adolf Shtandt as a candidate in Zolochiv, as early as 1906, took place for the following reasons: a) To prove to the Jews and non-Jews in Galitsia that we, the Zionists, receive authority and a permit from the Galitsian Jewry to protect its interests, and by doing that, present to the world our political visit card. b) To organize our party in all the cities, towards a new goal. c) To establish an apparatus capable of running a campaign, acquire experience in disseminating propaganda, something we were not used to doing, and draw out the national Zionist ideology from the halls of our union to the street. We also wanted to learn the tactics of our rivals. The 1906 election was like a dress rehearsal for what we faced in 1907.

The people of "Bar Kokhba" participated in that first battle along with the Zionist intelligentsia from Lviv and Eastern Galitsia. Waldman, Korngruen, Khartiner, Sirkes, and others were sent to Zolochiv. Their mission was to stay in Zolochiv until the end of the election, give speeches publicly, acquire voters "house to house" (in Yiddish "Fon man tsu man" [from one man to the other], and mainly to learn the ploys of the rivals we would meet when the real battle comes. We stayed in Zolochiv and worked day and night. Our Lviv friends from the organization "Emuna" ["Faith"] worked along with us. The work was tiring and not without risks. Once and a while, one of us got arrested and sent to jail. The gendarmes interrupted our gatherings and disallowed them for all sorts of strange excuses such as – the houses where the parliament representative, Shtoikher from Czernowitz, or Ernest Breiter, were slated to give a speech at, was about to collapse and other similar excuses. Obviously, corruption was represented by the local patriots, and the Polish terror won in the end. However, we won the hearts in the Jewish street. As early as 1906, people began to use the phrase - "Stand hat zikh di shtimung, un Guld – di shtimen" ("The sympathy to Shtandt, the votes to Guld). The war began, and the new election law brought about the conditions for it.

In 1907, the election for the Austrian parliament in Galitsia was held under the new election constitution. However, the request to institute a proportional election based on ethnic groups failed. Also, the Jews were not considered a separate ethnic group in the 1907 election. Obviously, the dreams about a national Jewish curia (and for that matter any national curia's), did not materialize. We, the Zionists, requested that but it was clear that the Galitsian Poles would never agree to that, and without the support of the Poles in the parliament, it was impossible to pass any reform in the election law. It was also clear that the Poles were supported by the Jewish assimilators and the religiously orthodox people who understood that their influence and their political and economic standing would break down if the election would be held under the framework of national curia's. They understood that the people would expel them, and the Austrian-Polish administration in Galitsia, with all its deceitful and hypocritical ways, would not save them.

[Columns 137-138]

Instead of the proportional election and the Jewish curia, the authorities created election districts deliberately intending to minimize the number of districts where a Jewish candidate had to be elected (for reasons of fairness, and the non-Polish world). That was a clear attempt to prevent the Jews from voting for a candidate they wanted to vote for instead of a candidate the Poles wanted. For that purpose, they divided the Jewish district of Zolochiv-Brody and added three small non-Jewish towns and several Polish villages to all the Jewish cities like Brody. Despite all the ploys, terror, and corruption by the authorities, and despite knowing that we were facing a difficult and risky campaign, we decided to participate in the election, with all of our energy. At the time, we did not think about mandates for the parliament, politics, or economy. None of us thought about our own personal status or personal benefit. We just came out enthusiastically to fight a holy war, exalt the horn of the Jewish nation, and bring about its national and cultural rights.

Mainly, we had one objective - To eradicate evil from among us - eradicate these sleazy characters, which took over the Jewish street, exploited the nation, and degraded its flag. In 1907, a holy war between Zionism and assimilation for the survival of the Jewish nation and its dignity erupted.

Obviously, the people of "Bar Kokhba" bore the campaign burden and work on their shoulders in the Ternopil's sector. The most prominent figure, the fighter on the front line, was Israel Waldman. At the time, (if I am not mistaken), he had already received a Doctor of Law degree. He was an outstanding speaker, daring and vigorous. Prominent figures and friends brought to Ternopil from all over Galitsia helped him in handling the propaganda. A month before the election, all of the association's members, who resided outside of Ternopil in near or far cities, received recruitment orders. We asked them to leave their offices and jobs, come to Ternopil, and stay there until the end of the election. None of them refused to obey the order, even if it meant losing one's job and livelihood. Nobody refused to work on the campaign or did not complete all the missions he was tasked with, even if they were dangerous or unpleasant. "Bar Kokhba" people were tasked with the propaganda work - a) In almost half of Eastern Galitsia outside of the Ternopil district b) In the city of Ternopil itself, where the Zionist candidate, Adolf Shtandt, ran against the assimilator, Gal. c) In the provincial cities around Ternopil that belonged to other districts, where our candidate Mahler, ran against a Polish noble. We divided the work with Waldman. He concentrated on the city of Ternopil, and I took on myself the area which belonged to Mahler's district - Mikulintsy, Terebovlya, and Chortkiv and its hundreds of villages. The district had two mandates. One mandate was to be elected by the majority of the votes (the votes of the majority – Ukrainian peasants). The other mandate was reserved for the candidate who was to receive more than a quarter of the votes (usually the votes of the Polish and Jewish minorities). The Polish nobles' plan was good, until we broke it, by positioning Zionist candidates. There was no hope for these candidates to receive a quarter of the votes. In Austria, these candidates were called "zählenkandidat" ("Counting Candidates"). They did not come from the leadership of the Zionist party. They were not of the caliber of people like Shtandt, Zipper, Braude, Thon, or Maltz. They were second or even third-level people. They were appointed only so that the Jews would have somebody to vote for, avoiding giving their vote to a Polish candidate, without evoking the hatred of the Ukrainians. The opposite was true. That was a kind of a neutral position, like a public announcement that we do not want to help one nation rule over the other. Also, it was a declaration that we demanded what is due to us – everything that is given to every other nation in the Austrian empire, meaning recognizing the Jews as a nation with its own language and culture. Obviously, there was no shortage of curiosities. Our political leaders were inexperienced. Like the Polish-Austrian administration, they had never faced the masses and did not know how to influence them and how to subdue the masses to their will using all sorts of ploys. Our leaders did not appreciate our nation's will in Galitsia. In the provincial cities and villages, The Jews demonstrated courage that even the most enthusiastic people among us could not foresee. With boundless enthusiasm, without regard to the possible undermining of their economic situation (as their livelihood depended on the wealthy Polish estate owners), they handed us their vote. And so it happened that in two of the districts - one in Chortkiv where "Bar Kokhba" worked, and the other in Pidhaitsi, where "Emuna" from Lviv worked, the Ukrainian candidate received the majority votes, but neither the Jewish candidate nor the Polish received a quarter of the vote. A run-off election ("stichwhalen") was called between the Zionist Jew and the Polish Noble. In that election, the Ukrainians voted for the Zionist candidates. In the district of Chortkiv, Professor Mahler (who was a Zionist but not from among us) was elected, and in Pidhaitsi, a Zionist candidate Dr. Heinrikh Gabel was elected. He never dreamed about being elected.

In Ternopil, Dr. Israel Waldman moved heaven and earth. We had never seen such intensive dissemination of propaganda in our city before. We conducted public gatherings where thousands participated, parades, posted posters, distributed newspapers, and published articles, which were distributed to every Jewish home. The days when Adolf Shtandt gave speeches became National celebrations. It was a year of enthusiasm and political awakening. Despite the terror by the district's Polish commissioner and the danger, we fought like lions. One day we found out that the voter cards had to be printed on a special paper. That paper was stored at the court in Vienna, and the district commissioner did not send to anybody suspected of supporting Zionism. So, Waldman organized a street demonstration

[Columns 139-140]

Delegates from Galitsia to the 9th Zionist Congress in Hamburg
(In the pictures: Most of the Members of The Galitsian Zionist Central Committee)

From right to left – Sitting: **Meir Henish, Dr. Khaim Tartokover, Dr. Ph. Korngruen, Maiblum, Dr. Yehoshua Thon, Mrs. Dr. Thon, Dr. Mordekhai Zeev Braude, Mrs. Sarah Ritterman from Stanislawow, Adolf Shtandt, Zilah Waldman Dr. Michael Ringel, Mrs. Dr. G. Gabel, Bentzion Fet, Dr. Israel Waldman, Dr. Alexander Hausman**
Standing: **Braude (Brother of Dr. Braude), Unknown, Joseph Zusman from Stanislawow, Moshe Waldman, Dr. Hirshorn, Eng. Sokal from Stanislawow, Dr. I. Lauterbach, Rabbi Dr. Nimrower, Herman Trop, Dr. Alexander Ritterman,**
Waldman from Drohobicz, Avraham Shenbach from Sanok, Dr, Heinrikh Gabel, Dr. Henryk Rosemarin, Yehoshua Washitz from Hamburg, Unkown, Dr. Warhaftig, Unknown

and a parade to the district commissioner under the watch of the gendarmery - a real revolution. Ernest Breiter, a parliament representative, a Polish democrat, and one of the world's righteous, who stayed in Switzerland at the time, bought the special paper for the voter cards and we distributed them throughout Galitsia's cities in a single sleepless week. Dr. Israel Waldman established an association for the hard working laborers and porters called "HaShakhar" ["The Dawn"]. From among its members, he formed a guard group. That group, along with people from "Bar Kokhba", guarded him and Adolf Shtandt from the attacks by the underworld thugs, who were hired by our rivals to "blow out" our gatherings by force. We fulfilled that mission faithfully and did not shy away from using force ourselves. In the meantime, the issues of the "Des Yiddishe Tagblat" newspapers were handed down from one person to another. Meir Khatiner published there his sequel article - "Knesset Israel BeTza'ar" ["Literarily – "Israel's Knesset in sorrow"] – written in blood and fire. It constituted a declaration of a merciless war against Jewish assimilation. If you have not seen Jews waking up at 4 o'clock in the morning and running to the train station to grab a copy of the newspaper where the articles were published, you have not witnessed a Zionist event. Shtandt himself said many times that these articles brought him half of the Jewish votes. However, despite all of the efforts, we only managed to conquer the people's hearts. We attracted the youths in all the Hasidic homes, the half-converted Jews, and the women. We caused a split in many Jewish homes and also acquired a popular and pure name for the Zionist Movement. However, Gal was elected over our candidate as the parliament representative. He was a half-converted Jew, a person lacking a national spine and knowledge of Judaism. He was what was named - "Ein gemesigter izrelit" ("a moderate Jew") without a Jewish spirit in him who joined the club of the young Polish representatives in the Viennese parliament. We were encouraged to hear that Adolf Shtandt was elected in Brody. In the evening when the results of the election became known, the porter association held a serenading party honoring Gal, after receiving two sacks of flour from his mill in Ternopil. However, the news about that party was overshadowed by the sea of joy and excitement than engulfed Ternopil Jews as a result of the election of Adolf Shtandt, who was the real Jewish winner.

In 1907, the first Zionist club in the Austrian parliament (and, for that matter, the first parliamentary Zionist in the entire world) was established in Vienna. The following people were the founding members of the club: Dr. Beno Shtroikher, Adolf Shtandt, Dr. Arthur Mahler, and Dr. Heinrikh Gabel. The real day-to-day activity of political Zionism began.

These lines are not the place to review who were the people that were elected instead of the more qualified and prominent people. It is also not the place to describe how the harsh reality, which offered too few possibilities to match the theory, hopes, and enthusiasm that rose during the election, trumped the theory. The parliamentary Zionist club brought us a big honor. We grew up, and the world began to treat us not as a group of idealistic students but as a popular movement with all of its advantages and disadvantages.

[Columns 141-142]

During that same period, the following people were elected as "seniors": Avraham Shwartzman, Alexander Rapoport, Leon Horwitz, Aba Auerbakh, and Moshe Fisher. In 1910, Ternopil Zionists and many other Jews who joined our camp participated in the big political battle for recognizing Yiddish as one of the formal languages in the Austrian empire. Formally recognizing the language would have allowed establishing Jewish schools and ensured government budgeted allocations to Jewish cultural institutions. The victory meant that tens of thousands of people could respond that their spoken language was Yiddish rather than Polish, in the census held in Austria every decade.

In 1910, the terror by the Polish-Austrian governors did not subside, but the stubbornness, will, and pride of the Jewish masses grew with it. Unfortunately, history caused all of the efforts, victories, dedication, and deep faith of the Jewish masses in Ternopil and Galitsia all the creations and the achievements sank in a sea of tears and blood. The majority of them were forgotten or about to be forgotten.

In 1911, new elections were held upon the dissolution of the central Austrian parliament. Dr. Israel Waldman managed the campaign in Ternopil again, and Adolf Shtandt was placed as the candidate in Ternopil and other locations. The campaign propaganda was managed vigorously and dedicatedly like in 1907, however, despite all the efforts, the results were negative, and the Zionist club in the Austrian parliament was dissolved.

The national political defeat did not undermine the influence of the movement. The opposite was true. Just then came the disillusionment and disappointment from the diaspora and anything associated with it. Even before the defeat in 1911 and more vigorously after it, the Zionist thinkers in Ternopil, like in the rest of Galitsia, turned their efforts towards a direct day-to-day work on settling Eretz Israel and the dissemination of the Hebrew language and culture. There was no shortage of harsh debates and crises at the [Zionist] Union and the central committee in Lviv about whether the Zionists needed to be involved in national politics. The person in the center of these debates was "Bar Kokhba's" member, Meir Khartiner, who zealously fought against the one who represented the view about national political involvement, Dr. Gershon Zipper. The quarrel was spilled over to the newspapers and the Jewish public opinions.

My memories about the events beyond 1911 are greatly blurred since I moved to Lviv in 1911 as the president of the Galitsia and Bukovina's Hebrew Schools organization replacing Dr. Shlomo Shiller z"l who made Aliya to Eretz Israel. In the same year, three Hebraic organizations (the Hebrew Culture Union, headed by Yehoshua Thon, Hebrew Teachers Association, headed by Rafael Superman, and Hebrew Schools Association, headed by D. Korngruen) announced the establishment of the "Day of the Hebrews", the first in Galitsia and the entire world, which was held in Lviv. This Hebrew conference brought with it an awakening of the Hebrew movement. Thanks to it thirty five Hebrew elementary schools in provincial cities were established, and a seminar for Hebrew teachers was founded in Lviv. In 1912-13 I moved to Berlin as the secretary for the limited executive committee of the International Zionist Union, and my connections with Ternopil

The membership (and guests) of "Bar Kokhba", New York (1952)

[Columns 143-144]

weakened. After the First World War, I was elected, along with Dr. Israel Waldman, Adolf Shtandt, Dr. Leon Reikh, and Mikhael Ringel as a representative to the "Commitè des Delegations Juives" ["Committee of Jewish Delegations"] in Paris. In 1920, I have already managed the central Eretz Israeli office that assisted tens of thousands of immigrants and pioneers in their Aliya to Eretz Israel. I attribute all of my activities there to my membership in "Bar Kokhba" in Ternopil. The last time I visited Ternopil was when I traveled along with my wife, Frida Korngreun (nee Zilberdik) to say goodbye to my parents before making Aliya to Eretz Israel.

* * *

I tried to describe our Zionist life in Ternopil, in the period of "Sturm und Drang" ["Storm and Passion"]. I know that I have only provided the outlines. The actual Zionist life in Ternopil was rich in many aspects, fruitful, alluring, authentic, and cultural.

Ternopil was a strong citadel of the international and the Galitsian Zionist Movement. Ternopil treated Zion and Zionism seriously. Zionist Ternopil could always be counted on to act dedicatedly without any doubt, disciplined without any deviations, believing in the vision. In Ternopil, the youth tried their best to unify Zionism with human culture and general humanity with the Hebraic and Jewish culture. We never disassociate ourselves from the Zionist and Jewish world. We succeeded in most of our endeavors. It is hard to remember all of the details: all of the balls, theatrical shows, scientific and popular lectures, Jewish history classes, Jewish schools, and many more. Etched in my memory are the visits by the generation's greats, Jewish and Christians. I remember the visits of people like Leah Rozin, who was a great actor in the imperial theater in Vienna, Morris Rosenfeld, the famous poet, and especially the visit by Shalom Aleichem.

"Bar Kokhba" Association was the only organization or institution in our city that continued its existence as an association of academic Zionists beyond World War II. Its center is in Tel Aviv with branches in Jerusalem, Haifa, and New York (after its branches in Warsaw, Lviv, and Krakow were closed). Its activities did not cease because of the two World Wars and other local wars. The spark was not extinguished. When the source was annihilated in Ternopil by the Nazi Holocaust, and the branches in Poland closed or emptied, the branches in Eretz Israel and America continued their activities. The name "Bar Kokhba" was never erased, and the connections among the members never ceased during good and bad times.

It is impossible to understand and appreciate Zionism in that portion of Galitsia, which bordered Russia, during those heydays before 1914, the days of Herzl, the awakening of the Jewish nation, and the creation of those values, ideas, slogans, and views, on which the founding state of Israel and its Hebraic culture are based, without describing "Bar Kokhba's Ternopil".

The Protocol

From the first congress of the Zionist Graduates of the Schools in Galitsia

Location: Ternopil
The meetings' location: The Social Club
Dates: 15 – 16th July 1901

The First Meeting

Member Korngruen opens the meeting at 10 AM, in the name of the conference's founders. He welcomes the participants and calls for fruitful work.

The presidential committee of the conference was elected based on the proposal by the special committee. The following members were elected unanimously:

Chairman: Member Ph. Korngruen (Ternopil).
First Vice-Chairman: Member Izik Bekher (Stanisławów – now Ivano-Frankivsk).
Second Vice-Chairman: Member Mark Vishnitzer
Secretaries: Members Yaa'kov Karp (Zolochiv) and Henrik Landsberg (Stryj)

The chairman takes his place at the head of the table and invites two members to keep order.
The chairman proposes to accept the proposal of the special committee:

1. To award to right of advisement to the academic members.
2. To award the right of advisement to Mrs. Roza Pomerantz, the chairwoman of the Ternopil district Zionist committee.
3. To adopt the bylaws of the Zionist conferences.

The proposals were adopted unanimously. According to paragraph no. 1 of the agenda, the chairman recognizes member Bekher to give a lecture about the subject: "Our Organization".

In the opening of his lecture, the speaker divides the youth into three types a. The assimilators b. Indifference youth c. The Zionist youth. In his description, he skips over the first type, as it is small, and in a sorry state. However, he recommends investing efforts to win the hearts of the youth of the second type. These efforts should rely on the mobilization of the Zionist youth, who is the most numerous among the Jewish studying youth. The speaker demands that the Zionist youth, exert not just an external effort but first and most of all, also penetrate and deepen the [Zionist] idea among the members. After talking about the obligation of the Zionist youth towards the movement, he concludes that only the unity of the youth and its consolidation into a single national organization would guarantee efficient actions. In the speaker's opinion, a free organization of "academic Zionists in Galitsia" should be established.

At the end of the speech, the speaker asked the participants to postpone the debate about his lecture until after the following lecture about methods of propaganda, which is related to his lecture.

In the discussion that followed Bekher's lecture, Israel Waldman claimed that we should separate the discussion about the form of the organization and the propaganda methods. On the other hand, Mrs. Pomerantz supported the speaker's proposal. In the vote that followed, Mrs. Pomerantz's argument was adopted, and the chairman recognized Izik Nussbaum to lecture about "propaganda".

In that lecture, the sincere desire of the studying youths to get involved in Zionist work was expressed. The Zionist movement should utilize them as the pioneers of the Zionist ideas to disseminate the Zionist ideas,

[Columns 145-146]

in words and actions to every corner and location in Galitsia. The number of people who can deliver propaganda is as large as the number of our members. The speaker divided the propaganda into four types according to the age group it could be assigned to members: a) Propaganda among the high schools' students (by establishing clubs for the fostering the study of history, literature, and the Hebrew language) b) Propaganda among the academic youth (by personal interaction and dissemination of Jewish studies) c) Propaganda among the intelligentsia (by organizing national holidays festivals, literary lectures, and distribution of political newspapers) d) Propaganda among the masses (by popular lectures and Yiddish newspapers).

Members Vishnitzer, Landau, Israel Waldman, Pomerantz, and Katzstein participated in the debate. Based on Mrs. Pomerantz's proposal, an organizing committee includes the members: Bekher, Vishnitzer, Shpindle, and Korngruen. Mrs. Pomerantz was elected as the chairwoman.

The second meeting was devoted to the problems of the propaganda, and the following proposals were adopted:

1. To establish an academic Zionist association in every city where conditions allowed.
2. The conference tasked its participants, to establish a "Toynbee Hall" (a popular university for the masses) in every location it was possible to do so.
3. The associations should organize public gatherings and send speakers to the provincial city.
4. The conference tasks the associations with the obligation to organize popular balls.
5. The association must establish clubs
6. The association must mobilize all of the Zionist studying youths to service the Zionist Union in all of its areas of involvement.

In the third Meeting – the committee submitted the following proposals:

1. The conference of the Galitsian Zionist graduates in Ternopil on 15 – 16 July 1901 is founding a Zionist academic in Ternopil in the name fraternity of "Bar Kokhba".
2. Graduates of high schools and people with an academic degree are entitled to join. Teachers of the Baron Hirsch school and elementary schools can join as non-regular members but with the obligation and rights of regular members. The association is allowed to elect honorary members (prominent figures with special achievements benefiting Zionism) for a conference and the association steering committee usually. Honorary members enjoy the same rights as regular members.
3. The fraternity would be headed by a steering committee. The steering committee would consist of members from the central office who would be assigned by the conference, and members who would be elected directly by the conference.
4. The location of the central office for the years 1901 and 1902 would be in Ternopil.
5. The central office would consist of three members, all from Ternopil. Four additional members from other cities would be elected directly by the conference.
6. The fraternity of "Bar Kokhba" would organize the conference annually, at a time that coincides with school graduation. The conference of the graduates and the general assembly of the association would be held together.
7. It is the responsibility of the steering committee to make sure that the conference resolution would be executed, however, the committee has the authority to pass its own resolutions, as long as they do not contradict the conference's resolutions.
8. The central office must execute the committee resolutions.
9. The committee and its members must execute the instructions by the central office.
10. At a frequency decided upon by the conference (in 1901 – 1902 – once a month), the representatives of the committees must send reports about the activities, situation, and general and specific proposals related to the location where they are operating.

The organization's proposal was adopted unanimously. The location of the main office was determined to be in Ternopil for the then-current year. The following members were elected to serve in the head office: Avraham Pomerantz, Landau, Mueller (Ternopil), and the representatives of the committees: Horn (Brody), Bekher (Stanisławów, now Ivano-Frankivsk), and Landsberg. (Stryj).

According to the proposal by member Korngruen, it was decided upon an annual membership of two Kronen (paid in installments of half a year). The president of the association would be elected from among then members of the central committee, by the central committee itself.

Lively debates, with the participation of all members, followed the lecture of member Vishnitzer about "Our Cultural Roles". The opinions of the participating teachers were heard.

The following decisions were adopted:

    a. Absolute prohibition of duels among members of the fraternity. Matters of honor between members of the fraternity and people on the outside should be resolved in peace. A dual would depend on specific cases.
    b. The first conference requires that the members of the fraternity, develop their physical abilities. For that purpose, members should establish clubs for athletics, fencing, and other sports.
    c. The conference demands that its teachers serving in schools, named after Baron Hirsch, pay attention to the development of the physical abilities of the school children (As proposed by the member Mrs. Khartiner).
    d. The conference believes that our Jewish culture must be based on morals. Therefore, the conference demands the cultivation of good Jewish attributes and ethics. The conference wishes to bring the youth closer to the Jewish masses by mending its views and widening its knowledge about Judaism, Jewish history, Yiddish literature, and Hebrew (Vishnitzer's proposal). It is forbidden to hurt the religious feeling of Jews and non-Jews (Mueller's proposal)
    e. [Members are encouraged to] establish Jewish social life and take interest in Jewish poetry and art.
    f. The conference requires that the central office with send memorandums to the management of the schools established by Baron Hirsch and all the high school religion teachers to demand that they author textbooks in the spirit of the National Jewish and Hebraic cultures and to pay special attention to the teaching of Jewish history and the Hebrew language, in a modern style (proposals by Shpindel, Werfel, Korngruen, Aftibutzer).

The conference ended with the singing of The Zionist hymns and the signing of a fraternal covenant.

The undersigners:

The Conference Chairman: Member Ph. Korngruen
The First Acting Chairman: Member Izik Bekher
The Second Acting Chairman: Member Mark Vishnitzer The Secretaries: Members Ya'akov Karp, Henrikh Landsberg

Author's Note:

    1. Details about Dr. Israel Waldman's personality and Zionist activity can be found on column 147 of the book

[Columns 147-148]

Dr. Israel Waldman
(A Biographic Note)

Translated by Moshe Kutten

Israel Waldman was born in a Zionist home in Chortkiv in 1881. His father, and especially his uncle Dudu Swartz instilled the Zionist spirit in him from his youth. Waldman studied in the State's Polish-Ukrainian gymnasium from 1891 – to 1897. In 1897, he was forced to leave the gymnasium since he was caught doing Zionist work in public, something that was forbidden for high school's students. He received a high school diploma in 1899 in Berezhany as an external student. In 1905, he graduated from law school in Lviv and received a law doctorate degree. He apprenticed as a lawyer with Dr. Holobovitz for seven years. The latter was from among the leaders of the Ukrainian National Movement of Western Ukraine (Eastern Galitsia). During that period, he connected with Western Ukraine's intelligentsia circles, whose first (and the last) prime minister was the same Dr. Holobovitz.

Dr. I. Waldman

Israel Waldman was a political Zionist during his entire life. The history of the Zionist Movement in Ternopil is inextricably linked to his name and personality. None of the Zionist activities in Ternopil took place without Waldman's participation as the initiator or executer.

Israel Waldman was a national Jew. For him, there was no difference between activities connected directly to Eretz Israel and the daily struggle waged by the Zionist Union for obtaining the national rights for the Jewish minority. As a speaker par excellence and an excellent organizer he managed, in Ternopil and the entire Eastern Galitsia, the elections to the Austrian parliament in 1906, 1807, and 1911. He also managed the 1910 fight for the recognition of Yiddish as one of the formal languages in Galitsia. He was always interested in politics and defended the rights of the Jewish workers, artisans, and merchants (the details of which are mentioned in the article about the Zionists Movement). Some of his important activities were - the founding of an organization of porters and workers by the name of "HaShakar" ["The Dawn"], the establishment of the first Galitsian national Jewish association for athletic and physical culture by the name of "Beitar", and the publishing of a local Zionist newspaper by the name "Slovo Zhidovska" ["The Jewish Word"]. These can be attributed to him directly. Waldman represented and headed the Zionist camp. His slogan was: I am a Jew, and there is no Jewish matter, which is of no interest to me".

He served in the Austrian army during the First World War, received a High Medal of Excellence, and rose to the rank of captain.

After the war, he sided with the Ukrainians because the Western Ukrainians recognized the Jews as a separate nation and were ready to award them national-cultural autonomy. Dr. Waldman was a candidate for the position of minister of Jewish affairs in the government, which was supposed to be established after the election if the people who supported the cooperation with the Jews would win. Although Waldman received an absolute majority, the victory by the Poles over the Ukrainians in 1919 put an end to the Ukrainians' dream about an independent state in Western Ukraine.

Waldman returned to Vienna and was active there as a Zionist and Democrat until he made Aliya to Eretz Israel in 1935. However, his health condition did allow him to actively participate in politics. He resided in the house he built, along with his wife Tzila (nee Otshert) who was known in Ternopil as one of the first women who knew Hebrew and was also knowledgeable about the Talmud. Her father, Engineer Otshert, was a veteran Zionist and a national Jewish public activist.

Israel Waldman died in Jerusalem after a serious illness on 19 September 1940.

[Columns 149-150]

The "Young Zionism" in Austria

by Meir Khartiner

Translated by Moshe Kutten

One of the most characteristic chapters in the history of Zionism in Imperial Austria, that the formal Zionism kept totally quiet about, came out of the Zionist youth. They revolted against Zionism's central leadership in Galitsia, close to the First World War. The revolutionary youth movement stood to capture the entire Jewish youth in Galitsia and Austria had it not been for the [First] World War. The war muddled all the national and Zionist values among the Eastern European Jews.

That movement was crystalized as the order of "Brit Bnei Khorin" ["Sons of Freedom Alliance"]. It was organized in cells called "Gideon" [after the biblical prophet and military leader Gideon and his war against the pagan god Ba'al– Judges 6-8]. The daring goal of the order was to organize the national intellectuals among the large Galitsian Jewry (consisting approximately of eight hundred thousand people) under a single association. It aimed to purify the international Zionist Union, contaminated by the diaspora's civilization, and direct it toward the Eretz Israel and Hebrew culture. Indeed, that movement was not born in a vacuum. It was founded because of the call of the hour.

There is no doubt that the enormous propaganda that the Galitsia Zionists disseminated during the election to the Viennese Reichsrat in the summer of 1907 brought the Jewish masses closer to the Zionist idea. I recall a phrase by Uri Tzvi Grinberg from 1909. He was still a kid when he said about the election: "It was the hummer that awakened the people to pray *Slikhot* [penitential prayers] …!" However, the Zionist victory did not bring any reprieve to the people, neither economically nor spiritually. As a minority lucking any influence in the parliament, the Zionist leadership deviated from the path of national and moral purity, which brought it the win. It ceased to attract the studying Jewish youth, known for their high intelligence., the youth that was then concentrated in various academic associations in the state's cities. Straying away from the public-moral purity resulted from the political war within the rotten autonomous Polish in Galitsia: The Viennese Reichsrat was the target and the Yiddish and Polish as means of propaganda. That war distracted the Zionist leadership away from Zion and the Hebrew culture. Apart from the meager collection of funds for the JNF, nothing was done to benefit Eretz Israel and the Hebrew movement. All the productive activities were carried out by "informal" activists such as Ph. Korngruen, Refael Superman, Yosef Tishler, Dr. Israel Rot, Tzvi Sharpstein, Khaim Tartokover, and [Meir] Khartiner. That was how the Galitsian "Hebrews Day" convened in Lviv in the summer of 1911 under the initiative of Ph. Korngruen, with the assistance of the people mentioned above. That was a large demonstrative gathering, which left an enormous impression on the entire Zionist world. The following would serve as examples: Bialik sent a congratulatory and enthusiastic letter from Odesa; "HaTzfitra sent a member of its editorial committee A. N. Frank as its representative to the conference; Dr. Yehoshua Thon came from Krakow and chaired the conference. However, the "official" Zionism treated the conference coldly, and a series of my propaganda articles on the approaching conference barely made it to publication in the official Zionist newspaper, "Tageblatt".

Whatever happened in the rest of Galitsia happened in Ternopil. The national glamor of our academic association, "Bar Kokhba", considered the true founder of Zionism in Eastern Europe during the first years of the century, dimmed by becoming addicted to the state and local politics.

An opposition against the non-Hebrew and non-Eretz Israel trend in Zionism was established in our association, which contained more than forty active members. Only four Hebrew-oriented members remained in our club: Yerukham Fishel, Korngruen, and Tzila Otshert-Waldman, Moshe Delugach (the son of the rabbi from Chemrinitz? in Russia), and myself. Almost all of the "Bar Kokhba's youth joined the opposition, crystallized around me. I was initially one of the most enthusiastic and active propagandists of

[Columns 151-152]

the Zionism's politics, as I considered it as the brave warrior against assimilation. I came out with my alarm call "*Knesset Israel BeTza'ar*!" ["Literarily – "Israel's Knesset in sorrow!"] A series of Zionist proclamations appeared as the main articles in the "Tageblatt" before the election mentioned above. They provoked an enormous national enthusiasm among the Galitsian Jewry. However, I became a total opponent of that Zionist politics from the day I realized, from within the confine of the top leadership circle, that the politics were not benefiting the voters but the elected. It also does not attract the diaspora towards Zion, but completely the opposite: Zion to the diaspora…

As opposed to that diaspora-based Zionism, whose official name was "*Gegenvart Arbeit*" ("The work at present"), which we called derogatorily - "diaspora work". I established a new system named "Neo-Zionism" or "*Yung Tzionismus*" ["Young Zionism"]. The following were its principles:

Nationality, in its perfect and ideal sense, consists of three factors: land, blood (race), and culture.

Zionism is nothing but the perfect nationalism of the nation of Israel: The religion of Moshe, Cenebium (Marriage), and the Land of Israel.

For that reason, it is, nationally and Zionistically, forbidden to abandon Moshe and Israel's religion, practice intermarriage, or sabotage any cause of Eretz Israel. At present, the nation of Israel is defective. The homeland factor does exist in theory but not in reality. The Zionist Union is not a proper mechanism to realize the missing.

The homeland is the earth that feeds the national life, and the political life is only one side of the national life.

By introducing politics in the diaspora into Zionism, we add a foreign element to our national compound and cause harm to the Eretz Israeli cause as follows:

a. The public and national energy are split. That energy is not aimed at building a single national center but many national centers.

b. The national element in Zionism ceased to be qualitative and unifying and homogeneous and became a harmful factor, just like conversion and intermarriage. It became an antizionist not less than the "Territorial Zionism" [e.g. Uganda proposal], in which the harmful element is the foreign land.

c. **Diaspora-based optimism instead of pessimism.**
Implementation of Zionism is not an administrative endeavor. It involves such elements as the ones required to establish a new business, which requires enormous financial investment and especially the participation of tens of thousands of immigrants. However, history teaches us that the Jewish masses only immigrate due to **catastrophic psychology** when they are expelled from where they reside. So, Zionism requires losing faith in the diaspora life, namely diaspora-based pessimism. However, Zionism based on diaspora politics invokes diaspora-based optimism, uprooting the Zionist idea at its mental core.

d. Diaspora's State Zionism has been adopted by most of the diaspora's Zionists. Adding the optimism factor to it, the Eretz-Israeli cause, which is distanced from and not essential for the diaspora's Zionists, would be pushed aside and eventually disappear.

The "Young Zionism" proposes the following corrections:

a. **Removing the state, diaspora-related work from the Zionist program.**
The diaspora-state politics should be done by whoever would do it- not by the Zionist Union.

b. **Conquering the intelligentsia.**
It is not a big concern if Zionism's influence on the masses would be reduced due to the removal of political involvement in the state. Our main goals of securing immense investments in Eretz Israel and mass immigration would not be achieved by propaganda anyway. We should not lose hope, for now, about these goals and concentrate on securing support from our nation's intelligentsia. The body would follow the head anyway.

c. **Creating catastrophic psychology.**
We should not wish, G-d forbid, for pogroms and the catastrophic psychology they cause. But we are allowed to create an alternative for it – creating internal catastrophic psychology within the Jewish intelligentsia by forcing a mental disconnect from the foreign land they reside in. Jewish academic or religious intellectuals would have to forgo their right to vote or be elected to non-Jewish public institutions. Since the ebullient youth would not agree to such a spiritual death, it would turn to the only path open for it – the path to Eretz Israel.

d. **The new organization.**
We should form, within the International Zionist Union, an organization for the Jewish intellectual youths, which would have the following plan: 1) Prepare the youths for Aliya to Eretz Israel 2) The Zionist Congress should impose

a prohibition on the Zionist unions, in the various countries, to be involved in state politics, a similar prohibition, which was issued to prevent involvement in Territorial Zionism [securing alternatives to Eretz Israel].

I gave a comprehensive lecture about these ideas (in the summer of 1910), to two inspired and honest members: Shmuel Reiter (killed in his youth in the town of Berezhany), and may he live long, Moshe Landau (today – Dr. M. L., Kfar Saba, Israel). We decided – a youthful act – to establish a secret "triumvirate" (three men rulers coalition). We aimed at making our association fight for the new idea and someday establish a federation like the "Mizrachi" [Religious Zionist movement] and "Poalei Tzion" ["Workers of Zion"].

We attracted about half of the members of our association and became an openly non-political opposition. Among the first "converted" members, I recall the following: Moshe Kleinberg, Shimon Atterman (today in Brooklyn, NY), Beinush Tunis (today in Newark NJ), Tzvi Parnas (today in Tel Aviv, Israel), Israel Glassgal, Pinkhas(Pini) Shapira-Diament, and Israel Retzenstein.

Endless arguments commenced, which were followed by quarrels. The political people evaded a formal public debate. We finally became suspicious that the central Zionist committee was involved in that. They brought us, especially me as the opposition leader, to a trial, in front of the entire assembly. The charges were: conspiracy and holding a secret meeting of the people who opposed politics, which was held without the knowledge of the senior.

The "trial" was stormy and lasted a few hours. The opposition proposed that if the political leaders of "Bar Kokhba" declare that they forgo their active and passive voting rights to the Austrian public institutions, the opposition would cease to exist. However, that proposal only heightened the storm. At that point, I took the floor and declared that the establishment of the opposition is nothing but breaking up idols we ceased to believe in. That was a long tradition of the nation of Israel and also Zionism.

[Columns 153-154]

I continued as follows: "Since I did not see any possibility for a compromise, and since I would never agree to the formal objective of "Bar Kokhba", I declare that I would not be a member of the association any longer. I stood up and left.

Eighteen members left with me. More than twenty remained. That happened on one of the nights in the spring of 1913.

The following day we all gathered at the home of member Elazar Retzenstein (he was killed as an Austrian officer at the beginning of the First World War), on Ruska Street in Ternopil. We formed the first "Gideon" association there.

Our "triumvirate" prepared the following plan:

We are founding an order ("orden", or as we first called it – a covenant) – "Bnei Khorin ["free people"], who free themselves from the diaspora. Any Jew with high or religious-Hebraic education. The people with an academic degree formed a cell called "Gideon" (named after the war by the biblical judge Gideon against Midian tribes and their god Ba'al. The people with religious education would form another cell with a different name. The two types of cells have equal rights and obligations, including the duty of knowing fencing and the use of weapons.

A candidate for "Bnei Khorin must swear three oaths: One oath toward the Jewish culture, another toward the Jewish race, and the third toward Eretz Israel. The member had also to take vows to the Torah, warfare, and making Aliya to Eretz Israel.

The swearing and vow making ceremony progressed as follows (the swearer-in denoted as SI, reads the sentence and the swearer – denoted as S, answers with a "yes or no" – according to the ancient Hebrew judicial ceremony in Israel):

SI – I am swearing you in, and you swear by your human honor.

S -Yes!

SI – You would never abandon the religion of Moshe and the people of Israel.

S – No!

SI – You would not marry a non-Jewish woman who had not converted.

S – No!

SI – You would bring your son into the "Covenant of Abraham, our Father".

S -Yes!

SI – You would not take roots in the diaspora land.

S – No!

SI- Therefore you are giving up your right as a citizen, to vote and be elected to any political institution in the diaspora's country.

S -Yes!

SI – you take a vow now.

S – Yes!

SI – You will be a practitioner of the Jewish religion and Hebraic literature all of your life.

S – Yes!

SI – You will learn how to become a warrior to defend our nation and our homeland.

S – Yes!

SI – You would try to hasten your Aliya to Eretz Israel with all of your might.

S – Yes!

SI – You are now Ben Khorin [A free man or woman]

We held a festive public ceremony, in the summer of 1913, in Ternopil. I was the first member to swear and take the oath. I then swore in and accepted the oath of all of my friends, one by one.

For ethical reasons, the triumvirate decided not to hold any leading position. The triumvirate proposed that our friend, medical student Tzvi Parnas, whom we knew as a vigorous and agile young man, as the first "senior" of the first "Gideon" cell of Ternopil. Later on, he headed the cell of "Gideon" in Vienna from 1913 – to 1914 until the outbreak of the First World War.

Thus, the idea of Young Zionism was born as a result of a spontaneous reaction to the diaspora-based deviation of the Austrian Galitsian Zionism. The idea widened and rose to the level of a comprehensive national movement. The goal was to protect the nation against the fundamental and serious dangers we faced at the beginning of the 20th century. These dangers included: A mass exodus of people from the Jewish religion, making them "people without religion", violation of Abraham's Covenant, intermarriages, and the worst of all dangers - the horrible ignorance. While the formal Zionism did not pay attention to those national dangers, the "Young Zionism" considered fighting them - a Zionist duty. It was the "Bnei Khorin organization that introduced the need for armament as a mandatory clause of the Zionist plan. They raised it a long time before Jabotinsky. It was raised since we anticipated a [independence] war in Eretz Israel.

At its core, the "Young Zionism" was a pioneering idea of the Jewish intelligentsia during the period before the First World War. It was conceived at a time when we could not even dream about general Trumpeldor-like pioneering of the diaspora's Jewish youth. And so, the "Young Zionism" served as an ideological passage between the diaspora-based Helsinkian political Zionism [Helsinki Zionist Conference held in 1906. Decisions were made there by the Zionist Organization on actions in its branches in various countries] before the First World War, to a pioneering Zionism, born after Balfour Declaration. A Zionism that prepares the masses for conquering the homeland. The ideological distance between the two approaches on one side, and the meteoric success of the Young Zionism in Austria on the other, can only support the above-mentioned metaphor.

Let me now mention some trifles from that time – namely the symbols that I adorned our members with. Our Gideon warrior icon was the letter G throwing a spear with a three-color ribbon (black - symbolizing the land, red – symbolizing the blood, or our race, and blue symbolizing the sky or Torah). I also authored our Gideon-ic anthem. With the help of other members, I began to write a booklet containing the fundamentals of "Young Zionism". My work was cut-off by the [First] World War and its horrific events.

The establishment of the order of "Bnei Khorin resonated throughout the Jewish students' circles in the state and the entire kingdom. The following "Gideon" cells were established before the war broke (August 1914): Lviv (the founder: medical student Dolio Pordes), Stanisławów [now Ivano Frankivsk] (the founder: law student Dolio Zusman), Sasiv (the founder: philosophy student Avraham Koritz), and in Vienna (the founders: medical students Parnas Tunis, and Rosenfeld, all form Ternopil).

I am not sure where did the Russian" Yevreskia Encyclopedia", published in the 1920s, received its information. In that encyclopedia, the entry of "Tzeirei Tzion" ["Zion Youths"] erroneously claims that the movement (which had similar objectives to ours) was established in Ternopil and Stanisławów [now Ivano Frankivsk]!

[Columns 155-156]

Based on the aspiration of forming a new Zionist federation, our members in Ternopil tried but failed to send me as the "Gideon's" representative to the 11th [Zionist] Congress in Vienna (1913). Despite that failure, I did participate in the Zionist Congress (since 1898) as the veteran representative of [the Jewish newspaper], "Hatzfira". I actually received two mandates thanks to two sources. One source was the International Zionist center in Berlin, whose president at the time was Nakhum**Error! Bookmark not defined.** Sokolov z"l. The other was Sokolov's religious secretary – the founder of the "Hebrew Day" may he live long, my friend Dr. Ph. Korngruen.

When the member of the Zionist Steering Committee, Dr. Shmaryahu Levin, visited Vienna in 1913, I and the "senior" of the "Gideon" cell in Vienna. Tzvi Parnas went to see him. We had requested him to formally provide moral support for our movement but encountered a brick Helsinkian wall. We came out of the meeting greatly disappointed…

The World War, which caused many casualties and destructions, ended. In August 1920, before we could start thinking about an efficient renewal of the "Bnei Khorin" order, I made Aliya to Eretz Israel with my wife. Our movement was left "without wind in its sails" …

In the meantime, enormous and fateful events took place in our Jewish world. The East shone, and the West darkened. The idea of autonomy for Eastern European Jewry went bankrupt. The main prerequisite for mass immigration, namely - "Catastrophic Psychology", was created by the war. Thus, the motivation behind the Young Zionism movement was no longer the need of the time. However, it was sorrowfully satisfied. History brought the justification for it …

The common platform for the quarreling brothers, "Gideon" and "Bar Kokhba", was recreated. The two organizations were able to reunite. The members of both organizations became candidates for making Aliya to Eretz Israel …

[Columns 157-158]

Memories from the period 1914-1919

by Dr. Khaim Gilad (Shmeterling)

Translated by Moshe Kutten

The Period of the Russian Conquest 1914-1915

The First World War broke out almost abruptly, and Galitsia became an atrocious battlefield from the beginning. Following some light border skirmishes, the Russian army launched a large-scale offensive and conquered Western Galitsia during the first few months of the World War (August – October 1914). That glorious and developed Jewry, who enjoyed equal rights in Austria (albite not totally free from antisemitism) found itself under Russian rule. Russia - the colossal country, publicly promoted special laws against the Jews. It was a country where Jews felt like second-class citizens.

The Jews were totally astonished upon the conquest of Ternopil, about two weeks after the break of the war. Life began to return to normal, as much as it was possible under a foreign and hostile military rule, only very gradually., The economic state of the Jewish residents deteriorated, and the community's activities substantially weakened, except for the essential services like slaughtering, burials, and alike.

After a short while, an aid committee, headed by Shperling, was formed. Dr. Shmeterling was nominated as the administrative manager. Financial assistance was received mainly from Kyiv's Jews.

When the Austro-German offensive commenced in May 1919, the Russians expelled many Jews from towns of Western Galitsia. A substantial portion of them arrived in Ternopil penniless. A large soup kitchen for the needy was opened. The financial means for the refugees' needs were provided by "Kyiv's Committee for the Support of the Jews Affected by the War[1]".

Russian rule became more liberal upon the break of Kranski's First Russian Revolution in February 1917. A professor from Kyiv University was nominated as the district and the province governor. A short while later, a public council was elected to assist the governor. Three Jews (among them, one Zionist – the author of this article), three Poles, and three Ukrainians were elected to the council. The Jewish representatives were elected in a well-attended public gathering.

The Ukrainian authorities allowed the opening of a Hebrew school in the city.

The offensive of the Austro-German armies in the direction of Ternopil began in the summer of 1917. As a result, the Russians were forced to retreat. Before their retreat, the Russian soldiers attacked the Jewish residents, robbing anything they could put their hand on, and in some cases committing murders and arson. Following several days of battles, the Russians left the city. Austrian rule was re-established after three years hiatus. Life returned somewhat to normal.

Activists and Staff of the Soup Kitchen for the Jewish Refugees from Russia

[Columns 159-160]

The community committee, headed by Mr. Lvov, was also re-established. The front was established not far east of the city.

The Expulsion of the Jews from Towns of the Ternopil District

The Austrian authorities were forced to expel the Jews from the towns of Terebovlia, Mykulyntsi, Strusov, and more, at the request of the German military's headquarter in Eastern Galitsia since those towns were closed to the front in the summer of 1917.

The writer of this article was summoned, one day, to the governor of the Ternopil district. The expulsion decree was explained to him there. As a representative of the Jewish community of Ternopil, he was tasked with handling the transport of those poor Jewish souls to Western Galitsia. After the community realized that there was no way they could annul the decree, they took on themselves to manage it. The civil government made cargo trains available for that purpose. When the expelled people found out about the expulsion order, they took the necessary belongings and some food and went on their way. Their morale was very low.

The writer of these lines disembarked the train in Lviv, along with some of the expelled people, and went into the city. He turned to the Jewish community. Thanks to the community's help, he purchased food for the small group under his supervision. They arrived at their final destination, Yavoriv, in the evening. The weak women and children were loaded onto wagons. The men and the rest of the women continued their way on foot. When they arrived in the city, the heads of the Jewish communities assisted in arranging their lodging in Jewish homes. Yavoriv's Jews welcomed the newcomers with open arms, love, and friendship. The writer of this article stayed in town for a few more days to ensure that everything was well organized and returned later to Ternopil.

The Disintegration of the Austrian Kingdom and the Ukrainian Rule

The Austrian Empire began to disintegrate in 1918. A Jewish conference was organized in October to discuss the situation. The conference was attended by representatives from the entire Austrian Kingdom. The writer of these lines participated as the representative of Ternopil's Jews. The discussion revolved around the state of the Jews in the various provinces of the Austrian Kingdom and the means for forestalling the impending evil.

With the dissolution of the Austrian Empire, towards the end of 1918, various national countries sprouted on its territories. In Eastern Galitsia, the Ukrainians established their own republic, with Ternopil as its temporary capital. Since the Poles did not recognize the Ukrainian government, they declared the entire state of Galitsia, including the Russian Ukraine, as part of the Polish Republic. Open war broke out between the Poles and the Ukrainians. It took place mainly in the central part of Galitsia. The Jews in Eastern Galitsia (the controversial territory) immediately declared neutrality. The Ukrainian government respected the fact that the Jews could not act differently without endangering the millions of Jews residing in the Polish territory. The government officially recognized the neutrality declared by the Jews. As a result, the Ukrainian government did not impose compulsory recruitment on the Jews of Eastern Galitsia. General recruitment decree to the Ukrainian military warring against the Poles was announced for the Ukrainian population there

In the meantime, dreadful news about the horrible pogroms conducted against the Jews by Petliura's army in the Russian Ukraine arrived in Eastern Galitsia. As a result, the Jews in Eastern Galitsia began to fear for their fate. However, the Ukrainian government treated the Jews fairly and even friendly.

In February 1919, a battalion consisting of several thousand new recruits, which was about to be sent to the Polish-Ukrainian front, concentrated in Ternopil. Antisemitic spirit began to spread among these recruits (probably under the influence of the propagandists in Russian Ukraine). The recruits complained about the fact that the Jews were exempt from compulsory military service. They claimed that there was no reason why the Jews would not join the army to defend the Ukrainian homeland. During one of the days in February 1919, the battalion soldiers exhibited a hostile attitude. They entered Jewish stores and took various merchandise without paying. Brawls accompanied by curses and expletives erupted when the soldiers encountered resistance from the Jewish shopkeepers. Those brawls heralded harsher events that erupted at night. The writer of these lines turned immediately, in the name of the city's Jewish community, to the Ukrainian police commander. The latter promised to restore order but did not fulfill his promise. The riots intensified more and more during the evening of the following day.

A stormy gathering of the Jewish residents commenced at the hall of "Yad Kharutzim" [the hall of the Artisans guild] on Berl Street. The security means needed to address the ominous signs were debated. Although the Jewish defense force was well organized and armed, it was decided that it could not battle against an army battalion. That battalion consisted of about four thousand soldiers armed with rifles and a machine gun. Besides, a resistance action could wreak havoc on the city's Jewish residents. As it turned out, that was a smart and correct decision.

Immediately after the public gathering, the community committee gathered in its offices on Sobieski Street to discuss the situation. The fear grew from one hour to the next as news about attacks by the soldiers in the various sections of the city, particularly in the city center, kept coming.

[Columns 161-162]

The news was also received about closed stores and multiple robberies of stores and Jewish homes. It was decided to send a three-person delegation to the military commander in the city, whose residence was in Sobieski Square, opposite the church.

The delegation crossed the snow-covered and empty street and entered the garden to pass through to the commander's office, located on the other side. To the delegation's surprise, it encountered fierce gunfire from the direction of the military headquarters' gate and from the right side. The delegation was forced to retreat. It was clear that the situation was more serious than previously thought. That was confirmed by the news that filtered into the community committee offices about additional attacks and robberies in various locations and the echoes of shouts and gunfire from different directions. The committee took shelter in its offices during the entire night. The writer of these lines came out in the morning to explore the situation in the city. A horrible scene unfolded before his eyes, at the first glitters of the dawn. All of the Jewish shops were broken into, and the merchandise was thrown out on the streets and sidewalks. Groups of drunken soldiers wandered around, here and there, and pulled various goods out of the merchandise piles. It turned out that soldiers broke into many apartments, robbed everything they could put their hands on, hit the residents, and forcibly undressed them naked. Fortunately, the soldiers did not use firearms. There was not a single murder or a severe injury, just brutality, abuse, and humiliation. During the hours of the mornings, groups of soldiers wandered around and fired their rifles (probably just to frighten the people into confinement). Life in the city ground to a halt and no living soul could be seen on the street.

When the writer of these lines turned to the district governor, located on Mitzkevitz Street, he found the office empty. On his way down, from the second floor, he saw the governor climbing up from the cellar. The governor told him that the battalion rebelled against the authorities, jailed the headquarters' military officers, and shut down the civil rule in the city. A meeting between the civil governor, the priest Gromnitzki, and the writer of these lines, was held at about 11 AM. The governor phoned the Ukrainian headquarters in the city of Khodorov, provided details about the situation (namely – the total anarchy), and requested help. At around 2 PM, trains filled with soldiers arrived at the city and returned order. A military court was held the following day. The court sentenced three of the rebels [leaders] to death. The sentence was executed immediately, and the battalion was sent to the front.

The colossal extent of the damages suffered by Ternopil's Jewish residents became apparent two days later. The Jewish community decided to send a delegation to the Ukrainian government (The government has moved to Stanislav {now Ibano-Frankivsk. The delegation consisted of Dr. Rapoport and the writer of these lines met with the interior minister and demanded full reparations for the damages. The Interior Minister apologized, blaming the events on a military insurrection. He stated that the Ukrainian government treated the Jews emphatically. However, in that case, the authorities were not able to prevent the attacks and robberies, because they were in danger. The minister proposed to provide the Jews in Ternopil with a train tanker filled with kerosene from Drohobych as compensation for the damages. He offered that the Jews would be able to sell the kerosene and thereby could pay for some of the losses. The delegation refused to accept the offer since the damages were on a totally different order of magnitude than the money, they could receive from selling the kerosene. The minister responded that the government did not have any other means of paying for the damages. The delegation decided that Dr. Rapoport would return to Ternopil. The writer of these lines traveled directly to Vienna to submit a report to the Jewish State Committee. The thought was to have the committee turn to Baron Vasilko, the representative of the Ukrainian government in Western Europe to request his help in securing compensation. That plan was carried out, but all the lobbying efforts by the Jewish State Committee in Vienna did not bear any fruits. A short while later, the Poles conquered Eastern Galitsia, which brought the end of Ukrainian rule in the area.

Author's Note:

1. See the chapter about Ternopil of Sh. Z. Anski "Khurban Galitsia" ["The Destruction of Galitsia"], col. 163.

[Columns 163-164]

Ternopil During the First World War

by Sh. Anski

From the book, "Khurban Galitsia" ["The Destruction of Galitsia"]

Translated by Moshe Kutten

Ternopil was the second-largest city in Eastern Galitsia after Lviv [formally Lemberg]. It was also one of the oldest, rich in historical gravestones, memories, prominent and great learned people, and scholars. The Ternopil synagogue, built from stone, was one of the oldest in Galitsia.

Ternopil almost escaped suffering directly from the battles as the Russian army approached. There were no destroyed or burnt houses. When I arrived in the city, it made an initial impression on me as a quiet city but vibrant. Its streets were crowded with passersby, all the businesses and shops were open, and the trade in the market was lively. However, when I looked closer, I noticed that the crowds in the streets, market, and train station, consisted mainly of military personnel, nurses, and regular Russian people. The Russian language could be heard in every corner. The civilian population was hardly seen. Missing was the bourgeois and the educated crowd, those people who are usually dressed like people who own the place, often elegantly and coquettishly. The rare passerby from among the intelligentsia circles was dressed in tattered and worn clothes. They walked hesitantly, and their facial expression was sad. They keep quiet like they are scared, and their faces are impoverished, tortured, and gloomy. Their glance was pondering and gloomy. Signs with distorted Russian were hung above all of the shops. Signs declaring "Russian Shop" could be seen at every turn. Indeed, Russians with typical Slavic faces sat in those stores. These were the "*Kuptzi*" (merchants) who flocked there from Kaluga, Tula, Moscow, and other Russian cities and made good business with the help of the authorities. The shops and businesses were open, but the trade was almost non-existent. There were no shops for gold products nor shops for luxury items. The shelves in the shops are empty. Dusted under wares or cologne bottles, which remained from past times, could still be seen in the shops' windows. Most of the merchandise in the market were food products: rolls, pork oil, and cigarettes.

Spending one day in Ternopil was enough for me to understand the mood in the occupied city. Before the war, it was a large cultural European city. After the conquest, the city was choked, chained, and helpless. It was as if they sucked its vigor out of it, and left it to die slowly from a malignant disease without outside help. I observed the same situation in all the large cultural cities in the occupied area. They all seemed to me to be dying.

I first made acquaintance with the local rescue committee. Like in other places, the committee consisted of people who joined indecently, without approval by the population. The representative of the [central] Rescue Committee in Kyiv made efforts to find in each location remaining prominent people, such as former activists in the community. The local rabbi was also invited to join if he did not leave town. The representative would discuss the situation in the city and establish a committee that would later be approved by Kyiv's [central committee]. Although most of the intelligentsia and the wealthy people left with the Austrians, many [of the remaining influential people] were taken as hostages, but some educated activists remained in each of the large cities, like Ternopil and Chortkiv. These people served as candidates for the local rescue committee, and the activity established in other cities could be organized through them.

Several prominent and influential community members joined the Ternopil committee, such as professor Rosenbaum, Yitzkhak Nakht, and Mr. Tauber. The chairman was Mr. Tauber, a pious Jew, and wealthy merchant. His son, an educated man, was active in the committee and helped him in his work.

The budget of the Ternopil's committee exceeded twenty thousand rubles, a bit less than half the budget of the entire province of Galitsia. However, the first words I received about the budget were that the amount was insufficient and must be increased. When I remarked that, in my opinion, it was unjustified for Ternopil to receive half of the overall budget, particularly since the city had wealthy people in Ternopil who could help the needy, Mr. Tauber responded:

[Columns 165-166]

"Indeed, a few people in the city still have some property or are earning money. These people donate to help the local needy that nobody else helps. The "Zhemsky" (the local self-rule authorities) and the Kyiv committee only support the refugees, numbering about ten thousand in the city. People from all directions, from towns and villages, escaped to the city. There were even some refugees from places now in the hands of the Austrians. Most of these people are those who came back from Russia and are not allowed to return to their former locations. About a thousand families from Rohatyn and about six hundred families from Pidvolochysk reside in the city. Altogether, there are refugees in the city from 120 different places. Initially, the "Zhemski" assisted five thousand three hundred families. They distributed a litra of bread for an adult and half a litra for a child, three pieces of sugar for two days, and a bit of porridge and beans. They later dropped all the people who "were able to work" (in actuality, they could not find work anywhere). So now, only three thousand and five hundred people receive assistance, among them 1700 refugees. Starting the 2nd of May until the end of July, the committee distributed cash money (18 kopeks per person) rather than food, for 27 thousand rubles a month. The refugees were satisfied with that arrangement; however, the governor forbade the distribution of money, and the organization began to distribute food products again. In actuality, the committee is forced to support even those who are "able to work". In addition, the number of needy continues to grow. People who donated half a year ago must now seek help, as their wealth has diminished. We also have owners of estates and homes in the occupied area, millionaires with huge accounts in Austrian banks, and they are dying from hunger. We must organize a credit union for them. Besides them, we have many people in the city who need shoes, clothes, firewood, shelter, and more."

He was obviously right. Most of the assistance from the committee was enhanced nutrition for the sick, old, and children. It distributes white bread, eggs, and sometimes meat. The [local] committee members insisted that it would be more convenient to support people with money rather than produce and asked me to convince the [central] committee in Kyiv to agree to that. They reasoned their claim by claiming that it was much easier to distribute money (twice a week) so that the needy would not need to wait long hours in lines. We did not agree with their claim since there was no guarantee that the needy would spend their money on products that had been distributed to them, and the goal of achieving increased nutrition would not be achieved.

The tragic fate of the children was particularly troublesome. During the eighteen months of the conquest, the schools were closed, and the children casted off the yoke. They ran around the city barefooted, torn, and tattered, their bodies thinned out, and their faces greened.

It took a lot of effort to convince the authorities to allow adults to "pray" with the children. Using that excuse, "kheders" were organized, which carried the name "houses of prayer". About 800 children registered, but only about eighty attended because the rest did not have clothes, or worse, they got so accustomed to the life in the streets that they could not be forced to go a kheder.

The "Zhemsky" organized a residence home where 300 girls were gathered, mostly saved from a life of prostitution.

I witnessed old Jews wearing long *peot* [sidelocks], standing and cleaning the street half-naked in a deep freeze.

"The clothing distress, particularly for those who were taken to forced labor and the children in the kheders was horrible", told the committee member who accompanied me. "They used to take five to six hundred people a day for forced labor, but it was not so awful in the summer. Today, they take 100-120 people a day. It is horrific to watch them freezing in the cold".

A conference of the Galitsia communities and rescue committee representatives gathered in Ternopil in June (1918). Unfortunately, I could not participate and could not even obtain detailed information about the participants, actions, and resolutions that passed there. I did hear that the mood in the conference was elated, and that it progressed intensively. Plans of action for the reorganization of the assistance activities were made based on new sound foundations.

I received the following telegram from the conference:

"The first conference of the representatives of the Jewish population in Galitsia and Bukovina, held in Ternopil, congratulates you as the first representative of the Russian Jewry in Galitsia and the first advocate of our brothers during these hard times, You were the first person who tightened the relationship between the Russian and Galitsian Jews, and proved once more the unity of the Jews around the world. We extend our warmest greetings and best wishes to you for the moral assistance you have extended to us".

Signed: The chairmen of the conference - Grinberg, Weinfeld, and Krop.

That telegram, which moved me greatly, was the last greeting I received from our brothers in Galitsia.

The Russian conquest in Galitsia began under the oppressive rule of the Russian dictator, with bloody pogroms in Brody and Lviv [Lemberg], and ended through the revolution and the disintegrating and barbarian army in bloody destruction in Kalush and Ternopil.

With these events, the end came to the three-year horrible epic of Russian rule. It resulted in the bloody destruction of the Jewish centers in Poland, Galitsia, and Ukraine.

[Columns 167-168]

From an Austrian to a Ukrainian Regime

by Ben-Tzion Fett

Translated by Moshe Kutten

When Emperor Franz Joseph died, Karl the 4th ascended to the throne. He proclaimed autonomy for Galitsia and other nations in the Austro-Hungary empire. It was clear that the end of the "union of nations" idea of the Habsburg kingdom had ended. The only question was when would the revolution come?

We, the Zionists who served in the Austrian army since the break of the war in 1914, faced a problem: What would be the fate of the Jewish minority upon the disintegration of the empire? We particularly feared for the fate of Galitsia Jewry, which found itself between the rock and the hard place, in the conflict between Poles and the Ukrainians in their struggle for power. At the time, I was in Przemysl. A few Jewish officers gathered one day in the hotel "City" to discuss what to do to protect the Jewish population in the city? We decided to establish a self-defense force. About two thousand Jewish soldiers and officers stationed then in the city were divided into companies. They received a clear order to gather at a specific location when certain events occurred and report to the militia command. It consisted of Captain Kaiser, Lieutenant Hertzbaum, and myself. On the 1st of November 1918, the Habsburg empire fell. The struggle of Galitsia Jewry for its existence has begun.

We received news about the riots by the soldiers of Polish General Haller and about the brave defense by our youth. The companies in Przemysl were placed on standby. We did not know anything about the situation beyond the San River.

On the 3rd of November, I left Przemysl, trying to reach Ternopil, which was not an easy feat those days. After three days of road tribulations, I arrived at my destination.

The city was in turmoil. Soldiers from different nations returning from Ukraine were concentrated in Ternopil. The officers of the various nations gathered their soldiers to send them back to their countries: Austrians, Czechs, Hungarians, Poles, Slovenians, and Slovakians all passed through Ternopil. Our boys too began to return to their homes.

Chaos prevailed in the city. A certain kind of Ukrainian rule had begun to organize, but among the Jews, despair and helplessness prevailed. The city lacked any self-defense, and we found it our duty to establish one. We founded the self-defense force in December 1918, under the agreement by the authorities. The militia was headed by officer Leinberg and myself. The authorities gave the self-defense force the authority to arrest any citizen and even a military person,

including officers, who would not obey their order. The militia was also awarded the right to judge, among the Jews, and the right to impose a jail term up to five days.

Ben-Tzion Fett and Abraham Leinberg, Commanders of the Jewish Militia

The command team of the defense militia announced a youth mobilization. The following is the text of the following proclamation:

Komandeh fun der Yudisher Militz
Oiffoderung [Apeal]
Mir foderen oif aleh yuden, vas zenen geboiren in di yahren 1892 – 1900, zikh tzi melden binen 3 tag bei der komandeh fun der yidisher militz, nakh abloif

[Columns 169-170]

fun 3 tag velen mir erheben ver es iz der oiffoderung nikht nakhgekumen.
Tarnapal, dem 18 detzember
Das komandeh fun der yudishsher mulitz

[The command of the Jewish militia:
We demand that all Jews born in the years 1892-1900, report to the Jewish militia headquarter within 3 days, after which we will find out who did not comply with the request].
Tarnopol, December 18, 1918
[The command of the Jewish militia]

The Jewish Militia in Tarnopol, 1919

Eight hundred people enlisted. The city was divided into areas, and a company guarded each area day and night. The militia received a few rifles and bullets from the authorities. We also found some hand grenades and a machine gun in the barracks. The militia [command] was situated in the seminary in Sobieski Square.

The very existence of the militia was not to the liking of the Ukrainian masses. They even tried to break into the seminary once. The mob later retreated because of their fear of the machine gun, which stood at the entrance to the building, and the permanent guard near it.

The militia command did not content itself with maintaining order outside. It considered its main task - the enforcement of order internally. The committee advocated the establishment of a managerial body for the Jewish public in the city, and that was how the National Committee was formed, headed by Dr. Aleksander Rapoport. All of the layers of the [Jewish] population were represented in that committee: Dr. Avraham Shwarzman, Dr. Shmeterling, Dr. Ya'akov Lippa, Dr. Yona Abend, Shmuel Margalit, and David Parnas represented the Zionist Union. David Lvov, Shmera'leh Eikhenbaum, Khaim-Wolf Markus, and Khaim Oks, represented the [religion] orthodox' s. Dr. Zlatkes was the representative of the socialists, and Dr. Belmer represented the unaffiliated.

The National Committee took on itself the management of the Jewish community. It was responsible for maintaining the militia whose members were fully enlisted and enforcing order in all parts of the city. All other organizations like "Yad Kharutzim", the merchants guild, "Bar Kokhba", and the Zionist Union with all of its affiliations resumed their activities in the city.

The Zionist representatives aspired to give the organization a democratic character by holding a general democratic election. The date for the election was set on the 3rd of March 1919, following the population census, which was held with the help of the militia.

During the election preparation, riots broke out one night in the city. On the 15 February a Ukrainian mob broke into the city and proceeded to rob shops, break windows, and attack homes. The militia got into a battle with the rioters and took control of the situation. Several militia members got wounded in the battle, among them, Ya'akov Planer[1], who was critically wounded.

The National Committee turned to the Western Ukraine government in a memorandum on 17 February 1919. The following was stated boldly:" In these conditions, not only Jewish property is subject to robbery, but the lives of the Jews are in danger. We demand that the government provide protection of lives and property. We state that the local authorities did not make any effort to find the people responsible for the riots".

A delegation consisting of Dr. Aleksander Rapoport and Dr. Khaim Shmeterling appeared on behalf of the National Committee before the interior minister and handed him the memorandum.

Dr. Makukh, the interior minister, blamed the communists, who reside in Ternopil in large numbers. He announced the death penalty for three of the rioters. He determined that a Pole named Pikhorsky and a Jew - Lafayovker were among the rioters. Concerning that Jew, it was later found out that he was a 19-year-old student from Lviv and that he did not take any part in the riots on 15 February.

The Ukrainian government promised the Jews reparations in a form of a kerosene train car, which would be handed over to the Jews in Ternopil to sell, without imposing transportation costs and customs. The National Committee never got it (see the memories of Dr. Gil'ad (Shmeterling), column 157).

Proportional free elections to the National Committee were held for the first time on the 3rd of March.

[Columns 171-172]

The following parties participated in the election: Zionists, Orthodox Jews, Jewish socialists, unaffiliated, Merchants and artisans ("Yad Kharutzim"). The Zionists received an absolute majority in the election. The author of these lines was elected as the chairman of the National Committee. The community approved a new by-law based on the principles of Zionism and democracy.

The National Committee faced the problem of organizing the schools because the Ukrainian regime planned the Ukrainization of the high schools where most students were Jewish. The National Committee turned to the government requesting to "maintain the learning language for at least one more year, according to the curriculum customary in the Austrian high schools.

During its existence, the National Committee introduced new arrangements in all aspects of life and carry out essential activities, some of which are listed below:

- The task of registration of births, which during the Polish regime was a private matter. The responsibility for that task was transferred to the National Committee and managed by the Committee's secretary, the teacher David Korngruen.
- A radical change in the organization of studies at Perl's school was implemented.
- The library named after Perl was established
- A prohibition on marriages and divorces held by a rabbi not certified by the National Committee was issued.
- A comprehensive operation against the pogroms of Petliura's soldiers in Eastern Ukraine. A memorandum was submitted to the Ukrainian government, calling for it to stop the distribution of antisemitic proclamations by Petliura's army.
- Help was provided to the pogrom victims in Proskurov [now Khmelnytskyi].
- New arrangements in organizing the rabbinate after the death of the *gaon* R' Yosale Baba"d were made.
- The Committee assisted the Eretz-Israeli branch in pioneers' *hakhshara* [training].

These are the outlines of some of the activities of the National Committee. These activities embodied all the aspects of Jewish lives. We should note that the committee members acted in complete harmony, despite the disagreement and the disparity in their political views.

I would like to bring up another affair, which brought honor to Ternopil's Jewry and its youth. When the Polish army approached Ternopil in its battle against the Ukrainians, a few hundreds of the Jewish militia members left the city with the Ukrainian army and arrived in Eastern Ukraine. The Jewish militia brought encouragement, assistance, order, and security to Eastern Ukraine's Jews. In various locations such as Khmilnyk, Balta, Zhytomyr, Vinnytsia, and others, Ternopil's people, along with the local self-defense members, participated in battles against the Petliura's thugs and succeeded in saving Jewish lives and properties. Many of Ternopil's people lost their lives defending the lives of their brothers on the other side of the border. The graves scattered around various cities in Eastern Ukraine attest to that. Our youth knew how to defend not only the Jews in Ternopil but also their brothers in faraway places. The national education administered to the youth was not in vain[2].

Author's Notes:

1. Ya'akov Planer, a member of the Kvutzat Shiller [Shiller Group, A kibbutz in Israel also called Gan Shlomo]. He died in Eretz Israel in 1944.
2. See the article by M. Guliger on column 175.

[Columns 173-174]

During the Days of the Ukrainian Regime

by A. Weisglas

Translated by Moshe Kutten

With the disintegration of the Austrian Empire at the end of October 1918, part of Galitsia that included the Ternopil district, Borislav areas, Drohobych till Sub-Carpathian Reisyn, and on the other side beyond the Zbruch River, became under the rule of "Western Ukraine" headed by the lawyer from Lviv, Dr. Holobovitz. The Jewish population was led by the "National Jewish Committee".

The Jewish youth, regardless of party affiliation, but mostly the Zionist youth, who participated in the [First World] War, reached the commissioned ranks, and even received medals of excellence, sensed that the antisemitism tendencies that so depressed them in the army were coming to an end. Even though the Jewish soldiers excelled in their diligence, hidden antisemitism persisted in the Austrian army.

However, all the hopes that the Jews pinned on the change of the regime, proved false very quickly. With the establishment of Ukrainian rule, antisemitism grew so much that the need to form an organized armed militia that would protect the Jewish population became necessary. The Poles and the Ukrainians who served in the Ukrainian army fanned the flame of antisemitism among the Ukrainian peasants and incited them to conduct pogroms and assaults.

After its defeat in Lviv, the Ukrainian army coalesced and a considerable improvement in the relations between the Ukrainians and the Jews became noticeable. The tendency to join the Ukrainian army prevailed among the Jews. The Ukrainians were comrades in arms of the Jewish soldiers in the Austrian army.

In 1919, the Poles conquered the district of Ternopil, and the malicious acts by the Polish army started again. The Jewish youth could not accept the contempt that the Poles have shown towards the Jewish population. That resulted in an increase in the tendency to join the Ukrainian army to fight the Poles together.

A few weeks later, the Polish army retreated from Ternopil, and the Ukrainian army returned. The Jews enlisted then in masses to the Ukrainian army. At the same time, a special committee was formed in Ternopil headed by officer Leinberg who organized a self-defense force (Probojewyj, Zydivskij Tarnopolsky Kurin). The force consisted of approximately 700 – 800 people. It participated in several successful battles near Skalat, Sataniv [Stanov], and Husiatyn. A cavalry unit headed by Ya'akov Planer, containing about 60 people, participated in those battles and "protected", along with two other companies, the retreat of the First Corp of General Tarnowsky (the Ukrainian army consisted of three corps).

When the Jewish unit crossed the Zbruch River, the situation changed, and the enthusiasm in its ranks diminished. It turned out that the Ukrainians now fought alongside Petliura and the rebels, so the Jews saw it as their duty to defend the Jewish population against the Ukrainian thugs. Not once did the intervention of the Jewish militia prevent riots (in Zhytomyr, Berdychiv, Vinnytsia, Uhniv [Uhnov], and more[1]). With the help of the local liaisons, it was placed in suitable locations. In emergencies, we did not hesitate to cross the front to take shortcuts to our destination. The Ukrainians treated us as their allies.

The Ukrainian army passed through several periods. Sometimes it fought side by side with Petliura and other times against it. Sometimes it fought alongside the Red Army and other times against it. In the end, part of the Ukrainian army joined the Red Army. It was called the "Chokha" (Czerwina Ukrainska Helycka Armia). The opponents of the Bolsheviks {in the Ukrainian Army"] fought against the Red Army when it entered Galitsia.

Quite a few Jewish soldiers lost their lives in Ukraine protecting the Jewish population. Some were killed by an ambush, and some during the forced recruitment of the Jewish youth to our battalion.

Author's Note:

1. See the article by M. Guliger on column 175.

[Columns 175-176]

Memories of A Jewish-Ukrainian Soldier

by Moshe Guligerr

Translated by Moshe Kutten

A. The Jewish-Ukrainian Battalion

After the European Jewry was annihilated, every tiny item or detail that survived attained a status of a holy remnant worth keeping. Since the Ukrainian-Jewish battalion was formed in Ternopil [Tarnopol] by the city's Zionist Movement (which maintained friendly relations and political cooperation with the Ukrainians, for a certain period), any memories related to the history of the battalion, filled with Jewish content, should be included in the book dedicated to memorializing Jewish Ternopil.

The Jewish battalion was attached to Petliura's corps before the latter became the overt enemy of Ukrainian Jews. The unit was slated to fulfill the role of a "storm unit". However, one of the main goals of the battalion, as presented by its commander at the time of its formation, was to assist Ukrainian Jews, as much as possible. That was a difficult mission due to the enormous enemy forces that the battalion faced. On one side - was a short tradition of political cooperation during the days of the imperial Austrian rule when the only thing that the unified Jews and the Ukrainians was their common struggle against the Poles' oppressive politics in Galitsia. On the other side, the numerous Petliura militias, for which the name gangs fit better than the army, carrying the old tradition of [the antisemite hetmans] Khmelnytskyi, Gonta, and Zalizniak. That tradition was reignited by the death of the Tzarism. Within Petliura's corps, we, the Jewish-Ukrainian battalion, constituted just a tiny part…

B. The Rescue of the Jewish City Berdichiv [Berdichev]

At the end of July 1919 was stationed in Kozyatyn, a large station on the railroad line between Zhmerynka and Kyiv. From there, a side railroad truck led to Berdichiv [Berdichev]. Hair-raising rumors were floating in the air. After Petliura allowed his army to take revenge on the Jews for their support of the Red Army, every town, which a Petliura's gang captured from the hands of the Red Army became a metonym for a pogrom against the Jews. Tens of Jewish communities, in towns across Podolia, Vohlyn, and Ukraine, were wiped out from the face of the earth. At the head of the list – the town of Proskurov [now Khmelnytskyi] acquired an "everlasting name" for the big massacre, when six thousand Jews were murdered in one day, on Shabbat, 15 February 1919.

We feared that the big city of Berdichiv, where most of the population was Jewish, would not experience the fate of Proskurov. Our fear was based on our knowledge that the military plan for the Perliura's army called for an approach to Berdichiv, then held by the Bolsheviks. Luckily, we were not far from the city as we could reach Berdichiv from Kozyatyn via a train ride of a few hours. Luckily, Hetman Petliura planned to pass through Kozyatyn. Therefore, the battalion's command decided to send a delegation to ask him to send our unit to attack Berdichiv, conquer it from the hands of the Bolsheviks, and enter it first. All of that was to prevent a certain pogrom against the Jews in the city.

The delegation consisted of three officers: the battalion commander, Leinberg, Oberleutnant [a rank equivalent to Leutnant Colonel] Pinkhas ("Pini'leh") Shapira-Diamant, one of the wisest people in the battalion, and myself (I served as the "doctor" of the battalion (not without success) based on several semesters of medicine studies).

Our delegation went out, during one of August's cool nights, to the train station in Kozyatyn, where we waited a long time for the train carrying Hetman Petliura to arrive. The Hetman hosted us close to midnight in his dedicated train car. Petliura treated us quite politely, even after we told him that we wanted to enter Berdichiv first to prevent a pogrom against the city's Jews. He did not want to openly admit that he allowed pogroms to proceed against Jews. However, he said that the central command

[Columns 177-178]

must keep its word and allow the first army companies that conquered a city to rule the city for a few hours. He admitted that some soldiers got drunk and robbed a "little bit", but these things were unpreventable. We responded that we would prevent these things from happening if he allowed us to take the city. He declared that he did not carry any grudge against the Jews however, he stated that it was difficult for him to control the feelings of wild soldiers, who learned to hate the Jews during the days of the Tzars. In the end, he gave us the permission we had requested and shook the hand of every one of us.

We came out happy from there and brought the news to our comrades. The battalion boarded the train cars without delay and traveled to Bedichiv as fast as possible, fearing that somebody else preceded us…

When we reached the city, we realized that our fear was not without reason and that there was a justification for our haste. The atmosphere was electrified. Flocks of crows gathered around the train station already, ready to plow onto the corpses... Hundreds of peasants - women, and men, from the neighboring villages carrying large empty sacks, sat down, lay down, and walked around the train station and the fields around it. They waited eagerly for the thugs, the Jewish slaughterers, to help them in the slaughter and looting.

When we got off the train, they began to celebrate. Our uniforms misled them. However, when they gathered around us they were bitterly disappointed: they received an order to hurry up, leave the city, and return to their villages. The peasants refused to obey our orders and remained in their place, grouching and cursing. Several soldiers headed by officer Ya'akov "Kuba" Planer, the heroic boxer among us who rode a horse, used their whips against the refusers.

The battalion was arranged in a spread formation and entered the city. The streets were deserted. No living soul was seen. We progressed carefully because we thought the enemy soldiers were hiding in the city's interior, in positions prepared in advance. We, the Jewish officers, marched on the front line ahead of the troops. We knocked on the closed shutters and gates and yelled in Yiddish that we were Jewish and that they should open up. We did not receive an answer. The fearful Jews thought that it was an ambush by the murderers' gangs. After all, they may have people who spoke Yiddish among them.

We did not receive any response from the enemy to the shots we shot in the air either. To convince the Jews that we were Jewish, we began to sing "HaTikivah". The shutters, gates, and windows opened immediately. Hundreds or even thousands of men and women burst into the street joyfully with tears in their eyes. Plenty of flowers were thrown at us.

The Jews in the city told us that the Bolsheviks left Berdichiv because they feared that their retreat may be blocked by the armies of [general] Denikin. Which were marching toward them from beyond the Dnieper River.

That was how the Ukrainian-Jewish Battalion prevented a certain pogrom in Berdichiv.

We stayed in Berdichiv for about a month, and from there we went up to Kyiv.

C. The "Snitches"

It was the end of August 1919. As early as the first days in Berdichiv, we found out how bad the repulsiveness of the [division], particularly the political division, prevailed in some circles of the nation. Anybody who had a grudge against his friend came to the central command of Petliura's army, which entered Berdichiv a short time after us, and blamed him for being a communist. The Ukrainian command sent the victims without any investigation to the city of Vinnytsia, where they were executed.

One night, a short time before we left Berdichiv, about 1 AM, when I was sleeping in my room on Makhnovskia, a delegation of Berdichiv Jews woke me up. They told me that "haters" snitched about the counselors of the [Zionist Movements] "HeKhalutz" and "HaShomer" that they were communists. Their proof was that they worked throughout the summer along with about thirty other youths in agriculture, dividing the profit among themselves…Was there any better sign of communism than that? These Zionist youths who intended to make Aliya to Eretz Israel simply participated in a "*Hakhshara*" [Training for people who intended to make Aliya to Ertz Israel]. Berdichiv Jews, for whom the Ukrainian-Jewish battalion was a source of light in the dark, hurried up to the Jewish "doctor". To try and save the lives of these youths.

Fortunately, I was a friend of the commander of Petliura's army that was stationed in Berdichiv. He resided in Makhanovskia Street, opposite my apartment. I hurried to see him, but I did not find him in his apartment, since he attended the joyful ball organized by the city's honorable people for the new rulers.

I ran to the tavern and found him there. When I convinced the commander that the two youths were not communists and on the contrary, they were Zionists who belonged to the same union that I belonged to, he issued a written order to free the two youths immediately. Around 3 AM, I went to the place the youths were jailed, but the two "criminals" were already on their way to Vinnytsia. There was no other way but for the youths' parents to hurry up and deliver the order to Vinnytsia. However, a trip to Vinnytsia from Berdichiv was too dangerous for Jews to take. It was decided, therefore, that I would take a wagon from my Sanitary unit and send the Jews in it to Vinnytsia.

When I turned to my commander, comrade Leinberg, about a license for that

[Columns 179-180]

he answered that it was not possible because he just got the order to leave Berdichiv and attack Kyiv. I told him then to forget about my request and proceeded to place the Jewish parents in the wagon. I took with me an armed soldier as if I was transporting prisoners to Vinnytsia. I left Berdichiv without the permission of my commander, Leinberg, and traveled to Kozyatyn station, and from there to Vinnytsia on a train. When I returned to Berdichiv, the battalion already left, but my people with the horses waited for me there. Two days later I found the Battalion in Sviatoshyn forest when it was in the midst of making preparations to interrupt its repose stop and advance toward Kyiv. The two youths were found alive, but when we reached them, they have already been mutilated, since the wild men who captured them, punctured their ears, so they remained deaf for the rest of their life

D. A Holy Remnant of a Jewish city

A Hebrew booklet, a holy remnant that remained in my possession, a memorial for the city that survived the "small" Ukrainian Holocaust. However, like the rest of the European Jewry, it did not have a savior during the big German Holocaust. I unusually attained the book, typical to Berdichiv of that time. I lost the book later but got it back miraculously, also in a way typical of that time. The story is worthy of telling.

The heart-warming news was heard in our city of Ternopil during the oppressive days at the beginning of the First World War. That news, which came from Russia, was about the material and moral assistance (organized by Sh. Anski), wonderous in its size and dedication, that Russia's Jews provided to the tens of thousands of the Jewish brothers from Galitsia. Those Jews who were expelled by the Tzarist army to Russia's interior and passed through the Jewish towns in Podolia and

Volhynia[1] Naturally, the idea of recompensing the Russian Jews were brought up when the wheel turned on our poor brothers in Ukraine. We, the Jews from Galitsian Ternopil, became the powerful people… That was how our secondary mission of helping our Jewish brothers, wherever we found them, became one of the main objectives that the Jewish battalion set for itself.

In Berdichiv, we were hosted in private Jewish homes. My good friend Leib'tsi Lehrer, a lieutenant in our battalion, had a room with one of the teachers in "Schwartzman Gymnasium", Khaim Ziskind. He was the brother of the rabbi in Chudniv [Chudnov]. The son of that rabbi, who converted his surname Ziskind to Matok [Sweet in Hebrew] early on, was one of the prominent teachers in Ternopil). Khaim Ziskind published an article in the [Hebrew newspaper] "HaTsfira". He also published articles in other Hebrew papers under his acronym - Khaza"k [his acronym spells like the word Strong in Hebrew].

I spent a substantial amount of time in the company of that fascinating man. He was depressed and heartbroken since his young son and daughter escaped with the Bolsheviks before our battalion entered the city. He told me that only after we became close friends. He and his wife lived destitutely and were happy when I could help them in their time of need. However, to not shame them with charity gifts, I bought books from him – for his benefit. Among those books, he gifted me a small Hebrew book by the name of "Ruth" a poetic story about the "chronicles of Elimelekh and his family" by the Head of a Yeshiva Mendel Baumgarten in Vienna, 5625 [1865]. The literary value of the book was not great but I liked it because of the few lines of dedication that Khaim Ziskind wrote with a quivering heart and trembling hand in that city and that time… I later left the books that I bought from him and other authors in Ukraine with an acquaintance in Proskurov so that I could retrieve them later ti.

Seventeen years after the Berdichiv affair, when the [First World] War ended and my fate brought me to America in 1936, I came to visit the city I was born in. A childhood friend, the Hebrew teacher Tzvi Greenspan, invited me on the first Friday evening of my stay in the city. Tzvi and his wife (nee Shitzer in Ternopil) prepared an unusual surprise for me at their home. Tzvi handed me a small book he took from his library and said: "Please make Acquaintance!"… I immediately recognized the small book I left that time along with my other books in Proskurov. Greenspan bought the book a long while ago, in Ternopil, from a peddler selling tattered rags and old papers in the market. As known, there was a second pogrom in Proskurov at the end of 1919…

With tearing eyes, I read the following lines on the first page:

"I gave this book to my loveable friend, Mr. Moshe Goligor "*Nero Ya'ir*"[literally –"his candle will shine" – a blessing for a long life], in my first moment of becoming acquainted with him as a Jewish man, speaking pure Hebrew, when he stayed in my home, at my time of troubles and distress. When I found out about his Hebrew name, I wanted to fall on his shoulder and cry, but I was lost for words and was tongue-tied. Fear and despair (in memory of my children who left and disappeared) but also joy and hope engulfed me, so I remained silent. I only took the book and gave it to him – as a memory while my heart was pounding, my pen shaking in my hand, my brain confused, and the thoughts overwhelming – therefore, please forgive me if my words are mixed up… I wish the rage would pass, and you would honorably reside in your city, happy and successful. I revere you,

Kh. Ziskind (Khaza"k)
(Translator of Krilov's Fables from Russian to Hebrew)

Berdichiv, holy Shabbat night, Torah portion "*Re'eh*" ["See, this day I set before you blessing (and curse)", Deuteronomy 11:26], "*Atere"t*"[2]

Author's Notes:

1. See the article by Sh. Anski on column 163.
2. That date corresponds to 26 Av 5679, 22 August 1919.

[Columns 181-182]

The Zionist Movement During the Years 1919-1939

by Dr. Tzvi Parnas

Translated by Moshe Kutten

A.

Substantial changes took place in the life of Ternopil following the First World War. A fierce battle for the control over the fertile Podolia province between the Ukrainians and the Poles erupted during 1919 – 1921. During that period, the western countries had already enjoyed peace. Even Russia, which still struggled with the labor pangs of the new revolution, did not give up on the region.

The Jewish population experienced a state of fear and depression. The horrible news about the pogroms in the nearby cities of Proskurov and Lviv, and the days of fear the population experienced in February 1919, made their mark on the people's mood. Making a living was very difficult, the trust in the government and the currency deteriorated, and the future remained uncertain. Although the Ukrainian government awarded the Jews cultural autonomy rights and made an effort to accomplish these rights, the hearts of the people were not into that because of the insecurity that prevailed then.

Only in one location in Ternopil - Mickiewicz Street, where the organizations - the "old" "Bar-Kokhbah" and the "young" "Gideon" were located, life was vibrant. The two groups reunited. The contrasts and disagreements that separated the brothers in 1912 – 1914 became irrelevant, and new missions of the time unified them again.

The first mission was to tighten the ties, severed by the war, with the world's Jewry in general and the Zionist Movement in particular. We have not received any newspapers from abroad for almost the entire time. The news from Eretz Israel, including news about the new management team, were irregular. The center of gravity moved to the United States and England. The political centers, which shaped the Movement's image, and delineated its international political policies, were located in those centers.

New life was breathed into the ranks of the Zionist Movement and the Jewish masses when the contact with the West was renewed. An "Aliya bureau" was established in Ternopil under the initiative of Dr. Parnas. The bureau set a target for itself to train and prepare youths and adults for Aliya. A few gardens were purchased in the city (getting out of the city was dangerous), agronomists were hired, and garden tools were purchased. The response was immense. Groups of youths and adults marched daily to work, carrying hoes on their shoulders and singing. A substantial number of "Bar Kokhba's" members participated.

That activity buoyed the depressed spirits, but not for long since the [Polish-Ukrainian] war front approached Ternopil. Twice during two weeks, the city changed hands from the Ukrainians to the Poles. In the end, Ternopil and its district were transferred to Poland, and the Ukrainian dream of establishing an independent state vaporized.

Dr. Aharon Abeles, the Community Preacher, Eulogizes the martyrs over the common tomb

The transition to the new reality paralyzed "Bar Kokhba's" initiative for months. Some of "Bar Kokhba's" members remained in the Ukrainian battalion. The national committee disintegrated[1]. However, the situation began to clear, and during August-September, a tight connection with the revived Jewish center in Lviv and the capital Warsaw was established. Newspapers began to arrive, particularly [the Jewish newspaper in Polish] "Khavila" from Lviv. The connection with the Zionist Union and its leader, Dr. Gershon Zipper, was also renewed. Again, it was "Bar Kokhba" who took over, according to their tradition,

[Columns 183-184]

the leadership helm of the Zionist Movement in the city and its environs.

The transfer of the regime into the hands of the Poles reinvigorated the assimilators, who were the dominant force before the war, and their allies, the orthodox people. The government-appointed *Komisars* [commissioners] were again appointed to head the Jewish community and municipality. The Zionists did not get any footing in the councils, which consisted of appointees. Since the resignation of the last elected chairman of the community, "President" Schitz in 1910, only appointed commissioners, headed the community. An attempt was made to hold elections a few years before the First World War. However, because two Zionist representatives (Landau and Margalit) were elected, the elections were invalidated.

The community leadership was at the hands of Dr. Yosef Parnas, on behalf of the assimilators, and the head of the municipality was Dr. Yosef Weissnikht. They were joined by the school teachers and clerks, such as Dr. Halperin, Mosler, and a short while later, Gottfried. The unaffiliated intelligentsia was represented by Dr. Mentel, Dr. Peiles, and Dr. Fisher. Some lesser representatives from among the merchants and the orthodox people, headed by David Lvov and Moshe Rozner were also elected. Because of their official standing as leaders of the community, the assimilators received the monies slated for welfare and rehabilitation from the [Jewish organizations] the "Joint" and "ICA". That strengthened their standing and influence in the city.

Under these new conditions, "Bar Kokhba's" activities concentrated mainly on organizing. An activity for the benefit of "Keren Kayemet" [KKL-JNF], which became, in a short time, a popular institution, a favorite by the masses. The "blue Box" was installed in every Jewish home and business was organized first. Later on, the turn of the "Keren HaYesod" fund [literally The Foundation Fund", the name in English- "United Jewish Appeal"]. The first activity for the benefit of "Keren HaYesod", was a large demonstration of love for Eretz Israel, and affinity for the modern Zionist idea. In particular, that was expressed by the collection of gold jewelry headed by Ya'akov Bertfeld. His generosity served as an example. There was hardly any Jewish home, that did not contribute to the fund.

Gatherings that assembled on events related to Zionist purposes, attracted crowds. The large demonstration following the Son Remo Resolution left an unforgettable impression. It became clear that the Zionist idea won the hearts of the masses, and the influence of the assimilators and the orthodox people lost their hegemony, despite being supported by the authorities.

The headquarter of the [Zionist] Movement was located in the [command post] of "Bar Kokhba" on 5 Sobieski Street. The unwritten constitution of the Zionist life in Ternopil, and later, also the general Jewish life in the city, stated that all principal problems of the Zionist Movement, and later (after "Bar Kokhba's" AHF took the leadership in the Jewish community), the rest of the public life issues, including political and local problems, were first discussed

Demonstration during Polish-Russian War (1920)

at the meetings of the committee of "*Alter Herren Farband*" ["Old Men's Committee" or AHP] of "Bar Kokhba". Only after the problems have been discussed at the AHF, they were transferred to the local committee of the Zionist Union. Most of the Zionist Intelligentsia's activists, who were already the majority of the local [Jewish] Intelligentsia. were members of the AHF. The local [Zionist Union] committee deviated from the AHF resolutions only on rare occasions. Obviously, in its deliberations, the AHF considered the thinking of the Jewish population. That was why its authority was established. The AHF decisions required approval by the assembly. That meant that several tens of disciplined youths stood ready to execute them.

The head of [both] the AHF and the [Zionist] Union was, at that time, Dr. Tzvi Parnas. That was before profound differences of opinions which stood to divide the [Zionist] Movement into separate factions. That division was to come later. "The Union" and the "HaMizrakhi" movements operated harmoniously with "Bar Kokhba". The tendencies for divisions coming from Eretz Israel have not reached us yet, and the diaspora problems did not cause divisions.

Only one [youth] movement, "HaShomer HaTza'ir", caused some worries in its extreme views, which it acquired under the influence of the Russian Revolution. In the "Bar Kokhba's" circles, the idea of establishing a new youth movement was ripened. However, before that idea could be realized, the "Bar Kokhba" organization set up a preparation program aiming at educating the youth in the spirit of the "old" organization.

Pilsudski's adventure in Kyiv in 1920 disrupted life again, just as life began to crystalize, and new troubles befell the movement and the population. The first priority was to save the youth that prepared to make Aliya. Thanks to a popular fundraising project, which brought in substantial sums, it became possible to proceed with the Aliya endeavor. The large shipments of clothing were distributed to the needy, particularly among the pioneers. That was how the first group of Ternopil's youth, "Bar Kokhba's" members among them, set sail on their way to Eretz Israel.

"Bar Kokhba" played a major role in the first country-wide conference,

[Columns 185-186]

held in Lviv at the end of the war between Poland and Russia. The [Zionist] Movement's plans of activities in Galitsia were delineated there, and the opportunity to have direct contact with the people who formed it was available. The conference became a turning point in the history of the Movement, which became the legitimate leading body of the Jews in the Ternopil District.

A large delegation, consisting mostly of "Bar Kokhba's" members, participated in the conference from Ternopil. Dr. Tzvi Parnas was elected to the state committee of the [Zionist] party. Since then, the Zionist Movement in Ternopil maintained a tight tie with the party's management. A new period had begun. The delegation returned to Ternopil with a strong feeling that indeed life was returning to normal. Finally, everyone could devote time to their own affairs and, at the same time, help establish a sound foundation for the Movement.

The Zionist Movement set a goal for itself to remove the assimilators from positions they acquired unjustifiably. After all, the opinion of the masses was against them. The Movement wished to take over the influence over the nation and educate it in the spirit of the national idea. Since the political positions were dependent on the will of the Polish authorities who supported the assimilators, nothing else could have been done except making efforts to take over institutions that were dependent on public opinion.

A credit cooperative by the name "Credit and Economic Self Help", was established and developed over time,

to the point that the assimilators were forced to abandon the credit fund supported by "JCA", headed for many years by the pharmacist Julius Frantsuz.

The second position transferred to the hands of the Zionists was the social institutions, which were initially supported handsomely by the "Joint" organization. The newly organized "District Jewish Committee for Orphans", became an important welfare program around which hundreds of dedicated people banded together. Dr. Liebergal, one of "Bar Kokhba's" activists, served as the general secretary of the institution for many years.

To manage the struggle against the assimilators, the need for a journal that would reflect the views of the Zionist Movement, not only toward the Jewish public but principally toward the Polish public, has surfaced. For the Polish public, which received its information from the assimilators and the Jewish youths educated at assimilators and orthodox homes, the concepts of the Jewish revival movement were foggy and distorted. It was decided, therefore, to publish the journal in Polish, under the name known before the First World War - "The Jewish Word" ("Slovo Zhidovska").

That was not an easy feat. Among the veteran authors, only Dr. Shwartzman remained in the city. However, his health was so frail that they could not rely on him to exert the required substantial effort. There were only a few among the Zionists who wielded the scribal rod. Among the veteran participants in the journal was Isenberg, who left behind his Zionist-labor past. A skillful person came to us from an unexpected source – from among the Yeshiva students: Mr. Hillel Zeidman. The entire load was placed on the shoulders of Dr. Tzvi Parnas who often had to fill all of the journal's pages besides his political and ideology papers in his own section.

The efforts invested in publishing the weekly journal were not in vain. Firstly, the Movement's rivals had to be careful about what they spoke about, if not, they would have been denounced by the weekly journal. Secondly, the weekly journal succeeded in clarifying some of the problems that weighed on the relations between the Jews and the Poles.

Over time, the burden of publishing the weekly journal was relieved off the shoulders of the Movement by publishing Lviv's journal "Khavila". The journal added a special supplement with its Ternopil's edition called "Khavila Ternopolska", which was dedicated to the city affairs and its problems.

B.

The first time the Zionist Movement faced a difficult test was during the election to the Polish Sejm in 1922, based on the new constitution and the democratic election law. The Ternopil election district encircled the southwestern part of Podolia province and accrued ten seats in the Sejm. That provided an opportunity to capture one seat for a Jewish candidate. Therefore, Ternopil bore the responsibility not only for the city itself but also for all the neighboring towns.

The situation in the district was particularly complicated because the Ukrainians decided to boycott the election in Eastern Galitsia. They had still not recovered from their defeat and had not come to terms with their vanishing dream after two years of independence. The Zionist Movement faced a difficult and delicate problem - how to proceed among the public and the Zionists. Many thought that the Jews should not intervene in the standing issues between the rival nations and their conflicts since the Jews may suffer from the two sides.

Vigorous debates were held in the district about that subject. However, in Ternopil, the opinion that the Jews should participate in the election came on top for the following reasons:

a. Participation in the election ensures a unified position of the Jewish population. Boycotting the election by the Zionists would allow the assimilators the possibility of announcing a unified front with the Poles and pushing the Movement to the margins.
b. Boycotting the election would be perceived by the Poles as a collaboration with the Ukrainians and most importantly:
c. The right of the Jewish nation to take an active part in shaping life in the country should not have been given up, even if it may be dangerous.

Ternopil made it easy for the party

[Columns 187-188]

by not offering its own candidate.

However, the disappointment was great when the candidate list on behalf of Ternopil contained people that nobody recognized. In the city with prominent candidates in the past (during the Austrian rule, Adolf Shtandt appeared twice on behalf of Ternopil), that decision invoked resentment, which almost reached a level of rebellion. Only with the effort of the Union, did the storm die down. In the end, members and residents were convinced that it was too late to right the wrong and that disobedience to the party's instructions may endanger the chance for the Jews in the election. In the end, discipline overcame local patriotism.

Another complication in Ternopil was Director Lenkiewitz, who headed the municipality for many years. He joined the [Polish] democratic party and appeared on its behalf as a candidate for the Sejm. To attract Jewish votes and strengthen his chances of being elected, he added a Jewish candidate, the assimilator Dr. Rudolf Mentel, to the second position on his list. By doing that, he hoped to win the votes of the assimilators and the orthodox people.

The members of the Zionist Movement set aside their bitterness and entered the campaign vigorously and with exemplary dedication. Hundreds of youths, among them members of "Bar Kokhba", became active in the propaganda campaign, first in the election to the Sejm and later to the Senate. Thousands participated in the campaign gatherings. The speakers were on a high level. The peak in the propaganda campaign reached the rally with the participation of Dr. Leon Reikh who charmed the crowd with his distinguished personality, no less than his brilliant speech.

Even before the official election results were published, it was apparent that Ternopil's Jews did not disappoint the hopes pinned on them. In that election, the Jews stood like a fortress wall behind the Movement. More than twenty-six thousand votes were cast for the national list no. 17 in the city and the district. That was enough for a hair below three representatives. The elected representatives who approved officially for the Ternopil District were Berl Hoizner and Tzvi Heller.

However, with that, the election chapter did not end. The party assembly was tasked to resolve complicated and difficult problems created by local ploys resulting in the election of some unqualified people. Ternopil, which did not offer its own candidate, could objectively serve as an arbitrator in the quarrels between the various factions with parochial ambitions. According to a proposal by the council, which was accepted, the candidates were obligated to return their mandates, and the council was allowed to determine who was the qualified person to represent the Jewish population of the Ternopil District, in the Sejm.

A committee consisting of three people confirmed Dr. Zomerstein, Dr. Einsler, and Roza Pomerantz-Meltzer as Sejm representatives. The latter was from among the founders of the Zionist Union in Ternopil who managed the social services in Lviv and the entire country.

The election cleared the political and public atmosphere in the city. It became obvious to everybody, even the Poles, that the assimilators lost their hegemony in the Jewish street, and the influence of the orthodox people lessened and became limited to religious affairs. The masses came out of the election encouraged and confident in their power.

The election results were felt in the city only a year later. The Jewish representatives used all of their influence to urge the government to end the rule of the *Komisars* and other appointees in the municipal councils and communities, who blocked the way for new people who had risen within the Jewish public.

It was not easy to break down the wall that the old rulers erected around the community, fearing the fall of the fort they ruled for decades. The prevailing relations in the committee were reflected in communities' law from 21 March 1890. The community authority was limited. It possessed a distinctly religious character. The authorities were given permission to intervene in all of the community's affairs. The elections were based on curia's and only taxpayers, whose number did not exceed 15% of the adult population (about 1 thousand people), were allowed to vote. Women and youths did not enjoy voting right. The election was not proportional but personal.

The community apparatus was in the hands of a few, and everything was done in secrecy. The powerful and "beautiful people" ruled tyrannically and trusted the authorities. They knew that "unconnected" people do not have access to the voters' list, and public supervision of the election process was not enabled. The old community leaders used all sorts of ploys to ensure their victory, with no consideration to public opinion since they knew the wealthy were on their side.

The Zionist propaganda undermined their complacency. The old leaders were shocked by the crowded gatherings. In those gatherings, harsh criticism was directed at their denial of the community's national goal, wasteful management of the community's finances, use of public money for private purposes, and the deprivation of the poor.

The public awareness campaign opened the public eyes to see how much the community leadership institution, which played principal roles in the past and was destined to accomplish great things in the future, had deteriorated. The demand for a democratic election, and public supervision of the community's finances, was acceptable to the people. The proof of that was the election results, which astonished the authorities and the community's old leaders alike. Among the 24 representatives, 21 were elected from the national list, and only three from among its rivals. One of the three was David Lvov, a respectable man, philanthrope and liked by the people.

[Columns 189-190]

He was caught in the assimilators' net because of his naivety. They used his name to capture votes. Their second elected person was Moshe Rozner, a representative from the young generation who later realized that the views of the national movement were closer to his heart. He later claimed that his inclusion in the assimilators' list was a result of a misunderstanding. The third elected representative was Khaim Oks, an independent in his views who did not always act along his party's lines.

The election proved that the assimilators' time had passed and that they did not represent public opinion. However, the assimilators did not want to yield their rule and prepared themselves for a possible defeat. In advance. During the campaign, they introduced forgeries that may lead to the disqualification of the election and the continuation of their appointed leadership. However, all of those ploys did not help them for long.

C.

In the meantime, tendencies for division deepened within the Zionist Movement, which did not have any objective basis in reality and only introduced divisions in the ranks. These divisions weakened the movement substantially.

The people of "Hamizrakhi" [orthodox religious Zionist Party], separated first. A short while later, the people of the "Hit'akhdut" [Socialist Zionists] separated. Instead of a single local committee, three committees were established. Every one of them settled in a separate office, organization, and center of the ideology of its own. With that, the unavoidable personal ambitions and exaggerated partisanship.

For "Bar Khokhba" [see Dr. Korngruen's article column 109], the separate factions presented an extremely severe problem since the organization was based on a unified ideology and discipline. "Bar Kokhba" achieved numerous successes thanks to those principles and it did not see the need to deviate from its way and become a lukewarm party. "Bar Kokhba" could not agree that its members would receive instructions from others (only a tiny number of members joined the "Hit'akhdut"). "Bar Kokhba" objected to the class views of the "Hit'akhdut", as it considered it an alien concept without a real footing in the social structure of the Jewish population. At the country conference in Lviv, "Bar Kokhba's" representatives sided with those who strove for ideology clarification, organizational unification, and removal of those Union members who caused the unhealthy situation in the organization. Despite the close personal relations among "Bar Kokhba's" members, the organization did not hesitate to expel the dissidents while maintaining good personal relations. That prevented destructive competition in activities related to the national funds. Similar relations were maintained between "Bar Kokhba" and the "HaMizrakhi" party, headed for many years by David Parnas and later, Yehoshua Parnas.

The national representatives to the Sejm exerted pressure on Ternopil's governor and convinced him to add the Zionists to the Jewish community management team. The Zionists agreed to join provided that a reorganization would be based on the actual power balance in the city. They also insisted that a new election would be called as soon as possible. Another condition was that the *Komisars*, appointed by the authorities, would manage the community affairs based on the council's resolutions.

Dr. Peiles was nominated by the authorities as the community's *Komisar*-commissioner, and Dr. Tzvi Parnas as his vice, both with the approval of the Zionists. The following people were elected to the council on behalf of the Zionists and "HaMizrakhi": Dr. Abend, Avraham Oks, Weisman, Nagler, Sh. Margalit, Meirberg, and Y. Parnas.

The Zionists decided to unite themselves into one faction, whose members were obligated to vote according to the majority view, to present a unified Zionist view. That strategy prevented splits that could have weakened the battle for the leadership of the community.

The improvements introduced in the community by the national [Zionist] faction did not distract the movement from the need to hold a new election according to the law. That need was not only aimed at demonstrating adherence to the principles of democracy but to refute any suspicion that lust for power pushed the Zionists to fight against the old leadership. On a side note, the relations with Dr. Peiles were good, and all the council resolutions obtained by the national majority have been executed faithfully and consistently.

The issue on the top of the Jewish public agenda in Poland was the attitude toward the government. Should the Jewish public enter into a negotiation with the government and arrive at an agreement ("*Ugoda*") or continue to oppose it? That was the period of the notorious Grabski. He was known for his discrimination against the Jewish population, in general, and particularly concerning taxes. The harsh quarrel about the agreement also affected the unity of the Jewish parliamentary coccus – the "*Kolo*". Some of the representatives of the "17" list, including their leaders, Leon Reikh and Dr. Yehoshua Thon, the representatives of the merchants, and the "Aguda" party, supported the agreement with the government. Most of the representatives of Congressional Poland were on behalf of the latter, however, only a minority from Galitsia,

Yitzkhak Gruenbaum, who conducted a fierce battle against the agreement, headed the opponents. The debate besieged the Jewish public and did not skip any city or town. The storm also besieged Ternopil. The vast majority of "Bar Kokhba's" members, particularly the young ones, were among the opponents of the agreement. To better understand the problems associated with that battle, the "Bar Kokhba" organization decided to invite Yitzkhak Gruenbaum to Ternopil and hear from him first-hand about his objections against to agreement. By that invitation, the "Bar Khokhba" organization allowed Gruenbaum inroads into Galitsia, which were not otherwise available before that.

Gruenbaum's, lecture expressed the view of those

[Columns 191-192]

whose national honor resided in their heart, supported by an iron-clad logic. He made a huge impression on his listeners. His lecture greatly influenced the formulation of "Bar Kokhba's" resolution against the agreement. It was the first time that opposition was at the AHF. It was an opposition of the old members with Dr. Abend and Dr, Nussbaum at its helm. That was too serious of an issue, to allow indecision. Final voting produced a majority for the people who objected to the agreement. But the vote also hastened the departure of many members, who could not, for some time then, come to terms with the organization's framework and found an excuse for the leave. Dr. Horowitz, Dr. Seret, and Dr. Dines, among others, left. Some members did not follow them but distanced themselves from the organization for some time. The deserters established their own voting block "Maccabiah" in the conference in Lviv. At that conference, which stood to decide the political battle, most of the Ternopil delegations voted against the agreement, causing a defeat to the official resolution. As a result, Dr. Reikh resigned although, efforts were made to word the resolution to avoid injury to Dr. Reikh, whom the movement considered its greatest leader. However, he did not want to impose his view on the majority or conduct a fight against it.

The "Bar Kokhba" party in honor of Y. Gruenbaum

Obviously, those frictions undermined the standing of "Bar Kokhba" in the city. Many among the old members ceased their activity or distanced themselves from it. Even its status within the local committee was more difficult than before, but here personal relations helped overcome the crisis.

D.

During the time of the weakening of the Zionist Movement in the city, the election to the community [council], was again on the agenda. Unfortunately, a fight between two rabbis about the rabbinical position took place. Rabbi Shalita relied on his family lineage: He was the son-in-law of the former rabbi, Rabbi Heshil BABa"D. The other rabbi was also a decedent of BABa"D, but not directly. Shalita was the rabbi of the simple people, clever, not zealot, and he enjoyed the support of his many relatives. Rabbi BABa"D was a famed learner and had a polite character. The Hasidim and the student scholars concentrated around him. In 1923 the election of the rabbi issue was pushed aside since other important issues attracted all the attention. In the election of 1926, a change in the mood took place. The masses who were disappointed with the issues related to "high politics", came back to worry about local problems closed to their heart. The assimilators and the orthodox people hoped that the quarrel between the rabbis would present an obstacle for the Zionists, since one could find supporters of either rabbi either within "HaMizrakhi" or other Zionist factions. Those supporters did not always consider what was best for the movement over their zealotry.

Other groups, such as the small businesses and "Yad Kharutzim", the organization of the craftsmen, began to show interest in the community council

[Columns 193-194]

and made efforts to be represented in it. Under these circumstances, there was a danger that the Zionists would fail. To prevent it a Zionist front was formed after a long and grueling negotiation. It consisted of the General, "HaMizrakhi", and "Hit'akhdut" Zionists. A special committee ran the election campaign. Concerning the economic organizations, it was decided to support their own Zionist candidates or members who were fans of the national Zionism.

During the year before the election the Zionists managed the community affairs and finances. The time was too short to introduce far-reaching changes. The Zionists were also careful not to change the distribution of taxes for the fear that any changes would hurt them in the election. In their campaign, emphasis was placed on the national requirements and cultural and social activities. Gatherings organized by the Zionists were attended by large crowds however, they lacked the enthusiasm and interest they generated in 1923. Luckily a reprieve and relief came from an unexpected source – the orthodox people.

In a large gathering held by the orthodox campaign at the municipal hall, with the participation of the Sejm representative, Rabbi Levin from Sambir [Sambor], most of the attendees were Zionists. All the proposals were approved. The orthodox people who pinned their hopes on that gathering, and mobilized all of their resources to ensure its success, were disappointed. Rabbi Levin convinced them to enter into a negotiation with the Zionists. In the end, an agreement between the Zionists and the orthodox party was reached. The rabbis had requested, and the Zionists conceded about preserving the rabbinical status quo. In terms of the city's prestige, BABa"D had a slight advantage. The Zionists agreed to let their members have a free hand in the election by voting their conscience because, as aforementioned, many of the Zionists and "HaMizrakhi" people supported Rabbi BABa"D. Against that, the orthodox people agreed to vote for a Zionist candidate for the community chairmanship. They also agreed to support the budget proposal to be submitted by the Zionists. As a side note, we should mention that two third of the national list was manned by the Zionist Union's people.

Naturally, the agreement, like any other agreement, was based on mutual concessions. For example, the Zionists agreed to add Dr. Peiles to the list. The latter treated the Zionists fairly during his service as a "*Komisar*". The Zionists agreed to include a paragraph in the community's by-laws, which determined that an election can only be held with a minimum forum of two third of the members. That paragraph caused the election to become dependent on non-Zionist members. That dependence made its mark, not once, in the days to come.

With the signing of the agreement, the tension in the city subsided. Rabbi Shalita's followers used that peace to add three of their candidates to the community [council]. Typical of the change in public opinion was that no group agreed to add the assimilators to its list. Their ruling period and influence in Ternopil, which served as their citadel for a long time, came to an end.

The authorities approved the election since there was no fault in them. However, difficulties were discovered when it came to electing the ruling committee and chairman. Dr. Peiles believed, in his nativity, that he would be elected the chairman. When he found out that the Zionist do not intend to present his candidacy for that position, he ceased coming to the [council's] meetings. The orthodox faction, probably under the pressure of the "Starosta" [District administrator], who could not come to terms with the fact that the community would be headed by the Zionists, came out with new demands. They demanded having an orthodox vice chairman and a guarantee that its candidate would be elected the rabbi. The difficulty in forming the management team could have placed the community's survival at risk since the authorities looked for any excuse to dismantle it. In the end, the difficulties were removed and in May 1926, when a quarrel took place between [Marshall] Pilsudski and the Witos's government, Tzvi Parnas was elected as the community's leader.

Ternopil enjoyed an elected community [council] only on rare occasions. Most of the time it was headed by the government–appointed *Komisars*. After a hiatus of twenty years, the community leadership was elected and headed, for the first time in the city's history, by a Zionist chairman.

E.

With the attainment of the majority in the community, the Zionists were poised to man essential roles. First, they strove to achieve their principal objective: the fulfillment of Herzl's motto of "Taking over the communities". The rule by the assimilators that lasted several decades and the developments that occurred in the 19th century undermined the community. The statute of the community, which served as Jewish autonomy's citadel for many generations, diminished and its influence impeded. The Zionists wished to restore its glory as much as it was possible under the new communities' law. Although the law emphasized the religious role of the community, it did leave some possibility to introduce some living content that would reflect the aspirations of the Jewish nation.

The character of every institution is reflected in its budget. The community's budget was based until then, mostly on indirect taxes and principally on the revenues from slaughtering. That was a distinct consumption tax, which put the load on the shoulder of the masses. The Zionists aim to widen the activities to include cultural and social areas. That necessitated substantial sums. The easiest way to get them was to increase the slaughtering taxes. However, that would mainly hurt the masses. The Zionists chose a different way – an increase in the direct taxes and the elimination of all the special "rights" enjoyed by the "connected". Also, the payments the rich paid for the gravestone increased (the cemetery was one of the community's main revenue sources).

[Columns 195-196]

Substantial improvements were also introduced in the management of the community offices and its officials worked more efficiently.

The slaughtering was leased, which brought in an additional sum of 25 thousand guldens annually without raising the taxes. The ritual bath was also leased, which resulted in annual savings of several thousand guldens. An additional source of revenue was the gravestone industry of the community, where efficient methods were introduced. In parallel to increasing the taxes on the rich, the community [council] tried to reduce the taxes on the middle class and the poor. The *Voivode* [governor] Kwashnivski supported the new budget policy and rejected all the appeals submitted by various claimants.

Thanks to those changes, the first budget was raised by 50%. That enabled the widening of the community activities into new areas. To express the community's inclination towards the national revival idea, a sum of 2400 guldens grants for Keren Kayemet [JNF] and Keren HaYesod [United Israel Appeal], was allocated in the budget. The Hebrew school received a grant of 5000 guldens. The social institutions also enjoyed the support of the community. The requests for financial support submitted by the yeshiva, synagogue [and other religious institutions] were also accommodated. The chairman had, at his disposal, a discretionary fund of twenty thousand guldens for urgent needs, and the needy when they needed support. The assistance for Passover – "Maot Khitin" ["matzo fund"] increased as compared to previous years.

New life enveloped the community and its institutions, which were reorganized in line with the new conditions. A renovation effort at the community house on Mickiewicz Street made it efficient and ostentatious. The house contained a 100-people meeting house, spacious offices, and waiting areas, fitting an institution representing the Jewish population.

Even the relations between the various factions were satisfactorily marshaled, and peace was established between the rabbis. On all religion-related issues the religious factions consulted with each other resulting in joint actions. For the first time in the history of the Ternopil community, the affairs of the "Batei HaMidrash" were put in order. The community [council] issued a special by-law that regulated the process of electing the *gabbaim* and the requirements for maintaining buildings and other properties. However, the Zionists were mainly interested in social and cultural activities and made sure to allocate the budget for them.

One of the most important institutions in Ternopil was the school named after Perl. The establishment of that school was like a revolution not only for Ternopil's Jews but for those in the entire area. However, as early as the end of the 19th century, and during the period before the First World War, the school lost much of its glory. That happened because state schools, universities, and technical colleges opened their gates to Jews. During the days of independent Poland, the school became a regular school, where the teaching language was Polish. The only difference between that school and the state schools was that it was closed on Shabbats and Jewish holidays. However, maintaining the school heavily burdened the community, which had to allocate about twenty thousand guldens annually. In fact, these sums had to come from the state treasury or local authorities.

That was the situation when the newly elected community management began its activities in 1926. The Zionists considered themselves the heirs of Perl's ideas concerning healing the social structure of the Jewish population. Therefore, they saw it as their duty to return the glory to the school and make it into an institution that would teach the Jewish youth, productive professions. They also wanted to introduce Hakhshara [training] towards Aliya - their guiding principle.

One of the first steps taken by the community [council] was to investigate the legal and pedagogical state of the school so that they would be able to make substantial changes in collaboration with the teaching staff, and the agreement of the education ministry. Initially, it seemed that it would be possible to arrive at reasonable solutions to the problems by ways of peace, however, when the community[council] began to inquire about the curriculums and teaching methods, investigated the status of the library, and requested reports from the school's management, it met with a flat refusal.

The school's principal claimed that, indeed, the community maintained the school financially, however, administratively, it was under the authority of the [district] schools' supervisor, who was the only person who was authorized to approve the requests. At the time, to free himself from the dependency on the community, [the school's principal], Mr. Gottfried, secured a financial allocation from the municipality, thanks to the support of the orthodox people and the assimilators. At that time, the Zionists supported the move, although they considered it a political maneuver.

Despite the obstacles, the community did not give up on its plan. It sent several teachers to the vocational schools of Dr. Tzetzilia Klaften, a native of Ternopil, who received her initial education at the school named after Perl. The teachers were trained in hand-crafts, a profession that the community wanted to introduce into the curriculum.

The fight by the elected council in this area, and others, continued tirelessly, however, the development of the political affairs in Poland reduced to naught all of the efforts to make the community [council], the representative of the Jewish population.

With the tide in the national movement, it was impossible to ignore it and prevent it from participating in the second autonomous in the city, meaning in the municipality. The actions by Dr. Lenkiewitz, who headed the municipality, were displeasing to the district "*Voivode Zetvo*" [district governor] and the Polish population. Dr. Lenkiewitz was not leaning on any specific party: his only supporters were the assimilators, and he reached his position

[Columns 197-198]

only because he was the most prominent Polish figure in the city.

With the subsidence of the influence of the assimilators and orthodox people, it was time to change the composition of the municipal council. The Polish authorities have also used their usual means at that council – nominating commissioners (with a high turnover, which harmed city affairs).

The municipality [council] was responsible for essential and important areas of operation. It is therefore clear why the Zionists could not have given up on their participation. The following people joined the council on behalf of the Zionists: Dr. Abend. Dr. Parnas, Dr. Horwitz, A. Ox, and more. The authorities did not desert their assimilating allies and nominated some of their representatives. Naturally, frictions formed between the representatives of the Zionists and the orthodox people and assimilators. All the efforts to find common ground with them, particularly concerning matters related to the Jewish population, were in vain.

To begin with, the Zionists flatly refused to accept any role the authorities wished to force on them. They refused to serve as the instrument of oppression at the hands of the Poles. The latter requested that the Zionists vote against the justified demands of the Ukrainians. They also fought against the autocratic methods at the magistrate and demanded to institute democratic ones. The Zionists fought a hard battle against the subservient and lobbying ways typical of the orthodox people and the assimilators and demanded vehemently equal civil rights for the Jews. They did not accept the discrimination of the Jewish population and requested the establishment of new institutions and an increase in the existing budgets. However, their actions in the municipality were not limited to criticism. They also made an effort to contribute positively to the handling of the city's affairs. Thanks to Dr. Parnas, a member of the oversight committee, a waste of municipal funds was discovered, which yielded the resignation of the regime-appointed commissioner, officer Novakovski. Dr. Parnas was tremendously active in using his experience acquired while serving as a member of the district's orphanage committee.

The Zionists demanded, at every opportunity, to hold a new election based on a democratic law. The first election, which was held based on the old law (based on the principle of the curia's), resulted in a substantial victory for the Zionists. However, the authorities did not approve of the election results because they have not yielded an absolute majority to the Poles. During the next election, the Poles were satisfied with the results, and the municipal [council] began its work. Dr. Abend and Avraham Ox joined the council, on behalf of the Zionists then. A short while later, the Zionists won representation in the magistrate, where Dr. Abend served as their representative. The economic organization justifiably requested representation in the municipal election. The Zionists ensured that representatives of these organizations would join the municipal council. However, suitable people for these roles were not always found. Therefore, the Zionists had to grudgingly agree to some of the candidates, they did not like. The assimilators and their supporters took advantage of that situation and succeeded in penetrating through those people and capturing important positions.

F.

The election to the Polish 2nd Sejm was held in 1928. It took place in much more difficult conditions than those of 1922. This time the Ukrainians did not boycott the election, and achieving a mandate for a Jewish representative was not that easy. Tzvi Heller, the Sejm's Zionist representative, managed to win the hearts of his voters, so there was no issue with selecting the candidate. The election campaign was very tense. The political opponents did not dare to come out with independent lists, since the Zionists had a decisive hold; The Zionists' victories in all areas of life in Ternopil and their brilliant victory in the Sejm election served as undisputable proof of that. The national list secured thirty-one thousand votes in the election.

In the local affairs, too, nothing was done without the cooperation of the General Zionists. The new Zionist parties established after their separation from the Zionist Union strengthened thanks to the position their central administration acquired with the support of the Jewish Agency in Eretz Israel. That also affected the parties in Poland. In Keren HaYesod, the General Zionists were in charge. However, at the KKL-JNF, the Hebrew school, and the [Zionist] Shekels [fund] Committee, friction arose, reaching a tense level. The dual existence of the movements "Bar Kokhba" and "Maccabiah" also weakened the position of the General Zionists. Although, with the establishment of the youth movements, "HaNo'ar" ["The Youth"], and "Akhva" ["Brotherhood"], "Bar Kokhba" strengthened numerically, the internal difficulties in coordinating work increased.

The growth of the movement in all of its factions had some benefits. The competition between the groups resulted in increased activity. The relations between the youth movement "HaNo'ar" and "Bar Khokba" were harmonious and they enjoyed tight cooperation between them. "Bar Kokhba"-organization supported the youth movement, and many of the young group's members joined the adult brother organization.

Brilliant talents rose out of the youth movement such as Edelstein (who died at a young age), Ekselbirt, Gotlieb, Khaim Parnas, and the "biggest gun" in the group - Israel Kurfuerst. The purchasers of the Shekels [membership certificate in the Zionist Organization] stood by the party at the election. Eighty percent of the population were loyal to the national movements in its factions.

However, the division among the factions made its mark during the preparation for the election for the community [council]. The elections were held following the end of the first council's term, which was elected after the [First World]. "Bar Kokhba" strove to form a unified Zionist front but encountered exaggerated demands from the new parties. HaMizrkahi considered the community as its natural area of activity

[Columns 199-200]

and did not want to be discriminated against by the non-Zionist orthodox people. The "Hit'akhdut" considered it their duty to represent Socialistic Zionism and put the emphasis on class-related slogans. Although the demands by "HaMizrakhi" seemed justified, it was difficult to realize them for a simple reason: They lacked the

charismatic figures who would attract voters. The friction among the Zionists encouraged the rivals, who hoped to build themselves at their expense. "Agudat Israel" [non-Zionist orthodox party] and the assimilators prepared themselves for a defeat by the Zionists. Their goal was to "capture" the institution named after Perl. Among the people who were not close to the Zionist movement, a perception was formed that "the Zionists fight each other". In the end, the division caused damage to the Zionists. The "Hit'akhdut" won only one representative (which was promised to them anyway). The lesson that could have been learned from those elections was that the "Hit'akhdut" overestimated its influence in the city. However, as seen in the election to the Sejm, it did not learn that lesson either.

The Wizo Committee in Ternopil

G.

The election for the community in 1930 was held based on the new Community Law, which imposed a proportional rather than personal election. That law somewhat limited the responsibilities of the community [council]. The community council had a chairman of its own, who approved the budget and supervised its implementation. The management was elected by the council and actually managed the community. It represented the council before the Jewish population, the local authorities, and the government. The Polish country's community council umbrella council was supposed to serve as the religious council. The Communities Law did not fulfill all the hopes and did not succeed to make the community the institution of Jewish autonomy as the Zionists wished, but it was a step forward. The election was democratic. Every Jews, 24 years and older, enjoyed the right to vote. The election progressed in a calm atmosphere, and the voters expressed their trust in the coalition that carried the burden of managing the community.

Dr. Parnas was elected again as the chairman of the community [council], and Shalom Podhortzer, from the religious wing and Ya'akov Meirberg of "HaMizrakhi", were elected as his vices. All the conditions existed for the council to continue its activity in harmony until the end of its term. However, that hope did not come to fruition. That time, the spoilers came from the management of the school named after Perl.

The *Voivodezetvo* [district governor], the highest authority over the school, notified the community management that the school, library, and the house of prayers were to be handed over to a directorate. Dr. Peiles, Dr. Weissnikht, Pepperish, and Gottfried were selected to be permanent members. The head of the community and a representative of the local school's oversight supervisor were slated as additional compulsory members. The directorate was given the authority to collect up to 4 guldens from the slaughtering fees to support the budget. The negotiations about these changes took place behind the back of the community, which was the interested party. That arrangement violated the will of the school's founder, as declared by Mikhael Perl.

The situation resulted in the handing over of the institution to a directorate that sabotaged the principle of Jewish self-rule. Firstly, the directorate was given the authority to impose taxes on the Jewish population. Secondly, a precedent was formed whereby a non-Jew (the school supervisor), would rule in the affairs of a Jewish religious institution. That dangerous precedent undermined the basic rights of the Jews. While it was difficult to pinpoint who was to blame, it was clear that the assimilators were the initiators of the resolution to further their own ambitions.

In a special session of the council attended by all members, a harsh protest against the assault on the rights of the Jewish population was issued. The council requested that the school management take all possible steps to nullify the resolution. It also decided the turn to the ministry of education and religions. A delegation headed by Dr. Reikh turned to the *Voivode* in Lviv, but he evaded giving a clear answer. The well-reasoned juridical-based appeal generated a big impression. The community planned to turn to the high court that dealt with the administrative affairs if they would not receive a satisfactory response from the ministry. The people at the ministry understood that, so they dragged the matter and avoided giving a clear answer. When the pressure on the ministry did not yield any results, it was decided to use other tactics to hasten the decision. The community came out with a harsh attack in the newspapers on the *Voivode* and later on the minister. Boycotting the articles by the authorities could have served as an excuse to submit a claim to the high court.

[Columns 201 202]

The authorities figured out that goal and did not boycott the articles. In the end, Lviv's *Voivode* got fed up, and he decided to get rid of the fighting community administratively by dissolving it and nominating a government-appointed commissioner to head a council of "disciplined" people. To make it look like a legal step, he ordered an investigation of the financial books of the community, which supposedly discovered embezzlements in the ledger and financial dealings. The consoler Pohoriles was nominated as the government commissioner, and a council of "disciplined" people served under him. The first step of the nominated council was to nullify the appeal submitted to the ministry so that they can implement the *Voivode's* plan.

Dr. Parnas, as the head of the community council, submitted a complaint [to the court] that his honor was harmed by the claims of embezzlement. By doing that, he hoped to uncover the forgeries made by the budget investigation, used as a basis for the council's dispersion. In addition, a delegation on behalf of the orthodox people traveled to the former Ternopil's *Voivode*, who served as the senate chairman at that time, to convince him to discuss the affair with the government. It was well known that Dr. Kwashnivski trusted Dr. Parnas and could not stand the assimilators. Dr. Kwashnivski was very influential during the Sanation Government, and his lobby bore fruit. A decree came out of Warsaw to reestablish the community council and punish the people who were responsible for its dissolution.

The Ternopil's *Voivode* invited Dr. Parnas and discussed a possible solution, namely, how to bring back to the community [council] operation without damaging the authority of the authorities. The following has been decided: 1) The *Voivode* would announce that following an additional detailed investigation (resulting from the appeal), he had not found any fault in the community activity. 2) Dr. Parnas would withdraw the complaint he submitted to the court. The official responsible for the dissolution of the community council was transferred a few weeks later and took another position. The community was content with the solution. The assimilators fortified themselves in the school's directorate. The assimilators' only revenge was that they did not call for any official directorate meeting. That way, they would need to rely on Dr. Parnas, as he was obliged to participate in all official meetings on behalf of the council.

The situation with the school named after Perl did not change, although, the new council notified the ministry that it insisted on its view that the directorate is illegal in its authority. The community council also denied the right of the government-appointed commissioner to go against its appeal and withdraw it on his own initiative. However, none of these complaints bore any fruits.

The situation in the community became more complicated when Dr. Parnas had to be away from Ternopil for several days per week in his role in the national organization. [Joining the Zionists] neither the orthodox people nor the *Voivode* approve of his resignation. In the end, a compromise proposal was approved: The community council's meeting would only take place with Dr. Parnas in attendance. It was also decided that every important step would only be done after consulting with him. The council secretary's office maintained tight phone contact with Dr. Parnas. He served as the head of the community even when he moved to Warsaw. At that time, he traveled to Ternopil two days a week.

In 1932, the district authorities organized an exhibition aimed mainly to demonstrate the district's achievements in agriculture and the agriculture industry. However, the room was reserved for cultural achievements by the population.

The preparations were already in the implementation stage when the organizers realized that they could not ignore the Jews who also lived in the district, particularly since it would harm its success because the insulted Jews would boycott the exhibition.

The *Voivode* invited Dr. Parnas and authorized him to arrange for a Jewish section at the exhibition. The special committee, established for that purpose, consisted of the members Yosef Halicher and engineer Hirshberg from the district authorities. A group of artists prepared diagrams, and other people participated.

The committee managed to collect rich materials such as Torah's *Atarot* [ornaments around the Torah scroll], *Parokho* [screens in front of the ark], valuable holy implements, printed works, and rare manuscripts, pictures of buildings, and artistic gravestones. Dr. Tzetzlia Klaften, artist Lilyan, and the visual artist Kahana from Lodz helped to arrange the articles and prepare the decoration in the exhibition halls. All the [Jewish] institutions in Ternopil participated in the exhibition. Only the school named after Perl was an exception and did not want to cooperate with the committee. In order not to provide a pretext to the haters of Jews, the committee agreed to allow the school to have its own booth.

The exhibition took place at the community's buildings. All of the visitors were very impressed, and the media (Jewish and non-Jewish) devoted appreciation articles to it. The exhibition provided proof of vast artistic treasures, collected over generations with love and reverence, and the richness of the Jewish artistic life. The number of visitors to the exhibition was huge. They came from far and near. The exhibition lasted eight days, and at the end, a conference of all the Ternopil district's communities was held. Artist Lilyan gave a lecture about the need to guard the artistic treasures and submitted a few particle proposals on how to preserve the antiques and art. Resolutions about preservation were obtained and the Ternopil community was tasked with their implementation. Unfortunately, the communities did not show much interest in that matter.

The term of the second elected council came to an end, but no new election was held. The authorities preferred to nominate a commissioner. The Polish regime deteriorated into a dictatorship and retreated from the democratic principles, which were the guiding light for the Zionists.

[Columns 203-204]

Among the officials, one could always find submissive people who were willing to fulfill the government's demands.

That was how the Jewish self-rule faded before the life itself was extinguished.

H.

In the meantime, the state of the Jewish population continued to deteriorate, and all the efforts to improve it were in vain. The masses turned their back to country-wide politics, which disappointed them, and there were no signs on the horizon about improvements in the future. Everybody felt that difficult days were ahead and that the evil forces were ganged against the Jewish people. Under those circumstances, the masses turned their aspirations toward the ancestry land. The struggle over every immigration certificate and fundraising for Eretz Israel captured the top positions on the agenda.

The fact that the aspiration to make Aliya strengthened among the ranks of "Bar Kokhba", was supported by statistics. During the period 1927 – 1938, about eight hundred people, most of them young, made Aliya. During the same period, the relations with the executive committee in Lviv, or more accurately with Dr. Reikh, improved. The "agreement" issue, which caused a storm in its time, was not an issue anymore. The only thing left for the Jewish population to do was to protect what little they had and to ward off the ploys aimed at driving them out entirely from economic and political life. Even that course of action did not stand a chance. The only conclusion was to train the youth and anybody who wanted to make Aliya and try to rehabilitate the poor classes, which were bound to stay where they were. Dr. Reikh's visit to Ternopil, by the invitation of "Bar Kokhba," culminated with a mass gathering, where he reviewed the situation and warn against optimism. with his assessment, he opened the eyes of the last few who deluded themselves that there was an outlet from the distressful situation.

At the same time, the Zionists faced a problem that could have affected their standing in the community and the district authority. The chief rabbinate position became vacant in Lviv. Rabbi Levin from the "Agudah" [anti-Zionist Agudat Israel Haredi party] wanted it. The Zionists objected to Rabbi Levin capturing that position for political reasons but they lacked a candidate who could compete against Rabbi Levin. Dr. Tzvi Parnas brought up the candidacy of Rabbi BABa"D, who opposed the "Agudah", and who also opposed any intervention of religious figures in political affairs. In the end, the issue of electing the chief rabbi was taken off the agenda under the pressure from the authorities.

The improvement in the relations between "Bar Kokhba" and Dr. Reikh, brought back the members who previously withdrew from the organization due to the difference of opinions concerning the "agreement" with the government. The following people returned to the organization: Dr. Shwartzman, Dr. Abend, Dr. Nussbaum, and others. It was a good sign since "Bar Kokhba's" 30th anniversary was approaching, and the opportunity to celebrate it under the spirit of solidarity and unity became available.

An important and honorable event in the city was the visit by Kh. N. Bialik. Bialik showed a particular interest in the school named after Perl. His interest in the school was so great that he found it necessary to prolong his visit so that he can become acquainted with the school and its library. Bialik found a high level of Hebrew in Ternopil. However, he resented the situation at the school named after Perl. Attending a gathering, he scolded the Zionists about the barbaric treatment of literary treasures, which resulted in the loss of important and valuable documents. Bialik expanded on Perl's influence on the Jews in Odesa and about a school founded based on Ternopil's example.

Bialik visited the old local cemetery and spent time in solitude at the grave of Perl, RN" K [Ranni Nakhman Kromkhel], and the rest of the Jewish great scholars. Before leaving town, he summoned the people of Pen International, Jews, and Poles and urged them to rescue Perl's library and archive. However. His warning was like a voice calling in the wilderness. The assimilators' gang managed to nullify all of his efforts, and "convince" the authorities, who were happy about every opportunity to strike against the national movement, to leave that cultural institute in its neglective state.

I.

In 1932, "Bar Kokhba" organization reached its 30th year. The preparations lasted many months, and attempts were made to attract all the members, scattered around the world. Indeed, the members of "Bar Kokhba" did not disappoint. They returned to their native city and raised memories from past days. The entire city celebrated, and the celebration lasted three days.

Following the celebrations, the dismal days returned with their troubles and fears. These were the days of Minsk and Przytyk pogroms and the riots [against the Jews] in the universities. It was also the days of the "*Piketim*" (guards standing by Jewish stores to prevent Polish buyers from entering), the days of the "*Obshem*" ("On the contrary" in Polish of [prime minister] Skladkovsky, who gave the economic boycott against the Jews its official status), and the days of pushing out the Jewish population from their sources of livelihood. Even during that daunting period, the Jewish youth proved that they knew how to defend the nation's honor. Its firm stand, without fear, strengthened the spirit of the masses. The Zionists' representatives in the community and municipality too, did not keep quiet. At every opportunity, they protested against the discrimination by the authorities. They announced explicitly and openly with a loud voice that the Jewish population would know how to protect its rights.

The election to the Sejm in 1930 was the last election that allowed public participation. However, the conditions were totally different [when the time came for the next election].

[Columns 205-206]

Kh. N. Bialik visiting Ternopil
From right to left – Standing: Abeler, Dr. Shwartzman, Dr. Abend, Dr. Horwitz, Dr. Orens
Sitting: N. Tversky, Kurfuerst, S. Schwartz, Kh. N. Bialik, Dr. H. Parnas, Dr. A. Rapoport

Reality proved (the jailing of the opposition in Brisk, Lithuania, and other events) that Pilsudski was striving for dictatorship. His party announced that it was the choicest and best in the country ("*Elita*"). Unfortunately, the Jews were divided among themselves. Unlike the previous election, the [Zionist] Union appeared as a unified block. However, the efforts by Yitzkhak Gruenbaum to establish a unified Zionist front. The Zionist left preferred to form a socialistic party. The "Aguda" and merchants appeared in separate parties, and Vetzlav, Vishlitzki, and Ignatzi Yaeger appeared in a "Nonaffiliated block", collaborating with the government (B.B.V.R.).

The Thirtieth Anniversary of the "Bar Kokhba" Organization, 1932
Seniors: Dr. H. Parnas, Pomeranz, Liebergal, and Dr. Sharfspitz

[Columns 207-208]

Galitsia Zionists also submitted their own list.

Ternopil Zionists demanded that their candidate would be a prominent figure who was trusted by the population. However, the "Hit'akhdut" found it necessary to replace Dr. Tzvi Heller, who represented the Ternopil's district until then, with Dr. Bristiger. Dr. Bristiger did not know how to attract the hearts of the masses, since he overemphasized the socialistic slogans, and thereby pushed aside the General Zionists and their voters. It became known to all that their Zionist camp is divided and weak, as happened in the election to the community [council]. The non-Zionist activists of the economic parties, headed by Hirsh Eikhenbaum seized on the opportunity. The Zionist gatherings were disrupted and dispersed by their opponents. The masses were indifferent toward the election, as they did not believe the Jewish representative's periluminal struggle can bring any results. The list received 17 thousand votes (compared to 31 thousand in 1928) and Dr, Bristiger failed.

The failure encouraged all of the General Zionists' rivals, to whom the revisionist group, which attracted several hundred votes, joined. The General Zionists participated in the reception of Ze'ev Jabotinsky during his visit to Ternopil, with clear reservations about his views. The existence of the revisionist group did not contribute to the strengthening of the Zionist Union. Just the opposite, it caused another division.

Avraham Shwartzman passed away after a long illness in 1933. He was one of the most prominent members of "Bar Kokhba" and his balanced view and cleverness helped the organization to pull out of difficult situations.

A greater loss was the death of Dr. Abend, who fulfilled responsible roles on behalf of the Zionists in the city. His funeral became a demonstration of love and appreciation for the prominent public figure.

Despite the recent failures, the public treated the Zionists with respect. Proof of that was the nomination of Avraham Ox, who managed to acquire a good name for himself, in his activities at the trade and industry bureau, to a consulter in that bureau.

With the death of Pilsudski in 1935, the Jewish situation worsened. The [government organization] "OZON" (The Camp of National Unity) came out openly with slogans, the inspiration for which came from Hitler's Germany.

The last important political appearance of the Zionists, was at the municipal election, held by mayor Vidatzky. The Poles tried their best to block the way to the municipality for the Jews and the Ukrainians. Their goal was to take over the municipality and leave only a few minority representatives without any influence. The Zionists received six mandates from the ten Jewish representatives. Among the four non-Zionist representatives, there was not even a single representative of the assimilators.

During the establishment of the new magistrate, the Poles tried to pressure the Zionists to give up on their candidate and demanded that they support the candidacy

of D. Shtekel, who was more acceptable to them. The Zionists rejected that demand. As a faction with six representatives, they were entitled to send a representative of their choosing to the magistrate. However, under the pressure from the Poles, who vigorously objected to the candidacy of Dr. Parnas (whom they perceived as an "extremist"), the Zionists decided to leave Dr. Nussbaum in that role. The latter previously fulfilled the role after the death of Dr. Abend.

The event that could testify about the relations with the Poles, was the arrest of a member of the committee to help Jewish refugees from Germany. It was well known that thousands of Jews with Polish citizenship were expelled from Germany and were detained in camp Zbaszyn at the border with Germany. The Polish authorities accused the committee members that they support communists. They did not shy away from using dirty provocations and proceeded to submit a political claim to the court against Dr. Tzvi Parnas. The trial took place in March 1939 and proved to all that the accusations were based on lies and were brought just to defame the Jewish activists. In the end, Dr. Parnas was acquitted of the charges.

The military [self-defense] group of Beitar, 1934

With worry and fear, the Jewish population looked at the heavy and dark clouds appearing on the west and east horizons. During those difficult months, the Zionists mobilized all of their powers and stood ready for what was to come. Large branches and a club opened on Ternovskigo Street. All the institutions worked under great tension as if the population wanted to distract themselves from the future. That future threatened each one individually and the entire population.

That was the situation when the Second World War erupted. Again, like in the years of the First World War, Ternopil Jews did not stand aside but helped their miserable brothers who found refuge from Hitler's army.

On 17 September, the first Russian tanks broke into the city. On the same day, the Zionist Movement in Ternopil ended.

At that time, nobody could anticipate that the fate of that magnificent community had been sealed. Nobody could anticipate that a few years down the road, we would write about Ternopil as a settlement that was, but it is no more.

Author's Note:

1. See the article by Ben Tzion Fett: "From the Austrian to a Ukrainian Regime", Column 167.

Parties
and Youth Movements

[Columns 211-212]   [Blank]

[Columns 213-214]

The Zionist Labor Party "Hit'akhdut" ["Union"]

by Arye Avnon - Bronstein

Translated by Moshe Kutten

A local party branch was established in Ternopil at the beginning of the 1920s, a short time after the international conference of the "Hit'akhdut" in Prague (1920). Among the founders of the branch were: Professor Sam, Avraham Zeltzer, Dr. Yehuda Tzellermayer, Dr. Shaul Orenstein, Avraham Taft, Avraham Rozenshtroikh, Shmaryahu Pechnik, Moshe Shtierman, Klahr, Gusta Steinberg, Israel Greenspan and others. These people held advanced political views. They considered the Zionist labor movement the most suitable conduit to educate the nation, organize it for the building of Eretz Israel, and train the youth for Aliya and self-fulfillment. They trusted the party to consolidate the Zionist ideology based on the experience acquired by the pioneers of the Second Aliya and the philosophy of the great Zionist Labor Movement's ideologues - A. D. Gordon, Yosef Aharonovitz, Yosef Bussel, Dr. Khaim Arlozorov, and others. In the meantime, the Third Aliya broke through to Eretz Israel via many routes. New types of settlements were formed, in addition to the organic kibbutz. The need to educate the masses about pioneering actions, based on the requirements of the time and the tremendous opportunities in Eretz Israel, became apparent. The distress in the diaspora was great, the days of Grabski approached, and thousands of Jews in Poland and Galitsia prepared themselves for Aliya.

The branch of the "Hit'akhdut" in our city prepared vigorously for the required actions. It penetrated circles, which were still far from Zionist ideology, organized hundreds of members, trained them, and showed them the route to Zionism, work, and fulfillment. The fields of activities by branch' were many and encompassed two major areas: Political-educational activity for working in Eretz Israel, and activity related to the present situation in the diaspora, in our city

The political-educational activity:

This was a new Zionist area of activity in our city. No more toeing the line with the old views and the modes of life inappropriate for the turbulent time of Zionism fulfillment and country revival. No more non-committing home owning. From now on, the center of attention would be directed at education. The education would be based on recognizing the diaspora's Jewish reality and the need to change it by preparing for Aliya and fulfillment as a group in Eretz Israel.

Our branch grew and encompassed wide circles of members. That allowed us to organize the district and activate the branches scattered throughout the neighboring areas. As a result, a "Hit'akhdut's" member, Dr. Tzvi Heller, was chosen as the candidate for the Polish Sejm. We reached that point through the fruitful work and spirit of volunteerism of all the members in the branch, and thanks to the accomplishments in all areas of activities. Dr. Heller was elected twice to the Polish Sejm. The third time, the election was held under a hostile political atmosphere toward the national minorities. At the same time, the political police and the district governor directed the votes… The terror that prevailed was unusual even in the Polish reality of that time. Every hall, rented for our campaign rally, was "checked" by the authorities' experts and was disqualified because of the "risk of collapse". In one campaign season, all the public halls in the city were disqualified. We received a license to hold a rally in a large field - in the open, but the police organized a gang of rioters to disrupt the rally. In the end, the police broke into the rally from the adjacent third gymnasium building where the policemen were waiting for every opportunity to disperse the crowd and "succeeded in restoring order".

The election was based on the principle of "division of votes". With the help of the police and the presidents of the district courts, the government seized, the votes cast for non-government parties and combined them into a fake unaffiliated "block for collaboration with the government (B. B. V. R.). Our candidate, Dr. Bristiger, received 31,000, however, the government "decided" that he received only 24,000 and therefore failed since the minimum number of votes was 27,0000[1]

According to the agreement,

[Columns 215-216]

all the Zionist organizations and parties were supposed to work without any reservations in support of our candidate. An explicit country-wide agreement was in place. However, we would not be lying by stating today what every child in the city knew then, that the rival parties did not act to fulfill that agreement. The entire burden of the campaign and the personal risk involved in handling the campaign fell solely on the shoulders of the "Hit'akhdut" members.

Our party city's secretariat organized annual district-wide rallies that no other party managed to organize or hold. Hundreds of members from all the towns and distanced places gathered for enormous Socialistic-Zionist demonstrations, organized tastefully, where the best of our country leaders gave speeches to large crowds of the party members and its fans. On the stage of these district rallies, the following people gave speeches: Dr. Avraham Levinson, Dr. Kopel Schwartz, Dr. Gur-Arye Terlo, Yosef Levi, Dr. Tartokover, Fishel Werber, and Dr. Tzvi Heller. The Ternopil district rallies acquired a name for themselves throughout the entire country.

In the election to the [Zionist] Congresses, our party broke the monopoly of the conservative parties and received a substantial number of votes (second place after the General Zionists). It also provided an essential contribution to the Eretz Israel labor faction. Dr. Orenstein was elected several times, as a representative to the Zionist congresses. The platform of the Eretz Israel labor movement penetrated the awareness of many of the Jewish community in the city, and they expressed their trust in the "Hit'akhdut's" Zionist activity. Just as our representative to the Polish Sejm knew to bring up new topics for debate in the Sejm (like the demand for the government's support of training the pioneers who were making Aliya, and for assistance to the movement for productization of the diaspora's Jews) so did our emissaries to the [Zionist] congresses know to fight for a change of values, and firming the democratization of the Zionist life.

Activities related to the present situation:

That activity occurred within the Jewish community, its institutions, and the municipality. Our community [council] representative, Dr. Y. Tzellermayer, fought vigorously against those who advocated the preservation of the old regime in the community. He demanded fitting that autonomous institution to the Zionist spirit and the needs of the working masses in the city. His brilliant speeches, with realistic content, built on the principles of the Zionist labor movement, made a huge impression and often led to the acceptance of our proposals. The old generation people were astonished to see the young doctor who dared to "break" the traditional line in the Jewish community, as was formulated in the past.

Dr. Orenstein, our representative at the municipality, where a harsh and hostile atmosphere toward the Jews prevailed, fought in the battles for the Jewish needy. He vigorously demanded the remedy of the perpetual injustice toward the Jewish neighborhoods in the city. He also demanded to award support to social assistance programs, employment of Jewish workers in the municipality's projects, support for the Jewish educational institutions, and improvements in the living conditions of the Jewish poor in the city. He condemned the indifferent attitude toward the sanitary conditions in the Jewish neighborhoods and the lack of roads and sewers - problems that the Christian city leaders never thought to address.

General social institutions:

When it was still possible (without interference by the political regime in the country), our members participated in the operation of the general city and district HMO. Avraham Goldenberg, Shmuel Kermish, and Yosef Brinstein were our talented elected representatives of the Jewish working class to that district supervision committee of that institution.

Members of the "Hit'akhdut" in Ternopil

[Columns 217-218]

They spoke on behalf of the public about introducing medical assistance to the Jewish working masses, improving the medical institutions, and easing the tax burden imposed on the workers.

Charity Fund:

Our members organized and established a charity fund by providing cash loans to the needy of the working class, for purchasing working tools, assisting poor artisans, and providing loans for the productization of many Jews in the city. The fund handled its activity quietly and humbly but was a blessing for an important class in the community.

Professional Unions:

A lot of attention was devoted by the "Hit'akhdut" to the establishment of professional unions among the Jewish workers in the city. Three such unions were established: trade workers and accountants, semesters, and porters. The establishment of these organizations boosted the image of the workers in the eyes of the public and in their own eyes. The possibilities associated with a unified and organized body raised the worker's self-confidence.

Activities within the Zionist institutions:

Our members captured principal positions in all Zionist institutions, and managed the activities dedicatedly and with pioneering volunteerism.

In the "Keren Kayment Le'Israel" [KKL-JNF], headed for many years by our member Schwartz, the following members were active: Miriam Slepter, Azriel Guliger, Dov Grueberg, Shmuel Kermish, Moshe Greenfeld, Yehoshua Sigal, and Arye Bronstein. These members visited homes, collected funds in synagogues, parties, weddings, and balls, and worked tirelessly to collect money for the fund of KKL-JNF. They invented new ways of establishing new far-reaching circles for the benefit of the fund. They were the life and soul of the fund activities in the city.

Our members Dr. Tzellermayer, Dr. Rottstein, and Dr. Orenstein worked for many years for "Keren HaYesod" ["Foundation Fund" or UIA - "United Israel Appeal"].

The Ternopil Committee of K.K.L. (National Fund)

The method there was a bit different. It was less involved with the masses and was based on contributions by wealthy individuals, such as rich merchants and owners of properties. Our members also solicited contributions from the middle class and people of means within the party. The members' public appearances on behalf of "Keren HaYesod" raised its image in the eyes of the public.

The fund for the workers of Eretz Israel was under the leadership of our member, Dr. Sh. Orenstein, and the fund's secretary was Arye Bronstein. District gatherings were held, and the activities of the funds widened

Cultural Activities:

In addition to teachers, our member Nathan Ostern was active on behalf of the "Hit'akhdut" in the organization "Tarbut" ["Culture"]. The students came from among the members of the "Hit'akhdut" and its branches, members of the "HeKhalutz" ["The Pioneer"] organization, and various youth organizations. The majority of the educational material was concentrated around Eretz Israel and the contribution of the labor movement to building the homeland.

The "Hit'akhdut" also organized a drama club headed by Shraga Mistrikh-Alufi. The club was active for several seasons and helped develop the understanding and appreciation of modern Jewish dramatic art.

The masterpiece of the cultural activity of the "Hit'akhdut" party was the library of the "Gideon" organization, under the management of Dr. Orenstein, Mendel Nisbaum, Avraham Goldenberg, Moshe Greenfeld, Azriel Morkes, and others. Everyone worked to foster that project.

The "Hit'akhdut" experienced an important turning point with the establishment of the pioneering youth union "Gordonia", the student union "Kadima" ["Forward"][2], and the Aliya organization of the craftsmen "HaOved" ["The Worker"]

During the years of big Aliya, the "Hit'akhdut" party organized the craftsmen and people of various professions in an Aliya organization, "HaOved". The organization was headed by our member Shmaryahu Pechnik. The time was insufficient to develop a wide-reaching activity because our horrible enemy put an end to everything. The organization generated excitement and interest among the craftsmen, but only a few were lucky to make Aliya.

Another branch of the "Hit'akhdut" party was the "Boslia" organization. The goal of that pioneering union was to organize "Hakhshara" [Training] for the party members and its fans and thus prepare a pioneering reserve unit for the party. The training enabled the trainees to make Aliya in unified groups, based on the common experience, of living together at the branch and the "Hakhshara". "Boslia" union developed during the 1930s increased the pioneering excitement in the city and also succeeded to train many pioneers for Aliya. The first nucleus of "Bolsia" unified and settled in the kibbutz "Kiryat Anavim".

Our members, Y. Sigal, M. Greenspan, G. Katz, Margalit, and others, headed the organizational and education activities in "Boslia".

Author's Notes:

1. See the article by Tzvi Parnas, columns 198 and 207.
2. See next chapter

[Columns 219-220]

"Poalei Tzion" ["Workers of Zion"]

by Tzvi Weisbersht, Dr. A. Avishur (Werber)

Translated by Moshe Kutten

The Socialistic-Zionist activity, which was later embodied by the "Poalei Tzion" party, began with a small group called "Ahavat Tzion" ["Love of Zion"] headed by its members, Sirkes, Sapir, and Tzinker. That group was active before the death of Herzl. Over time Weisbersht, Bilfeld, Lorber, Glazer, Shaper, and others joined the group. After the death of Herzl, the group changed its name to "Bnei Herzl" ["The sons of Herzl"]. For some time, it was hosted by "Bar Kokhba", and later on moved to its own apartment on Ruska Street.

That was a period of frenzy. Some Jewish youths were members of the PPS ["*Polska Partia Socjalistyczna*", or "Polish Socialist Party"]. But many who were called "separatists", fought for an independent Jewish socialist party like the PPS. The studying youth established the "Bar Kokhba" organization. However, some youths did not find their place in either of these movements and wished to combine the [Zionist] idea of national revival with the socialistic ideology, similar to the ZPS ["*Zydowski Partia Socjalistyczna*"]. They searched for a Socialistic-Zionistic home. In the beginning, these were just quite foggy ideas and were not shaped into a formal ideology. That lasted until a refugee from Russia, a carpenter by the name of Tabachnik, who was a member of the Russian "Poalei Tzion", arrived at Ternopil. He escaped the pogrom in Kishinev and breathed a new life into the ranks of the movement's followers in Ternopil[1].

The founding conference, which laid down the foundations for the "Poalei Tzion" movement in Galitsia, gathered in Lviv a short while later.

The first steps of the new party were not easy. At the time, an arduous struggle by the workers was taking place. The workers demanded improvements in their working conditions, shortening of the work day, which lasted 14 – 16 hours then, increasing the pay, etc… The existing socialistic movements PPS and ZPS led the struggle, and the masses followed them.

However, the "Poalei Tzion" movement did not have a party's literature, which defined its goals and views. The literature was needed to give the members the ideological weapon to fight its rivals, the PPS and the ZPS, who were equipped with rich folklore and scientific-based socialistic literature.

Luckily, relief came in the form of Dr. Daniel Pasmanik's book: "The Theory and Practice of "Poalei Tzion". Dr. Pasmanik, who visited Ternopil, generated excitement with his lectures, which contained an excellent deep analysis of the fate of the Jewish nation in the diaspora, its place in the economic system, and the dangers that a socialistic win may bring to the Jewish masses in the diaspora"[2]. The book of Dr. Pasmanik, his lectures, and the publishing of the weekly magazine "Yiddisher Arbeiter" ["The Jewish Worker"] offered a substantial contribution to the dissemination of the "Poalei Tzion" ideas and to the widening of its influence among the masses. Reinforcement of the movement arrived when the war between Russia and Japan broke out. Many Jews escaped Russia, including some excellent speakers, who helped in the development of the party with their skills and experience.

The following people were among the activists at that time: Shwartzapel (in New York at the date of publication), Tzuger (New York), Bahara"l [R' Avraham Yosef (?), Son of Rabbi Leib], Avram Shterholtz, Sobel, Goldstein, Vestel, Pendler, Shtekel, and others. Many of the school's students joined the party. Among them were Shimon Peler, who excelled in his knowledge of socialistic literature and served as an expert on theoretical issues, and A. Werber (today, A. Avishur).

What made "Poalei Tzion" viewed favorably by the masses was the party's positive attitude toward the Yiddish language. In their conference in Chernivtsi [Czernowitz] a resolution was obtained about the Yiddish being the national language of the Jews. Among the many of the participants of that conference who visited Ternopil were prominent figures like Sh. Asch, Y. L. Peretz, Z. Reizen, H. D. Nomberg, and others. They strengthened the national [revival] idea among the youth in their lectures.

After a relatively short period, representatives of the city intelligentsia, such as Dr. I. Waldman. M. Khartiner. Dr. Ph. Korngruen, Dr. Tzin, and Dr, Bigel, drew near the movement and helped it with their education and speeches, which conquered the hearts of their listeners.

Slowly, the area of influence of "Poalei Tzion" widened, and branches of the party were established in all the towns of the district.

Author's Notes:

1. See the article by Dr. P. Korngruen, Column 124.
2. Ibid

[Columns 221-222]

The Z. P. S – "Bund"
The Jewish Socialist Party

by Arnold Himelbrandt & Israel Grinberg

Translated by Moshe Kutten

The Austrian Socialistic party ruled the workers' movement until the end of the 19th century. Citizens of the nations that populated the Austrian Empire were all members of its ranks. The tendency to establish national socialistic parties that would operate among the masses, in their own language, and according to their national aspirations and special needs heightened with the trend of strengthening the national consciousness.

To allow for these tendencies, which undermined the foundation of the Austrian empire, to express themselves the congress of the Austrian socialistic party, held in Bern in 1899, announced "the principle of national and cultural autonomy for every nation and people". As a result of that announcement, the Polish Socialistic Party - *Polaska Partia Socjalistyczna* or P.P.S. and the Ukrainian Socialistic Party or U.P.S. were established.

A Jewish socialistic party has not yet been formed then because the national ideology spread among the masses under the influence of the Zionist movement and the "Bund" in Russia. The Galitsian Jewish members of the P.P.S. objected to that idea since most of them were assimilators who rejected the whole idea of a Jewish nation. A while later, under the pressure from the Jewish public opinion and reality, the PPS had to relent and agree to establish professional guilds for the Jewish workers under the authority of the center of professional guilds in Vienna. Over time, the guilds became the nucleus of the Jewish Socialistic Party, Z.P.S. (*Zydowska Partia Socjalistyczna*).

The struggle against the negative attitude of the leaders of the Polish and Austrian socialistic movements against the demands of the Jewish masses to establish their own socialistic party lasted until 1905. Dr. Henrik Grossman from Krakow, the initiator of the idea of a Jewish Socialistic party, headed that struggle. He was aided by Dr. Eintzigler, R. Birenbaum, A. Fakh from Lviv, and Dr. Brass from Krakow. These people ran a vigorous propaganda campaign. In that campaign, which they ran in Yiddish, the language of the masses, they pointed at the harsh conditions under which the Jewish masses lived and the need to form a Jewish socialistic party to represent the working Jews and fight for their right to improve their social and national standing.

Like in other cities of Galitsia, a special committee of the Jewish party, headed by Dr. Zlatkes, Dr. Nusbrekher, Y. Birpas, Y. Goldstein, and Tepperberg, was formed in Ternopil. The committee in Krakow managed the entire activity.

The foundation for the ZPS party was laid in the congress of the Jewish Socialistic Party gathered in Lviv in June 1906. Israel Grinberg, Y. Birpas, Y. Goldstein, and A Tepperberg participated in that congress from Ternopil.

The professional guilds active at that time joined the party however, they continued to report to the center of the professional guilds in Vienna.

That situation lasted until the break of the First World War. With the establishment of the Polish state, the need to unify the socialistic movement throughout the country arose. At the time, the "Bund" was active in Congressional Poland, and its influence among the masses was substantial. At the congress in Krakow, held in 1920, it was decided to unify the "Bund" and the ZPS. The unified party was headquartered in Warsaw.

The unique conditions prevailing in Galitsia after the war and the administrative pressure by the authorities worked against the socialistic movement particularly since the working class in that agricultural region was very small and its influence among the population was insignificant.

Being between the rock [Polish authorities) and the Ukrainian hard place and the choking atmosphere of antisemitism and national oppression, the masses were not attracted to the ZPS ideology. The party's ideals seemed to be divorced from reality or, at a minimum, valid only sometime in the future. They were attracted by the ideas of the national and socialistic revival in Eretz Israel. The propaganda of the Zionist-Socialistic with all of its branches, could point to real political achievements (Balfour Declaration, San Remo Declaration, agricultural settlements in Eretz Israel, etc..), had a fertile land to grow - an alert national spirit and a strong yearning for redemption from the poor social and national state. On the other side - some (albite only a few) were attracted by the Communist Party's propaganda.

That propaganda excited the imagination with the achievements of the Russian Revolution and promised to solve all the economic and national problems immediately.

[Columns 223-224]

"HaMizrakhi"

by Tova Sanhedrai (Dimend)

Translated by Moshe Kutten

The Ternopil "HaMizrakhi" movement with all of its branches included its youth movements "Torah VeAvoda" ["Torah and Work"], "HeKhalutz Mizrakhi" ["Mizrakhi Pioneer"], and "Bnei Akiva" ["Sons of Akiva"].

The "HaMizrakhi" party reorganized in 1920, was a lively and ebullient Zionist movement that fought vigorously for the Zionism idea and Aliya to Ertz Israel.

The road of the founders was not rosy. The Zionist idea was not popular among specific circles of Polish Jewry, particularly among the religious Jews. However, due to the dedication and vigor of the trailblazers, the idea stroked roots and slowly conquered hearts.

The activists of the "HaMizrakhi" and "Torah & Avoda" movements placed propaganda, Hebrew-based education, and revival of the Hebrew language at the center of their Zionist activity. They established a network of Hakhshara [Training towards Aliya] kibbutzim. In 5686 [1925/6], they founded a Hebrew school by the name of Mata"t (acronym of MeTzion Tetze Torah - [from out of Zion the Torah will come]). The school network was spread over the entire Eastern Galitsia area. Hundreds of graduates came out of the school in Ternopil. Besides gaining knowledge of the Hebrew language, they were imbued with a deep religious Zionist conviction. Many of them made Aliya.

For the adults, "HaMizrakhi' organized lectures and lessons about Zionism, the Hebrew language, education, science, and more. These cultural activities influenced wide circles in the city. The movement grew and gained popularity with the public. We should note here that "HaMizrakhi" exerted a substantial influence on the Husiatyn Hassidim, so much so that they eventually began to send their youth the Eretz Israel. That fact is noteworthy in light of the negative attitude of most of the Hasidism movement toward the Zionist idea.

The members of the "HaMizrakhi" took a substantive active role in every Zionist activity in the city, including activities that benefitted the "KKL-JNF", "Keren HaYesod" funds, and more.

During the same time, the "HaMizrakhi" movement founded the bank of "HaMizrakhi" in Eretz Israel. The organization in Ternopil saw it as their honorable duty to help in the development of that economic institution in Eretz Israel and devoted itself to disseminating the stocks of that bank among its members and fans.

The religious youth was organized in "HaMizrakhi Youth", and those who planned to make Aliya in "HeKhalutz HaMizrakhi". The latter maintained agricultural training kibbutzim in provincial towns and crafts kibbutzim in the city.

It wasn't easy for the religious youth in those days, particularly the Yeshiva students, to transfer to collective and working life. Tremendous mental powers were required to leave home, against the parents' will, and move on new life.

The Local Committee of "Mizrakhi"

From right to left – sitting (center): Z. Wahler, Teikhman, D. Parnas, I Biller, I. Walfish, Friedberg, A. Meiberger, I. Parnas, M. Fessel
Standing: Stolzenberg, Urbakh, Z. Ginsburg, Wallakh, Milgraum

At the training camps, the members received physical and spiritual training. Quite a few members were absorbed in the religious settlement in Eretz Israel.

The adolescents were organized in the "Bnei Akiva" movement. In addition to the religious-Zionist education and the Hebrew language, they also received training in scouting and sports. These youths participated enthusiastically in any Zionist activity, particularly in collecting monies for the KKL-JNF.

"HaMizrakhi" ensured that it was represented in the community [council]. Its representatives exerted a great influence there and benefitted the Zionist movement.

The best of the adult and young members prepared for an Aliya to Eretz Israel, but only a few were fortunate to fulfill their aspirations. The rest met a bitter fate when the Holocaust befell the Polish Jewry.

We need to mention some of the activists who distinguished themselves the most.

[Columns 225-226]

The Committee of "Mizrakhi" Youth-Organization

From right to left – sitting: Joseph Landau, Khaviva Glikman (Ganz), Khaim Baron, Tzipora Shiferman, Hirsh Lindman
Standing: Israel Messing, M. M. Margolis, Yehuda Feld, Moshe Wolfenhut, Yehoshua Wasserman

In their activities, and contributed greatly, from their ideas and time to the work of the movement. Unfortunately, it was not possible to memorize them all, and we have undoubtfully skipped over many dedicated activists. We ask for their forgiveness.

Yitzkhak Walfish. He was attracted to the religious Zionist idea in his youth and was among the first organizers of "HaMizrakhi". At the time of the book's publication, in Canada.

Zusia Wahler Z"L. A native of Ternopil. A scholar. Dedicated to the Zionist idea and to the dissemination of the Hebrew language among the youth. He was the principal of the Mata"t school, and the secretary of the "Tarbut" school

Avraham Meiberger Z"L. One of the first members and founders of the movement. He was the "HaMizrakhi's" representative in the community council.

Yitzkhak Biller Z"L. One of the activists. He handled the organization of the middle class towards Aliya.

Tzvi Friedberg Z"L. The chairman of "HaMizrakhi". Educated his son in the spirit of religious Zionism. They were all members of the "Torah & Avoda" youth movement. One of his sons was killed during Israel's Independence War.

Dr, Eliyahu Markus Z"L. A native of Ternopil. He was a scholar student. He organized the Hebrew school after the First World War, while he was still young. In 1924, he moved to Krakow and became the chairman of "HaMizrakhi" in Western Galitsia. At 28, he was elected as "HaMizrakhi's" representative to Krakow's city council. He returned to Ternopil with his family during the Holocaust to liquidate his businesses and perished there.

Mordekhai Fessel. A native of Ternopil. One of the activists of "HaMizrakhi and "Torah & Avoda". He was ordained as a rabbi by Rabbi Steinberg from Brody. He was the vice chairman of HaMizrakhi. He was in Israel at the time of the book publication.

Yehoshua Parnas Z"L. The son of the rabbinical judge Rabbi Israel Parnas Z"L. He was a native of Ternopil and the "HaMizrakhi's" representative to the community council.

Gedalia Kornberg Z"L. A scholar. He was one of the initiators of the committee for Aliya and agricultural settlement by the name of "Ternopil Estate".

Sander Goldberg Z"L. Dedicated to his friends. His home was a distinguished Zionist home, where the Hebrew language ruled.

Mikhael Shiferman Z"L. A scholar student. He fulfilled the ideology of "Torah & Avoda" in all aspects [except one]. He did not make Aliya to Eretz Israel.

Tzipora Shiferman Z"L. A native of Ternopil. One of the prominent leaders of "Torah & Avoda" in the city. She attained high education in Hebrew and served as a Hebrew teacher. She also taught the language in many other clubs. She was the life of the movement's leadership. Her only wish she could not fulfill was to join the movement of "HaPoel HaMizrakhi" ["The HaMizrakhi Worker"] in Eretz Israel. She passed away tragically.

Shmuel Weissman Z"L. One of the leaders of the movement "HaMizrakhi youth". He was a scholar student and an educated man. One of the central pillars of the movement. He was a Hebrew teacher. During the [Second World] War, he went into exile in Russia, and we lost all traces of him.

Yehuda Feld. One of the leaders of "Torah & Avoda" and one of its prominent activists. At the time of publication, he was in the U.S.

Rivka Feld (Tarif) Z"L. One of the activists, Dedicated to the movement's ideas and activities.

Tova Dimend (Sanhedrai). A native of Ternopil. One of the leaders of "Torah & Avoda" and "HeKhalutz HaMizrakhi". The movement's representative to the conference in Lviv in 1932. Responsible for managing the pioneer *Hakhshara* [Training for Aliya] around the city. At the time of publication, in Israel.

Mendel Haiman Z"L. A scholar. A Hebrew teacher. The student of Rabbi Baba"d ZTz"L. One of the central pillars of the movement.

[Columns 227-228]

Khaim Baron Z"L. For many years, a member of the management team of the movement "Torah & Avoda" and one of its distinguished activists.

Ze'ev Wilner Z"L. "HaMizrakhi's" secretary and one of its prominent activists.

Eliyahu Shwartzman Z"L. Headed "Bnei Akiva", and one of the excelled activists of the KKL-JNF work in the city.

The following are the members of the committees who managed the daily work:

Itamar Teikhman Z"L, Pesakh Tzvi Katz Z"L, Kopel Yaffe Z"L, Khana Glikman Z"L, Mendel Margalit Z"L, Israel Messing (in Israel at time of publication), Yisaskhar Friedberg Z"L, Yehoshua Wasserman Z"L, Shmuel Tzoref Z"L, Khava Gernik Z"L, Tzipora Shikler Z"L, Ze'ev Rethoiz Z"L, Eliezer Neigeboren Z"L, Moshe Wolfhoit Z"L, Yosef Landau and Khaviva Glikman (Ganz) (in Israel at time of publication), Hirsch Lindman Z"L, Moshe Altzofrom (In Israel; at time of publication), Shmuel Tirkel Z"L, and others.

"Tif'eret HaDat" ["The Splendor of Religion"] and "Agudat Israel"

by Dr. Hillel Zeidman

Translated by Moshe Kutten

The drive for unification within the religious Jewry became apparent during the last years before the First World War. That was the period of the establishment of "HaMizrakhi" (1902) and "Agudat Israel" (1912). The echoes of these organizations reached Ternopil after the Zionist unions, such as the academic "Bar Kokhba" (1902), were already active. As a mimicry of competition, the religious Jews began to organize themselves. They wanted to defend against the new movements and act to strengthen the religion.

The idea of establishing an organization of Haredi Jews with a local characteristic (without an affiliation with the country-wide or worldwide movements such as "HaMizrakhi" or "Agudat Israel"), surfaced in 1913. The name of that organization was "Tif'eret HaDat". Its founders, activists, and Haredi donors were: R' David Lvov, R' Ya'akov Breitman along with his sons-in-law, and the distinguished scholars - Rabbi Meir Shapira (who later gained fame as the Rabbi of Lublin), R' Moshe Rozner, R' Leibush Arak, and R' Baruk Veksler. The other founders were: R' Lippa Tirkel and his sons, Feivel, Yekhiel, Shmuel, and Shlomo, R' Shmeril Eikhenbaum, R' Mordekhai Eingler, and more. Most of them were traders, rich estate owners, or otherwise wealthy. They donated substantial sums to purchase the building of "Tif'eret HaDat". The building, located on the corner of Sobieski Square, was one of the most splendid mansions in the city. Before that, a Catholic teachers seminary was housed in it.

During the First World War, it was not easy being a homeowner due to the oppression exerted by the conquering Russian regime. The leaders of "Tif'eret HaDat" had to sell the building. However, toward the end of the war, the value of the money obtained from the sale of the building diminished due to the devaluation of the currency, and the leaders regretted selling the building, which was carried out improperly under duress. After long negotiations and a judgment by the rabbinical court, the leaders received the building back. However, their worries were not over since the largest hall in the building was occupied by the academic organization "Bar Kokhba". After negotiations, "Bar Kokhba" left the large hall on the second floor and moved to another hall on the first floor. "Tif'eret HaDat" moved to the large hall vacated by "Bar Kokhba".

The housing of "Tif'eret HaDat" in a spacious and splendid hall served as a tremendous push for the development of that union. It acquired large numbers of members. The union was subjected to the influence of "Agudat Israel" through its leaders, who were members of "Agudat Israel" [party]. That influence was exerted, particularly through R' Moshe Rozner and his son Yehoshua, R' Shmeril Eikhenbaum, R' Horowitz, and others, The local branch of "Agudat Israel" was also housed in the building in the same hall where the religious school for girls "Beit Ya'akov" was housed. As a result, the boundaries between the apolitical "Tif'eret HaDat" (some of its members belonged to "HaMizrakhi") and "the party of "Agudat Israel" became blurred until the two organizations unified.

An important activity was carried out by "Tze'irei Aguadt Israel" [The Youths of Agudat Israel"], founded in 1927 by Tzvi Horwitz, the grandson of R' David Lvov". He was an educated and skilled scholar. Unfortunately, he was killed in a train accident in Nowy Sacz [Santz], in 1931.

Thanks to the leaders of "Agudat Israel" and "Tze'irei Agudat Israel", the party became an important factor in the public life of Ternopil's Jews between the two World Wars. It achieved a substantial representation in the management of the community and all the public institutions.

[Columns 229-230]

Youth Movements

"HeKhalutz" ["The Pioneer"]
A Turning Point for the Ternopil's Youth

by A. Mesh

Translated by Moshe Kutten

With the issuing of the Balfour Declaration and the conquering of Eretz Israel by the British, the Zionist activities in the cities of Poland and Galitsia deviated from its limited and amateurish framework in favor of specific Aliya-related activities, carrying its ideology into practice.

Ternopil was known to experience organized Zionist activities many years before that. However, like in other country districts' cities, the Aliya issue was not placed at the center of private or public life.

However, following Balfour Declaration, deep national excitement surrounded the Jewish youth, who strove for action. Although Eretz Israel was still subjected to military rule and its gates locked to large Jewish Aliya, pioneers began penetrating through the first opened cracks. These pioneers flocked to Eretz Israel, overcoming many obstacles and hindrances on their way, like trailblazers starting a new life for their homeland.

* * *

The enthusiastic stories about the few brave pioneers who stole borders and arrived in Eretz Israel were heard with intense jealousy among the national youth. Even before the establishment of "HeKhalutz" and before an organized Aliya became possible, a group of academic students and high school graduates was crystalized in the city. They raised the flag of Aliya among the local youth and saw the first seeds for a large Zionist movement.

That year, tens of youths who earnestly planned to learn Hebrew underwent agricultural *Hakhshara* [training for Aliya]. They planned to eventually make Aliya and began to crystalize around the first Zionist cell - the "HaShomer" ["The Guard"]. Over the years, that movement changed its character and organizational framework, and through various transformations, it became a cell of the "HaShomer HaTzair" movement, originally an educational youth movement with no specific political affiliation.

A framework was required for the daring ones among the local youth who prepared themselves for a major change in their life. They needed a place where they could concentrate their will and initiative. "HaShomer" organization, which raised the motto of self-fulfillment, found its way to the hearts of these youths.

There was an "out of place' aura around the appearance of the Ternopil's youth pioneers who spoke about Aliya and manual work. They looked for places to be trained in the neighboring agricultural farms. The general atmosphere in the Jewish street

The first "HeKhalutz" Group in Israel

From right to left – sitting: Avraham Neuman, Jacob Teikhman, Aba Schweig
In the center: Yetka Yampoler-Neuman., Meir Kestenbaum, Debora Boberstein-Levion
Standing: Yehoshua Grosskopf, Eliyahu Kaspi, Mordekhai Brum, Mager, Moshe Kaspi, Jacob Doner, Zvi Hershkowitz, Shmuel Kahane, Itzkhak Tenenbaum, Ze'ev Silber

[Columns 231-232]

was not ready for "dreamers" and "non-conformists" who advocated a change of values and wished to set an example by their own doing.

Most parents whose children "fell into bed ways" and were "caught by the fulfilling pioneering" were astonished. The call for manual work and Aliya sounded to them as the call of immature and inexperienced boys and girls whose fever of their faith drove them to lose their minds.

* * *

With the news that the group arrived in Eretz Israel a second group was organized in the beginning of 1921. That group was organized on its own without any guiding hand. Most of the members of that group were about seventeen years old, students before their graduation. Among them were A. Berger, brothers Shitzer, Sh. Knopholtz, Y. Schweig and others.

The first group of pioneers that made Aliya in 1920 after only limited preparations included more than one hundred young men and women. Their Aliya was a leap of the spirited and generated awe and admiration in the city. The group contained the following people: A. Neuman, Y. Groskopf (changed his name to Rimoni), Yetka Yampoler, Tova Schweig, Dvora Biberstein, and others.

Hakhshara on their own initiative. They went around the villages and Jewish estates in the district, looking for opportunities for agricultural work for meager food to ensure a minimum survival.

It was not easy for these youth, who had never experienced manual work before, to work among the sturdy Ukrainians, natives of the villages. Many did not find work on agricultural farms. They had to find other sources for survival until the date of their Aliya. They worked in wood cutting and tree chopping for the city Jews. That was how they trained themselves in manual work on the cusp of a substantial change in their life.

The Aliya of that group was legal. They received entrance visas to Eretz Israel from the British consul in Warsaw, with the help of the Eretz Israeli office there. However, they were responsible for the transportation on land and sea. They had to do that without help from their parents, who considered Aliya of their children, an adventure of irresponsible youths.

The Aliya of the Ternopil's third group materialized under arduous conditions for various unrelated reasons. The group contained brothers Zilberman, Sh. Goldstein Z"L, A. Tenenbaum, A. Mager and others. Although they did receive certificates [entrance visas], they could not get transfer visas [through other countries]. Most of them had to steal borders and travel tens of kilometers before reaching the port. Most did not have the opportunity to train themselves in agriculture, construction, or stone cutting, so they worked during their wanderings in simple incidental manual jobs to accustom themselves to manual work and save some money.

I was a "bench hugger" [student] in "Beit HaMidrash" [a school for religious studies]. The yearning for our ancestral land among the students of "Beit HaMidrash" was deeply rooted. It was fed from the holiness of Eretz Israel that we received at home and from religious studies. However, that yearning was limited to the imagination and was far from any concept of realization.

The fact that some youths in the city dared to organize as pioneers and make Aliya against the will of their parents shocked the yeshiva students. It caused a revolution in their young souls. It raised their hope that they would be able to join the pioneers soon.

The effect of the action by that small group of youngsters who made Aliya was much more pronounced than the speeches by Zionist preachers in the Zionist gatherings and meetings.

A similar process took place among the student population. Before that process, they considered their high school and university studies as their life mission. In that, they were supported by the parents who made substantial efforts to help their children graduate.

The Polish high schools in the city, where hundreds of Jewish children studied, served as the citadels of the assimilators' circles. These people alienated themselves from the national aspirations of their nation. They fought against the Zionists and their strengthening public standing. However, the redemption idea, which conquered the youth in a storm, also penetrated these Polish schools. The events presented the Jews among them, with the question: "Where [are you heading]?"

* * *

The "HeKhalutz" branch in Ternopil was organized in 1923. The branch maintained an organizational connection with the center in Lviv and spread its propaganda among various youth circles already involved in the process of the national awakening. The "HeKhalutz" format attracted youths from different social classes under the same roof, where the idea of living in communes unified them all and made them into a fulfilling congregation.

Any person who witnessed the partitions that separated the workers and the poor from the "wealthy high school students" and the children of the "homeowners". couldn't help but appreciate the enormous social contribution of the "HeKhalutz" movement. Upon joining the movement, the members had to peel off the customs and routine manners of their previous lives. All the members wore uniform khaki clothing and did their best to blur the symbols separating the classes. The discussions about Zionism and agricultural work in communes in Eretz Israel, the trips outside of the city, and the district's gatherings that brought together hundreds of pioneers, all in their most exciting age, all helped in crystalizing the image of the new youths. They saw themselves as the central force in the building of the homeland.

[Columns 233-234]

The Branch of "HeKhalutz" in Ternopil, 1924

Pini Zilberman (aka Pinkhas Kaspi Z"L, who died a few years before this book's publishing in Kiryat Khaim, Israel) was among the outstanding characters who joined "HeKhalutz" when the organization widened its range of activities. His revolutionary step generated great awe among all the public classes in Ternopil. Pini Zilberman was a tall and good-looking young man. He wore a black suit and an overcoat like the refined and mature young men the matchmakers were running after with their proposed matches. He was known to everybody as a dealer in the stock market on Ruska Street and was socializing with respectable religious circles. Unexpectedly, he experienced a great spiritual transformation following the Aliya of his two brothers. He abandoned his businesses and substituted his fashionable with simple working outfits. Passersby saw him going to his chiseling job at the cemetery, carrying his tools bag on his shoulders, like an apprentice learning a profession with the gravestone craftsman.

That step by Pini Zilberman was so revolutionary and daring that many of the people who rejected the "HeKhalutz" movement and Zionism claimed that he was possessed by a "Dibuk" [an evil spirit]. Therefore, they claimed that the change in him would not last long. But he nevertheless continued tirelessly in his new way.

While the personal example is often used as an educational and influential factor, it can also serve as a symbol for many in its spiritual sincerity. Pini felt the joy of life awakening in him when he joined "HeKhalutz".

* * *

With the widening of the range of the activity and the increase in the number of new members, the small temporary room provided to the organization as a favor by other institutions and associations was not big enough. The organization was forced to find an apartment that fitted its needs. The apartment rent was financed by the organization's membership fees since it did not have any other sources of revenue. Although "HeKhalutz" influence in the city grew, there was still a lack of appreciation of its importance and even the Zionists did not find it their duty to support it financially. The branch moved around through many apartments until it was handed to the "Hit'akhdut's" club in the Austronskego alley, near the large wood storage warehouse of the Oks family. The club hardly contained all the clubs and groups but it enabled regular energy-filled and wide-ranged activity.

The "HeKhalutz" headquarter looked at the development of the Ternopil's branch favorably and with satisfaction. From time to time, the headquarter sent representatives to visit and discuss. The process of organizing groups for agricultural "*Hakhshara*" in Jewish farms in Eastern Galitsia began.

A lengthy debate was taking place throughout the "HeKhalutz" organization during those days: Agricultural *Hakhshara* or vocational *Hakhshara* - what would better fit the needs of Ertz Israel? It was agreed by all, that an Aliya should not be allowed without prior physical training. The living conditions in Eretz Israel were harsh. Pioneers who were not mentally and physically prepared for the absorption pangs, and hardships of striking roots would not be effective in a country that was only beginning to build itself. Preference was given to agricultural training of large groups without rejecting individual vocational training.

[Columns 235-236]

A substantial portion of the agricultural farms in Eastern Galitsia was owned by Jewish estate owners, who employed thousands of villagers. After negotiations, they agreed to absorb groups of pioneers during the working seasons and allow them to work in their fields for food and some coverage of expenses. They fitted houses and warehouses to lodge the pioneers, which included kitchens. The outing to the farms from the "HeKhalutz" took place on a large scale.

The organized outings of tens of Ternopil pioneers to "*Hakhshara*" farms before their Aliya served as an expression and demonstration of the power of the movement, which continued to grow and establish branches. It penetrated various youth circles and thereby fulfilled an exceptional Zionist mission. Ternopil's Jews, who could never imagine Jewish girls and boys, Torah learners, and loafers dependent on their parents, would be farmers in Eretz Israel, in the future. They witnessed in awe the enormous change created by "HeKhalutz" in its call for self-fulfillment.

While a few of Ternopil's pioneers learned construction professions in the city and most received agricultural training in the villages, the pioneers of the provincial towns put an emphasis on manual labor. Ternopil city served as a place for "physical training" for pioneers from other Galitsian towns, who were lodged in the city as communal groups in rented apartments. They worked chopping firewood on the city's streets, like the Ukrainian hewers, who made a living in that profession for generations.

Tens of youths from wealthy homes, fine men, yeshiva students, and students from Brody, Zolochiv, Ozerna [Jezierna], Strusiv [Strosov], Khorostkiv [Khoroskov], Mikulice [Mikulnitza], Terbovlia [Trembobla], and Pidvolochysk [Podvolichysk], stayed in Ternopil for many months. The Jews in the city looked at them astonishingly as they chopped wood near their homes in the days of ice and snow and wondered about the "abnormal phenomena", which they could not explain.

We should also credit the Ternopil "HeKhalutz" branch for the achievement in dissimilating the Hebrew language among the national youth as a living language of the individual and the public. Although a branch of the "Tarbut" ["Culture"] organization, which later contributed greatly to this area, opened in the city in 1924, its activity was limited initially and did not include many members. "Tarbut's" activity was limited to Shabbat and aimed only at people who already knew the language. "HeKhalutz" enacted the Hebrew language as the official language of the branch and forced the joining members to fully use the language for group discussions and trips, individually and in public gatherings. The Hebrew tone became an organic part of the pioneering folklore in the city.

As the number of pioneers from the Ternopil branch who made Aliya grew, so did the number of new members, and the range of influences widened. After the Aliya of the large fourth group, headed by Pini Zilberman, the branch membership doubled and tripled. The youth movement, "HeKhalutz HaTza'ir" ["The Young Pioneer"] was established. That organization encompassed more than one hundred boys and girls. Their '*Hakhshara*" was scheduled to last three calendar years. At that time, the management team was enlarged. It was headed by Nakhum Greenspan (Aka Nakhum Tzfoni Z"L, a member of Kfar Gil'adi kibbutz who died in 1950), who possessed amazing organizational skills. He was one of the best and most loyal city pioneers, respected and appreciated by all in the city and the headquarter.

Nakhum Greenspan was a yeshiva student. He studied in Jezierna *Kloiz* on Bogata Street. He was sharp and knowledgeable in religious studies. His father anticipated that he would someday serve as a rabbi in one of the towns. However, like many of his friends, he was "caught" by the Zionist and pioneering ideology. He joined the branch and became a central figure there. He directed all of his internal fervor to organizational and propaganda-related activities. He succeeded in enlarging the groups, conducting regular cultural activities, and creating the basis for the adult "*Hakhshara*" outings.

The "HeKhalutz" branch reached a peak in its development at that time. It became an important factor in the national public activity in the city. Instead of disregard and disrespect, people began to respect and appreciate the organization. Sending off a pioneering group for Aliya was an event that gathered hundreds of Jews, singing "HaTkivah" enthusiastically. It also attracted the attention of the Christian population to the idea of the Jewish national revival, which caused a stir in the Jewish street.

Among the groups that went out to agricultural "*Hakhshara*", at the beginning of 1925,

The Agricultural "Hekhalutz" "circle", Autumn, 1925

From right to left – Standing: Yehoshua Groskopf (Rimoni), Eliyahu Kaspi, Brum, Abraham Mager, Moshe Kaspi, Diner, Lande (Hirshkowitz), Shmuel Kahane, Jacob Tenenbaum, Silber
Sitting in the center: Yetka Yampoler-Neuman, Meir Kestenbaum, Debora Biberstein-Levion
Sitting below: Abraham Neuman, Jacob Teikhman, Aba Schweig

[Columns 237-238]

the "club", for which work was arranged for it in the village of Mlynivtsi [Mlinovtza] near Zboriv [Zborov], left a big impression. The stay was scheduled for the summer only, but it continued until after the [fall Jewish] holidays. The "club" contained 20 youths from wealthy homes whose parents were forced to surrender when they faced the "rebellious" children. I recall the ploys employed by the club members to take their belongings to the farm while facing objections from their parents. One girl, a daughter of a Hassid known for his objection to "HeKhalutz", planned her "escape" to take place when both parents were out of the house. With the help of her friends. She went out through a window, carrying the bundle she prepared ahead in secrecy.

With the Aliya of the best leaders of the Ternopil branch who served for several years, the pace of activity slowed because of the depletion of organization and guidance personnel. However, the "HeKhalutz" was like a young tree. It grew new branches and was not affected by the fall of its leaves. The members of the "Young Layer", who were guided and trained by their predecessors, harnessed themselves to the yoke. With the help of the headquarter, they ensured the continuation of the activities at the branch.

The "HaKhalutz" pioneers and activists in Eretz Israel continued to diligently correspond with the branch and helped ensure its activities. They also assisted in forming new groups for Aliya. Many people in Eretz Israel followed the development of the branch with interest and vigilance. They have invested the fervor of their youth and the innocence of their faith to form that branch and grow it.

During my visit to Ternopil in 1931 (6 years after I made Aliya), I found out that the branch has weakened greatly. The reason for that was the Aliya of its founders and the depletion of the organizers and counselors. However, from the point of view of the number of members, its value was still substantial. It served as the single address for youths who looked for a way to save themselves and their nation. The importance of the Ternopil "HeKhalutz" enterprise in the implementation of Zionism in the city, disseminating the Hebrew language, and raising the self-fulfillment motto as a personal obligation for any Zionist individual was immeasurable.

One could find the hundreds of Ternopil pioneers who made Aliya in all types of settlements, all professions, and even in prominent public positions.

In the face of the Holocaust and the annihilation of Ternopil, the "HeKhalutz" organization will remain in our memory as the entity that induced a revolution among the youth. It was also an organization that warned against the approaching catastrophe. As part of its international structure, the organization called its nation to abandon life in the diaspora and to involve itself in building a new homeland. Among all of the Zionist organizations that acted to advance the idea of national revival in our city, "HeKhalutz" captured an honorable position. It saved hundreds of youths from the teeth of assimilation and degradation. It planted the national and social national idea in their heart and ordered them to personally fulfill that idea as pioneers who go in front of their camp.

HaShomer HaTzair" ["The Young Guard"]

by Avraham Amernet

Translated by Moshe Kutten

Once again, my glance goes back to the place of my childhood and youth. Once again, a host of sights float before my eyes, sights that any Ternopil native carries in his or her heart forever. From the fogs of my memory, the streets and the alleys of the Jewish suburbs rise up. Lives flew, and folklore and fables were woven there. These fables were about Ternopil, a "mother Jewish city". That synagogue, a giant box, and an old fort were given to the city's Jews by King Sobieski as an appreciation for the heroism in defending Ternopil against the attacking Turkish corps. Gray and ancient was the synagogue, but shining between its bricks was the glory of heroism, exuding pride in the hearts of the Jewish youths in Ternopil and straightening backs.

The sleepy Seret River flows slowly, not far from the synagogue, and whirling its water southward to the Dniester. On summer nights, boats slide on it. Hebrew tunes are sounded and carried over to its bank from the boats, passing through reeds island, bridges, and the white hills of Petrikov. The space is filled with strange echoes: "The yearning of the *Shomer'ic* [Guard] youth for a distanced homeland, on the banks of the Jordan River, and for a new Hebraic life.

And the echo is pulsating and coming from the groves of Yanovka, Kodkovtza, Gaia, and Charni Las, and from the Shakespear Valley, near the sources of the failing stream, Rodka. Groups of *Shomrim* [male guards] and *Shomrot* [female guards] are immersed in a heated discussion about the yearned tomorrow in the homeland: Tent camp…, desolate landscape…, howling of the jackals…, homeland.

On the opposite side – is the boardwalk of Mitzkevitz Street. That is the street of the masters, seeded with many lights in the evenings and rich in playhouses. That's where Ternopil's golden youth is wasting its life in bad taste. Nearby the line "A-B" passes. That's the dark track that runs parallel to the boardwalk and continues along the sidewalk on the side of the barracks, home of the district manager, and courthouse. That's where the *Shomrim* and the pioneer would meet in the evening to continue their discussions. These youths are in a hurry.

[Columns 239-240]

They count the days remaining until the date of their Aliya. How long would they remain here?

* * *

1913. The first Jewish scouts appear in the city streets. Their uniform attracts attention. Gray shirt with rolled up sleeves, above the left breast pocket, a white badge with Hebrew inscription in azure letters – "HaShomer". Colorful strips drop down from the shoulder, a colorful tie, a rope, a whistle, a leather belt, a green scout hat tight with a strap under the chin, blue shorts, an iron-clad stick, and a backpack on the back. The Jewish high school students showing off in this outfit. With this naive coquettish appearance, they announce that the Jewish youth, like his gentile counterpart, is entitled to have a youth movement of his own. This movement advocates a sound mind in a sound body and stands for returning a healthy fresh-looking face and upright and proud standing to the Jewish youth sitting with a bent back engrossed by a book. The commandment of guarding human and national pride must be etched in the youngster's heart.

Here march the *Shomrim* towards the Gaia Vilieka Forest. They are singing a Hebrew march (in most cases, the singers would not understand the lyrics). The Jews caress the youths with affectionate glances: How comely our scouts look! How nice the appearance of these youths was in the 20 Tammuz convocation memorial to the "Founder of Zionist Union"! With such youth, the Zionist vision would not remain a fairy tale.

The idyll lasted only a short period until the break of the First World War.

The Jewish refugee families who escaped Ternopil from the Russian invasion wandered to Vienna. The war accentuates the pointlessness of the Jewish reality in the diaspora. The Jews are fighting on the fronts of other nations and for interests of other people. A man shoots bullets at his brother. The Jewish youth in Vienna is defending itself against the degradation which now engulfs the crumbling Austrian empire. The youth is rising to defend itself and dreams about another future - his redemption in a different reality. The echoes of the "HaShomer" heroism and the Jewish working fighters in Eretz Israel accompany the birth of the first new Jewish youth movement. Its name would be "HaShomer HaTza'ir". Many Ternopil native youngsters who stayed in Vienna during the war joined the new movement.

1917. The war is ending. The flow of the returnees from Vienna brings the news about the new movement to Galitsia's dispersions. The first cell of the "HaShomer" branch was established in Ternopil in the fall of that year. The images of its founders are already hiding in the shadows of forgottenness. Here is the first head of the branch: Kenyuk, the leadership members Hammer, Berger, and Karu, and the leaders of the battalions: Keppel, Moshel, Fisher, Khana Biberstein, and more and more.

The new center of the Jewish youth in Ternopil is feverish and noisy. It had been just founded, and it became like a kingdom encircling the entire life of the youngster. The branch is swarming like a beehive, full of vitality. Here is where trips would start. Here is where impressive musters would take place. Here is where they would sit down, congested, every group in its own corner, and study the history of the Jewish nation and geography of Eretz Israel. Here, they would also talk about moral values, responsible behavior, and *Shomer*'s ten commandments. They would learn that a *Shomer* is a loyal son or daughter of their nation and that their language is Hebrew. They would be taught that a *Shomer* helps the weak, is a nature lover, and keeps his thoughts and behavior pure. This is where Hebrew singing is being heard. Exultant laughter and joyfulness enliven the youngsters to play. Parties entice the camp. Here is where they print the branch's newspapers. In short – a whole world.

Over there, in the house wing in the yard, Hebrew lessons are conducted. A duty and condition for membership in the branch - diligence in studying the language is required. All commands and instructions are given in Hebrew. One day a week is dedicated entirely to Hebrew. Woe to the youth who would not study the language. His or her membership is at risk.

In the house cellar – the workshops. Armature woodworkers work with wood, shoemakers fix the shoes of the branch's members, bookbinders bind the books of the *Shomrim*, and *Shomrot* is sewing and embroidering. Working becomes the symbol of rich folklore and enriches the life of the Jewish youngster. The house on Valova Street is like a magnetic rock for Ternopil's youths. The branch is too small for hosting everybody. Additional apartments are to be rented. New areas of activities are to be initiated. The Dream of a youth who shapes his own life rose and became a reality in Ternopil.

The period is stormy. Some states are drowning, others are floating. Turbulent waves of events flood the city. A smell of pogrom is in the air. A self-defense force is being established. The graduates of the *Shomer* branch are the life and soul of the self-defense force. War fronts are created again, this time between the Poles and the Ukrainians. The armies conquer and then retreat. Hopes shutter and evaporate. Bitter disappointments strike Ternopil's Jews. The city that used to rule over the trade roads leading east was disconnected entirely from its sources of livelihood and now became a distant town.

The Ukrainians establish their own republic. Holobovitz's temporary government resides in Ternopil.

[Columns 241-242]

The Jewish youth enthusiastic about Balfour Declaration sympathized with the Ukrainians and their struggle for their political revival. Like them, we strive for independence. Now, the Ukrainians are battling the Poles. They promised national and cultural autonomy to the Jews. The Ukrainian republic would stretch out to include Odesa. Many of the "HaShomer HaTza'ir's" members enlist in the Ukrainian army and reach the shores of the Black Sea. In Odesa, they come closer to the shores of Eretz Israel.

Youths arrive daily at the "HaShomer" club from the neighboring towns. They go out east, on a way filled with obstacles. They first aim at Odesa, where the "HeKhalutz" has begun to operate. From there, in a tumultuous effort – to Eretz Israel. The first leader of the "HaShomer" branch in Ternopil is among the wanderers. The hardships of the road, the Typhus epidemic, and cruel battles wreak havoc on the brave group. Kenyuk dies somewhere in the Ukraine prairies. The members of the "HaShomer" branch bow their heads in memory of their leader.

Petliura's Kozaks appear and with them the news about the Proskurov Pogrom. Pogrom refugees arrive in the city. The "HaShomer" youth stand ready to help the needy. The Poles return to conquer the city – and take revenge on the Jews. They close and seal the club of the "HaShomer" on Valova Street. They confiscate the equipment and property. At night, however, the branch members break into the club through the windows. They transfer the library and the workshop equipment to hideouts in the attics of Jewish homes. "HaShomer HaTza'ir" branch goes underground. The activity is more romantic now. Small groups gather here and there in the women's section of the synagogue, river bank, attics, and remote communities near the city's "New Park". The youth is fascinated by the danger and adventure. The movement ember is preserved that way. The *Shomer'ic* loyalty is forged and hardened. The young ones become counselors, and the graduates prepare for Aliya.

1920 – 1921. Among the first going are Khana Biberstein, Yetka Yampoler, Schweig, Zilber, Berger, Pechnik and more. They are considered heroes by all. The echoes of the battle in Tel Khai arrive in the city. Eretz Israel becomes close to our hearts - perceptible. It excites the soul of the youth, magical and alluring. So much so that many among the members do not appreciate the cruel truth: they must harness enormous power to transfer from the reality of the Ternopil diaspora to the pioneering way of life in Eretz Israel. Desertion tendencies are rising among the first group of pioneers. Some boys return to Ternopil, hopeless and bitter. They bury their looks in the ground when they encounter other members. The lesson is fetid and shameful. Indeed, the big prosaic reality cannot be conquered by casual romantic adventure. The pioneer must be trained to withstand the test.

The" HaShomer" branch continues its activity. It comes out from the underground again and is housed now in the street named after Baron Hirsch. This is also a house with a big yard adjacent to a huge wood warehouse, a sustenance area for the joyful "HaShomer" community. The branch isolates itself, more and more, from the outside world and its influences. It is like a zealots' sect, that opposes the street with its manners and charms. That street leads to a career, emptiness, assimilation, and defilement of the Zionist idea.

In the branch, the Hebrew language and poetry are being revived. That is a result of the self-education of the youth. The goal is to forge a character and knowledge of the nation and its homeland. The Shomrim collects fables and folklore stories and participates in the Simkhat Torah's dances at the kloiz of the Husiyatin Hassidim. In the old cemetery, you can find them sitting around the graves of the city's Jewish greats, Rabbi Nakhman Kromkhel and Yosef Perl, and listening to chapters of the national history. That is how the Jewish youth absorbs the roots of Jewish Ternopil to take it with them for the rest of their lives.

Over there, in the street named after Baron Hirsch, the flame is kept alive. These are the last days of the Third Aliya. Some high school students abandon their studies and acquire a profession on the road that leads them to Eretz Israel. This is the place to mention some of these young people: Tzvi Shitzer, Biller, Morgenstern, Feingold, and *Shomeret* Lunka Blaustein, who surprised the branch members with her decision to learn carpentry. With that, she proves that the emancipation between the sexes is expressed by material things. Lunka Blaustein learned the entire profession and became an artisan in carpentry. However, she fell sick with a disease that ended her life.

The pace is fast: Study groups, lectures, flourishing scout folklore, rhythmic commands pacing a column of youths on trips. Time to play scouting games. In the summer and winter, at the entrance to Pshevolikha, bonfires are lighted. It is Hannukah. The youngsters light a strange menorah. It is extremely cold and the Shomrim are jumping from one leg to the other, singing "*Maoz Tzur Yeshuati…*"

That is how life is flowing - the workers work diligently in the club's rooms, and there are parties, choruses, and a drama club. Large and beautiful is the *Shomer'ic* world in the street named after Baron Hirsch.

The crises arrived fast…

1922. The branch remained without leadership. The leaders are leaving the city. A few make Aliya, and some leave to study in universities. The rest are just abandoning the *Shomer'ic* game upon the arrival of their adulthood.

* * *

[Columns 243-244]

Is it possible to extinguish the incredible flame in the heart of the youth? In 1923, a small group of 16-17 old youth rise and take it upon themselves to revive the *Shomer* branch.

And the branch is revived. A unique camp gathers around the branch's flag. The fifteen-year-old youths counsel the twelve- and thirteen-years old youngsters. The self-education enthusiasm of the youths who carry a vision in their heart produces miracles. However, the branch experiences a turning point. The counselors who reach the critical age (18-19) concluded that there is no sense in education, particularly Zionist education, without the principle of self-fulfillment. There is also no completeness in a *Shomer'ic* education of a person without leading the youngster to a life conducted according to a moral value of equality, cooperation, and mutual aid. The *Shomer'ic* group, where every member is a brother to others, serves as the first step toward an Aliya to Eretz Israel, and life in a kibbutz. The education slogan is: "from a *Shome'ic* group in the diaspora to a guard of the homeland in a kibbutz" That change, which now generates a revolution in the Ternopil's branch, resulted from the influence of the pioneers of the *Shomer'ic* Aliya, who founded kibbutzim, and brought their life examples back to the diaspora, as an instruction for the future generations of "HaShomer HaTza'ir". The affiliation with the national union, managed by the leadership in Lviv, also strengthened the branch in Ternopil.

Slowly, the *Shomer'ic* cell in Ternopil has established an exemplary branch. Its beginning was in a small room in Memritz alleys and then continued through the hall in the market square and the spacious ground floor in Isenberg's house on Lvovska Street, near the old synagogue. The branch became a center radiating influence over the Jewish youths in the provincial towns. The members of the local leadership go out and establish *Shomer'ic* branches in Terebovlia [Trembovla], Mikulintsy, Pidvolochysk [Podvolochiska], and Zboriv. District leadership is formed in the city. The youths publish newspapers and go to meetings, mutual visits, and mutual trips. In the summertime, The Ternopil branch, in collaboration with the district's cells, organizes a *Shomer'ic* summer colony in the heart of the forests. Life is lively and full of interest. The Shomrim excelled in activities benefiting the Zionist funds. The annual branch balls are held in the theater hall of "Bertztvo Mishtzenskia". They become worthy events because of the Hebraic - Zionist character (We should mention the play "Masada") and due to their artistic and scouting nature. The branch's graduates, who join the ranks of "HeKhalutz", participate in managing the branch. They enrich the folklore of the pioneering youth there.

Every year, tens of Shomrim go out to Hakhshara. They learn agricultural tasks during the summer in the estates, working as seasonal groups. Some travel to the Carpathian Mountains. There, in the sawmills of Nadvorna, Tatariv [Tatrov], and Brosznów, they get used to hard physical labor and commune life, as an actual preparation for the kibbutz life in Eretz Israel…

* * *

1930. From now on the branch experiences a period of ebb and flow. The Aliya waves empty the branch of its counselors until new counselors rise from among the apprentices rise and take over.

That is how the history of the *Shomer* branch flows until the tragic end when the entire Jewish population tumbles down into the annihilation abyss of the Holocaust.

* * *

The history of the young generation is woven into the history of the *Shomer'ic* branch. From its early days at the end of the First World War, the branch served as a trusted sanctuary for youths who sought to escape the disgrace of degeneration and the shame of disintegration. The branch was a youthful inn with a healthy character, imbued with hope, opened for the redemption beats. The *Shomer'ic* branch was a school of life for hundreds of youths who sought to pave the road for their future.

"HaNoar HaTzioni" ["The Zionist Youth"]

by A. Dolin

Translated by Moshe Kutten

In 1929, the studying youth union "HaShakhar" ["The Dawn"], experienced ideological turbulence and was facing a turning point. The opinion that the movement should move from only educational work to activities of fulfillment won. As a result, it was decided to contact similar Zionist organizations of the General Zionists in Galitsia and establish a unified Zionist movement.

Representatives of all the General Zionists who advocated the Zionist ideology gathered in the same year in Lviv. Representatives from Lviv, Przemysl [Pshemishel], Rohatyn, Sambir [Sambor], and Ternopil participated. The leader of the Hebrew Youth Union represented Krakow. Munio Migden, a talented speaker, who described the "HaShakhar" sanctified activity,

[Columns 245-246]

and the last chairman of "HaShakhar", Aharon Doliner (Dolin), represented Ternopil at that conference. The scouting-pioneering youth movement "HaNoar HaTzioni" was established at that conference. The leader of the new organization, Yitzkhak Steiger, visited Ternopil to clarify the ideology platform of the movement and the plans of action. He also selected a leadership team that consisted of the following members: Shlomo Gotlieb – head, Aharon Doliner – vice, and Max Mondschein – secretary.

The Conference of the "Zionist Youth" in Ternopil, 1932

Thanks to the vigorous action of the leadership team, who operated enthusiastically and dedicatedly, the member ranks increased. As early as the first summer vacation, ten members were sent to a counselors' colony in Bustryk, in the Tatra Mountains, and thirty young members to the summer colony in the Carpathian Mountains. Gotlieb and Doliner became members of the pioneering group who took part in founding Kibbutz A' of the "Zionist Youth". The members of that kibbutz now reside in the Kibbutzim Usha and Tel-Yitzkhak (named after Yitzkhak Steiger Z"L).

General Zionist pioneers were a new phenomenon in the Jewish street and generated favorable curiosity among the movement's supporters. However, its rivals projected a failure for it. These rivals were mistaken. Although, in general, pioneering was weak at that time, the pioneering club of the "Zionist Youth" expanded. A pioneering *Hakhshara* [Training for Aliya] was founded in Dolzhinka near Ternopil with an Eretz Israeli atmosphere that impressed all visitors. The Ternopil branch, located on the ground floor in Sobieski Square, was also a lively place. Eretz Israeli songs could be heard there until the late hours of the night.

In the meantime, the "Zionist Youth" movement expanded and grew, and its local organizations were founded in many countries throughout the diaspora. The central leadership, whose activities greatly expanded, required people. They found them from among the movement activists in Ternopil. Shlomo Gotlieb, who headed the "HeKhalutz" made Aliya. He returned a year later as an emissary and was elected as a representative for two of the Zionist conferences. Leizer Khoben organized the movement's summer camps. Avraham Overman, who possessed outstanding leadership skills, became one of the movement leaders. Max Mondschein, a skillful organizer and speaker, dedicated all his energy and enthusiasm to the movement until his bitter end. Moshe Tarif was appointed the editor of the international movement newspaper, "HaNoar HaTzioni", which appeared in Warsaw.

The Ternopil branch continued its activities, and many members, who dedicatedly managed the day-to-day work, stood out. Among them: were Moshe Fuchs Helrikh, the head of the branch and his vices, Petrushka, Moshe Kenner, Yosef Biller, Dvora Spindel, and many who did not make Aliya: Gusta Tarif, Selka Wahler, Ya'akov Nives, Moshe Ingler, Max Mondschein, Tonka Parnas, and Israel Altshiller. The latter was the educator of all "Zionist Youth" layers. He was dedicated to the movement in his heart and soul and worked for it for many years. Another member, the vigorous Tonka Parnas, died in the forests as a partisan. Many other dear members dedicated their energy to the Ternopil branch. Most of the branch members made Aliya, and some were from among the founders and builders of Kibbutzim Usha and Tel-Yitzkhak.

[The following section was moved from the end of the article for consistency]. After laying down the foundations of the Ternopil branch, the organization of another twenty other branches in the provincial towns had begun. The following members headed the activities in the Ternopil district in separate periods: D. Khoben, A. Doliner, M. Mondschein, Y. Altshiller, Y. Nives, Tonka Parnas, Klara London, and Ya'akov Winterfeld.

The educational work in the "Zionist Youth's" branches was conducted in three layers. The scouting layer received special attention. It was headed by prominent members such as Pesakh Weizer, Ze'ev Shikler, Y. Nives, and Y. Merbakh. Public shows than included artistic appearances were held under the name "Eretz Israeli Evenings".

These appearances were prepared by Khaim Biller, Munek Spitzer (aka officer Golan), A Soldner, Tarif, Veska Ballet, and others. These evenings attained an outstanding artistic level and attracted crowds. The accomplishments of the crafts club were also exhibited in various exhibitions and amazed the visitors.

The branch disbanded under the decree by the authorities upon the entrance of the Russians to Ternopil in 1939. The last leader of the branch, Kuba Nives, was jailed but was released later on. The youths gathered and decided to find their way to Eretz Israel, in all ways possible. Their fate was bitter. They were caught at the Romanian border, and the heads of the group, Klara Spitzer and Munio Hirschhorn, were arrested and sentenced to ten years in prison. Upon the eruption of the war between Russia and Germany, they were released. Hirschhorn died as a martyr in the battle of Warsaw. Klara Shpitzer made Aliya to Eretz Israel.

Ze'ev Shikler and Henka Fuchs, in collaboration with branch members Moshe Kurtz and Brunek Libergal, established a living memorial to the movement. Leaning on their vast experience in the Ternopil's branch, they established the farm, "HaNoar HaTzioni", in the Jerusalem mountains.

[Columns 247-248]

"Gordonia"
by Arye Avnon-Bronstein
Translated by Moshe Kutten

"Gordonia" [youth movement], was formed just a short time after the "Hit'akhdut". In the beginning, it was a youth union considered ancillary to the party. However, over time, it became independent but always remembered its source.

The appearance of "Gordonia" in the Zionist arena was timely. The single youth movement in the 1920s, "HaShomer HaTza'ir" was almost completely closed to youths who did not study. Without another choice, the youths turned to Communism or were apathetic toward Zionism." Gordonia" turned to the working youth, the children of the workers, and the poor. It organized and educated a generation of people who made Aliya to Eretz Israel. The unreserved and undisputed principle of self-fulfillment in a commune in Eretz Israel yielded a clear and consistent educational program that fitted the requirements of Zionism and the state of the youth in the diaspora.

"The thirteen attributes" of Gordonia were decided upon at the international conference of "Gordonia" in Gdansk [Danzig]. They became the basis for the entire educational program of the movement.

The activity of "Gordonia" in Ternopil was crowned with success. A large number of youths found a social, ideological, and educational atmosphere that matched their needs and views. In addition to the ongoing educational activity throughout the year, we organized district-wide summer camps, and the graduates participated in the state-wide camps. The camps' activities were practical and introduced a new breath of fresh air into the branch's ranks. "Gordonia's" members were active in all areas of the Zionist activities appropriate for their age, such as "KKL_JNF", "Ezra" ["Assistance"] (a fund that supports the activities of "HeKhalutz"), and more. Since our members came from poor homes, we had difficulties

maintaining the club (on 3 Doli Street). The self-sacrifice and volunteering spirit among the youths became apparent. Every member brought firewood or pennies, from his or her meager salary, for rent or maintenance of the club. Modesty, simplicity, and pioneering appearance were the attributes of "Gordonia" members. It was a pioneering movement of the common people, by its way of life, educational methods, and views. It absorbed all of that from its source – the workers' movement in Eretz

Israel and its philosopher A. D. Gordon. The aspiration to form a new life regime based on a commune in Eretz Israel, and the educational commandment of self-fulfillment were the principles of the movement education.

The Committee of "Ezra" in Ternopil, 1929

[Columns 249-250]

A small group of members formed the branch in our city. Among them, we should note the first and the last branch activists and counselors: The teacher Gusta Steinberg, Sara Tzoref, Leah Druk, Nushka Berger, Ze'ev Sternberg, Miriam Slepter, Dov Gruberg, Azriel Goliger, Avraham Finkelstein, Arye Bronstein, and other activists dedicated to the movement and its way, with all of their hearts.

Many of the "Gordonia" members were made Aliya to Eretz Israel. They were scattered among various settlements such as Khulda, Degania, Kiryat Anavim, Kvutzat Shiller [Gan Shlomo], Ayanot, Afikim, and more.

Dear members of Gordonia of Ternopil died or fell during the independence War and even before that: Arye Druk died in the Arab attack on Kfar HaKhoresh, Sara Tzoref died from malignant disease in Kfar Vitkin, Yehudit Marder died from a severe malignant disease

in Khulda, Shalom Diner-Putashnik died in Jerusalem battles during the operation to save the children of Kiryat Anavim.

They were all loyal members whose thread of life was cut before its time and did not live to witness the establishment of the State of Israel, their life goal. May their memory be blessed. May their soul be bound up in the bond of the life of the nation.

The Leadership of "Gordonia" in Ternopil, 1934

"Histradrut HaNoar HaLomed"
["The Union of Young Students"] –"HaShakhar" ["The Dawn"]

by A. Dolin

Translated by Moshe Kutten

In 1922, an operational hiatus of the scouting union "HaShomer" occurred. Replacing it, the studying youth, headed by Mordekhai Hammer, and Pushko Kopler, organized studying in clubs of self-education. When the members matured, they unified with the studying youth union "HaShakhar". Based on the bylaws of the porters' organization "HaShakhar" (located now in the archive of the Zionist Union).

During the first period, the members of "HaShakhar" hold gatherings in the large hall of "Bar Kokhba". Later on, they moved to their own apartment in the market.

Zalman Marzend was elected to be the first chairman of the union. He was then a student in the seventh grade of high school, energetic, and a skilled speaker and lecturer. Energetic and enthusiastic members, such as Munio Migden, Ludvik Akeslbirt, Munio Gotlieb, Selka Gottfried, Moshe Fiol, Leizer Khoben, and others, gathered around him.

Over time, the activists circle expanded and included the following: Brothers Krigesfeld, Israel Altshiller, Milek Amernet, Lebek Gottlieb, Hela Zuberman, David Weinstein, Beko Biller, Rozka Loifer, Zekharia Merlin, Tzipka Yakov, Netka Krisberg, Ya'akov Winterfeld, Max Mondshein, Mania Lekher, Libek Wertzber, Kuba Fischer, Shlomo Shikler, and Aharon Doliner.

All the weighty problems on the top of the agenda of the Zionist world were debated upon at the stormy union's gatherings. Not once did these gatherings end with the departure of single members or even whole groups who disliked the views of the majority.

The first to leave the union were former members of "HaShomer" ["The Guard"] to form the "HaShomer HaTza'ir" ["The Young Guard"] youth movement. A year later, another spilt took place. At that time, a large group departed and established the "Kadima" ["Forward"] union.

Although these divisions weakened the union,

[Columns 251-252]

they also resulted in competition and envy, which caused an increase in the actual and ideological activity in all areas (e.g., collection of contributions for the various funds).

When the members of "HaShakhar" matured, they established the graduate section. Some joined "Bar Kokhba", "Maccabiah", or "Hertzelia" organizations without relinquishing their memberships in "HaShakhar".

A Group of "HaShakhar" Members 1926/7

From right to left – sitting: Avraham Neuman, Jacob Teikhman, Aba Schweig
In the center: From right to left – sitting: M. Balmer, M. Herzog, M. Herlikh, M. Migden, D. Weinstein, A. Doliner, L. Ekselbirt
Standing: M. Tauber, I. Gruen, Z. Merlin, Rosenman, K. Fischer, B. Lande. I Fuchs, L. Gotlieb, L. Landstein, L. Waritschewer

The period of existence of "HaShakhar" was not that long. It disintegrated in 1929, and most members joined the "HaNoar HaTzioni" movement (see column 243). However, during its short period of existence, it left its mark on the youth movements in the city. Also, many members of the Zionist movement, with all of its branches and affiliations, came out of its rank.

"Histadrut HaNoar HaLomed"
["The Union of Young Students"]
"Kadima" ["Forward"]

by Khaim Harari (Goldberg)

Translated by Moshe Kutten

Those were the days of agitation and ideological struggle among the studying youth in our city. The time – the end of the 1920s and the beginning of the 1930s.

Histadradrut HaNoar HaLomed "HaShakhar" grew, branched, and encompassed hundreds of youths without a Zionist affiliation. Clubs for learning the history of our nation and Zionism were organized. For those who wanted to join our union, we arranged tests in these subjects.

In the union itself, committees for the national funds were established, and balls, parties, and lectures were held. It seemed at the time that the organization's life would proceed calmly. However, the stormy debates about the essence, and the way to construct Zionism, engulfed the public, penetrated our union and it raised the temperature. So much so that the need to open windows to the winds blowing in the Jewish street was recognized.

When the debates began within our union, a group of members showed affection for the labor movement in Eretz Israel and the "Hit'akhdut" party. Among the first members in that group, the following members should be mentioned: Shmuel Shteirman, Azriel Goliger, Dov Gruberg, Avraham Finkelstein, Ya'akov Reber, and more, whose names I do not remembers, those who were fortunate and live among us today, and those whose fate did not allow them to live in the revived homeland, such as Marzend, Izenberg and others who died, and in their death, they commanded us life.

At first, our members demanded to remain unaffiliated. Others joined the "General Zionists" party. However, with time, when we realized that we would not be able to keep

[Columns 253-254]

when we realized that we could not keep a non-affiliated status within "HaShakhar", we decided to establish a new organization - the non-affiliated Histadrut HaNoar HaLomed – "Kadima". I would not be mistaken to say now, many years after the split, that our intentions were pragmatic and that there were truly no hidden intentions at first about an affiliation. However, the time has done its thing. We later arrived at the conclusion that at times like those, non-affiliation was not possible and that "Kadima" too, must define itself clearly as an affiliated Union of Young Students.

Some of us who were members of the "Hit'akhdut" party joined "Gordonia" and "HeKhalutz". We decided to abandon our studies and fulfill our aspiration in Eretz Israel, among the family of workers in the city or in an Israeli village. Those who fought to give "Kadima" a character of political affiliation had to arrive also at another conclusion – joining one of the fulfilling pioneering movements.

With pride and satisfaction, we should note that there isn't a place in Eretz Israel where pioneers from Ternopil settled, where there are no former "Kadima" members. They were and are active today in the kibbutzim and the cities during days of self-defense and struggle and days of peace and building. It is not coincident that the founders of "Kadima" and its first counselors settled in Khulda, Ramat David, and Degania. They participated in guarding and defense efforts. The same principles that guided the founders of "Kadima", found their realization in Eretz Israel. Those who were not satisfied with that ideology left and went to where ever they went – some to other Zionist unions and others outside of the Zionist ideology.

We did not consider "Kadima" as a target on its own. We saw it as a conduit through which we could instill the working Zionism ideology to those who were not ready to realize that ideology at that time. We wanted to make these youth into an element that appreciates labor and into a pioneering factor that would serve as an example by their own doing.

We remember affectionally those discussions and debates within the walls of "Kadima" on Austrokeskigo Street about the "Religion of Labor", of A. D. Gordon and the value of individual fulfillment. The results of those debates gave us the best counselors and activists for the sister movements of "Gordonia" and the "Hit'akhdut", the sister party of "HaPoel HaTza'ir" ["The Young Worker"].

When we raise the memory of the Ternopil community along with all of its unions and associations, we should not forget to mention "Kadima", which contributed so much to instilling the pioneering Zionist spirit among the studying youth in the city.

[Columns 255-256] [Blank]

[Columns 257-258]

The Religious Life

[Columns 259-260]   [Blank]

[Columns 261-262]

The Rabbis of Ternopil

The Rabbis of Ternopil During the 18th and 19th Centuries[1]

by Hillel Zeidman

Translated by Moshe Kutten

Rabbi Yehoshua-Heschel BABa"D, the author of "Sefer Yehoshua"

Among all the rabbis of Ternopil, we have details only about the last eight remained, starting with Rabbi Yehoshua Heshel BABa"D , the author of "Sefer Yehoshua".

Rabbi Yehoshua Heshel BABa"D served as a rabbi in Ternopil toward the end of the 18th century and the beginning of the 19th century. He was a descendant of some of the great rabbis in Poland - the author of "Meginei Shlomo", MIRSh"A [Rabbi Yehoshua Hechel], and ReM"A – (R' Moshe Isserles).

He served at first as a rabbi in Lublin, but because of his inclination toward Hassidism, he got involved in a dispute with the "*Mitnagdim*" ["people who oppose Hassidism]. They snitched on him to the authorities that he was not an Austrian subject, therefore, was not allowed to reside in Lublin. He was then forced to leave the city. He was later accepted as a rabbi in Ternopil. He lived a long life in that position and died there at the old age of 100.

His book "Sefer Yehoshua" was admired by the rabbinical world of the 19th century and was considered and cited by the "*Poskim*" as a reliable source.

Rabbi Shlomo Yehuda Leib Rapoport (SHI"R)

Rabbi Shlomo Yehuda-Leib Rapoport, known by his pen name, SHI"R [the word shir means a song in Hebrew], served as the rabbi in Ternopil for a short period, from 1837 – 1840. He was the son-in-law of the author of "Ktzot HaKhoshen" ["The Ends of the Breastplate"], about "Shulkhan Arukh – Khoshen Mishpat". He was nominated as the rabbi under the lobbying of Yosef Perl, the Enlightened Movement's pioneer in Galitsia.

SHI"R was born in 1790 and was raised in Jewish tradition. He later studied Mishnah and *Poskim* and also secular sciences. He was the first rabbi who used historic aspects in critiquing Talmudic and Rabbinical literature. He was, therefore, considered one of the founders of "Khokhmat Israel" ["The Science of Judaism" – an intellectual movement that examined critical religious issues using scientific tools].

Among his books and research papers, we can find the research of Sa'adia Gaon, Nathan Ben Yekhiel, Hai Gaon, Eliezer Kalir, Khanan Ben Khushiel, and Nisim Bar Ya'akov. Six of his biographies were published in the journal "Bikurei HaItim"

["First Fruits"] (1821 – 1831). He corresponded with [The Italian Jewish scholar] Shmuel-David Luzzatto (SHaDa" L). These letters were published in the book "Igrot Yehuda". He also published poems.

He had to leave Ternopil due to disputes between the enlightened and the orthodox. He moved to Prague, where he served as rabbi for 27 years, from 1840 until he died in 1867[2].

Rabbi Yosef BABa"D , Author of "Minkhat Khinukh" ["Offering of Education"]

Rabbi Yosef BABa"D is the most famous among Ternopil's rabbis thanks to his book "Minkhat Khinukh". The book was written as a commentary on the book "Sefer HaKhinukh" ["The Book of Education"], authored by one of Spain's greatest scholars, R' Aharon Levi of Barcelona. In fact, the book "Minkhat Khinukh" is more than a commentary. The rabbi from Ternopil used the book "Sefer Khinukh" only as a basis for his huge Talmudic structure and his innovations and explanations of all 613 commandments. "Minkhat Khinukh" is an original creation on its own, however, the rabbi from Ternopil demonstrated uniformity of thinking with the scholar from Barcelona. "Sefer HaKinukh" and its commentary were adopted by all yeshivas.

"Minkhat Khinukh" was published in several editions since it was first published in Lviv in 5629 [1869/70]. The book was published in New York in a magnificent scientific edition as late as 5712 [1951/2] by the publisher – the brothers Shulsinger.

Rabbi Yosef BABa"D wrote the book, not for publication but to teach his son. He actually wrote it in the introduction: " to encourage my young son and his friends, to study the commandments every week…".

[Columns 263-264]

The book excels in its ease of language and clarity of its style. The atmosphere of supreme morality, logic, and cleverness that surround it made the book popular. The "commentary" by the rabbi from Ternopil, which surpassed "Sefer HaKhinukh" in depth and sweep of visionary scholarly, made [the combination] "Sefer HaKhinukh" and "Minkhat Khinukh", a helpful textbook set to those who study. So much so that the greatest of Lithuania's rabbis. So much so that the greatest of Lithuania's rabbis, Rabbi Soloveichik, ZTZ"L of Brisk [Brest] said about it: "I do not understand how is it possible to explore a Mishna subject in the Gemarah without first studying the issue in "Minkhat Khinukh".

Today, students in all the Yeshiva's in Israel and America, and in every place where Mishnah and *Poskim* are being learned, study the book. It is also a good blend of the Sephardic and Ashkenazi methods of learning.

R' Yosef BABa"D was born in 5550 [1800] to his father, Rabbi Moshe BABa"D of Przeworsk, Galitsia. He was the grandson of Rabbi Yehoshua Heschel BABA"D , the rabbi of Ternopil and author of "Sefer Yehoshua". R' Yosef BABa"D was first the rabbi of Oskov and Zbarizh, He was accepted as a rabbi of Ternopil during the "cultural conflict" between the enlightened people headed by Yosef Perl, and the orthodox people. His predecessor was Rabbi Shlomo Yehuda-Leib Rapoport (SHI"R"). He served as a rabbi until he died on 24 Elul 5634 (1874).

Rabbi Shimon BABa"D and Rabbi Yehoshua-Heschel BABa"D

After the death of R' Yosef BABa"D in 5634, his son R' Shimon BABa"D took his position. He served as the city's rabbi until 1909. He was a distinguished scholar and published emendations to his father's book, "Minkhat Khinukh", which left a big impression.

After him, his son, R' Yehoshua Heschel BABa"D , was appointed. He served in that position until he died in 1919. He was gifted with noble virtues, kindheartedness, love of Jewishness, and hospitality.

Rabbi Menakhem-Munish BABa"D , the author of "Khavatzelet HaSharon" [The Rose of Sharon]

R' Menakhem-Munish BABa"D , a relative of R' Yehoshua Heschel BABa"D , was the second rabbi of Ternopil while the latter was still alive. Before that, he served as a rabbi in Yavoriv near Lviv.

He was an extraordinary figure – a genius in the Torah, studious, and exceedingly knowledgeable. He possessed noble virtues. He was endlessly diligent in his studies. He taught the Torah and educated many students.

After the First World War, he began regular teaching from 4:30 am to 9:30 am every day and even during Shabbat and holidays. He taught the Mishnah. However, in the course of teaching Gemarah, he clarified *Sdarot* and *Shitot* ["methods and series] in *Poskim Rishonim* and *Akhronim* [first and last], utilizing logic and extraordinary proficiency. His teaching method was different from the custom in Galitsia and Poland. It was more similar to the methods used in the yeshivas of Lithuania, meaning: Deeper delve into the spiritual, straightforwardness, common sense, deep analysis of the intentions of the sages, and a wide review that encompasses all the sides of the problem under discussion, and the assumption related to it.

Rabbi M. M. BABa"D

The essence of R' Menakhem-Munish BABa"D's life was learning the Torah. That's where all of his aspirations and experiences were. He was not interested in any affairs outside of the Torah world. He hated covetousness and, therefore, he served in the rabbinical court unwillingly since it took him away from his learning. He distributed monies from his salary to the poor.

He was among the first who responded to Halakha-related questions. His responses were gathered in the book "Khavatzelet HaSharon", which was received favorably by the learners. His unique character is highlighted in that book: His rulings are clear and to the point. His responses are coherent, without any attempt to boast about his proficiency. His exalted virtues are revealed incidentally and on their own from his humility. He was humble by nature, far from any trace of aggression. He never demanded to accept his view due to his authority as a *Posek* [A legal scholar who determines the position of Halakha] but made an effort to clarify the problem at hand so that the conclusion would be self-evident.

The entire family of Menakhem-Munish consisted of rabbis. His five brothers were all rabbis: Rabbi R' Yitzkhak BABa"D Head of Rabbinical College [ABD] of Tartakiv, Rabbi R' Leibush, ABD Pidvolochysk, Rabbi R' Shalom, ABD Variazh, Rabbi Yosef, a rabbinical judge in Mykulyntsi, and Rabbi R' Nakhman, ABD Halych. His sister Ratzi was the wife of the rabbi from Strusiv. His four sons-in-law, who married his daughters, were rabbis: Rabbi Elimelekh Frenkel-Teomim, who superseded him in Yavoriv, Rabbi Aharon Sheneh [?] from Tluste, Rabbi Feivel BABa"D, the rabbi in Bodaniv [Bodzanov], and Rabbi Yehoshua BABa"D the nephew of R' Leibush, who took the place of his father-in-law as a rabbi in Ternopil, after his death.

Rabbi Munish BABa"D died at seventy-two in Sivan, 1938, in the retreat town Tatariv[?] [Tetrov] near Dolyna, after a long illness. His entire family – his brother, sisters, and sons-in-law rabbis perished in the Holocaust during 1942 -1943.

Rabbi Menakhem-Munish, one of the Last *Poskim* was a prominent figure in Galitsia's Jewry. He was considered on the same level as the famous rabbis, Rabbi Meir Aran from Buchach and Rabbi Menakhem-Mendel Shteinberg from Brody, both of whom were crowned with the title of *Gaon*.

[Columns 265-266]

Rabbi Ya'akov Shalita

Rabbi Ya'akov Shalita served as a rabbi in Ternopil between the two World Wars (1919-1942). He served together with Rabbi Menakhem-Munish BABa"D, who was appointed when Rabbi Heschel was still alive and with his approval.

In a city as big as Ternopil, there was certainly room for two rabbis, and there was sufficient work for both of them, together and separately. That was the case when Rabbi Yehoshua-Heschel BABa"D served together with Rabbi Menakhem-Munish BABa"D. However, in 1921, the Polish government issued a rule that only one rabbi may serve as the head rabbi of the community. That's where a problem and the controversy started – who is the head rabbi? Rabbi Shalita was younger than Rabbi BABa"D but he could claim that he had the "right" for the rabbinical position by being the son-in-law of the late Rabbi Yehoshua-Heschel BABa"D and that he was awarded the position as a dowry and by inheritance. On the other side, Rabbi Menakhem-Munish BABa"D was much older in age and service and was known to be a Torah great.

Each rabbi had a group of supporters within the population and the community council. The quarrel also affected the election to the community's institutions[3], at least among the Haredi Jews. It lasted until the death of Rabbi BABa"D.

The Rabbi from Husiatyn at the railway station of Ternopil, 1936

Rabbi Yehoshua-Heschel BABa"D was then appointed as a replacement and the community resigned itself to the service of two equal-level rabbis, despite the Polish law. Both rabbis were experienced, possessed skills and manners, and had good virtues and wisdom.

Rabbi Ya'akov Shalita was the son of Rabbi Ben-Tzion Shalita, the rabbi of the community of Zboriv (located between Zolochiv and Ternopil). He was a learner and proficient in the Mishnah and *Poskim*, gifted with sharp apprehension and wise in the ways of the world. Husiatyn Hasidim were among his supporters. Firstly because of the loyalty to the rabbi of Husiatyn Hassidim and his dynasty, and secondly, because Rabbi BABa"D was a Belz Hassid, while Rabbi Shalita was a supporter of the Rabbi from Husiatyn.

Rabbi Shalita perished with his family in 1942 while showing supreme heroism. His only son, Shimon, was killed by the Ukrainians in 1941.

Rabbi Yehoshua Heschel BABa"D

Rabbi Yehoshua-Heschel BABaâ€□D, the son-in-law and nephew of Rabbi Menakhem-Munish BABa"D, and the son of Leibush BABa"D from Pidvolochysk [Podvolichysk], took his father-in-law position in 1938. He was a great scholar, educated, thinker and modest, social, and gifted with virtues. His wife was also educated. He perished with the Jewish community in 1942, along with his entire family. His parents had ten sons and daughters, and nobody survived.

Rabbi Dr. Shmuel A. Taubles

Rabbi Dr. Shmuel A. Taubles was the [last] preacher in the "Temple" established by Yosef Perl, where the enlightened people and the assimilators prayed. He was also a teacher of religion in the city's high schools (the first and the third gymnasium). He died in 1940 in Terebovlia [Trembowla] near Ternopil.

Author's Notes:

a. See the article by Dr. N. M. Gelber about Ternopil Rabbis during the 18th and 19th centuries (column 30).
b. Ibid column 75 – a detailed description of the feud around SHI"R.
c. See the article by Dr. Tzvi Parnas, column 192, chapter D.

[Columns 267-268]

R' Ya'akov Kapil Landman ZTz"L

by Rabbi Zusia Landman *Av Beit Din* Bucharest

Translated by Moshe Kutten

The famous *Tzadik* Rabbi R' Ya'akov Kapil Landman ZTz"L was born in the city of Strilyshcha [Strelisk] in 5600 [1839 / 1840], to his father, *Gaon Tzadik* R' Tzvi Hirsch Landman. The latter was Av Beit Din [Head of the rabbinical court – ABD] of the holy community of Strilyshcha, and the son-in-law of the holy Rabbi R' Uri of Strilyshcha, known as "The Seraf of Strelisk".

Rabbi Ya'akov Kapil Landman

He studied the Torah diligently from his youth and was Torah great. He was certified to teach by the *Gaons Tzadikim* Rabbi Yosef BABa" D ZTz"L from Ternopil, the author of "Minkhat Khinukh", and Rabbi Tzvi Orenstein ZTz"L of Lviv.

In 5620 [1859 / 1860], he settled in Ternopil, where he acquired a name for himself. Many flocked to see him because of his teaching, fear of G-d, and Hassidism.

He authored valuable books:

    a.   "Heshiv Lev Avot" ["He Shall Turn the Hearts of the Parents"]. The *Gaon* author of "Minkhat Khinukh" wrote in his approbation to the book wrote the following:

    "The Tora great, ruler of the Halakhah, the famous Tzadik R' Ya'akov Kapil Shalita from Ternopil, knowns to the Hassidim masses as a shepherd of the Jews in his wisdom and knowledge. Say thanks to him, as he is respected by all and filled with a blessing by G-d, and respected with his pure and delightful phrases, by the way of *Deras*h [interpretation], and the occult. Anybody who would study the book would find everything they need since it is filled with delights".

    b.   "Sefer Ya'akov" ["The Book of Ya'akov"] is about Psalms, written in the way of *Derash* [exposition or interpretation], and the Kabbalah [study of the occult].

    c.   "Beit Ya'akov" ["the House of Ya'akov'] about the system of the 22 letters in the way of the Kabbalah. The book remained in a written format and it was never printed.

Rabbi Ya'akov Kapil Landman was known as a "*Ne'im Zmirot*" ["pleasant singer"], who attracted listeners with his prayers, songs, and melodies. His voice was pleasant and powerful. When he prayed in public, people from different synagogues and Batei Midrash of Ternopil came to enjoy the melodies.

He died in 5679 [1919]. May his memory be blessed.

Ternopil – A City of "Minkhat Khinukh"
["Offering of Education"]

by Dr. S. B. Feldman

Translated by Moshe Kutten

Ternopil attained merit when the classic Talmudic book "Minkhat Khinukh" was published. No other book like it was ever published, before or after its publication.

The uniqueness of the book is in its universal character. It encompasses the whole sea of the Talmud in the true sense of the word. Whoever dealt with the Talmudic literature knows that it is more appropriate to talk about the ocean of the Talmud than a sea of the Talmud. Authoring a book that encompasses such an ocean is truly a miracle in the world of books.

The "Minkhat Khinukh" book is like a commentary on the book "Khinukh" of R' Aharon HaLevi. It contains all 613 commandments according to the order they appear in the Torah. The R"Y [Rabbi Yosef] BABa"D's commentary is spread over three hundred and seventy pages (seven hundred a forty folio pages). The text of the "Khinukh" occupies one-thousandth of that area. "Minkhat Khinukh" deals with only short comments of the "Khinukh" book.

R"Y BABa"D intended mainly to provide commentary on all the 613 commandments and not a summary of all the Halakha rulings with their details and pedantries. Those details can easily be found in the books of the RAMB"M, [Karo's] "Shulkhan Arukh", and their commentators. Indeed, R"Y did not wish to repeat things known to people who deal with the Halakha. In his commentary, he expands on the wide and branched ambiguity of the Torah commandments.

The ambiguities are of different types.

First, he provides a precise and succinct description of the Halakha principles for every commandment. Then he brings up cases controversial among the *Poskim* themselves and provides a guide for resolving them based on *[Poskim] Rishonim* [First] *and Akhronim* [Last]. In the end, he raises problems that he is considered an expert in uncovering. These are problems not discussed by any author. He attaches practical guidance, wonderous in its clarity. With that, he demonstrates unprecedented sharpness and proficiency.

[Columns 269-270]

Incidental to presenting the principles and proposing the problems, there are also surprising comments accompanying each commandment, predicaments that are really astonishing. R"Y ends his presentation on some issues with the acronym "ra"s" (required additional study). More than 80 years later, none of the predicaments have been resolved.

The style follows the one used in other Talmudic books of the latest generations. However, the book transcends in its concise presentation. It is easily readable by whoever is used to reading *Pilpul* [casuistry] books. The clear and concise delivery, its excellent order, and original and surprising comments attract the reader.

For yeshiva students and all the other Torah learners who wish to delve into Talmudic problems, the book's educational value is enormous. The learner feels that is shown how to fathom a Talmudic enigma and is taught the correct way to approach its resolution.

The book was first published in Lviv in 5629 [1968/9] when the author was already old. If I am not mistaken, he was about eighty years old at that time. It is not known how much time the author devoted to writing the book but we know that it was the period when the rabbis and the learners were heavily engaged in *Pilpul* of "Contradictions" (called "*Peshtel*" in Yiddish). That was a method of an exaggerated sharp-wittedness, like a chain of connections, which cannot withstand the criticism of logical thinking. The R"Y BABa"D knows the art of *Pilpul* and sharpness, but he distances himself from exaggeration and sharp-wittedness. His *Pilpul* is fresh and based on common sense and only adds grace and magic to his writings.

Overall, the book provides a series of Talmudic essays as many as the number of the commandments. Whoever reads the whole book experiences the taste of the whole Torah. Readers and learners wonder how can a single book contain so much Talmudic knowledge.

It is well known that the Lithuanian Yeshivas boasted about their learning methods against those of *Pilpul*-based methods customary in Poland. Yet, not even a single book was ever published from the Lithuanian Yeshivas that could be compared to the "Minkhat Khinukh", in content, style, and logical structure of its essays. The fact is that high-level students read the book frequently, enjoy it, and make an effort to follow its Torah teachings.

It is logical to assume that the "Minkhat Khinukh" would continue to be the standard book guiding future generations. That is, as long as there are learners of the Halakha and people who judge according to the Halakha.

Rabbi Reuven Cohen Rapoport, one of the generation's scholars who served as a rabbinical judge and teacher of righteousness in Ternopil, handed the book to the publisher- Salat publishers in Lviv.

The following is written on the front of the book:

"The book is a wide commentary of the "Khinukh" book, using tremendous *Pilpul* and wonderous proficiency, a wonder of the truth of the Torah. It was authored by one of the distinguished, holy, and pure Gaons of our time, may his light shine.

"Published with the promotion and effort of Rabbi R' Reuven Cohen Rapoport".

The author's name was omitted in the original book, which was new. Only in the later editions published after his death, his name was mentioned.

R' Yoseli BABa"D the author of "Minkhat Khinukh", was known not only as a Talmudic genius but also as a great Tzadik. I can tell you two stories about him:

The first story, my father Z"L, R' Israel from Zboriv, told my brother, Yehoshua Redler-Feldman (R' Benyamin). Rabbi BABa"D had some differences of opinions about public matters with the community leaders (I do not have any details about these matters). When the community leaders threatened him (I do not have any details about these threats either), the author of "Minkhat Khinukh" told them: "There is no meaning to your threats. The little porridge that I eat here every day, I can eat in any Jewish city or town".

The second story is more personal: In the fall of 5678 [1917], I stayed several days in Ternopil. On that occasion, I entered the "Ohel" [mausoleum], where the grave of the R"Y BABa"D is located. I found the nice gravestone by the grave with a long inscription written on it. However, the stone was tilted to one side. When I asked why they don't fix the gravestone, I received an answer: "No Jew would dare to touch the stone for the fear that it would disturb the body of the Tzadik". The heads of the community and *Khevra Kadisha* [burial society] also avoided fixing the gravestone. So, the stone is tilted on the grave, which harbors such a prominent figure - one of a kind in his generation.

[Columns 271-272]

Haredi Jews in Ternopil

by Hillel Zeidman

Translated by Moshe Kutten

In memory of my father and teacher, Avraham Zeidman, my brother Moshe, a student in the yeshiva "Khakhmei Lublin" ["Lublin's Wise Men"], my sisters, Sara and Rakhil, teachers at the "Beit Ya'akov" school, my sister Rukhama and her husband, Moshe Blaustein, and my brother Anshil – Victim of the Holocaust, 5702 [1941/2] – 5704 [1942/3].

When I remember the Haredi Jews of Ternopil, a sharp pain fills my soul, and a glow that radiates from their faces lights my way among them. However, that is not the light at dawn, the sunlight at noon, or even not the golden light before sunset. It is the light emanating from the flame on the altar where they were sacrificed and vanished with no trace or gravestone. Filled with eternal yearnings, love of the Torah, and longing for the messiah, they are now covered by the darkness of death and the truth that the "glory of eternal of Israel will not fail" [Samuel I, 15:29]. However, they were annihilated and there are no more. Their graves were only erected within our souls. Let's raise their memories as they appear in front of our eyes.

When looking for a point of view to look at the victims etched in my memory, I return to the trip that I made with my father-teacher Z"L in the evening before Yom Kippur, from our home at Lelwela Street, near Tarnovskiego Street, to the Husiatyn Kloiz on Podolska Nizsza Street, closed to Lvovska Road, which crossed almost the entire city from east to west. I will describe that trip and record the people I met on my way.

On Lelwela Street, near the corner of Tarnovskiego, resided R' Shalom Podhortzer, who served, for a long time, as a member of the community council and was the vice leader of the community on behalf of the Haredi Jews. As we leave Lelwela Street onto Tarnovskiego Street, we find, on our right, the house of R' Moshe Rozner, a Haredi leader and one of the city's prominent figures. He was the vice president of the community council, vice chairman of "Agudat Israel", and the chairman of "Tif'eret HaDat" ["The Glory of Religion"]. He was the native of Bukovina, the son-in-law of R' Ya'akov Breitman, and the brother-in-law of Rabbi Meir Shapira, the famous rabbi of Lublin. His sons, R' Yehoshua and Dr. Mordekhai, were among the activists of "Agudat Israel". Dr. Mordekhai Rozner was a teacher in the seminary for religious teachers in Warsaw, on Gnesha[?] Street, and one of the editors of the Yiddish newspaper "The Yiddisher Tagblat". He was a relative of Professor Salo Baron from Columbia University, a native of Tarnov, Galitsia. R' Moshe Rozner was a scholar, a gentle, noble, and honest man, and so was his family, of whom nobody survived the Holocaust.

That is the place to dwell about the Breitman family, which was close to the Rozner family. It was one of the most prominent families in our city. R' Ya'akov Breitman had four sons-in-law, all scholars and respected people: R' Leibush Arak, a Torah great; Rabbi Meir Shapira, the Rabbi from Lublin and the head of the Yeshiva "Khakhmei Lublin" (1922 – 1926). The latter was also the representative of the Polish Sejm and one of the leaders of "Agudat Israel" in Poland; The aforementioned, R' Moshe Rozner, and R' B. Weksler. The sons of R' Ya'akov Breitman were Daniel, Fishel, and more. The Breitman family owned the estate of Zrobinitz near Zbarazh. The brother-in-law of R' Ya'akov Breitman was Yehudah Ber Zeidman, the owner of the Kamionka estate near Ternopil. His sons were R' Avraham, Shlomo, and R' Mordekhai. They owned a large home on Koscielna Street. The sons of R' Leibush Arak were all distinguished scholars. His sons - Shlomo and Avraham (who died in his youth), were both distinguished students of Rabbi M. M. BABa"D. They were all respected people of the Chortkiv Hasidim.

We continue our trip. At Ritna Street, we pass near the home of R' David Lvov, a distinguished scholar, noble-spirited and dignified man with pleasant manners, educated, and philanthropist, one of the special people in Galitsia. Everybody in our city treated him with reverence. He was one of the leaders of "Agudat Israel", a confidant of Rabbi M. A. BABa"D, member of the community council and municipal council. He had three sons and two daughters. His sons were: Yosef, Nathan, and Meir. His sons-in-law were R' Khaim Horwitz and Sh. D. Kahana. All were respected people and among the leaders of "Agudat Israel". His grandson, Tzvi Horwitz, a distinguished scholar of the Torah, was educated and extremely talented. He was one of the founders of "Tzeirei [Young] Agudat Israel", and their leader. He was killed in an accident in Sanz. His brother, Arye, was one of the distinguished students of Rabbi BABa"D.

[Columns 273-274]

"HaMizrakhi" People

When on Ruska Street, we passed near the home of R' Avraham Meiberger. We will dwell a bit on this activist and his work: R' Avraham Meirberger was the president of "HaMizrakhi" in Ternopil. He was educated and a Torah learner and possessed pleasant manners. He was a vigorous activist, the vice chairman of the community council in Ternopil, and a member of the state institutions in Galitsia.

The "HaMizrakhi" leaders in our city were: R' Yitzkhak Ginsburg from Rzeszow [Raysha], R' Gedalia Kornberg, Zisha Wahler, a Hebrew teacher and Torah reader at the big synagogue (he was superb at this holy work), and Itamar Teikhman. However, the spokesperson of "HaMizrakhi" was the party's excellent speaker and author, R' Yitzkhak Walfish, now[1] one of the prominent figures of the community in Toronto, Canada).

"HaMizrakhi" in Ternopil was active in many areas and received many votes in the election to the community council. In the election to the Polish Sejm in 1922, one of the two representatives from the Ternopil district was "HaMizrakhi" leader, Dr. Bernard Hoizner (The other representative was Tzvi Heller). Dr. Hoizner and Rabbi Dr. Shimon Federbush visited Ternopil and appeared in "HaMizrakhi" gatherings.

"HaMizrakhi" in Ternopil participated actively in the management of the Hebrew school, made its mark on that institution, and directed it toward religion. "HaMizrakhi" cooperated with the Zionist Union in all political affairs and money collection activities for Eretz Israel funds.

"HaMizrakhi" in Ternopil boasted about the "HaMizrakhi" country leader, Dr. Simkha Bunem Feldman, who served as a lawyer in Ternopil before the First World War. He made his mark on the association there. Among the representatives of the "HaMizrakhi" in the community institutions were the council president, Mr. Meirberger, R' Yitzkhak Walfish, R' Gedalia Kornberg, R' Zisha Wahler, R' Mordekhai Fessel [now in Tel Aviv], and Rabbi R' Ya'akov Shalita, who was one of the fans of "HaMizrakhi".

The Learned and Scholars

Ternopil learned concentrated mainly around Rabbi Menakhem Munish BABDa"D. His student later became Rabbis in various communities. I will mention some of them, my friends with whom I studied. Each one of them excelled in a unique area.

Rabbi Shimshon Weissman served as a rabbi in Lupatyn, near Lviv. He was a wise, deep learner and a very honest man. He was endowed with distinguished virtues. (His brother, Rabbi Yitzkhak Weissman-Sharf, is now a rabbi and Yeshiva teacher in Brooklyn New York); Rabbi Dov (Bercho) Katz, the rabbi in Dobromil, the son of the cantor at the big Beit HaMidrash, Reuven Katz. He was persistent, diligent, and pious with a strong will; Rabbi Tzvi Schwartz, the rabbi in Yezupil [Yezopol], the son of R' Pinkhas Shwartz; Rabbi Wolf Mond from Lancut [Lantzut], Yeshiva teacher in Mukacheve [Munkatch]; Rabbi Moshe Bloy from Dukla; Rabbi Y. Landau, a rabbi in Burshtyn; Rabbi Bendelman from Rzeszow [Raysha], and more.

Among the distinguished students of Rabbi Menakhem M. BABa"D was his nephew, Rabbi Asher BABDa" D, the son of the rabbi from Tartakiv. Rabbi Asher now serves as a rabbi of the "Minkhat Khinukh" congregation in New York. Rabbi Shaul D' Katz-Margaliot, who once served as a rabbi in Torest[?], Belzyce [Belzitz], and Pruszkow [Proshkov] near Warsaw, now serves as a rabbi in Brooklyn. R' Mendel Igli now serves as a Kosher slaughterer and inspector in New York. Rabbi Meir Shapira, who once served as a rabbi in Narol, is now a member of Belz Hassidim in New York. Rabbi Elimelekh from Vienna is now in London Rabbi Neistein is now in the Weinland, a town near New York. Rabbi Avraham M.BABa"D, the nephew and brother-in-law of the rabbi from Ternopil, requires a special mention. Today he is a prominent rabbi in England and the rabbi of Sunderland. He is also the head of the Yeshiva there. He is a member of the "Council of Torah Greats" of "Agudat Israel", and one of the leaders of "Agudat Israel".

My brother Moshe Zeidman who was a student of Yeshiva of "Khakhmei Lublin", taught Torah to the students there for free.

Some distinguished learners were proficient in the Mishna and Poskim who never served as rabbis and were more knowledgeable than many Rabbis. R' Shmeril Eikhenbaum, an exceptionally wise man whose aphorisms became famous. He had an outstanding memory and knowledge (His son was Shlomo Eikhenbaum. His grandson was a graduate of the "Institute for Jewish Studies" in Orsha. The latter was a religion teacher in Ternopil's high school). R' Hersh Leib Thaler, an inspector of lungs adhesion and decider in matters related to Kosher and Treifa [Non-Kosher]. He is very knowledgeable; R' Yosef Popresh, the grandson of [Rabbi Yosef BABa"D the author of "Minkhat Khinukh". His sons were exceptional learners: R' Avraham Delitz, a Melamed, and R' Tzvi Manheim who is a Husiatyn Hassid; There were many more.

From the old generation - R' Manis (Manila), a Maggid [preacher] who taught many students.

Closure

In conclusion, I must note that much more was hidden within the religious public in Ternopil than what such a review can contain. Many deserving people and events were not mentioned here because of the lack of notes and material - the community documentation and notes were destroyed when the community itself was annihilated. However, there is also another reason why such a review cannot be complete. That is common to the entire Jewish religious public in Poland. The majority of the Jews followed the commandment "Walk humbly with G-d" [Micha 6:8]. They did not stand out in public. The publicity did not reach them, and they did not need publicity. Their life was a matter between them and G-d. Therefore, they possessed hidden powers. From the outside, only their exteriority was shown. To discover the brightness of their light, you had to penetrate their soul. Whole worlds were destructed.

Translator's Note:

a. Here and wherever the text refers to the current time, it means the time of publication February - 1955.

[Columns 275-276]

The Synagogues in Ternopil

The Old Synagogue[1]

by Engineer, Architect Zeev Porat (Oks)

Translated by Moshe Kutten

Not once did the Ternopil's community fall victim to provocations and calamities. It is, therefore, not surprising that Ternopil's community built its synagogue in the style of a fortress-like building. It was similar to synagogues built in other Jewish communities like Lutsk, Brody, Rzeszow [Zheshuv], Leshniv, Zhovkova [Zolkiew], Lyuboml, and Brzeziny [Bezhezhin]. The building could serve as a fort to protect the life of Jewish residents during wars and other dangers.

Due to their unique architectural exterior and original interior design, these citadel-like synagogues acquired a name in the art world.

The square shape of the building is emphasized in these synagogues. The solid construction is expressed in the exterior of the monumental and mighty building with its large measures (compared to its renaissance-style square predecessor) and the thick walls (in Ternopil, the thickness of the walls reached almost one meter and a half). It was supported from the outside by auxiliary walls and the middle columns - those mighty support pillars that held the dome.

The Old Synagogue

The citadel-like synagogue is adorned outside by a roof banister forming a beautiful gallery. The gallery is a classic example of outdoor decorations of most of the 16th and 17th centuries baroque-styled synagogues in Poland. It was also used in other majestic buildings in Poland that remained from the Krakovian renaissance period and beyond.

The gallery is undoubtedly the architectural element that most characterizes the Krakovian renaissance construction. The renaissance artists tried to emphasize the classical architecture format. The horizontal and continuous lines of the building are in contrast to the gothic style with its rising lines. Those artists could accomplish their style easily using the long gallery, particularly during that period of construction of attractive public buildings sporting a fairly wide front. The tall ledge of the Krakovian gallery adorns the roof of the building while hiding it. It distinguishes itself in its graceful architecture, made of protruding minarets and sunken arcades held between two ledges.

In contrast to the smooth and vast exterior walls with their large windows, the blind arcade that encircles the main portion of the building presents a single architectural element having a unique stylistic character.

With its rich profile, the gallery suggests a shape of a crown, and since it is located at the head of the building, it actually becomes like the wreath of the house, presenting the most decorative part of the synagogue [exterior].

A reference to the gallery tradition can be found in the Torah commandment

[Columns 277-278]

about building a banister for the house roof: "When you build a new house, you shall make a parapet for your roof…" (Deuteronomy 22:8). There is also a reference included in the description of the Temple in the book of Ezekiel.

The gallery consists of four main parts, characteristics of most citadel-like synagogues. a) The lower ledge that separates the gallery from the building itself b) The gallery itself with its decorations shaped like a blind arcade and half circle arches of blocked and sunken windows separated from each by flat columns. Guns' embrasures, like the ones in Ternopil, were often placed in these sunken windows. c) The upper ledge. d) The upper part is usually made of toothed wall steeples with shooting slots between them.

The interior of these types of synagogues is adored by the composition of the walls. It is also a result of the square shape of the building. The decoration of the walls was mostly the same. The walls are divided into three main areas, separated by three decorated half-circled arches, three windows, and two pilasters. That division is the natural result of the dome structure with its nine squares. Only the eastern wall that houses the holy arc is different from the other walls. In that wall, only two windows were cut out on the two sides of the arc, and sometimes there is an additional small circular window.

Usually, we do not know who were the architects of the citadel-like square synagogues. There is no doubt, however, that the style of these synagogues was influenced by Italian construction. During the reign of Queen Bona Sforza [d'Aaragona, 1494 – 1557], the [second] wife of King Sigismund I, Italian architects arrived in Poland. It is conceivable that some of them were Jewish and that they may have designed synagogues. The Ternopil synagogue serves as a classical example of citadel-like synagogues because it embodies all the architectural lines that characterize that unique construction.

Author's Note:

1. For historical details, see the article by Dr. N. M. Gelber, column 25, etc…

Houses of Prayer, and *Batei Midrash*

by Dr. Hillel Zeidman

Translated by Moshe Kutten

When I set to begin the sacred work of writing (instead of etching the words on gravestones) for my city Ternopil, especially for the keepers of religion in it, the dear and near images of the murdered, tortured, and burned figures, rise up my memory and light up the darkness of that period with the brightness of their souls.

From the big synagogue, the building that looks like a fort from the 16th century, ancient and rich with tradition; From the Husiatyn *Kloiz* filled with Hassidim and learners; From the R' Yanka'leh's *Kloiz* of the honorable people; from the *Beit HaMidrash* enveloped by the kindness of the simple people; From Ozherna *Kloiz*, where praying learning took place days and nights, seven days a week; From the praying house of the rabbi from Medzhybizh [Mezhbuzh], Rabbi Avraham Yehoshua Heschel, the grandson of [Rabbi Yehoshua Heschel] the author of "Ohev Israel" from Opatow [Apta]; From the parrying house of R' Yose'leh, the grandson of the Rabbi [Tzvi Hirsh] from Zidichov, and the follower of the Zidichov's style of praying, with its unique sweet sadness tone and soft melody – from all the synagogues, *Batei HaMidrash* houses of prayer, and *Kloizes* – the melodies of the cantors, and prayer leaders are rising within our souls. Their voices are delectable, glorious in their appearance, and amicable. The prayers of the holy congregations yearning for salvation are echoing and rising - the congregations of diversified crowds, the smallest of which is filled with good deeds and the lesser of which possesses supreme virtues. Everybody is firm in their faith and dedicated to the Torah and the sanctities of the Jewish people.

The last sigh of the holy congregation of Ternopil, a mother city for the Jewish people, is rising from the torturous abysses and the annihilating gas chambers of Belzec. The dying cry of the large congregation who always waited for the messiah penetrates the depths of our souls. The sigh of the Mishnah scholars and *Poskim*, the Jews of the Psalms and Mishna chapters, penetrates our depths. The bitter fate united them all - the humble and the proud, Hasidim and "bourgeoises", rich and poor, learned and simple people – who were united in spirit and faith, became equal in their calamity.

No more holidays would be celebrated at the home of the rabbi from Medzhybizh, on Tarnovskiego Street. People would no longer celebrate at the homes of the local rabbis, R' Ya'akov Shalita, and Rabbi R' Heschel BABa" D in Simkhat Torah. People would no longer meet at the *Beit HaMidrash* of the butchers and water carriers and would not gather any longer at the *Kloiz* Husiatyn and *Kloiz* Chortkiv. We would never be able to hear R' Yosel'eh's Zidichov's style effusion of the soul during the Days of Awe around the big synagogue and the commercial streets of Ruska, Rynek, and Sobieski. No longer would people observe the Shabbat and holidays. The whole community became desolated, passed, and disappeared as if it never existed. The entire community was sacrificed on the altar by a nation of beasts and sank into the abyss of tortures and annihilation without a trace, grave, or gravestone. Our childhood and youth, the magical dreams of our youth, were washed away by the blood of the mass killings. Cruel strangers settled in our houses where we were born to love the Torah and where we were educated to be faithful.

Whatever was precious and holy was desecrated and destructed. Only the survivors of our community,

[Columns 279-280]

the remnants of the annihilated generation, carry their memory with grief. We must guard the ember of memory, write the names and history, and erect gravestones on graves floating in the air.

The Jewish Ternopil with its pious Jewry, was, like most other Jewish cities, a city inside a city – a Jewish enclave within a gentile city, alien corn in the diaspora land. Jews who were strict with the commandments encircled the Jewish enclave with erub of limits (R' D. Ber dealt with that diligently and guarded the wires lest they were cut off). The faithful Jews lived their lives within that Jewish enclave, far from any foreign culture. These were Jews with a resilient character, and the spirit of times and the gentile surrounding could not change them. They built their own life, sourced within the Judaism treasures, in a unique Jewish atmosphere, around the Jewish holidays: Passover Eve, Days of Awe, fasts, and celebrations.

The lives of the pious Jews, the keepers of the Torah and commandments, concentrated around the houses of prayer, *Kloizes*, and *Batei Midrash*. These were the centers of congregations, denominations, and Hasidic groups. Every one of these houses of prayer had its own character. None was the same as the other. The people who prayed in each of these houses of prayer made their mark on them and were influenced by them.

So, let's try to make a list of the houses of prayer of the Ternopil community. It was believed that there were 52 such houses. However, a detailed list did not survive, and we are forced to rely on our memory.

The Big Synagogue. That was a stone fort-like building from the 16th century. Famous cantors lead the prayers, accompanied by choruses organized tastefully. The last cantor, Hillel Hershaft, was murdered by the Germans in 5702 [1941/42]. The Ba'al Koreh [Torah reader] was the exceptional Hebrew teacher, Zisha Wahler. He performed his work with precision, knowledge, and remarkable competence. His reading of the Torah was like art.

The Old *Beit HaMidrash*. Learned homeowners prayed in it, Ashkenazi style. Scholars conducted lessons there about weekly Torah portions, Bible rabbinic teachings, and the Mishnah. The last prominent scholar was Shmeril Eikhenbaum, a distinguished scholar who was sharp-minded, knowledgeable, wise, and witty. He was a confidant of Rabbi Menakhem-Munish BABa"D. He managed, for the rabbi, the politics at the community council and its management, where he was a member for many years.

Kloiz **Husiatyn**. The *kloiz* was located near the old *Beit HaMidrash* and the big synagogue. The people who prayed at that *kloiz* were scholars. Some of them were distinguished scholars, knowledgeable in the Mishnah and *Poskim*, such as the Melamed, R' Avreme'leh Delitz, and the merchant, R' Pinkhas Schwartz. The most prominent figure in *Kloiz* Husiatyn was R' David Lvov, a wealthy Hasid philanthrope with noble virtues and character. He was a Boyan Hasid but prayed at the *kloiz* of the Husiatyn Hasidim. He held the highest authority among the Haredi Jewry and was elected as its representative for the community council.

The *Kloiz* of Rabbi Yekl'leh (named after the founder R' Ya'akov Podhortzer, the grandfather of the mayor of Safed). The *kloiz* attracted wealthy homeowners and some scholars. Rabbi Menakhem-Munish used to pray at that *kloiz* during the Days of Awe. He was the Ba'al Toke'ah [The person who blows the Shofar]. With his prayers before the blowing of the Shofar, he caused quivers in the hearts of his audience.

Kloiz **Chortkov**. The *kloiz* served as a center for wealthy people and famous scholars. Hasidic estate owners R' Yehuda-Ber Zeidman and his sons R' Avraham-Shlomo, R' Mordekhai and R' Ya'akov Breitman, and his prominent son-in-law, Meir Shapira, prayed in that *kloiz*. The latter gained fame as the Rabbi of Lublin and the founder of the Yeshiva of "Khakhmei Lublin". He became the leader of "Agudat Israel", and one of its representatives for the Polish Sejm. The rest of R' Ya'akov Breitman's sons-in-law were also famous scholars, like Leibush Arak, the relative of Rabbi Arak of Buchach, and R' Moshe Rozner, the deputy head of the community council and the chairman of the Haredi union "Tif'eret HaDat".

Ozerner *Kloiz*. The *kloiz* was located on Podolska Wizsza Street, which was parallel to Ruska Street. Perhaps because of its central location or its other virtues, the *kloiz* was filled with praying people and diligent learners. It held several *Minyans* in the morning and evening prayers. From among the people who prayed, I remember R' Leib Hersh Thaler, "HaRo'eh" (the inspector of the lungs and the decider between a Kosher and Treifa [non-Kosher] meat). He was exceptionally proficient in the Mishna and Shulkhan Arukh. His proficiency spanned beyond the limits of his profession. I also remember R' Yitzkhak Walfish, who now[1] resides in Toronto Canada. He was an educated man, excellent speaker, and preacher, and one of the flag carriers for "HaMizrakhi".

R' Neteh'leh's *Kloiz*. It was located across from the Big Synagogue and was one of the oldest houses of prayer in the city. It was found 150 years ago by a pious merchant, Neteh'leh, who did not have sons and thus dedicated all of his fortune and house to the community. The *kloiz* had two floors. R' Yehoshua Heschel BABa"D, the author of the famous "Sefer Yehoshua" lived on the second floor. After his death, both floors served as houses of prayers.

Katberg's *Beit HaMidrash*. It was located near the old synagogue. The people who prayed there were learned homeowners.

R' Efraim Soshe's *Kloiz*. Also, a house of prayer for wealthy homeowners.

R' Nekhemchi's *Shulakhel* [small *shul* –small synagogue]. It was located across from *Kloiz* Husiatyn on Podolska Nizsza. A house of prayer for the craftsmen.

R' Nathanieli's *Kloiz*. The people who prayed in this *kloiz* were wealthy merchants and enlightened but pious.

The house of prayer of the bakers (*Das Bekerrisheh Shulakhel*).

[Columns 281-282]

Not only bakers prayed there but also other craftsmen.

The New *Beit HaMidrash*. Near Baron Hirsch Street.

The House of Prayer at the Jewish Hospital. It was located on Ostrogskiego Street.

The House of Prayer at the Old Cemetery. It was also located on Ostrogskiego Street (also called Mikulintzer Street).

The *Minyan* If R' Yose'leh. The house of prayer of R' Yose'leh Eikhenstein who was related to the Zidichov [Hasidim]. It was located near the big synagogue.

Mezbuzher *Minyan*. The house of prayer of Rabbi Yehoshua-Heschel from Medzhybizh [Mezbuzh], related to the Afta family, son-in-law of the rabbi of Kapischnitz.

The House of Prayer of the Water-Carriers. It was located near the Big Synagogue. On Shabbat and holidays, it was crowded with the common people, who prayed there, and in the afternoon, attended lessons taught by volunteer *melameds*.

The House of Prayer of the Coal Handlers. The house of prayer of the craftsmen.

The House of Prayer of Rabbi Menakhem Munish BABa"D. It was located at the rabbi's home on Perl Street. The rabbi studied there on weekdays with his students, and on Shabbat and holidays, people prayed there in public.

The House of Prayer of R' Yekl'leh. It was located on Yosef BABa"D Street. The brother-in-law of Rabbi Yosef BABa"D and the son of the rabbi of Mikulintsy [Mikolnitz] resided in that house. People prayed there in public on Shabbat.

The Tempel. Named after Yosef Perl and was located on Perl Street. It was the house of prayer of the enlightened and serve as the "fort" of the assimilators. That synagogue does not belong to the chapter of Haredi Jews and requires a separate review.

Translator's Note:

1. Here and wherever the text refers to the current time, it means the time of publication February 1955.

Cantors and Cantorship

by M. Sh. Geshuri

Translated by Moshe Kutten

With the progress in Torah education, its cantorship also developed. Starting in the 16th century and later, some Jewish congregations had famous cantors, some of whom were mentioned in the literature, particularly on their gravestones. The Jewish audiences were eager for music and a good cantor, and known cantors served in the Big Synagogue in Ternopil. Unfortunately, we did not receive any information about Ternopil's cantors before the 17th century. In the 17th century, Ternopil was influenced by the western world through Vienna, Austria, which captured a central role in music. The greatest composers resided there, whose compositions spread throughout the entire cultural world. The other influence came from the east, big Russia with its millions of Jews, which served as an important center for the traditional emotional cantorship. Russia's cantors visited Galitsia from time to time. Obviously, the traditional-learned Ternopil was interested in listening to great cantors whose singing carried artistic value. Big Russia had many such cantors who did not belittle Ternopil, which was remote geographically. Cantors did not consider Ternopil a unique city. The best of Russia's cantors, the most famous of them "Little Yerukham (Blindman)" visited Ternopil.

* * *

Little Yerukham (1798 – 1891)

Little Yerukham, called little because of his short stature, was one of the fathers of the traditional cantorship in Eastern Europe in the 19th century. Ternopil was fortunate to have Yerukham serving in it for about nine years as a cantor and even established a school for cantorship, where his famous chorus came from. That chorus laid the foundation for traditional music in the diaspora. Yerukham erected a fence around his cantorship to protect it from the influence of western music coming from Vienna. Yerukham was a courageous fighter who possessed all of the required attributes for a battle and win.

From Ternopil, he moved to Berdichev, where he served as a cantor for fifty years. He died there in 1891 at the age of ninety.

Yehoshua (Pichi) Abrass

Ternopil enlightened people who wished to make changes in the synagogue, would not dare to establish a "Temple" based purely on the German modernization movement, due to the resistance by most of the pious city residents to any radical changes. However, they did not hesitate to establish their "temple" based on the "corrected" original singing, according to the harmony rules, and to unify the two styles as much as possible (called Soltzer's method).

[Columns 283-284]

The "temple's" activists began looking for a cantor loyal to Soltzer's method.

Fortunately, they found such a cantor by chance "from the heavens". A "Temple" activist visited with a local Brody banker, Moshe Kalir, on his business. A young cantor by the name of Yehoshua (Pichi) Abrass, one of the senior students of Soltzer, visited the same banker with a letter of recommendation. He sang a few compositions of Betzalel from Odesa for the activist. The latter was fascinated by Abrass's voice. After he heard that Abrass was one of Viennese Soltzer's students, he did not let him go and literally dragged him to Ternopil. The "Temple' gabbais listened to his voice and offered him the cantor position in the new choral-style synagogue. Abrass stayed in Ternopil for two years and amazed many listeners, who never tired of listening to him. Undoubtedly if it was up to Pichi himself and his employers, who were more than satisfied with him, he could have stayed in Ternopil for many years.

He stayed in Ternopil until 1842 but was forced to leave for personal reasons. He moved to Lviv and was accepted as a cantor in the big synagogue there.

Pichi was one of the reasons the Ternopil zealots spread libels against Rabbi SHI"R as he sang for SHI"R in Shavuot. It happened very early in the morning following the all-nighter "Tikkun Leil Shavuot" [The practice of staying up all Shavuot night to study Torah[1]].

If cantor Pichi had written his memoir, he would have covered details about life in Ternopil during his stay, especially about the status of the Jewish music in the city.

Kalman Lev

Kalman Lev was one of the most influential cantors of our generation. He was a composer and composed wonderful recitatives that the cantors used successfully.

Kalman Lev was born in Ternopil in 1862 and received a traditional Jewish education. He sang with the greatest cantors who served in Ternopil. He sang as a tenor for Little Yerukham, while the latter served as a cantor in Ternopil. He moved to Kherson and sang for Pinkhas Minkovski. Later, he moved to Odesa and was accepted to the "Cold Synagogue" there. Two years later, he moved to the larger Nikolayev synagogue. From there, he moved to Nikopol, where he served for fourteen years, accompanied by a beautiful chorus. In the end, he left Europe and moved to America.

He composed many Jewish-styled compositions and educated many students, poets, and cantors who continue his work in promoting today and help in lifting the image of the cantorship. He died in New York in 1914 at the age of 52.

Isidor Edelsman

Born in Otyniya (Galitsia) in 1886. His parents were merchants. His father was a great scholar and a hearty prayer leader without making it a profession. Isidor began to sing, as an assistant to the cantor, at the court of the rabbi from Vyzhnytsya [Vizhnitz], R' Rabbi Khaim Hager. In 1897, after the passing of his father, he traveled to his uncle in Austria, where he was a prominent merchant. His uncle sent him to a conservatorium in Vienna under the supervision of the chief cantor, Bauer. He later served as a cantor in Hungary, and from there, he moved to Ternopil. Immediately in his first appearance, he captured the hearts of his listeners in Ternopil. His voice, which was clear as a crystal, electrified the audience. In addition, he was knowledgeable in music. In 1929 he left Europe and settled in America, where he accepted a cantor position in Boston.

Shaul Brandes (1866 – 1929)

He was born in Ternopil in 1866 to poor peddling parents. He had a pleasant alto voice and sang for prominent cantors, including Nisan Belzer (Spivak). He liked the theater and moved from cantorship to the theater and back to music, several times.

David Hirsh

He was born in Khyriv [Khyrov], near Przemyœl [Pshemishl] in 1870 and sang with many cantors. Little Yerukham took him to Ternopil, where he sang with his chorus. He was enrolled there in school to study music. He resided in Ternopil for three years until the famous cantor, Ya'akov Bekhman, took him to Lviv.

Avraham Trakhtenberg

He was born in Kamyanets Podilskyy [Kamenets-Podolsk], in 1861. He was 16 years old when his family moved from Russia to Austria. He joined the chorus of Little Yerukham in Ternopil and in a short period, managed to learn the musical notes and become professional until he became the conductor of the chorus. He served in that position for two years.

Shmuel Kavetzki

Was born in Vinkivtsi [Vinkovitz], in Podolia province. In his youth, his voice was a soprano. Served as a singer with the cantors Shlomo Wlochisker, Avraham Klikhnik, Shumel Weinman, and others. He showed great talent in composing his own compositions and conducting choruses, In the end, it turned out that his talent as a chorus conductor was no less than being a cantor.

[Columns 285-286]

He served in Ternopil as a conductor at the Big Synagogue for a short while.

Ze'ev-Wolf Wilder

Ze'ev-Wolf Wilder was born in 1860 in Stanislavchyk, near Brody. He studied in his father's Yeshiva, who was a known *Ba'al Tfilah* [leader of the prayer]. Later, he was accepted as a singer in Little Yerukham's chorus in Ternopil and served there successfully for three years. Only when he lost the soprano voice he returned home. He studied kosher slaughtering and, at the end of eighteen, became a cantor/slaughterer. Cantor Wilder gained fame in the Jewish world for his mighty voice. He published twenty of his compositions, which were accepted enthusiastically by the cantors. Wilder served as a cantor in various countries, including America, England, and Africa. Today[a], he resides in America and serves as a cantor there

Levi Liuberer

Cantor Levi Liuberer, who gained fame as a great "*Ba'al Tefillah*", was also known by the name of "Levi Ternopoler" or "Levi Balter", after the cities of Ternopil and Balta. He was a unique recitator and a great scholar. Many cantors taught him in Ternopil, some of whom gained fame. All of his students were proud of their excellent teacher.

Moshe Goldbaum

He was known in Ternopil as "Moshe Khazan [cantor]. He prayed with his own chorus in the "Temple" on Perl Street for many years. He was the last of the cantors, a student of Soltzer and other western-style cantors, and diligently guarded their melodies. The "Temple" in Ternopil, at the time it was established, was slated to be a modern house of prayer. It was aimed to unify the religious spirit with the beauty of the external form of the 19th century and the first decades of the 20th century. It was far different from the reform "temples" of today. It had more order, quietness, and politeness in the way people prayed than in the "*Shitbalakh*" [Small houses of prayer, less formal than a synagogue]. However, that did not affect the inspiration. Unlike all other cantors, Moshe Khazan and his family were residents of Ternopil throughout their entire life, a symbol of Perl's period. He maintained that tradition with the caretaker who was a descendant of Perl's family and the only descendant who did not become a gentile.

Hillel Hershaft and M. Kotzik

In 1933, two new cantors came to Ternopil to replace their predecessors who left the city. Hillel Hershaft served at the Big Synagogue and M. Kotzik at the Chorus Synagogue. In 1938, cantor Weintraub from Lviv replaced Kotzik.

Nisan from Odesa

At the end of the 16th century, a famous cantor, Nisan Odisser served at the Big Synagogue. He sang with a chorus of ten singers. During the Days of Awe, 4000 people who enjoyed his pleasant prayers came to the synagogue.

* * *

These are the names of the cantors I managed to collect from Ternopil natives. Obviously, many names were lost. It is worthwhile for Ternopil natives to write down the names of the cantors so they would be remembered for eternity.

Author's Note:

1. See the article by Dr. N. M. Gelber, column 84.

Translator's Note:

a. Here and everywhere else where the author relates to the current time, it means the time of publication of the book – February 1955.

[Columns 287-288] [Blank]

[Columns 289-290]

Educational and Cultural Institutions

[Columns 291-292] [Blank]

[Columns 293-294]

Hebrew Educational Institutions in Ternopil

"Tarbut" ["Culture"] School

by Mordekhai Deutsch

Translated by Moshe Kutten

When I arrived in Ternopil in 1924, I found a cultural field of action – The Hebrew school. That school was founded before the First World War through the efforts of pioneering activists. With the break of The First World War, many activists left the city, which was close to the Russian border. They elected to move to the capital city Vienna until the fury passed. The young ones enlisted in the Austrian army. The old-timers never returned to their native city. Some remained in Vienna, and others moved to Congressional Poland. There was ample space for cultural work.

The war handed Ternopil a heaping plate of troubles, calamities, pandemics, and destruction. Schools were closed because the state of the Jews was grievous. following days of the foreign and hostile regime and the continued war around and within the city for three years. Then came the Ukrainian regime, which lasted half a year, and in the end, the entrance of the Poles. All of those events impoverished the Jewish population. Only a handful of people dedicated themselves to the idea that the youth must receive a Hebrew education. They recognized early that there was no future for the Jewish youth in the diaspora, and therefore, they must be educated in pioneering [for settling in Eretz Israel], and be provided with the knowledge of the Hebrew language, a common language needed for the ingathering of the exiles in the homeland. These people invested substantial energy and efforts to revive whatever needed revival and fix whatever needed fixing.

Their way was not paved. They faced many obstacles.

Poetess Elisheva with the Committee of the Hebrew School

[Columns 295-296]

Founders of "Tarbut" in Ternopil, 1926
From right to left –sitting: Weisman, Tukhman, R. Berger, Greenspan, Simon
Standing: Z. Wahler, M. Deutsch, I. Kurfuerst, A. Meiberger

However, these pioneers possessed a strong will, which won over their initial ability. We often faced challenging problems. For example, the search for a place for the school. We took over rooms in Perl's school, which were slated to be rented to shop owners. That school was under the control of the assimilators, and they did not want to let the Hebrew school have a foothold in "their" school. We waged a fierce battle against them until they were forced to yield to public opinion. It was also helpful that we were already situated in the school, and it was not easy to get rid of us. However, they reminded us at every opportunity that we forced our way in as if Perl's school was their private property.

Balancing the budget was one of the most severe problems we faced. Often, we could not pay the teachers their wages on time, but we have always managed to overcome the crisis. Our elected members in the municipality council helped us tremendously by securing a monthly financial allotment from the municipality. That enabled us to continue our operation and even widen and improve the school. We were not satisfied with what we had; We wanted to enlarge the framework and connect with the center in Poland.

When the state-wide organization of the Hebrew elementary and high schools was established in Poland under the name "Tarbut", the schools won their proper recognition. When Tzarist Russia ruled Poland, it looked unfavorably at the existence of a modern education system in Poland. The Tzarist government often interfered with the efforts of the local authorities to establish new schools. When Poland secured its freedom, its government turned to establishing a modern educational system for Polish children. The Polish authorities did not object to Jews establishing their own schools based on their own customs. In Galitsia, a sophisticated educational system of the Austrian government has already existed. It was difficult for us to follow our brothers in Congressional Poland and establish independent elementary and high schools according to their format since it required investing substantial expenses. Our parents were still far from the idea that their children need a complete Hebrew education consisting of both Jewish and general studies. We, therefore, began at the foundation and established the first Hebrew kindergarten. Our hope was that when the children graduate, they will be ready for elementary school. We also hoped that sometime in the future, we will be able to establish a high school. We joined the "Tarbut" system and elected a special committee to handle the affairs of the kindergarten. The members of the committee were: Ostren, Rekka Oks, and Penka Shekhter and they invested substantial energy and effort in it.

The second thing we found proper to establish was evening Hebrew lessons for youth and adults. A few months later, people started to talk Hebrew in Ternopil, and debates and discussions in Hebrew could be heard. A while later, Dr. Ledder founded a "Tarbut" branch in the city. The following members were elected to the committee: Kurfuerst, Edelstein, Weisman, Wahler, Saraf, Ginsberg, Meiberger, Berger, and Deutsch. The school won the parents' confidence due to the dedication of the teachers to their role, and the time and effort they invested to improve and elevate that institution.

With our lobbying, prominent figures from Eretz Israel visited our city. The author Shmuel Tchernovitz (aka "Sfog") gave lectures about educational and cultural problems. He was impressed with Ternopil and wrote an article about the city and its cultural situation in the weekly "HaOlam" ["The World", the official journal of the international Zionist Union]. Even the great author Sh. Y. Agnon [later a Nobel Prize winner] was our guest at the school while he stayed in the city.

[Columns 297-298]

He even participated in a trip with us. Dr. Tzvi Feffer Z"L accompanied the author to show him the city's antiquity and Perl's library. We also invited poet Elisheva when she toured Polish cities to learn about Polish Jewry. She read from her poems in front of a large crowd in the "Betztvo" hall. We were also fortunate to bring the giant of Hebrew poetry, Kh. N. Bialik, to our city. The culture committee exerted a substantial effort until we managed to bring the poet to our city. Bialik lectured about "National Culture Problems". He was very interested in seeing Perl's library and visited the remnant of that prized asset. The neglect in the library, particularly the ancient manuscripts, depressed the poet. I have already mentioned that Perl's school and the library were under the control of the assimilators, and they did not allow any foothold for the Zionists. The proposal about moving the library to the Hebrew University in Jerusalem met with a total refusal. In the evening, at the gathering, Bialik's speech was filled with bitterness about that neglect. He called in sorrow: "What is culture?", he asked, and answered: "A person of culture is not the one who dresses in a nice shirt that others made from him, but a person who knows how to create new things for himself". At night, we held a small party among our people and fans. Here we met a completely different Bialik, the man of the people. He lectured us about Mendelson's Enlightened Movement. Bialik explained that that movement targeted Torah learners and yeshiva students who knew Hebrew. The Hebrew language served them as means through which they aimed to reach the German language. Their translation of the holy scriptures helped these young men to learn German. The final objective was total assimilation. Opposite that movement was the Galitsian Enlightened Movement, which targeted the masses to be able to teach them to read the holy scriptures. Their objective was to translate the bible into the spoken language [Yiddish] so that even a commoner who cannot read the source would be able to appreciate the beauty of the translated Book of Books. They hoped to attract the masses toward the source. That was why Mendel Lefin translated the books of Psalms, Proverbs, and Job into Yiddish. He wished to bring the bible close to the commoners. From there, just a short jump to the root, the source. Bialik spoke with admiration about Galitsia wise men, RN"K [R' Nakhman Kromkhel], SHI"R [Shlomo Yehuda Rapoport], Lefin, Perl, and their colleagues.

We tried our best to increase and strengthen to school. During the last few years of its operation, the student body reached seven hundred. The Hebrew evening lessons were also filled with students. We wished that the center of Torah studies would fit the name the city acquired for itself throughout the diaspora. Although according to the size of its population Ternopil was considered an average city, much like many other average cities in Galitsia, it was known as great in Torah, education, and loyalty to Zionism.

Then came the oppressor and destroyed everything. Nothing was left from the cultural richness. The dear members who devoted days and nights to the dissemination of the Hebrew language are gone: Israel Kurfuerst, who ran to do any meritorious deed., Tzvi Greenspan, the dedicated teacher, Saraf, Zusia Wahler, Mrs. Shitzer, and Mrs. Steinberg, all teachers, and counselors, whose heart was dedicated to the education of the young generation toward Eretz Israel. The activists Meiberger, Yehoshua Parnas, Ya'akov Feffer, Knopholtz, Primer, Weisman, Shalom Fisher, Kopel Yaffe, Friedberg, Tzvi Ginsburg, Rekka Oks, Dr. Tzellermayer. The defiled hand of the Nazi beast of prey annihilated everything.

The students who live in Israel will never forget the teachers and activists who were so dedicated to the dissemination of the Hebrew language because the school was the element that pushed them to leave the diaspora and make Aliya to Eretz Israel.

"Tarbut" Association and its Activities

by Nathan Ostern

Translated by Moshe Kutten

An important and unforgettable page in the chronicles of Ternopil was the fruitful work in the field of the Hebrew culture.

Under the management of the teacher Peled, the Hebrew school, which contributed significantly to learning the Hebrew language (using the Ashkenazi pronunciation) and its culture, served as a spiritual center for the community as early as 1909. Later on, other famous teachers joined such as Matok and Wittenberg Z"L, and with unified forces, disseminated knowledge and taught Hebrew and general education to many local Jews.

The First World War and the prohibition by the local authorities caused a severe reduction in a school activity. However, even then, teaching did not cease. Some people always managed to organize underground Hebrew courses despite the strict prohibition. In that affair, we should particularly commend Eliyahu Shitzer, who was very active until his Aliya to Eretz Israel, where he became one of the founders of Kfar Yehoshua.

[Columns 299-300]

With the end of the war, the school officially reorganized and renewed its operation with more vigor. That time, Greenspan Z"L took the helm. Assisting Greenspan was a group of skilled and enthusiastic teachers. We should note Hadasa Shitzer (Greenspan's wife), Saraf, Gusta Steinberg Z"L, and others. In 1920, the first kindergarten was established in our city. The "Tarbut" association, which set a goal for itself to disseminate the Hebrew culture among the masses, was established in 1924.

Before the "Tarbut" association was formally established and received recognition by the authorities, another association, by the name of "Ivriya", was already active in Ternopil. It fulfilled all "Tarbut's" roles (except for the evening lessons). When the "Tarbut" organizations were formed in all Polish cities, we simply changed our name from "Ivriya" to "Tarbut" and widened its operation.

Two big halls in the famous "Schloss" building ("The Castle") were rented. They served the goal of the association – the dissemination of the Hebrew culture. All the obstacles faced by the association, including the financial difficulties, were resolved with substation efforts.

A whole branched network of activity was established. Hebrew lessons for the youth and adults were organized, lectures were given by invited lecturers, and prominent guests were brought over for a visit. Among these prominent people were: Bialik, Mossinson, Elisheva, and Agnon. Over time, a Hebrew library and a reading room were established. The "Tarbut" union became a center for a rich community life, which created institutions that glorified the entire Jewish community.

The way "Tarbut" revived the local kindergarten after a halitus of two years (1921-22) deserves to be mentioned. The activists copied from the birth lists all the children aged 4 – 6. After visits with the parents and explanations, the kindergarten was revived with 25 – 30 children. They were nurtured with love by dedicated and skilled kindergarten teachers.

The activity network required a substantial budget. The school and kindergarten tuition covered only 50 – 60% of the budget. The activists had to knock on many doors – among them doors of institutions that were hostile to "Tarbut's" activities – to collect sufficient allotments and contributions to enable the operation of the many activities. The successful annual balls in Purim and Hannukah also brought some money to the budget.

From the group of "Tarbut" union activists, the noble and modest image of the chairman, Israel Kurfuerst, stands up. He acquired a lot of respect and affection from people from all walks of life. He was very active and together with others bore the burden consistently and decisively out of recognition of the role and the mission.

Over time, many other people joined "Tarbut", among them students of the *Batei Midrash* who played a major role in the development of the movement in the city. These people contributed their vigor and education to the success and proliferation of "Tarbut", which penetrated all layers of the population, particularly the assimilators' circles. It is deserving to mention some of these people. Zusia Wahler was an educated man who served as a "Ba'al Koreh [Torah reader] at the big synagogue, the secretary of the Hebrew school, and a teacher at the evening lessons. His Shabbat afternoon lectures in front of the association members excelled in their content and format and attracted a large crowd.

"Maccabi" Hebrew School, 1909

[Columns 301-302]

Haiman arrived at "Tarbut" almost directly from the *Beit HaMidrash*. He was a single son of pious parents, received religious education, was a man with great skills, and was very perceptive. He excelled in his wit and ability to analyze problems, on which he lectured in "Tarbut" clubs. Weihraukh, Zeidman, Baras, and others were among "Tarbut" activists, who did not spare their time and energy for the association's activities. It is no wonder, therefore, that emissaries from Eretz Israel, authors, and journalists, found fertile ground in Ternopil for their cultural activities. Through their visits they enriched the Hebrew atmosphere in Ternopil. Journals and weekly newspapers could be found not only in the reading hall of Tarbut but also in tens of private homes. Hebrew books enjoyed wide distribution in Ternopil.

Many of the activists managed to make Aliya, however, the connection with the members who remained in Ternopil was not cut off, and the fruitful work did not cease. The school principal, Greenspan Z"L, barely restrained himself from his passion for making Aliya since he recognized his essentiality in the city and his responsibility for the continuation of the cultural work in Ternopil.

In 1937, the author of these lines received a letter from Greenspan with a fiery soul outpouring filled with yearnings for Eretz Israel. Greenspan wrote about his strong desire to make Aliya and continue his activity in our homeland. However, the hand of the vile murderers got him. He and the rest of the activists and the best of the youth were annulated. The Holocaust put an end to their dream.

Their body was annihilated, but their spirit is hovering with us. They have been memorialized by their cultural ventures, which took root deep in the hearts of those who worked with them or were fortunate to learn the Torah from them and who made Aliya Israel. May their memory be blessed along with the rest of our nation's martyrs who were cut off before time by the barbarian murderers.

Committee of the Hebrew School in Ternopil, 1929
From right to left – sitting: Friedberg, Primer, Deutsch, Yaffe, Luner
Standing: Knopholtz, Tz. Greenspan, Wahler, Margolis

The Kindergarten of "Tarbut"

by Masha Ostern

Translated by Moshe Kutten

I will raise some memories from the kindergarten of "Tarbut" in Ternopil. When I arrived in 1930, I had already found a kindergarten operated for several years. It was located in the "Zamek" [Castle], a large house that served as a king's castle in the past, but nothing left of its magnificence. It was populated by many residents, most of whom were artisans, and small shopkeepers, who hardly made a living. When one of the residents' children became ill with a contagious disease, the kindergarten had to move out and look for a temporary apartment for a certain period.

[Columns 303-304]

The kindergarten's apartment served as a class of Hebrew lessons during regular days, and on Shabbat for gathering of "Tarbut" members. The furniture color faded from use, and the rest of the equipment was impoverished. Most of the children came from poor or middle-class homes, and their mother tongue was Yiddish and Polish. When I asked where are the children of the Jewish intelligentsia, I was told they are in the Christian kindergarten. I recall the painful impression That this answer made on me. My first visit was to Christian kindergarten.

The Committee of the Kindergarten, 1934

From right to left: Kurfuerst, Z. Schekhter, Prin, Tutoress, Ostern

It was arranged very nicely in a decent apartment but I was shocked to see the Jewish children kneeling at the picture of the holy mother, together with the Christian children for morning prayer. I decided then to try my best to take our children from the Christian kindergarten.

I first began to improve our kindergarten to be worthy of its name. "Tarbut" rented two large and long rooms. After a long battle, explanations, and pleas, I finally managed to convince the cultural committee of the need to dedicate one of the rooms solely for the use of the kindergarten. I painted all the furniture myself, and the floor I painted red. I decorated the walls with pictures and placed pots and flowers on the windows. Unfortunately, there was no room for a garden because we did not have a yard. I gradually introduced all sorts of games and instruments. I followed Montefiore's method, whereby I built most of the instruments myself with the help of the children. I established a workshop for wood and other crafts. My goal was to begin the education of good pioneers for Eretz Israel at an early age.

I must note that I found understanding and dedication from the kindergarten committee. In the beginning, the number of children was low, and the tuition fees were insufficient to cover the expenses. The committee organized various activities to balance the budget. The main activity was the show by the children in the "Sokoll" hall in Hannukah. The educator in me objected strongly to the appearance of the children as "artists" in such a large hall full of strangers. I fought against such a show but did not prevail since it had already become a tradition. It also served as propaganda. The kindergarten committee overruled me. The Christian kindergarten also conducted a public show once a year.

The appearance of the children was successful in several aspects. After the show, dances and games were organized in the large hall with the participation of guest children. There was a rich and nicely organized snack bar, a large orchestra of wind instruments, and many other surprises. The women of "Tarbut" invested a substantial effort in organizing the ball. "Tarbut" halls were bustling like beehives, with members who came to help in the preparations for the ball. Everyone wanted that ball to succeed. Indeed, the ball covered all the deficits of the entire year.

I started an educational activity among the potential parents by conducting individual discussions, home visits, parents' gatherings, lectures about education in early childhood, national education, and value of our national holidays, the education towards work and social life, mutual aid, and more. I have to mention, with feelings of gratitude, Mrs. Shmorek, who was our regular lecturer at the parents' gatherings. She lectures on topics that I had difficulties with. As a result of these activities, a flow of the children of the Jewish intelligentsia ensued. They realized that even "Tarbut" can organize a kindergarten according to hygienic and pedagogical principles. We also were privileged to be visited and praised by the Christian supervisor from the government's education department. The number of children exceeded all estimates, and we were forced to hire a helper.

I should mention here a daring trip that I organized on the "Lag BaOmer" holiday. I rented several cabs, and we decorated them with our national flags. Every child was dressed in white and was holding a bow decorated in blue and white. We invited the available mothers, sat down in the cabs, drove through streets with deafening singing, and went to the "Gaia" (A forest distanced several kilometers from the city). We spent several hours there, playing games, eating a festive meal, and singing. We went back home in high spirits. That daring trip was a subject for conversion by all.

The kindergarten was a big center for the youth, members of "Tarbut". I had many volunteers helping to prepare instruments and games before every celebration. We spent many pleasant evenings on improvement and enhancement work. Dear and delightful youth grew up in Ternopil, dedicated to national ideas.

During my four years of work in Ternopil, I became attached and fell in love with the city. Some of my students reached Eretz Israel as children with their parents, and I also followed their progress here. However, most of them were annihilated by the defiled hand. May their memory be blessed.

[Columns 305-306]

The Jewish Theater in Ternopil

by Dr. Moshe Fiol

Translated by Moshe Kutten

Ternopil, the district city of Ternopil of forty thousand people, did not have regular Polish or Ukrainian theaters. From time to time, some troupes bothered to appear in our city from the outside, but with little success. Their success was limited because they stayed with us only a short period and were not popular except for the intelligentsia circles. The approach of the Jewish public to the theater was completely different. Ternopil Jews got to see different troupes, from popular troupes to the best representatives of the theater world. The Jewish artists sometimes stayed whole seasons in the city, and when they were about to leave, new troupes were waiting at the gates, announcing their future shows. I remember seasons when two troupes appeared at the same time. Besides theater troupes, prominent artists appear from the outside, as well as local semi-amateurish artists.

Before the First World War, the shows were mainly held in a hall, which the people called the "Schloss". After that, they usually rented the Ukrainian theater building "Bratztva Mishchenskia" for the shows until the building became the permanent location for the Jewish theater. The Polish theater "Sokol" was also made available for Jewish artists after the First World War. Only when the state of the Jews became more distressed, the Jewish theater had to move to the movie theater and the Polish workers' club "Gaviazde".

The remarkable appreciation the Jewish public in our city had shown toward the theater, either as spectators or by working on the stage, can be attributed not only to the fondness for the spoken Jewish language, jokes, and folklore but also to the unique geographical position of the city.

Ternopil was located not far from Galitsia's capital, Lviv, which served as the center for many theaters. Also, the short distance to the Russian border was an advantage, as Russian Jewish artists considered Ternopil their first artistic stop on their way abroad. The fondness the wandering artists received from us in Ternopil influenced their decision to elongate their stay in the city. As an example, we should mention the artistic couple Felpeda who, after the First World War, intended to just pass through the city to other places and even held contracts from Jewish theaters in the US. However, from the first moment of residing in Ternopil, they felt the warm cultural atmosphere that encircled them. The local artists held on to them for two seasons and appeared together. When the couple left the city, the local troupe continued with more vigor and energy in its theatrical activity.

That theatrical club, which took the initiative in its hands, was close, in its spirit and status to the professional guilds. The actors were commoners, who worked in workshops during the day, gathered in the evenings, and busied themselves with their artistic work, which they considered a holy mission. Here is the place to praise those dear people who did not let any political element take over their artistic aspirations. They did not separate between proletarian and any other art. They even assisted other drama clubs we will mention below.

We will remember these dear people in their heartfelt simplicity. How high-souled these commoners were! With deep intuition and sincere love for the art, they fulfilled their aspiration. These were: The brothers Strusler, Emil Schorr, Kaufman, Hennig, Weizer, and Mrs. Luftig. May their memory be blessed.

The years following the First World War brought with them the formation of a new theater in the Jewish world. The echoes of Vilna Troupe and the artistic theaters in Warsaw, Moscow, and New York arrived in the city. Only a short while later, these famous theaters appeared in Ternopil. People from all walks of life visited the popular theaters and enjoyed

[Columns 307-308]

Goldfaden's plays "Akedat Yitzkahk" ["Binding of Isaac"] and "Shulamith". The intelligentsia preferred the new artistic theater. That was the first time the words of the great dramatists, such as Romain Rolland, Hayermans, Nikolai Gogol, Moliere, and others, could be heard from the stage in Yiddish. That was also the first-time people in the city saw the original plays and comedies by Ansky, Asch, Wajter, Nomberg, Shalom Aleikhem, and others.

The high artistic level of the new theater impressed the intellectual spectators, so much so that a group of students who wished to follow the artistic theater was organized. That was how the academic drama troupe "Ansky" was established. Jewish male and female students who were originally distanced from the Jewish national language and culture immersed themselves in serious artistic work. To gain experience on the stage, they began showing easy plays. After acquiring the language and stage experience, they became a meaningful studio that no longer ascribed importance to the number of plays but their quality. Thus, the preparations began for the famous play - "HaAverkh MeVilna" ["The Young Man of Vilna", or in Yiddish - "Der Vilner Balebesl"] by Mark Arenstein. The play was chosen not only due to its great literacy value but also because of the large number of characters, which allowed many actors to gain experience. Among the participants in that play, some had already endeared themselves to the audience with their acclaimed talent. First and foremost, we should mention Emil Blishtift Z"L. That assimilating student, who initially did not even know Yiddish, became an enthusiastic follower of the Jewish culture. He distanced himself from any other occupation and dedicated himself, without any reservation, to the Jewish theater. The others etched in my memory were: Levinkron, Liebergal, the brothers Gelber, Mrs. Simi Ger, and Mrs. Nagler, may their memory be blessed, and Kornblit and Kinstler, may they live long, who headed the troupe. We should also mention the former professional actor Mr. Peled Z"L who served as the volunteer director for some time. We should also note the academic association "Bar Kokhba, where most of the participants came from, and also allowed the club's rehearsals to be held in their hall.

The intelligentsia and other layers of the Jewish population flocked to see these shows. Professional actors from the professional Jewish and Polish theaters often attended the shows. There is no doubt the repertoire of the drama clubs greatly influenced the repertoire of the professional theaters. Thus, advertisements for the plays by Ansky - "The Dybbuk" and "Day and Night", Gutzkov - "Uriel D'akosta" and Asch - "Esh Nekamot" ["God of Vengeance"], and others began to appear.

During the time when the two drama clubs experienced successes, the idea came about that for the advancement of the common goal it would be

beneficial to unify. That was how the partition between the two clubs fell, and a unified troupe, under the management of the author of these lines, was established. The first and only literary theater began its operation in the city. Credit must be given to the theater for a whole series of successes. It would be sufficient to mention part of its repertoire to get some idea about the amount of work. In the winter season of 1927, the following plays appeared: "Two Hundred Thousand" and "It is hard to be a Jew" by Shalom Aleikhem, "The Eternal Wandering Jew" and "The Singer of His Sorrow" [In Yiddish - "Der Zinger fun zayn Troyer"] by Osip Dymov [pseudo name of Isidorovich Perelman], "The Last Days of our Lives" by Andreyev, "Motkeh the Thief" [in Yiddish - "Motkeh Ganev"] by Asch, "The Village Boy" [in Yiddish - "Yankel Boyle oder Der Dorfs-Yung"] by Kobrin, and "The Wall" [in Yiddish- "Di Vant"] by Segalovitz. Besides the big plays, we organized, on various occasions, literary evenings, where we played poems and stories by Bialik, Peretz, and others. We also showed plays in Polish for the youth who did not understand Yiddish.

Students of the Dramatical Troupe "Ansky" in Ternopil, 1923

[Columns 309-310]

At some point, Polish actors turned to us with a proposal to collaborate on showing the "Dybbuk" in the Polish language. However, the general atmosphere was unsuitable for such a collaborative project. At that same time, clouds appeared in the sky of the Polish Jewry. The air became thicker and thicker, and the approaching storm was felt. The Poles stopped renting halls for Jews. The censor demanded to receive a Polish translation of every play. Hopelessness prevailed, and the youth began to dream about leaving the country. The Zionist organizations grew from one day to another, and the desire to immigrate strengthened. The gray days blackened until the 1st of September 1939, when the end to everything came.

The Dramatical Club "Hatikvah", 1925

[Columns 311-312]

Wolfstahl Family

"Wolfstahl Orchestra"

by M. Sh. Geshuri

Translated by Moshe Kutten

Ternopil people are boasting, until today, about the musical Wolfstahl family that gave great pleasure to the people of Ternopil with its music. The founder of the family, Khoneh Wolfstahl (1851 – 1924), was born in Tysmenytsia near Stanislaw [today Ivano-Frankivsk] to his cantor father. The latter was a good player and loved music. Instilled that love in his seven sons. Troubled by worries about their livelihood, the family settled in Ternopil, where they organized themselves as the "Wolfstahl Orchestra".

As a child, Wolfstahl sang in a chorus with his brothers under his father, the cantor. Thanks to his compositions, the band, which traveled around and played in rich people and Admors' courts, acquired substantial fame in Galitsia, particularly in Ternopil, where it played for many years.

Wolfstahl was autodidact in music. He did not receive any music education until his service in the [Austrian] army as a military musician. During his military service, Wolfstahl composed several military marches, waltzes, and other dance melodies. His compositions were played by military orchestras throughout Habsburg's kingdom.

For his brothers to play his compositions, he was forced to send them to foreign composers. Only after these compositions were issued under foreign names, the brothers could include them in their reportorial. Wolfstahl did not publish these compositions in print. Only a few were preserved by some orchestras. Most of them were forgotten or remained under the name of other composers.

Wolfstahl's true passion was discovered in the Jewish theater when he served as a conductor of Ya'akov Ber Gimpel's chorus. He wrote compositions for the theatrical operettas: "Satan as a Savior" by Moshe Schorr, "R' Yehuda HaLevi", "Bat Yerushalaim" ["Jerusalem Daughter"], and "Bustanai" ["Orchardist"] by Yitzkhak Auerbakh, and "Queen Sheba" and "HaNeshef Hakomi" ["The Comical Ball"] [the name of the play in the article - "The Comic Bal" seems to be erroneous]. These operettas held on for years as part of the repertoire of the Jewish theaters in Eastern and Western Europe. Many of Wolfstahl's melodies were sung by the people as folklore melodies.

Due to his poor financial situation, he was forced to play day and night. Wolfstahl was forced to organize his own ensemble, have a tour throughout Galitsia and Bukovina, and also played in Budapest and Berlin. In the end, the ensemble disbanded and he settled with his family in Lviv. During the First World War, Wolfstahl resided in Vienna and conducted the Jewish theater Orchestra there. After the war, he returned to Lviv and played at weddings and cafes. During the pogroms in Lviv, the artists café, where he usually played, was destroyed, and he was left without a means to make a living.

Marcus Wolfstahl

Marcus Wolfstahl was a great musician from the same family, who resided in Ternopil, and gave music lessons, including cantors. One of his students was the cantor Mordekhai Shnormakher, a native of Drohobych. The latter studied with Marcus to play the contrabass. When he gained a bass voice, after losing his young voice, he began to sing with the local cantor in Ternopil, Nisan from Odesa, who was a great musician. Marcus Wolfstahl resided in Ternopil for a long time. From there he moved to Lviv, where he learned to play the piano with the Polish pianist Yartzki. He also studied harmony and other musical areas with the conductor of the Lviv Orchestra, Badenstein. After he learned to speak German, he moved to America and served as a cantor there.

[Columns 313-314]

Khone Wolfstahl

by Karl Rothaus[1]

Translated by Moshe Kutten

Many eventful years have passed in my life, which I devoted to music. I began playing in my childhood. I still remember those initial days when a good angel stood by my cradle – a man with a royal beard, in the style of [the emperor] Franz Joseph. His blue eyes shined on a pleasant face that sang melodies, with a nicely carved nose, and a forehead of a distinguished musician.

The man was respectable and possessed good manners. His hands caressed me like warm father's hands, and his fingers were musician's fingers proficient in all instruments, especially the violin and cello.

Sometimes, during the snow and freeze-filled fall mornings, I encountered Khone Wolfstahl while passing through Sobieski Square, marching home. He entertained the audience during the entire night and played dance melodies with his band until the light of day. Then, with the violin half-hidden under his coat's wings, close to his heart, he marched home while his big galoshes creaked in the snow. I greeted him, feeling guilty: I went out on my way to school following a pleasant sleep and a hearty meal, while my uncle had to earn his living "in that way". There was always an apologetic undertone in his response since he knew that people did not appreciate his work.

When I started my daily studies of Greek, Roman, and history literature, Khone would arrive home, drink coffee, and rest for a few hours. His apartment, situated within our spacious house, was very small: one bedroom and a small kitchen. When he was resting from the endless rehearsals playing Waltzes, Polkas, and quartets, his wife Sara, would sit down idle to avoid disturbing him. She did not even dare to read a book. Indeed, who wants to read a book in the morning? A while later, she would glance at her watch and sneak quietly out to go shopping. Upon her return, she would already find him sitting at the kitchen table writing music notes. Composing music brought comfort to his delicate soul but also the curse of obsession, passion, and meager living.

Khone Wolfstahl

Khone Wolfstahl never got the chance to study music. His entire music education was acquired while serving in the [Austrian] army. That was where he learned how to play all of the instruments, organize and conduct an orchestra, and compose his new compositions.

In his civil life, while he played as a member of a "Kley Zemer" [musical band], he became a father of four. He was then tasked with the difficult role of making a living for his family by music involvement only: playing violin and cello, solo or in a band, playing dancing music, playing classical and classical-like music on orchestra's instruments, and composing music on commission. For a fee of ten coronas, he would organize a band of four musicians. To best harmonize the tones, he would incorporate a violin, flute, harp, and double bass. For an additional charge of 4 coronas, he would add some players, for example, one or two violins, a double bass, and a flute. Concerning the program, Khone would incorporate music from different backgrounds: old melodies, Jewish songs, parts of modern operettas, and ending with mazurkas. Khone would prepare the program for every band and perform the following night.

He would compose melodies deep in his heart, filled with the warmth and dedication of a true artist. Everything he touched, was involved music: Roses' Waltz for his daughter's birthday, a polonaise-styled glorification song for a Polish noble (Prince Sapieha), and story tales using amusing rhymes for a little child.

Khone considered receiving money for music compositions, an insipid matter. He was tortured by sleeplessness, lived in poverty and under pressure, and swallowed his wife's silent reprimands, only to be able to sit down and compose his melodies.

He struck luck when the manager of a Jewish theater, where he and his orchestra often played, noticed him. The head of the theater in Lamberg [Lviv] decided to allow Khone the opportunity to show his ability;

[Columns 315-316]

The theater captured the heart and mind of the music composer.

Allow me to note that I am not seeing the Jewish theater with an evil eye. The "Brody Singers", and the folk plays by Gordin were etched in my memory as the birthplace of pure Jewish art. As a youth, I experienced the events and experiences of life's light and shadows at the Gimpel's theater. There was where I learned to laugh and cry with the play's characters.

When Khone was tasked with the new role, a bountiful spring of melodies, hymns, waltzes, and polkas was awakened in him. The new theater of "*a drameh mit tantz un gezang*" (Jewish drama with dance and singing) was born. Khone prepared the libretto, composed the music, and wrote the music notes. Rehearsals were conducted and repeated, and the performance was entirely at the hand of my uncle, Khone Wolfstahl. I recall the plays: "Bat Yerushalaim" ["Jerusalem Daughter"], "Bustanai" ["Orchardist"], and "Shalosh Matanot" ["Three Presents"].

The musicals were ordered and the wage was paid in cash. According to my memory, Gimpel paid 200 coronas for each musical, and he gained all rights to it. The sum was agreed upon when Wolfstahl was ordered by his physician to travel to Carlsbad for four weeks of therapy. The costs associated with such a trip, including the taxes, physician's fees, and travel expenses, were estimated to be 200 coronas, and that was the sum requested by Khone as a wage for his work. He did not request a penny more.

The publishers did not show any interest in these compositions and plays, so Khone did not gain any additional encouragement or publicity. However, the songs, melodies, and ideas, began to appeal to the Jews in all countries Jews resided. Sometimes, Khone Wolfstahl's name was mentioned, however, his name was omitted. Nobody paid attention to that except Khone's wife, whose heart was broken because of that. However, she learned to stay silent and share the fate of the true artist and skillful composer. Besides, she knew that it was beyond Khone's ability to change things around and that he was happy with what he got.

The circumstances and events occurring over time changed his life, in a way they did for the entire world. During the First World War, I saw Khone among the refugees in Vienna as a wonderer and homeless, but he also enjoyed the atmosphere of musical Vienna.

When the war was over, he returned to his city, Lamberg [Lviv]. I visited him there. His apartment was located in a gloomy building in the corner of the yard. Metal scraps were scattered all over the yard and a sign was hung on the wall: "The office of Robfogel Zonena and Partners". The door opened on the second floor into a narrow and dark room. From beyond the table, I saw the kind face of my uncle, Khone Wolfstahl. I spent hours with him, his wife, and his daughter Rosa. I felt that the time came for the publication of his compositions. I hind as much to him, but he was undecided and hesitant in his response, so the matter was postponed.

* * *

Ternopil, the birth city of Khone (and mine), the city in the Austro-Hungary kingdom, ceased to exist. Since then, it transferred to the hands of the Poles, Ukrainians, and Poles again, conquered by the Germans and then, the Russians, who were rumored to name the city Tomashinkgrad. And the Jews, whom Khone lived among, and for whom he composed his music, where are they? Many of his generation, his friends and admirers, perished in the Holocaust. Only a few survived. Some are scattered in European countries, and some arrived in New York, but, most of the surviving remnants reached the safe shores of our homeland in Israel. The time has come for us to gather his compositions and publish them so that they remain in the hands of the nation in Israel.

Book Editor's Note:

    1.   When this hearty article about Khone Wolfstahl was prepared for print (December 1954), we received the news about its author's death. Karl Rothaus, a native of Ternopil, was a prodigy. He played the piano from the age of five, and composed his first musical composition at the age of seven. His name is associated with an unbreakable bond with the history of the modern Hebrew theater due to his famous composition he wrote for the play "Uriel Acosta", and the less–known music for "Shylok" played at [Israeli National Theater] "HaBima". He composed many symphonies, chamber compositions, operas, and ballets. With the eruption of the Second World War, he moved to the US. He taught and guided a whole generation of young musicians, and served as the vice president of the International Music Corporation for Modern Music.

[Columns 317-318]

Folklore Chapters

As Told by the People

by A. Landfish

Translated by Moshe Kutten

From time immemorial, it was customary at the Old Synagogue, before the concluding prayer on Yom Kippur, to hang on the ark a white elongated *Parokhet* [a curtain for the ark]. The writing on that *Parokhet* was embroidered with diamonds and gems: "*Yom Miyamim Hukhas – Yom Kippur HaMeyukhas*" [A great importance was attributed to that day – Yom Kippur an honored day – a hymn sang as part of the Musaf prayer of Yom Kippur].

My father, Alter Landfish Z"L, was born in 1835 [may be an error M.K.]. He was a pious and G-d fearing man. We used to pray for many years at the Old Beit HaMidrash, however, after his oldest son died, he moved to the Old Synagogue because they used to dance and sing at the Old *Beit HaMidrash*.

The Old Synagogue was an old stone building in which the chill was always present. An atmosphere of seriousness enveloped it. They did not dance or sing there, even during *the Simkhat Torah holiday*, like in the other houses of prayer.

Aba [father] once told us the history of the *Parokhet*:

A wealthy, pious, and honorable Jew, R' Shalom Dankner, used to pray there at the western wall for many years. During the Days of Awe, the *custom* was to "auction off" the Torah *Aliya's* [the blessing before and after Torah reading] and other honoring functions, except at the opening of the Ne'ila prayer [concluding prayer], which R' Shalom Dankner was always honored with. Nobody dared to encroach on his role even after he lost his wealth. When the *Gabbai* would announce:" A gulden for the opening of Ne'ila – the first call!" the crowd remained silent, and nobody thought to compete with R' Shalom Dankner.

However, an unprecedented event occurred once. When the *Gabbai issued* his customary auction announcement, one Jew named Sapiluk, a commoner who became rich, raised his two fingers – signaling that he was willing to pay more. Embarrassment encompassed the synagogue, and everybody jumped on their feet to see who dared to break the tradition. Shouts and threats were heard. Following a short discussion, the *Gabbais* decided to continue the auction to allow for winning it for R' Shalom.

However, when the auction price reached a substantial sum, a small bag filled with jewelry fell on the *Gabbais*' table. R' Shalom Dankner's wife threw it from the women's section since she could not bear to see her husband's sorrow and humiliation. At that point, Sapiluk could not overbid, and R' Shalom Dankner won the auction.

After Yom Kippur, the *Gabbais* decided to return the jewels to Mrs. Dankner and offered that she would only pay a symbolic sum. However, she refused to receive her Jewels back. It was then decided to sew a *Parokhet,* embryoid the writing using diamonds and gems, and hang it every year before the opening of the Ne'ila prayer. Two *Gabbais* stood by and guarded the *Parokhet* during the prayers and hid it in a safe place after the prayers.

When the First World War erupted, the *Parokhet* was transferred to Vienna, and I do not know its fate.

* * *

In 1896, a Zionist organization by the name of "A'havat Tzion" ["Love of Zion"] was established in Ternopil. Young men and women gathered, read newspapers, and played chess; A lecture was organized from the to time. A ball called "*Neshef HaMacabbim*" [Macabbees Ball] was organized on Hanukkah, and sometimes an amateur play was shown.

At the same time, a Jewish scholar lived in Ternopil called Mania Maggid. According to people's opinions, he could have served as a rabbinical judge, but he did not come from a good lineage. Mania Maggid was an opponent of Zionism, but his daughter, a beautiful girl of 17, joined the Zionist organization and visited its club without her parent's knowledge. There she met a nice youth with a pleasant voice, a painter, and they fell in love with each other. It was clear that R' Mania would not agree to the match under any circumstances.

Once, in Purim, we heard the drums beating and the flutes playing. A group of Purim actors went from house to house, as was customary in those days, to play short sketches about biblical subjects. And here, the group approached

[Columns 319-320]

R' Mania's home and following them was a large crowd of boys and girls. When the actors entered the house, the entire crowd forced themselves in, me included. R' Mania was sitting at a set table, with [his family and] a few guests. The actors played the scene from the Book of Esther: King Ahasuerus marries Esther. The merrymaker began to sing, and the gathered youth repeated after him. With all the noise and tumult, nobody noticed that R' Mania's daughter disappeared from beyond the table and mixed with the crowd. One of the couple's confidants handed the daughter a mask, dress, and crown. "King Ahasuerus" approached her then, took out a ring, put it on her finger, and said in a loud voice [the Jewish wedding vow]: "*Harei aat mekudeshet lee…* ["Behold you are consecrated unto me…"]. Everybody laughed and yelled "*Mazal Tov*" and served the couple wine. Then "King Ahasuerus" and Queen Esther" took off their masks. To the embarrassment of the parents, "Queen Esther" turned out to be none other than their daughter, and "King Ahasuerus" was none other than the painter… Panic arose in the room. R' Mania set motionless like a fossil. His wife fainted, and they had to call a doctor. The entire crowd disappeared. The city was agitated and tumultuous. The Zionists' opponents used the case to gore the movement and defile it. The parents and the rabbinate tried to convince the painter to divorce his wife, but all their efforts were in vain. The couple could not see any other way out except to leave the native city and immigrate to America.

* * *

Sixty years ago[1] , the price of a litra of veal in Ternopil was fourteen cents [hellers?], However, one Jewish villager brought veal to the city daily and sold it for twelve cents. There were many, particularly among the poor, who jumped at the bargain and bought all their meat from that villager. That lasted for about three years. One day, the gabbais announced, in all the synagogues and houses of prayer, that anybody who bought meat from that villager must throw away the pots and kitchen tools since they were forbidden. They also disallow selling them to the gentiles. Embarrassment descended on the city since most of the people who bought the meat from the villagers were poor. In addition to their sorrow for eating *taref* [non-Kosher] meat for years, they had to throw away the tools they used to cook it. The rabbinate decided to excommunicate the person who failed the city by supplying *taref* meat.

I still see the scene of the ex-communication in front of my eyes. At 3 p.m. on Wednesday, a caretaker passed the streets and used his hammer to knock on the shutters of stores and homes. It was a signal for everybody to gather at the synagogue. A crowd of several thousand Jews gathered shortly while later. Black candles were lit and Rabbi Shimon BABa"Da Jew with a majestic appearance, spoke about the wrong that was done to the city Jews. He later read the "Rebuke Torah Portion*",* and the audience responded with "Amen". When the rabbi finished the rebuke, he ordered the Jewish villager to leave the synagogue and never come again among the Jews. With dead silence and the people standing on both sides of the aisle, the villager walked crying. Excommunicated by his fellow Jews, the villager had to leave the village and escape to America.

Translator's Note:

1. Here and wherever the text refers to the current time, it means the time of publication - February 1955.

Words in the Name of their Sayer
[Verbatim Quotation]

by M. Deutsch

Translated by Moshe Kutten

As well known, Yosef Perl was not kind to the *Tzadikim*; On the contrary, he did not shy away from using the police to expel a *Tzadik* who happened to stop by Ternopil.

One of the dignitaries in the court of the Zhydachiv Hasidim came out with a cunning idea: "I will go to Ternopil, and Yosef Perl will expel me by the force of the police. Thus, I will become famous among the Hasidim". He dressed in a silk gown and wore a "*Spodik*" on his head, traveled to Ternopil, and walked around by the home of Yosef Perl. Perl noticed him when he went out on his terrace and said:

"You are walking around here in vain, I will not expel you from Ternopil by calling on the police. I do not intend to make you a rabbi".

* * *

Yosef Perl tried his best to ensure that the Jews attained equal rights compared to the rights enjoyed by other citizens. He had some success. His son was the first Jew to study pharmacology. When the son completed his studies, he planned to open a pharmacy. He needed a license for it, and he could not obtain one despite his many inquiries. Yosef Perl was forced to turn to the king and requested to speak with him. The king accepted his request, and Perl got to see the king and plead his wish. The king responded: "So what, let him begin working in another profession, and he will be fine". Perl answered: "Yes your honor the king, but even Your Majesty can not give my son back the years he spent studying".

[Columns 321-322]

* * *

Yitzkhak Pasternak was one of the famous Chortkiv Hasidim and spent all his days in the company of the Hasidim in a tavern on a cup of honey water and stories telling the praises of the *Tzadik* and words of the Torah.

He made a living by brokering between the estate owners and the merchants. He once entered the home of an estate owner to talk about some business. He did not find him at home because the estate owner spent his days in the tavern. His wife was angry about her husband, who neglected his work, and she ran to the tavern to fetch him. When Pasternak saw her from afar, he asked the barman to pour a cup of "honey water" from "that very old wine. When she entered, he welcomed her kindly, and before she opened her mouth, he told her: "First, please drink this cup of honey water since today is the anniversary of the death of the holy *Tzadik*, may his memory protect us". The woman drank the honey water, became dizzy, and had to sit down and rest. She fell asleep a minute later. When she woke up, her husband told her: "You see? That is how we are being tortured for years!"

* * *

Shmerl Eikenbaum interpreted the phrase written above the synagogue of the enlightened people: "This is the gate of the LORD; *Tzadikim* shall enter through it" [Psalms 118:20] as follows: "Like righteous come through the gate, so it is the gate of G-D".

He interpreted the name: "Balak ben Tzippor" [King of Moab - Numbers 22:2] as "Ba Lock ben Tzippor" [In Hebrew – "A lock, the son of Tzippor, is coming" or] in Yiddish (in Ashkenazy accent) – A Jew with "leken" (curly sidelocks) is coming.

He said:" I thought that this was somebody like a son of a Tzadik*[In Hebrew* – ben means son], but I found out that he is the son of a bird [in Hebrew, tzippor means a bird] – so he is a free bird or a free man.

* * *

Mykulyntsi [Mikulnitza] is a small town located not far from Ternopil. A Jew who resided there used to walk every day, very early in the morning, with a *Talit* and *Tefilin* to pray. One day, a wagon harnessed to four horses stopped by him. The *Paritz* [wealthy man] sitting in the wagon asked the Jew:"

"What *Paritz* owns this town?". The Jew answered:" Before Rozhin people came here, the town belonged to the *Tzadik* from Stratyn, however after the people from Rozhin came, the town is divided into two: A half belongs to the *Tzadikim* from Rozhin and another half to the *Tzadikim* from Stratyn".

* * *

Three grandsons of famous *Tzadikim* resided in Ternopil, and many from the lower classes were among their followers.

During one of the winter nights, one of the *Tzadikim* hears knocks on the door and a voice calling: "Rabbi – open!". The rabbi gets off his bed, washes his hands, wears warm clothing, and sits on his chair. Two poor women come in and begin to cry: "Rabbi, we have a woman in our family, who has difficulties in her childbirth, and we come to ask you to pray for her". The rabbi sits down and expects to see the redemption money but does not see anything in a form of a coin. He ponders in his mind – what should he do? Did he get off his bed in the such cold for nothing? No money? He tells the women: "Please know that a harsh sentence hangs over that woman, and I cannot do anything for her myself. Go and wake up the two ther *Tzadikim* in the city, and the three of us will try to avert that sentence".

To the Khupa

by Meir Khartiner[a][1]

Translated by Jerrold Landau

The entertainment makes noise and raises a tumult.
We have almost forgotten,
The bride and groom are fasting – oh no!
Everyone wants to eat!
The jester shouts like a goy:
"Beloved *mekhutanim* [in-laws]!
The crowd is not at this point
They are falling on their faces!
It is time to conduct the khupa, the khupa, the khupa
It is time to set up the khupa – the khupa, let's get on with it already!"

[Columns 323-324]

Thank G-d they stopped fighting
Already the two sides:
Let's go Jews, lets move
To the khupa – hooray!
Waiting already in front of the synagogue

Is the Society of Good Deeds: [a group to help with the festivities at the wedding]
Young girls, young men – so many! –
Playing pranks, laughing, crying –
Suddenly voices: Be quiet already! They are already coming – they are already coming!
Suddenly voices: Be quiet already! They are already coming, hey hey hey!

Come forward, first class musicians:
Moshe Rimpel the fiddler
Meilech Buhay with the bass,
Berl with the cymbals.
Avraham'el raps on the drum,
Yona on the cymbals:
Wolf blasts the trumpet.
It resonates through the streets:
Tom tadrata tata, ta tata, ta tata!
Tom tadrata tata – tadrata tata ta!

A crowd, a large group!
All in their Sabbath clothes:
The groom's side is few,
How large is the bride's side.
Coming first is a fine Jew
Ship among ships!
His belly is completely immersed
In the tractate of gizzards [i.e., he is corpulent, and seemingly well fed] –
It is the bride's father, the father, the father!
It is the bride's father – the father, ho ho ho!

Behind him is a young lamb [The Hebrew translates it as tail]
The clothes of great feeding [i.e., of wealth],
Royal garb, with a *streimel*
The first product of the needle: [i.e., the finest tailoring]
Two or three hairs in his beard,
His *peyos* are in good form –
It seems that he is very preoccupied
He is reviewing his speech –
Hooray, the groom is coming, the groom, the groom!
Hooray, the groom is coming – the groom very exquisite!

[Columns 325-326]

Right and left, on every side
The entourage is coming!
Brother-in-law Mekhtshe, a proper Jew
Yentkhe the regal:
Drags himself like a pest
A sort of ruddy sort.
Instead of a *streimel*, he had a regular cap.
A cane with a *gulke* [a walking stick?] –
It is our rabbi, the rabbi, the rabbi!
And indeed, it is our rabbi – the rabbi, ti di da!

And the Jews are marching en masse
Fie! A large camp:
The relative Zerach, the relative Zetz
The relative Shalom Shakhna
A woman with a double chin rejoices
As wide as Noah's ark,
Moving like the Czar's horses
Who is the woman?
Mazel Tov, the mother-in-law, the mother-in-law, the mother-in-law!
Mazel Tov, the mother-in—law – the mother-in-law, dear groom!

A variegated crowd moves along
All are decked with gold:
Relatives without number,
Girls and tall men!
They lead, like a blind cow
Some girl,
Her face is covered with a veil,
Behind her they follow –
O, the beautiful bride, the bride, the bride!
O, the beautiful bride – the bride, without invoking the evil eye!

But – is the girl lacking grace,
Is she not happy?
There is something that cannot be understood –
Jews, go slowly!
Now it almost seems to me,
She wipes her eyes – –
The flute plays from afar,
It wishes to ask her:
My bride, why are you crying, why are you crying, why are you crying?
My bride, why are you crying – why are you crying? *Oy, oy, oy!*

[Columns 327-328]

Why are you crying now
Before the khupa circle? –
O, you beautiful, sweet child
Do you love another boy!
O, the one young of years knowns
Perhaps you are!
The fiddle sighs, so sweet,
It moves the soul:
Sweet you were – you were, *oy vey zmir* [woe is me]!
Sweet you were – you were, *oy vey zmir* [woe is me]!

Perhaps G-d will make a miracle,
As is in books –
My girl, questions, questions,
Out of childhood!
See you mother, with the girdle,
Your father, with fine pedigree – – –

The bass calls out,
Angry like a thousand winds:
A Jewish girl is buried, buried, buried!
A Jewish girl is buried – the spirit of a good year!

It is already not far from here,
My girl, your grave!
The khupa stands, the groom
Does not even move a limb…
There are numerous differentiations!
Cantor, o, a song!
She will circle seven times [at the wedding ceremony, the bride circles the groom seven times]
She will put on the ring –
Trakh! A glass shatters – a heart – a glass
Trakh! A glass shatters – a little heart, a little one. [Trakh is onomatopoeia]

And the Khupa is now over
With the ten *Hamelech's* [probably a custom to recite *Hamelech* – the king – ten times]
The musicians start up again
And they play a happy song.
Jews form
A hearty circle,
Women tap on the cans
They have married off a girl!
Merry and joyous, and joyous, and joyous!
Merry and joyous – and joyous – *oy vey vey*!

[Columns 329-330]

    Khana, Khaya the gabbai's wife
    Dances to the point that her kerchief vibrates
    The mother-in-law gestures
    The father-in-law with the belly (sings):
    "Praised is He forever,
    Who lives forever!
    With good *mazel* [good fortune] I am again a father-in-law
    I have married off the *mezinke* [youngest daughter]!
    Mazel tov to us all, to us all, to us all!
    Mazel tov to you all – to all *Mazel Tov*!"

Editor's Note:

a. The song "To the Khupa" was a famous popular song in Galicia from its Jewish sources. Its Hebrew translation was produced later by the author. The song and its melody were composed by M. Khartiner in 1905 for his friends in the Bar Kochba academic society in Ternopil, to sing on the wedding day of Dr. Yisrael Waldman of blessed memory.

Translator's Note:

1. This English translation is based on the Yiddish, from the left side (even columns) of the pages.

Notes for the song – To the Khupa by Meir Khartiner

Ternopil Throughout the Year

by Avner Avnon-Bronstein

Translated by Moshe Kutten

Through the thin fog formed after my departure, now approaching twenty years, Ternopil, my childhood and youth city, is standing tall in its beauty and charm. In actuality, it is a city like any other, but for me, it is a city unlike any other. My intimate "me'" is tied to its calm view and, at the same time, lively life, with thousands of threads. These threads differentiate it entirely from any other city in the world. It is my soul city. Every street, house, and person was absorbed in my heart and became part of it. Today, "after the great disaster", my heart is aching for all of the people who shaped my life at the beginning of my journey on earth. My emotion grows and explodes seven-fold when I remember the tragic and painful fact that all of that "was, and it is no more".

There is a will and need to rescue the memories of the past etched in my heart since time immemorial from oblivion. Perhaps doing so would bring healing and relief to the heart mournful for the life that passed and faded away forever…

Here is the amazing street named after Yosef Perl. When I returned from my wandering life in Vienna and Hungary in 1918, I went to that street. We settled in a house bordering Perl's school with its "Temple". I found my first friends on that street. That was where I spent my free and quiet time and contracted world after years of wondering. I was enrolled to study at Perl's school. Within its walls, I met the essence of the Jewish poor. We studied in a large class of eighty-seven students, seven on each bench. That was during the Ukrainian regime. The other schools were closed and therefore, Ukrainian and Polish children flocked to our school. The class educator was the old teacher, Glassgal, who served in this role for forty-three years. He was a noble-spirited man, one of the people one never forgets. I will always remember him affectionately and with admiration for his fatherly treatment of every child.

[Columns 331-332]

Our school principal, Okser, gave us a speech. I remember only one sentence from that speech: "You are young today, however, when you grow up, you will be proud that you were fortunate to study in the school named for Perl". We were ten years old then and did not understand the meaning of those words. However, over time I learned to understand their meaning well. I recall the teachers' lounge. A big picture of Yosef Perl hung at the center of the wall, a noble figure wearing an impressive uniform adorned with excellence awards medals on his chest. We thought the picture was of the emperor, but the caretaker corrected us: "This is Yosef Perl", he said. In reverence, we drew back…

The thick books in Perl's library made a huge impression on us. "May it be so for us to know the secret concealed within those books.

Perl Street obtained a unique character during the Days of Awe. The "temple", which was closed during the year except for holidays and Shabbat, was filled with people. We, the children, observed the many people, different from those we used to see in our street on weekdays, with curiosity. We knew they were important people who lived on Mitzkeivitz and Tarnovski streets. We always tried to get in and listen to the prayer, the cantor, and the chorus singing. We especially liked listening to the sermon by Dr. Taubles. He seemed to us as an ancient prophet (as much as we knew about prophets) with his style of speech and enthusiasm. We listened to him eagerly when it came to memorializing deceased exalted people who lived in the city and prayed in that "Temple": Yosef Perl, SHI"R, Nakhman Kromkhel… The entire audience became emotional when those names were mentioned. After so many years, it became clear that the distance between the audience and the people Dr. Taubles mentioned, was immense, and not just in time…

Almost opposite the Temple, on the other side of Perl's Steet, the middle-class people gathered in their house of prayer: Merchants, accountants, and trade workers. At least, that's what the golden sentence written on the front of the house said. Their *Tallitot* were larger than the ones in the "temple". A few houses further, the house of prayer "Yad Kharutzim" ["The Hand of Diligent"] was located. The following people prayed in that house of prayer: Craftsmen, kiosk owners, small merchants, and Jews without any specific trade, the commoners whose faces showed signs of worrying about their existence and hard work. Their *Tallitot* were big and showed a clear sign of old age…And again, a few houses down the street, the Minyan of Rabbi BABa"D, the rabbi from Yavorov, was located. During the long breaks in Days of Awe's prayer, the praying people got out onto the street. The view was spectacular. The holiday clothing, the various *Tallitot*, and the peaceful discussions during an easy stroll gave the street an unforgettable perspective. Only the people from BABa"D house of prayer did not mix with that crowed and kept a reasonable distance. These were the "silk Jews", who diligently boycotted the "Temple" and made sure not to pass it. Fate was "cruel" to them. The home of their rabbi was located on the "loathed" street carrying the name of their hated person - Yosef Perl… At the end of the break, the people returned, every person to their own house of prayer. Only the voices that emanated from the windows testified that there, on Perl Street, G-d gathered Jews from all classes to worship. The epitome of Ternopil's Jewish population prayed in that street.

The street looked entirely different on regular days. Here is the proud image of Rapoport, the owner of the bookshop, located across from the "Temple". Inside the store, there was a darkness of a typical antiquarian, evoking curtesy in the hearts of his visitors. That was a respectable store, far from external glitter, arousing a sense of eminence. The furniture warehouse of Mr. Katz was located in the neighboring house. And here is the owner of the warehouse, the elegantly dressed Jew, paunchy with his eternal cigar between his lips. Warming in the summer sun he seemed to me as the perfect advertisement for his furniture…

The Market

And here nearby is the grocery store of Cohen. A dark shop in the building "Yad Kharutzim", filled with merchandise in boxes, tin bins, drawers, barrels, and jars, but mostly empty of buyers… further, an empty yard and the workshop of Drexler. An old Jew, wearing glasses, a yarmulka on his head, agile, always running here and there and nobody knows why. His turnery wood creations amazed all. And so on – shops and workshops of all kinds and types, a textile workshop, barbershop, Zilber's shoemaker shop, the leather workshop of Winkler, Helman's pharmacy, the hatter shop of Podhortzer with the amazing cat in the windows, and more, and more. All of those shops were located on that small street. Life was peaceful but filled with worries about making a living. Quietly and without commotion, life continued.

[Columns 333-334]

Everyone carried their hardship silently and tried to show a smiling face so as not to be seen as a downer… It seemed that the glorious past helped them overcome the difficulties of the present. Despite being located among crowded and noisy markets, between Kazhimzhovski [Kazimierzowski?] Square and the central market, that cultural street was unique with atmospheres of regular days and holidays, and with its own soul…

On the other side of Perl Street w as the park, surrounded by four rows of houses, shops, and institutions – and Sobieski Square. Strange, but this was a park used by both Jews and soldiers. In the early hours of the summer mornings, the school children scattered through the park's corners, trying to improve their standing and memorize their lesson one last time before the test. They concentrated on their work, and every moment was dear. They "swallowed" compositions and "covered the material" in a hurry.

Following the students, old women appeared, slowly, slowly, mostly coming two at a time, sitting on the park's benches, enjoying the fresh air before the day's warmth began to oppress. Wearing sleepers, holding walking sticks, their faces wrinkled from the toil of life. They conducted conversations about days gone by, about physicians like Dr. Leibelinger who knew the secret of Carlsbad, and the healing seasons they spent in that enjoyable place in the distant past.

Later on – like in all other world parks - mothers appeared pushing children's carriages for a morning stroll. In the evenings, the park became the domain of another authority: The garrison's soldiers met there with their girlfriends, the maids. A different atmosphere prevailed in the Jewish Park named after Sobieski.

Surrounding the park – were four rows of buildings with a [unified] style and shape. Diversified private and public life, trade, and institutional life took place in these buildings. One front of the school named after Yosef Perl faced Sobieski Square. In that wing, a Hebrew school opened towards the end of the First World War. Hundreds of children acquired the Hebrew language there. Three or four idealistic teachers conducted the teaching. They were pioneers in the best and most sublime meaning of the word. They worked hard there for many years under difficult conditions without any external support. They seeded the idea of the national revival in the hearts of the Jewish children and youth in the city.

I can still see the clear images of these dear Hebrew teachers. Here is the teacher Greenspan, a flawless man with deep knowledge of the Hebrew cultural treasures. He was somewhat hasty and untidy but strict and boundlessly dedicated to his educational mission. He educated many generations of Hebrew-speaking youth. His spouse and partner in his educational mission was teacher Shitzer-Greenspan, a hearty woman with a tender approach to every child. And how can we forget teacher Gusta Steinberg and the innocent smile on her accommodating face? She was a woman that found all of her happiness in teaching and dedicated her life and future to it. She was a pioneer teacher. I have not found a person like her. I fondly remember teacher Sharaf, who came to us from afar and taught in our Hebrew school. Those teachers were the first to excite the children's imagination with the views from Eretz Israel. Here in the dark classes of Perl's school, Bialik's "heralding bird" flew for the first time for us bringing a greeting from the "valley, ravine, and top of the mountains" … Here we learned about the dreamers and the fighters of the Second Aliya. Here we absorbed Eretz Israel's atmosphere and the views of its fields and vineyards.

In the same classes, the Jewish self-defense headquarter was located during the days of horror between the various invasions during the horrific years 1918 – 1920. Here were the Jewish students and workers, who wore stripes on their arms and worked vigorously to gather rifles and ammunition. They then distributed them among the areas exposed to the danger of the attacks by the antisemitic gangs who wandered around and looked for the opportunity to conduct pogroms among the Jews. That was a period of lawlessness. We were children at the time, and I remember the excitement with which we accompanied every armed jew, going out to his mission and guard, thirty years before the establishment of IDF (Israel Defense Force)

On the other side of Sobieski Square – "Bar Kokhba", the Zionist association of the Jewish students and intelligentsia was located. In our generation, between the two World Wars, we have not always understood the character and role of that association as part of the city's public life. However, to its credit, we must mention its activity among the assimilating academic youth, saving many by enlisting them to be under the Zionism influence.

A short distance away, in the structure of the Polish "castle-fort" [Zamek], was the center of the Zionist activity in the city. The large public assemblies and conferences of all the Zionist parties were held in its large hall. Here was where saber-rattling by the rivals in the election for the Zionist Congresses took place. Here was where political life took shape. In the same hall, armature theater troupes tried their luck – Zionists, communists, and just people who were "crazy about" the theater.

The second floor of the castle building housed the evening lessons of the Hebrew union "Tarbut". Hundreds and thousands of youths and adults studied Hebrew here, taught by the best teachers in the city. Here, in parallel to the Hebrew school for children, was the circle of the Hebrew language, and its culture was closed. The Zionist idea received an original character among the learning crowd. In addition to the teachers, several individuals worked hard to develop the Hebrew lessons network in the city, In particular, we should credit Mr. Kurfuerst and Zusha Wahler.

[Columns 335-336]

Despite the propaganda of the [right-wing antisemitic "National Democratic Party" of the] Andakies to "rescue" the historic castle from the hands of the Jews, the blessed and efficient operation of the Jewish national movement took place there until the Holocaust.

At the side wing of the castle, operated, educated, and sparkled the Zionist union of the "No'ar Tzioni" ["Zionist Youth"]. That movement formed relatively late after the youth movements "HaShomer HaTzaier" ["The Young Guard"] and "Gordonia". However, it managed to attract the bourgeoisie youth and join them into the Zionist education circle in the diaspora and onto the fulfillment of the Zionist ideology in Eretz Israel.

The orphanage of Mrs. Oksenhorn was located in a tightly closed house, in the same Sobieski Square, opposite the park, near the city military headquarters. Tens or perhaps hundreds of Jewish children lived in that tightly closed house. They only came out for a short stroll in the street, marching as a group and under the strict supervision of a few women matrons and helpers. We never saw these children playing freely in the park across from their houses or visiting some other entertainment venues in the cities. These places were outside their boundaries, which lay in the margin of the economic lives of the children and youth in the city.

A big fair, named after "Holy Anna", took place annually in Sobieski Square and adjacent streets. Hundreds of families relied on that fair to remedy their miserable state during the rest of the year. Anyone who could not find work during the year looked forward to the fair and held onto it like a drowning person clutching a straw. Small merchants in the city and the nearby area, and even from far-away places, brought all sorts of bargains for sale at the fair. The merchants and their assistants announced, in loud voices, about the "opportunity given to buying this bargain only on that day". The announcers amazed the masses with their rhymes, composed haphazardly to praise the cheap merchandise and its shaky quality. The announcers' hoarse voices led to the frightening commotion that prevailed at the fair. Buyers and just curious people crowded the square. They all turned that usually quiet corner into a raging sea, where waves of people moved continuously and aimlessly. When the fair ended, the square returned to its calm.

A small and clean Jewish restaurant of Mrs. Sara Rosenberg-Goldberg was located on Kozhminski Street, one of the side streets off Sobieski Square. The owner was a unique figure in the city: she spoke Hebrew. She looked like somebody who was copied from the enlightened circle, people of the early generations, and placed in that restaurant to serve her customers. She surprised people with her kind manners and eloquent and enlightened language. She induced an atmosphere of culture and distinctive grace in anybody lucky to meet her. Mrs. Sara was a modest woman, tied to her place of work, but her soul was far away from that physical place – her soul was in Eretz Israel. She corresponded with Dr. Herzl and was among the first people that got hooked on the Zionist idea at the dawn of the national movement. She dreamt about making Aliya to Eretz Israel as early as the beginning of the 20th century but fate changed the path of her life and dreams and confined her to her small restaurant until her last day. While she was deprived of fulfilling her own aspirations to make Aliya and live in Eretz Israel, she knew to transfer her love for Hebrew and Eretz Israel to her only son. She hoped that he would take revenge on her cruel fate that prevented her from fulfilling her dream. With all the warmth in her heart, she dedicated herself to educating her son about the same goal she could not reach. Mrs. Sara taught her son Hebrew from his childhood. A while later, she was happy to see him joining the fulfillment movements of "Gordonia" and "HeKhalutz".

Mickiewicz [Mitzkevitz] Street

And just as Mrs. Sara was the only woman in her generation that spoke Hebrew daily, so was her son. He was a prodigy. He was one of a kind who used his early Hebrew education in practice every day. Both mother and her small son strolled the city streets, speaking Hebrew between them.

Some streets were a unique world on their own and unlike any other. Here is the main street of the city – Mitzkevitz Street. Large Jewish shops, elegant cafes, movie theaters, hotels, the municipal building, a district court with a jail in the yard, the Jewish community building, and more. The essence of the Jewish youth was reflected in that street. On the one side, students and unaffiliated youths spent their free time. The other side was the meeting place of the youths from the youth movements and "HeKhalutz". After their meetings at the various Zionist unions, they appeared in that street in the late hours of the evening for a short stroll and meetings with youths from other organizations. The section between the "Polonia" hotel and the end of the military hospital's wall was the pioneering meeting section.

[Columns 337-338]

In that section, some listened to the music of the Goldring orchestra, which played at the "Polonia" café. Obviously, they listened to the music while standing outside…

In the morning hours before noon, in the same street, near Ingler newspapers kiosk, a diversified crowd gathered to wait for the newspapers arriving from Lviv and Warsaw. Near that kiosk and the triple-faced clock, world and country news published in [the Warsaw Yiddish newspaper] "Haynt" ["Today"] and [the Lviv Polish Jewish newspaper] "Kvila" ["Minute"], were spread for everybody to read.

At the community building, the various representatives, Zionists, Haredi, and assimilators wrestled with each other about the image and operation of the Jewish community. A building in which all the Jewish community's public activities were managed stood at the center of that street. Dr. Parnas headed the Jewish community and oversaw all its beneficial activities for many years until the Second World War. He was the man who fulfilled the Zionist directive to take control of the Jewish communities. He carried his role proudly, guided by the principles of democracy and caring for public interests. As a person who possessed European manners t and culture, he was able to heal the tears caused by the divided public. He educated it to aspire for great deeds and directed his substantial vigor toward a productive channel. He did all that while his Zionist spirit enveloped that entire ancient community.

When you turned from Mitzkevitz Street onto Tarnovski Street, you entered the world of the free professions. Most Jewish lawyers, physicians, and engineers resided on that street. I knew them all from my work on behalf of the Keren Kayemet LeIsrael [JNF-KKL]. All the refugees who escaped to Russia before the city was conquered by the Nazis, passed through that street directed west to east.

Our city spread over a large area and consisted of purely Jewish communities, mixed communities, and Christian areas where only a few Jews resided. A Jew from the Polish community of Zrodzia was considered by us a person from another town. Christian-dominated communities were scattered in various corners of the city, such as near and around the "new" public park, Polish hospital, train station, and more. Jews who resided in these areas formed Jewish islands in a sea of gentiles. They certainly did not have an easy life there.

Against that, the atmosphere in Ostrogski was Ukrainian-Jewish. On the side of the Jewish hospital stood the "Bertztvo" building – the center of the Ukrainian national operation in the city. However, the building also served as a place for cultural and public activities of the Jewish parties, often more than the activities of the Ukrainians themselves. The Jewish residents of that street were mainly middle-class people, shopkeepers, and wood merchants. That street led to the two Jewish cemeteries. One of them, the old cemetery, was located in the middle section of the street. That cemetery is the resting place of the city's Jewish community greats from past generations. Yosef Perl, Nakhman Kromkhel, and others were buried there. We would pass that place with admiration and apprehension. Every public activist from outside the city and every emissary from Eretz Israel used to visit the cemetery and commune with the memory of our city's greats. The new Jewish cemetery was located down the same street outside the city. The street witnessed many tears shed at the Jewish funerals when they passed through it on their last way.

There was also a large center for the Jewish poor. It encircled all of the streets on the southwestern side of the city, with the Seret River bordering it on one side, the market square on the north side, and Kaziemizovski on the east. The center's heart was located in the streets around the old synagogue. Here, leanness and poverty combined most convincingly. The rest of the big center's streets were also settled by people of the middle class – artisans and Jews without any obvious classification: porters, waggoneers, small shops merchants, peddlers, owners of a stall in the market, or people who were unemployed chronically and who "died" from hunger ten times a day. These people lived in dire poverty in the streets, Podolska Nizsza, Podolska Wizsza, Czacki, Baron Hirsch, Bogota, Lwowska, and in the allies that branched off these streets. Children rolled in the muck, mothers constantly looking for food for their children, and heads of families ran around like ants, carrying the unbearable heavy burden of existence… Thousands of Jewish children were born, grew up, suffered, and carried in their hearts the insult of their miserable, oppressed, and degrading childhood for the rest of their lives.

Within the sea of small lapidated houses, prone to collapse, inside the center of poverty stood the fort-like synagogue. It was built in the early stages of Ternopil as a house of prayer but also as a fort defending the Jewish settlement from attacks by the Turks and Tatars. The Dominican church was built at the same time for the Christian population. That old synagogue was built as a building copied from one of the countries in the east. The style, the basalt stones, the flat roof, with its guard rail containing slots for cannons – all of that gave the building a unique grandeur. The whole building portrayed resilience and rooting by the Jews. The prayers of thousands of Jews emerged from that glorified temple, during the Jewish holidays. The atmosphere of the grayish fort synagogue was an appropriate background for the gray life of the crowded Jewish community. The building witnessed some moments of exaltation when the Zionist greats, such as Dr. Khaim Arlozorov, Dr. Meir Giar, and many others, appeared on the stage and enthused a crowd of thousands. That fort was the pinnacle of the Jewish assets in the city. What was its end?

And there was a river in the city – the Seret River. Hundreds of boats carrying

[Columns 339-340]

youths sailed into the bosom of nature. Here was where residents of poor neighborhoods, youths of the suburbs, and young workers, gained some of their peace of mind back. Youth movements' leadership meetings and discussions with emissaries from their headquarter or Eretz Israel were also held on these boats. The atmosphere there was pleasant and convenient for public activities. In those boats on the Seret River, the best of the pioneers and the Jewish youths made their plans for Aliya and education in Eretz Israel.

At the extreme edge of that Jewish center, on Ruska Street – two worlds operated in one corner, near the café of Shtekl: One of the worlds was the currency "black market" and the other, the parking lot of the Jewish waggoneers and porters. Those worlds were the two poles of the Jewish ways of making a living in the diaspora. On one sidewalk near the café, unnerved Jews ran around, in the summer or winter, searching endlessly for a "client" who wanted to buy foreign money or do a bartering business in foreign currency. Their eyes projected worry and fear. Worry about the profit, a few guldens to feed their family, and fear from the policemen who always bothered them. Most of the" black marketeers" were once shop owners or other businessmen. However, during one of the financial crises, they lost their wealth and had no choice but to become "black marketeers". Near them, waggoneers and porters stood all year round waiting for a miracle from heaven – an order to haul freight from one location to another to make a few measly pennies. The work was so arduous for such a meager wage, and the families at home were hungry and in need of clothing… The whole tragedy poor economic state of the Jews was reflected in all of its cruelty in that one corner of Ruska Street.

There were some city corners in which a single youth union branch or a cultural institution was located. These institutions often exerted an unforgettable influence on their neighborhood, directly or indirectly.

The members of the club "Yehuda", showed their power in sports, mainly soccer. They carried the flag of the Jewish sport and fought to protect its honor against the Polish and Ukrainian gentile clubs. A large crowd of sports fans flocked to the stadiums outside the city to watch the games. The hidden hatred toward the Jews often rosed up and floated on the surface in these stadiums. The national sentiment of a group of Jewish pickpockets would flare up in full force. They were the first to break into the pitch to defend the "Yehuda" players and pay the attackers back what they deserved. Indeed, these destitute people had a stormy national consciousness, and they often defended the honor of Israel proudly and bravely. Who can plunge into the depths of a Jewish soul?

The Jewish community in Ternopil, scattered in the various city neighborhoods, came to political gatherings, cultural appearances, lectures, and theater plays, after a whole day of hard work. Jews from all classes found some relief from the daily distress and dove into the spiritual world. Crowds filled up the concert halls and theaters, not only of the Jews but also those of the Poles and Ukrainians. Many would free themselves on Sunday, the Christian Sabbath (enforced by the regime), for a short trip with their family to the neighboring areas (Petrikov, Zagrobela, Gaia Vilieka [Velyki Hai?]) to enjoy the beauty of Podolia's nature and the expanse of the fields and forests.

That was a large community, lively and bubbly, with noble virtues and an open heart towards national affairs. It fought its battles under a difficult economic situation while the hope for national redemption guided it at every step. There were rich and poor Jews, however, the sense of brotherhood united them all in sorrow and joy. The feeling of respect and mutual responsibility guided all of them. The Jewish community in Ternopil was a settlement with a glorious past and quite a grayish present but possessed supreme ideas. It handled its battles through courtesy toward its rivals, where persuasion and explanation were its only weapons. We did not have political hooligans, and rivals' assemblies were not busted. There were no provocateurs in our camp. We conducted our discussions pleasantly and preferred common sense over demagoguery. Our community consisted of great human beings who were calm and possessed good manners. We also had a superior dedicated, and loyal youth. It had Jewish and general education and sublime aspirations. That youth filled up the workshops, shops, various schools in the city, and universities throughout near and far European countries. We had hoped that with the help of that youth, we could change the state of the Jewish population. However, the horrific fate of millions of Jews in Poland also hit Ternopil's Jews. Our dear and beloved people, institutions, and undertakings were all annihilated – only our memories remained…

[Columns 341-342]

The Sports Clubs in Ternopil

The Athletic and Physical Culture Zionist Association "Beitar"

by A. Landfish

Translated by Moshe Kutten

"Beitar" - the Zionist Association for Athletic and Physical Culture, the first of its kind in Galitsia, Austria, and the whole world, was established in Ternopil in 1904 by Dr. Israel Waldman.

"Beitar" resided in the "*Retztvo Mishtzenska*" and its counselor was the Ukrainian gym teacher Tchubaty. Members who came out from that association were active later on in all of Ternopil's sports movements[1].

"Beitar" Association at the time of its establishment

Sitting – Center: Dr. Israel Waldman
To his right: Tchubaty – Ukrainian gym teacher, Dr. Kapel, Dr. Abraham Shwarzman, Joseph Spanier
To his left: Jacob Tzin, Jacob Likhtigfeld, Dr. Weisglas, Hollender

Author's Note:

1. For details see the article by Dr. Korngruen, column 126.

The Sports Club "Yehuda"

by Dov Niman

Translated by Moshe Kutten

At the end of the First World War, when the members of the "Yehuda" sports club, headed by Ya'akov Planer, returned from their service in the Austrian army, they turned to reestablishing the sports movement in the city.

The beginning was hard since the old timers lost their ability to participate in sports activities, and there was a need to train a new generation of athletes.

The first sports appearance of the club was in a soccer game against a student team in Zolochiv.

[Columns 343-344]

The win by the Ternopil team aggrandized the club in the eyes of the public, which mobilized to help it by donating money and equipment.

The club went from strength to strength. For a while, it played as part of the third-level league. However, after the spectacular wins in Ternopil and surrounding areas, the club moved up to the second-level league. The sports team from Ternopil acquired a name for itself. Its number of fans grew, not only among the Jews. The Ukrainians and Poles also respected it.

Fondly remembered is the wheat merchant, Avraham Ketcheh, a Haredi Jew who helped the club with his substantial contributions. He contributed to the club to thank it for the pleasure his children, who were among the outstanding athletes of the club, brought him.

"Yehuda" did not own its own athletic field until the engineer, Mundek Weisglas, took it upon himself to build it on the site of the "*Blonia*" [?]. He invested a lot of energy in that project until he saw the fruits of his work. Since then, the Ternopil Jewish youth had an athletic field of its own.

A few years before the Second World War, the club succeeded in climbing to the first-level league.

When the antisemitism in Poland strengthened, many members of the club joined the "Hekhalutz" movement to fulfill their life's dream of making Aliya to Eretz Israel. Those members who were not fortunate to do so lost their lives along with the rest of the Polish Jews.

Football Team "Yehuda", 1924

[Columns 345-346]

Economy and Welfare

[Columns 347-348]   [blank]

[Columns 349-350]

On the Economic and Social Image of Ternopil

by Dr. Tzvi Parnas

Translated by Moshe Kutten

A. The Economic Structure of the Population

Ternopil is located in Podolia, a region with a distinct agricultural character. Agricultural production of some products there exceeded local demand. For example, 12.5% of all wheat, 20% of all buckwheat, 18% of all beans, 46% of the corn, and 35% of the tobacco produced in Poland, came from Podolia. These were just some of the numbers provided for illustration. Podolia was not only an export center for agricultural crops but also for eggs, milk, meat products, and even forest woods, as evident by the official statistical data.

The vast majority of the population made a living in agriculture. A million and six hundred thousand lived in the Ternopil area (namely Podolia) in 1931, among them not more than 185,500 (16.8%) in cities and towns. That was after the population in the cities grew faster than in the villages. On average, the population grew at a rate of 1% per year, during 1870 – 1900, while in the cities, the growth was 1.4% per year. In the last few years before 1931, the gap between the population growth in cities and the villages was even wider.

The Jewish population in Ternopil Voivodeship [province] in 1931 numbered 134,000 people (8% of the entire population). More than 70% of the Jewish population resided in towns and cities, and close to 30% in villages. The Jewish community in Ternopil numbered 15,000 people in the city and 3,000 more in the neighboring villages. In the city, the Jewish population constituted 44% of the population of 33,900 people, while in the entire province, the Jewish population constituted only 34.7% of the population. Ternopil contained the largest percentage of Jews than any other city in Podolia. Although the Ternopil city's Jews constituted only about 1/10 of the entire Jewish population in the province, their influence was decisively beyond their actual numbers.

An important factor in shaping the demographic character of Podolia's Jewish population was immigration. According to the data of the Bureau of Statistics in Warsaw, the natural growth of Podolia's Jews during the ten years 1921 – 1931 was 13,000. However, only 5,000 remained in Podolia after 8,000 people immigrated. During 1927 – 1938, 2900 Jews from Podolia made Aliya to Eretz Israel from the Ternopil province. Among them, about 800 people from the city of Ternopil.

What were the occupations of Ternopil's Jews? According to the census, the Jewish occupations were:

Jews:

Agriculture	200	1.3%
Trade	6600	44.2%
Industry and craftsmanship	4100	27.3%
Transportation and freight	1000	6.6%
Miscellaneous Occupations	3100	20.6%
Total	15000	100.0%

The group of "Miscellaneous Occupations" included free professions, office staff, public and religious institutions employees, landlords, and people who lacked any occupation.

The professional distribution of the non-Jewish population was entirely different as depicted in the following table:

Non-Jews:

Agriculture	2350	12.4%
Trade	1200	6.3%
Industry and Craftsmanship	3100	16.3%
Transportation and Freight	2650	14.0%
Miscellaneous Occupations	9600	51.0%
Total	18900	100.0%

The largest group of non-Jews was the "miscellaneous occupations". That group included the officials in the offices of the government, courts, police, etc. The group also included the housemaids, who were mostly Ukrainians.

The economic division between the Jews and non-Jews is demonstrated in the following table:

[Columns 351-352]

Occupation	Jews	Non-Jews
Agriculture	8.0%	92.0%
Trade	84.7%	15.3%
Industry and Craftsmanship	57.0%	43.0%
Transportation and Freight	27.4%	72.6%
Miscellaneous Occupations	24.4%	75.6%

These numbers prove that the Jews had numbers superiority in Trade, Industry, and Craftsmanship, while the non-Jews concentrated on transportation. This is reasonable since transportation was run by the state, and all of its employees were employed by the state. The same was true for the post office's employees and the telegraph office. Against that, the Jews were in the majority in private transport.

The numbers mentioned above do not fully reflect the situation, without reviewing the social structure of every occupation, namely, who headed the economic pyramid who was the base, and who made their mark on economic life and delineated its path?

We start with agriculture. The 200 Jews (which included the head of the family and his family) were all owners or lessees of estates, which in Podolia (and particularly in the former province of Galitsia) formed a considerable group with a substantial influence over agricultural production. The city of Ternopil was surrounded by farms owned or managed by Jews, such as Biala, Kotpoptza, Proniatyn, Dragnovka, Zagroblia, Smikoptza, and others. It is worthwhile to devote research about the role of the Jews in Polish agriculture since they were negligibly mentioned in the official publication because of the overwhelming majority of the non-Jews in that area.

The following is the social structure of the people who made a living in agriculture:

	Total	Jews	Non-Jews
Independent	1900	200	1700
Non-physical workers	150	-	150
Physical laborers	500	-	500
Total	2550	200	2350

As aforementioned, all the 200 Jews who made a living from agriculture were independent, and 25% of the non-Jews were employed either as non-physical workers or as manual laborers.

The social structure of the people who made a living in trade was more complicated:

	Total	Jews		Non-Jews	
Independent	6400	5900	89.4%	500	41.8%
Non-physical workers	400	350	5.3%	50	4.1%
Manual Laborers	1000	350	5.3%	650	54.1%
Total	7800	6600	100.0%	1200	100.0%

The huge gap in the social structure of the people who made a living in trade between Jews and non-Jews is highlighted in this table. While the independents constituted about 90% of the Jews, they amount to only 42% for non-Jews, and about 60% were employees.

During the last few years before the Second World War, the income tax offices maintained the list of taxpayers according to their ethnicity. The numbers were published after the war, and they provide an illuminating description of the role the Jews played in trade. The 971 trade licenses purchased in Ternopil, were divided according to their types:

	Total	Jews	Non-Jews
Types 1 & 2	103	92	11
Type 3	400	385	15
Types 4 & 5	468	368	100
Total	971	845	126

Among the Jews, businesses with the highest turnover (types 1 – 3) constituted 56% of the total number, while among the non-Jews, only 20%.

The businesses were divided according to their character into three major groups:

    a.   Businesses for purchases
    b.   Businesses for sales
    c.   Services

The following businesses were included in the first group:

	Jews	Non-Jews
Purchases of grains	35	5
Purchases of fruits	10	-
Purchases of cattle	25	25
Purchases of leathers	10	-
Miscellaneous Purchases	10	-
Total	90	30

The following businesses were included in the second group:

	Jews	Non-Jews
Sale of food	300	40
Sale of clothing	170	10
Sale of furniture	10	-
Sale of chemical products	35	5
Sale of paper	10	5
Sale of construction materials	45	5
Miscellaneous Sales	85	5
Total	655	70

The following businesses were included in the third group (services):

	Jews	Non-Jews
Hotels and restaurants	60	20
Currency exchange	10	-
Offices	5	-
Transport	10	-
Miscellaneous Services	15	6
Total	100	26

[Columns 353-354]

In the first group, the Jewish businesses constituted 75% of the total, in the second group – more than 90%, and in the third – about 80%.

In 1938, the turnover of the Jewish businesses reached 28 million guldens (5.6 million dollars). The turnover of the non-Jews businesses amounted to only 3.6 million guldens, namely 11% of the total turnover. The revenues of the Jewish businesses, which served as a basis for the tax assessment (except the part which was tax-exempt), reached about 2 million guldens. These numbers prove that the share of the Jews in the Ternopil's trade was decisive.

The following was the situation in the Industry and Craftsmanship section:

	Total	Jews		Non-Jews	
Independent	3800	2400	58.5%	1400	45.2%
Non-physical workers	400	300	7.4%	100	3,2%
Manual laborers	3000	1400	34.1%	1600	51.6%
Total	7200	4100	100.0%	3100	100.0%

In this professional section, the independent people among the Jews also constituted a most significant share, although as much as among the merchants.

There were about a thousand workshops and factories in Ternopil. However, only 233, which employed more the five workers, were required to purchase industrial certificates according to the law,

110 plants carried a distinct character of factories, while the number of workshops was about 900. According to the law, every craftsman had to pass a test at the craftsmanship bureau to receive the title of a craftsman. There were 550 craftsmen in Ternopil. The largest group among them was the carpenters (22%). After them, came according to their numbers, butchers, tailors, and shoemakers.

In the Industry group, the following businesses held a prominent position: Flour and buckwheat mills, factories for making drinks (among them the big beer factory in Podolia), factories for making sweets, and large metal products workshops. The tax offices estimated the total value of the products of the large factories (types 1 -7) to be seven million guldens. Plants under Jewish hands manufactured products estimated to be six million guldens.

The following are the numbers for the "Transportation and Freight" group:

	Total	Jews		Non-Jews	
Independent	750	700	70.0%	50	2.0%
Non-physical workers	500	100	10.0%	400	15.0%
Manual Laborers	2400	200	20.0%	2200	83.0%
Total	3650	1000	100.0%	2650	100.0%

That table proves that 93% of the private Transportation and Freight businesses were in the hands of Jews. The state transportation and transport businesses employed the largest number of employees. The share of Jews among the employees was negligible.

The group "Miscellaneous Occupations" was divided as follows:

	Total	Jews		Non-Jews	
Independent	2300	1100	35.4%	1200	12.5%
Independent without an occupation	1500	900	29.9%	600	6.2%
Non-physical workers	3400	600	19.3%	2800	30.0%
Manual laborers	5500	500	15.4%	5000	51.3%
Total	12700	3100	100.0%	9600	100.0%

Based on the explanations about the "Miscellaneous Occupations" group above, it is no wonder that the "Independent" group constituted more than 65% of the Jews and less than 19% of the non-Jews. The group "Independent without Occupation:" included wealthy people who made a living off their stocks or interest, people receiving pensions, landlords, and people who were supported by welfare institutions, etc. There were about a thousand landlords, who owned half of the apartment buildings in the city valued at twenty million guldens.

In conclusion, we should bring some numbers for comparison to understand the economic image of Ternopil residents and draw some general conclusions about the roles played by different groups.

We start with the main group, "Independent":

Independent:

	Total	Jews		Non-Jews	
Agriculture	1900	200	1.8%	1700	31.2%
Trade	6400	5900	52.8%	500	9.2%
Industry and Craftsmanship	3800	2400	21.4%	1400	25.6%
Transportation & Freight	750	700	6.2%	50	0.9%
Miscellaneous occupations	3800	2000	17.8%	1800	33.1%
Total	16650	11200	100.0%	5450	100.0%
Total in %	100.0%	67.3%		32.7%	

From that table, we learn almost 53% of the Jewish independent people concentrated in trade, and relatively small portions in Industry and Craftsmanship, free professions, and non-physical work. Transportation and Agriculture portions constituted very small portions. The first place of the non-Jews belonged to the group "Miscellaneous Occupations" (free professions, pension receivers, and the wealthy with no specific profession). After that group came the Agriculture and Industry groups.

[Columns 355-356]

The Trade and Industry groups captured a negligible portion.

Among the independent people, the Jews constituted about two-thirds, although their percentage of the total population was about 44%. These numbers speak for themselves.

When we move to the second group: office and non-physical workers, the following picture is drawn:

Office and non-physical workers:

	Total	Jews		Non-Jews	
Agriculture	150	-	-	150	4.3%
Trade	400	350	25.8%	50	1.4%
Industry and Craftsmanship	400	300	22.2%	100	3.0%
Transportation & Freight	500	100	7.4%	400	11.4%
Miscellaneous occupations	3400	2600	44.6%	2800	79.9%
Total	4850	3150	100.0%	3500	100.0%
Total in %	100.0%	27.8%		72.2%	

The characteristic of this group was the group "Miscellaneous Occupations" took the top place both among the Jews and the non-Jews. These were the state and community officials, office workers in the public, religious institutions, lawyers' firms, and the rest of the free professions.

Among the Jews, the non-physical workers and the workers in Industry and Trade occupied the top places. Among the non-Jews, the government office workers of the railway, post, and telegraph offices, took first place. In the group of non-physical workers, the Jews constituted a modest part of 27.8%. That was the direct result of the policy of driving the Jews out of government offices but also reflected the passion of the Jews for economic independence.

To complete the picture, we bring the numbers for the physical laborers. We have taken out the housemaids, as they represented a special type of worker:

	Total	Jews		Non-Jews	
Agriculture	500	-	-	500	5.2%
Trade	1000	350	14.2%	650	6.5%
Industry and Craftsmanship	3000	1400	57.3%	1600	16.1%
Transportation & Freight	2400	200	8.1%	2200	22.1%
Miscellaneous occupations	5500	500	20.4%	5000	50.1%
Total	12400	2450	100.0%	9950	100.0%
Total in %	100.0%	19.8%		80.2%	

Among the employees in Ternopil, the Jews constituted about 20% of the workforce, most as apprentices and only a negligible portion

Union of Commercial Workers

[Columns 357-358]

were employed in larger industrial plants. The "Miscellaneous" group captured second place among the Jews. Workers of the institutions such as the community, *Batei Midrash*, public welfare, and religious, and a small portion of Jewish housemaids belonged to that group.

Among the non-Jews, the "Miscellaneous" group took first place. Houseworkers and housemaids numbered 3000 were the majority in that group. The rest were workers who worked in public and religious institutions, caretakers, and assistants for free professionals.

The railroad workers and the physical laborers in telecommunications constituted the majority in the "Transportation and Freight" group. Only a small portion worked in private transportation companies.

The non-Jewish industrial workers were employed as assistants and apprentices with the craftsmen and in large industrial factories. We should note that most of the workers in the industry came to work in Ternopil from the neighboring villages, and they do not appear as such in the table. That means that the number of Jewish workers was proportionally even smaller than the number in our table.

Based on the aforementioned analysis we can now get a clear picture of the social structure of the Ternopil population, particularly the split between the owners of plants on one side and hired workers on the other. That problem generated many arguments before the break of the Second World War.

	Jews		**Non-Jews**	
Independent	11200	74.7%	5450	29.0%
Employees	3800	25.3%	13450	71.0%
Total	15000	100.0%	18900	100.0%

From these numbers, we see that Jewish independents constituted 75% of the total and only 25% were employees, who depended economically on an employer. Among the non-Jews, the proportions were the opposite. We should also note that the Jewish independents did not use hired employees, and the vast majority worked by themselves or with their own family members. Therefore, there was no friction between employees and employers among the Jews.

We can draw the following conclusions from this short analysis, based on the statistical information mentioned above:

What we had was a dynamic and robust community. That community was the initiator and the organizer of all essential economic areas. It constituted the majority number of people in trade, craftsmanship, and the free professions. It exported agricultural products to the rest of Poland. It was the one that built apartment buildings in the city and lived in them. It was the main tax-payer of city and state taxes. It made a living on its own without hiring employees. It was a diligent social and economic element, socially with great virtues.

B. Credit Unions and Banks

Like all other Jewish communities, Ternopil was blessed with institutions of welfare and charity for every needy. These institutions were managed according to customs that were inherited from one generation to the other. However, the social and cultural revolution among the Jewish population during the 19th century also made its mark in that area. A new layer was established – the Jewish bourgeoisie, made of merchants, contractors, wealthy landlords, and people with free professions. That layer, which captured the leadership of the Jewish public, excelled in its momentum. During the 1860s, several welfare institutions were established, and the community established a new a hospital[1]. These institutions were modernly managed but did not deviate from a philanthropic charter.

An additional development in the area of welfare operation took place in the 20th century. A new type of social activist rose, who was not content with just providing assistance but also tried to remedy the sources of the problem. Although the objective conditions that allowed annulling the source problem did not always exist, at least efforts were made to ease the distress by providing collective assistance. The goal was no longer just philanthropic but also to provide rehabilitation of the sufferers and assistance that would bring with it the economic independence of the dependent.

The first credit institution, which was based on a business foundation, but with public orientation, was the bank "Kupat Milveh" ["Loan Fund"], established by the JCA [Jewish Colonization Association]. The bank did not seek profits. Its objective was to serve as a loyal support organization for the craftsman and the small business owner. The credit union was founded based on the Austrian corporation law allowing financial activities on a mass scale for social purposes. These credit unions were established from the member fees, and their general assembly delineating their activities. The number of votes of each member was counted according to the number of "stocks" they owned. Since the JCA organization invested a sum of several thousand guldens in the credit union, it owned the majority of the "stocks". Therefore, its representative had a decisive opinion in every assembly.

The credit union provided loans of fifty and up to a hundred guldens for a biweekly payment of one to two guldens. The interest charged was minimal, just to cover costs and accumulate some small reserves.

[Columns 359-360]

Dr. Mark Parnas, the first representative of JCA in the fund served for many years. He was also the head of the fund's management team. After his death, pharmacist Julius Frantsuz served in that position.

The fund served hundreds of people from among the small business owners, craftsmen, and owners of stalls in the market. It was characterized as a transitional stage between a charity fund to a cooperative credit institution.

Indeed, a public-oriented credit institution with a wide field of activity was also established. It was the "Onia Kreditova" ["Credit Union"], which was founded by Ternopil Zionists to serve as a source of credit with favorable terms for the members of the movement and the public at large. The founders used the bank in Lviv as an example. That bank, which carried the same name, assisted the Ternopil bank in the first stages by providing credit. The "Onia" bank served middle-level merchants and small craftsmen who suffered from a shortage of credit because existing banks were not fully available for them. The Apothecary Bank mainly financed trade in agricultural products, and the Municipal Saving Fund served the city's numerous officials and the owners of neighboring farms.

M. Fisher headed "Onia Kreditova" bank. His assistants were Mark Schwartz and Fleishman, members of [the Academic Zionist organization] "Bar Kokhba". They executed the "Economic Policy" of the movement. The two banks: "Kupat Milveh" of the JCA and "Onia" were different in their characters. The "Onia" was more democratic in its character since it did not answer to just a single owner. The extent of its activity was wider, and the loans it awarded were higher. The "Onia" developed nicely, and its credit activities grew more and more until the break of the First World War, which turned everything upside down. The economic life faltered, most activists left the city, and the bank ceased to exist.

In 1921, the Zionists renewed their efforts to establish a credit institution. Dr. Tzvi Parnas and Ben-Tzion Fett led that effort, this time based on the modern Polish corporative law. Large sums of money were collected, particularly from the various business circles and mainly among the Zionists. The bank, headed by Tzvi Parnas, opened at 5 Sobieski Street, handled a broad activity, and maintained close contact with respected Polish economic institutions. In parallel to the bank named "Independent Economic Assistance and Credit", the JCA fund continued with its measly operation. Life in new Poland did not return to its normal course. The value of the Polish mark deteriorated, and inflation, which ruined all the banks and financial institutions, including the cooperative bank, prevailed. The entire fortune of the bank was lost, except for its apartment, into which large sums were invested.

The "Organization for Supervision of the Jewish Cooperatives" ("Revizons Farband") came to the rescue. That organization was funded by the "Joint" [JDC – "Jewish Joint Distribution Committee"]. JCA center joined in, and together with the "Joint", they established a dedicated organization to assist the Jewish cooperative institutions named the "Foundation".

After negotiations, it was decided to unify the "Loan Fund" of the JCA and the "Bank for Self Help" into a single bank. The by-laws of the new bank were approved by the general assembly held in 1924. In these bylaws, the principle of equality, in the bank management, between the two rescuing organizations was approved. Dr. Tzvi Parnas was elected to head the new bank and Dr. Weissnikht to the supervision committee. That principle did not last long. With the strengthening of the national movement, the number of assimilators' supporters of the JCA diminished more and more.

Thanks to a credit of fifteen thousand guldens the bank received from the ["Foundation"] organization and the sums deposited by the members, a large capital was accumulated, which enabled vigorous activity.

With time, the "Popular Bank" as it was called by the people, secured the trust of the people, deposits grew more and more, and the loan amounts were raised.

The Committee of the Cooperative Bank, 1922
Dr. Tzvi Parnas, Eng. Schekhter, Eikhenbaum, Sperling, and Clerks: Mrs. Horowitz and Gelber

[Columns 361-362]

In the first conference of the credit cooperatives in Galitsia, assembled in Lviv, Dr. Tzvi Parnas was elected to the presidency of Lviv representation. The direct contact with the central institutions was a blessing for the bank, which turned into a flourishing institution with eight hundred members. The bank activists worked dedicatedly and managed it without favoritism (according to their own resolution, they could not obtain a loan from the bank). When bullies from various circles tried to seize control, they were alert to prevent any assault on the bank.

The craftsmen and small merchants presented a unique problem. The doors to the banks were closed for them since they lacked surety. They were initially helped by the loan fund of the JCA. However, with the closure of that fund, they were left with no source of credit. The vacuum was filled by "Tzekabah" [?] (the center for all the welfare funds of the "Joint"). The fund in Ternopil was established in 1926. Most of its customers were craftsmen and small merchants. The Zionism [political] left showed interest in it for political reasons. The fund received its foundation capital from the "Tzekabah". The principle based on which the fund operated was providing loans of twenty-five guldens (and higher sums in exceptional cases) without interest and with small monthly payments.

The fund's committee included Dr. Tzellermayer, Dr. David Rottstien, Yehoshua Parnas, and Isenberg. The hundreds of people who benefited from the fund served as a support mechanism. Many of its customers established themselves over time and moved to the cooperative bank.

In addition to that fund, there were some small funds affiliated with *Batei Midrash*, companies, etc. but the scope of their activity was small and limited to a small circle.

The year 1932 was a record year in the history of the cooperative bank. Although it was not the largest bank in the city, it was undoubtedly the liveliest. The bank's capital with its reserves reached more than sixty thousand guldens. The total amount of loans and rediscount credit was about one hundred thousand guldens. The inkaso document file – about five thousand guldens per month.

The changes in the economic conditions in Poland during the years before the Second World War, the crisis phenomena, the impoverishment of the Jewish population due to the policy of discrimination, and also the lack of suitable people resulted in the deterioration of the bank over time. The savings dwindled, and the bank equity decreased due to deficits. Despite all of that, the bank continued with its activities, until it was abolished with the takeover by the Soviets. The capital, amounting to substantial sums of hundreds of thousands of guldens, was transferred to the Soviet government bank.

Ternopil excelled not only in banking cooperatives. One of the first production cooperatives in Poland – the cooperative of the carpenters, was established there. As aforementioned, the number of furniture and construction carpenters was substantial in the city. Ternopil's carpenters not only met the city's demand but also the needs of the neighboring villages. The villagers bought standard doors and windows in the city and furniture for their houses. During the inflationary period that followed the collapse of the Polish mark (currency used until the end of the First World War), the buying power of the villagers and their needs increased. However, just then, a competitor to the Jewish carpenters rose from among the non-Jews. The youth in the villages studied carpentry in modern vocational schools. The villagers did not need the city's Jewish carpenters any longer, as they found professionals locally. The crisis erupted in full force with the appearance of the new currency – the Polish gulden, issued as part of the economic stabilization efforts. The population's buying power decreased, and the only way out was to strengthen the competitive standing of the Jewish carpenter. That could have only been achieved through mechanization and the introduction of mass production. The JCA assisted the carpenters by purchasing a system of machines and making it available for the Jewish carpenters. For a minimal fee, a carpenter could produce the parts for his products and assemble them in his workshop. Thanks to that arrangement, the Jewish carpenters in Ternopil were rescued from economic collapse.

A few years later, the carpenters met with another severe crisis. With the worsening of the economic situation in Poland, the demand for furniture decreased, and the prices fell. The carpenters became impoverished, and many could not afford to buy the wood needed for production. They became dependent on retailers who took advantage of their distress and dictated poor working conditions. A group of carpenters established a production cooperative, and their situation greatly improved within a short period.

The cooperative consultant, Dr. David Rottstein, assisted the cooperative and contributed tremendously with his experience and energy. He often helped the cooperative to overcome problems it got itself into.

New opportunities for the carpenters opened with the establishment of the "Rehabilitation Fund" of the "Tzekbah". That fund assisted production cooperatives not only by providing loans but also by handling the sales of the products abroad. Thanks to the initiative of the Jewish institutions and their connections with the Jewish public abroad, the doors of the international market opened for Polish products.

[Columns 363-364]

One of the most respected social institutions in the city was the orphanage, founded by the pharmacist Fleishman. Before his death, he donated a substantial sum to establish an orphanage. He also donated the revenues from his pharmacy on Perl Street to cover the maintenance of the orphanage. In 1908, a nice building on Sobieski Square was built. About 30 girls found shelter in it, and in time of need, even more.

The pharmacist's widow, Mrs. Julia Fleishman, forwent her private life and devoted herself with all her heart and soul to the orphanage. A unique organization took care of its maintenance. It was headed by the dedicated activist, Mrs. Anna Oksenhorn, the wife of Dr. Herman Oksenhorn and the sister of Edmond Rauk, the Galitsian representative in the Austrian parliament and later the Polish Sejm.

For tens of years, these two great women managed that institution and handled its budget, which was paid via membership fees, donations, and revenues from the charitable organization's traditional annual ball. The elite participated in that ball, and its revenues were a substantial portion of the orphanage budget.

Many of the institution's graduates captured a respected part of the city's life, which testifies to the orphanage's atmosphere and high education level.

The assimilators ruled that institution for many years. That was one of their last fortresses in the city, to the dismay of the Zionists who warned day and night about the lack of national education in the institution. However, the new winds blowing in the Jewish street finally penetrated the orphanage. Mrs. Fleishman and Mrs. Oksenorn could not ignore any longer the revolutionary changes in public opinion, so the orphanage's children were swept by the turbulent current of life around them.

The First World War wreaked havoc on city life. During 1914 – 1920, the city rulers changed seven times. Many of the city's residents, most of which from among the intelligentsia and the wealthy, found refuge in Vienna during the Russian invasion and later during the war with the Bolsheviks. The city was robbed, and many of its neighborhoods were burnt. Unemployment and hunger prevailed. As a result of the poor sanitary conditions, an epidemic broke out, which cut down a horrific portion of the population, particularly among the poor. The aid committee, headed by Shmuel Margalit, and the group of physicians worked day and night to rescue the sick and to prevent the spread of the epidemics. The Ukrainian regime, which ruled Ternopil and its surrounding areas then, was powerless and did nothing to improve the situation.

As a result of the war's hardships, the number of orphans and neglected youth in the city grew and became a severe social problem. Ternopil's activists did their best to ease the distress however, a turn for the better happened only upon the establishment of the "Tzentus" corporation ("The Central Corporation for Taking Care of Orphans"), which organized district committees. The district committee in Lviv handled the districts of Lviv, Ivano-Frankivsk [formerly Stanyslaviv or StanisŁawow], and Ternopil.

At the beginning of 1924, the first conference gathered in Ternopil. The representatives of thirty committees and institutions that took care of orphans and neglected children participated in that conference. The conference elected a "District Committee for Orphans" headed by a presidium consisting of the members – Dr. Tzvi Parnas, chairman, Engineer Berl (from Zloczow), vice chairman, and Yosef Libergal, general secretary. Dr. Tzvi Parnas was elected for the district office in Lviv and together with Dr. Shaf represented Lviv's district committee at the central assembly of "Tzentus" in Warsaw.

The number of orphans under the care of the district committee reached about a thousand two hundred. About a hundred and fifty in Ternopil alone. Closed institutions initially existed in Ternopil, Brody, Zloczow, and Berezhany. Over time, additional institutions were established in Zalishchyky, Skalat, and Chortkiv. The majority of the orphans - about 80% – were handed over to families. That arrangement was put in place not only for savings purposes but also for educational and social reasons. Experience has shown that although closed institutions had some advantages (such as better hygiene and culture), they lack the homely atmosphere, joyful occasions, and worries of normal life. The children in these institutions were detached from reality, and a huge psychological gap opened up between them and their brothers and sisters who grew up outside of the institutions.

Dedicated supervisors made sure that the children who grew up with families were safe and that the allowance provided to the families was fully utilized for their care. Children who had relatives, maintained relations with them. Only orphans who did not have any relatives were housed in the institution.

The "Tzentus" in Warsaw published a monthly magazine named "Das Kind" ("The Child"), and the district assembly in Lviv published the magazine "The Public Review" ("Przeglad SpoŁeczny"). The activists and educators found useful material, which served as a source of guidance and inspiration in their daily work.

The "Taz" corporation (The Corporation for Maintaining Health) took care of the children's health, which was perilous for most of them. "Taz" organized summer camps, and its physicians treated the children throughout the year.

A special problem arose when the children reached adolescence. The talented among them continued their studies in school, however, in most cases, the children were placed as apprentices of craftsmen when they reached the age of 14 to 15. A dedicated committee (called "*Patronant*") made sure

[Columns 365-366]

that the children learn the profession from superior craftsmen. The "Vozet" [?] corporation, headed by Dr. Tzetzilia Klaften, also opened the gates of its schools for the students of the institution and the orphans handled by the council. The boarding house dormitory where the students were lodged played a major role.

Workshops for knitting and needlepoint were also established within the institution. They did not only serve as learning workshops but also as a source of revenue for the institution.

The activities among the orphans were financed from several sources. During the very difficult initial period, the "Joint" covered about 70 percent of the budget, and not only that, but it also provided moral support. The manager of the "Joint's" department for handling orphans, Leib Neustadt, invested a lot of energy and love in his work. Dr. Bernard Kahan, the head of the "Joint" in Europe, showed strong interest in the problems encountered by the activists, taking care of the orphans and neglected children.

With the economic recovery of the population, the portion of the "Joint's" contribution in the budget decreased, and the one covered by [local] donations increased. In that respect, we should mention fondly the estate owners in Ternopil surrounding, who donated their agricultural produce to the institution, and the city's merchants who contributed from their inventories, especially fabrics for clothing.

Starting in 1926, the community allocated monthly allotments for the institution and the orphans. Even the municipality fulfilled its obligation to a certain extent, particularly after the establishment of the committee for social work, by providing financial assistance. The boarding house also received an allocation from the government. Over time, it was almost possible to free the "Tzentus" and "joint" from the need to support the social institutions in Ternopil and its surrounding. In the years 1937-38, the 17 cities, members in the district council, received a symbolic sum of two thousand guldens [from the "Tzentus" and "Joint" organizations] against the sum of ten thousand guldens they received in 1925.

The following are the numbers that paint the picture of the situation in 1937:[a]

In private care:

	1925	1937
Total in the district	207	212
From them in Ternopil	19	26

In Institutions:

	1925	1937
Total in the district	101	87
From them in Ternopil	--	16
Total in the district	308	299
From them in Ternopil	42	19

The numbers in the table do not include the orphanage (22 girls), which retired from its membership in the council due to the reduction in its allocation membership.

We should mention the assistance extended by Galitsia natives in the USA to their native city's residents in general the social institutions in particular. The council maintained a tight connection with the organization of Galitsia natives in the USA and submitted two proposals for solving the orphans' problem: a) Adoption of orphans by families in America b) Fundraising to establish a vocational school including all the needed equipment,

Among the organizations that responded kindly to the request of their townspeople, were the organizations of Zolochiv natives and Skalat natives. In Skalat a magnificent orphanage was built, thanks to the contribution of the American organization, and its budget was guaranteed for years.

A representative of the Ternopil natives' organization, Mr. Greenspan, visited his native city and was very impressed with the social institutions in the city and particularly the care provided to the orphans. When he returned to the US, he continued to show interest in that field and acted and urged Ternopil's natives to act for the benefit of the social institutions in the city.

The Committee of the Tarnopoler Landsmanschaft in U.S.A.

From right the left: Top row – S. Marmorek, Dr. Schuster, Dr. Migden, Wunderlikh, and Atterman
Center row – Dr. Goldwasser, Mrs. Rottenberg, M. Guliger, Racker, Dr. Fish, and Bazas
[Names of people on the bottom row are missing in the article]

Space is limited to mention here all the people who dedicated their time and energy to ease the lives of the ill-fated. We at least mention some who showed a superior noble spirit and endless dedication in the holy work they took upon themselves.

[Columns 367-368]

People demonstrated great spiritual virtues of love for others, unbelievable energy, and dedication in that work.

* * *

"Taz" (the corporation for the preservation of health) had an important role in the area of health. Close cooperation was maintained between the orphans' council, community, and "Taz", which benefitted the city.

The war left Ternopil a grim "inheritance" in the form of many deceases, such as tuberculosis, trachoma, boils, and more, which were brought by improper nutrition and poor sanitary conditions.

"Taz" began a concentrated effort to eradicate the diseases. In parallel, it conducted a vigorous information campaign in poor communities. Sanitary supervisors visited individual homes and distributed soap, disinfectants, and tickets to the public bath (which were made available by the community). They also distributed informative pamphlets with hygiene instructions for the prevention of diseases and other information. Competitions were announced with prizes for the houses that excelled in their cleanliness. "Taz" also organized public lectures about topics in hygiene and infectious diseases.

Great importance was attributed to the activity of "Taz" helping pregnant women and babies. They organized clinics where young women received training and babies were taken care of. As a result of that activity, infant mortality decreased, and their health improved.

"Taz" was headed by Dr. Hersher, the head of the municipal hospital. All the Jewish physicians assisted him, particularly the young among them. Dr. Hersher's secretary, Dr. A. Korenweitz, whose great dedication should be praised here, carried the burden of the enormous organizational effort.

Ternopil had a hospital of the Jewish community established thanks to the generosity of some people, among whom were the members of the Lazarus family who established several charity funds in Lviv and Ternopil. The hospital was built in a suitable location, and the arrangements in it were satisfactory.

The hospital played a major role in the city. Jewish patients did not like using the services of the municipal hospital because it lacked Kosher food, and the atmosphere there was church-like. The patients there were taken care of by nuns, who not always showed sympathy and understanding toward Jewish patients. That situation did not change much, even during the reign of Dr. Hersher as the hospital manager, and the service by Dr. Feit as the head of the district's health department.

With the establishment of independent Poland, open antisemitism increased in all areas of life. Antisemitism did not pass over the municipal hospital either. To all of that, we should add the obstacles encountered by the Jewish students who graduated the medical school but were not always admitted into the government and municipal hospitals as residents. The Jewish hospital admitted them with open arms. Jewish nurses could also receive residency training in their profession.

The community's elected council, headed by Dr. Tzvi Parnas, a physician, showed an understanding of the needs of the [Jewish] hospital and demonstrated a true concern for its medical level. The "Taz" corporation also came to the hospital's aid and made the most modern medical devices available for it. The community built new special buildings to house them.

To assure an efficient treatment of the sick people, a budget was allocated for hiring a resident physician and an additional nurse.

A clinic located inside the hospital took care of tens of poor patients who came to seek help every day.

A nursing home was located near the hospital. It was not very elegant, and the conditions inside were quite modest. However, about a hundred lonely people found shelter there. A dedicated committee took care of their health and living conditions on behalf of the hospital.

Representatives of the old people took part in the management of the nursing home and the supervisory committee. Be that, the feeling of responsibility toward the institution increased, and feelings of distrust, which often poisoned the atmosphere in institutions of that kind, were prevented.

A special association handled the budget for the hospital and the nursing home. D. Shpigelglass, V. Shtekel, and Zeidfeld were some of the most active and dedicated committee members who performed the holy work faithfully and wholeheartedly.

The community also maintained a public bath, which played a major role in the hygienic preservation of the masses.

* * *

In 1930, the "District's Orphan Council" established a boarding house. Although close contact between it and the orphanage was maintained, the boarding house was defined in its bylaws as an independent institution. For a short time, Dr. Tzvi Parnas, who, as mentioned above, served as the head of the council, headed the committee overseeing the school. However, even after he left that position and the two institutions were managed by other activists, the close contact between the two institutions continued.

The boarding house was housed in a dedicated building surrounded by gardens. The building was leased

[Columns 369-370]

for the orphanage in the Zarodia neighborhood, and was modified to fit the school's needs. Twenty-five boys were educated there. They were elected from among the candidates recommended by the local councils that handled the care of orphans.

During the first three years of the existence of the boarding house, the district council for orphans covered the budget of the boarding house. Later on, a dedicated committee overseeing the boarding house was established, which received allocations from the community, municipality, and government.

The committee tried to register its students into the two-year vocational school in Ternopil, known for its high level of studies but encountered difficulties. The problem resulted from the prerequisite for acceptance to the school: a candidate had to complete eight years of elementary education. Only part of the boarding house's students did. Also, the number of students at the vocational school was limited as it was the only vocational school in the district. In addition, another problem arose. When a group of Jewish students was admitted by the school, the Polish and Ukrainian students announced that they were boycotting them and refused to interact with them in classes and laboratories. Intervention by the principal, who was liberal, was in vain. When the Polish and Ukrainian students realized, a short while later, that they did not achieve their goal – the Jewish students continued their studies, and they moved to fistfights. The Jewish students did not sit idle and returned a double portion. In the end, two of the bullies were expelled, and order was restored. The Jewish students from the boarding house became among the best students in the vocational school.

The rest of the boarding house students were sent to superior workshops in the city. They also received continuing education studies in their profession and in general and Jewish topics by participating in evening courses. These evening courses were conducted on a high level, particularly during the reign of the principal Dr. Berger. He was a gifted educator with a public orientation. Because of these virtues, he endeared himself to his students who had nothing but feelings of appreciation and respect toward him.

The Committee of the Boarding House for Orphans

In 1935, the boarding house moved to the community house on Miskiewicza Street. In the meantime, management passed from Mrs. Salka Schwartz, who made Aliya to Eretz Israel in 1933, to Dr. Zlatkes. The same harmony that prevailed in the past did not reign in the new committee. Friction arose between the members of the committee and Dr. Zlatkes and Eikhenbaum. However, in the end, the sense of responsibility toward the institution and its students won, and good relations were restored.

* * *

In 1938 the Polish government issued a law that revoke Polish citizenship from Polish natives who stayed abroad, claiming that their connections to Poland were shaky, so to speak. The sting of the law was directed toward the Jewish citizens of Poland who resided abroad. Hitler's government found an excuse to harass the Jews and the Poles, with whom the relations had already deteriorated, despite the friendship covenant between them. Within twenty-four hours, tens of thousands of Jews holding Polish citizenship were deported from Germany toward the Polish border near the Polish town of Zbąszyń [Zbonshin]. At that point, the refugees were arrested by the Polish government, which refused to admit them into the country. "Joint" took care of the huge camp established in Zbonshin, and the Jewish communities gave their share. With the worsening of the relations between Germany and Poland, at the beginning of 1939, the Polish authorities dismantled the Zbonshin camp, and several thousand refugees were transported to Ternopil. A committee consisting of Dr. Tzvi Parnas, Dr, Nussbaum, Dr. Horwitz, Dr. Seret, Kurfuerst, and Ekselbirt was established to help the refugees.

Miss Salka Schwartz among the alumni of the boarding house before her departure for Palestine, 1933

The tasks that the committee faced required a great effort. The refugees arrived naked and destitute. The committee was tasked with finding them a roof over their heads, food, and clothing. The refugees' legal status complicated the situation and caused difficulties,

[Columns 371-372]

since most of them lacked certificates proving their Polish citizenship.

The increase in population made its mark in all areas. The food prices rose, and so did the apartment rents. The Polish population, which was antisemitic, to begin with, did not hide its resentment and dissatisfaction with the "invasion" by those "guests". The Jewish population, too, showed signs of impatience. Contributed to that was the boastful attitude of the "German" Jews, who treated their local "culturally inferior" brothers with contempt.

The tension in the city grew because of a refugee who tried to infiltrate Russia. He was caught by the Polish border guards and was accused of spying. The Polish authorities jumped at the case like one who finds great spoil. They used it to excite hatred against the activists who headed the committee. They were blamed for aiding the communists. Only thanks to their firm stand the baseless libel was refuted.

That was the situation when the Second World War broke out. Before the people could comprehend what happened, the city was flooded by thousands of refugees from western Poland, Bielsko-Biala, Katowice, and Krakow, who escaped from the Nazis. There was a need again to take care of lodging the refugees and provide for their needs. Ternopil's residents showed again their great generosity. They hosted the refugees in their homes, and a soup kitchen distributed meals for a symbolic fee was established. The population in the city doubled in just a few days. Large military units camped in the city, and refugees from the Polish areas conquered by the Nazis arrived daily. Highly ranked officials, state ministers, and ambassadors passed through Ternopil on the way to neighboring Romania. The tension increased in the city. The disintegration of the fronts did not leave room for any illusion. People realized that the end of the Polish regime has come, and everybody nested the fear of tomorrow in their hearts.

* * *

On 17 September [1939], the first Soviet tanks reached Ternopil and following them, large military corps. Although the destruction of war passed over Ternopil, nobody knew what the new regime would bring.

After a few days of chaos, life returned to the so-called "normal". The refugee problem was again high on the agenda, and it was necessary to find out the position of the new rulers. Captain Zhukov, whom the refugees' committee representative turned to, explained that principally, there was no room for such a committee since the government was supposed to provide work to all its citizens. However, in the meantime, until a civil regime is established in the city. The committee is allowed to continue its activities. The officer also promised that in the case rationing would be enacted, the committee would receive food for the soup kitchen.

Under the new conditions, the refugees needed to organize and find work. The first initiative began by the shoemakers, whose number was substantial among the refugees. A large workshop equipped with machines was arranged at the merchant union's hall, and the cooperative bank gave a group of shoemakers a loan. The shoemakers' productive cooperative was formed with by-laws that addressed the new conditions. Magister Rostel headed the cooperative, which included about thirty people. It became clear very quickly that the cooperative was a solution not only for the refugees but also for the shoemakers in the city since the independent shoemakers did not receive allocations of leather. Within a short time, the cooperative expanded to the size of a factory that employed hundreds of people. Assistance for the factory also came from abroad. Dr. Sh. Hirschhorn, a representative of the "Joint" organization, arrived at Ternopil and brought substantial sums of money to aid the refugees. The money was allocated to production plants. Obviously, the name of the donor was not mentioned in the books.

Other craftsmen, such as tailors, tinsmiths, and carpenters, followed the shoemakers. They formed cooperatives that made substantial progress within a short time. So much so that the Ukrainian head of the cooperative operation, who arrived in Ternopil in November, could not hide his amazement at the Jewish cooperatives, their methods of work, and organization.

With the settling of the refugees, the committee's mission ended. That was the swan song of Ternopil's activists, who fulfilled their mission faithfully for generations until the destruction of the glorified community, famous for its prominence.

Author's Note:

1. See the article by N. M. Gelber, "The History of Ternopil Jews", columns 104 – 105.

Translator's Note:

a. The heading for the table is missing in the original article. I am assuming that the numbers represent the difference between 1925 and 1937..

[Columns 373-374]

Destruction and Holocaust

[Columns 375-376] [blank]

[Columns 377-378]

Yizkor

by Meir Khartiner

Translated by Moshe Kutten

From the Holy City, I remember my holy community, the crowning city-Ternopil,
in tears I remember you from the land of the Jordan River and Mount Khermon!
I left you on a cloudy day when the diaspora land began
to tremble under the feet of Israel.
Then the laws of nature changed, and dawn came from the west
and David's violin began playing songs of glory to Zion:
"There is light there and joy, Torah and singing, the foreign land's darkness is forgotten…"
Oh, who knew that we would remember you laminating,
like remembering a wretched and tormented mother!

* * *

You were like a mother to us, a mother city in Israel,
an old and honorable community, educating her sons to good and glory:
Jewish souls, two millennia in the midst of you, set their eyes on G-d of Israel;
Luminaries-teachers, Torah greats shined in you with a heavenly light from the darkness of the diaspora;
World's scholars and great authors lighted the candle of wisdom in you
to evict darkness from people's hearts.
And a new generation rose in you, flying over a thousand years of diaspora abyss.
And with smoky firebrands around the ruins of Tel Khai, lighted the torch of freedom and revolt –
Lifting the banner of the Son of a Star [Bar Kokhbah] – they went and still going to Jerusalem!

* * *

Six million, one of every Jewish soul, the cannibals - decedents of the Vandals, annihilated,
Hundreds of Jewish communities were destroyed – for all of them we tore our clothing and souls.
Double the tears for your destruction, mother! Because we knew your treasures.
And we know - in our enormous grief, may we be comforted:
You, like all the other killing fields, serve as a warning,
so the world filled with heavenly treasures would never sink into the abyss again.
There would be a day when the feeling of vengeance for the incinerator-burnt bones would rise
And in a still voice, more powerful than an atom bomb, and war thunders,
would announce to the astonishing world that an old nation rose from its grave
to tear Satan, the nations' gobbler, and declare peace for all –
because G-d has spoken.

Ruins of the old synagogue in Ternopil after the war

[Columns 379-380]

Ternopil During the Second World War

by Avraham Oks

Translated by Moshe Kutten

Under the Soviet regime

A.

Hitler's rise to power and the out-of-control antisemitism in Poland, which reached new heights under the influence of its western neighbor, foretold bad news to Polish Jews. They found themselves in an unbearable situation with no outlet. The ground dropped from under their feet, and not a single ray of light was visible on the horizon. However, the news about Hitler's invasion of Poland and the beginning of the war came down like a heavy blow. The heart prophesied evil, and it knew what was predicted.

During the 1939 summer months, the illusion that the war was preventable prevailed among the Polish residents. The events in Europe since Hitler entered the Saarland, and the signing of the Munich agreement, strengthened that illusion. No one predicted that Hitler would dare to challenge the western powers, who signed a defense treaty with Poland. Even less than that, nobody expected that the end of Poland would be decided in just a few days. The quick disintegration of the country, which declared from the crack of dawn to late in the evenings, of its strength and readiness (*silni, zwarci, gotowi*) astonished and depressed everybody. In a few days, the glory of Poland wallowed in the dirt, with its spine crushed. "If the mighty have succumbed…" thought the astonished Jews. They still haven't had time to shake off their confusion when the news about the conquest of the eastern part of Poland by the Soviet army. Poland invested a fortune in fortifying its eastern border. Everything was in vain because the calamity came from the west, from the "friendly Germany".

The Soviet army was once in Ternopil in 1920. Its miserable look arose ridicule and repudiation. In those days, the Soviet regime looked like a creature born during the swirl of war and was doomed to disappear once life returned to normal. However, twenty years passed, and at that time, the Red Army was a regular army equipped with modern weapons and possessed exemplary discipline. Everybody felt that the Russian regime came to stay permanently.

The feelings of the Jewish population toward the ways things have developed were mixed. The initial response was a relief since the nightmare of a Hitlerian conquest was averted. The horrible news about the atrocities committed by the Nazis in Germany, Czechoslovakia, and the first days of the conquest in Poland reached Ternopil. Although the Soviet rule brought some dangers to the Jewish population, they were dangers of a different type. It was clear that the end has come to the lives before the war and that new lives began. Within a short time, with one swoop, the structure, built by generations, was obliviated. The community, movements, parties, and various organizations that Ternopil was blessed with, were paralyzed. The city activists who dedicated their lives to public activity were pushed aside, and new people, whom nobody knew, surfaced. All of a sudden, communists, in numbers beyond anybody's expectation, appeared and openly declared their affinity for the new regime and claimed that they were always loyal to the ideas of the revolution. The homes of the movements, parties, and organizations were confiscated and transferred to the hands of the new institutions that bore strange names. During the chaos of the first few days, "Bar Kokhba's" people managed to rescue their archive and hid it in a safe place until calamity passed. Public activity continued only in a very few areas, and the activists illusioned that these areas would remain available for them to work on: assistance to the refugees who escaped there from all corners of conquered Poland, the orphanage, and the hospital.

The first weeks of the new regime brought with it an economic awakening. Thousands of military personnel and officials, who flocked to Ternopil from Russia and neighboring areas, pounced on the goods

[Columns 381-382]

in the stores and bought the entire inventory higgledy-piggledy. However, the merchants sobered up when they realized that the value of the currency was low and in addition, it was not possible or advisable to replenish the inventory due to the lack of merchandise in the market and the negative attitude of the authorities toward private trade. That position by the merchants brought upon them the response from the authorities who began to use pressure means toward them. The authorities conducted searches in their homes, and suspects blamed for hiding goods were arrested. The authorities also "organized" a movement against the merchants they called "The Nation's Anger". Subsequently, the merchants were tried in show-off trials and sentenced to long jail times.

The regime formats and methods began to take shape slowly out of the chaos that prevailed in the first few days after the entrance of the Soviet army. The first blow was the deportations. In the Ternopil, the families of Jewish officers who served in the Polish army were arrested and sent as prisoners to Russia. Although there were only a few cases, it was enough to evoke fear among the Jews. People wished to prove that they were not related to the Polish regime.

The fate of other areas conquered by the Soviets, formally under Polish rule, was also sealed at that time. A special conference of the representatives of the professional unions, representatives of the factory workers, and others gathered in Lviv. The conference representatives decided to turn to the Soviet authorities and ask them to annex these Polish areas to the Soviet [Western] Ukraine and institute there the Soviet regime. A referendum held a short while after the conference aimed only to approve the conference's resolutions. Nobody dared to evade their participation or to voice their objections for the fear of risking one's life.

The only remaining connection to the outside world was the radio. Everybody listened to London broadcastings and believed that the western powers would begin a major offensive that would defeat the Germans and restore the situation, which existed before the war.

B.

In the meantime, the Jews tried to get used to the new conditions and reality. The social revolution began. One after the other, old occupations were transferred to the hands of the government. The government stores, opened every day, drove the merchants out. The merchants did not receive allocations of goods [like the government stores] and had to make a living from what they had in their inventories. Their days were numbered.

A real revolution took place in the education field. The authorities launched a propaganda campaign to transfer the Jewish children to Yiddish-based schools that were established then. The propaganda found fertile ground. For years, the Polish Jews waged battles for their right to have Yiddish and Hebrew schools, but they achieved very little. And here, the regime granted them the rights they always wanted. There were no illusions about the character of those schools. However, just the fact that Jewish children would study together with Jewish teachers sounded positive, and the opinion that they should not miss the opportunity and overcome all difficulties, such as the lack of teachers who knew Yiddish, won. The Jews hoped that the schools would attract children of assimilators who did not even know the shape of a Hebrew letter, thereby they could serve as a barrier to assimilation.

Dark clouds began to gather on the horizon from many sides. Rumors spread in the city that Zionist leaders were ordered to go to the NKVD - [a service of the] Interior Ministry [called "The People's Commissariat for Internal Affairs", later the Soviet regime's secret police]. The rumors said the leaders were interrogated there at length about the Zionist party's activities and its activists. The interrogees were sworn to secrecy. However, they did not hesitate to tell Dr. Tzvi Parnas the details since his personality was the center of these interrogations. Dr. Lippa, Dr. Horwitz, Kurfuerst, Ekselbirt, and in the end, also Dr. Parnas. A while later, Dr. Tzellermayer brought the news from Lviv about the arrests of the Zionist activists. This served as a warning to Ternopil's activists. The tension in the city increased, and the activists spent the night outside their homes any time suspicious preparatory activity was apparent since the arrests took place only at night.

There were mass arrests among the Poles, who were sent to inner Russia and central Asia. Officials, police staff, and officers were among the first to be deported. These arrests generated fear in the city and infused a depression in it.

The problem of the refugees from the western parts of Poland was on the agenda. Cut off from their families, discouraged by the gloomy reality, and filled with longing for their relatives who remained across the border, they seized the idea of returning. They were encouraged when the authorities announced the possibility of a population exchange of people who "got stuck" abroad.

When the mixed committee of population exchange was established, many refugees expressed their wish to return home during the census. However, it did not take long for the illusions to evaporate. The Germans refused to accept a large number of Jews, and the Soviet authorities considered these refugees, who refused to obtain Russian citizenship, a hostile element. During the night, mass arrests took place among the refugees. They were taken out of their beds, transported onto train cars prepared for them, and transported to inner Russia, east and north. These horrific nights made a somber impression on the local population, who shared in the sorrow of poor refugees but at the same time worried about their own fate, witnessing the cruelty and rigidity of the regime.

C.

The reality also slapped the face of the Jews in other areas. The illusion of the system of Yiddish schools did not last long.

[Columns 383-384]

On a fine day, people found out that pressure was exerted on the school principal, Professor Hirshberg, to make Ukrainian the teaching language. The authorities did not heed the wishes of the parents, expressed in a special assembly, to manage the school in Yiddish. A short time later, the school disappeared, and Ukrainian schools replaced it.

In the meantime, the process of nationalization proceeded at a quick pace. All stores and industrial plants were transferred into the hands of the government, and their owners were left without resources and sources of income. Their bourgeois past played against them, and they could not secure a job in a plant or office. A rent level was established for every class. Subtenants, most from among Russia's officials and their families who flocked to the city in mass, were introduced into large apartments.

The suffering of the Jewish population reached a peak with the issuing of the passports decree and the decree of the nationalization of private property. According to the new law, every citizen residing in Russia had to have a passport. However, these certificates were unequal to all citizens and they were used as a means of supervision. Most of the Jews received a passport marked with the symbol: "Clause 11". It was forbidden for a holder of such a certificate to reside in central cities, the location of district offices, large industrial plants, etc… Ternopil was such a city.

An owner of such a passport could not hold a major position in any important office. Thousands of Jews were decreed to abandon their residences and move to small towns. They encountered difficulties finding places to live due to a shortage of available houses. A bigger problem was finding work. There were no large plants or offices that could absorb all the newcomers. Lack of work affected not only the livelihood of these people, but the lack of work carried the bigger danger of being deported to inner Russia.

The second decree was the nationalization of private property, such as furniture, clothing, and linen. Special committees went from one house to another and confiscated whatever they desired. That was an operation of exploitation and oppression.

The Jews proved again their ability to adapt, probably the result of the diaspora's hardships. Most of them joined all sorts of production cooperatives, government stores, and offices. As productive citizens, they avoided being marked with "Clause 11" in their identification documents. The former activists were careful to avoid any activity that would arouse suspicion by the authorities, thereby avoiding being subjected to oppression and persecution throughout the Soviet rule encountered by many. In actuality, none of the Zionist activists was jailed or deported.

The Ternopil Ghetto and its Destruction

A.

The Jews did not have enough time to recover from all the shocks they had experienced during the last few years since the outbreak of the Second World War, and once again, a surge of violence was unleashed on them, surpassing in their horror everything that had happened until now.

On 22 June 1941, Nazi Germany attacked Russia surprisingly, and since then, events progressed at a dizzying pace. The Soviet army retreated, and high-ranked officials fled the town in a panic. Several hundred activists who collaborated with the Soviet regime and were afraid of Nazi revenge, Dr. Tzvi Parnas among them, were recruited by the Soviets, escaped as well. Those who stayed behind witnessed with anxiety and fear, the Nazi troops entering the city on the twelfth day of the war. The power of the German army and its dizzying victories brought depression and despair to the Jews. However, even the wildest imagination could not foresee the suffering, torture, and cruel deaths that awaited them.

The Ukrainians welcomed the Nazis with open joy, hoping that their day had come. They became friendly with the Germans and falsely accused the Jews of everything that happened during Soviet rule. The Germans handed the Ukrainians to city management and the organization of the civil militia. The Germans also appointed a Ukrainian mayor.

Three days later, bloody pogroms, unprecedented in the history of Ternopil, took place.

On Friday, July 4, companies of the German army, headed by officers, entered Jewish streets, armed with weapons and hand grenades, shouting: "Get out, Jews!". They called out the men, positioned them at the wall, and killed them in cold blood. The Germans pushed the Jews toward the market from all sides, near the old bath house on Zatzerkevna Street, near the carpentry shop on Ostrogskiego Street, near Gorpin house on Lvovska Street, in Zarodia, and in Sienkievicza Street. They abused the poor people, forced them to dig pits and throw the corpses of the people who were choked to death or shot into those pits. Some of the Germans turned to the houses of prayer and Beit HaMidrash. There, they broke the Holy Arks, took out the Torahs, and desecrated them. After tearing them up, they threw the Torahs into the garbage. They burnt five hundred Jews who gathered in *Kloyz* Yekel'eh, alive. The tinsmith Klarnet and Sh. Kantzuker perished there. A sea of flames surrounded the *Kloyz* and the neighboring houses, and cries of the victims tore open the heavens. The listeners twisted in pain because they could not help the victims.

Hundreds of Jews were tortured in the cellars of Gorpin's house and were later killed.

[Columns 385-386]

Many Jews who found themselves under a pile of corpses tried to save themselves by waiting for the end of the slathering. Under the cover of darkness, they later escaped to their home in an indescribable state.

Following the "formal" slaughtering, which lasted for a few days, the Ukrainians conducted their own pogrom. The fact that several tens of corpses lay in the jail yard on Mickiewicza Street served as an excuse for that pogrom. Hundreds of Jews had to pay for a sin they did not commit. They were dragged to the jailyard and were ordered to wash and clean the corpses, and perform additional deranged tasks under the mockery and joyful eyes of the executioners, who abused and tortured them. In the end, the Ukrainians cruelly killed them all. At that time, some people among the Jews dared to hurl blunt accusations in the face of the murderers. It was told about the old man, Izik Kopler, who prophesied the animals, shaped like men, their bitter end for the atrocities they committed when the day of revenge came.

The corpses lay in the city's streets for many days, and paddles of frozen blood covered the sidewalks and roads.

B.

When the wave of pogroms subsided, men who managed to survive came out of their hideouts to identify their relatives among the victims, which was not very easy to recognize. Human language is inadequate to describe the horrific scenes that happened there, and the cries and shouts that tore open the heavens. Thousands of people walked around in the streets, and when they found their relatives' corpses, they had to take care of the burial themselves. There was no home where there wasn't somebody who died there. Hundreds of families lost their loved ones. Heartbroken and torn, everyone was looking into their own soul and feeling their own pain, with no one to comfort them. The martyrs were buried in the old cemetery without a ceremony since neither "Khevereh Kadisha" [burial society] nor community council existed.

About five thousand Jews were killed during those ten horrific days. A heavy blow befell the community and its leaders, shocking them to their core. Overwhelmed by pain, wrapped in sorrow and grief, the Jews walked around. The Jews lost their trust in man. They also lost hope of a possible way out of the horror.

That mood did not change when posters, on behalf of the German authorities, were hung in the streets proclaiming that the Aryan revenge against the Jews, ended and that from that day on, it was forbidden to rob or kill them. However, in parallel to these announcements, the authorities published instructions that put limits on the rights of the Jews, in all areas of life and disassociate them from the rest of the residents. Forced labor jobs for the army and the state and communal institutions were imposed on the Jews. Their food was rationed in meager quantities that were insufficient to vitalize one's soul. These arrangements placed the Jews as inferior people, deprived of any human rights.

The Jews did not have enough time to get accustomed to these miserable lives, and the company of the "Einsatz Reinhard" (The Gestapo's military arm, attached to the front armies [dedicated to the annihilation of the Jews]) arrived in the city.

At the beginning of July, the teacher Gottfried was invited and ordered to establish a committee of the Jews consisting of at least sixty Jewish intellectuals. According to the order of the "Einsatz's" officer, the candidates should come to the "voivudzetvo" [district offices] on Shvinto-Yenska Street, dressed up in holiday clothes, where they were supposed to be nominated as the representatives of the Jews.

When the candidates assembled, the Germans began to make fun of them and abuse them. And before the poor men understood what was happening, they were loaded onto trucks and transported outside the city to the foot of "Dogs' Napes" (*Hitzles Berg*) Mountain. They were tortured there and ordered to dig graves. They were murdered one by one. Among the slain people were: Sh. Margalit, the teacher Bentzion Kapon, Dr. Shlomo Horwitz, Yul Kaner, and the two sons of Dr. Shwartzman.

The objective of the "operation" was clear: To remove from the hearts of the Jews any illusion that normal times would return, and that order was restored. It was also aimed at annihilating all those who could lead the Jewish public as leaders in distress and serve as spiritual and moral support.

C.

As early as in August, the German authorities organized the civil management of the District of Ternopil (*kreizhauptmanshaft*) and nominated a dedicated official for Jewish affairs - the Nazi Palfinger, who became an "expert" in Jewish affairs during his service in Warsaw.

Palfinger began his activity by imposing a forced "contribution" of million rubles on the Jews. The Jews had to deposit the money in a savings bank managed by the Ukrainians in eight days.

The Ukrainians used the money to restore the Ukrainian building "*Bertzvo Mitzetzenskia*", the destruction for which the Jews were blamed. In addition to the money, Jews were forced to work on the restoration for free. The foreman was Dr. Stephen Brukovitz, who enjoyed, not once, in the past from the political and financial help of the Jews.

[Columns 387-388]

Now, he probably wanted to atone for his "sins' by abusing the Jews, his benefactors.

Among the decrees introduced by the district officer Hager, was the special symbol that the Jews had to wear, limiting the rights of the Jews and their ownership of their properties, forcing them to abandon their residences, and cutting their rations.

To execute the German orders, a special committee was established by the Gestapo called "*Judenrat*" (the Jews' committee). Many of the candidates for the "*Judenrat*", including the writer of these lines, avoided their participation using different excuses. In the end, the lot fell on Dr. Fisher to serve as the chairman and Dr. Ya'akov Lipa as his locum tenens. Among the rest of the committee members were Dr. K. Pohoriles, Dr. Sh. Hirshberg, Izik Klinger, M. Brenzon, Ya'akov Labiner, Dr. Baral, Dr. L. Dretler, F. Helleriekh, Eric Shafkopf, and L. Ekselbirt.

In the beginning, the population trusted the "*Judenrat*", hoping that it would help to introduce order back to lives, and perhaps sweeten their fate.

The Jews could contact the authorities only through the "*Judenrat*". That allowed it to concentrate in its hands, all the Jewish affairs, to the extent that the Gestapo allowed it. It was the "*Judenrat*" that distributed the food rationing vouchers and identification certificates, managed the registration of births and deaths, referred the sick to the hospitals and welfare institutions, and provided licenses to stores, workshops, and apartments (in case there was a need to move to another apartment). Every Jew needed to turn to a sorting committee of the "*Judenrat*", where he received instructions about where and how long he would need to do forced labor work, and what kind of taxes he was obliged by the authorities to pay. The range of authority of the "*Judenrat*" was quite wide. It ruled the lives of the Jews, and their fate was in its hand to a certain extent. The most responsible role fell on the lot of the department of work assignment ("*Arbeit-Einzats*"), which directed the victim to hard labor in hostile areas. Every outgoing to work was dangerous since only a few returned in peace.

The Jews served as a target for the Germans and the Ukrainians who exploited them in every way sucked their lifeblood in hard labor and robbed them of anything they wanted.

D.

On September 1941, an order to establish a Jewish ghetto was published. In the beginning, the ghetto included the following: Part of Kazimierzowski Square, the market [rynek] and the streets Dolna, Perl, Lvovska, Podolska, Nizczia, and Miodowa, part of Szeptytzkich square to Serberna Street, Chatzki and Shkolna Streets, part of Ruska Street and the small market.

According to the "*Judenrat*'s" registration records, 12,500 souls were crowded into this narrow area. In the past, that was the poor area where five thousand Jews resided in poor sanitary conditions. Obviously, when the crowding more than doubled, the conditions became unbearable. The people that were forced to move there from places outside the ghetto experienced the worst. Ukrainian thugs attacked them on the way to the ghetto, robbed their movable property, and abused them.

The ghetto was surrounded by fences and barbed wire. The entrance was from two gates: near the Russian church on Ruska Street and at the intersection of Miodowa and Szeptytzkich Streets. It was no wonder that under the crowding conditions, without sufficient water supply (a tiny number of wells) and without gardens or open areas, the ghetto was prone to decease and epidemics from its beginning.

A sign that said "Danger of epidemic - entry to non-Jews is prohibited", hung above each gate. That was a bitter mockery since it was the Germans who crowded thousands of people into such a small area and created by their own doing the conditions that yielded decreases.

Life in the streets of the ghetto was nearly halted. The noise was silenced and no laughter could be heard. It was especially depressing to see the children running around hungry and dirty. A struggle for existence commenced. The old sources of livelihood dried out. The gaps between rich and poor and between the educated and uneducated blurred. Everyone was shoved into poverty's melting pot.

Day by day, the hungry, tired, and frail Jews went out to forced work for the Germans. Despite the pain and the disgrace, they also had to give a ransom to their torturers – expensive gifts of silver, gold, and fabric. The Jews arranged parties for Germans, either by force or out of a desire to bribe them. However, the latter was insatiable and extorted the Jews continuously and without limits.

In the meantime, the hunger in the ghetto was getting worse. Amounts of food products decreased, and bread was nowhere to be found. People collapsed from starvation in the streets. The typhus epidemic spread, yielding a horrific "harvest" of victims. Unfortunately, it was necessary to hide the disease cases from the eyes of the Gestapo for fear that they would kill the sick people. There was a shortage of physicians and medicines. The number of non-Jewish physicians was small, even on normal days. Now, the Jewish physicians were recruited to the Aryan side. The "*Judenrat*" established a department that handled funerals and kept order in the cemetery. However, when the typhus epidemic broke out, that department was overwhelmed. There was also a shortage of wood boards for coffins and cloths for shrouds.

Assistance to the sick was going on all the time, but, at one point, the Nazis suddenly published an order on behalf of the Gestapo about the need to establish a clinic for the sick,

[Columns 389-300]

an institute for neglected children and orphans, and a nursing home. Behind that seemingly humanitarian step, malicious intents were hidden. The intent was to receive lists of the frail people who burdened the public, as it were. To accelerate the death by starvation, the Nazis began to strictly guard against any infiltration of food into the ghetto above the rationed quota. The price of food products in the ghetto rose substantially, and the state of the poor was desperate.

At the end of November 1941, a fire broke out at the old *"Beit HaMidrash"*. It was clear to all that the Nazis set fire to it. The people who found shelter there – and their number was quite large - remained without a roof over their heads. They were naked and destitute since all their belongings were burnt in the fire. That was the Nazis' satanic plot. To top that, the "*Judenrat*" was fined a huge sum of money for the "neglect" – for not acquiring equipment for putting off fires…

Fate did not spare the Jews any humiliation. When the harsh winter started to affect the Nazis' armies, the Jews were again ordered to pull them out of their misery. In December, an order was published that every Jew must hand over any furs they owned. Anybody who disobeyed the order would be killed. Twelve hostages were jailed by the Germans, and the Jews, who froze for lack of firewood, were forced to hand over their fur, even those hidden on the Aryan side. That operation was executed with unprecedented cruelty. The following case will testify to that: During an audit visit to Schwartz bakery on Chatzki, several months after the publication of the order, the Gestapo found several useless pieces of fur that even the bakery's owners did not know about them. Five people were tortured for that and later executed.

E.

In that period, the Jewish militia began to capture an important role in the life of the ghetto. The militia was organized by the "*Judenrat*" to keep order. In actuality, it was under the direct mastery of the Gestapo. The following officers served in the militia in various periods: Sh. Kopler, Weinstein, Dr. Rotenberg, and Greenfeld. It was usual for changes to occur in the militia's leadership. The Gestapo demanded absolute discipline that not everybody could withstand, and the orders became harsher and crueler as time progressed. For that reason, Dr. Gustav Fisher and Dr. Ya'akov Lipa were replaced over time. Replacing them was Dr. Karol Pohoriles, who was a submissive servant to his Nazi masters and executed all their orders without reservation.

Initially, the "*Judenrat*'s leaders still illusioned themselves and others that following the Gestapo orders blindly would prevent a much greater calamity – the annihilation of the Jews. Their motto was not to anger the Germans, appease and lobby them with gifts, and interest them personally in the existence of the ghetto, which served as a source of work and money for them. The goal was to save whatever was savable, to dig in until the storm blew over since the final defeat of the Germans was beyond any doubt. The news arriving from the fronts strengthened that belief. The main thing was to survive until the end of the war. The supreme imperative was to save the youth, which constituted the nation's future. The belief that it was possible to save the youth had some basis since the Germans were interested in the able workforce, and they could only find it among the youths.

The new people in the "*Judenrat*" with Dr. Pohoriles at the top (after the war he changed his name to a Polish name: Buchinski), did not even try to cover up their actions with any ideological excuses, so to speak. They served as instruments in the hands of the Nazis, with only one objective guiding them – to save their own lives.

Fear and horror befell the Jews when the news about the establishment of labor camps arrived at the beginning of 1942. The task of establishing the camps, along with their equipment, huts for the workers, and apartments for the Ukrainian policemen and the German officials in charge of the camps, was imposed on the Jews.

The camps were established in Kamionka on the road to Pidvolochysk, Velykyi Hlybochok near the quarries, and Zahrebellya.

Young people were taken or kidnapped suddenly and sent to the camps. The people in the ghetto were tasked with keeping them with money, clothing, whites, and tools. Strict discipline prevailed in the camps. Every sign of fatigue or slowing down the pace of work brought harsh punishments, including death. Many workers could not withstand the harsh conditions, and their end was bitter. High mortality in the camps required a steady flow of new workers. Jews from neighboring towns were also brought to the camps.

The camp in Zahrebellya was located not far from the bridge on the Seret River, near the edge of the ghetto. The workers at that camp received food and clothing packages from their relatives in the ghetto. Obviously, bribing the guards were required to allow the packages into the camp.

With sorrow and pain, the Jews performed works that involved blasphemy. They were ordered to smash the fences around the cemetery, uproot gravestones, and pave the streets with them. The workers toiled from dawn to night, in the pouring rain, freezing cold, and hot sun, and woe to a worker who showed fatigue or weakness. The foreman conducted a review daily and checked every worker. He eliminated on the spot whoever did not please him. People went to work sick and tried to hide their illnesses from the eyes of the executioner foreman

[Columns 391-392]

(By the way, he was sentenced to death by a Polish court in Bytom).

These holy places still stand desecrated today, and the bones rolled in the dirt and demanded to avenge their insult. The tombstone of Rabbi Munish BABa"D z"l was miraculously saved and remained whole until today.

Besides the aforementioned camps, the Jews also worked in the army barracks. A few Jews worked near Janowska in building an airport. Luckily for that group, the work there was managed by a Polish engineer from Poznan. He was an exceptional man, and did his best to sweeten the fate of the workers. Thanks to that engineer, several people from that group survived, among them a child which was born to the Ginsburg family, a day before the annihilation of the camp's Jews.

F.

The worsening of the situation for the Jews was heralded by the news, spread in March 1942, that the "handling" of the Jews was transferred directly to the hands of the Gestapo. Its people broke into the ghetto day and night and caused panic among the frightened Jews. They robbed and looted everything, confiscated all the firewood found among the Jews, and ordered the destruction of fences and buildings.

The Jews sunk under the load of the hard work imposed on them from all sides. They were forced to work on the barracks renovation and other despicable jobs in the houses of the Gestapo men. The Gestapo Komendant, Obersturmführer Miller, was an animal in the shape of a man. His assistants were the Gestapo officers Laks, Maye, Reiman, and Reinish. Their frequent visits to the ghetto were accompanied by hits, kicks, and brutal abuses, ending with shooting. For every small deviance from the "law", the most severe punishments were imposed. That was how Miller murdered the former mill owner, Shalom Finkelstein, when they found some firewood in his home, how the electrician Lama Epstein was murdered along with his wife and child, for eating cherries during work, and how the waggoneer Izik Keller was killed in the forest because the killers thought he was going to slow.

However, even during that dark period, when everybody fought hard for their survival, some people worried about others. Dr. Yehuda Friedman, Professor Khaim Hirshberg, Sh. Rosner and others established a soup kitchen for the poor that distributed hot meals to the needy. A committee of several people, among them Avraham Margalit, Avraham Oks, Moshe Wahl, and I. Feldman, collected money to support rabbis and other honorable needy.

G.

The most horrible period in the history of the ghetto began on 25 March 1942: The period of the "recruitment of the souls", as it was called by the people. The Gestapo demanded from the "*Judenrat*" six hundred people: old, sick, handicapped, and "anti-social elements" to transfer to "other places". The fate destined for those poor people was already known. That was why some of the "*Judenrat*" members tried to avoid fulfilling that order. However, the head of the committee pressured and threatened the hesitating until the list was finalized. The *"Schupo"* (*SchutzpolizeiJudenrat*'s) list. The eyes of the latter were open then, who did not understand, at the time, why would the Germans had pushed for the establishment of nursing homes, hospitals, and orphanages. Like inanimate objects, the victims were thrown onto trucks and transported like sheep to the slaughterer, to Janowska.

The news about the horrible slaughter, which could not have been hidden from the public, felt like a shock to everybody. It evoked mourning and anger against the men the "*Judenrat*", particularly against Dr. Pohoriles, N. Halperin, and the convert Dr. Baral. However, people were powerless, had to swallow their sorrow and pain, and could not show the feeling of nausea they felt toward those traitors.

There was no illusion anymore that indeed, the fate of the Jews was sealed, that after the first "Aktzia", there would be more, that the "*Judenrat*" was an instrument at the hands of the executioners, and that no help should be expected from anywhere.

The non-Jews deepened the feeling of powerlessness and isolation with their nonhuman behavior toward the Jews. Not only did they show no trace of sympathy to the persecuted Jews or participation in their grief, but the opposite – they rejoiced at the Jews' calamity and collaborated with the executioners against the Jews. The Ukrainians and Poles handed over to the hands of the Gestapo, anybody who was suspected in their eyes to be a Jew. There is no doubt that without that treatment, many Jews would have been able to evade the Nazi executioners on the Aryan side, since the Germans, in most cases, could not distinguish between a Jew and a non-Jew just by their looks. Abandoned by the whole world, surrounded from all sides by predatory animals ambushing their soul and life, they lost all hope, and bitter despair settled in their hearts.

The Jews did not have radios, since the Germans confiscated them immediately after entering Ternopil. However, German newspapers were smuggled into the city. People learned to read between the lines. Sometimes, Jews who transported cattle to Warsaw brought news. In Warsaw, people knew more about what was happening in the world. The news about the German defeats consoled the people, however at the same time people knew that they "may expire till redemption comes": whoever survives starvation and epidemics, would be killed by the Nazis. Goebbels' venomous propaganda, and the news about the gas chambers and annihilation camps, did not leave any room for illusion, but there was no way out. However, before they departed from that gloomy world, they had to yield the last of their energy to their torturers.

[Columns 393-394]

One of the many Jewish common graves in the vicinity of Ternopil, found after the War

Several workshops were established in Ternopil during the spring months. The "*Judenrat*" provided the raw materials for these workshops. Women worked there too. Nobody was illusioned that they would save themselves by working there. Although they were all already hopeless, they did try to lengthen their lives. The will to live was so strong that it sometimes suppressed the accepted feelings, such as the feeling of family or national unity. By that reasoning, we can explain (although to justify) the behavior of the men the "*Judenrat*" and the Jewish militia, whose actions showed unprecedented hardness of the heart and cruelty. That small group of people was the one that stained the entire ghetto and formed an erroneous perception of moral deterioration. In actuality, the Jews, who stood the difficult test, showed great qualities of devotion and courage, and most remained true to the human ideals they were educated about.

The Germans exerted efforts to break the spirit of the Jews, separate between brothers, and imbued demoralization among their ranks. However, before the death blow fell on them, the Jews did not succumb to the Germans' ploys. The contemptible people among the Jews constituted a tiny minority. It is wondrous to realize how minute the results of the satanic activities by the Nazis were, which meant to prove to the world the inferiority of the Jews and their moral retardation. By doing that, they meant to justify, to a certain extent, the horrific actions they carried out. Although we cannot point to individual acts of heroism in the ghetto, the Jewish community, as a whole, showed courage and respect. The Germans did not see fear or hopelessness in the eyes of Jews as they led them to their death. Instead, they saw contempt and nausea toward their murderers.

H.

In August 1942, advertisements appeared on the Aryan side of the city. They were signed by the main executioner of Lviv District, General Katzman. The ad announced the transfer operation that would be held in the ghetto. The non-Jewish population was warned not to assist the Jews. Anybody caught hiding a Jew or helping Jews in any way to evade the Germans would be shot.

The Jews prepared for that event and used any means available to them, to save themselves. A feverish activity of building hideouts commenced. People built false walls behind which there were rooms, corridors, perforations, attics, and alike. These people demonstrated an exceptional innovative ability to evade the claws of the Nazi beast.

On the morning of Monday, August 31, Gestapo men, military, and Ukrainian militia surrounded the ghetto from all sides. By the command of the Germans, the "*Judenrat*" people appeared with their families. Jews were chased after when they were caught. The Gestapo thugs and their collaborators busted doors and broke into apartments yelling "*Juden, Heraus!*" (Jews, Out) and hurried the frightened Jews, chasing them toward a concentration location. The Jewish militia, who knew the location of the hideouts the Jews built, helped the thugs to discover them and pull out of the hiding.

In a span of a few hours, thousands of Jews were concentrated in the market and *Bander* [?]. They were ordered to crouch, and whoever dared to move was shot on the spot. The Gestapo officers and their assistants checked everybody and their work permit. Permission to return home was given only to those who worked for the S.S. and the Gestapo.

[Columns 395-396]

On that horrific day, the Gestapo commander showed his cruelty. The Jewish militiamen followed after him.

Among the thousands of victims, the Germans pulled out the young ones, able to work. The rest - elderly, women, and children, were pushed with hard hits into trucks and transported to the train stations. In the train cars slated to hold a maximum of 40 people, they shoved one hundred. Some train cars were already filled with Jews from Zbarazh, Strusiv, and Mikulintsy. There, the "operation" was held two days earlier. The poor people sat down in the crowded and packed train cars for two days without water or food.

The train that carried the phrase: "all the wheels are moving toward victory", traveled through Zolochiv and Lviv to Belzec, the death factory. Despite the strict guarding, many dared to drill holes in the cars' walls and jump from the moving train. Many fell under the train wheels, ran over, and were killed. However, there were some a succeeded in escaping. Most of them were robbed by the Ukrainians and handed over to the Nazi executioners. Only a few managed to escape and infiltrate back into the ghetto.

The fate of the wretched people brought to Belzec is known: They were choked to death in the gas chambers and burnt in the crematories.

The operation on 31 August "swallowed" 1300 people. Those who survived began to look for their relatives but soon realized that the hand of the murderers reached them.

The living, if these could be called life – returned to their "routine". Those people were hopeless and were waiting for their bitter end, which nobody could escape.

I.

At the beginning of September, an order was published to reduce the size of the ghetto. People who lived around the market, on the streets of Pola, Berk Yoslevitz, and Lvovska (till the big river [Seret River]), and on the streets of Zatzerkevna, Doli, Shpitizki, and Bloniya (on the same side of Ruska Street), were ordered to abandon their homes. They were given three hours to do so. Obviously, they could not have to salvage much of their belongings. The distress of thousands of people, squeezed into the reduced ghetto, deepened again. Their situation was like a chased animal

seeing the encirclement getting tighter and tighter.

A day without "visitors" at the ghetto was rare. When news spread about an imminent visit by Miller, the streets emptied. The "*Judenrat*" operation almost stopped. People did not know where and when the next blow would come. People took turns guarding the ghetto at night so that warnings could be sounded. People went to sleep with their clothing on. They improved their hideouts based on the experience acquired from past operations. Even the babies knew that they had to be quiet so no sound of life could be heard by the people who were seeking their lives.

In the second half of September, the people in charge of houses were required to submit lists of elderly people, older than 60, to the "*Judenrat*". Despite knowing what to expect if they got caught, they did not hesitate to edit the lists and "correct" the dates of birth. Only a few names from among those brave people remained in my memory: Moshe Wahl, Barukh Hirshhorn, N. Kozover, and M. Kalman, and they were not the only ones. To frighten the Jews and the "*Judenrat*", Miller ordered to erect of gallows on Bogata Street near the Jewish militia.

Common grave of tortured Jews discovered in the vicinity of Ternopil

[Columns 397-398]

He announced that anybody who would not obey him and would not execute his orders would be hanged. The militiamen did what they were tasked with diligently.

On 30 September, Miller's deputy, Laks, showed up with a company of the *"Schupo"* (*Schutzpolizei*) and demanded that a thousand Jews be handed to him. The "*Judenrat*" probably knew about that ahead of time because Laks collected the Jewish militia people and gave them prepared lists. Pohoriles collected several hundred Jews over several hours and concentrated them in the building of Tarif's mill. The militia people were not idle until the number of Jews reached 750. They then sent the Jews to Belzec.

Several days later, the Gestapo men appeared again, that time in civil clothing, and pull-out Jews from their homes. In that aktsia and other similar "aktsias" that took place until mid-November, about 2400 new victims were sent to Belzec. The method of kidnapping the victims exceeded in its cruelty everything that happened before.

The criminal opportunism of the "*Judenrat*" did not help them. Miller did not consider them reliable enough and suspected them to be too soft. For that reason, he brought over from Zbarazh the famous executioner, Greenfeld, and appointed him the head of the "*Judenrat*". To be able to execute his "mission", Greenfeld was also nominated as the head of the Jewish militia. The last stage of the ghetto's existence had begun.

A harsh winter began. The Jews went to work every day dressed in torn and worn clothing that did not protect them from frost. Much to the bitter mockery, the Jews were forced to unload coal while, at the same time, they could not get heating materials for themselves. When they returned home from their hard labor, they sat in the cold and the dark. The municipality was forbidden from providing electricity to the ghetto.

Every object that remained in the hands of the Jews was sold for a slice of bread. The deportations stopped for some time, so the worries of daily life rose again to the top of the worry list. News began to arrive about the Germans' defeats in Stalingrad and North Africa. The Jews saw on the horizon the final defeat of the Germans and took comfort in the fact that although they may not live to see with their own eyes the day of revenge, that day would surely come.

J.

At the beginning of winter 1942/43, Sturmführer Rokita who headed the Janowska [forced labor concentration] arrived in Ternopil. The account of his cruelty has long since reached the city, and fear and anguish took hold of the ghetto residents.

Rokita appeared at the "*Judenrat*" and requested to provide him with everything needed to establish a forced labor camp. That request meant that fundraising and recruitment of people would be required again. All the homes around the new bath house on Podolska-Niszsa Street were emptied and made available to the camp. The Jews who worked on the Aryan side were concentrated in these houses. A kitchen, bakery, warehouses, and clinic were established near the camp's workshops. It was forbidden to leave the camp under the threat of a death sentence. About 3000 people from Ternopil's ghetto and the neighboring towns concentrated in the camp. Above the entrance gate to the camp, the mocking phrase was hung: "Work sets you free". Strict discipline was enacted in the camp. At a headcount, held twice a day, the Jews were forced to stand for hours in the frost. Rokita robbed the Jews of their money and clothing and dressed them in rugs and shoes with wooden soles. Every "offense" was punished with the death penalty. Those who possessed valuables bribed Rokita and managed to free themselves from the camp. The Jews remaining in the camp toiled in hard labor. This time they did not have any illusion that they could save themselves by doing that.

In the beginning the month of February, the Gestapo began a campaign of extermination of the remaining Jews in the ghetto. The "*Judenrat*" and the Jewish militia handed over to the Gestapo all those who did not report to work. Blood of the innocents was shed daily.

The last chapter of the Jewish community in Ternopil approached its end. Whoever managed to save some jewelry and valuables and possessed a non-Jewish Aryan appearance acquired from himself and his family, Aryan documentation, and counterfeit birth certificates and identification papers. However, only a tiny number of these "Aryans" survived. The Ukrainian and Polish population showed great "vigilance" so no Jew would evade the Nazi's claws.

The lack of response by the world and the world Jewry undermined the faith of the Jews and broke the strength of their resistance. They stood in front of a gaping abyss and the world was silent. Nobody hurried up to help them.

On 9 April, the Gestapo men surrounded the reduced ghetto, pulled out a thousand Jews, and moved them to the camp. They chose the young people, took the rest through the bridge and Petrikov's brick kilns, and killed them all.

A unique event happened when the respected teacher Hirshberg, spoke insolently to the Germans. He foreboded a bitter end for them because of their cruel crimes. The Germans were thunderstruck, remained silent, and did not respond for several minutes.

The Rabbi from Medzhybizh [Mezhybozhe] exhibited honorable behavior and courage when he rejected Rokita's offer to stay in the camp while his family and his followers were led to their death. The rabbi sacrificed himself when he joined the people who were led to their death. [The Jewish militia's man] Leib Fiol refused to follow the order to arrange the victims in rows of four and protested against the disgraceful role the Germans wanted to force him to perform. The policeman

[Columns 399-400]

Katz tore off all of his police decorations when he saw his family members among the people sentenced to death and joined them.

K.

There was no quiet day with no kidnapping or victims between April 9th and June 20th, the day of the final extermination. Many families committed suicide without waiting for the executioners. Prices of poisonous drugs rose tremendously during that period. The rope around the necks of the Jews got tighter and tighter. The hope that somebody would save them from death diminished. The searches for bunkers and hideouts were held using the cruelest means. Painfully, some Jews did not stand the test and, in a moment of weakness, revealed the entrances to the bunkers to the Gestapo. The "*Judenrat*" and Jewish militia lost control of the situation. On the contrary, by their actions, they accelerated the end of the Jews and their own end. In their despair, the Jews clutched at the only straw left for them: "the Rokita's" camp. And just like a few months earlier, they may have made exceptional efforts to evade the camp so now, they stood and begged to be accepted there.

Every time groups were brought to the camp from the "aktsias" for a selection, the ghetto residents envied the "lucky" people in Rokita's camp with their hearts trembling and contracted by fear.

Everyone was looking for their relatives among the people who were led to death. In many cases, when they saw them, they preferred to die with their families over staying alive without them.

An extraordinary case happened to Engineer Winter, who worked in Rokita camp's bakery. Upon seeing his wife and children among the people condemned to die, he joined his family without hesitation. Rokita, who appreciated Engineer Winter's professional expertise and organizational skills, wanted to leave him in the camp. However, the engineer insisted, rejected the temptations offered by Rokita with disgust, and went with his family to his death.

Not only the living Jews were exterminated. According to the order by the Gestapo, all the Jewish certificates of Ternopil and neighboring areas, including birth certificates, were brought to Ternopil and burned. The Nazis wanted to annihilate not only the Jews but any trace of them.

L.

On 30 June, formal announcements appeared, on behalf of the district military governor (*Kreishauptmann*), that Ternopil was declared a city without Jews ("*Judenrein*"). Only a few Jews, who possessed Aryan papers, escaped to Lviv, Krakow,

Warsaw, and other large cities. There they did not fear encountering non-Jewish acquaintances, who were more dangerous than the Nazis. Indeed a few among those people survived.

On 21 July 1943, the Gestapo surrounded the camp, pulled out about 2500 people, and led them to their deaths. The rest were annihilated two weeks later. The Nazis destroyed the bunkers and hideouts they did not discover until then.

During the same period, the only substantial resistance by a group of Jews in Ternopil occurred. To their surprise, when the Nazis discovered a bunker on Baron Hirsch Street, they encountered armed resistance. The people in the bunker were ordered by the Gestapo to come out. The Jews responded with a barrage of gunfire and hand grenades.

Unfortunately, we do not have details about the heroic act since none of the people in the bunker survived. According to information from the event, the resistance lasted about 24 hours, and several Gestapo men were wounded. The head of that daring act was a young baker named Zelinger z"l.

Only a few managed to save themselves thanks to the help of non-Jewish acquaintances who risked their life, sometimes because of their generosity and some other times greed. That was how the family of the author of this article survived. They were saved in their kiln, located on the road to Smykivtsi [Smikovtza].

Many physicians who worked in the hospitals joined the Ukrainian partisan movement. Over time, the Ukrainians were disappointed with the Germans, who did not fulfill their promise concerning the Ukrainian national aspirations, and revolted against them. The Bandera's men ("Bandervitzi") organized [as a militia] from among these partisans. They were distinct antisemites but required the assistance of the Jewish physicians and sought their help. However, when it seemed to them that they managed without the Jewish physicians, they did not hesitate to exterminate them. Many families who escaped to the forests were exterminated by the Polish and Ukrainian partisans.

This is the place to infamously mention the Polish priest, Deacon Volenga. He did not hesitate to sermon from the pulpit, during the cruelest against the Jews, that the hand of G-d justifiably reached the Jews. He further included in his sermon that everybody who helped the Jews violated the G-d's will. The sermons of that antisemite in the pretentious cover of a religious man embarrassed the few who did not want to make their religion a fraud.

M.

Out of the eighteen thousand Jews residing in Ternopil when the Germans arrived, only 139 survived. That number was registered by the Jewish committee ["*Judenrat*"] during the period of May – July 1944 (after the liberation of Ternopil by the Soviet Army). Additionally, about 200 people survived among those who were deported to Russia or recruited into the Soviet Army.

After the end of the war, several Gestapo men who served in Ternopil fell into the hands of the Poles. Among them: Doka, the *Komendat* of the camp in Zahrebellya, the Gestapo official Karuf, who "excelled" in his cruelty during the "aktsias", Angeles, the Gestapo official in charge of the "aktsias" in the Lviv district official, and Reiman, the person in charge of the Jewish affairs in Ternopil district.

[Columns 401-402]

Some of Ternopil's survivors, among them - Dr. Pohoriles, testified in the trial against Reiman. The latter hurled the terrible accusation against him: "After all, you have collaborated with the Gestapo". All the Gestapo men were sentenced to death – a little comfort for those who survived.

The glorious Ternopil Jewish community that brought out of its midst, people of Torah, wisdom, and action was destructed and annihilated most cruelly. The city that proudly carried the Judaism flag became a pile of rubble. The life that flourished for generations was destroyed.

The Names of "Bar Kokhbah's" Members who Perished in the Holocaust

Translated by Moshe Kutten

Dr. Nathan Nussbaum	Anna Abend	Herman Farber
Dr. Yitzkhak Keron	Dr. Ya'akov Lippa	Nathan Schwadron
Dr. Wilhelm Landau	Ludvik Ekselbirt	Magister Manes Baumrin
Dr. Zigmont Mandel	Magister Herman Freizman	Norbert Preiss
Dr. Zigmond Braund, Judge	Magister Marc Lilla	Aharon Teomim
Philip Kopler	Oskar Fleishman	Avaham Kritz
Magister Ludvik Lebenkron	Magister Wolf Kelber	Ya'akov Nagler
Mendel Kacher	Dr. Jonas Rosenkrantz	Yitzkhak Deutsch
Dr. Rudolf Sharfshpitz	Eng. Max Belmer	Shlomo Kharp
Dr. Ludvik Klinger	Yosef Shtekel	Aba Auerbach
Magister Yosef Libergal	Yosef Yarichover	Magister Meir Arenkrantz
Magister Ya'akov Rosenman	Eng. Yosef Schwartz	Israel Kurfuerst
Magister Moshe Gelber	Magister Avraham Pal	Regina Pfefer-Kurfuerst
Magister Karol Gelber	Engineer Leon Arak	Panka Brif
Dr. Israel Zeinfeld	Sabina Arak-Greenfeld	Peppa Roseman
Magister Markus Keller	Max Karmelin	Rosa Doliner
Eliyahu Kenigsberg	Leah Karmelin-Barban	Tonka Tzimet
Eng. Mikhael Biller	Oskar Teitel	Klara Ginsburg
Dr. Maxemilian Herzog	Shmuel Kacher	Yetka Milgrom
Dr. Adlof Herzog	Magister Zekharia Merlin	Yonia Berg
Dr. Eduard Kelber	Shmuel Fuks	Klara Lifshitz
Eng. Shlomo Khoben	Anna Tzeiler-Fuks	Ernestina Lifshitz
Eng. Shmuel Khoben	Maxemilian Rosenzweig	Ernestina Zeidman
Zigmont Kessler	Magister Gustav Lenda	Prof. Herman Enzelberg
Eng. Ya'akov Biller	Dr. Moshe Sapir	Maria Enzelberg
Dr. Wilhelm Biller	Dr. Fredrik Sheinberg	Etka Shtadler
Zekharia Merlin	Leon Sheinberg	Mina Segal
Magister Henrik Goldberg	Wilhelm Shapira	Anna Epstein
Magister Shmuel Abend	Yitzkhak Farber	Zhenia Perser

[Columns 403-404]

From the Depths…

Translated by Moshe Kutten

The author of the following letter, Slomia (Mushia) Luft, was born in 1912. After graduating in 1929 in Vienna, she settled with her parents, Shalom and Khana (nee Oks) Luft, in Ternopil. She became proficient in music and served as a piano teacher in the music school. In 1937 she married David Oks, a philosophy dr. and a teacher in the high school in Brisk de Lita [Brisk-Litovsk]. The couple spent the summer months of 1939 in Ternopil when the war broke out and they stayed there.

The author gave the letter to a Polish acquaintance, who hid it in a tin box in his cellar. When the Red Army approached Ternopil in 1944, the acquaintance gave the letter to the author's brother (Bobbie) who was hiding from and it was he who brought it to Israel after the war.

The author of the letter hid with Poles. However, they handed her over to the Germans on 4th July 1943. She was imprisoned and executed on 20 July 1943.

Bobbie and Tzila, mentioned in the letter, are the author's brother and sister. Tzila perished. Bobbie – today Shmuel (Luft) Ben-Shalom – made Aliya to Eretz Israel, and serves in IDF at the rank of captain.

The author of the letter hid with Poles. However, they handed her over to the Germans on 4 July 1943. She was imprisoned and executed on 20 July 1943.

Ternopil, 7 April 1943

My Dears,

Before I leave this world, I like to write a few words to you. If this letter would reach you someday, I and everybody else here would not be alive. Our demise is approaching. We know and feel it. We are all destined to die like all

Slomia (Luft) Oks with her husband z"l

the innocent people had already been executed. The turn of the few who survived the slaughtering will come very shortly (in days or weeks).

This is terrible, but it is the whole truth. Unfortunately, there is no escape or way out from the horrible death.

I could tell you so much more, but how can I describe all the nightmares and suffering we endure. The pen cannot describe our nation's tragedy in this bloody land; the suffering, cruelty, and manipulated cruelty to hurt people, oppress, chase, degrade, and then kill. First, they squeezed us like lemons, sucked our blood to the last drop, and then threw it into a sewer ditch. They robbed us of our human feelings and instincts. After they converted us into animals who operate mechanically, they killed us en masse. No, you would not comprehend that, and could not feel what we feel. A normal-thinking human would never believe that a person can withstand such tortures and that such horrible things can occur in the twentieth century.

I will try the describe our fate since July 1941. At the beginning of July 1941, five thousand people were murdered, including my husband, David. He left home on 7 July (12 Tamuz 5711) and did not return. He volunteered to become a member of the "*Judenrat*" which is about to be organized. Despite my objection, he found it his duty, as a candidate for becoming a rabbi, to offer his service. He wanted to be an advocate for his nation. About six weeks later, after five days of searching, I found him among the corpses brought to the cemetery from the kiln (the killing location). My life stopped on that day, as there was no point to continue living. Even in my youth dreams, I could not have found a better and more loyal friend than my husband. I was given two years and two months to live a truly happy life with him. Strangely, it happened exactly two years and two months after our wedding (7 May 1939 - our wedding day to 7 July 1941, the day of our separation). There is no point in prolonging the discussion about my torments, and

[Columns 405-406]

my bleeding and injured heart, at the time that I had to bury him with my own hands, the person I love, the person who understood me, my beloved and loyal husband. How can I describe you being exhausted from the many searches until we were "happy" to find "our" corpse among the many forsaken corpses? How can I convey all of that in words?

Here is a woman bereaving her husband, the second woman, her only son, and above all, a woman who bereaved her husband and children. Can one describe a brimful of so much sorrow and pain? And that was shared by thousands of people.

So, David is gone. He is "lucky" in that everything has passed for him. He would not have to see the coming two horrific years. The bullet of death is still waiting for us. In the beginning, I thought that I would not be able to live without him. But alas, the human being is a tenacious creature. I continued to live. How? It is hard to say. The deep and bleeding wound does not have a cure. It is so sad to live alone, particularly because I was so pampered by my loyal husband and because I got so used to our peaceful and carefree home. But we continued to live.

In September 1941, we were sent to the ghetto. Imagine that we were surrounded by fences. It was possible to enter the Aryan communities only with licenses awarded to workers. A large gate guarded by German or Ukrainian policemen constituted the "border". Food items were smuggled into the ghetto with many difficulties and fear. I accepted a job in September with a German company as a secretary and typist. I was lucky because the office was located in our former home. The dining room served as an office. The desk stood where our piano used to stand. Instead of playing the piano, I began "playing" the typewriter. I should not complain. I had a good job. The employer and the staff were good, and their attitude toward me was decent. They treated me like a human being, not like a Jew. My father and brother Bobbie got a job in the same plant.

I was initially very depressed by the ghetto. However, we slowly get used even to these conditions.

The winter of 1941/42 was exceedingly cold and harsh. It became difficult to survive. People died from hunger and cold. However, despite the robbing visits, searches, growing hunger, and cold, life continued. From time to time, people sold their belongings, clothes, and linens and somehow survived until March 1942. Then the nightmare began. On the night of Saint Bartholomew's Day (23 March 1942) the "*Judenrat*" was ordered to supply a "quota" of seven hundred "pieces of people" to be murdered. What? You don't want to believe that? Indeed, it did happen. Our brothers - the Jewish policemen, were the ones who transported the people toward their death. The concentration location of the victims was the former synagogue. It was warm there so the victims did not suffer from the cold before being transported to their death. They were also provided bread and jelly. Later on, they were loaded onto trucks and transported to Janovka [concentration camp]. Everything there was ready: graves, a machine gun, and that was the end of it. It was a horrible night, but that was just the beginning. Quiet again, if that could be called as such. The forced labor camp's nightmare, the unending fear of what the next day brings. Despite all of that, we continue to live in distress and fear.

In July 1942, [my sister] Tzila was taken to the forced labor camp Jagielnica because she did not work anywhere. Her condition was not bad.

On 31 August, the "Big *Aktsia*" began. [The "*Judenrat*" was requested] to provide three thousand victims. The exact number of people who lost their lives in that *aktsia* is estimated at two thousand five hundred if not more.

That was when we lost our good, loving, and dedicated mother. The murderers used a new ploy – the working people and their families received special stamps from the police containing details about themselves and their work. The working people and their families were safe from being selected in an "*aktsia*". At that time, the *aktsia* was supposed to include only people who were not working and children. Our Jewish policemen searched again for their victims in apartments and hideouts. Bobbie and I went to work, leaving father and mother at home. After all, they possessed the "Stamps of Life". They stopped us at the gate and transported us to the "place of trouble". We were convinced that we were slated to die. However, we did not stay long at the concentration location: We successfully managed to escape. Many people got shot at that location. Luckily, I reached the office. A lot of work was waiting for me. I sat at the office while thousands waited outside for their death.

[Columns 407-408]
Thus, we continued our life without our mother – that good soul, the loyal and dedicated mother. Alas, we miss you so much at every step.

In October, Tzila returned from the forced labor camp in Jagielnica. In the meantime, the daily worries and the arduous but futile existence continued. We had to move again because the ghetto was reduced since the apartments of the murdered were vacated. We moved to 22 Szeptyckikh Street. Three houses on that street were within the limits of the ghetto (numbers 20, 22, and 24). We continued to live our lives.

On the 3rd and 5th of November, the *aktsias* were renewed. People were pulled out from all possible hideouts, and we had to move again. At 11 in the morning, the ghetto was suddenly surrounded, and the devil's dance began again. Luckily for me, without knowing about the *aktsia*, I left the ghetto precisely 10 minutes before it was surrounded. My fate would probably be to leave the ghetto on the last convoy.

We were forced to move again to a new place. We were ordered to evacuate whole streets again, and the crowding in the ghetto increased. Over time, we got so used to everything that we lived as fools. We did not respond anymore when we lost the people close to us. Nobody cried; We were no longer humans; We lived like stones, without feelings; No news made an impression on us; We lived in silence even when we were led to die. The people at the concentration square were restrained and silent.

In January 1943, we were transferred from the firm to the labor camp. We were subjected to a military barrack regime. Women and men were separated. It was now forbidden to appear on the street alone, only in groups accompanied by a policeman. We became prisoners of [forced] labor.

Father and Bobbie resided in the men's section and I and Tzila in the women's section. I forced my father to come with us to the camp while he was sick with kidney disease. I wanted to be together and die together. Many of our acquaintances escaped to the big cities. They were equipped with "Aryan" papers. Many were captured, and only a few evaded [the enemy].

From January to April 1943, quiet prevailed. We continued with our life again and got used to our troubles, all the census operations, etc...

Everything started again in April 1943. A small number of people, about twenty, were pulled out of the ghetto and murdered somewhere. On Thursday, fifty people were murdered, and so on.

26 April

I am still alive and would like to talk about what happened from 7 April until today.

The common opinion is that time has come for "Everything". Galitsia must become free of Jews ("*Judenfrie*"). First, the ghetto would be annihilated by the 1st of May. Seven hundred people remain in the ghetto.

Thousands of people were shot during the last few days. People are transported to their death "officially". Before it was called Ansiedlung [settlement], or Umsiedlung [relocation]. No such names are used now. The latest events were horrible again. The concentration point was located in our camp. Here, the victims, pulled out from their hideouts by the Jewish policemen, were sorted out and then transported to their death. We could observe everything from our windows at the camp. Alas, those scenes, those images! How can I describe them? We ceased to be human, became animals, and lost all human feelings. Sons brought their parents to the place of killing, fathers brought their sons, and women tried to escape leaving their babies behind. And that scene again – children join their parents, although they could save themselves for some time, being able to work. We observe the square being filled up with people sentenced to death. This time the graves in Petrykiv [Petrikov] were ready ahead of time. The victims were forced to leave their outer clothing behind. Men were forced to strip to their underwear and were led to their death on foot. After all, it was very close, why waste gas for the trucks, and why bother with the trains? After all, it's simpler to get rid of harmful elements locally. When they transported people on a train, a few escaped from the train cars. There is no such opportunity now. In my opinion, it is easier to die locally instead of traveling for two or three days, knowing that the destination is death. It is horrible both ways, but at least dying locally is done quickly.

In Petrikov, the whole operation progressed as follows: People strip naked at the grave, then kneel down and wait for the shot. The rest of the people stand ready, waiting for their turn. Between each group, they pause to arrange the corpses to ensure that the place is utilized fully. The operation does not last long. Half an hour later, the clothes of thousands of people arrive at the camp.

This is really too much. My nerves cannot take it anymore. If somebody would have told me, ahead of time, that I would be able to experience so much agony, I would not imagine that. Where do I get the power for all of that when I know that everything I do is in vain? There is no rescue. waste to have an illusion that one can escape this mass murder operation. We do not have any hope. We live from one day to another, or more correctly from one hour to another.

On 9 April 1500 were murdered. There was quiet for two or three days after that and then everything started again. This is Endless.

[Columns 409-410]

[Columns 411-412]

Today only seven hundred are left in the ghetto.

I have to add that the" *Judenrat*" received a bill of thirty thousand guldens following the "*aktsia's*", for "used bullets". Interesting, isn't it?

We, the people in the camp, are forced to enter the victims' apartments and rob their belongings. What a disgusting job. How horrible all of this is? Remnants of a whole nation. Those empty apartments, deserted streets, the dead city. Oh, how much it hurts, and why does it have to be so? Why can't we scream and or get weapons to defend ourselves? How can we see so much innocent people's blood spill and not say or do anything but wait for death till it comes and claims us too? That is so horrible. I am thinking about exploding, but we do not explode. We live – if we can call this life. And the world knows that we are being murdered, and nothing happens. Nobody wants to help us; nobody wants to rescue us. So miserable and abandoned, we descend to Sheol. Do you think we want to end our life like that? No and no. We do not want to, despite everything that happened to us. On the contrary, the will to live is stronger now - as death comes closer, the will to live becomes stronger.

Oh, how much do we want to live? We want to see, with our own eyes, the revenge of the millions of victims for the unimaginable suffering. Unfortunately, we would not live to see the day of the revenge.

My dears, you must take revenge; You must do something to take revenge for the injustice and the horrible and inhumane acts.

In fact, revenge is impossible since whatever happens, it would be very little, almost nothing, compared to our fate, since whatever was done to us is incomprehensible.

I cannot continue writing any longer. Even if I fill in additional pages, you would not understand. I will, therefore, finish.

My beloved David lies in the cemetery, and I do not know where my mother is. She was transported to Belzec. I do not know where my grave would be – Petrikov, Zagrobek, or Zarodzin. If you would ever come here sometime after the war, ask our acquaintances where the latest camp convoys went.

It is not easy to say goodbye forever. However, we are going to die soon with a smile on our lips.

Live in peace and flourish, and if can, someday, take revenge.

Mushia

[Columns 413-414]

My Experiences in Ternopil Ghetto

by Janet Margolis

Translated by Moshe Kutten

Between a nightmare and death

The Germans entered Ternopil on 2 July 1941, after short battles. The city residents sat in the bomb shelters, and only a few dared to be shown on the street. The Jews preferred to seclude themselves at home.

At dark, a group of Germans arrived at our house gate. It was pouring rain. The German knocked on the gate. However, after a short discussion, the residents decided not to open the gate for them. Then, the Germans began to storm the gate, trying to break it with the butts of their rifles. They failed to do so. We had a night of horrors.

The following morning, we opened the gate when nobody was in front of the house. The streets were filled with military personnel, cars sped on the roads, and urban mob looted the stores.

Restlessness was in the air. A rumor was spread at noon. It claimed that corpses were discovered at the jail and that the Jews were at fault. The Germans gathered the National Ukrainian Committee to discuss the "technical problems" associated with the Ukrainians' plans for the pogroms against the Jews. Pharmacist Bilinski, teacher Khomoba, and others participated in that meeting. The houses' courtiers were ordered to provide details about all the residents. Gangs of thugs were organized to conduct pogroms in the city.

On Friday, 4 July, at about 9 am, machine guns were placed on the street corners, and companies of S.S. soldiers appeared dressed in their black uniforms adorned with skulls. The courtiers stood by each house gate to provide details about the house residents. The residents were pulled out of their houses. They were told they were going to "work", but instead, they were shot on the spot. Mass killings took place in the yards and the cellars (e.g. in Me'ika's).

When pogroms raged in all their terror in the Jewish neighborhood, the Jews in other areas did not know about them. We also did not know about the happenings until the sound of gunshots reached us and until we saw the first dead casualties. Only then we closed the gate in panic and hid in various hideouts. A short while later, we heard knocks on the gate. We did not open the gate at that time either. The Germans tried the break through the gate, but all their efforts were in vain. Instead, they broke the glass windows and entered our home through the windows. The Germans searched and rummaged throughout the apartment, but fortunately, they did not find our hideout. They proceeded to rob the apartment and loaded themselves with all sorts of items they left the house.

We women went down in the evening and closed the gate. Shocking scenes were revealed before our eyes. Killed people lay down crowded with their heads ruptured, filled with blood and mud (after the rain). The cars steered their course through the corpses.

The following day, the Jews were ordered to bury the dead in the yards because of the stench that poisoned the air. The mass murder renewed in the afternoon. On the same day, Saturday, 5 July, my father was murdered in jail.

On Sunday, announcements appeared in the streets that forbade acts of violence and murder. They threatened anybody who defied the order with a court marshal. Calmed down somewhat, the Jews began to come out of their hideouts. A short while later, Ukrainians appeared at the houses and promised that the acts of murder would stop, and now they are only taking people for light work. Many fell for their solicitations and went out to work. At the end of the work, they were led to the jail and other locations and were murdered there. Only a few Jews survived that day and returned home.

On the same day, a mass murder took place in the yard neighboring our house. Thirty-seven people were murdered there, among them, also my mother.

The following was the chain of events that day:

The S.S. soldiers broke into our house and discovered all the hiding men except my husband. They ordered the men to carry heavy crates

[Columns 415-416]

filled with weapons. Among the people recruited for that work was my only son.

Ignoring all the dangers, I ran after them and begged the Germans to allow me to help my son in his work, but they drove me away and threatened that if I did not go away, he would kill me. Suddenly, the Germans blocked the street, and I could not do anything but return home.

During my absence, the Germans pulled my mother out to carry corpses. I saw her for the last time, pulling a corpse. She was all red from the extreme effort. I wanted to go and help her, but at that moment I heard screams coming from our house. These were the screams of my neighbor, who tried to defend herself from the Germans who abused her. Her two children stood by weeping. I went to help her. When the Germans noticed me, they left her alone and began to loot the apartment.

When the Germans left the house, I looked into the yard through my neighbor's apartment window to see where my mother was. I saw a group of Jews standing in front of the Germans with their arms up. I feared showing myself again to the Germans, so I just followed what was happening. Suddenly I heard gunshots. A few moments later, the Germans returned from the yard, and one of them said: "finished". I realized that my mother was no longer alive.

I was crushed. Yesterday, my father was killed, and today – my mother was. To top of that, my son was also missing. All of a sudden, I heard a voice calling me: "Mother! Here I am". Not everybody returned. Our neighbor was murdered because he walked too slowly. I was so happy to see my son that I was distracted from all the disasters that had befallen me in the last 24 hours.

One of our neighbors returned from work together with my son. My husband came out of his hideout. Only two families remained in our house. My son and the neighbor were ordered to return to work the following day.

Dark fell in the room. We did not taste anything. We simply forgot that we had to eat. We sat down and debated what to do the following day. Should the men go out to work, or should they hide? Our neighbor thought that they should go. I objected. After a long debate, they decided to go to work. We didn't sleep a wink. I lay down in my clothes and hugged my son. My husband lay down below and held us both as if he feared of losing us.

We woke up early. I prepared something to eat, but again nobody tasted anything. My husband shaved and shaved my son too. They dressed up and prepared themselves to go to work.

Before they left, I went to the neighboring yard to the place where my poor mother was murdered. I encountered a shocking scene. I saw a large open grave filled with men and women corpses, and above them, I saw the frozen figure of my mother with her face down. German soldiers stood on the side and took pictures. They probably thought I was not Jewish and had the audacity to ask me who did it. I brazenly lashed out at them: "You did".

I ran away home, and there I could not repress my pain any longer and burst into tears. My son and husband joined me in crying.

The neighbor began to urge them to go to work. I wanted to say goodbye to them, but they decided to save me the agony and left without saying a word. I decided to accompany them and followed them at a distance.

The concentration point was in front of the jail. The men were positioned in a row and were forced to perform military maneuvers under the guidance of one of them. I stood among the non-Jews who stood by to look at the scene. When the men entered the jail, panic got hold of me. I feared for their fate, and I decided to act to try to save them. However, everywhere I went, I encountered apathy and helplessness. When I realized I could do nothing to rescue them, I went back home.

The hours passed lazily. Our neighbor returned in the evening – alone without my son and husband. I understood that their fate was sealed. I hurled heavy accusations against the neighbor, who persuaded them to go to work and caused their death, but what has been done could not be undone. I hit the wall with my fists and head. I wanted to commit suicide but people watched after me. They gave me brandy to drink, but which did not help much. There was no medicine for my grief.

Dead and more Dead…

At the same time, my sister arrived from Velyki Hai [Gaia Velyeki]. She brought the bitter news that all the Jews there were murdered, including my brother-in-law and my son-in-law. The corpses lay in the forest and were still not buried. My pain was endless. I saw everything around me collapsing. I remained almost alone without all of my close relatives. Six people from among the people closest to me were dead. I stopped eating, lit candles, and sat down for a "Shiva". People came to console me, saying that they saw my husband and son. I ran to go look for them but in vain. These were fabrications, trying to cheer me up and bring me out of my despair.

After a week of pogroms that lasted from Friday, 4 July, until the following Friday, 11 July, things calmed down somewhat. Five thousand Jews were murdered during that bloody week. Among them, about eight hundred women and children. During the same week, the city's Jewish intelligentsia was slaughtered, who were the natural candidates for the first "*Judenrat*". It happened as follows:

The Germans summoned teacher Gottfried and tasked him with gathering several tens of Jews from among the city's honorable. The excuse was that the gathering would aim at establishing a "*Judenrat*". Gottfried went from one house to another and promised no harm would come to the people. The gathering was slated to take place in the "*Vovidezetvo*" [the district government] building. When the people gathered at that place, the Germans loaded them onto trucks, brought them to the brick kilns, and murdered them. Gottfried himself was careful

[Columns 417-418]

not to attend that gathering[1]. Rumors were spread in the city that the victims were sent to work somewhere until several weeks later when their mass grave was discovered.

In the meantime, a wave of decrees befell the Jews. All the men were required to appear and register with the labor office, which referred them to perform physical work. The Jews were ordered to wear a Star of David on their clothes and purchase a special sign for 100 zlotys to hang on an easily seen place in their house. Dr. Fisher, a lawyer, was ordered to collect among the Jews, within just a few days, a contribution of a million and a half zloty. Otherwise, the Germans threatened that they would jail hostages in the synagogue and burn them alive. Panic rose in the city; It seemed impossible to collect such an enormous sum. People sold jewelry and all other valuables. The Christians capitalized on the opportunity and bought everything from the Jews at close to nothing. Despite all the efforts, Dr. Fisher failed to collect the money by the deadline and had to ask for an extension. Several benevolent Christians came to the help of the Jews (e.g. Dr. Benshovitz and other anonymous contributors). The Germans were not satisfied with only the money and continually stole other goods, such as furniture, carpets, and more.

A rumor spread suddenly that the Germans would allow, for a certain amount of money, to exhume the dead and rebury them. I managed to receive such a license and came together with several other women, with the sanitary committee in attendance, to exhume my mother's body from her temporary grave. It was an extremely difficult task to do the work because of the stench emitted from the grave. The committee ordered us to stop our work after about ten corpses for two reasons: Firstly, they claimed that too many people gathered to look at the horror, and secondly, because of the terrible stench that spread in the air. Luckily, I had already exhumed my mother's body and transferred her to the cemetery.

I felt depressed and bitter. I almost stopped eating. I went to my mother's grave every day. There, I met many sisters in distress, who like me, came to cry over their family members and pour their hearts. I returned to my dark and gloomy home in the evening. I was lonely. People avoided meeting me. My husband's friends, who used to visit us often before the war, evaded seeing me in the street. Even my cousins ceased exchanging letters with me. I remained alone with my pain, leaning only on my own resources.

While thinking about my situation, I began to believe that I was saved from the claws of death for a reason: to fulfill a mission. My mission was to find my beloved murdered father and son and bring them to a Jewish burial. I turned all my thoughts and energy to that. I wandered around in every place where a mass grave was discovered hoping to find the bodies of my husband and son.

A while later, I found out how my husband and son were murdered. They were told to transport the slain Ukrainians from the jail to the Christian cemetery. While my husband was busy with his work on the cart, the Germans pulled my son and other Jews and began to brutally abuse them. They chased after them and hit them with sticks and batons. My son stood up suddenly and turned to his torturers: "You do not have the right to hit and torture us. We are innocent. Kill us, but don't torture us." Hearing that, they hit him harder until he collapsed and died. When my husband saw that, he passed out. The Germans began hitting him with murderous blows until he had to stop working. When he showed some signs of being alive, a German approached him and "finished" him by shooting him dead.

That story crushed me again. I felt that I was losing my mind. The tortured image of my son stood before my eyes, day and night, and I felt the physical pain he suffered as if I was beaten and tortured myself.

About ten weeks after the disaster, a mass grave was discovered in the cemetery. The corpses were already in a state of decomposition. Most were covered with only undergarments, and their hands and feet tied with a barbwire. On the first day of my search, I did not find my husband or my son. My son came to me in my dream that night so tangibly that I felt him near me. I woke up early in the morning and ran to the cemetery. In the meantime, they moved the corpses to the cemetery morgue. I entered the room and noticed suddenly a familiar pair of pants, a shirt, and undergarments. Their colors faded, but I recognized the zipper right away. My son, my dear son, my beloved…

As I was stood there, bitterly mourning my son, they called me that they had found my husband. They identified him based on the certificates he had with him. I saw him several times but did not recognize him. He changed so much.

I buried my husband and my son, one near the other. The only thing left for me to do is to find my father. However, despite all my great efforts, I could not find him.

The establishment of the ghetto

In the meantime, life did not stand still. A ghetto was established in Ternopil, the first in Galitsia. One of his organizers was Fierstenberg, a Jew from Bedzin [Bendin], who arrived in the city wearing the uniform of an officer in Warsaw's Jewish militia. He was lodged with Shmuel Cooper. Furstenberg convinced people to join the militia and organized its first company. He also praised the idea of a ghetto, pointing at the Warsaw ghetto as an example. He intermediated between the frightened and confused "*Judenrat*" and the Germans and in the end

[Columns 419-420]

it was "agreed" to establish the ghetto. A special committee set its borders, and Jews were ordered to move into it from their various places of residence by the end of September.

The crowding in the ghetto was horrible, but even there, one could easily distinguish between the wealthy and the poor. While the wealthy lived relatively comfortably and had plenty to eat, the poor resided in small rooms and died from hunger. Although a soup kitchen that provided hot soup daily was organized, the people who benefitted from it and other social assistance programs were the first to suffer from any calamity. Therefore, the ghetto's needy preferred to forgo assistance, which could have cost them their life. In addition to the hunger and crowding, the poor suffered from the cold, which was one of the harshest hardships that claimed many victims.

Except for the searches and kidnapping for forced labor, life in the ghetto was quite monotonous. One day was similar to another, and one worry chased after the other.

I decided to start working in public service. The teachers planned to open a school and gathered several times to discuss their plans. However, the parents objected to assembling too many children in the same place. In the end, small groups of 5-8 children gathered and studied in private homes.

At the same time, the "*Judenrat*" organized social work department and a hospital. Donations were collected to maintain an orphanage and nursing home, which were later established. A kindergarten was also planned. The hospital was located in Me'ika's home in the old market and the orphanage in *Beit HaMidrash*. The children at the orphanage lay down on bunks and were hungry most of the time. The institution was managed by Professor Joachim Hirschberg, who headed a group of workers; however, a lack of resources and food hindered their work. The nursing home was also located in *Beit HaMidtrash*. The state of the poor elderlies aroused pity in the hearts of all who saw them. The kindergarten was not established since the building slated for it housed the jail of the Jewish militia.

Those who destroy and ravage you…

The population began to look for ways for making a living. One man opened a coffee house and the other – a workshop. Many baked pastries for the shops. Children sold cigarettes in the streets. Those who went out to work outside of the ghetto smuggled food products.

There were also "big" merchants in the ghetto, such as Teikhman and Haus. They worked in selling jewelry and even accumulated wealth. These people were just a few individuals. Most of the people suffered from hunger.

There were also "intermediaries" who did good business. These people included: Cooper, the Jewish militia officer; Fleishman, the contact man of the Gestapo; Dr. Baral, the camp physician; Eisner and Rosa Schwartz, the workers at the labor department, militiamen, and others. Pharmacist Freudenthal's house served as the place of residence for the top people and was called "the palace". The Gestapo people gathered there with their lovers and their Jewish adjutants, gorged and drank, played cards, and did all sorts of shady businesses.

Among the leeches who sucked the ghetto's blood was Labiner, the manager of the supply department of the ghetto. The ghetto residents received 70 grams of bread per day and a tiny portion of jelly. A portion was allocated for social institutions, and the rest disappeared into Mr. Labiner's pocket. Obviously, he did not deprive the "*Judenrat's*" members. He provided them generously. All of that was done at the expense of the poor since the wealthy managed themselves.

Baral sorted out the candidates for the labor camps, and since he did not object to receiving gifts, the poor were again the victims.

Rosa Schwartz headed again the women's department. She was not content with all sorts of extortions but used her position for all sorts of private services at her home, which people had to do after a full day of hard work.

That was how some "agile" people and parasites thrived and lived at the expense of their brothers' hardship.

The first "*Aktsia*"

A rumor spread at the beginning of 1942, that the Germans demanded to be supplied with a "blood donation" of about a thousand Jews. Negotiations between the "*Judenrat*" and the Gestapo were conducted, and it was decided that the "*Judenrat*" would execute the "*aktsia*" in collaboration with the Jewish militia. They prepared the list of the people who were "sentenced" to die, and Dr. Dretler approved it.

At the head of the list were the residents of the orphanage (except the staff) and the nursing home. It also included all those who depended on any form of social assistance - again, the poor and the needy.

Although the "*Judenrat*" tried its best to keep all the preparations secret, the population knew that something was about to happen. They just did not know when. One day, the militia and the "*Judenrat's*" officials were summonsed. They have been divided into groups of three. Every group received a list of victims and was tasked with bringing them to the old synagogue using various excuses. The operation began at the curfew hours in the evening, when going out to the street was forbidden. It was supposed to end at five o'clock in the morning. The Germans did not intervene and relied on their caddies from the "*Judenrat*" and the [Jewish] militia. When the messengers failed to deliver the "quota"

[Columns 421-422]

until 4 a.m., Dr. Baral ordered to capture of people on Podlska- Nizsza Street (the section of the poor people).

It was a horrific night. The screams and wailings rose to the heavens. I heard the calls: "mother, don't cry. I am going with you. Don't be afraid, your daughter will not leave you".

The transport of the victims from the synagogue to Bianov forest began at exactly 5 a.m. The Germans loaded the victims on trucks. They lay them down in layers upon layer and covered them in tarpaulin. The S.S. troupes stood on the top and trampled the victims with their boots and machine guns. The convoy began to move toward the forest. The "*Baudinst*" (construction service) has already prepared mass graves in the forest. The victims were ordered to strip naked. Men, women, and children were separated. The children were murdered first before the eyes of their parents.

Great was the resentment among the ghetto residents when the news about the "*aktsia*" became known. Under what authority did the "*Judenrat*" take it on itself to be the ultimate judge in determining who would live and die? People raised other cities as examples where the leaders of the "*Judenrat*" chose to commit suicide than serve as stooges at the hands of the Germans, spilling their brothers' blood. The people of the "*Judenrat*" had only one response: the murdered did not have any chance to stay alive in the conditions of the ghetto, and people should not be sorry about the barn when the house is on fire…

People learned a lot from that "*aktsia*". They had no more illusions concerning the role the "*Judenrat*" and the Jewish militia play. Everybody tried their best to avoid falling into their hands, entrenching, and escaping their claws at a time of fury. Feverish hideouts and bunkers' construction activity began.

The stranglehold is getting tighter…

The first Passover holiday in the ghetto was very gloomy. The "*Judenrat*" forbade baking matzas, and the ghetto residents baked them at home. The rabbi allowed them to eat porridges, legumes, and beans. During the holiday a group of prisoners was brought to Bianov forest and executed there. "Operations" such as this became routine.

Rumors spread that anyone between the ages of 14 and 60, men and women, would be recruited to work. The work would be allocated by the labor bureau, which would equip every worker with the letter "A" [for *Arbeit* – work] in the middle of the Star of David. Those rumors became a reality very quickly.

People without that sign could not move around, not even stand in front of the house for a breath of fresh air. People were persecuted from all sides. It was forbidden for a lone Jew to appear outside of the ghetto (the objective was to prevent any contact with the Christian population). Within the ghetto, it was forbidden for even the owners of the signs to move around during work hours, except for people equipped with a special license from the doctor. The city looked like a ghost town during the day. People ran around in a panic to stock up on food and water only during the evening,

All of a sudden, news spread that women would be recruited to a camp to work in the natural rubber orchards. [The Germans] usually kidnaped women when they went or came back from work. Therefore, the women avoided going out. Many women were kidnapped from their own houses and hideouts. After work, they were transported to Belzec's crematoria.

In July 1942, a rumor spread that the work certificates had to be stamped and that anybody who would not get the stamp would go to the "*himelkomando*" ("sky command"). The family members of the stamp owner would also be protected from kidnapping.

A "stamp panic" commenced. The provider of the stamps was Shmuel'ke Cooper, a former militia officer. When he appeared in the street, people surrounded him from all sides and begged with tears in their eyes to award them the "stamp of life". The truth is that Shmuel'ke helped many, particularly his acquaintances.

In the meantime, the news about "Operation August" in Lviv arrived in Ternopil. There, stamps were accommodated. That news amplified the panic.

People predicted that an "*aktsia*" would begin in the city at any moment. The famous "*Rollbrigade*", which "toured" the cities and sent Jews to Belzec, was supposed to arrive in Ternopil. With fear in their hearts, people ran to the train station every day, to check whether the "death cars" have arrived.

"Operation August"

On 31 August in the morning, I heard a voice: "Lulek, wake up! It is starting" They called the "*Judenrat*" person - Lulek Pohoriles. I saw through the window that the ghetto was surrounded, and many Gestapo troupes were positioned in the market. We hurried up and hid in our hideout. It was a room located behind a closet and a moving wall. We could see what was happening in the market through the room's window.

The market was full of people. Trucks arrived continuously, and people were loaded on them and transported under a guard equipped with a machine gun to the train station. It was very hot that day and people passed out of thirst. Sounds of screams, wailings, and gunshots reached us. The militia pulled people from all sides. The people of the "*Judenrat*" operated in an official capacity in the two concentration points (a second location was at the "*Umshlagplatz*" [transshipment square] in the horse market near Targowica Street).

The Germans came to our house twice but

[Columns 423-424]

by a miracle did not find us. Five thousand people were murdered in that operation.

The ghetto shrunk. Now, people were ordered to abandon the streets of Perl, Lvovska, and Berek Yoselevitz Streets, as well as one side of the market.

People predicted that another big "*aktsia*" would occur again in October. People looked for new ways to hide. Some passed to the Aryan side even then. The supplier of the faked Aryan papers was a Jew by the name of Weinstein, who was captured in the end and murdered. Aryan papers were now the dream of everybody. However, only a few managed to get them, and even fewer use them. Aryan appearance, Christian acquaintances, etc., were conditions only a few could meet.

About a thousand Jews were annihilated at the end of October's operation. After that operation, the Jews were ordered to abandon the Kazimierzowski market. The ghetto now extended from Ruska Street down to the [Seret] river.

On the way to death

On 8 November, while I was busy transferring my belongings to my new apartment, I noticed a panic in the street and the sound of gunshots. I realized that an "*aktsia*" began again. We ran with the rest of the neighbors to the hideout in the cellar. The entrance was not camouflaged sufficiently, and I immediately felt that this time, I was entrapped. However, it was too late to do anything about that.

The Germans broke into the cellar a short while later, together with militia people. They robbed our money, rings, and watches stating: "You would not need these things any longer". They yelled and kicked us out of the cellar. I received a few strong blows to my back and found myself in the square by Kazimierzowski Street.

Many people were already in the square, but new ones were brought in continuously. Many slain people lay in the street. The headquarter of the gestapo was located on Baron Hirsch Street. About a thousand people were crowded into that building. We stood there, pressed to each other. All of a sudden, they ordered us to sit down. Because of the crowding, this was impossible to do. However, as we absorbed blows from the rifles' butts until blood was drawn, we fell on the floor without paying attention to each other. The living sat on the dead and trampled them. The guard changed continuously because of the stench.

We sat like that for two days without any food or water. In the meantime, the "*Judenrat*" people pulled out their confidants and brought over other victims to replace them since the number had to be preserved…

In the evening of the second day, we were taken out to the street. The Germans and the militia people arranged us in groups of ten and led us to the train station.

I said goodbye to the familiar streets and the cemetery that could be seen from afar. I tried to walk fast to avoid the beatings inflicted on people who lagged behind. We were surrounded by the Jewish and Ukrainian militias and the Gestapo troops. Miller himself marched at the head of the convoy. Christians stood on the side of the road and looked at us curiously. Their glances were apathetic and even mocking. We walked in silence, concentrating on ourselves. Everybody said goodbye to the city where they were born, educated, and spent beautiful days.

A policeman approached me on the way and whispered in my ear to try to join the group of young people as they entered the train car. On the way to the station, the men were pulled out, and we, the women, were turned toward the train cars. I noticed a group of young women, and I pushed myself into the car with them. The car was locked quickly behind us.

A leap into life

We were about eighty women in the car. There was a hatch on top of the car that was grilled and latticed with barbed wires. A short while later, we found out that somebody had smuggled a file to cut the grilles. I organized the work. A few women stood by the hatch, and a few others stood on their backs and filed the grilled. The train raced forward. The jumps commenced when the grilles were removed. The "jumping contender" would climb on her friend, take her leg out through the hatch, hold on to the lintel, let go of one hand and jump in the direction of the racing train.

I followed each of the jumpers. Most of them were killed immediately, and others were run over by trains traveling in the other direction. Some women were shot by the Gestapo guards. Those who survived the jump were captured by special guards of the train workers, who handed them over to the Gestapo. If I am not mistaken, I was the only one that survived out of all the jumpers.

I hesitated to jump for a long time. I thought that it did not make any sense. I thought that even if I survived the jump, and returned to the ghetto - and then what? They will capture me again, and I will have to endure the seven Halls of Hells again? I looked through the window and saw an abyss gaping before my eyes. However, when I realized that out of the eighty women, only a few remained, I thought about what would happen to these poor women who would be charged with helping the escapees. I decided then to jump.

A few minutes later, I was already hanging on the other side of the hatch, ready to jump. I felt that I was caught by the barbed wires. I started to scream out of fear, and at the same moment, I felt that my body was leaping forward and falling. A bullet struck my head. Fortunately, it was only a light scratch. The guards missed their target. I had not recovered yet from the jump when I saw a locomotive-speeding toward me. I rolled over in a flash

[Columns 425-426]

to a nearby pit. All of that lasted just a few seconds

I was saved, but I was beaten and wounded. Blood trickled from my head and hands. I tore off some frozen weeds and put them on my wounds. The blood stopped. I later wiped my face and arranged my clothes.

While I was taking care of myself, two young Ukrainians appeared before me. "Hay Jew, come with us to the Gestapo!", they welcomed me. When I asked them how did they know I am Jewish, they responded that only Jews jumped from trains, and my condition indicated that I was not a tourist. I preached morals to them. I told them who is what the Germans were, betraying and cheating the Ukrainians, etc. One of them was probably an honest man, and he whispered to the other to leave me alone. However, that man demanded a ransom from me. I tried to argue that I did not have any money, but in the end, I gave them 20 guldens. Before we parted, they explained where we were: about fourteen kilometers from Lviv and there are two ways leading to the city: one through the forest and another on the road. I chose the road.

On the "Aryan" side

It was early in the morning and cold (I wore a summer coat) when I arrived at a village. I saw a woman farmer milking a cow in one of the cowsheds. I approached her, greeted her, and asked whether she agreed to sell me some milk. She looked at me suspiciously. To calm her down, I made up a story that I was a peddler from Lviv. I told her that I carried some belongings to the village to barter them for food products, and the despicable driver robbed me and threw me out of the car. I was almost killed. Now I have to return home destitute. My story probably made an impression on her, and she invited me to her home and offered me soup.

I went for three days without food and drink, so I ate with a great appetite, everything she offered me. During my meal, I thought about the poor people who reached the end of the trip and the suffering they endured. I could hardly believe that I was sitting quietly and eating.

After eating, I felt tremendously tired and asked the landlady to allow me to rest a bit. She agreed. I lay down on the bench and fell asleep.

My nerves did not allow me to sleep for a long time. I woke up, washed, fixed my socks and the torn coat, and ate something again. The farmer told me about a truck passing through the village that evening, transporting workers to Lviv. She told me that I could join them. I expressed my joy, but in my heart, I knew it was not joyful information. I began to converse with my host and tried to test whether she would agree to host me for a few days. She absolutely refused. I only secured her permission to stay for the night. I lay down on a straw bunk and felt that I was experiencing a miracle.

In the following days I convinced the landlord to transport me to Lviv in his cart. I obviously paid handsomely for it. The landlady lent me a large shawl. I wrapped myself in it and sat down in the cart.

During the journey, I thought about how to use my host to help me settle in Lviv among Christians. I entered into a small talk conversation with him. Suddenly, I turned to him, addressed him in a mysterious tone, and asked whether he was a good Pole and a patriot and whether I can rely on him. When he answered in the affirmative, and I got the impression that he was a decent man, I told him that I was a a member in the Polish underground in Ternopil and that I was running away from the Germans. I told him I need to hide, for a certain amount of time in Lviv, since they would be looking for me in Ternopil. I mentioned the names of several clergies, my so-called friends, who cooperated with me and would be willing to cover my expenses. They would also pray for those who would help in my time of need.

My story made an impression on the farmer. He thought about it, and in the end, he said that he had a relative in Lviv who was a strange man but would probably be willing to lodge me for a handsome fee.

When we reached our destination, the farmer entered his relative's house and stayed there for a short while. I sat on the cart and felt as if my fate was being determined during those minutes. A short while later, the farmer appeared with his relative and invited me into the house. Two women welcomed me. One of them, as it turned out, was the landlady, and the second one, chubby and made-up, turned to me and said: "We were sure that there is a Jewish woman in the cart, but instead, we see you, etc…"

After a short negotiation, we agreed on the conditions. I also asked the landlord to recommend a physician who could take care of my wounded hand, which was swallowed and covered with black spots.

The two of us, the tenant woman and myself, sat down for lunch. She presented herself as a Ukrainian from Buchach. During the meal, I asked her to send a telegram in my name to my relatives to notify them that I arrived peacefully in Lviv. She did not take her eyes off me and said: "Don't be afraid. I know you are Jewish, and I also guessed you jumped off the train. You played your role well. Please know that I am also…Jewish. They call me Yula here. I have papers, and I was even registered in the registry office. I will help you too. We will tell the neighbors that my acquaintance came from a provincial city to recuperate. In the meantime, lay down and rest and be strong".

It was like a dream for me. The woman's words slowly penetrated my consciousness. I felt a kind of warmth pouring through my body and faith filling my heart.

Author's Note:

1. According to other sources, Gottfried did come to that gathering but was released with two others due to their advanced age.

[Columns 427-428]

Common grave for the martyrs of Ternopil

With the signing of the book of remembrance, we collectively raise the blessed memory of Ternopil veterans - dreamers, and fighters, the last and first, who were brought out of a foreign land by their redemption aspirations and rooted in the land of our homeland; People of all ages and classes, intellectuals and commoners, that the love of their nation and homeland brought them to the shores of Eretz Israel, and perished in it in the campaign of work, guard, defense, and the great independence war.

The state of Israel, the fulfillment of the nation's dream for generations, is the living memorial who escaped and made aliya in a youthful storm and gave their energy and blood to lay the pillars for its formation.

Honor and glory for their memory

[Columns 429–440]

Name Index

* These names appear in the Notes: following N. M. Gelber's article in columns 21 –108.

Please note the page numbers of this list refer to the original *[column numbers]*

Prepared by Moshe Kutten

A

Abeler	205
Abeles Aharon	182
Abend Anna	401/402
Abend Shmuel	401/402
Abend Yona Dr.	169, 190, 191, 197, 203, 205, 207, 208
Aberman Aba	102
Aberman Meshulam	102
Abramson	123
Abrass Yehoshua (Pichi), cantor	Notes: 143*, 177*, 282, 283
Aftibutzer	146
Agnon (Sh. Y.)	296, 299
Aharonfreiz Mordekhai Dr.	107
Aharonovitz Yosef	213
Ahasuerus, biblical king	319

Aikhel Yitzkhak	Note: 155*
Akhad Ha'Am	119, 120
Aleikhem Shalom	133, 144, 307, 310, 370
Alexander I, Tzar	51, Note: 66*
Almantzi Yosef	77
Altshiller Israel	246, 247, 250
Altzofrom Moshe	228
Amernet Avraham	237
Amernet Milek	250
Angeles	400
Ansky Sh.	162, 163, 179, 180, 307, 308
Apter Melekh	79
Arak Avraham	272
Arak Leibush R'	227, 272, 280
Arak Leon	401/2
Arak Meir	280
Arak R' from Buchach	280
Arak Shlomo	272
Arak-Greenfeld Sabrina	401/402
Aran Meir R'	264
Arenkrantz Meir	401/402
Arenstein Mark	307
Arlozorov Khaim Dr.	213, 338
Arye-Leib son of David	51
Arye-Leib son of Shaul	31, 33, 34
Asch (Shalom)	220, 307, 308, 310
Ashkenazi (nee Perl) Mrs.	93, 96
Ashkenazi Menakhem-Mendil R'	25
Ashkenazi Shimon	Note: 49*
Ashkenazi Tzvi, khakham	31
Ashkenazi Ya'akov (Ya'avetz) R'	31, 33

Atlas Rakhel	Note: 60*
Atlas Ya'akov Dr.	101, 102, Note: 186*
Atlas Yitzkhak-Leib	46
Atterman Shimon	152, 366
Auerbakh Aba	113, 141, 401/402
Auerbakh Eliyahu	95
Auerbakh Ya'akov	54
Auerbakh Yitzkhak	311
Augustus Fredrick, king	29
Augustus Sigismund, king	21, Note: 1*
Avishur A. Dr. (see Werber)	

B

BABa"D Asher R'	274
BABa"D Avraham R'	274
BABa"DAvraham-Arye R' ABD	31
BABa"D family	30, 31
BABa"D Feivel R'	264
BABa"D Leibush R'	264
BABa"D Menakhem-Munish R'	263-266, 272-274, 279-281
BABa"D Mordekhai	30, 31
BABa"D Moshe R'	31, 263
BABa"D Nakhman R'	31, 34, 264
BABa"D Nathan R'	31, 34
BABa"D Ratzi	266
BABa"D Sara	Note: 15*
BABa"D Shalom R'	264, 320
BABa"D Shimon R'	263, 319
BABa"D Ya'akov R'	31, 34
BABa"D Yehoshua Heschel R' (son of R' Lebush))	31, 263, 265, 266
BABa"D Yehoshua Heschel R' (son of R' Yitzkhak)	30, 31, 35, 55, 75, 77, 79, 90, 263, 264, 265
BABa"D Yehoshua Heschel R' (son of Shimon)	264

BABa"D Yehoshua-Heschel R' (author of "Sefer Yehoshua") R'	30, 31, 33, 34 261-265
BABa"D Yitzkhak R'	30, 31, 34, 264
BABa"d Yosef (Yosa'le) R' (author of "Minkhat Khinukh")	30, 31, 103, 172, 262, 264, 268, 270, 274, 279 282, 318, 391
BABa"D Yosef R', judge	31, 264
Badenstein	312
BaHaR"L [R' Avraham Yosef, son of R' Leib]	220
Bakh	Note: 186*
Balaban Meir Dr.	Note: 4*, 72*
Balfour (Lord)	156, 222, 229, 241
Ballet Veska	246
Balmer M.	251/2
Bandera (Stepan)	400
Baral Dr.	387, 392, 420
Baras	301
Barasch Julius Dr.	Note: 172*
Barman Yisaskhar	25
Baron Khaim	225, 227
Baron Salo Prof.	271
Bartosiewicz Pavel	45
Bauer, cantor	284
Baumgarten	180
Baumgarten Mendel	180
Baumrin Manes	401/2
Bavari Baron	Note: 46*
Bavorovski Duke	Note: 9*
Bazas	366
Beer Peter	Note: 108*
Beigel A.	127
Beigel Ze'ev-Wilhelm	122, 123
Bekerman	122, 123

Bekher Izik 143	146
Bekhman Ya'akov, cantor	284
Bellegarda Friedrich-Heinrich, Graf	43
Belmer Dr.	169
Belmer Max	401/2
Belter Mrs.	367
Beltukh Wolf	111, 112
Belzer (Spivak) Nisan, cantor	284
Ben Ze'ev Yehuda-Leib	Note: 156*
Bendelman R' from Rzeszow	273
Benshovitz Dr.	417
Benyamin, son of Avigdor from Zbarazh	54
Ber D.	279
Berel	364, 367
Berer Dr.	369
Berg Yonia	401/2
Berger A.	231, 240, 241
Berger Leizer	241
Berger Nushka	250
Berger R.	295
Bernstein Arye-Leib R'	Note: 15*
Bernstein family	81
Bertfeld Ya'akov	183
BESHT (Ba'al Shem Tov)	69, Note: 108*
Betzalel of Odessa	283
Betzalel of Zhovkova	32
Bialik Khaim-Nakhman	150, 204, 205, 294, 297-302, 310, 334
Biberstein Dvora	231, 236
Biberstein Khana	240, 241
Bigel Dr.	220
Bik Emil Dr.	105, 130, 134, 135

Bik Meir	Note: 191*
Bik Ya'akov-Shmuel	47, 86, 87, 89, 90, Notes: 107*, 108*, 156*
Bikhovski Elisheva poetess	294, 297, 299
Bilfeld	219
Bilinksi Leon Dr.	Note: 46*
Bilinski (nee Bronstein) Malvina	Note: 46*
Bilinski Victor	Note: 46*
Bilinski, pharmacist	413
Biller Khaim	246
Biller Mikhael	401/2
Biller Wilhelm	401/2
Biller Ya'akov	401/2
Biller Yitzkhak	224, 225, 242
Biller Yosef	246
Binder Yoakhim Dr.	107
Birenbaum Dr.	107
Birenbaum R.	221
Birpas Y.	221, 222
Blaustein Lunka	242
Blaustein Moshe	271
Blaustein Mrs.	367
Blautein (nee Zeidman) Rukhama	271
Blazer Nisan (Spivak), cantor	284
Blindman Yerukham (Little Yerukham), cantor	281-285
Blishtift Emil	307
Blokh Shimshon	47
Bloy Moshe R'	273
Blumenfeld Berish	86
Blumenfeld Yosef Dr.	93
Boberstein-Levion Dvora	230
Bodek Hirsh	86

Bodek Israel	86
Bodzianowski Jacob	21
Boistein Betzalel	108
Bozhik	308
Brandes Shaul, cantor	284
Brass Dr.	221
Braude Markus Dr.	110, 118, 130, 135, 138
Braude Max Dr.	130
Braude Mordekhai-Zeev Dr.	139
Braund Zigmond Dr., judge	401/2
Brauner	127
Breitbein	102
Breiter Ernest	136, 139
Breitman Daniel	272
Breitman family	272
Breitman Fishel	272
Breitman Ya'akov	227, 271, 272, 280
Brenzon M.	387
Bretfeld Ya'akov	102
Brif Panka	401/2
Brinstein Yosef	216
Bristiger Dr.	207, 214
Brod Hertz	79
Broiner Zigmont	112, 118, 125
Bromberg-Bitokovski Z. Dr.	109
Bronstein (nee Falkenfeld)	Note: 46*
Bronstein Ignaz Yitzkhak	43, Note: 46*
Bronstein Leib	Note: 60*
Bronstein Leon	Note: 46*
Bronstein-Avnon Arye	213, 217, 247, 250, 329
Bronstein-Avnon Avner	43, 329

Brotziner-Trakhtenberg	86
Brukovitz Stephen Dr.	386
Brum Mordekhai	230, 236
Buber Martin	120
Buchinski	see Pohoriles
Bukhner Ze'ev	86
Bush Y.	92
Bussel Yosef	213

C

Cherkevski	105
Cohen R'	103
Cohen Shalom	77
Cohen Yosef Dr.	104
Cohen, store owner	332
Cohenberg Mendel	55
Cooper Sh.	418, 419, 422
Czartoryski	89
Czartoryski Adam	47
Czartoryski family	90

D

Dankner Mrs.	317, 318, 367
Dankner Shalom	317, 318
Dankovitz Shimon Dr.	105
Davidovitz David	23
Delitz Avraham	274, 279
Delugach Moshe	150
Dembitzer Khaim-Nathan R'	Note: 14*, Note: 16*
Dement Zeev	92
Denikin	177

Dessauer Julius-Heinrich Dr.	Note: 140*
Deutsch Mordekhai	293, 295, 296, 301, 319, 320
Deutsch Yitzkhak	401/2
Dinaburg Ben Tzion	Note: 113*
Diner	236
Diner-Potashnik Shalom	250
Dines Dr.	191
Dinish Menakhem	50
Dinish Yitzkhak	Note: 60*
Dizenfeld Zusia	112
Dobbes Yekhezkel	87
Doka	400
Dokash Yekhezkel	400
Doliner (Dolin) Aharon	242, 243, 245, 247, 248, 250, 251/2
Doliner Rosa	401/2
Donayevski	105
Doner Jacob	230
Dreifinger	123
Dretler L. Dr.	387, 420
Drexler	332
Dreyfus	110
Druk Arye	250
Druk Leah	250
Dukash Yekhezkel	93
Dykeh von Baron	43, 44
Dymov Osip (Perelman Isidorovich)	310

E

Edelsman Isidor Cantor	284
Edelson Isidor	284
Edelstein	198, 286, 296

Eibeschitz Jonathan R'	Notes: 19*, 22*, 24*
Eikhenbaum	360
Eikhenbaum Hirsh	207, 360, 370
Eikhenbaum Shimon	274
Eikhenbaum Shlomo	274
Eikhenbaum Shmeril	169, 227, 228, 274, 279, 321
Eikhenbaum Ya'akov	see Gelber -Eikhenbaum Ya'akov
Eikhenstein (Zhidachover) Tzvi-Hirsh R'	67
Eikhenstein Yose'le R'	277, 281
Eingler Moshe	227, 246
Einsler Avraham Dr.	187
Eintzigler Dr.	221
Eisner	420
Eizenshtetter Hirsh	41
Ekselbirt Ludvik	198, 249, 251/2, 370, 382, 387, 401/2
Elimelekh R' from Vienna	274
Eliyahu son of Arye-Leib from Kovrin R'	31
Emden Ya'akov R' (Ya'avetz)	Notes: 17*, 19*, 22*
Enzelberg Herman Prof.	401/2
Epstein Adolf	105
Epstein D.	64
Epstein Lama	391
Erter Yitzkhak Dr.	47, 66, 86, 87, Notes: 64*, 96*
Esther, biblical queen	319
Ettinger Hertz	64
Ezkiel, biblical prophet	277

F

Fakh A.	221
Falkenfeld Moshe-Pinkhas R'	33, 34, 42, Notes: 24*, 46*
Falkenfeld Rakhel	Note: 46*

Falkenfeld Shmuel R'	33, 34, 42, Note: 46*, 79
Falkenfeld Yosef R'	33, Note: 25*
Farber Herman	401/2
Farber Yitzkhak	401/2
Fedder Gutman Tuvia	89, Notes: 155*, 156*
Fedder Tzvi-Hirsh	89, Note: 155*
Federbush Shimon	273
Feffer Tzvi Dr.	297
Feffer Ya'akov	298
Feibel Berthold	120
Feigenbaum	308
Feingold	242
Feit Dr.	368
Feld (nee Tarif) Rivka	226
Feld Yehuda	225, 297, 308
Feldman Israel R'	270, 391
Feldman Simkha-Bunem Dr.	267, 273
Feller	122
Felpeda	305
Ferdinand, emperor	99
Fessel Mordekhai	224, 225, 226, 273
Fett Ben-Tzion	139, 167, 168, 208, 359
Fibotzki Dr.	98
Fierstenberg	418
Finkel Ludwik	Note: 7*
Finkelstein Avraham	250, 252
Finkelstein Shalom	391
Finlesh Yosef Dr.	Note: 194*
Finlish (nee Perl) Sheindel	83, 95, Notes: 154*, 169*
Finlish Arye-Leib	54
Finlish David	54

Finlish Nakhman	54, 55, 83, 84, 88 and 96. Notes: 71*, 138*, 154* and 169.
Fiol Leib	398
Fiol Moshe Dr.	249, 305
Fischer Kuba	249, 251/2
Fish	366
Fishel Yerukham	150
Fisher Gustav Dr.	183, 387, 389, 417
Fisher Moshe	118, 120, 122, 127, 141, 249, 359
Fisher Shalom	298
Fishler Yitzkhak	75
Fleishman	359, 419
Fleishman Julia	363
Fleishman Oskar	401/2
Fleishman, pharmacist	363
Flohen Karl	93, 103
Fogel Israel	102
Fogel Shabtai	111, 112, 113
Frank A. N.	150
Frankfurter Michael	105
Frantsoiz Leah	Note: 60*
Frantsuz Julius	185, 359
Franz Joseph I, emperor	43, 57, 58, 63, Note: 194*, 167, 313
Freizman Herman	401/2
Frenkel Aharon	75, 77, Note: 123*
Frenkelfeld Dr.	92
Frenkel-Teomim Elimelekh R'	264
Freudenthal Shimon Dr.	Note: 194*
Freudenthal Shlomo	Note: 194*
Freudenthal, pharmacist	420
Friedberg Tzvi	224, 225, 298, 301
Friedberg Yisaskhar	228

Friedman Israel R' of Rozhin	70, 75, Notes: 120*, 121*
Friedman Philip Dr.	68. Notes*: 58 65, 99, 101 and 108.
Friedman Yehuda Dr.	112, 113, 125, 133/4, 391
Friedrich-Heinrich Bellegrada Graf	43
Friehling Alex Dr.	92
Friehling Moshe	50, 51, 64, Note: 89*
Frühling Moritz	Note: 194*
Fuchs I.	251/2
Fuerst Dr.	80

G

Gabel Heinrikh Dr.	138 – 140
Gabel Mrs.	139
Gal M.	132, 139, 140
Gaon Sa'adia R'	261
Garfinkel Khaim	93
Garfinkel Nathan	93
Geiger Avraham Dr.	86, 87, Note: 161*
Gelber	360
Gelber brothers	308
Gelber Karl	401/2
Gelber Moshe	401/2
Gelber Nathan Michael Dr.	21, 266, 278, 286, Notes*: 27, 32, 34, 54, 115, 120, 132 and 195
Gelber-Eikhenbaum Ya'akov	Note: 64*
Gelman	124
Ger Simi	308
Gerber Shaltiel	Note: 155*
Gernik Khava	228
Gershon son of Nathan	31, 32
Geshuri M. Sh.	281, 311
Ghirondi Mordekhai-Shmuel	87

Giar Meir Dr.	338
Gideon, biblical prophet	153
Gilad (Shmeterling) Khaim Dr.	157, 169, 170
Gimpel Avraham Dr.	Note: 186*, 315
Gimpel Ya'akov-Ber	311
Ginsburg David	85
Ginsburg Dov	47
Ginsburg family	391
Ginsburg Klara	401/2
Ginsburg Shaul	Note: 119*
Ginsburg Tzvi	224, 296, 298
Ginsburg Yitzkhak	273
Ginsburg Z.	224
Glassgal Hirsh	103, 330
Glassgal Israel	152
Glazer	219
Glikman (Ganz) Khaviva	225, 228
Glikman Khana	228
Gogol Nikolai	307
Golan	see Spitzer-Golan
Goldbaum Moshe, cantor	285
Goldberg Adolf Dr.	Note: 194*
Goldberg Henrik	401/2
Goldberg M.	55
Goldberg Sander	226
Goldberg, orchestra's owner	337
Goldenberg Avraham	87, 216, 218
Goldenberg Berish	94, 108, Note: 157*
Goldenberg Hirsh	87
Goldenberg Shmuel-Leib	84, 86, 87, 93, Notes: 63*, 144*
Goldfaden (Avram)	307

Goldhaber Avish	55
Goldstein Sh.	231
Goldstein Y.	220, 221, 222
Goldwasser Dr.	366
Golitsyn, prince	43
Golokhovski Agnor Graf	Note: 186*
Gonta	175
Gordin	315
Gordon A. D.	213, 247, 249, 254
Gordon David	94, Note: 163*
Gorpin	384
Gotlieb Lebek	250, 251/2
Gotlieb Munio	249
Gotlieb Shlomo	198, 245
Gotlober A. B.	Note: 155*
Gottfried Mark	Note: 198*, 183, 196, 200, 386, 416, 426
Gottfried Selka	249
Grabski (Władysław Dominik)	190, 213
Grass Shalom	93
Grass Yosef-Benyamin	93
Greenfeld	389, 397
Greenfeld Moshe	217, 218
Greenspan (nee Shitzer) Hadasa	180, 298, 299, 333
Greenspan (nee Shitzer) Hadasa	299, 333, 367
Greenspan Israel	213
Greenspan M.	218
Greenspan Refael	116
Greenspan Tzvi	180, 280, 295, 298-300, 302, 333, 366
Greenspan -Tzfoni Nakhum	236
Grinberg Israel	166, 221
Grinberg Uri Tzvi	149

Grold (Goldberg) Yosef	Note: 194*
Gromintzki priest	161
Groskopf-Rimoni Y.	231
Gross Shalom	93
Gross Yosef Benyamin	93
Grossman Henrik Dr.	221
Gruberg Dov	217, 250, 252
Gruen I.	251/2
Gruenbaum Yitzkhak	190
Gruenberg Avraham	112, 113
Gruenberg Yitzkhak	120, 127, 190, 206
Guld Dr.	132, 135, 136
Guliger Azriel	217, 250, 252
Guliger Moshe	107, 172, 175, 180, 366
Gutzkov	308

H

Haberman A. M.	Note: 72*
Habsburg, Royal House	35, 98, Note: 1*, 131, 167, 311
Hager	387
Hager Khaim R'	284
Hai Gaon (Hai ben Sherira) R'	261
Haiman Mendel	226, 301
HaLevi Aharon	103, 268
HaLevi David	30
HaLevi Shmuel	30
HaLevi Yehuda	54, 311, 315
Halicher Yosef	202
Haller	167
Halperin George	120
Halperin Israel	Notes*: 10, 11, 19 and 20

Halperin N.	392
Halperin Ya'akov Dr.	108, 183
Hamer Mordekhai	240, 249
Handek Khaim	Note: 42*
Harari (Goldberg) Khaim	251
Hartman A.	107
Haslavski	30
Hauer Franz von, Baron	51, 55, 56, 66, 68, 69. Note: 108*
Haus	419
Hausman Alexander Dr.	139
Hayermans (Herman)	307
Heller Tzvi Dr.	187, 198, 207, 214, 215, 273
Helleriekh F.	387
Henish Meir	139
Hennig	306
Herlikh-Fuchs Moshe	246, 251/2
Hershaft Hillel, cantor	279, 286
Hersher Dr.	367, 368
Hershkowitz Tzvi/Zvi	230
Hertzbaum	167
Hertzenstein brothers	86
Herzl Theodor Dr.	109-112, 114, 116, 119 – 122, 125, 126, 129, 130, 143, 190, 210, 335, 372
Herzog Adolf Dr.	401/2
Herzog Maxemilian Dr.	251/2, 401/2
Heschel Avraham Yehoshua R' from Opatow	278
Heschel Israel R'	24
Heschel R' of Krakow	30
Hilferding Jan	45
Himelbrandt Arnold	221
Hirsch de Baron	129, 145, 146, 242
Hirsh David, cantor	284

Hirsh Shlomo Tzvi	93/4
Hirsh Yosef	Note: 60*
Hirshbein Peretz	308
Hirshberg Eng.	202
Hirshberg Khaim Prof.	391, 398
Hirshberg Sh. Dr.	387
Hirshberg Yoakhim, Prof.	383, 419
Hirshhorn Barukh	396
Hirshhorn Munio	246
Hirshhorn Sh. Dr.	139, 372
Hirshhorn Ya'akov Dr.	Note: 194*
Hoizner Berl	187
Hoizner Bernard Dr.	273
Hollender	341
Holobovitz Dr.	147, 173, 240
Holstein Christian	95, 96
Homberg Hertz	41, 42, 48, 49, 61
Horn	146
Horowitz Avraham HaLevi R'	46
Horowitz Dr.	191, 197, 382, Notes*: 59, 71, 79, 82 and 146
Horowitz Selah	360, 366
Horowitz Sheftel	46
Horowitz Shmuel di (Shmelkeh)	130, 132
Horowitz Yeshaia R' (SHELAH)	46, 47, 48
Horwitz Aha'leh	86, 93
Horwitz Arye	272
Horwitz Khaim	228, 272
Horwitz Kona	91, 92
Horwitz Leon Dr.	113, 127, 141, 205
Horwitz Nathan Dr.	91, 92, Note: 108*
Horwitz Pinkhas	55

Horwitz Shaul-Katriel	93
Horwitz Shlomo Dr.	386
Horwitz Tzvi	228, 272
Hutton Ulrikh von	69

I

Igli Mendel R'	274
Ingler Mordekhai	227
Ingler Moshe	246
Ingler, kiosk owner	337
Inlander Moshe	86. Notes: 138* and 169*
Inzler Avraham Dr.	187
Isenberg	186, 243, 361
Israel, Maggid	24
Israel-Isrel from Zhovkova	Note: 24*
Isserles Moshe R'	261
Izenberg	102, 252, 361

J

Jabotinsky Ze'ev	154, 207
Jakobson Israel	49, 83
Jospeh II, emperor	37
Jost Dr.	80, 84, Notes: 111*, 140* and 141*

K

Kacher Mendel	401/2
Kacher Shmuel	401/2
Kahan Bernard Dr.	365
Kahana David	Note: 17*
Kahana Sh. D.	272
Kahana, artist	202

Kahane Shmuel	230, 236
Kaiser	167
Kalil Pasha	29
Kalir Eliezer	261
Kalir family	81
Kalir Moshe	283
Kalir-Ziskind Alexander	see Ziskind
Kalman M.	396
Kaminker-Wakhman	112, 113
Kaner Yul	386
Kantz Wilhelm Dr.	Note: 194*
Kantzuker Sh.	384
Kapel Dr.	341
Kaplansky	124
Kapon Bentzion Dr.	386
Karl IV, emperor	167
Karmelin Max	401/2
Karmelin-Barban Leah	401/2
Karmin	101
Karo Yosef R'	268
Karp Ya'akov	144
Karuf	400
Kaspi (Zilberman) brothers	231
Kaspi (Zilberman) Pinkhas	233, 235
Kaspi Eliyahu	230, 236
Kaspi Moshe	230, 236
Kassel David	87
Katz David (Dzionio)	112, 113
Katz Dov (Bercho) R'	273
Katz G.	218
Katz Moshe Khaim	86, 93, Note: 146*

Katz Pesakh Tzvi	228
Katz Reuven	273
Katz Simkha Dr.	Note: 122*
Katz, furniture warehouse owner	332
Katz, militia policeman	399
Katzman	394
Katz-Margaliot Shaul D'	see Margaliot
Katzstein	145
Kaufman	306
Kavetzki Shmuel, cantor	284
Kelber Eduard Dr.	401/2
Kelber Wolf	401/2
Keller Izik	391
Keller Markus	401/2
Kenigsberg Eliyahu	401/2
Kenner Moshe	246
Kenyuk	239, 241
Kermish Shmuel	216, 217
Keron Yitzkhak Dr.	401/2
Kerpel Adolf	107
Kerpel Aharon	108
Kessler Zigmont	401/2
Kestenbaum Meir	230
Ketcheh Avraham	343
Khaim Zelig son of Nathaniel, cantor	24
Khanan son of Kushiel	261
Kharif Yosef R'	Note: 15*
Kharp Shlomo	402/2
Khartiner Meir	122, 124, 126, 136, 139, 142, 149, 150, 220, 321, 330, 377
Khayut Tzvi Hirsh R'	81, 92, Note: 159*
Khayut Tzvi Peretz, Prof.	Note: 15*

Kheimesh Avraham R' from Lublin	Notes: 21*, 24*
Kheimesh Moshe-Pinkhas	Note: 24*
Khmelnytskyi	175
Khmilenker	102
Khoben D.	246
Khoben Leizer	245, 249
Khoben Shlomo	401/2
Khoben Shmuel	401/2
Khomoba	413
Khorin Aharon	87
Kinderfreind Aryeh-Leib	51, Note: 64*
Kinstler	308
Kita'ee Rakhel	Note: 194*
Kittel	102
Klaften Tzetzilia Dr.	196, 202, 365
Klahr	213
Klarnet	384
Kleinberg Moshe	152
Klikhnik Avraham, cantor	284
Klinger Izik	387
Klinger Ludvik Dr.	401/2
Kluger Shlomo R'	77, 81
Knopholtz Sh.	231, 298, 301
Kobrin	310
Koenigsberg Alexander	122, 123, 127
Kolischer (nee Korenfeld) Rosa	Note: 194*
Kolischer Emil Adler von Dr.	Note: 194*
Kolischer Julius Dr.	64, 92, 105, 131, 135
Kolischer Karl	Note: 194*
Kolischer Nathan	64, 95
Kolischer Sh. D.	272

Kolka Rocznik	Note: 7*
Koniecpolski Alexander	22
Kopler Izik	385
Kopler Philp	401/2
Kopler Pushko	249
Kopler Sh.	389
Koreh Meir	50
Korenweitz A. Dr.	367
Koritz Avraham	154
Korkis brothers	110
Kornberg Gedalia	226, 273
Kornblit	308
Korngruen (nee Zilberdik) Frida Mrs.	143, 146, 372
Korngruen David	103, 107, 142, 171
Korngruen Philip Dr.	109, 112, 113, 117-120, 122, 125, 127, 133/4, 139/40, 142, 144, 150, 154, 189, 220, 342
Kortum Bogopel	43, Note: 28*
Korytowski Franciszek	23, 42, 45, 48, 90, Note: 43*
Kotzik M., cantor	286
Kozover N.	396
Krakover Sara	Note: 15*
Krakover Yitzkhak R'	30, Note: 15*
Kranski	157
Kratter Franz	55
Krieg	134
Krigesfeld brothers	250
Krilov	180
Krisberg Netka	250
Kristianpoller Michael R'	81
Kritz Avraham	401/2
Kromkhel Avraham	92

Kromkhel Nakhman (RN"K) R'	47, 76, 87, 90-92, Note: 159*, 119, 203, 242, 298, 331, 338
Kromkhel Shalom	86
Kron	122, 127
Krop	166
Krzysztof Jan	21, 22
Kurfuerst Israel	198, 205, 293, 295, 296, 298-300, 303, 334, 370, 382, 401/2
Kurtz Moshe	246
Kwashnivski Dr., governor	195

L

Labiner Ya'akov	387, 420
Lafayovker	170
Laks	391, 397
Landau HaLevi Tzvi-Hirsh R'	Note: 22*
Landau Leon	Notes: 57*, 58*
Landau Manish	94
Landau Menakhem-Mendel	93
Landau Moshe Dr.	84, 94, 152
Landau Tzvi Hirsh R'	Note: 22*
Landau Wilhelm Dr.	112, 112, 117, 127, 145, 401/2
Landau Y. R'	273
Landau Ya'akov son of Yizkhak R'	33, 84
Landau Ya'akovka	86
Landau Yekhezkel R'	Note: 25*, 84
Landau Yitzkhak R' son of Tzvi Hirsh	Note: 22*, 33
Landau Yosef	225, 228
Lande (Hirshkowitz)	236, 251/2
Landfish Alter	317, 339
Landfish Moshe	317
Landman Tzvi-Hirsch	267

Landman Ya'akov-Kapil R'	267, 268
Landman Zusia R'	267
Landsberg Henrik	143, 146
Landstein L.	251/2
Lauterbach I. Dr.	139
Lazarus family	367
Lazarus Oscar Dr.	Note: 194*
Lebenkron Ludvik	401/2
Ledder Dr.	296
Lefin Menakhem-Mendel	47, 48, 88-90, 119, 298, 302 , Notes*: 53, 71, 108, 157 and 158
Lehrer Leib'tsi	179
Leibel Shimon	37
Leibelinger Dr.	333
Leinberg Avraham	168, 174, 176, 178, 179
Lekher Mania	250
Lenda Gustav	401/2
Lenkiewitz Dr.	187, 196
Leszczynska Victoria	29
Leszczynski Jan	46
Leszczynski Stanislaw	29
Letris Meir Dr.	47, 92, 93, Notes: 53*, 156*
Lev Kalman, cantor	283
Levenstein Bernard	107
Levi Aharon from Barcelona R'	262
Levi Yosef	215
Levin R' (from Sambir)	193, 203
Levin Shmaryahu	155
Levinkron	307
Levinson Avraham Dr.	215
Levinzon Yitzkhak-Dov-Ber (RIVAL)	88, Notes: 63*, 122*, 148*
Levi-Yitzkhak of Berdichev R'	73

Liebergal Brunek	246
Liebergal Yosef Dr.	185, 206, 308, 364, 401/2
Liebling Philip	103, 107
Lifshitz Ernesta Libergal	401/2
Lifshitz Klara	401/2
Likhtigfeld Ya'akov	112, 113, 341
Lilla Marc	401/2
Lilyan, artist	202
Lindman Hirsh	225, 228
Lippa Genia	367
Lippa Ya'akov Dr.	169, 382, 387, 389, 401/2
Lippa, student	Note: 59*
Lippe Ch. D.	Notes: 196*, 197*
Liske Xawery	Note: 8*
Liuberer Levi, cantor	285
Lobkowitz, prince	64, 74
Loifer Rozka	250
London Klara	246
Lorber Berl	102, 219, 367
Löw (Lef) Leopold	87, Note: 140*
Lowenstein Bernahrd R'	107, Note: 196*
Lowenstein Dr.	132
Lozatto Moshe-Khaim (RAMKHAL) R'	Note: 19*
Lub	367
Ludvik, king	Note: 1*
Luft (Ben Shalom) Shmuel	403
Luft Bobbie	403, 404, 406, 407
Luft David	404
Luft Khana (nee Oks)	403
Luft Shalom	403
Luft Slomia (Mushia)	403-412

	Luft Tzila	403, 406, 407
	Luftig Mrs.	306
	Luner	301
	Luzzatto Samuel-David (SHADAL) R'	77, 84, Note: 152*, 262
	Lvov David	157, 183, 188, 227, 228, 272, 279
	Lvov Meir	272
	Lvov Nathan	272
	Lvov Yosef	272

M

	Mager Avraham	231, 236
	Mahler Arthur Dr.	137, 138, 140
	Mahler Mendel Dr.	88, 89
	Mahler Refael Dr.	73, Notes*: 105, 112, 117, 120, 121, 122, 127 135 and 136
	Maiblum	139
	Maimonides Moshe (RAMBAM) R'	268
	Makukh Dr.	170
	Maltz David	108, 138
	Mandel Zigmont Dr.	401/2
	Manheim Tzvi	274
	Manis/Mania (Manila), maggid	274, 318, 319
	Mannheimer Noah R'	83, 101
	Marder Yehudit	250
	Margaliot Markus	64
	Margaliot Mordekhai-Berish	63, 64
	Margaliot-Katz Shaul D' R'	274
	Margalit Avraham	391
	Margalit Mendel	228
	Margalit Shmuel	169, 190, 218, 363, 386
	Margolis Jennet	413
	Margolis M. M.	225, 301

Maria Theresa, empress	37
Marks Karl	124
Markus Eliyahu Dr.	225
Markus Khaim-Wolf	169
Markus Reis	Note: 194*
Markus Shmuel (Shapel Marian-Igen)	Note: 194*
Marmorek S.	366
Marmorek Yosef	Note: 194*
Marzend Zalman	249, 252
Masita Zalman R'	90
Matok (Ziskind) Khaim, teacher	179, 180, 297
Maye	391
Me'ika	419
Meiberger Avraham	224, 225, 273, 295, 296, 298
Meir Ba'al Haness R'	74, 75, 87
Meir R' ABD Przeworsk	33
Meir R' from Lublin	26
Meir Ya'akov	67
Meirberg Ya'akov	190, 200
Meirovitz Moritz	103
Meizes Y. L.	87
Meltzer (nee Pomerantz) Roza	see Pomerantz Roza
Meltzer Isaac	116
Mendelson	85, 89, Note: 140*, 297
Meniyes Yitzkhak-Michael	50, Note: 63*
Mentel Rudolf Dr.	107, 183, 187
Merbakh Y.	246, 248
Merlin Zekharia	250, 251, 401/2
Mesh Y. A.	229
Mesharet Tzvi-Hirsh	75
Messing Israel	225, 228

Mesuta	103
Metternich, chancellor	64
Migden Munio Dr.	244, 249, 251/2, 366
Milgraum	224
Milgrom Yetka	401/2
Miller, Obersturmführer	391, 396, 397, 424
Minkovksi Pinkhas, cantor	283
Mistrikh-Alufi Shraga	218
Mohar A. M.	88, 89
Moliere	307
Mondschein Max	245, 246, 250
Montefiore	303
Mordekhai son of Tzvi-Hirsh	51
Morgenstern	242
Morkes Azriel	218
Moshe-Shaul R', ABD Kalish	Note: 15*
Mosler Anton	Note: 36*, 183
Mossinson (Ig'al)	299
Mueller Albin	112, 113, 127, 146
Mund Wolf R'	273
Munis Yitzkhak-Mikhael	50, 86, 87, 92, Note: 63*

N

Nagler	190
Nagler Mrs.	308
Nagler Ya'akov	401/2
Nakhman from Braslav (MAHARAN) R'	Note: 111*
Nakht J. Dr.	Note: 100*
Nakht Yitzkhak	164
Nakhum, prophet	93
Naphtali R' from Ropshitz	67

Napoleon	43
Nathan, son of Yekhiel from Rome R'	Note: 145*, 261
Nathanieli R'	280
Nathanzon	81, 86
Nathanzon Dov-Ber	Note: 153*
Natkis Avraham-Benyamin-Tzvi	Note: 96*
Neigeboren Eliezer	228
Neiger Avraham	88
Neiman Ya'akov	50-53, 55. Notes: 58* and 61*
Neistein R'	274
Nekhemchi R'	280
Neteh'leh R'	280
Neuman Avraham	230, 251/2
Neustadt Leib	365
Niman Dov	341
Nimrower Dr. R'	139
Nirenstein M.	86
Nisbaum Mendel	218
Nishka, preacher	Note: 106*
Nisim Bar Ya'akov	261
Nives Yaa'kov (Kuba)	246, 248
Nomberg H. D.	220, 307
Nossig Alferd	120, 121
Novakovski	197
Nusbrekher Dr.	221
Nussbaum Dr.	191, 203. 208, 370
Nussbaum Izik	112, 113, 122, 144
Nussbaum J.	127
Nussbaum Nathan	111, 112, 113, 116, 117, 401/2

O

Odisser Nisan (Nisan from Odesa), cantor	286	
Oks Avraham	190, 207, 379, 391	
Oks David Dr.	403, 404, 412	
Oks Khaim	169. 189,190, 197, 207	
Oks Rekka	296, 297, 298	
Oks Shalom	403	
Oksenhorn (nee Rauk) Anna	335, 363	
Oksenhorn Herman Dr.	363	
Okser Shalom Dr	108, Note: 198*, 331	
Oksman Yitzkhak	Note: 119*	
Orens Dr.	205	
Orenstein Shaul Dr.	213, 215, 216, 217	
Orenstein Ya'akov R'	60, 66, 77, 267	
Ostern Masha	296, 302, 303	
Ostren Nathan	218, 296, 303	
Ostrogska-Zamoyski Katarzyna	22	
Ostrogski family	21	
Ostrogski Konstanty, prince	21	
Otshert Yosef	107, 148	
Ovadiah, prophet	93	
Overman Avraham	246	

P

Pal Avraham	401/2	
Palfinger	386	
Paries Aharon Dr.	Note: 95*	
Parnas David	75, 169, 189, 224	
Parnas H. Dr.	205	
Parnas Israel	109, 224	
Parnas Khaim	198	
Parnas Mark Dr.	359	

Parnas Tonka	246
Parnas Tzvi Dr.	152, 154, 155, 180, 181, 184-186, 190, 197, 199, 201-203, 208, 266, 337, 349, 359-361, 364, 368, 370, 382, 384
Parnas Yehoshua	189, 226, 298, 361
Pasmanik Daniel Dr.	124, 126-128, 220, 306, 308
Pasternak Dr.	126
Pasternak Yitzkhak	321
Patrila	21
Pechnik Shmaryahu	213, 218, 241
Peiles Dr.	183, 190, 193, 194, 200
Peled	297, 308
Peler Shimon	220
Pendler	220
Pepperish	199
Peretz Y. L.	220, 310
Perl Imanuel	103
Perl Mikhael	77, 83, 95, 96, 103, 104, Notes: 181*, 194*, 200
Perl Miryam	70
Perl Tauba	Note: 181*
Perl Todros R'	46
Perl Yosef	46-96, 103, 119, 124, 125, 171, 199 201, 204, 242, 266, 281, 284, 295, 297, 301, 319, 320, 330-333, 338. 363 and 387, Notes*: 51, 42, 54, 58, 60-63, 66, 71, 79, 88, 93, 100, 101, 104, 106, 108, 111, 121, 122, 130, 131, 138, 140, 141, 146, 154, 158, 161, 168 and 181
Perl Zelig	55
Perlmutter	102
Perser Zhenia	401/2
Pestor Yehuda	Note: 96*
Petliura	160, 172, 174, 175, 176, 178, 241
Petrikov	398
Petrushka	246

Phillipson Dr.	80
Pikhorsky	170
Pilsudski, Marshall	184, 194, 207
Pinsker Simkha	87
Pirutzki Arzem	Note: 186*
Planer Ya'akov (Kuba)	169, 172, 174, 177, 341
Pleva	121
Podhortzer Shalom	199, 271
Podhortzer Ya'akov (Yeke'leh) R'	278, 280, 281, 384
Podhortzer, hatter	332
Podles	108
Pohoriles	201
Pohoriles (Buchinski) Karl (Lulek) Dr.	387, 389, 390, 392, 397, 401, 422
Pollak	109
Pomerantz Avraham	111, 112, 113, 116, 127, 145, 146
Pomerantz family	112
Pomerantz Mendel	108
Pomerantz-Meltzer Roza	116, 120, 143, 144, 145, 187
Popresh Yosef	274
Porat (Oks) Zeev Eng.	275
Pordes Dolio	154
Portis (Khazak) Yitzkhak Dr.	Note: 21*
Portis Zalman	Note: 21*
Posros A.	125
Potocki (Potowtski) (nee Leszczynski) Victoria	29
Potocki (Potowtski) family	23, 28, 29, 45
Potocki (Potowtski) Joseph	29
Potocki (Potowtski) Stephen	28
Poznan	391
Preiss Norbert	401/2
Primer	298, 301

Prin	303

R

Rabidowitz Sh. Dr.	Note: 159*
Racker Dr.	366
Rapoport	127
Rapoport Aharon	Note: 194*
Rapoport Alexander Dr.	Note: 137*, 112, 141, 162, 169, 170, 205
Rapoport Johan	Note: 194*
Rapoport M. A.	103
Rapoport Shlomo-Yehuda-Leib (SHI"R) R'	47, 76-87, 91, 93, 95, 97, 119, 261, 263, 261, 263, 263, 266, 283, 298, 331, Notes*: 86, 96*, 11, 124, 143, 145, 146 and 159
Rapoport Ya'akov Dr.	64, 82, 162
Rapoport-Cohen Reuven R'	270
Rauk Edmond	363
Razenstein	113
Reber Ya'akov	252
Redler-Feldman Yehoshua (R' Binyamin)	268
Regel Falk	Note: 60*
Regenbogen Henryk	112, 113, 118
Regenbogen Tzvi	118
Reggio I. Sh.	86, 87, 93, Note: 165*
Reikh Leon Dr.	118, 143, 187, 190, 191, 200, 203
Reikhman Rosen Nusia	367
Reikhman Yosef	112
Reiman	391, 400, 401, 402
Reinish	391
Reis Markus	Note: 194*
Reis Shimon	50
Reiter Shmuel	152
Reitman Hirsh	65, 66, 92. Notes*: 88, 147 and 161

Reitman Hirsh	65, 92, Notes: 88*, 147*, 161*
Reitman Mark	112, 113
Reitman Yosef	118
Reizen Z.	220
Rethoiz Ze'ev	228
Retzenstein Elazar	153
Retzenstein Israel	152
Retzenstein Ya'akov	112
Rienthal I.	106
Ringel Michael Dr.	139, 143
Ritterman Alexander Dr.	139
Ritterman Sarah	139
Rodnik Y. D.	108
Roikh	132
Rokita	397-399
Rolland Romain	307
Roseman Peppa	401/2
Rosenbaum, Prof.	164
Rosenberg-Goldberg Sara	335
Rosenbush Yeshayahu	Note: 42*
Rosenfeld Morris	144, 154, 370
Rosenkrantz Jonas Dr.	351
Rosenman Ya'akov	251, 401/2
Rosenmarin Henryk Dr.	139
Rosenstein Ziskind	102
Rosenthal Shlomo	84
Rosenzweig Maximilian	401/2
Rostel	132, 372
Rot Israel Dr.	150
Rotenberg Dr.	382, 389
Rotenberg Mrs.	366

Rothause Karl	313, 316
Rothschild Edomnd de, Baron	109, 119,
Rottstein David Dr.	217, 361, 362
Rozenshtroikh Avraham	213
Rozin Leah	144, 372
Rozner Mordekhai Dr.	271
Rozner Moshe	183, 227, 271, 272, 280
Rozner Yehoshua	227, 271

S

Sakher Karl Von	65, 75, 77, 80, 82, 84
Sakher-Masoch Leopold-Ritter Von	Notes: 123*, 129*, 133*
Sam Prof.	213
Sanhedrai (Dimend) Tova	223, 226
Sapiluk	317
Sapir Betzalel	102
Sapir Israel	102, 219
Sapir Moshe Dr.	401/2
Sapir Zeev-Wolf	103
Saraf	296, 297-299, 334
Sas Avraham	112, 113, 123, 127
Schekhter Z.	303, 360
Schitz	183
Schleikher Max	123
Schmidt Anton Adler	86, 87
Schorr brothers	86
Schorr Emil	306
Schorr Mendel (Emil)	80, 306
Schorr Moshe	312
Schorr Schacher	Note: 134*
Schorr Yehoshua Heschel R'	80, 86, Notes: 134*, 141*

Schuster Dr.	366
Schwartz	205, 217
Schwartz Eizner	420
Schwartz Kopel Dr.	215
Schwartz Mark	359
Schwartz Pinkhas	273, 279
Schwartz Rosa	420
Schwartz Salka	205, 366, 367, 370
Schwartz Tzvi R'	273
Schwartz Yosef, Eng.	401/2
Schwartz, bakery owner	389
Schweig Aba	230, 236, 251/2
Schweig Tova	231, 241
Schweig Y.	231, 236
Sedlinitzky, graf	64, 65, 69, 73, 74
Segal Mina	401/2
Segalovitz	310
Seret Dr.	191, 370
Seyfarth Karl	73-75
Sforza Bona (d' Aragona), Queen	277
Shaf Dr.	364
Shafkopf Eric	387
Shalita Ben-Tzion R'	265
Shalita Shimon	266
Shalita Ya'akov (Yeke'leh) R'	192, 193, 265, 266, 273, 277, 280, 282
Shaper	219
Shapira Meir R' from Lublin	227, 271, 272, 280
Shapira Meir R' from Narol	274
Shapira Wilhelm	401/2
Shapira-Diament Pinkhas (Pini)	152, 176
Shapiro Yitzkhak	122, 127

Sharfshiptz Rudolf Dr.	206, 401/2
Sharpstein Tzvi	150
Sheinberg Fredrik Dr.	401/2
Sheinberg Leon	401/2
Shekhter Penka	296
Shenbach Avraham	139
Sheneh Aharon R'	264
Shenkar	107
Sheremedez Gzhagozh	23
Shiferman Mikhael	226
Shiferman Tzipora	225, 226
Shikler Shlomo	250
Shikler Tzipora	228
Shikler Ze'ev	246, 248
Shiller Shlomo Dr.	110, 142
Shimon bar Kokhba	114, 123, 125, 126
Shimon Bar Yokhai	88
Shimon-Hirsh	37
Shishman Ibrahim Pasha	22
Shitzer brothers	231
Shitzer Eliyahu	236, 298
Shitzer Hadasa see Greenspan Hadasa	
Shitzer Tzvi	236, 242
Shmeterling Khaim (Gilad) Dr.	123, 157, 169, 170
Shmorek Mrs.	304
Shmuel of Ternopil	30
Shmuel son of Feibish R'	24
Shmuel son of Ya'akov (Jakobovitz)	33, Note: 23*
Shnormakher Mordekhai	312
Shpeizer Aharon	Note: 194*
Shperling	157

Shpigelglass D.	368
Shpindel	145, 146
Shpitzer Klara	246
Shpitzer Munek	248
Shponberg David	Note: 194*
Shraga Shlomo	55
Shtadler Etka	401/2
Shtandt Adolf	110, 111, 118, 122, 130, 1
Shtandt Carl	108
Shtekel D.	208, 220
Shtekel V.	368
Shtekel Yosef	401/2
Shtekel, café owner	339
Shterholtz Avram	220
Shtierman Moshe	213
Shtierman Shmuel	252
Shtroikher Beno Dr.	136, 140
Shulbaum Moshe L.	51, 93
Shulsinger brothers	262
Shwadron Nathan	401/2
Shwartzapel	220
Shwartzman (Dr.)' sons	386
Shwartzman Avraham Dr.	141, 169, 185, 203, 201, 205, 207, 341, 386
Shwartzman Eliyahu	227
Shwartzman Shmuel	Note: 119*
Shyemanovska Elizhbieta	51
Sigal Yehoshua	217, 218
Sigismund I, king	21, 277
Silber Ze'ev	230, 236
Silberfeld	Note: 130*
Simon	295

Sirkes Moshe	124, 133
Sirkes Yosef	124, 127, 133, 136, 219
Skladkovsky	204
Slepter Miriam	217, 250
Smolenskin Pertez	93-95
Smolska Franciszek Dr.	94
Sobel	220
Sobieski family	23, 26, 28
Sobieski Jan (John) III, King	26, 237, 333
Sobieski Maria Kazhimiera Queen	23
Sobieski Ya'akov (Jacub) King	26
Socrates	88
Sokal, engineer	139
Sokolov Nakhum	155
Soldner A.	246
Soloveichik Khaim R'	263
Soltzer, cantor	282, 283, 285
Spanier Joseph	341
Sperling	360
Spindel Dvora	246
Spinoza	92
Spitzer Klara	246
Spitzer-Golan Munek	246
Starzynski Mikhael	45
Steiger Yitzkhak	245
Stein Imanuel (Munyo)	126
Steinberg Gusta	213, 298, 299, 333
Steinshneider Moritz Dr.	98
Stern Betsalel	66, 92, 93
Sternberg Ze'ev	250
Stöger Michael	Note: 39*

Stolzenberg	224
Strusler brothers	306
Superman Rafael	142

T

Taaffe	105
Tabachnik	123, 124, 219
Taft Avraham	213
Tahun graf	101
Tarif Gusta	246
Tarif Moshe	246
Tarif, mill's owner	397
Tarnopoller Aharon	24
Tarnopoller Gelah	24
Tarnopoller Meir son of Yitzkhak R'	23-25
Tarnowski Jan	21, 23, Note: 1*
Tarnowsky, general	174
Tartokover brothers	135
Tartokover Khaim Dr.	120, 139
Tau Yosef	Note: 35*, 137-141, 143, 187
Tauber M.	164, 251/2
Tauber Sh. D. R' Dr.	Note: 196*
Taubles Shmuel R' Dr.	107, 108, 266, 331
Tchernovitz Shmuel	296
Tchubaty	126, 341, 342
Teikhman Itamar	23, 43-46, 48-52, 54, 59, 63, 273
Teikhman Ya'akov	224, 230, 236, 251/2, 419
Tenenbaum A.	231
Tenenbaum Itzkhak	230
Tenenbaum Jacob	236
Tenenbaum Moshe	Note: 155*

Tepperberg O.	221, 222
Terlo Gur-Arye Dr.	215
Thaler Hersh-Leib R'	274, 280
Theyls Ignatzi	23, 43-46, 48-52, 56, 59, 63
Thon Mrs.	139
Thon Yehoshua Dr.	107, 110, 138, 139, 142, 150, 190
Tirkel Feibel	227
Tirkel Lippa	227
Tirkel Shlomo	227
Tirkel Shmuel	227, 228
Tirkel Yekhiel	227
Tirkes Yosef	122
Tishler Yosef	150
Tornauer Levi	Note: 42*
Torre Hillel Dalla	87
Trakhtenberg Avraham, cantor	284
Tratokover brothers	135
Tratokover Khaim Dr.	120, 139, 150, 215
Trop Herman	139
Trumpeldor (Yosef)	154
Tukhman	295
Tunis Beinush	152, 154
Tutoress	303
Tversky N.	205
Tzellermayer Yehuda Dr.	213, 216, 217, 298, 361, 382
Tzimet Tonka	401/2
Tzin Izidor	111, 112, 122, 126
Tzin Ya'akov	123, 341
Tzinker	219
Tzoref Sara	250
Tzoref Shmuel	228

Tzuger	220
Tzuntz Leopold Dr.	86, 87
Tzvi Hirsh R' from Zidachov	277

U

Unter Karl	112
Urbakh	224
Urban Hirsh	Note: 42*
Uri of Strilyshcha R'	267
Uspitz Mordekhai	86
Ussishkin (Menakhem)	121-123

V

Valerstein Mordekhai-Shlomo	94
Valerstien Nathan	94
Vasilko Baron	162
Vestel	220
Vidatzky	207
Vishlitzki Vetzlav	206
Vishnitzer Mark	143-146
Vita	121
Vitah Shmuel Dalla Volta	87
Volenga	400

W

Wachs	107
Wahl Heinrikh	Note: 194*
Wahl Moshe	391, 396
Wahler Selka	246
Wahler Zusia/Zisha	223/4, 225, 273, 279, 295, 296, 298-301, 334
Wajter	307, 308

Waldman (nee Otsheret) Tzila/Zilah	139, 148, 150
Waldman from Drohobitz	139-113, 116, 118-121, 125-127, 136-139, 141, 143-148, 150, 156, 220, 329, 341
Waldman Israel Dr.	111
Waldman J.	127
Waldman Moshe	139
Walfish Yitzkhak	224, 225, 273, 280
Wallakh	224
Warhaftig Dr.	139
Waritschewer L.	251/2
Washitz Yehoshua	139
Wasserman Yehoshua	225, 228
Weihraukh	301
Weinbau Salo	102
Weinberg Julius	Note: 194*
Weinfeld	166
Weinlez Israel	Notes*: 43, 51, 57, 58, 86, 89, 102, 114 and 131
Weinman Shmuel, cantor	284
Weinstein	389, 423
Weinstein David	250, 251/2
Weintraub Yitzkhak-Hirsh	Note: 60*
Weintraub, cantor	286
Weisbersht Tzvi	219
Weisglas A.	173
Weisglas Dr.	341
Weisglas Mundek	343
Weisman	190, 295, 296, 298
Weisman Shimshon R'	273
Weisman-Sharf Yitzkhak R'	273
Weissberg M.	Notes: 66*, 83*
Weissman Shmuel	226, 398
Weissnikht Yosef Dr.	183, 199, 360

Weisstein Shmuel	93, 103
Weitzman Khaim Dr.	120
Weizer	306
Weizer Pesakh	246
Weksler Barukh R'	227, 272
Werbel Mordekhai-Eliyahu	93
Werber (Avishur) A. Dr.	122, 127, 219, 220
Werber Fishel	215
Werdum Ulrikh	25
Wertheimer Joseph	Note: 94*
Wertzber Libek	250
Wiesenfeld Z.	113
Wilder Ze'ev-Wolf, cantor	285
Wilner Ze'ev	227
Winkler Bernard	112, 113
Winkler, leather workshop owner	332
Winman Shmuel	284
Winter Ya'akov	399
Winterfeld Ya'akov	246, 250
Witos (Wincenty)	194
Wittenberg	297
Wladyslaw	22
Wlochisker Shlomo, cantor	284
Wolf Gershon	Note: 94*
Wolf R' of Skalat	Note: 15*
Wolfenhut Moshe	225
Wolfhoit Moshe	228
Wolfson Aharon	Note: 155*
Wolfstahl brothers	133/4, 311
Wolfstahl family	133, 311
Wolfstahl Khoneh	311-316

Wolfstahl Marcus	312
Wolfstahl Roza	316
Wolfstahl Sara	315
Wunderlikh	366
Wurmser Christian, graf	43

Y

Ya'akov (Lorberbaum) from Lissa R'	79
Ya'akov from Dubno R'	87
Yaeger Igantzi	206
Yaffe Kopel	228, 298, 301
Yakobson	123
Yakov Tzipka	250
Yampoler-Neuman Yetka	230, 231, 236, 241
Yarichover Yosef	401/2
Yartzki	312
Yastrov Mordekhai Dr.	105
Yehoshua-Heschel from Medzhybizh [Mezbuzh] R'	281
Yekel'eh/Yankel'eh R'	see Ya'akov Podhortzer
Yekeles Dr.	105
Yelink Aharon	87
Yerukham little	see Blindman
Yetlis Yehuda	77
Yosef Michael	37
Yula	124
Yustus Sigfrid I	73, 75

Z

Zaks (Sachs) Shneur	87
Zaks Mikhael Dr.	84, 86
Zalizniak	

Zaltz Avraham Dr.	109, 213
Zamoyski Tomasz	21, 22
Zamoyski-Ostrogska Katarzyna	22
Zangwill (Israel)	121
Zankovski	45
Zeidfeld	368
Zeidman Anshil	271
Zeidman Avraham	271, 272, 277, 280
Zeidman Ernestina	401/2
Zeidman Hillel Dr.	186, 227, 261, 271, 277
Zeidman Mordekhai	272, 280, 301
Zeidman Moshe	271, 274
Zeidman Rakhil	271
Zeidman Sara	271
Zeidman Shlomo	272, 280
Zeidman Yehuda-Ber	272, 280
Zeife Shlomo	133
Zeinfeld Israel Dr.	401/2
Zelinger	400
Zeltzer Avraham	213
Zerakh from Nadvorna	Note: 21*
Zhukov	372
Zilber Ze'ev	230, 236, 241
Zilber, shoemaker	332
Zilberdik	143
Zilberfeld	77
Zilberman (Kaspi) brothers	see Kaspi
Zilberman (Kaspi) Pinkhas (Pini)	see Kaspi
Zilberman Herman Dr.	Note: 194*
Ziltz F.	113, 116
Zin Ya'akov	127

Zipper Gershon Dr.	110, 130, 135, 141, 182
Ziskind Khaim	179, 180
Ziskind Kalir Alexander	81, 86
Zk"sh Avraham	84
Zlatkes Dr.	169, 170, 221, 370
Zlatkes Mark Dr.	112, 113, 169
Zoltzer	282, 283
Zomerstein Dr.	187
Zonena Robfogel	316
Zuberman Hela	250
Zusman Dolio	154
Zusman Joseph	139

This index is for the English edition

NAME INDEX

A

Abarbanel, 64
Abeler, 134, 286
Abeles, 119, 286
Abend, 111, 124, 125, 129, 133, 134, 135, 136, 268, 286
Aberman, 56, 286
Abramson, 81, 286
Abrass, 67, 189, 286
Afta, 188
Aftibutzer, 95, 286
Agnon, 196, 198, 286
Aharonfreiz, 60, 286
Aharonovitz, 139, 286
Aikhel, 68, 287
Akeslbirt, 167
Akhad, 287
Almantzi, 41, 287
Altshiller, 164, 167, 287
Altzofrom, 150, 287
Amernet, 159, 167, 287
Andreyev, 204
Angeles, 267, 287
Annals, 43
Anski, 106, 107, 116, 117
Ansky, 203, 204, 287
Apter, 42, 287
Arak, 150, 181, 187, 268, 287
Arak-Greenfeld, 268, 287
Aran, 175, 287
Arbass, 70
Arenkrantz, 268, 287
Arenstein, 203, 287
Arlozorov, 139, 224, 287
Arye-Leib, son of David, 27
Asch, 144, 203, 204, 287
Ashkenazi, 10, 15, 44, 53, 287
Atlas, 22, 56, 63, 70, 288
Atterman, 100, 245, 288
Auerbach, 268
Auerbakh, 27, 52, 73, 74, 91, 206, 288
Avishur, 144, 288
Avnon-Bronstein, 165, 218
Avot, 178

B

BABa"D, 14, 15, 16, 28, 35, 41, 42, 49, 57, 126, 133
BABa"D, 219

BABa" D, 177, 186, 187
Baba"d, 112, 149
BABa"D, 172, 173, 174, 175, 176, 178, 179, 180, 181, 182, 187, 188, 261, 288, 289
BABa"Da, 212
Badenstein, 206, 289
BaHaR"L, 289
Bahara"l [R' Avraham Yosef (?), Son of Rabbi Leib], 144
Bakh, 70, 289
Balaban, 61, 62, 64, 289
Balk, 62
Ballet, 165, 289
Balmer, 168, 289
Balter, 191
Bandera, 267, 289
bar Kokhba, 81
Bar Kokhba, 82
Bar Ya'akov, 172
Baral, 258, 261, 279, 280, 289
Baras, 199, 289
Barasch, 69, 289
Barman, 10, 289
Baron, 148, 149, 180, 289, 302, 321, 328
Baron de Hirsch, 85
Baron Hirsch, 95, 161, 162
Baron Vasilko, 106
Bartosiewicz, 22, 289
Bauer, 190, 289
Baumgarten, 26, 117, 289
Baumrin, 268, 289
Bavari, 63, 289
Bazas, 245, 289
Beckerman, 83
Beer, 37, 65, 289
Beigel, 80, 81, 83, 289
Bekerman, 80, 81, 289
Bekher, 93, 94, 95, 290
Bekhman, 190, 290
Bellegarda, 290
Bellegrada, 21, 298
Belmer, 111, 268, 290
Belter, 290
Beltukh, 73, 74, 290
Belzer, 190, 290
Ben Khushiel, 172
Ben Petakhya, 37
Ben Yekhiel, 172
Ben Ze'ev, 290
Bendelman, 182, 290
Ben-Shalom, 269

Benshovitz, 277, 290
Ber, 290, 315
Ber Gimpel, 206
Ber Levinzon, 63, 66
Bercl, 290
Berer, 290
Berg, 268, 290
Berger, 154, 160, 161, 166, 195, 196, 247, 290
Berl, 243
Bernstein, 44, 61, 290
Bertfeld, 119, 290
Betsalel, 15, 63
Bialik, 98, 133, 134, 196, 198, 204, 221, 290
Biberstein, 154, 160, 161, 290
Biberstein-Levion, 158
Bigel, 144, 290
Bik, 23, 47, 49, 58, 65, 68, 70, 85, 86, 87, 290, 291
Bikhovski, 291
Bilfeld, 143, 291
Bilinksi, 291
Bilinski, 63, 275, 291
Biller, 147, 148, 162, 164, 165, 167, 268, 291
Binder, 60, 291
Birenbaum, 59, 145, 291
Birpas, 145, 291
Blaustein, 162, 180, 291
Blautein, 291
Blazer, 291
Blindman, 189, 291, 331
Blishtift, 203, 291
Blokh, 23, 291
Bloy, 182, 291
Blumenfeld, 47, 51, 291
Boberstein-Levion, 154, 291
Bobrovsky, 49
Bodek, 47, 291, 292
Bodzianowski, 7, 292
Boistein, 60, 292
Bozhik, 292
Brandes, 190, 292
Brass, 145, 292
Braude, 72, 78, 85, 87, 89, 90, 292
Braund, 268, 292
Brauner, 83, 292
Breitbein, 56, 292
Breiter, 88, 90, 292
Breitman, 150, 180, 181, 187, 292
Brenzon, 258, 292
Bretfeld, 292
Brif, 268, 292
Brinstein, 140, 292
Bristiger, 135, 139, 292
Brod, 292
Broiner, 74, 78, 82, 292
Bromberg-Bitokovski, 72, 292
Bronstein, 21, 63, 139, 141, 142, 166, 291, 292

Brotziner-Trakhtenberg, 47, 293
Brukovitz, 258, 293
Brum, 154, 158, 293
Buber, 62, 79, 293
Buchinski, 260, 293, 318
Buhay, 215
Bukhner, 47, 293
Busch-Letteris, 70
Bush, 51, 293
Bussel, 139, 293

C

Cherkevski, 58, 293
Cohen, 41, 57, 58, 220, 293
Cohenberg, 28, 293
Cooper, 278, 279, 281, 293
Czartoryski, 23, 49, 293

D

Dankner, 211, 293
Dankovitz, 58, 293
Davidovitz, 8, 293
Delitz, 182, 187, 293
Delugach, 98, 293
Dembitzer, 61, 293
Dement, 51, 293
Denikin, 115, 293
Dessauer, 67, 294
Deutsch, 194, 195, 196, 200, 213, 268, 294
Dimend, 146, 149, 321
Dinaburg, 66, 294
Diner, 158, 294
Diner-Potashnik, 294
Diner-Putashnik, 166
Dines, 125, 294
Dinish, 28, 63, 294
Dizenfeld, 74, 294
Dobbes, 47, 294
Doka, 267, 294
Dokash, 294
Dolin, 163, 167, 294
Doliner, 163, 164, 167, 168, 268, 294
Donayevski, 294
Doner, 154, 294
Dreifinger, 81, 294
Dretler, 258, 279, 294
Drexler, 220, 294
Dreyfus, 294
Druk, 166, 294
Dukash, 51, 294
Duke Bavorovski, 61
Dykeh, 21, 294
Dymov, 204, 294

E

Edelsman, 190, 294
Edelson, 294
Edelstein, 130, 196, 294
Eibeschitz, 61, 295
Eikenbaum, 213
Eikhenbaum, 111, 135, 150, 182, 187, 241, 248, 295
Eikhenstein, 35, 188, 295
Eingler, 150, 295
Einsler, 123, 295
Eintzigler, 145, 295
Eisenberg, 56
Eisner, 279, 295
Eizenshtetter, 20, 295
Ekselbirt, 130, 168, 248, 255, 258, 268, 295
Elimelekh, 117, 175, 182, 295
Elisheva, 195, 196, 198
Emden, 15, 61, 295
Emperor Ferdinand, 54
Emperor Franz [Joseph], 21
Emperor Franz I, 29, 33
Emperor Franz Joseph, 70, 109
Emperor Josef II, 62
Emperor Joseph II, 18
Empress Maria-Theresa, 18
Enzelberg, 268, 295
Epstein, 33, 57, 261, 268, 295
Erter, 23, 47, 48, 63, 65, 78, 295
Ettinger, 33, 295
Euler, 48, 63

F

Fakh, 145, 295
Falkenfeld, 16, 20, 42, 63, 292, 295, 296
Farber, 268, 296
Fedder, 48, 49, 68, 296
Federbush, 181, 296
Feffer, 196, 197, 296
Feibel, 79, 296
Feigenbaum, 296
Feingold, 162, 296
Feit, 246, 296
Feld, 148, 149, 296
Feldman, 178, 181, 261, 296, 319
Feler, 83
Feller, 80, 296
Felpeda, 203, 296
Fessel, 147, 149, 181, 296
Fet, 90
Fett, 109, 110, 137, 240, 296
Fibotzki, 53, 296
Fierstenberg, 278, 296
Finkel, 61, 296
Finkelstein, 166, 169, 261, 296
Finlesh, 71, 296

Finlish, 27, 28, 44, 53, 64, 67, 68, 69, 296, 297
Fiol, 167, 202, 266, 297
Fischer, 167, 168, 297
Fish, 245, 297
Fishel, 98, 297
Fisher, 78, 79, 80, 83, 91, 119, 160, 197, 240, 258, 260, 277, 297
Fishler, 40, 297
Fleishman, 240, 242, 243, 268, 279, 297
Flohen, 51, 57, 297
Fogel, 56, 74, 297
Frank, 98, 297
Frankel, 42
Frankfurter, 297
Frantsoiz, 63, 297
Frantsuz, 121, 239, 297
Franz Joseph, 206, 297
Freidman, 74
Freihling, 49
Freizman, 268, 297
Frenkel, 41, 297
Frenkelfeld, 51, 297
Frenkel-Teomim, 175, 297
Freudenthal, 71, 279, 297
Friedamn, 83
Friedberg, 147, 148, 150, 197, 200, 297
Friedman, 63, 65, 66, 73, 82, 261, 298
Friedrich-Heinrich, 298
Friehling, 25, 51, 57, 64, 298
Frühling, 71, 298
Fuchs, 165, 168, 298
Fuerst, 43, 298
Fuks, 268
Fürth's Rabbi – Shmuel son of Feibish, 10

G

Gabel, 89, 90, 91, 298
Gal, 86, 89, 90, 298
Ganz, 148, 150, 299
Gaon, 172, 298, 301
Garfinkel, 51, 298
Geiger, 47, 48, 68, 298
Gelber, 7, 62, 63, 66, 67, 71, 177, 185, 192, 203, 241, 250, 268, 286, 298
Gelber -Eikhenbaum, 295
Gelber-Eikhenbaum, 63, 298
Gelman, 81, 298
Ger, 203, 298
Gerber, 68, 298
Gernik, 150, 298
Gershon son of Nathan who was the son of the tax collector, 15
Geshuri, 189, 205, 298
Ghirondi, 48, 298
Giar, 224, 299

Gilad, 299
Gimpel, 208, 299
Ginsberg, 196
Ginsburg, 23, 46, 147, 181, 197, 261, 268, 299
Gintsburg, 66
Glassgal, 57, 100, 218, 299
Glazer, 143, 299
Glikman, 148, 150, 299
Goebbels, 262
Gogol, 203, 299
Golan, 165, 299
Goldbaum, 191, 299
Goldberg, 28, 70, 71, 149, 169, 268, 299, 301, 302
Goldenberg, 46, 47, 48, 51, 52, 60, 63, 65, 67, 68, 140, 142, 299
Goldfaden, 203, 299
Goldhaber, 28, 300
Goldstein, 144, 145, 155, 300
Goldwasser, 245, 300
Goliger, 166, 169
Goligor, 117
Golokhovski, 70, 300
Gonta, 114, 300
Gordin, 208, 300
Gordon, 52, 68, 139, 166, 170, 300
Gorpin, 256, 257, 300
Gotfried, 71
Gotlieb, 130, 163, 164, 167, 168, 300
Gotlober, 68, 300
Gottfried, 119, 128, 131, 167, 257, 277, 284, 300
Gottlieb, 167
Grabski, 124, 300
Grass, 51, 300
Greenfeld, 141, 142, 260, 265, 300
Greenspan, 76, 117, 139, 143, 157, 195, 197, 199, 200, 221, 245, 300, 323
Greenspan -Tzfoni, 300
Grinberg, 97, 109, 144, 145, 300
Grold, 70, 301
Gromnitzki, 106
Groskopf, 154, 158
Groskopf-Rimoni, 301
Gross, 301
Grosskopf, 154
Grossman, 145, 301
Gruberg, 166, 169, 301
Grueberg, 141
Gruen, 168, 301
Gruenbaum, 79, 125, 134, 301
Gruenberg, 74, 83, 301
Guld, 86, 87, 88, 301
Guliger, 113, 114, 141, 245, 301
Guligerr, 114
Gutman, 48, 296
Gutzkov, 203, 301

H

Ha'Am, 68, 79
Haberman, 64, 301
Hager, 190, 258, 301
Haiman, 149, 199, 301
HaLevi, 57, 178, 206, 301
Halicher, 132, 301
Haller, 109, 301
Halperin, 60, 61, 79, 119, 261, 301, 302
Hamer, 302
Hammer, 160, 167
Handek, 62, 302
HaNes, 48
HaNess, 40
HarArzot, 61
Hartman, 60, 302
Haslavski, 14, 302
Hauer, 26, 28, 29, 35, 36, 37, 65, 302
Haus, 279, 302
Hausman, 90, 302
Hayermans, 203, 302
Heller, 123, 129, 135, 139, 140, 181, 302
Helleriekh, 258, 302
Helman, 220
Helrikh, 164
Henish, 90, 302
Hennig, 203, 302
Herlikh, 168
Herlikh-Fuchs, 302
Hershaft, 187, 191, 302
Hersher, 246, 302
Hershkowitz, 154, 302
Hertband, 60
Hertzbaum, 109, 302
Hertzenstein, 47, 302
Herzl, 72, 73, 75, 76, 79, 80, 82, 84, 85, 93, 127, 143, 222, 302
Herzog, 168, 268, 302
Heschel, 9, 14, 186, 188, 302
Hilferding, 22, 302
Himelbrandt, 144, 302
Hirsch, 224
Hirschberg, 279
Hirschhorn, 165, 250
Hirsh, 63, 186, 190, 302, 303
Hirshbein, 303
Hirshberg, 132, 255, 258, 261, 266, 303
Hirshhorn, 70, 264, 303
Hirshkowitz, 158, 309
Hirshorn, 90
Hoizner, 123, 181, 303
Hollender, 227, 303
Holobovitz, 96, 113, 161, 303
Holstein, 53, 303
Homberg, 20, 24, 31, 303

Horn, 95, 303
Horowitz, 23, 63, 64, 68, 85, 86, 125, 150, 241, 303
Horwitz, 23, 28, 47, 49, 51, 63, 65, 73, 74, 83, 91, 129, 134, 150, 181, 248, 255, 258, 303, 304
Hutton, 304

I

Ibrahim Shishman Pasha, 7
Igli, 182, 304
Ingler, 164, 223, 304
Inlander, 47, 69, 304
Inzler, 304
Isenberg, 121, 162, 241, 304
Israel, 304
Israel-Isrel, 61, 304
Isserles, 172, 304
Izenberg, 169, 304

J

Jabotinsky, 102, 135, 304
Jacobson, 45
Jakobovitz, 323
Jakobson, 24, 304
Jan Krzysztof, 7
Jost, 43, 65, 67, 304

K

Kacher, 268, 304
Kahan, 244, 304
Kahana, 61, 132, 181, 304
Kahane, 154, 158, 305
Kaiser, 109, 305
Kalil, 13, 305
Kalir, 44, 47, 172, 189, 305
Kalir-Ziskind, 305
Kalman, 264, 305
Kaminker-Wakhman, 74, 305
Kaner, 258, 305
Kantz, 71, 305
Kantzuker, 257, 305
Kapel, 227, 305
Kaplansky, 81, 305
Kapon, 258, 305
Karl IV, 305
Karl the 4th, 109
Karmelin, 268, 305
Karmelin-Barban, 268, 305
Karmin, 55, 305
Karo, 178, 305
Karp, 93, 95, 305
Karpel, 60
Karu, 160
Karuf, 267, 305
Kaspi, 154, 156, 158, 305, 332

Kassel, 48, 305
Katarzyna Ostrogska Zamoyski, 7
Katz, 47, 51, 66, 68, 74, 143, 150, 182, 219, 266, 305, 306
Katzman, 263, 306
Katz-Margaliot, 182, 306
Katzstein, 94, 306
Kaufman, 203, 306
Kavetzki, 191, 306
Keidanover, 9
Kelber, 268, 306
Keller, 261, 268, 306
Kenigsberg, 268, 306
Kenner, 164, 306
Kenyuk, 160, 161, 306
Keppel, 160
Kermish, 140, 141, 306
Keron, 268, 306
Kerpel, 60, 306
Kessler, 268, 306
Kestenbaum, 154, 158, 306
Ketcheh, 228, 306
Kharif, 61, 306
Kharp, 268, 306
Khartiner, 80, 81, 82, 83, 88, 91, 95, 97, 98, 144, 214, 217, 218, 252, 306
Khatiner, 90
Khayut, 44, 51, 61, 68, 306
Khaza"k, 117
Khazak, 61, 318
Kheimesh, 16, 61, 307
Khmelnytskyi, 112, 114, 307
Khmilenker, 56, 307
Khoben, 164, 167, 268, 307
Khomoba, 275, 307
Khorin, 48, 307
Kinderfreind, 25, 63, 307
King Frederick Augustus, 13
King Ludvik, 60
King Sigismund I, 7, 185
King Sigismund-Augustus, 7, 60
King Sobieski, 159
Kinstler, 203, 307
Kita'ee, 71, 307
Kittel, 56, 307
Klaften, 128, 132, 244, 307
Klahr, 139, 307
Klarnet, 257, 307
Kleinberg, 100, 307
Klikhnik, 191, 307
Klinger, 258, 268, 307
Kluger, 41, 44, 307
Knopholtz, 154, 197, 200, 307
Kobrin, 204, 307
Koenigsberg, 80, 81, 83, 307
Kohenberg, 63
Kolischer, 33, 51, 53, 58, 70, 86, 87, 307

Kolka, 61, 308
Koniecpolski, 7, 308
Kopler, 167, 257, 260, 268, 308
Koreh, 25, 308
Korenfeld, 307
Korengruen, 74
Korenweitz, 246, 308
Koritz, 102, 308
Korkis, 72, 308
Kornberg, 149, 181, 308
Kornblit, 203, 308
Kornfeld, 70
Korngreun, 92
Korngruen, 57, 59, 72, 73, 77, 78, 79, 80, 82, 83, 87, 88, 90, 91, 93, 94, 95, 98, 102, 112, 124, 144, 227, 308
Kortum, 21, 62, 308
Korytowski, 20, 22, 23, 62, 308
Korytowsky, 49
Korytowvski, 8
Kotzik, 191, 308
Kozover, 264, 308
Krakover, 14, 61, 308
Kranski, 103, 308
Kratter, 28, 308
Krieg, 67, 308
Krigesfeld, 167, 308
Krisberg, 167, 308
Kristianpoller, 44, 308
Kritz, 268, 308
Kromkhel, 23, 41, 47, 49, 50, 51, 78, 133, 162, 197, 219, 224, 308, 309
Kron, 80, 83, 309
Krop, 109, 309
Krzysztof, 309
Kurfuerst, 130, 134, 195, 196, 197, 198, 201, 221, 248, 255, 268, 309
Kurtz, 165, 309
Kutner, 57
Kutten, 1
Kwashnivski, 127, 132, 309

L

Labiner, 258, 279, 309
Lafayovker, 112, 309
Laks, 261, 265, 309
Landau, 16, 46, 47, 51, 52, 61, 63, 74, 78, 79, 80, 83, 94, 95, 100, 119, 148, 150, 182, 214, 268, 309
Lande, 158, 168, 309
Landfish, 211, 227, 309
Landman, 177, 178, 309, 310
Landsberg, 93, 95, 310
Landstein, 168, 310
Latitzover, 37
Lauterbach, 90, 310
Lazarus, 71, 246, 310

Lebenkron, 268, 310
Ledder, 196, 310
Lef, 48, 311
Lefin, 23, 33, 48, 49, 63, 64, 65, 68, 78, 197, 310
Lehrer, 64, 68, 69, 117, 310
Leibel, 310
Leibelinger, 221, 310
Leinberg, 109, 110, 113, 115, 116, 310
Lekher, 167, 310
Lenda, 268, 310
Leniak, 61
Lenkiewitz, 122, 128, 310
Leszczynska, 310
Leszczynski, 13, 63, 310, 318
Letris, 23, 51, 63, 68, 310
Lev, 190, 310
Levenstein, 51, 310
Levi, 140, 173, 310
Levin, 102, 126, 133, 310
Levinkron, 203, 310
Levinson, 140, 310
Levinzon, 68, 310
Libergal, 165, 243, 268
Lichtigfeld, 74
Liebergal, 121, 135, 203, 311
Liebling, 57, 59, 311
Lifshitz, 268, 311
Likhtigfeld, 74, 227, 311
Lilla, 268, 311
Lilyan, 132, 311
Lindman, 148, 150, 311
Lipa, 63, 258, 260
Lippa, 111, 255, 268, 311
Lippe, 71, 311
Liske, 61, 311
Liuberer, 191, 311
Lobkowitz, 33, 311
Loifer, 167, 311
London, 164, 311
Lorber, 56, 143, 311
Lorberbaum, 42, 331
Löw, 48, 67, 311
Lowenstein, 59, 71, 86, 311
Lozatto, 311
Lub, 311
Luft, 269, 311, 312
Luftig, 203, 312
Luner, 200, 312
Luria, 16
Luzatto, 41
Luzzatto, 46, 47, 61, 66, 68, 173, 312
Lvov, 104, 111, 119, 123, 150, 181, 187, 312

M

Mager, 154, 155, 158, 312

Mahler, 39, 61, 66, 67, 89, 91, 312
Maiblum, 90, 312
Maimonides, 312
Makukh, 112, 312
Maltz, 60, 89, 312
Mandel, 268, 312
Manheim, 182, 312
Mania, 167, 211, 310, 312
Manila, 182, 312
Manis, 312
Mannheimer, 45, 55, 312
Marder, 166, 312
Margaliot, 33, 34, 306, 312
Margaliot-Katz, 312
Margalit, 111, 119, 124, 143, 150, 243, 258, 261, 312
Margolis, 148, 200, 275, 312
Maria Kazhimiera d'Arquien, 8
Marks, 81, 313
Markus, 70, 111, 149, 313
Marmorek, 245, 313
Marmurek, 71
Marzend, 167, 169, 313
Masita, 49, 313
Matok, 117, 197, 313
Maye, 261, 313
Me'ika, 313
Meiberger, 147, 148, 181, 195, 196, 197, 313
Meir, 313
Meirberg, 124, 131, 313
Meirberger, 181
Meirovitz, 57, 313
Meizes, 47, 313
Meltzer, 76, 313
Menakhem Munish, 181, 188
Mendelson, 46, 48, 67, 196, 313
Meniyes, 63, 313
Mentel, 60, 119, 122, 313
Merbakh, 165, 313
Merlin, 167, 168, 268, 313
Mesh, 153, 313
Mesharet, 40, 313
Messing, 148, 150, 313
Mesuta, 57, 314
Metternich, 33, 314
Migden, 163, 167, 168, 245, 314
Milgraum, 147, 314
Milgrom, 268, 314
Miller, 261, 264, 265, 282, 314
Minkovksi, 314
Minkovski, 190
Mistrikh-Alufi, 142, 314
Mohar, 48, 49, 314
Moliere, 203, 314
Mond, 182
Mondschein, 163, 164, 314
Mondshein, 167

Montefiore, 201, 314
Mordekhai, son of Tzvi-Hirsh, 27
Morgenstern, 162, 314
Morkes, 142, 314
Moshe Khazan, 191
Moshel, 160
Moshe-Shaul, 61, 314
Mosler, 62, 119, 314
Mossinson, 198, 314
Mueller, 74, 83, 95, 314
Mund, 314
Munies, 25
Munis, 47, 48, 50, 314

N

Nagler, 124, 203, 268, 314
Nakht, 65, 107, 314
Nakhum, 314
Naphtali, 314
Napoleon, 21, 315
Nathanzon, 44, 47, 68, 315
Natkis, 65, 315
Neigeboren, 150, 315
Neiger, 64, 315
Neiman, 25, 27, 28, 63, 315
Neistein, 182, 315
Nekhemchi, 315
Neteh'leh, 315
Neuman, 154, 168, 315
Neustadt, 244, 315
Niman, 228, 315
Nimrower, 90, 315
Nirenstein, 47, 315
Nisbaum, 142, 315
Nishka, 65, 315
Nisim, 172, 315
Nives, 164, 165, 315
Nomberg, 144, 203, 315
Nordau, 80
Nossig, 79, 80, 315
Novakovski, 129, 315
Nusbrekher, 145, 315
Nussbaum, 73, 74, 77, 80, 83, 93, 125, 133, 136, 248, 268, 315

O

Odisser, 191, 316
Oks, 111, 123, 124, 156, 184, 196, 197, 253, 261, 269, 311, 316, 318
Oksenhorn, 222, 242, 316
Oksenorn, 243
Okser, 71, 218, 316
Oksman, 66, 316
Orens, 134, 316
Orenstein, 31, 35, 41, 139, 140, 141, 142, 177, 316

Ostern, 142, 197, 200, 201, 316
Ostren, 196, 316
Ostrogska-Zamoyski, 316
Ostrogski, 316
Otsheret, 60, 329
Otshert, 97, 316
Otshert-Waldman, 98
Ovadiah, 316
Overman, 164, 316
Ox, 129, 135

P

Pal, 268, 316
Palfinger, 258, 316
Paries, 65, 316
Parnas, 40, 60, 72, 100, 101, 102, 111, 118, 119, 120, 121, 124, 127, 129, 130, 131, 132, 133, 134, 135, 136, 143, 147, 149, 164, 177, 197, 224, 231, 239, 240, 241, 243, 246, 247, 248, 255, 256, 316, 317
Pasmanik, 81, 83, 84, 144, 317
Pasternak, 83, 213, 317
Patrila, 7, 317
Pechnik, 139, 143, 161, 317
Peiles, 119, 124, 126, 127, 131, 317
Peled, 197, 203, 317
Peler, 144, 317
Pendler, 144, 317
Pepperish, 131, 317
Perelman, 204, 294
Peretz, 144, 204, 317
Perl, 16, 20, 22, 23, 24, 25, 26, 27, 28, 29, 30, 31, 32, 33, 34, 35, 36, 37, 38, 39, 40, 41, 42, 43, 44, 45, 46, 47, 48, 49, 50, 51, 52, 53, 56, 57, 58, 59, 63, 64, 65, 66, 67, 68, 69, 70, 71, 73, 78, 82, 112, 128, 130, 131, 132, 133, 162, 172, 173, 177, 188, 196, 213, 218, 219, 221, 224, 287, 296, 317
Perlmutter, 56, 317
Perser, 268, 317
Pestor, 65, 317
Petliura, 105, 112, 113, 114, 115, 116, 161, 317
Petrikov, 266, 317
Petrushka, 164, 317
Phillipson, 43, 318
Pikhorsky, 112, 318
Pilsudski, 121, 127, 134, 135, 318
Pinsker, 48, 318
Pirstein, 86
Pirutzki, 70, 318
Planer, 111, 113, 115, 228, 318
Pleva, 80, 318
Podhortzer, 131, 180, 187, 220, 318, 331
Podles, 60, 318
Pohoriles, 131, 258, 260, 261, 265, 267, 281, 293, 318
Pollak, 72, 318
Pomerantz, 60, 73, 74, 76, 77, 79, 83, 93, 94, 95, 313, 318

Pomerantz-Meltzer, 123, 318
Pomeranz, 135
Popresh, 182, 318
Porat, 184, 318
Pordes, 102, 318
Poros, 66
Portis, 61, 318
Posros, 318
Potocki, 8, 318
Potowtski, 8, 10, 11, 13, 19, 22, 318
Poznan, 61, 318
Preiss, 268, 318
Primer, 197, 200, 318
Prin, 201, 319
Prince Golitsyn, 21
Prince Konstanty [Wasyl] Ostrogski, 7
Prince Lobkowitz, 40
Prince Sapieha, 208

Q

Queen Bona Sforza, 185
Queen Marie Casimire Louise, 8

R

R' Arye-Leib, son of Shaul, 15
R' Benyamin son of Avigdor from Zbarazh, 27
R' D. Ber, 186
R' David, son of Shmuel HaLevi, 14
R' Gershon Nathan, son of Betsalel, 15
R' Israel, son of Shmuel, 14
R' Khaim Zelig, 9
R' Levi-Yitzkhak of Berdichev, 39
R' Mania, 212
R' Manis (Manila), a Maggid [preacher], 182
R' Meir, "Master of the Miracles, 40
R' Ovadya, 39
R' Todros was a wine merchant, 22
R' Ya'akov from Dubno, 48
R' Yisaskhar Berish, 61
Rabbi [Tzvi Hirsh] from Zidichov, 186
Rabbi Aharon Sheneh [?] from Tluste, 175
Rabbi Asher, 182
Rabbi BABa"D, 175, 176
Rabbi Eliyahu, son of Arye-Leib from Kovrin, 15
Rabbi Heschel, 15, 16, 175
Rabbi Israel of Rozhin, 66
Rabbi Meir Aran from Buchach, 175
Rabbi Menakhem-Munish, 175, 176, 187
Rabbi Nakhman of Bratslav, 66
Rabbi Naphtali from Ropshitz, 35
Rabbi R' Leibush, 175
Rabbi R' Nakhman, 175
Rabbi R' Shalom, 175
Rabbi R' Uri of Strilyshcha, 177
Rabbi Shalita, 126, 175, 176

Rabbi Wolf of Skalat, 61
Rabbi Yosef, a rabbinical judge in Mykulyntsi, 175
Rabidowitz, 68, 319
Racker, 245, 319
Rapaport, 68, 83
Rapoport, 32, 44, 45, 47, 49, 51, 52, 54, 60, 67, 70, 74, 78, 91, 106, 111, 134, 172, 173, 179, 197, 219, 319
Rapoport-Cohen, 319
Rappaport, 23, 41, 66, 67
Rappoport, 33, 65
Rauk, 242, 316, 319
Razenstein, 74, 319
Reber, 169, 319
Redler-Feldman, 180
Regel, 63, 319
Regenbogen, 74, 78, 319
Reggio, 47, 48, 51, 68, 319
Reikh, 78, 92, 122, 124, 125, 131, 133, 319
Reikhman, 319
Reiman, 261, 267, 319
Reinish, 261, 319
Reis, 25, 70, 319
Reiter, 100, 319
Reitman, 34, 64, 68, 73, 74, 319, 320
Reitmann, 50
Reizen, 144, 320
Rethoiz, 150, 320
Retzenstein, 73, 100, 320
Rienthal, 58, 320
Rietman, 78
Rimoni, 154, 158
Rimpel, 215
Ringel, 90, 92, 320
Ritterman, 90, 320
Rodnik, 60, 320
Roikh, 86, 320
Rokita, 265, 266, 320
Rolland, 203, 320
Roseman, 268, 320
Rosemarin, 90
Rosenbaum, 107, 320
Rosenberg-Goldberg, 222, 320
Rosenbush, 62, 320
Rosenfeld, 92, 102, 320
Rosenkrantz, 268, 320
Rosenman, 168, 268, 320
Rosenmarin, 320
Rosenstein, 56, 320
Rosenthal, 46, 320
Rosenzweig, 268, 320
Rosner, 261
Rostel, 250, 320
Rot, 98, 320
Rotenberg, 260, 320
Rothaus, 206, 209
Rothause, 321

Rothchild, 79
Rothschild, 72, 321
Rottenberg, 245
Rottstein, 141, 242, 321
Rottstien, 241
Rozenshtroikh, 139, 321
Rozhiner, 40
Rozin, 92, 321
Rozner, 119, 123, 150, 180, 181, 187, 321
Rubianus, 37
Rubin, 68

S

Saba,, 100
Sachs, 48, 331
Sakher, 43, 44, 321
Sakher- Masoch, 67
Sakher-Masoch, 66, 67, 321
Sam, 139, 321
Sanhedrai, 146, 149, 321
Sapiluk, 211, 321
Sapir, 56, 57, 143, 268, 321
Saraf, 196, 197, 321
Sas, 74, 81, 83, 321
Sasiv, 102
Schekhter, 201, 241, 321
Schitz, 119, 321
Schleicher, 81
Schleikher, 321
Schmidt, 47, 321
Schorr, 43, 47, 67, 203, 206, 321
Schuster, 245, 322
Schwadron, 268
Schwartz, 134, 140, 141, 182, 187, 240, 248, 249, 260, 268, 279, 322
Schwartzman, 66
Schweig, 154, 158, 161, 168, 322
Sedlentzky, 36
Sedlinitzky, 322
Sedlintzky, 34, 36, 40
Segal, 268, 322
Segalovitz, 204, 322
Seret, 125, 248, 322
Seyfarth, 40, 322
Sfog, 196
Shaf, 243, 322
Shafkopf, 258, 322
Shakhna, 216
Shalita, 126, 175, 176, 178, 181, 186, 322
Shalom Aleichem, 92
Shalom Aleikhem, 203, 204
Shapel, 70
Shaper, 143, 322
Shapira, 150, 180, 181, 182, 187, 268, 322
Shapira-Diamant, 115

Shapira-Diament, 100, 322
Shapiro, 80, 83, 322
Sharaf, 221
Sharfshiptz, 323
Sharfshpitz, 268
Sharfspitz, 135
Sharpstein, 98, 323
Sheinberg, 268, 323
Shekhter, 196, 323
Shenbach, 90, 323
Sheneh, 175, 323
Shenkar, 60, 323
Sheremedez, 8, 323
SHI"R, 219
SHI"R, 172, 173, 177, 190, 197, 319
Shiferman, 148, 149, 323
Shikler, 150, 165, 167, 323
Shiller, 72, 91, 323
Shimon bar Kokhba, 323
Shimon Bar Yokhai, 323
Shimon-Hirsh, 323
Shishman, 323
Shitzer, 117, 154, 162, 197, 300, 323
Shitzer-Greenspan, 221
Shlomo-Tzvi, son of Simkha Hirsh, 51
Shmertling, 81
Shmeterling, 103, 111, 112, 299, 323
Shmorek, 202, 323
Shmuel of Ternopil, 14, 323
Shnormakher, 206, 323
Shpeizer, 70, 323
Shperling, 103, 323
Shpigelglass, 247, 324
Shpindel, 95, 324
Shpindle, 94
Shpitzer, 165, 324
Shponberg, 71, 324
Shraga, 28, 324
Shtadler, 268, 324
Shtandt, 60, 72, 76, 78, 80, 85, 88, 89, 90, 91, 92, 122, 324
Shteinberg, 175
Shteirman, 169
Shtekel, 136, 144, 247, 268, 324
Shterholtz, 144, 324
Shtierman, 139, 324
Shtoikher, 88
Shtroikher, 91, 324
Shulbaum, 25, 51, 324
Shulsinger, 173, 324
Shwadron, 324
Shwartzapel, 144, 324
Shwartzman, 91, 121, 133, 134, 135, 149, 258, 324
Shwarzman, 111, 227
Shyemanovska, 25, 324
Sigal, 141, 143, 324

Sigfrid Yustus, 40
Sigfrid Yustus the First, 40
Silber, 154, 158, 324
Silberfeld, 67, 324
Simon, 195
Sirkes, 81, 83, 88, 143, 325
Skladkovsky, 134, 325
Slepter, 141, 166, 325
Smolenskin, 51, 52, 325
Smolska, 52, 325
Sobel, 144, 325
Sobieski, 8, 10, 13, 325
Sokal, 61, 90, 325
Sokolov, 102, 325
Soldner, 165, 325
Soloveichik, 173, 325
Soltzer, 189, 191, 325
Spanier, 227, 325
Sperling, 241, 325
Spindel, 164, 325
Spinoza, 51, 325
Spitzer, 165, 325
Spitzer-Golan, 299, 325
Spivak, 190, 290, 291
Starzynski, 22, 325
Stavitski, 21
Steiger, 163, 164, 325
Stein, 56, 80, 83, 325
Steinberg, 139, 149, 166, 197, 221, 325
Steinshneider, 54, 57, 325
Stern, 34, 50, 51, 63, 325
Sternberg, 166, 325
Stöger, 62, 325
Stolzenberg, 147, 326
Strusler, 203, 326
Stryj, 93, 95
Stutterheim, 28
Superman, 91, 98, 326
Swartz, 96

T

Taaffe, 326
Taaffe-Donayevski, 58
Tabachnik, 81, 143, 326
Taft, 139, 326
Tahun, 326
Tarif, 149, 164, 165, 265, 296, 326
Tarnopoller, 8, 9, 326
Tarnowski, 7, 8, 60, 326
Tarnowsky, 113, 326
Tartokover, 79, 87, 90, 98, 140, 326
Tau, 71, 326
Tauber, 71, 107, 168, 326
Taubles, 59, 60, 177, 219, 326
Tchernovitz, 196, 326

Tchubati, 83
Tchubaty, 227, 326
Tehun, 56
Teikhman, 147, 150, 154, 158, 168, 181, 279, 326
Teitel, 268
Tenenbaum, 68, 154, 155, 158, 326
Teomim, 268
Tepperberg, 145, 327
Terlo, 140, 327
Ternopoler, 191
Thaler, 182, 187, 327
Theyls, 8, 21, 22, 23, 24, 25, 26, 28, 30, 33, 327
Thon, 60, 72, 89, 90, 91, 98, 124, 327
Tirkel, 150, 327
Tirkes, 80, 327
Tishler, 98, 327
Tornauer, 62, 327
Torre, 48, 327
Trakhtenberg, 190, 327
Tratokover, 327
Trop, 90, 327
Trumpeldor, 102, 327
Tukhman, 195, 327
Tunis, 100, 102, 327
Tutoress, 201, 327
Tversky, 134, 327
Tzar Alexander I, 25
Tzellermayer, 139, 140, 141, 197, 241, 255, 327
Tzfoni, 157
Tzimet, 268, 327
Tzin, 73, 74, 80, 81, 83, 144, 227, 327
Tzinker, 143, 327
Tzipka, 167, 331
Tzoref, 150, 166, 327
Tzuger, 144, 328
Tzuntz, 47, 48, 328

U

Umanir, 37
Unter, 74, 328
Urbakh, 147, 328
Urban, 62, 328
Ushitz, 66
Uspitz, 47, 328
Ussishkin, 80, 328

V

Valerstein, 52, 328
Valerstien, 328
Veksler, 150
Verkhibekker, 37
Vestel, 144, 328
Vetzlav, 134
Vidatzky, 135, 328
Vishlitzki, 134, 328

Vishnitzer, 93, 94, 95, 328
Vita, 80, 328
Volenga, 267, 328
Volta, 48, 328
von Hutten, 37
von Sakher, 41, 46
Von Sakher, 34, 53

W

Wachs, 60, 328
Wahl, 67, 69, 70, 261, 264, 328
Wahler, 147, 148, 164, 181, 187, 195, 196, 197, 198, 200, 221, 328
Wajter, 203, 328
Waldman, 73, 74, 77, 78, 79, 80, 82, 83, 84, 88, 89, 90, 91, 92, 93, 94, 95, 96, 97, 144, 217, 227, 329
Walfish, 147, 148, 181, 187, 329
Wallakh, 147, 329
Warhaftig, 90, 329
Waritschewer, 168, 329
Washitz, 90, 329
Wasserman, 148, 150, 329
Weihraukh, 199, 329
Weinbau, 56, 329
Weinberg, 71, 329
Weinfeld, 109, 329
Weinlez, 62, 63, 64, 65, 66, 67, 329
Weinman, 191, 329
Weinstein, 57, 167, 168, 260, 281, 329
Weintraub, 63, 191, 329
Weisbersht, 143, 329
Weisglas, 113, 227, 228, 329
Weisman, 124, 195, 196, 197, 329
Weissberg, 63, 64, 329
Weissman, 149, 182, 329
Weissman-Sharf, 182
Weissnikht, 119, 131, 240, 329
Weisstein, 51, 330
Weitzman, 79, 330
Weizer, 165, 203, 330
Weksler, 181, 330
Werbel, 51, 330
Werber, 80, 83, 140, 143, 144, 288, 330
Werdum, 10, 330
Werfel, 95
Wertheimer, 65, 330
Wertzber, 167, 330
Wiesenfeld, 74, 330
Wilder, 191, 330
Wilner, 149, 330
Wincenty, 330
Winkler, 74, 220, 330
Winman, 330
Winter, 266, 330
Winterfeld, 164, 167, 330

Witos, 127, 330
Wittenberg, 197, 330
Wladyslaw, 7, 330
Wlochisker, 191, 330
Wolf, 65
Wolfenhut, 148, 330
Wolfhoit, 150, 330
Wolfson, 68, 330
Wolfstahl, 205, 206, 207, 208, 209, 330, 331
Wunderlikh, 245, 331
Wurmser, 21, 331

Y

Ya'avetz [Rabbi Ya'akov son of Tzvi Ashkenazi], 15
Yaeger, 134, 331
Yaffe, 150, 197, 200, 331
Yakobson, 81, 331
Yakov, 167
Yampoler, 154, 161
Yampoler-Neuman, 154, 158, 331
Yarichover, 268, 331
Yartzki, 206, 331
Yastrov, 58, 331
Yekeles, 58, 331
Yekl'leh, 187
Yelink, 48, 331
Yerukham, 189, 190, 191, 331
Yetlis, 41, 331
Yitzkhak son of Yehuda Halevi, 27
Yokhai, 48

Z

Zaks, 46, 47, 48, 331
Zalizniak, 114, 331
Zaltz, 72, 332
Zamoyski, 7, 332
Zamoyski-Ostrogska, 332
Zangwill, 80, 332
Zankovski, 22, 332
Zeev Braude, 90
Zeidfeld, 247, 332
Zeidman, 121, 150, 172, 180, 181, 182, 186, 187, 199, 268, 291, 332
Zeife, 332
Zeinfeld, 268, 332
Zeitung, 69, 70
Zelinger, 267, 332
Zeltzer, 139, 332
Zerach, 216
Zetz, 216
Zhidachover, 35, 295
Zhukov, 250, 332
Zidichov, 186
Zilber, 161, 220, 332
Zilberdik, 92, 308, 332
Zilberfeld, 41, 332
Zilberman, 71, 155, 156, 157, 305, 332
Ziltz, 74, 76, 332
Zin, 332
Zipper, 72, 85, 87, 89, 91, 119, 333
Ziskind, 117, 305, 313, 333
Ziskind-Kalir, 333
Zk"sh, 333
Zlateks, 73, 74
Zlatkes, 111, 145, 248, 333
Zolochiv, 93
Zoltzer, 333
Zomerstein, 123, 333
Zonena, 208, 333
Zuberman, 167, 333
Zusman, 90, 102, 333